ENCYCLOPEDIA
OF
NATIONALISM

D0927762

ENCYCLOPEDIA
OF
NATIONALISM

LOUIS L. SNYDER

Professor Emeritus
Ph.D. Program in History
The City University of New York

PARAGON HOUSE
New York

First edition, 1990

Published in the United States by

Paragon House
90 Fifth Avenue
New York, NY 10011

Library of Congress Cataloging-in-Publication Data
Snyder, Louis Leo
Encyclopedia of nationalism / by Louis L. Snyder.—1st ed.
p. cm.
ISBN 1-55778-167-2
1. Nationalism—Dictionaries. I. Title.
JC311.S5484 1990
320.5'4'03—dc20 89-8690
CIP

Manufactured in the United States of America

The paper used in this publication meets the minimum
requirements of American National Standard for Information Sciences—Permanence of Paper for Printed Library Materials, ANS1Z39.48-1984.

TO
FAYE S. LIEBERMAN
With much brotherly affection

Preface

In the early twentieth century, before the outbreak of World War I, British publicist Norman Angell made this striking statement, "Political nationalism has become for the European of our age, the most important thing in the world, more important than humanity, decency, kindness, pity, more important than life itself." Allowing for a modicum of exaggeration, there is much in this comment that rings true for the entire century. Because history is concerned with a process of change, it may be assumed that over the course of the century nationalism could well have been in decline, and that it was being superseded by internationalism of one kind or another. However, the experience of the Soviet Union and Soviet China runs counter to this belief: both peoples have subjugated any belief in internationalism to the more powerful factor of nationalism. Where the countries of Western Europe have united in a Common Market for their mutual economic interests, they have no intention of abandoning their political sovereignty in favor of control by the European Parliament.

Nationalism today retains its place as a powerful factor in human affairs. In the January 2, 1989, issue of *Time*, its editors refrained from the tradition of naming a Man of the Year and designated Endangered Earth as Planet of the Year for 1988. Warning about the very survival of the species, the editors stated: "Now, more than ever, the world needs leaders who can inspire their fellow citizens with a fiery sense of mission, not a nationalistic or military campaign but a universal crusade to save the planet."

The subject of nationalism is filled with enormous complexities—with inconsistencies, contradictions, and paradoxes. It seems that the field is still inchoate, burdened with conflicting definitions, approaches, and explanations. A frustrated scholar speaks of "the purportedly fleeting, regressive, immature nature of nationalism." The literature on the subject—from scholarly to popular—is tremendous. Yet, it is necessary to continue study of this elusive subject.

This book is designed to present some guidance to those interested in this historical phenomenon. It is based on a lifetime of attention to the meaning, characteristics, and development of nationalism. Its entries are designed to give a succinct summary without annoying detail on many aspects of this important historical force. Ideas on nationalism are presented without taking sides on the historical controversies that surround the subject, some of which are based on strong differences of opinion. Attention is given to a wide range of scholars, from the pioneer experts such as Carlton J. H. Hayes and Hans Kohn, to the intermediate commentators such as Hans J. Morgenthau and Karl W. Deutsch, to the more recent experts such as Boyd C. Shafer, Konstantin Symmons-Symonolewicz, and Walter Connor. To avoid the extension of this book into many volumes, each entry is condensed into a brief space, but a short bibliography is appended to each one for additional consultation. In some cases I have drawn upon my previously published work in presenting factual material.

I wish to express my thanks to Ken Stuart, senior editor at Paragon House, who alerted me to the necessity for this encyclopedia, which has never been done before. I am grateful to Juanita Lieberman of Paragon House for her encouragement as well as to Eric Greenfeldt of the Princeton Public Library, who has always been of assistance to me in my work. The staff of the Firestone Library at Princeton University has been graciously helpful in the production of this encyclopedia. Most of all, I express my warmest thanks to my wife, Ida Mae Brown Snyder, who has worked on this project from beginning to end and who is responsible for many improvements in style and substance.

LOUIS L. SNYDER
Princeton, N.J.

Introduction

British philosopher Isaiah Berlin said it succinctly: "In all a great array of elaborate, statistically supported serious futurology mingled with free fantasy, there took place one movement which dominated much of the nineteenth century, for which no significant future was predicted, a movement so familiar to us now, that it is only by some effort of the imagination that one can conceive of the world in which it played no part. . . . The movement is nationalism."

American sociologist Feliks Gross noted its importance: "Nationalism . . . permeates every political philosophy be it national, pan-national, imperialistic or international. The sentiment of national consciousness has entered a crusading phase so powerful that every dogma of the state and of peoples in general is linked with it. It has taken on as complete a hold on modern thinking and attitudes as did religion and theology on the thinking of the Middle Ages."

Thus is recorded the reaction of contemporary scholars on the importance of nationalism in our society today. Though there are many conflicting views on the meaning of nationalism, it may well be said to be that state of mind in which the supreme loyalty of the individual is felt to be owed to the nation-state. It remains the strongest of political emotions. Throughout the world, national consciousness has been molded into dogmatic philosophies and ideologies. In current society the most important question of our time—the quest for peace—is a search for solutions to problems of conflicting nationalisms.

Nationalism, it is said, the exaggerated and unjustified tendency to emphasize national interests, has turned out to be the curse of the century. Critics condemn it as an outmoded, deep-seated disease which plagues mankind and which cannot be healed by incantation. Its generative element is described as egotistic: all those living in a given country belong to one and the same in-group, which is distinct from the out-groups surrounding it. This mode of living gives protection to the in-group and requires little or no attention to others. From the viewpoint of critics, it is a sad state of affairs when nationalism, by dividing humanity into squabbling states, places excessive and exclusive emphasis upon the value of the nation at the expense of moral and ethical values. Its keynote is the overestimation of one's own nation and the simultaneous denigration of others. By its very nature nationalism has turned into a kind of religious faith. It is easily transformed into aggrandizement and oppression. Nationalism, it is said, breeds imperialism, and the latter, in turn, produces nationalism in the very people it subjects to its control.

It is well said that nationalism reflects the chaos of history itself. It is always in flux, and changes according to no preconceived pattern. It is multifaceted, murky, disheveled, irreducible to common denominators. It is partly real, partly myth. It intermingles both truth and error. The myths associated with nationalism are so strong that they have a way of perpetuating themselves and of becoming both true and real. Functioning in a milieu of historical paradox, nationalism is notorious for producing strange myths, which come to be accepted uncritically as normal and rational.

Nationalism works in a multiplicity of forms, some sharp and undisguised, some vague and hidden; some directed to cultural integration, others to political ends; some democratic in character, others tending towards authoritarianism or dictatorship. Among its many variations:

A force for unity. Nationalism may be the means by which politically divided nations achieve unity in a single state. There may be integration and consolidation of a country's territory and the nation acts as a unit (Italy, Germany).

A force for disruption. Nationalism may be the means by which a conglomerate state consisting of many ethnic units break down into component parts of varying nationalities (the Austro-Hungarian Empire).

A force for independence. Nationalism may result from the zealous desire of a mini-nationalism for self-determination and to break away for independence (Poles, Ukrainians, Balts, Finns).

A force for fraternity. Nationalism may represent the striving of irredentists to win union with the same in-group (*Italia irredenta*, Serbs, Rumanians, Bulgarians).

A force of colonial expansion. In the late nineteenth century of imperialism, nationalism was the road by which the imperialist powers sought to enhance their colonial position (Great Britain, France, Portugal, Spain, Belgium, the Netherlands).

A force for aggression. For the "have-not nations," nationalism represented a means by which they could acquire greater territory, greater wealth, peoples, and power (Wilhelminian Germany, Nazi Germany, Fascist Italy, militarist Japan).

A force for anti-colonialism. Following the mid-twentieth century, nationalism became the force which promoted the creation of new nation-states in the former colonies in Africa, Asia, and the Middle East. It was transformed from a movement of opposition and defiance to a movement of nation-building (Ghana, Nigeria, Congo, India, Indonesia, Syria, Jordan).

A force for economic expansion. Nationalism accompanies the attempts of the more powerful economic powers (United States, Japan, Federal Republic of West Germany) to extend their economic position on the world scene.

We see then how nationalism remains an extraordinary twentieth-century phenomenon, in many ways, one of the most powerful forces in the world today. It emerges again and again in one of its manifestations. It is behind the formation of new states on the map and it is persistently at work to bring about the breakdown of established states. As Carlton J. H. Hayes, pioneer scholar of nationalism, pointed out, nationalism may be a blessing or it may be a curse. It may be a blessing in its drives for cultural unity, but it may be a curse in its enhancement of political rivalries. It takes on an evil connotation when it drives for territorial expansion at the expense of already established states.

Modern nationalism began its historical journey in Europe, and a determined effort to end it has arisen on that continent. But it has been a lame and weak attempt to halt the development of a live and powerful force. The advocates of a combined Europe hail the formation of a European legislature, as if that body signals the weakening of nationalism and the formation of a European national state. Realistic observers conclude that economic union, as manifested in the Common Market, does not mean political union. European statesmen pay eloquent tribute to the successes of the Common Market, but they have absolutely no intention of relinquishing their political independence. Economic agreement, they say and let it be known, does not mean political unity or the end of the national state. They have no intention of compromising their political independence—and their accompanying national spirit, to the goal of united Europa.

Centralization versus Ethnic Nationalism

The extraordinary hold nationalism has on society today may be seen in the confrontation of two forms of nationalism: (1) the centralized nationalism of the Soviet Union; and (2) the demand of self-assertion and independence by many ethnic groups inside the U.S.S.R. For some seventy-two years these ethnic nationalities have remained inside the Soviet Union, not by choice but by the power of the tank. They have been held in what they regard as captive form not by special love of the Kremlin nor by regard for the ideology of communism, but by sheer force—power and might. They have seen the meaning of the Russian tank in Prague, Budapest, and East Berlin. They have remained quiescent only in the face of Soviet power. Their sense of national consciousness is muted, but it has not been destroyed. They would await the time for freedom. They would exist as "captive nations," but one day they would express their desire for self-determination and they would break away from the Soviet mold.

Then came two extraordinary and unexpected developments at the beginning of the seventh decade of the Soviet Union. Its economic system began to slide into disarray. The masters of the Kremlin, convinced that the capitalist world would seek to destroy it, had constructed huge military forces to protect the country. There was optimism that the Soviet system would win the struggle: Nikita S. Khrushchev made it plain: "We will bury you."

Yet there was something seriously wrong with the Communist experiment. The country was faced with everything from strikes to food shortages to nationalist unrest. The nation could not even be properly fed. Meanwhile, capitalist Japan and the Federal Republic of West Germany, losers in the great conflict of World War II, rushed on to unprecedented prosperity and the rest of the capitalist world surged forward. Mikhail Gorbachev, the new President, saw reform as absolutely necessary to rescue the Soviet Union from its economic slide. He introduced two new approaches to meet the crisis: *glasnost* (openness) and *perestroika* (restructuring). He would ease the rigid dictatorship of the hard-liners and give a new existence to the ailing Soviet Union. He would save the structure of Soviet communism.

For the many nationalities of the Soviet Union, the Gorbachev reform program presented an opportunity to throw off the shackles of centralized control. It was an opportunity not to be missed. With a more open society, ethnic dissenters, who had been forced into the underground for years, began to express their demands without fear of the secret police. From one end of the country to another, nationalists pressures began bubbling over. Bruising constitutional crises with Moscow arose over the critical matter of sovereignty. For years the ethnic nationalities had become inured to the idea of the Communist Party's monopoly of power. Now the demand arose that the party could have power only so long as the people trusted it. Nationalist ethnic clashes erupted in Armenia, Azerbaijan, Uzbekistan, Georgia, Moldavia, and the Ukraine. It had been just two years since the Gorbachev reforms allowed the ethnic nationalists to speak out openly and organize popular fronts.

A sense of emergent nationalism also penetrated deeply into the lives of the three Baltic peoples of Estonia, Latvia, and Lithuania. In 1939 Hitler and Stalin had agreed to the Nazi Soviet Pact, by which the three states noted for their fierce sense of independence, were thrust unwillingly into the Soviet orbit and incorporated into the Soviet Union. Faced with the overwhelming power of the Kremlin, the Baltic peoples remained restless under Soviet domination. In the new era of *glasnost* and *perestroika*, the Baltic peoples began to speak openly of their desire for independence.

The Baltic peoples began an intense campaign for full independence. The movement spread quickly. The new password became "Freedom!" In the late summer of 1989, more than a million Baltic peoples, in an unprecedented act of defiance against the Kremlin, held hands in a human chain stretching 370 miles across their Baltic homeland. Each individual in turn passed the word "Freedom" until it traveled across the three Baltic areas. Loud-speakers blared out nationalist songs as men, women, and children raised their hands to the sky and swayed to the music.

For the Kremlin this was the spread of the dangerous "virus of nationalism." Its own centralized nationalism obviously was good, but that of the Baltic peoples was unacceptable. Gorbachev actually contributed to the strengthening of Baltic nationalisms by appointing a commission to examine the disputed 1939 pact by which the Baltic states had been incorporated into the Soviet Union. The commission added to additional local national pride by acknowledging the long-denied protocol that had brought the Baltic republics into the Soviet sphere.

The Kremlin soon revealed its anger at the dangerous developments in the Baltic countries. In its estimation this was the first line of Soviet defense, with its important port facilities, missile installations, and many thousands of troops stationed in the area. To give independence to the Baltic peoples would encourage similar drives elsewhere throughout the U.S.S.R. Moreover, there was the problem of the many Russians sent into the Baltic countries, who claimed that independence would act as a threat to their own rights. Past performance of Soviet power indicated that the Kremlin would crack down before it gave independence to the Baltic peoples.

Baltic nationalists admitted the possibility of the Kremlin's decision to strike back but, convinced of the justice of their cause, they were determined to press on. They were inspired by the cascading events in Poland, where there was an epochal shift in political power. For the first time, a Communist regime was peacefully ousted there. Both Poland and the Baltic states had been the victims of other peoples for centuries. During the nineteenth century, the Polish people did not even have a territorial base, but the consciousness of Polish nationalism persisted. Poland was driving to recover its lost sovereignty under the leadership of the Solidarity movement, which only a few years earlier had been under official ban.

The conflict between centralized nationalism and the ethnic nationalisms throughout the Soviet Union has not been resolved at the present writing. Whether or not the Kremlin will use its military strength to stem the outburst remains to be seen. That was the choice of the hard-liners in Communist China, when they met the huge demonstrations for democracy by students in Tiananmen Square in Beijing with a massacre that sickened the world. The Chinese masters then denied that a single student had been harmed.

National Confrontation

The national confrontations throughout the Soviet Union are not unique in contemporary society. Throughout the world there are similar clashes between centralized nationalisms and mini-nationalisms, which hew to the cause of self-determination and independence. The new states of Africa recapitulate the experiences of the older national states and dedicate themselves to the sacredness of flag and anthem. Peoples everywhere with different languages and religions are bound together in artificially created national states, but they still yield to the demands of their own national consciousness. The force of nationalism remains powerful at both the central and local levels and the differences between them are seldom resolved. Many scholars, although they are averse to the dangers of prophecy, believe that these confrontations will continue into the twenty-first century. Nationalism remains one of the most powerful of all human emotions.

The twentieth century has seen two bloody world wars, in the origins of which nationalism played a most important role. Millions of lives have been sacrificed in the clash of nationalisms and the property damage has been enormous. Further gigantic wars of this kind have been discouraged in the atomic age, where the possibility of mutual destruction would be present and where it becomes decidedly inconvenient to settle accounts by use of atomic power. Yet, nationalism remains as one of the most powerful factors in life and the conflicts generated by it remain extremely difficult to resolve. It is not a pleasant situation. It is still the most powerful sentiment in the contemporary world. It remains a tough fact of life, fed by deep roots in man's need to hold on to the values he deems good.

Emergence of Modern Nationalism

Far from being a new and distinctive phenomenon, modern nationalism is a revival and amalgamation of older trends. It existed in the form of tribalism among primitive peoples. Later, the sense of tribal union was submerged for the most part in metropolitanism, the attachment to a city-state or cultural center, or localism, loyalty to village or region, akin to modern ruralism. Ancient peoples, such as the Athenians or Spartans gave their allegiance to the city-state. Rome developed into a huge empire, which forced the loyalty of peoples throughout Europe.

Although the Middle Ages saw the disintegrative factors of feudalism and manoralism, elements of nationalism persisted among peoples with similar languages, customs, and traditions. Feudal lords gave their allegiance to kings, not countries, but they retained a kind of sentiment which made them different from other peoples. Yet, the sort of group cohesion they favored was more akin to localism than the tenor of modern nationalism. Nationalism began to take on its modern form in the fifteenth, sixteenth, and seventeenth centuries with the formation of the European national states. In the medieval era, one did not consider himself primarily a Frenchman, German, or Briton, but he was, on the contrary, a Catholic Christian with his sense of loyalty reserved for Rome. The sense of nationalism was crystallized as the modern nation-state emerged, when loyalty to country became the dominant political concern of Europeans. The urge was there but the formation was modern.

The formation of the national state, indicated by the break of Henry VIII from Rome, was a basic factor that marked the end of the Middle Ages and the beginning of modern times. In this new historical process, the Roman Catholic Church lost its dominant position in the governing structure of Europe and was succeeded by a combination of units called nation-states. From the political point of view, the transformation saw a change from kinship to a new kind of governmental structure. Economically, the process was conterminous with the Commercial Revolution. Socially, the development ran parallel with the surge to prominence of the bourgeoisie, or middle class. From the point of view of religion, the older international religious society changed dramatically into a secular society.

Accompanying the rise of the national states were the great events of the Renaissance and the Reformation. Though the movement was inchoate, it went in a common direction. Europeans still maintained their regard for town, village, or region, but they gradually moved in a larger direction. There was nothing natural, preordained, or inevitable about the movement to nationhood. It just happened that way. Actually, it was accidental and unplanned. The emergence of modern nationalism was an artificial process. There is no scientific evidence to show that the sort of cleavages that distinguished nationalism are normal or even desirable.

Unfortunately, the rise of modern nationalism was accompanied by such tragic implications as confrontations, barbarities, and war. Nationalism has always been associated with warfare and the warrior tradition. The struggle was always the insider against the outsider, against the foreigner, against those who spoke different languages and had disparate traditions and an alien culture. Adherence was to territory, family, flag, and anthem. Those who defended the community against the outside took on the status of heroes, as defenders of what was sacred in life. Those who neglected the community or turned their services over to other peoples were condemned as traitors and subjected to the scorn of their fellow-citizens. Those who "belonged" to the union formed the heart of nationalism. They were expected to give it all their loyalty and strength. The individual hewed closely to his own family and was expected to see his larger family in the existence of the national state. To the present day, this sense of loyalty to the larger community was elevated by a strong belief in the rightness of nationalism. Through custom and training this view was transformed into the claim: "My country, right or wrong!"

Nationalism and the English Experience

By the early seventeenth century, those elements which together form the marrow of nationalism were already present in England. The roots of nationalism were already embedded in the English national character. The sense of national pride was strong. Shakespeare recognized the spirit. In *Henry V*, the King speaks to "you good yeomen, whose limbs were made in England," and urged the cry "God for Harry! England! and St. George!"

On the Continent, feudalism had taken on a disintegrated form but in England it was consolidated and hence more conducive to the formation of a national state. From Chaucer and Shakespeare a common language was molded, a literature appeared; common traditions and a knowledge of a common history, as well as common heroes, helped the consolidating process. The Reformation in England merged into a national issue. All these drives culminated eventually into the formation of a strong sense of national consciousness and the appearance of a full-blown English nationalism.

The religious situation contributed mightily to the formation of English nationalism as well as its extension throughout Europe. When Henry VIII broke with Rome, he established what amounted to a national church. This new religious movement was cast in a revolutionary mold. It was an intensely practical religion, independent, interested in whatever took place on English soil. It was concerned with government, banking, social welfare. The Bible-reading Englishman took pride in his social activism: he believed implicitly that his stand against tyranny had divine sanction. There was undoubtedly a drift toward secularism, which modern nationalism stimulated throughout the world.

From its beginnings, English nationalism was imbued with a spirit of liberty. In its modern form it came to a country already territorially unified, to a nation whose classes were distinguished by a strong patriotism that had withstood even the ravages of revolution. This special concept within the framework of historic liberties was studied and emulated throughout the world. English institutions of law and justice were respected everywhere.

Behind English nationalism was a long tradition of love for the land and for the nation. In the early eighteenth century, Henry St. John Bolingbroke, statesman and political philosopher, wrote of his secret pride in being a Briton. He added to his humanitarian nationalism a streak of expansionism by collaborating on the anthem: "Rule Britannia, rule the waves; Britons never shall be slaves." In the late eighteenth century Edmund Burke (q.v.), statesman and political writer, defended traditional English nationalism; he saw the strongest instinct, both natural and moral, that exists in man, as love of country. In 1830 Jeremy Bentham, philosopher and jurist, called for a properly directed liberal nationalism that would function in the family of nations.

Battered by civil strife in conflict between king and Parliament, the English, nevertheless, tended to become even more nationalistic. Both sides—royal England and Puritan England—were thoroughly saturated with the sentiment of national pride. The English national character was shaped largely by John Locke, philosopher and rationalist. In his *Two Treatises of Government* (1690) he defended the right of ultimate sovereignty in the people. That same year he issued his first of several *Letters of Toleration* calling for religious liberty. His work was vital in shaping the character of English nationalism.

Liberal nationalism, based on the security of the process of law, emerged in the English Revolution of 1688. Here was the basis for the kind of nationalism Englishmen preferred. It was destined to carry on for several centuries. Its message was extended to many other countries. It is noteworthy that English liberal nationalism emerged at the time of an essentially religious revolution. English Puritans occupied a role similar to that of the Jacobins in the French Revolution. There was a temporary halt in the Restoration, but the Puritan concept managed to prevail.

The English retained the special character of their nationalism, namely the liberal thrust and the close relationship to the religious matrix from which it rose. In the words of Hans Kohn: "It never made the complete integration of the individual with the nation the sin of nationalism: it always put a great emphasis upon the individual and the human community beyond all national division." Indeed, the British engaged in power politics. But along with it went the promise of liberty and justice under law, which they regarded as their special contribution to civilization.

The French Revolution and Nationalism

The ten years from 1789 to 1799, the era of the French Revolution, truly marked one of the great turning points in history. Dynamic forces were unleashed in France, forces which created a new state out of an outmoded, creaking structure. Indeed, there are historians who claim that the French Revolution really brought the beginning of the modern era, because only then was the system of feudalism overthrown.

Change was the keynote. It covered the entire spectrum of life in

France. Politically, the French Revolution meant the coming of age of modern nationalism. The old monarchy was abolished and a new state was placed on a national foundation. From the religious point of view, the Roman Catholic Church lost its powerful position in French society and was forced to serve national ends. Socially, the privileges of aristocracy and the clergy were abolished, while the middle class, the bourgeoisie, won its way to a dominant position in the power structure. There would be a new economic world with the concomitant First Industrial Revolution.

These great historical changes took place in a milieu of revolutionary fervor. Frenchmen intended to change the world and they did. They surged ahead to the *Marseillaise* and they gave the world a new watchword: "Liberty, Equality, Fraternity." From the dramatic storming of the Bastille in 1789 to the overuse of the guillotine culminating in the execution of Robespierre in 1794, events in revolutionary France exploded in a torrent of emotion. The effects would be European-wide as well as world-wide.

Behind the fireworks of the French Revolution was an extraordinary intellectual trend. The way for activism was prepared during the preceding Enlightenment, the Age of Reason, whose champions projected a new way of life. French *philosophes* prepared the way for the explosions at the barricades. Dissatisfied with the Old Regime, with their environment and society, they denounced the stratified system of privileges. They called for a greater sense of justice and toleration. They denounced the medieval, feudal, and manorial structures and called for a new social attitude. They turned from the one-time powerful medieval church and recommended a secular society. Aristocrats toyed with the new ideas in elaborately formalized salon sessions. The demand for reform was easily translated into understandable language for the common man, who rushed to the barricades and demanded the formation of a new society.

Three *philosophes* presented the essence of the demanded reforms—Montesquieu on the law, Rousseau on the socio-political structure, and Voltaire on the Church. Revolutionary France turned with delight to these new ideas—and the nationalism that went along with them.

In 1748 Charles-Louis de Secondat Montesquieu, after fourteen years of preparation, published his *L'Esprit des lois (The Spirit of the Laws)*. In this extraordinary work he presented an analysis of the relationships between political and social structures, religion, and economics. He noted the close connection between love of country and the republican form of government. "In republics," he wrote, "education ought to inspire a sentiment, which is noble but hard to maintain—namely, that disregard of one's own interest whence arises the love of one's country." Montesquieu's work won him great national and global fame.

Similarly, Jean-Jacques Rousseau, philosopher and political theorist, wrote novels and treatises that inspired the leaders of the French Revolution. He rejected aristocracy in favor of democracy as the most favored core of the nation. He urged every citizen to love his country. The people must be conscious of their national unity. He saw love of country as peculiar to democracies, for in democracy alone the government is entrusted to private citizens. "Now a government is like everything else: to preserve it we must love it."

Voltaire (real name François-Marie Arouet), crusader against tyranny and bigotry, famous for his wit and critical capacity, spoke strongly against what he called the "superstition" of the Church and papacy. He directed his harshest criticism against religion and sought to ridicule it out of existence. Voltaire's works became the inspiration for the anti-clerical movement in France. He did much to separate church and state in France and championed the nationalism that went along with it.

The big three of the French Enlightenment and others who held similar views contributed much to the rising sense of French national consciousness, the revolutionaries translated their ideas into the activism of the barricades and the guillotine. The Jacobins, with their advocacy of individualism and democracy, left a strong imprint on French nationalism.

The citizens of the French Revolution were so overcome by their new democratic nationalism that they decided to bring its glories to the rest of Europe. They had a new army, the *levée en masse*, which would defend the revolution against the despised *émigrés*. In December 1792 the National Convention expressed it in a decree. The revolutionaries would invade neighboring states and bring them the blessings of Liberty, Equality, and Fraternity. "The French nation . . . will not lay down its arms until after the establishment of the sovereignty and independence of the people whose territory the troops of the [French] Republic shall have entered and until the people shall have adopted the principles of equality and founded a free and democratic society."

Napoleon: Traveling Salesman of Nationalism

French citizens had precise ideals, but the Revolution itself was chaotic. France was in great trouble as the revolutionaries turned on one another and escorted leaders to the guillotine. More and more

Frenchmen began to feel that they needed a strong man who could maintain the achievements of the barricades and at the same time stabilize the country and win law and order. They found their man in a young Corsican who saw himself as a political and military genius, a wizard of diplomacy, and masterful statesmen. He was absolutely sure of his great destiny. He was driven by ambition, for himself, for his family, and for France—in that order. Napoleon rose to power, harnessed the dynamic forces of the Revolution, gave France a decade of glory, and then suffered the tortures of a humiliating exile.

Not until the shadow of Adolf Hitler darkened the world was a man so roundly hated as Napoleon. An ode by Southey (1810) revealed the contempt held for him by his enemies:

> Who counsels peace, when Vengeance like a flood,
> Rolls on, no longer now to be repressed:
> When innocent blood
> From the four corners of the world cries out
> For justice upon one accursed head?

After pushing his way to supreme power in France, Napoleon regarded himself as the logical successor of the enlightened monarchs. However, he departed from the role when he saw himself as the master, not the servant, of the state. He did not understand the meaning of liberty nor the sense of national consciousness that accompanied the Revolution. He would have been astonished had he been told that he would be the catalytic agent responsible for planting the seeds of nationalism throughout Europe. His main interest was conquest for the glory of his own name, not in disseminating a new historical force for the benefit of other peoples. He took the revolutionary nationalism, which had already been weakened under the Directory, infused strength into it under the Consulate, and began the business of seeking to sponsor "new nations" under his will.

Other Europeans—Italians, Spaniards, Prussians, Russians, were not inclined to bend to Napoleon's will. For them the conqueror was an outsider, who was seeking to subjugate them for the glory of France. Wherever Napoleon led his armies, he left the imprint of his iron heel, but he also stimulated the rise of a hostile nationalism in his wake. Europeans throughout Europe came to the defense of their own rulers and resisted what they called "a revolution gone crazy" in the hands of a Corsican adventurer. Frenchmen were impressed by the glory of Napoleon's conquests; others reacted strongly against what they regarded as the depredations of a power-mad dictator.

Napoleonic power resulted in the intensification of nationalism as a historical movement of the nineteenth century.

Until he died in exile at St. Helena, Napoleon remained unaware of his decisive role in the spread of nationalism. What he really wanted to do, he explained, was to bind the nations in a United States of Europe. He would incorporate thirty million Frenchmen, fifteen million Spanish, fifteen million Italians, and thirty million Germans into one nation. "That," he said, "would have been a noble thing." What he did not add was his intention of placing the whole of Europe under his own control, as well as that of his family and loyal adherents. He thought himself worthy of this glory, of "the grand, magnificent spectacle," and of "the perspective of power, greatness, happiness, and prosperity." Others did not. It never occurred to Nepoleon that non-Frenchmen might prefer their own way of life to the unsure blessings heaped upon them by the contemplated imperial presidency of a United States of Europe. Instead of unifying Europeans under his banner, the Corsican, without actually desiring the consequences, extended the force of nationalism into a dominant position in nineteenth-century in Europe. From there it spread its tentacles throughout the world.

Research on Nationalism

The importance of nationalism is so great in the contemporary world that much more scholarly research is indicated to help explain the ramifications of a complex historical phenomenon. There are no simple formulas accepted by all scholars. There are differences of opinion on the inconsistencies and contradictions of nationalism. Researchers in many disciplines are involved—historians, political scientists, sociologists, psychologists, and psychoanalysts. All approach the study from the viewpoint of their own specialities, which is to be expected. But more and more knowledge about the nature of this powerful historical force remains an absolute necessity.

Closer cohesion between the varied scholars of nationalism would do much to clarify the meaning, characteristics, and development of nationalism. Because of the psychological roots of nationalism, psychologists should be urged to devote more attention to it. Sociologists, too, with their interest in the we-group, could do much to help explain the meaning of nationalism. Analysis of nationalism is by no means the exclusive property of the historian, who is concerned primarily with its development. It is an interdisciplinary task and an important one.

ENCYCLOPEDIA
OF
NATIONALISM

A

A-B-C PARADOX.   An incongruity in nationalism proposed by the political scientist Hans J. Morgenthau (q.v.). Morgenthau saw a self-contradiction in the nature of nationalism: nation B invokes the principles of nationalism against nation A, yet denies them to nation C, in each case for the sake of its own survival. It is an unresolved paradox.

Morgenthau regarded nationalism and the internationalism of Marxism as the last great original contributions of the West to political thought and actions. Nationalism, in his view, sought two freedoms—collective, or freedom of a nation from domination by other nations, and individual—freedom of the individual to join the nation of his choice. But instead of advancing the common good of peoples, nationalism became a threat to civilization, a scourge of political anarchy, and a mockery of political morality. It was assumed that the triumph of nationalism would bring peace, order, and justice. Instead, Morgenthau explains, what happened was that the oppressors and the oppressed merely changed roles:

> There are no inherent limits to the application of the principles of nationalism. If the peoples of Bulgaria, Greece, and Serbia could invoke these principles against Turkey, why could not the people of Macedonia invoke them against Bulgaria, Greece, and Serbia? . . . Thus yesterday's oppressed cannot help becoming the oppressors of today because they are afraid lest they be again oppressed tomorrow. Hence, the process of national liberation must stop at some point, and that point is determined not by the logic of nationalism, but by the configuration of interest and power between the rulers and the ruled and between competing nations.

For Morgenthau this was the practice of nation B invoking the principles of nationalism against nation A and then denying them to C. Added to this paradoxical development was that the process became even more involved because of the difficulty of applying it consistently to mixed populations. The whole issue of nationalism thus became confused by minority problems. There were clashes between the ideas of collective and individual freedoms: the individual's rights to property and the pursuit of happiness turned out to be incompatible with the right to choose his own government according to his preference as a minority member. He could not enjoy both rights simultaneously: he had to sacrifice one or the other.

According to Morgenthau, fragmentation of nations was prevented from degenerating into anarchy by political power that halted the process at a convenient point. There are hundreds of regional areas throughout Europe and the world, each with distinctive cultural qualities. But instead of thousands of nations there are relatively few, composed of diverse cultural groups herded around fixed political centers. Those nations become successful when they have absorbed diverse minority groups within their borders, even though each minority believed it deserved national self-determination (q.v.). National disintegration might be allowed up to a certain point, but the process was always halted just short of chaos.

Morgenthau maintained that the very existence of the national state is paradoxically a denial of nationalism to others. It is an artificial situation when national states which often include particularistic cultural groups, each demanding its own right to a separate existence, are denied their national identity. The world is endangered by the A-B-C paradox when modern national states become adept in the task of denying to minor nationalities that very same nationalism which they have in the past demanded for themselves.

Bibliography: Hans J. Morgenthau, "The Paradoxes of Nationalism," *Yale Review*, 46, No. 4 (June, 1957), 481–488.

ACTION FRANÇAISE. The principal nationalist and reactionary movement in France during the first half of the twentieth century. Originating in 1899, the strongly nationalist, right-wing anti-Republican *Action Française* reflected the views of the anti-Dreyfusards in the conflict engendered by that famous case. Its nationalism was clothed with anti-parliamentarianism and anti-Semitism. Led by author Leon Daudet (q.v.) and publicist Charles Maurras (q.v.), the movement supported the doctrine of integral nationalism. (*See* **HAYES' CLASSIFICATION.**) It favored the restoration of the French monarchy, which it saw as the only institution capable of unifying French society torn by strife.

Leaders of the *Action Française* advocated provincial autonomy, a corporate state, and a privileged position for the Roman Catholic Church. In 1940, after the defeat of France by Nazi Germany, the *Action Française* supported the pro-Nazi government of Gen. Henri Pétain. Because of its association with the collaborationist Vichy government, the movement was suppressed by the de Gaulle administration after the liberation of France in 1944.

The *Action Française*, with its advocacy of extreme nationalism, served as a symbol, guide, and role model for similar movements in other countries of Fascist persuasion.

Bibliography: André Mirambil, *Le comédie du nationalisme intégral* (Paris, 1947); Edward R. Tannenbaum, *The Action Française* (New York, 1962); Eugen Weber, *Action Française: Royalism and Reaction in Twentieth Century France* (Stanford, Cal., 1962); Samuel S. Osgood, *French Royalism Since 1870* (The Hague, 1970).

ACTON, JOHN EMERICH EDWARD DALBERG (1834– 1902). Historian, moralist, and philosopher, Acton was Regius Professor of Modern History at Cambridge University, original editor of the *Cambridge Modern History*, and co-founder of the *English Historical Review*. In 1862, as editor of the *Home and Foreign Review*, he wrote a famous essay on nationality. A state, he wrote, which identifies itself with any single object, either one class or a nationality, may well become absolutistic. However, in a multinational state, a nationality could become both a limit to the excessive power of the state as well as a bulwark of self-government. A nationality inside a multinational state, he believed, when the state was based on freedom, could counteract the worst effects of absolutism.

To Lord Acton, the theory of nationality was more absurd and criminal than the theory of socialism. But he admitted that it has an important mission in the world and marks the final conflict and end of two forces that he saw as the worst enemies of civil freedom—the absolute monarchy and the revolution. (*See also* **NATIONALITY.**)

Bibliography: John Emerich Edward Dalberg Acton, *The History of Freedom and Other Essays*, ed. by J.N. Figgis and R.V. Laurence (London, 1922); David Mathew, *Lord Acton and His Times* (London, 1968); John Emerich Edward Dalberg Acton, *Selected Writings of Lord Acton* (Indianapolis, Ind., 1985).

AFRICAN NATIONALISM. The 1950s saw a new phenomenon: the entrance of Africa, the last continent, into the age of nationalism as an active partner in world history. The peoples of Africa did not wish any longer to be objects of history made by others, and began to feel themselves as active agents of their own history. In sub-Saharan Africa, ancient and primitive tribal societies were transformed. African natives learned about nationalism from their colonial masters.

The formative years of African nationalism were in the two decades between World War I and World War II. Actually, there was little to be seen on the surface, but pressures for African emancipation and the introduction of nationalism built up speedily at the end of World War II. The humiliating defeats of the white man at the hands of Japan had an extraordinary effect on colonial nationalism. The blacks of Africa began to see that their white masters were not the gods they were supposed to be. The psychological effect on the African was powerful. He began to see what he had called his "betters" suffer one defeat after another. The veil between him and the white man began to disappear. The white man's magic spell began to wear off. Ndabaningi Sithole expressed this view of the new African:

> The emergent African nationalism, in many ways, represents the degree to which the white man's magic spell, which at the beginning of the nineteenth century had been cast on the African, is wearing off. As long as this myth was thick and impenetrable, the African adjusted himself as well as he could to what he thought were gods, though gods that ate corn. As long as the white man was able to hold up his pretensions to the African as real, the African was scared, and never challenged the white man as his national ruler. Alas, the externals have had their day, and reality has taken its place; but few white people in Africa realize this extremely important change. Most of them still have the picture of the African who worships the white man as god, and they refuse to face the fact that Time and Eternity are beckoning to them to come down from their ivory towers and dwell among their fellow-creatures for their own sake and for that of their fellow-creatures.

Once the process of nationalism began in the great continent, it proceeded with astonishing speed. The maturation of nationalism took place as one newly independent state after another emerged, as the colonial powers, one after another, began to leave Africa. New African leaders, such as Kwame Nkrumah (q.v.) in Ghana, Jomo Kenyatta (q.v.) Tom Mboya in Kenya, and Sékou Touré in Guinea had been educated in Europe and had learned the basics of nationalism. They now returned home to demand national emancipation. At first, they were opposed by native tribalism (q.v.), itself a form of nationalism, but in the long run, they applied Western forms of nationalism to their own African homelands.

There were savage battles throughout Africa as the new nationalism emerged. Few of the new national states in Africa were established on linguistic or ethnic lines: they simply retained the old colonial boundaries set up by the parent imperial powers. The result was often chaos, but the process of nationalization, nevertheless, continued on.

For the natives of Africa, the emergence of the new nationalism meant a remarkable and, at times, frustrating change. The modernization of African tribal society meant a break with ancient and restrictive traditions. There followed a new individualism, much greater equality, and social mobility. There were differences of nationalism among various African peoples, according to their social and cultural interests, but essentially nationalism had come to stay. The state of mind that distinguished nationalism is the same everywhere, in Europe, Asia, Latin America, and Africa. The basic quality is that a people no longer wishes to be the object of history made by others, but insist that they, themselves, must make their own history. The call of nationalism is explicit: those affected by it are not willing to accept the thesis that their own traditions cannot be changed.

The peoples of Europe went through long struggles before they became integrated nations. It is to be expected that a similar process will take place in Africa as the change from traditional tribal to modern national society is implemented. Thus far, the transition in Africa has been relatively smooth. It has been called the last stage of the revolutionary transformation of world society in the long drive to the unity of mankind.

The unity of all Africans in a Pan-Africanism (q.v.) seems to be far off and cannot be expected in the forseeable future. There is an extraordinary variety in traditions, customs, religion, and language in sub-Saharan Africa, and it will take time for nationalism to overcome these differences. All efforts to federate the new African nations have failed. Meanwhile, African nationalism continues to function as the new states transform their ancient tribal societies in Africa and enter world society as viable national entities.

Bibliography: T. Walter Wallbank, *Contemporary Africa* (Princeton, N.J., 1956); Ndabaningi Sithole, *African Nationalism* (New York, 1960); Rupert Emerson, *From Empire to Nation: The Rise of Self-Assertion in Asian and African Peoples* (Cambridge, Mass., 1960); James Coleman, *Nigeria: Background to Nationalism* (Berkeley, Cal., 1965); Robert I. Rotberg and Ali A. Mazrui (eds.), *Protest and Power in Black Africa* (New York, 1970); Anthony D. Smith, *State and Nation in the Third World* (New York, 1983).

AL-FATAH. Palestinian guerrilla unit working for the independence of the Palestinian people. The name *Al-Fatah* is an acronym of the organization's full title: *Harakat al Tahir al-Falaston*, Arabic for "movement for the Liberation of Palestine." The initials HFT form the Arabic word for "death." The reversed initials FTH spell *Fath*, Arabic for "conquest." *Al-Fatah* was originally one of many similar organizations, but it soon became known for its fierce militancy. It had allegiance to no one country, but received attention from all. In recent years it has functioned as an extremist group of the Palestine Liberation Organization led by Abu Nital, who gained global attention by his acts of terror. (*See also* **PALESTINE LIBERATION ORGANIZATION.**)

ALFIERI, VITTORIO (1749–1803). Italian dramatist, precursor of the *Risorgimento* (Resurrection), patriot, and nationalist. Alfieri believed firmly that leadership in civilization belonged to the Italians, not to the French. Living in France at the time of the French Revolution, he hailed the taking of the Bastille with a triumphant ode. But he later turned on the French, returned to Italy, and spent the rest of his life in Florence. In 1879 he published his *Missogallo*, a collection of violent polemics in prose and verse in which he expressed his hatred of all things French. His fiery work represented a change from eighteenth-century Italian humanitarianism to what was later to become the Italian version of xenophobic nationalism. (q.v.).

Alfieri damned the French as "haughty insects":

> I, though born in the dullest winter of
> Italy,
> Italy, torn asunder and ignorant of arms,
> Yet did I swear hatred for the French. . . .
> In the meantime, may the putridity
> of these haughty insects be revealed,
> This putridity which extols virtue and
> stifles it in all its manifestations.

Bibliography: Gaudence Megaro, *Vittorio Alfieri: Forerunner of Italian Nationalism* (New York, 1930).

ALSATIAN NATIONALISM. Added to Breton, Basque, and Corsican separatisms, the centralized French state is faced with an Alsatian autonomous movement. Alsace and Lorraine, the provinces on the border between France and Germany, have been in contention between the two major countries for a thousand years. Alsace, occupied by the Romans in the first century B.C., became a Frankish duchy in the fifth century. From the tenth to the seventeenth century it was a part of the Holy Roman Empire. Full French control came in the early eighteenth century during the final days of Louis XIV.

During the eighteenth century the French royal house gave a measure of autonomy to the Alsatians, thereby setting a precedent for Alsatian particularism. (*See* **PARTICULARISM.**) The Alsatian people customarily spoke two languages—French and German; the upper classes preferring mellifluous French, the lower classes the guttural German. In the critical days of the French Revolution the role of Alsace as a separate province was ended. It was then incorporated into France.

With the Treaty of Frankfurt ending the Franco-Prussian War in 1871, Alsace and the contiguous province Lorraine were made a part of Otto von Bismarck's (q.v.) Second German Empire. Even though Alsatians spoke German, they felt themselves to be French and protested loudly against what they called the "mutilation" of their country. They resented the ensuing process of Germanization; they added their voices to French calls for *revanche*—revenge for the humiliation of 1870–1871.

By the Treaty of Versailles in 1919, Alsace-Lorraine was returned to France. Immediately, Germanization was succeeded by Frenchification. Paris would allow no "foreign tongues"—Basque, Breton, Corsican, or German. Along with the course of Frenchification came the emergence of an Alsatian home-rule movement in the 1920s. Alsatians would not go so far as to demand independence, but they did choose the alternative of more autonomy inside the French Republic. They were also motivated by religion: they opposed the anti-clerical measures adopted by the *Cartel des Gauches,* the leftist post-World War I French government. Moderate Alsatians urged the formation of a federal state in which they would have their own special rights and privileges. To Frenchmen, already emotionally attached to their own nationalism distinguished by pride in the glories of France, even this kind of appeal was sullied by what they called "a blind for German fostered sedition."

Germanization began all over again when Hitler and his Third Reich re-annexed Alsace. More than half a million resentful Alsatians left their homes and took refuge in French cities and towns to avoid the deadly embrace of the Nazi dictator. After Hitler's suicide in 1945, successive French governments were careful to modify the harsh prewar measures against Alsatians in the older Frenchification process. The new attitude led to withdrawal of the earlier anti-clerical steps taken against the strongly Catholic province.

The result of the new French treatment of Alsatians was dramatic. Alsatian separatism was not completely eliminated, but it was muted and no longer formed a threat to French centralism. Alsatian separatists did not resort to terror, to bombs and bullets to promote their cause, as did Basques and Corsicans. For most Alsatians, the Nazi era had a decidedly sobering effect. They would settle for a satisfactory place in the French democracy. Like the Welsh and Scots in the United Kingdom, they had some reservations about the extent of centralization and their unsatisfactory place in the national economy, but they believed moderate autonomy was far preferable to the violence of terrorism.

Bibliography: D.W. Brogan, *The Development of Modern France, 1870–1939* (New York, 1966); Arnold Martin, *The Co-ordination of Regional Plans for Alsace, the Rhineland-Palatinate, Baden, and Northwest Switzerland* (Strasbourg, 1977); Jean-Claude Streicher, *Impossible histoire des idées autonomiste* (Paris, 1982).

AMERICAN NATIONALISM. From its very beginnings, American nationalism took on a different form from that on the European continent. In Europe, nationalism was based partly on common descent and common religion, as well as the territorial imperative. (*See* **TERRITORIAL IMPERATIVE.**) But neither biology nor religion was paramount in the formation of American nationalism. Most important in the development of nationalism in the New World was a process of amalgamation of peoples of different backgrounds and cultural characteristics.

The new American nation was born in the late eighteenth-century Enlightenment, the Age of Reason, which produced in Europe such minds as Locke, Rousseau, Montesquieu, Hobbes, and Malthus. The ideas of liberty, equality, and fraternity, constitutionalism, and parliamentarianism crossed the Atlantic and influenced the Founding Fathers in their creation of a new nation. Those immigrants who came to the New World had little use for medieval, feudal, manorial, or ecclesiastical strictures. For them the key to a decent life lay always in the idea of individual liberty—the inalienable right of every individual to life, liberty, and the pursuit of happiness.

From the time of the early New England settlers and the Catholic immigrants in Maryland, to the Vietnam boat people, the United States has been the haven for peoples from many different countries. All formed a kind of "Melting Pot" of those of varying backgrounds, fused into a new nation proud of its multiple heritages. For the poorer classes of Europe burdened by political and religious limitations, this was, indeed, the Promised Land. Infused with a spirit of individualism, buoyed by the hope that their children would not be subjected to the dreary life they had led in Europe, they entered enthusiastically into the rough frontier life. They acted unconsciously in the sense of the simple, natural man envisioned by Rousseau. They abolished monarchy and aristocracy, separated Church and State, and forged a union based on liberty. In the process a nationalism, which reflected their own interests and desires, emerged.

These early molders of a nation were blessed with great leaders— from Washington to Jefferson to John Adams, Hamilton, and Franklin. All were enlightened *philosophes*, who called for a clean break from the entanglements of European politics. They created an extraordinary Constitution, which continued from then on to be the fulcrum of American life. They were optimistic rationalists who projected the vision of a great future for the nation-in-being. John Adams, in a letter to Thomas Jefferson sent in 1813, expressed this glowing sense of optimism: "Our sure, virtuous, public-spirited republic will last forever, govern the globe, and introduce the perfection of man."

Throughout their history, Americans revealed an affinity for both patriotism (love of country, *patria*) and nationalism (independence and unity of the nation, *natio*). (*See* **PATRIOTISM.**) From the days of the American Revolution to the present Atomic Age, Americans made clear their love of country and their willingness to defend its independence. From the many thousands of expressions of such sentiments, only a few examples suffice to indicate this feeling in the early days of the Republic:

In 1758. Nathaniel Ames of Boston, in his popular almanac, *Astronomical Diary*, published a glowing salute to the glorious future America: "As the celestial light of the Gospel, was directed here by the finger of GOD, it will, doubtless finally, drive the long Night of Heathenish Darkness from America."

In 1774. Patrick Henry exclaimed impulsively to the Continental Congress: "The distinction between Virginians, Pennsylvanians, New Yorkers, and New Englanders, are no more. I am not a Virginian, but an American."

In 1778. On his Fourth of July oration on the second anniversary of the American Declaration of Independence, David Ramsay of South Carolina glorified the qualities and destiny of America in terms that were unmistakenly nationalistic: "We have laid the foundations of a new Empire, which promises to enlarge itself into vast dimensions, and to give happiness to a great continent. It is now our turn to figure on the face of the earth and in the annals of the world."

Hector St. John Crèvecoeur, born in France, came to the United States and settled on a farm in New York State. His book of impressions, *Letters from an American Farmer*, achieved great popularity. He saw the American environment changing the European immigrant from peasant to freeholder. In 1782, he published his "What is an American?"—which reflected the essence of the new American nationalism:

What attachment can a poor European have for a country where he had nothing? The knowledge of the language, the love of few kindred as poor as himself, were the cords that tied him: his country is now that which gives him land, bread, protection, and consequence: *Ubi panis ibi patria* [where one earns his bread, there is his country] is the motto of all emigrants.

What, then, is the American, this new man? He is either an European, or the descendant of an European, hence that strange mixture of blood, which you will find in no other country. I could point out to you a family whose grandfather was an Englishman, whose wife was Dutch, whose son married a French woman, and whose present four sons have now four wives of different nations. *He* is an American, who leaving behind him all his ancient prejudices and manners, receives new ones from the new mode of life he has embraced, the new government he obeys, and the new rank he holds. He becomes an American by being received in the broad lap of our great *Alma Mater*.

Here individuals of all nations are melted into a new race of men, whose labours and posterity will one day cause great changes in the world. Americans are western pilgrims, who are carrying along with them that great mass of arts, sciences, vigour, and industry which began long ago in the east; they will finish the great circle.

The Americans were once scattered all over Europe; here they are incorporated into one of the finest systems of population which has ever appeared, and which will hereafter become distinct by the power of the different climates they inhabit. . . .

The American is a new man, who acts upon new principles; he must therefore entertain new ideas, and form new opinions. From involuntary idleness, servile dependence, penury, and useless labour, he has passed to toils of a very different nature, rewarded by ample subsistence,—

This is an American.

Consciousness of nationalism was strengthened by the War of 1812 against Britain. This was followed by the era of Western expansion. The problem of maintaining a national unit became critical. Would there be one American state or many? Would there be a unified nation or disintegration into many states? The response, sealed in blood, came with the tragic Civil War between the industrial North and the agricultural South. The South was defeated by force of arms as well as by its persistence in holding on to the outmoded vestiges of feudalism. Sectional differences vanished, and a unified national state was retained based on individual liberty and tolerance. After 1865 the unity of the nation was never again threatened.

At mid-nineteenth century, American nationalism took on a liberal tinge. It was best expressed by Carl Schurz, soldier, statesman, and diplomat, who had emigrated from Germany after the unsuccessful Revolution of 1848. In speech after speech, he spoke of "True Americanism," and of "The Great Empire of Liberty." He used lyrical terms: "This nation will not be false to her great destiny. . . . In every pulsation of the popular heart, in every breeze, there is victory. . . . There stands the National Will, undisturbed, in monumental repose. For the Great Empire of Liberty, forward!"

Schurz's liberal nationalism was supported by many Americans, but toward the end of the nineteenth century other American nationalists turned to a more integral view ("My country, right or wrong!"). The idea of Manifest Destiny (q.v.) began to take hold on many American nationalists. In some cases nationalism was combined with biological racialism. In 1885 Josiah Strong, a Congregationalist minister, called it the historical mission of the Anglo-Saxon "race" to bear the ideals of civil liberty and spiritual Christianity to peoples in the remote areas of the world. In 1900, American naval officer and historian Admiral Alfred Thayer Mahan wrote a series of books in which he urged Americans to "look outward" and understand that they were destined for expansion in Asia as reasonable for "national progress." In that same year Albert J. Beveridge, Senator from Indiana, informed the world that the United States had rescued the Filipinos from "a savage and bloody rule," and insisted that it was plain that they preferred "the just, humane, and civilizing government of the United States" to that of Spain. God, he said, had selected the American people as "His chosen nation to lead in the regeneration of the world."

This kind of nationalism was advocated by President Theodore Roosevelt in what he called the "New Nationalism." (*See* **ROOSEVELT, THEODORE.**) In 1932, publisher William Randolph Hearst assured the American people that "today the most envied honor in the world is to be an American citizen."

Thus, American nationalism took two forms. One retained its emphasis upon the Melting Pot and the egalitarian formula. This liberal nationalism presented the best of humane, pluralistic concepts, combining love of country and the dignity of the human individual. On the other side was the xenophobic, expansionist nationalism stressing integral nationalism and calling for force to extend the American dream to other peoples in the world.

Bibliography: Henry Steele Commager, *The American Mind* (New Haven, Conn., 1950); Hans Kohn, *American Nationalism* (New York, 1957); Michael McGiffert (ed.), *The Character of Americans* (Homewood, Ill., 1964); Hans Kohn and Daniel Walden, *Readings in American Nationalism* (New York, 1970); Rebecca Grumer, *American Nationalism, 1783–1830 (New York, 1970);* Richard W. Van Alstyne, *Genesis of American Nationalism* (Waltham, Mass., 1970); Henry Steele Commager, *Jefferson, Nationalism and the Enlightenment* (New York, 1975); Erich Hula, *Nationalism and Internationalism: European and American Perspectives* (Lanham, Md., 1984).

ANGELL, NORMAN (1874–1967).　English journalist, economist, worker for international peace, and strong critic of nationalism. Born Norman Angell Lane, he dropped the last name when he became world famous as the author of *The Great Illusion* (1910). Its theme was that in the final analysis war is generally unprofitable even to the victors. Knighted in 1931, Angell was awarded the Nobel Peace Prize in 1933.

Angell was one of the first publicists to call attention to the critical nature of nationalism. He saw it as "the most important thing in the world, more important than civilization, humanity, decency, kindness, pity; more important than life itself."

Bibliography: Norman Angell, *The Great Illusion* (London, 1910); *The Defense of the Empire* (London, 1937); *After All: The Autobiography of Norman Angell* (London, 1951); J.D.B. Miller, *Norman Angell and the Futility of War* (Basingtoke, Hampshire, 1986).

ANTHEMS, NATIONAL.　Patriotic hymns or songs expressing national sentiment. They are either adopted by governments as official national hymns or they are elevated to a prominent place in society by popular choice. The tunes may be original or borrowed from other countries. They are sung on ceremonial occasions, always with the goal of enhancing a spirit of national consciousness. In contemporary society some 159 nations, from large to small, have their own national anthems, which are sung with pride in the Fatherland or Motherland.

National anthems are of comparatively recent origin. The British *God Save the Queen* (or *King*) was first performed in London in 1745 to celebrate a resounding victory at Prestonpans. The original tune was adopted or adapted by other countries with special words suited to the patriotism of the people. In Germany it was sung to *Heil dir im Siegerkranz (Hail to Thee in Victor's Garland)*. In Switzerland it was used in *Rufst Du, mein Vaterland* (You Call, My Fatherland). The American national air, *My Country 'tis of Thee,* is sung to the same tune, with words by Reverend Samuel Smith (1843). Denmark and other countries adopted the same tune. Beethoven used it in his *Battle Symphony.*

National anthems often use a specific event as a stimulant. The French *La Marseillaise,* often considered to be the most dramatic of national anthems, was written, both words and music, by an army engineering officer, Claude-Joseph Rouget de Lisle, on the night of April 24, 1792. Troops from Marseilles sang the stirring tune as they stormed the Tuileries on August 10, 1792. Thereafter, it became popular as a song of revolution. The United States national anthem, *The Star-Spangled Banner,* was written by Francis Scott Key as he observed the bombardment of Fort McHenry from a British ship on which he was being detained. The melody was the song of the Anacreontic Society. This became the official national anthem, while *My Country, 'tis of Thee* was accepted as the unofficial national anthem. In recent years Irving Berlin's *God Bless America* has taken on popularity as another unofficial national song.

On occasion, other countries may have a series of official and unofficial national anthems. Thus, in Imperial Germany, *Heil dir im Siegerkranz* was adopted in the 1790s. In the 1840s, *Deutschland, Deutschland über Alles ("Germany, Germany, Above All"),* with words by H. A. Hoffmann von Fallersleben and music by Joseph Haydn has been used to the present day. After 1870, *Die Wacht am Rhein ("Watch on the Rhine")* became enormously popular in Germany as an unofficial national anthem.

In Nazi Germany, as elsewhere, a special national anthem was considered to be of important propaganda value. For some time Dr. Joseph Goebbels, Reich Minister for Public Enlightenment and Propaganda, had been searching for a poet who could provide him with a dramatic song. He found his man in Horst Wessel, son of a Protestant chaplain, a Nazi student and a Storm Trooper. A mixture of idealist and street-brawling ruffian, Horst Wessel became a drop-out and went to live in the slums of Berlin. In February 1930, a gang instigated by Communists invaded his room and killed him. Horst Wessel left behind him a marching song of three stanzas, which skillfully pieced together several Nazi slogans. It became the special song of the Nazi Party and later the second official anthem of

Germany after *Deutschland über Alles:* The tune may have been adapted from a Bohemian comic song. Its words revealed the strident nationalism of the Nazi movement from 1933 to 1945:

1.

Hold high the banner! Close the hard ranks serried!
S.A. marches on with sturdy stride.
Comrades, by Red Front and Reaction killed, are buried,
But march with us in image at our side.

2.

Gangway! Gangway now for the Brown Battalions!
For the Storm Trooper clears roads o'er the land!
The Swastika gives hope to our entranced millions,
The day for freedom and for bread's at hand.

3.

The trumpet blows its shrill and final blast!
Prepared for war and battle here we stand.
Soon Hitler's banners will wave unchecked at last,
The end of German slav'ry in our land!

The powerful strength of nationalism appears in the national anthems of small as well as large countries. Tribute is paid to the land and the people—the essence of nationalism. Several examples:

Royal Portugal: O Patria, O Rei, I Povo (Country, King, People).
Costa Rica: Noble Patria tu Hermosa (Noble Country so Beautiful).
Chile: Dulce Patria (Sweet Country).
New Zealand (National Song): *God Defend New Zealand.*

Even the mini-nationalisms (q.v.) are proud of their special national songs. The Welsh, while accepting British sovereignty, express their pride in *Mae hen wlad fy nhadau ("Land of my Fathers").* In general, national anthems express accurately the national sentiment of any people.

Bibliography: Martin F. Shaw (ed.), *National Anthems of the World* (New York, 1978); Marjory Alyn, *The Sound of Anthems* (New York, 1983); Alan H. Levy, *Musical Nationalism* (Westport, Conn., 1983); W.L. Reed and M.J. Bristow (eds.), *National Anthems of the World* (New York, 1985).

ARAB NATIONALISM.   *See* **PAN-ARABISM.**

ARAFAT, YASIR (1929–   ).   Leader of the Palestine Liberation Organization (q.v.) and active promoter of Palestinian nationalism.

Born in Jerusalem, Arafat claimed descent from Palestinian nobility. At an early age, he joined the Holy Struggle Army fighting against Israel. At the end of the 1948–1949 war against Israel, in which Israel defeated the Arabs, Arafat moved to Cairo. There he became chairman of the Palestine Student Confederation. He fought against the British and French in 1956, serving in the Egyptian army as a demolition expert. In the next decade the Arab world began to hear the name of Arafat.

In 1964, leaders of Arab states sanctioned the formation of the Palestine Liberation Organization. The 1967 war against Israel, resulting in another Arab loss, left the Arab armies shattered and disillusioned. Disgruntled Arabs began to look to Arafat's guerrillas as offering some hope for relief in a humiliating situation. They were impressed with his confidence: "I have no time to spare arguing over left foot and right. What is important is action and its results. We believe that the only way to return to our home and land is the armed struggle. We believe in this theory without any complications, and that is our aim and hope."

Arafat by 1969 gained control of *Al-Fatah* (q.v.), the largest and most effective of the Arab guerrilla units. By this time he was also leader of the P.L.O. He now emerged as a liberator who was fighting for his people. He and his followers would continue the struggle against the Israelis. Arafat scarcely cut the figure of a dashing guerrilla leader, but to his followers he was an immensely heroic figure. They started a campaign of terror against Israel. They ambushed Israelis, assaulted *kibbutzim* (Israeli settlements), and placed mines on roads and bridges. They attacked Israelis in market places, movie houses, and school buses. They encountered swift retribution from the Israeli army.

Arafat made headway in polishing his image. On October 14, 1974, the United Nations General Assembly invited representatives of the P.L.O. to participate in the debate on the Palestine question. A month later Arafat addressed the U.N. General Assembly, which passed a resolution stating that Palestinians had a right to self-determination (q.v.) and national sovereignty. Israeli officials replied that they would, under no circumstances, negotiate with the P.L.O.

The P.L.O. continued its campaign while at the same time changing to a diplomatic offensive. It called itself a government-in-exile. Backed by rich Arab oil princes, the P.L.O. established some eighty offices throughout the world. It now set its goals: (1) to put an end to inside rivalries that had plagued the movement for years, and (2) to win international recognition. However, moderates and extremists inside the movement continued to struggle for dominance.

Arafat continued to insist that his cause was a just one: "There are birds which fly around the world but come back to their original homes. There are fish that swim from the rivers to the sea, but their sons go back to their original sources. Home is something in the heart of every human being. In appearance, perhaps, I look happy, but in my heart something has cracked. I live the tragedy of my people. But I am optimistic because sooner or later my people will achieve their goal."

Bibliography: Thomas Kiernan, *Arafat: The Man and the Myth* (New York, 1976): Alan Hart, *Arafat: Terrorist or Peacemaker* (London, 1984); Shaul Mishal, *The PLO Arafat: Between Gun and Olive Branch* (New Haven, Conn., 1986).

ARMENIAN NATIONALISM. One of the most persistent mini-nationalisms (q.v.) in the world. Armenian sense of independence survived centuries of conquest by Assyrians, Macedonians, Persians, Mongols, Turks, and Russians. With their own language, literary and cultural traditions, a deep-rooted attachment to Christianity, and a sentiment of national identity, Armenians endured decimation and spoliation but never lost their urge for independence.

The supreme event in Armenian history was conversion to Christianity in 301 A.D. After resisting onslaughts by many conquering peoples, the Armenians came under Ottoman control in the nineteenth century. They were strongly influenced by the century's current of nationalism. The new Armenian middle class, impelled by the Industrial Revolution, sought energetically to better their position under Turkish domination. Armenians, in general, were not satisfied with Turkish control but moved only slowly in the direction of separatism. Their national spirit was displayed by philosophers, poets, artists, teachers, and musicians, all dedicated to the glories of their ancient past.

For Sultan Abdülhamid II, Armenian nationalism was equated with treason. Beginning in 1894 and continuing for two years in its first phase, there came a serie s of Armenian massacres that aroused global attention. Desperate Armenians turned to the Young Turk reformers in the belief that they would get help from that quarter, but it was a vain hope. Under the Young Turks, 20,000 Armenians died in the Adana massacres in 1909. In 1915 even more devastating slaughter took place. The Turks seemed to be intent on destroying the Armenian peoples altogether in order to prevent any possible chance of Armenians acquiring autonomy then or at any future time.

There was another period of Armenian martyrdom during the four years of World War I and the immediate postwar years. The Turks mercilessly suppressed any Armenians who spoke up for the Allied cause. Others managed to desert to the invading Russians. Many were deported to the deserts, where they perished. It is estimated that between 800,000 and a million Armenians died at the hands of Turks in the long series of massacres.

During the postwar years, the Allies proposed to establish an independent Armenia, but the goal was never achieved. The Turks, recovering their strength after the war, successfully countered the formation of an independent Armenia on what they regarded as their own sacred soil. Meanwhile, Armenians, much against their will, drifted into the Russian sphere of influence. As early as October 1917, the victorious Bolsheviks declared Armenia to be a part of the Transcaucasian Federation. On December 20, 1920, Armenian Communists proclaimed a new Soviet Republic. Dissenters were eliminated by the Kremlin. In 1936 Armenia became one of the fifteen constituent republics of the U.S.S.R.

The Soviet Union immediately revived its old process of Russification in dealing with dissenters. Armenians refused to eliminate their traditions. They insisted on using their own language. They discouraged intermarriage with Russians. They often used subtle ways to express their sense of national identity. On gala occasions they made it a point to display their own flag—a gold hammer and sickle split by a blue stripe—in preference to the Soviet national flag—a red background with hammer, sickle, and star. In May 1977 the famous Armenian Dance Ensemble, the pride of Armenians, performed its own national dramas in Victory Park, Yerevan, before a 150-foot statue of Mother Armenia. Dancers were careful to face the 17,000-foot snow-capped peak of Mount Ararat, a beloved Armenian symbol lost to Turkey but never forgotten by Armenians. In a state devoted to atheism, Armenians held enthusiastically to their Christian beliefs. They attended some 35 churches and joyously baptized their infants. Soviet authorities thought it best not to interfere with Armenian Christians in the practice of their faith.

Armenians have never forgotten their "Hundred Years' War" against the Ottoman Turks. Armenian death squads have operated throughout the world to take revenge for what they regard as the genocidal slaughter of their people. In 1973 the Turkish vice-consul in Los Angeles was gunned down. In 1975 the Turkish Ambassador to Austria was killed and the same year saw the assassination of the Turkish envoy to France. In 1979 the son of the Turkish Ambassador to the Netherlands was shot and killed. The Armenian Secret Army claimed some 136 attacks against Turks from 1975 to 1981.

Armenians insist that they are a nation with all the characteristics of a national state. Whether the domination be Turkish or Russian, Armenians do not intend to trade their sense of nationalism for existence as a people under foreign control. They maintain their national identity through war, conquest, dismemberment, and transplantation.

An extraordinary development in Armenian nationalism occurred in late February 1988, when the largest nationalist demonstration in the seventy-year history of the Soviet Union took place in the mostly Orthodox Christian Republic of Soviet Armenia. Encouraged by Mikhail S. Gorbachev's new twin policies of *glasnost* ("openness") amd *perestroika* ("restructuring"), tens of thousands of Armenians marched through Yerevan, their capital city, and demanded that the Nagorno-Karabakh Autonomous Region be incorporated into Armenia. This was an Armenian area inside Azerbaijan, where there was a bitter difference of religion: most Armenians are Christian, most Azerbaijanis are Muslim. The mountainous province of 150,000 inhabitants is inhabited mostly by Armenians.

Such demonstrations in the past led the Kremlin to send tanks and overpowering forces to crush any signs of rebellion, as, for example, in the Democratic Republic of East Germany and in Czechoslovakia. The Soviet Union is composed of more than 100 ethnic groups, which were united, in some cases by force, under Communist rule in 1920. The Party's Old Guard, the army, as well as the K.G.B. viewed this development in Armenia, as well as similar outbreaks in the Baltic states (*see* **BALTIC NATIONALISMS**), with shock and anger. For Gorbachev this was the most severe crisis of his tenure. The Armenian protests were only one of the minority problems facing him. Crimean Tatars, Latvians, Estonians, Lithuanians and others mounted protests in the more tolerant Gorbachev era. The dispute in the obscure mountain region went far beyond its contested borders. Gorbachev said that the redrawing of borders would constitute "an abuse of democratization fundamentally at variance with the aims of *perestroika*." He claimed that "it would poison public mentality with nationalist venom and thereby spoil relations between the people for many, many years to come." The Soviet Presidium announced that it was rejecting the demand of the Armenians and that its patience was exhausted. The Soviet Union, dominated by Russians who are but half the population of the country, appeared to be vulnerable to the rising tide of nationalism exemplified by disturbing events in Armenia.

Bibliography: R.P. Jordan, "The Proud Armenians," *National Geographic* (June, 1978), 846–873; David Marshall, *The Armenians: A People in Exile* (Boston, 1981); Adriano Alpago Nivello, *The Armenians* (New York, 1986).

ARNDT, ERNST MORITZ (1769–1860). German writer, poet, and patriot, one of the earliest advocates of German nationalism. Born on December 26, 1769, at Schoritz-bei-Garz, now in East Germany, he was appointed to the chair of history at the University of Greifswald and in 1810 came to the University of Bonn. He projected the idea of combining all German-speaking peoples into one politically powerful union. In pamphlets, poems, and songs he aroused a sense of nationalism in his countrymen against the French conqueror Napoleon. He denounced the German princes for "selling their people into bondage" and demanded that the French "stranglehold" be broken.

Arndt's stirring war songs, which brought him fame as "the poet of the War of Liberation," were designed to promote the consciousness of a common German Fatherland. He urged his countrymen to cherish their national spirit. Typical was this final stanza of his *Was ist des Deutschen Vaterland? (Where is the German's Fatherland?):*

> All Germany that land shall be,
> Watch o'er if God, and grant that we,
> With German hearts, in deed and thought,
> May love it truly as we ought.
> Be this thy land,
> All Germany shall be the land!

German resentment against Napoleonic domination burst into the War of Liberation in 1813. Arndt recorded the intense outburst of emotion against this domination in a famous passage. It was later incorporated into German textbooks again and again throughout the struggle for national unification: in the Second German Empire from 1871 to 1918, during the Weimar Republic from 1919 to 1933, and during the Third Reich from 1933 to 1945. This passage has been quoted often as an example of fervent nationalism in action:

Fired with enthusiasm, the people rose, "with God for King and Fatherland." Among the Prussians there was only one voice, one feeling, one anger and one love, to save the Fatherland and to free Germany. The Prussians wanted war; war and death they wanted; peace they feared because they could hope for no honorable peace from Napoleon. War, war, sounded the cry from the Carpathians to the Baltic, from the Niemen to the Elbe. War! cried the nobleman and landed proprietor who had become impoverished. War! the peasant who was driving his last horse to death. . . . War! the citizen who was growing exhausted from quartering soldiers and paying taxes. War! the widow who was sending her only son to the front. War! the young girl who, with tears of pride and pain, was leaving her betrothed. Youths who were hardly able to bear arms, men with gray hair, officers who on account of wounds and mutilations had long ago been honorably discharged, rich landed proprietors and officials, fathers of large families and managers of extensive businesses—all were unwilling to remain behind. Even young women, under all sorts of disguises, rushed to arms; all wanted to drill, arm themselves and fight and die for the Fatherland. . . .

The most beautiful thing about all this holy zeal and happy confusion was that all differences of position, class, and age were forgotten . . . that the one great feeling for the Fatherland, its freedom and honor, swallowed all other feelings, caused all other considerations and relationships to be forgotten.

Bibliography: Ernst Moritz Arndt, *Das preussische Volk und Heer* (1813), quoted in *Geschichte für Mittelschulen*, ed. by P. Jennrich, K. Krause, and A. Viernow (Halle, 1941), 111–112; Alfred George Pundt, *Arndt and the Nationalist Awakening in Germany* (New York, 1935); Hans Kohn, "Arndt and the Character of German Nationalism," *The American Historical Review*, 54, No. 4 (July, 1949), 787–803; Gustav Sichelschmidt, *Ernst Moritz Arndt* (Berlin, 1981).

ASIAN NATIONALISM.   Similar to the African experience, Asian nationalism reflected a deep-rooted racial context. Asians resented the white man. The early imperialists had succeeded in eliminating some traditions that had kept Asians in a strangle hold, but their attitude of superiority aroused resentment. The first whites who came to Asia had been accepted as equals, but the fraternization did not last. Soon, fortresses began to outnumber trading posts throughout Asia.

The nationalism that infected the Asian masses was supercharged with hostility. It existed in xenophobia, hatred of the stranger and the foreigner, often close to irrationality. It expressed itself in three forms—political, cultural, and religious. Politically, the peoples of Asia generally distrusted and feared the West. A kind of residual resentment bound them in a loose and cumbersome alliance against a renascence of the old imperial drives. Even stronger and more enduring than the political was the cultural xenophobia. For some centuries the peoples of Asia had endured colonial rule and had been made to feel that they were inferior. To many Westerners, Asian culture was barbaric or quaint. Foreigners often suppressed the temple schools run by Buddhist monks, custodians of the national culture, a situation that angered Asians. There was also a religious xenophobia. Asian religions expressed a hard core of exclusiveness, very much as did other religions. Asians, too, tended to exclude non-believers, and this became a tenet of their national sentiment.

The unexpected triumph of Japan over Russia in 1905 gave nationalism in Asia a tremendous boost. The huge Russian Empire was revealed to all as a giant with feet of clay. The Japanese, as early as the seventeenth century, had shown a kind of nationalism, but they learned much more about its new form after their country was opened to the West in the nineteenth century. Modern nationalism, with its structure of systematic propaganda in schools and family, in military service, and in the popular media, became highly popular in the early nineteenth century. After the end of World War I it spread throughout Asia.

One Asian country after another began to discard the chains of Western imperialism. The process was uneven, but it existed. Britain, which had bequeathed a sense of liberty and constitutionalism to Asia, gave independence to India, Pakistan, Ceylon, and Burma. China, where a theoretical autocracy had already crumbled under the impact of nationalism, eventually became prey to another kind of autocracy. India, which had been a jewel in the crown of the British Empire, was a special case. As early as 1885, Indian leaders called the first Indian National Congress in Bombay to seek union of all the hostile peoples in the vast subcontinent. For the first time in Indian history, a serious attempt was being made to eliminate differences in caste, religion, and language. The language problem alone in India was a thorny one; how could differences be resolved between rival linguistic nationalities, which included Indo-European (Hindi, Bengali, Marathi, and Urdu), Dravidian (Tamil, Telegu), and Munda? Eventually, some 438 million people, speaking a total of 14 languages and 800 dialects, were brought together in a new national state, a kind of federation held together with loose reins. The only common language was English used by the educated classes.

In China, too, nationalism became a driving force. In 1885 a young Chinese medical doctor named Sun Yat-sen (q.v.) began preaching the importance of nationalism for his country. He had received a Western education and his revolutionary principles came from the American and French Revolutions. His Three People's Principles (Nationalism, Democracy, and Livelihood) were intended as a kind of paraphrase of Abraham Lincoln's "government of the people, by the people, for the people." For Sun Yat-sen, Chinese nationalism was of the utmost importance: "Nationalism is that precious treasure which makes possible the subsistence of humanity. For instance, of what implement does a scholar make use of in order to earn a living? He uses the pen which he has in hand. Just as the pen is the means of livelihood to the student, so nationalism is to humanity the means of subsistence."

In this way, Sun Yat-sen expressed an attitude to nationalism that gained headway throughout Asia in the twentieth century. Asians in the past had lost their sense of freedom to foreign oppression. Nationalism as an idea became a most powerful political phenomenon through all of Asia. For Asians it was seen as a liberating force to win liberation from the white man.

Bibliography: Rupert Emerson, *From Empire to Nation: The Rise to Self-Assertion of Asian and African Peoples* (Cambridge, Mass., 1960); Clifford Geetz (ed.), *Old Societies and New States: The Quest for Modernity* (New York, 1963); Elie Kedourie (ed.), *Nationalism in Asia and Africa* (New York, 1970).

ATATÜRK, KEMAL (1878–1936).   Soldier, statesman, creator and leader of the new Turkish nationalism. As a young man, his proficiency in mathematics led his teacher to give him the name of "Kemal," an Arabic term meaning "perfection." During his youth, he bitterly criticized the despotism of Abdülhamid II. As a young Turk conspirator, he worked to set up a modern constitutional government. He would relieve the country from the blight of Western imperialism. He proclaimed "Turkey for the Turks," a slogan which became the guideline for his political life.

After World War I, Mustafa Kemal showed his distrust for the old Ottoman Empire by organizing the Republican People's Party. He announced a six-point program: (1) republicanism; (2) secularism; (3) populism; (4) nationalism; (5) statism; and (6) continuous reform. These goals, he said, would regenerate his country. As leader of the new Turkish nationalist movement, he became the heart and soul of Turkish national resistance. He rejected Pan-Ottomanism, Pan-Turanism, and Pan-Islamism (qq.v.) in favor of a powerful Pan-Turkism (q.v.). It was wrong, he said, to associate the Turkish name with tents, horses, armies, wars, and massacres. Turks should only follow the example of their historic ancestors, "the first cultured people of the world." He insisted that it was time for the world to understand that for thousands of years the Turks had been leading agents of culture and progress except when subjugated by foreigners. In his view there must be a renaissance of the Turkish "race."

While he favored the retention of the Islamic religion, Mustafa Kemal opposed Pan-Islamism (q.v.) as unsuitable for the Turkish people. Islam must be secularized in the new Turkey, and Muslim religious law must be replaced with a legal code borrowed from the Swiss. He would abolish religious schools in favor of civil education. He would close shrines and dervish houses. He would forbid polygamy and outlaw wearing of the fez. He would make Sunday rather than Friday the day of national rest.

Once Kemal Atatürk came to power in Turkey, these secular reforms became more than mere objectives—they were instituted. The Kemalist Revolution meant a new Turkish nationalism and a new process of Westernization. Kemal Atatürk was intent upon creating a pure Turkish language purged of Arabic elements, because these were foreign in origin. He abolished the diffuse Arabic script and replaced it with a Latin-type alphabet. He took the title Atatürk (Father of the Turks) for himself. For the Westernization process, he maintained that Turkey must reject her medieval raiment and take advantage of Western culture. There must be continuous *Devrin*, or overturning. He emancipated women and adopted the Western Gregorian calendar.

Elected President of Turkey in 1923, Kemal Atatürk pursued these secular policies zealously and successfully. He made certain that all Turkish children would learn that true Turks were not those enslaved by foreigners, by his own tyrannical rulers, or by religious obscurantism, but they must know that their ancestors had laid the foundations for civilization in Central Asia for thousands of years.

Bibliography: Dagobert von Mikusch, *Mustafa Kemal* (New York, 1931); Harold C. Armstrong, *Grey Wolf, Mustafa Kemal* (London, 1932); Ernest C. Ramsaur, Jr., *The Young Turks* (Princeton, N.J., 1957).

AUTONOMY.   The term "autonomy," derived from the Greek *autonomia*, means self-government. Specifically, it refers to the quality, or right, or state of being of self-government. The goal is a small or large granting of localized control of politics and administration. An autonomous people is able to administer its own government without absolute centralized control from the capital of the nation-state. Autonomy thus gives a special political status inside the national state.

In the mini-nationalisms or ethnonationalisms there are generally two very different kinds of dissidents against centralized control: moderates and extremists. Moderates may well be satisfied by inclusion in the centralized nation-state, but they demand regional rights, such as their own assemblies and executives. They may call for more economic autonomy, control of urban projects, and direction of their own culture. Against the moderates' request for more authority in local rights are the demands of extremists, who reject autonomy and call for outright independence. They may turn to terrorism to achieve their goal. The Welsh in Britain provide an example of a mini-nationalism stressing autonomous rights; the Basques in Spain, regarding themselves as liberators and not as terrorists, use bomb and bullet to win the status of complete independence. (*See also* **MINI-NATIONALISMS** and **ETHNONATIONALISM.**)

B

BALTIC NATIONALISMS.   As border populations, the people of
the three Baltic states, Latvia, Estonia, and Lithuania, have long been
under control of neighboring powers. In Latvia and Estonia, the
Teutonic Knights left a landowning class of barons, while Polish
influence was strong in Lithuania. Russian rule was extended to all
three provinces in the eighteenth century. In the late nineteenth
century the natives, encouraged by reforms in the Russian Empire,
began to assert their own sense of nationalism. During World War
I, the Baltic provinces seized the opportunity to work for the establishment of independent states. German and Bolshevik troops fought
bitterly for control of the area.

   After World War I the provinces of the former Russian Empire
were formed into independent states, and their new status was
recognized by Soviet Russia. All three peoples set up republican
forms of government to frustrate Hitler's Germany. However, in 1939
the Soviet Government forced them to concede occupation of important military bases. The next year they were completely occupied,
annexed, and transformed into constituent republics of the Soviet
Union. Despite their traditional anti-German attitude, the deporta-
tions and Russian terror led large sections of the population to
welcome German troops as liberators in 1941. The Germans occupied
the three areas until 1944. Western nations, including the United
States, have never recognized the Russian annexation of the Baltic
States.

The Baltic states are small but have important natural resources. Latvian S.S.R., occupying 24,695 square miles on the Baltic, has a population (1985) of 2,604,000, with its capital at Riga. It has timber and peat resources and produces dyes and fertilizers. Estonian S.S.R., also on the Baltic, occupies 17,413 square miles and has a population (1985) of 1,530,000, with its capital at Tallinn. It has textiles, shipbuilding, timber, and mining. Lithuanian S.S.R., on the Baltic, is 26,173 square miles, with a population (1985) of 3,999,000, and its capital at Vilnius. It produces cattle, hogs, and electrical appliances. In 1921 the new states were admitted to the League of Nations as independent states, but this status was lost when the Russians took over control.

Neither Latvia, Estonia, nor Lithuania has willingly accepted Russian domination. The people of all three states speak of the loss of their own culture. They have a sense of territory and the feel of history, essential ingredients of modern nationalism, and they resent the end of their independence. The belief in nationhood lies behind nationalist movements in all three countries. In 1988, in the era of *glasnost* (openness) and *perestroika* (restructuring), initiated by Mikhail S. Gorbachev, there has been an upsurge of nationalism in the Baltic states. For nearly five decades they have been restive under Moscow's domination. Now they seem inclined to challenge the Soviet control of their affairs. They are testing the primacy of the Communist Party and, eventually, hope for a restoration of their independence. In all three countries the fear exists that their own languages, customs, and traditional religious practices are being controlled by a foreign country, and they want their freedom. Like other peoples throughout the world, Latvians, Estonians, amd Lithuanians are affected by the currents of nationalism, and they want to be emancipated from Moscow.

Aware of the resentment in the Baltic states, the Kremlin has attempted to stifle nationalism there. It has granted a small measure of cultural autonomy to Lithuania in an effort at appeasement, but it has set strict limits to this concession. It has sought to rewrite Lithuanian history for schools in an effort to conform them to Soviet ideas. Soviet textbooks used in all Lithuanian schools emphasize annexation by the U.S.S.R. as a glorious chapter in Lithuanian history. Such tactics only inflame the cause of nationalism. Lithuanians prefer their own hero, the Grand Duke Gediminas, under whom Lithuanian power was extended from the Baltic Sea almost to the Black Sea and eastward to the Dnieper River.

The resurgence of nationalist activity in the Baltic states was due to the formation of political-action groups. Encouraged by *perestroika* and believing that the entire political and economic system of the Soviet Union is being changed by the new program, this grass-roots activity stresses Baltic nationalisms as the wave of the future. On July 9, 1988, more than 100,000 Lithuanians attended a rally led by the Initiative group in Vilnius. The Baltic peoples have never forgotten the national flags they used during their years of independence and they resent the ban on those emblems. Officials of the states have demanded an end to the Russian prohibition of their flags. Voices that have been mute in the past now demand that the Kremlin explain why many thousands of Latvians, Estonians, and Lithuanians were sent to Siberia during Stalin's repressive rule.

The Baltic peoples have long resented Stalin's interference in their affairs. Their resurgence of nationalist sentiment has been due in large part to their belief in how Stalin obtained control of their lives. On August 15, 1988, their suspicions were confirmed when they were told for the first time by the state-run press of the secret agreement between Stalin and Hitler that paved the way for the Soviet take over of the three Baltic states. This first official disclosure gave details of the Molotov-Ribbentrop Pact, signed on August 23, 1939, which included a secret agreement making clear that Latvia, Estonia, and Lithuania were forcibly occupied by Soviet troops. For the Baltic peoples this was aggression that destroyed their independence. Publication of the secret pact led the Baltic people to hope that Moscow, in the spirit of openness, was preparing to acknowledge that the Baltic areas had been occupied against their will. These hopes faded when the Soviets denied the existence of any secret protocols.

The Kremlin's effort to counter the call of nationalism in the Baltic states included sending Russian families into the area. These Russians now find themselves endangered by the rising nationalism and worry about their future safety and welfare. Nationalists in the Baltic states call for an end to the Russian migration and the recognition of their right to independence. Nationalism here, as elsewhere, has become a prime factor in the political life of the Baltic peoples. Moscow denounced these Baltic independent movements as caused by "the virus of nationalism."

Bibliography: Endel Kareda, *Estonia in the Soviet Grip* (London, 1949); Emanuel Model, *Estonia: Nation on the Anvil* (New York, 1963); Herbert Grant Watson, *The Latvian Republic* (London, 1965); Uytautas Vaitiekunas, *Lithuania, Program by the Committee for a Free Lithuania* (New York, 1965); Bronis J. Kaslas, *The Baltic Nations: The Quest for*

Regional Integration and Political Liberty (Pittston, Pa., 1976); Jonas Kinkus (ed.), *Lithuania: An Encyclopedic Survey* (Vilnius, 1986).

BANCROFT, GEORGE (1800–1891).   American historian, diplomat, and nationalist. In the nineteenth-century Age of Nationalism, historians in most countries expressed their sense of nationalism in their major works. Thus, the three great masters of the Prussian school of professor-patriots, Johann Gustav Droysen, Heinrich von Sybel, and Heinrich von Treitschke (qq.v.), waved the Prussian banner and praised the Hohenzollern monarchy. This disposition toward nationalism was also evident in major countries elsewhere. In the United States, George Bancroft and other American historians depicted the rise and character of the American people and revealed a sense of pride in their history.

Bancroft was graduated from Harvard in 1817 and took his doctorate at Göttingen. He was the first American trained in the German scientific school of historical scholarship, and he later applied this approach to his own historical writing. As Secretary of the Navy from 1845 to 1846, he established the U.S. Naval Academy at Annapolis. In May 1845, as Acting Secretary of War, he sent General Zachary Taylor across the border, an act followed by the war with Mexico. He was U.S. Minister to Great Britain from 1846 to 1849 and to Germany from 1867 to 1874. In Germany he developed a cordial relationship with Chancellor Otto von Bismarck, reminiscent of Bismarck's intimate friendship during his student days with John Lothrop Motley, who later became a distinguished American historian.

During his career as statesman, Bancroft gathered material and published from 1834 to 1876 his monumental *History of the United States*, covering the span from the discovery of America to the close of the Revolutionary War. This famous work, although little read today, is considered to be an important landmark in American historiography. It is strongly anti-British and it expresses a powerful sense of American nationalism. Bancroft made clear his deep regard for American democracy, for which he became a passionate advocate. The first scholar to produce a comprehensive study of the nation's history, he was greatly influenced by the German nationalist school of historians. Subsequent American historians, such as James Ford Rhodes, John Bach McMaster, and Frederick Jackson Turner, shared Bancroft's fond regard for his country in their own major works.

Bibliography: George Bancroft, *History of the United States of America* (6 vols., Boston, 1879); Russel Blaine Nye, *George Bancroft* (New York, 1964); Robert H. Canary, *George Bancroft* (New York, 1974).

BANSE, EWALD (1883–1953).   German scientific geographer, military writer, Professor of Military Science at the Brunswick Technical College after appointment by Hitler, and advocate of expansionist nationalism. His major work, *Raum und Volk im Weltkriege (Space and People in World War)* (1933), was later distributed widely in translation by the British as an effective instrument of propaganda against Hitler's aggressive policies.

In the preface to his book, Banse praised nationalism as "self-respect and healthy egoism." He denounced internationalism as "self-abandonment and a degeneration of the tissues of a people." "The internationalist is a bastard in blood and a eunuch in intellect. Man's greatest works always spring from the national soil even when they are not actually directed to national ends."

Banse saw Germany's salvation only in militarism:

> The sword will come into its own again, and the pen, after fourteen years of exaggerated prestige, will be put in its place. The sword has lain rusting in the corner for fourteen years in the German countries, while the pen has had the stage to itself; and as a result we have gone to the dogs. Certainly, the pen is good, but the sword is good too and often far better, and we want both to be equally honored among the German people. A man can only protect himself against assault with the sword; if he tried to do it with the pen he would only make himself ridiculous and get the worst of it!

In similar trend of thought, Banse compared the active warlike man with the pacifist, with sympathy for the former:

> The actively warlike man is the man who does not fight to live, but lives to fight. War is his element. His eagle eye is ever on the alert for chances and opportunities of fighting; with his slight frame, which looks as if it were built for cutting through obstacles, he comes down like a wolf on the fold. This born warrior hurls himself without thinking into the mêlée; so far from trying to avoid or mitigate a quarrel, he looks for it and greets it with a cheer. For him battle is the everlasting yea, the fulfillment and justification of existence. He is hopelessly handicapped for the work of civil life; wherever swords are being sharpened in the world, there you will find his clear-cut profile. If he had his way, there would always be trouble somewhere. He will even put his sword at the disposal of a foreigner, if he provides him with a good fight. The essential Nordic original aristocracy of the West and beyond it has always been the largest contributor to this class, and has shed its blood on every battlefield in the world. Fighting for fighting's sake, not in defense of hearth and home, is the watchword of this kind. . . .
>
> How utterly different . . . is the peace-loving man, the pacifist! Peace is the only state for which he is fitted and he will do anything to preserve it; he will endure any humiliation, including loss of liberty and even the most severe damage to his pocket, in order to avoid war. His dim, lusterless eye betokens servility (which does not rule out impertinence), his clumsy body is obviously built for toiling and stooping, his movements are slow and deliberate. This type is the born

stay-at-home, small-minded, completely flummoxed by the smallest interruption of the normal course of events, looking at the whole world from the standpoint of his little ego and judging it accordingly. To this bourgeois or philistine, the warrior is the sworn foe, the deadly enemy who only exists to destroy his miserable rest. It remains a source of mixed wonder and horror to him that anybody can jeopardize his peace and security from mere pugnacity or on idealistic grounds. That is just the essential difference: the warrior . . . wagers his whole habitual existence, all he possesses, on the point of his sword, when it is a matter of maintaining his ego, his point of view, in a word, his honor, which is more to him than his individual life; the man of peace, be his muscles weak or strong, values honor and renown less than his own little life, which seems so great and important to him; he sets the individual destiny above the destiny of the nation.

As a champion of extreme German nationalism, Banse called for a German renaissance with two important missions: (1) to summon the soul of Germany to the cultural and political task assuring that all thought, all action, and all speech on German soil would be German; and (2) to combine German territory throughout its whole extent into a unified and, therefore, powerful state, whose boundaries would be far wider than those of 1914. The preparation for future wars, he wrote, must not stop at the creation, equipment, and training of an efficient army, but preparation must go on to train the minds of the whole people for the war and must employ all the resources of science to master the conditions governing the war itself and the possibility of endurance.

Banse's views lent the credibility of a German military expert to substantiating the ideas implicit in Hitler's *Mein Kampf.* (*See* **HITLER, ADOLF.**) There is little doubt that the Nazi *Fuehrer* approved the ideas expressed in Banse's book, but at the time Hitler was anxious to prove to the world his peaceful intentions. When an English translation of the book appeared, German officials announced: "This book has unfortunately given anti-German propaganda abroad occasion to throw doubt on the peace policy of the German Government. The book is, of course, only the private work of an irresponsible theorist and is in no wise directive for the policy of the Government. For the rest, the strategic theories developed by Professor Banse in this book are so absurd that they are not to be taken seriously by German public opinion. Nevertheless, the book has been confiscated. The German Government desires thus irrefutably to show that it formally disclaims these senseless babblings, and is resolved not to allow its policy of peace to be in the least disturbed by the propagandist exploitation of such private works."

Unfortunately for Germany, Hitler's policy of "peace" subsequently went squarely in the direction of Banse's nationalism and militarism. British propagandists distributed copies of Banse's book to demonstrate the real character of Hitler's aggressive designs.

Bibliography: Ewald Banse, *Germany Prepares for War: A Nazi Theory of "Self Defense,"* trans. by Alan Harris (London and New York, 1934).

BARKER, ERNEST (1874–1960). English publicist, historian, and classical scholar. Barker believed that national character, in its formation and manifestations, was consistent with the character of the individual. He saw national character as a reality:

> National character is the sum of acquired tendencies, built up by leaders in every sphere of activity, with the consent and co-operation, active in some, but more or less passive in others, of the general community.

In support of his view, Barker held that each of us, in his or her moral growth, starts from the raw stuff of original nature that is partly a matter of temperament, as determined by bodily structure and its peculiarities, and partly a matter of instincts common to our general kind of inherited predispositions. The raw stuff is shaped into a general form. That settled form is character, the sum of acquired tendencies built upon native bases. In much the same way, a nation starts from the raw stuff of its material basis: it builds a sum of acquired tendencies and settles into the unity and permanence that we call by the name of national character. Barker expressed his agreement with Eduard Meyer: "National character is something which we can never explain scientifically in detail, but must accept as a thing which is simply given; and yet it is just this individual and particular element which determines the peculiarity and innermost essence of every historical process."

Barker's concept of national character brought him into a dispute with Hamilton Fyfe (q.v.), who denounced the entire idea as an illusion. According to Fyfe, Barker did not begin by asking if there was such a thing as national character, but took it for granted and expected his readers to do the same. "Prof. Barker does not include inherited tendencies, but these, as factors of national character, are proclaimed more insistently than elements acquired or implanted by schooling and patriotic propaganda. By ignoring them Prof. Barker showed that he had a clearer understanding of his subject than he set down in his book. But only by inference could the reader gather this." (*See also* **NATIONAL CHARACTER.**)

Bibliography: Ernest Barker, *National Character and the Factors in Its*

Formation (New York and London, 1927); Hamilton Fyfe, *The Illusion of National Character* (London, 1940).

BARRÈS, AUGUSTE-MAURICE (1862–1923). French politician, man of letters, and an outstanding advocate of integral, or extreme, nationalism. Born on August 19, 1862, at Charmes-sur-Moselle in French Alsace, he completed his secondary studies in Nancy and then went to Paris to study law, but instead turned to literature. At the age of twenty-seven he began a tumultuous political career distinguished by an increasingly intense nationalism.

The nationalism of Barrès grew into hatred for Germany, which he had never forgiven for acquiring all of Alsace and eastern Lorraine in 1871. Even his enemies were impressed by his superb writing style and his power of analysis. He advocated ego worship as a product of scientific naturalism. His trilogy, titled *Le Roman de l'énergie nationale* (1897–1902), presented his nationalistic views. In these works he showed an individualism based on a deep attachment to the soil of France. He emphasized nation, soil, and ancestors as repositories of national power. His prose style brought him to election to the *Académie Française* in 1906.

For Barrès, French national energy was grounded on such traditional elements as the Catholic faith, the army, and the monarchy. He praised Catholicism and attempted to show how Catholicism and nationalism had been integrated. In a lecture to the League of the French Nation in 1902, he expressed his opposition to the liberal nationalism of republican France. His countrymen were impressed by his emotional adulation of France:

> To attain this national, realistic view of the Fatherland, we must develop sentiments which already exist naturally in this country. . . . To create a national consciousness we must combine with a dominant intellectualism whose methods the historians teach, a less conscious, less deliberative element. . . .
>
> Nothing is more valuable in forming a people's soul than the voice of our ancestors. Our soil gives us a discipline, for we are only the continuation of the dead. . . .
>
> The dead! What would a man mean to himself if he represented only himself alone? When we look backward, we see an endless train of mysteries. Their recent embodiment we call France. We are the products of that collective being which speaks in us. Let the influence of our ancestors be enduring. Let the sons be vigorous and honest. Let the nation be one.
>
> The naturalized foreigner swears that he will think and live as a Frenchman. But in vain! In vain has he tied his interests with ours. Blood will follow the laws of nature against all vows, against all laws. He is our guest—this son from beyond the Rhine or the English Channel. We offer him safety and our generous friendship.

But we do not owe him a share in the government of the country. Let him feel our pulse, and, from roots that grow, nourish himself from our soil and from our dead. Indeed, his grandchildren will be genuinely French, not merely through a legal fiction.

Barrès' nationalistic views remained consistent. In 1917, in the midst of World War I, he delivered a stirring patriotic address in London at the Hall of the Royal Society of the British Academy. He saw the war against Germany as the apotheosis of his doctrines. He commended "the undying spirit of France" in highly emotional terms and glorified the honor of dying for France:

Millions of Frenchmen have entered this war with a fervor of heroism and martyrdom which formerly, in the most exalted epochs of our history, characterized only the flower of the combatants. Young or old, poor or rich, and whatever his religious faith, the French soldier of 1916 knows that his is a nation which intervenes when injustice prevails upon the earth, and in his muddy trench, gun in hand, he knows that he is carrying onward the *Gesta Dei per Francos.*

Roland, on the evening after Roncevaux, murmurs with dying breath: "O Land of France, most sweet art thou, my country." It is with similar expressions and the same love that our soldiers of today are dying. *"Au revoir,"* writes Jean Cherlomey to his wife "promise me to bear no grudge against France if she requires all of me."—*"Au revoir,* it is for the sake of France," were the dying words of Captain Hersart de La Villemarqué.—*"Vive la France,* I am well content, I am dying for her sake," said Corporal Voituret of the Second Dragoons, and expired while trying to sing the *Marseillaise.*—Albert Malet, whose handbooks are used in teaching history to our school children, enlisted for the war; his chest is pierced by a bullet, he shouts: "Forward, my friends! I am happy in dying for France," and sinks upon the barbed wire in front of the enemy's trenches.—*"Vive la France,* I die, but I am well content," cry in turn, one after another, thousands of dying men, and the soldier Raissac of the Thirty-first of the line, mortally wounded on the twenty-third of September, 1914, finds strength before expiring to write on the back of his mother's photograph: "It is an honor for the French soldier to die."

For his followers, Barrès breathed the soul of contemporary France. He, thereby, captured the hearts of his generation. For patriots of other countries, he was the prototype of the patriotic Frenchman. German poets, publicists, and novelists echoed his sentiment of extreme nationalism and spoke in similar terms for their own country.

In his political career, Barrès joined Charles Maurras (q.v.) in defending the doctrine of French nationalism. Until his death in 1923, he remained a champion of extreme nationalism and he continued his impassionate stand on the glorification of France.

Bibliography: Maurice Barrès, *Scènes et doctrines du nationalisme* (Paris, 1902); Maurice Barrès, *The Undying Spirit of France,* trans. by Margaret

W. Corwin (New Haven, Conn., 1917); Maurice Barrès, *The War and the Spirit of Youth* (Boston, 1917); M. François Burns, *Maurice Barrès, Myth-Maker of Modern French Nationalism* (Washington, D.C., 1968); Anthony A. Greaves, *Maurice Barrès* (Boston, 1978).

BASQUE NATIONALISM.   National separatism in plurinational Spain and France. Four Basque provinces (Vizcaya, Guipúzcoa, Alava, and Navarra), with some 750,000 Basques, are in the industrial heartland of northern Spain. Three Basque provinces (Labourd, Basse Navarre, and Soule), with about 150,000 French Basques, live on contiguous territory in southwestern France. Each combination forms a mini-nationalism, one in Spain and one in France. Both are known for their vigorous sense of independence, though the Spanish Basques have won global attention because of the violence of their extremists. Basque nationalism calls for a union of all seven principalities, although the French Basques are less restive than their brothers across the Pyrenees.

Even in their early history the Basques resisted all attempts by Romans or Visigoths to assimilate them. In the early tenth century the Basques south of the Pyrenees were brought into the kingdom of Navarre, but they managed to retain self-rule in their *fueros* (assemblies). Spanish Basques held these privileges for centuries, but lost them in 1873 because of their pro-Carlist stand in the Carlist Wars. Angered by this loss of what they regarded as precious rights, the Basques thereafter lent their support to any movement that opposed the centralism of Madrid.

Proud of their singular institutions, Basques were determined to maintain their unique integrity. Central to their existence was their language, which they regarded as a binding cement. The Basque language, indeed, played a major role in the formation and development of Basque nationalism. *Euskera*, one of the most distinctive of non-Castilian languages, is also one of the most complex of all tongues. Guttural, relating to no other language, the Basque language is a favorite of linguistic experts, who are fascinated by this consistently agglutinative tongue. It has its special phonology, grammar, and vocabulary. It bypassed the sort of cultural diffusion by which languages influence one another.

In addition to their special language, Basques enjoy a cultural affinity. During the course of centuries, the Basques developed their own special dress, customs, traditions, and folkways, all of which they guarded zealously against the inroads of foreigners. Neither Romans, Goths, Visigoths, nor Carolingians were able to overcome the special manifestations of Basque culture. Living in a countryside unlike the arid fields of southern Spain, Spanish Basques were active as fishermen, shepherds, and sailors. Immensely fond of choral singing, they held that "one or two Basques are nothing much, but three Basques always form a choir." Their favorite game is *jai alai*, in which players use scoops attached to their hands to throw balls at great speed. Young Basques play the game either with bare hands or with primitive wooden bats. Community games, including such trials of strength as lifting boulders, splitting logs, chopping wood, cutting hay, and towing heavy boats through rough seas, are always hotly contested. All such cultural activities strengthen Basque nationalism and the desire to maintain the independence of the Basque way of life. This is, indeed, a proud and highly sensitive nationalism.

During the Spanish Civil War lasting from 1936 to 1939, the Basque provinces formed an isolated Republican enclave in all probability because the Republicans gave them autonomy at the beginning of the conflict. The Basque Republic lasted just eight months. With the collapse of the Spanish Republic in 1939 and the beginning of the Franco dictatorship came a long period of martyrdom for the Basques. They were not happy about the plan of the Spanish dictator to mold a plurinational Spain into a united national state directed from Madrid. Franco discouraged regional languages and culture and especially any movements for separatism. Basques were punished by removal of privileges or by restrictions aimed at education, press, song, and dances. Often the Basque provinces were declared to be in a state of emergency.

Proud, stubborn, and militant, the Basques reacted strongly against such repressions. Many Basques gave up in disgust and emigrated to Argentina, Mexico, and Cuba. More than 12,000 Basques settled in the Boise region of Idaho and brought along with them their old traditions and customs. Basque nationalism was kept alive by an émigré government set up in Paris as well as by the Basque Nationalist Party (P.N.V.) functioning inside Spain. Basque resistance to Franco increased from 1940 to 1950. Franco retaliated with a series of harsh emergency measures. Proclaiming a "State of Exception," as legal justification, he ordered the Civil Guard to suppress Basque dissidents mercilessly. Basque activists were hunted down, turned over to harsh judges, and then subjected to torture or execution for "military rebellion."

In 1959, young Basque militants, reacting fiercely against the more moderate stance of their elders, organized the *Euzkadi ta Azkatasuna* (E.T.A.), or Basque Homeland and Liberty. Mostly from middle-class families, E.T.A. activists adopted their own version of Marxist-Leninist ideology. As the first generation of Basques to be free from the traumatic memories of the Spanish Civil War days, these young dissidents turned to violence and direct action to win Basque freedom.

From this time on, Basque separatism turned to terrorism. The Basque struggle for independence, now under the direction of E.T.A. militants, soon won a reputation as among the most violent mininationalisms in the world. In the summer of 1968, Meliton Manzanas, the dreaded police chief of Guipúzcoa Province, was killed in daylight apparently by E.T.A. fanatics. He had been, said one young nationalist student, "the butcher of our people." "We set up our own tribunal and sentenced him to death. Our central committee has decided on other executions." This became standard operating procedure among E.T.A. terrorists. They intensified their attacks. The angered police, annoyed by such revolutionary tactics, and armed with pistols, chains, and clubs, attacked E.T.A. units similarly armed. In 1978, Basque demonstrators turned Pamplona into a bloody battleground. There were scores of such confrontations between police and nationalist Basques.

E.T.A. violence continues to the present day. Basque extremists prefer the way of the Irish Republican Army (I.R.A) (q.v.), the Palestine Liberation Organization (P.L.O) (q.v.), the Red Army faction in the Federal Republic of West Germany, and the Red Brigade in Italy. Hard-line E.T.A. terrorists believe that an independent Basque homeland can be achieved only through violence—never through negotiations. Moderation, from the viewpoint of these nationalists, is the way of weaklings and fools.

Bibliography: Stanley G. Payne, *Basque Nationalism* (Reno, Nev., 1975); Robert P. Clark, *The Basques: The Franco Years and Beyond* (Reno, Nev., 1979); William A. Douglass (ed.), *Basque Politics: A Case Study in Ethnic Nationalism* (Reno, Nev., 1985); Christian Rudel, *Euzkadi, une nation pour les Basques* (Paris, 1985); Roger Collins, *The Basques* (New York, 1987).

BENTHAM, JEREMY (1748–1832). Philosopher, jurist, prophet of utilitarianism, herald of social and legal reform, and prominent British liberal nationalist. Bentham recognized that national feeling was present and operative, and that it was both a blessing and a bane. Properly directed, he said, nationalism would concern itself with the nation in a family of nations; love of country would become virtually synonymous with love of mankind. That was the essence of a liberal nationalism that would become weakened later in the century.

Bentham warned that when "oppressed" nationalities become free, they soon transform themselves from lambs into lions. He believed that one must go beyond mere love of country, which might be an example of "a malevolence exercized on a wide scale, . . . which sometimes takes the name of *esprit de corps*, of nationality: sometimes the high name of patriotism." He pointed to the model drawn by Fenelon, "I prefer my family to myself, my country to my family, and the human race to my country."

Bentham emerged as the early proponent of liberal nationalism between Jacobin and traditional nationalism. (*See* **HAYES' CLASSIFICATION.**) He fervently commended its role in history: if every suppressed nationality were free and possessed its own national language, educational system, army, and press, it would be able to live in peace with its neighbors. It was an optimism not fully justified by Europeans heading into the maelstrom of two world wars.

Bibliography: Elmer Louis Kayser, *The Grand Social Enterprise: A Study of Jeremy Bentham in Relation to Liberal Nationalism* (New York, 1932); Charles Warren Everett, *Jeremy Bentham* (London, 1966); Nancy L. Rosenblum, *Bentham's Theory of the Modern State* (Cambridge, Mass., 1978).

BERLIN, ISAIAH (1909–   ).   English philosopher, historian, and critic of nationalism. In his writings, Berlin ridiculed the idea of a supposedly objective march of history. He rejected the Marxist theories of internationalism and economic determinism, and held that "moral values are not just a subjective gloss unworthy of consideration on the great hard edifice of historical construction."

Like Normal Angell (q.v.), Berlin recognized the enormous importance of nationalism as a movement in modern history:

> In all [a] great array of elaborate statistically supported serious futurology mingled with free fantasy, there took place one movement which dominated much of the nineteenth century, for which no significant future was predicted, a movement so familiar to us now, so decisive both within, and in relationships between nations, that it is only by some effort of the imagination that one can conceive of a world in which it played no part. . . . This movement is nationalism.

Berlin saw nationalism as emerging particularly in France in the form of the defense of the customs and privileges of localities, regions, corporations, and states, and then of the nation itself. It developed against the encroachments of some external power, such as Roman law or Papal authority, or against such related forms of universalism as natural law and other claims of supranational authority.

   Bibliography: Isaiah Berlin, *Essays on Liberty* (New York, 1970); Isaiah Berlin, "The Bent Twig: A Note on Nationalism." *Foreign Affairs*, 51, No. 1 (October, 1972), 11–30; Isaiah Berlin, *Against the Current* (London, 1979).

BIAFRAN NATIONALISM.   The global pattern is a mosaic of linguistic pride, economic interests, political drives, cultural imperatives, psychological needs—and mini-nationalisms seeking identity. In Africa these factors are complicated by a persistent tribalism, which does not vanish from the scene. The continued existence of tribalism in the new Africa is that continent's counterpart of mini-nationalisms elsewhere. As colonialism melted away, the clash of central authority and the new nationalisms became more and more important in the evolution of Africa's history. The African experience was motivated by the same aspirations as that of the European. At its roots was a need for freedom, for the right of a people of similar likes and dislikes to function freely as extended family units.

   The Federal Republic of Nigeria presents a classic case of the struggle between the new nationalism and the older tribalism in Africa. Located on the western coast in an area of 356,699 square miles, more than twice the size of California, Nigeria has a population of 77,080,000 people (1980 estimate). The people have some 250 languages and dialects of which the most widely spoken are Hausa, Yoruba, Ibo, and Edo. Religious affiliation is along tribal lines; Northern Nigeria is mostly Muslim, southern Nigeria mostly Christian, and there is widespread practice of tribal religions such as animism. A country of extraordinary potentiality, with oil and agricultural diversity, Nigeria has been faced with troublesome problems.

   Nigeria won its independence in 1960 and became a republic in 1963. The business of welding antagonistic tribes into a viable centralized state was to have dangerous consequences. The critical issue was who would control the new government. The differences resulted in violence. The federal elections of 1964 were marred by voter intimidation and stuffed ballot boxes. The people had severely limited experience in democracy, and for them victory in elections was viewed not as a mandate for exerting political influence, but as a license for political domination. Nigeria was divided into mutually suspicious regions separated by tribes each with its own notion of independence.

   On May 30, 1967, the Eastern region seceded from the state and proclaimed itself the Republic of Biafra. The country was soon plunged into a bloody civil war, during which more than a million lost their lives. These included Biafrans, mostly Ibos, who died of starvation despite international efforts to save them. Negotiations between Biafrans and Nigerians dragged on, with no real results. The secessionists lost ground steadily and capitulated on January 12, 1970. They were integrated into national life although there was a strong residue of resentment.

While the Biafran secession failed, it indicated the intensity of regionalism in Nigeria. The British, when in control of the area, had created a situation in which neither a common Nigerian state nor the many diverse nationalities, especially the Biafran, could grow. Nigerian leaders, each impelled by tribal considerations, added to the problem. The Biafran revolt indicated the strength of tribal communities in African life. It was repeated, with variations, across the entire continent. The instinct or urge to fragmentation had a weakening influence on the process of nation-building in Africa as it had earlier in Europe. (*See also* **TRIBALISM.**)

Bibliography: W.H. Bascom, "Tribalism, Nationalism, and Pan-Africanism," *Annals of the American Academy of Political and Social Science,* 342, (July, 1962), 21–29; Frederick Forsyth, *The Making of an African Legend: The Biafra Story* (London, 1983); Bernard Odohwu, *No Place to Hide: Crisis and Conflicts Inside Biafra* (Enugu, Nigeria, 1985); Paul Harrison, *News Out of Africa* (London, 1986).

BISMARCK, OTTO VON (1815–1898).   Statesman and father of German national unification. Throughout his career, Bismarck was a strong anti-liberal, whose basic aim was to bring about the unity of Germany under Prussian leadership. He reorganized the Prussian state to insure its efficiency, important in the future wars of national unification against Denmark in 1864, Austria in 1866, and France in 1870–1871. Early in his career, he made an extraordinary statement: "It is not by speechifying and majorities that the great questions of the day will have to be decided . . . but by iron and blood." Transformed into "blood-and-iron," this phrase followed Bismarck throughout his life. He was regarded widely as a man of iron, unscrupulous, utterly ruthless, and extremely emotional.

Bismarck's dynamic personality was associated closely with all that we understand by the words "traditional nationalism." He was an ideal champion for those Germans who resented talks about "the fundamental rights of the German people," about liberty, equality, and fraternity, about freedom of speech, press, and assembly. The most conservative of conservatives and always loyal to his Junker upbringing, he became the reactionary genius of Europe. He defended all that was traditional in German history, its feudal, aristocratic monarchist features, with the same utter fearlessness that characterized his entire life. He was well aware of the force of nationalism and he aimed to take full advantage of it. His goal was always the unification of Germany under Prussian auspices and the simultaneous strengthening of the Hohenzollern monarchy.

The traditional nationalism represented by Bismarck was indelibly impressed upon the German people during his stormy career. He had little use for the liberal nationalism of Jeremy Bentham (q.v.) in Britain, François Guizot (q.v.) in France, and Giuseppe Mazzini (q.v.) in Italy. He was responsible for stamping out any trend of liberal nationalism in Germany after the unsuccessful revolution of 1848. A thorough aristocrat, he was opposed to any weakening of the class system in Germany. He ignored the feelings of his fellow countrymen.

Bismarck was successful in whipping into a national union the conglomeration of German states and principalities that had been regarded throughout Europe as "a geographical expression." Under his stewardship, nationalism became a force of inestimable importance in the historical development of modern Germany. Under Frederick the Great, the French language, art, literature, and institutions enjoyed great popularity; under Bismarck the philosophy of Germanness crystallized and became the essence of German nationalism.

In the final analysis, the structure Bismarck built laboriously rested on a weak foundation and had an element of artificiality. The middle and lower classes, backbone of the Second German Empire, supported his system as long as "blood-and-iron" gave it strength and character. The apolitical German people, trained to obedience and veneration of authority, were eventually led along the path of destruction by William II in World War I and by Adolf Hitler in World War II.

Bibliography: Otto Pflanze, "Bismarck and German Nationalism," *The American Historical Review,* IX, No. 3 (April, 1955), 548–566; Erich Eyck, *Bismarck and the German Empire* (New York, 1964); Louis L. Snyder (ed.), *The Blood-and-Iron Chancellor* (Princeton, N.J. 1967); A.J.P. Taylor, *Bismarck: The Man and the Statesman* (London, 1974).

BLACK NATIONALISM.   *See* **PAN-AFRICANISM, DU BOIS, WILLIAM E.B.,** and **GARVEY, MARCUS.**

BOLINGBROKE, HENRY ST. JOHN (1678–1751).   British statesman and writer, early advocate of English nationalism. During his
youth Bolingbroke acquired a reputation for his dissipation and
extravagances, but later he settled down and became an outstanding
statesman. His writings often expressed a strong sense of patriotism,
such as his essay on *The Spirit of Patriotism* and a treatise titled *The
Patriot-King*, then used as a textbook seeking to teach George III
before his accession to the throne the elementary principles of kingship. Bolingbroke was also the collaborator in writing the famous
anthem:

> Rule, Brittania, rule the waves,
> Britons never shall be slaves.

   Bolingbroke's aristocratically tinged nationalism was political and
cultural. He had a deep pride in being British: "I feel a secret pride
in thinking that I was born a Briton; when I consider that the Romans,
those masters of the world, maintained their liberty little more than
seven centuries; and that Britain, which was a free nation about
seventeen hundred years ago, is so at this hour."
   At the same time, Bolingbroke saw his own consciousness of
nationalism as humanitarian in scope. He believed that every nationality was entitled to its own development and its particular genius.
Each nation should attend to the business of its own advancement
and should take the kindest and most tolerant sentiment toward
other peoples striving for similar ends. Bolingbroke's ideas merged
into the liberal nationalism popular in Britain from the nineteenth to
the twentieth centuries.
   Bibliography: The Works of Lord Bolingbroke (4 vols., Philadelphia,
1841); Isaac Kramnick, *Bolingbroke and His Circle* (Cambridge, England, 1968); Simon Vary, *Henry St. John, Viscount Bolingbroke* (Boston,
1984).

BOLÍVAR, SIMÓN (1783–1830).   Called *El Libertador* (The Liberator), hero of South American independence, Bolívar was a passionate and headstrong patriot and nationalist. He was descended on
both sides from noble Venezuelan families. Studying in various
European capitals, especially in Madrid, he became an ardent follower of the teachings of Jean-Jacques Rousseau (q.v.). He witnessed
the final scenes of the French Revolution. Returning home, he joined
the party of independence in Venezuela. He took part as a brilliant
tactician in many strategic battles for independence. Leading an

enthusiastic force, he drove the royalists out of New Granada, Venezuela, and Ecuador.

As a national activist, Bolívar charged that Spain, unable to win the loyalty of South Americans, had resorted to devious behavior as a means of forcing its "ignominious yoke" on a people hungry for freedom. He urged patriotic Venezuelans to struggle against a government whose incentives were "a death-dealing sword and the flames of the Inquisition." Madrid, he said, has a government "that wants not domains, but deserts, not cities but ruins, not vassals but graves." His zealous leadership ended forever Spain's domination of the New World.

On February 15, 1819, the hero of liberation made a speech at Angostura in which he praised the concept of national sovereignty:

> The declaration of the Republic of Venezuela is the most glorious, most heroic, most worthy act of a free people; it is one that with the greatest satisfaction I have the honor to offer Congress, being already sanctioned by the unanimous will of the free people of Venezuela.
>
> Deign, Legislators, to accept with indulgence the profession of my political faith, the highest wishes of my heart and the fervent prayer which on behalf of the people I dare address you: Deign to grant to Venezuela a government preeminently moral, which will hold in chains oppression, anarchy and guilt. A government which will allow righteousness, tolerance, peace to reign; a government which will cause equality and liberty to triumph under the protection of inexorable laws.
>
> Gentlemen, commence your duties; I have finished mine.

Bolívar was successful in creating a new spirit of independence and nationalism in South America, but his later adoption of high-handed, even dictatorial methods, caused much murmuring against his power. He was widely accused of imperial designs and there were revolts and separatist movements against him. He died poverty-stricken and bitterly hated. Today, he is revered as the greatest of Latin American heroes and as a champion of Latin American nationalism.

Bibliography: Gargard Masur, *Simón Bolívar* (Albuquerque, N.M., 1948); John B. Trend, *Bolívar and the Independence of Latin America* (New York, 1951); John J. Johnson, *Simón Bolívar and Spanish American Independence, 1783–1830) (Princeton, N.J., 1968);* Dennis Hepman, *Simón Bolívar* (New York, 1985).

BRETON NATIONALISM.   Along with Basque separatism, Breton nationalism is one of the more important French mini-nationalisms. Brittany, an old province in the extreme northwestern peninsula of France, has revealed throughout its history a persistent trend toward regional independence. Geography has played a decisive role in the Bretons' way of life. Separated from the rest of France, their isolation contributed to their distinctive customs. Their language is of major significance. The basic Breton tongue belongs to the Cymric division of Celtic, which forms one group of the Indo-European family of languages. Throughout their history and well into the nineteenth and twentieth centuries, Bretons have held fast to their sense of uniqueness. Conservative in nature, they preferred their own traditional social structure and religious belief. They supported the French Revolution at the beginning, but outraged by the execution of aristocrats, they turned on the Revolution and remained royalist and anti-Jacobin. They were loyal to Paris in World War I, but in the background was a firm particularism and urge for independence.

The conflict between Breton regionalism and French centralism became strained in the mid-twentieth century, when Paris adopted a new policy on the language question in Brittany. The government issued orders making it plain that the children in Brittany were not to use the Breton language in primary and secondary schools. Older Bretons were angered because most of their countrymen were literate only in French. Breton intellectuals expressed their dismay about the very survival of their language. The language issue, as in many countries, brought about a heated confrontation between the central authorities and those Bretons leaning toward regionalism and eventual independence.

The tenor of Breton nationalism took on two forms: a literary movement and militant action. The literary movement, confined to about 10,000 intellectuals both inside and outside of Brittany, was concerned mostly with the effort in Paris to follow an official policy of gradually outlawing the Breton language. Breton intellectuals, disturbed by the language problem, began to call for more autonomy so that they could maintain their own language with its long historical background. For centuries, Bretons had resisted the efforts in Paris to impose centralization policies, and they did not want to allow the government to dictate to them on the language question.

The second form of Breton nationalism was led by dissatisfied militants, who saw themselves as patriots and liberators. Like the Basques of Spain, they preferred direct action to what they saw as useless negotiations. In 1966, young Breton activists formed the Breton Liberation Front (F.L.B.). In their underground publications, they denounced "French imperialism," and called for independence. Their program was in the classic tradition of mini-nationalisms everywhere: (1) the Breton people are oppressed; (2) the land of Brittany is occupied by foreign French military camps; (3) the evidence of Breton language and culture is discouraged by French imperial power; and (4) Bretons want an end to their humiliating status of submission to Paris and they demand full independence. Their goal was similar to that of the Irish Republican Army (I.R.A.) (q.v.) in Northern Ireland.

In its early stages, the Breton Liberation Front worked on a modest scale as its members plastered handbills or scribbled graffiti on accessible walls. They wanted merely to bring attention to their cause. Harmless puerile raids soon degenerated into dangerous guerrilla attacks. In early July 1978, Breton extremists attracted global attention when they planted a bomb at Versailles, where some 50,000 people had come to witness a fireworks display to celebrate the arrival of summer. A time bomb secreted in the south wing of the magnificent palace went off at 2 A.M. The blast left a large hole in the floor of a hall devoted to Napoleonic art panelling. Nothing comparable had ever happened before in France. The French public was shocked and angered. It was one thing for Bretons to demonstrate in their own territory, but it was regarded as an atrocity for these dissidents to strike at the heart of French culture. A government official called the bombing "a deplorable injury to the essential part of the French heritage." Versailles was not only an important tourist attraction, but for most Frenchmen it represented the glory and prestige of their country. Two Breton guerrillas were arrested, tried in November 1978, and given jail sentences of fifteen years.

From 1966 to 1979, Breton activists attacked more than 200 targets in France, including military and police barracks, radio installations, even a nuclear power plant at Plogoff. Hotheaded Breton activists continued their campaign for independence on the assumption that Paris had forsaken them, lied to them, and allowed them to remain poverty-stricken compared to the rest of France. Yet, despite its militancy, Breton nationalism received little mass support inside Brittany, even though there was much sympathy for its aspirations.

Bibliography: Thiébaut Flory, *Le mouvement régionaliste français* (Paris, 1966); Jack E. Reece, *The Bretons Against France: Ethnic Minority Nationalism in Twentieth Century France* (Chapel Hill, N.C., 1977); Maurice le Lannow, *Le Bretagne et les Bretons* (Paris, 1978); Bertrand Frelaut, *Les nationalistes Bretons de 1939–1946* (Paris, 1985).

BURKE, EDMUND (1729–1797). Statesman, political writer, and traditional nationalist, Burke looked with horror on the French Revolution and its excesses. He saw little but evil in the rebellion of a disorganized mob against the rule of law and order. Liberty, he believed, was inextricably tied up with order; it could not be reconciled with attacks by "the swinish multitude." His attitude was emotional:

> France, by the perfidy of her leaders, has utterly disgraced the tone of lenient council in the cabinets of princes, and disarmed it of its most potent topics. She has sanctified the dark suspicious maxims of tyrannous distrust; and taught kings to tremble at (what will hereafter be called) the delusive plausibilities of moral politicians. . . .
> Laws overturned; tribunals subverted; industry without vigour; commerce expiring; the revenue unpaid, yet the people impoverished; a church pillaged, and a state not relieved; civil and military anarchy made the constitution of the kingdom; everything human and divine sacrificed to the idol of public credit, and national bankruptcy the consequence.
> Were these dreadful things all necessary? Were they the inevitable results of the desperate struggle of determined patriots, compelled to wade through blood and tumult, to the quiet shore of a tranquil and prosperous liberty? No! Nothing like it.

Burke's own sense of nationalism was based on tradition and history. He expressed his love of country in a speech on the impeachment of Warren Hastings, the first Governor-General of British India:

> Next to the love of parents for their children, the strongest instinct both natural and moral, that exists in man, is the love of his country:—an instinct, indeed, which extends even to the brute creation. All creatures love their offspring; next to that they love their homes; they have a fondness for the place where they have been bred, for the habitations they have dwelt in, for the stalls in which they have been fed, the pastures they have browsed in, and the wilds in which they have roamed. We all know that the natal soil has a sweetness in it beyond the harmony of verse. This instinct, I say, that binds all creatures to their country, never becomes inert in us, nor ever suffers us to want a memory of it.

Burke's nationalism was aristocratic in nature. He saw the happiness of humanity as dependent more on the history of classes (especially the aristocracy) than on the masses. Englishmen, he said, look upon the legal hereditary succession of their crown as among their rights, not their wrongs, as a benefit and not a grievance, and as a security for their liberty, not as a badge of servitude.

Bibliography: Edmund Burke, *Reflections on the Revolution in France* (London, 1790); *The Works of Edmund Burke* (3 vols., New York, 1851); George M. Fasel, *Edmund Burke* (Boston, 1983); Iain Hampsher-Monk, *The Political Philosophy of Edmund Burke* (London, 1987).

C

CANADIAN REVIEW OF STUDIES IN NATIONALISM. The only scholarly journal devoted exclusively to the comparative interdisciplinary study of nationalism and related subjects. It prints regional and theoretical articles, review essays, and reviews of new books on nationalism. Founded in 1973 by Thomas Spira, Professor of History at the University of Prince Edward Island, Canada, the journal publishes an annual supplement, the *Annotated Bibliography of Works on Nationalism*. It is supported by the University of Prince Edward Island, as well as by the Social Sciences and Humanities Research Council at Ottawa, Canada.

The journal has an editorial board consisting of thirty-two scholars in the humanities and social sciences, especially those who have devoted their careers to the study of nationalism:

CARBONARI. Italian "charcoal burners," members of an Italian secret society that played an important role in the emergent nationalism on the Mediterranean peninsula. Organized in the latter days of the Napoleonic Empire, it was formed by Neapolitan republicans during the reign of Joachim Murat. It carried over after 1815 into the era of Austrian domination.

The goal of the *Carbonari* was to free Italy from foreign domination and to win constitutional liberties. It aimed to further the *Risorgimento* (Resurrection) movement and to champion Italian nationalism. It attracted a wide membership, including army officers, nobles, landlords, government officials, workers, peasants, and priests. Those who joined the *Carbonari* circulated forbidden literature and maintained a revolutionary ferment designed to promote Italian unity. The movement spread throughout the south of Italy. Among the foreigners who joined the *Carbonari* was Lord Byron. During his early years, Louis Napoleon was implicated in its activities.

Carbonari units tended to use Christian and liberal phraseology in their constititions. "Carbonarism teaches the true end of moral existence, and gives rules of social life. It is the sacred rights of equality that the Good Cousins *(bien cugini)* must especially attach themselves." *Carbonari* societies used a fantastic and mysterious symbolism designed to appeal to the masses. Members preferred a secret and seemingly impenetrable correspondence, by means of a dictionary of words referable to others of real meaning. A mystic religious language was used to explain the aims of the society, such as "cleaning the woods of wolves," alluding to Christ as a lamb torn by wolves. Members were initiated by a complex ritual intended to impress them with the dire effects of betraying secrets. Each new member was required to take a sacred oath:

> I promise, and swear upon the general statutes of the order, and upon this steel, the avenging instrument of the perjured, scrupulously to keep the secret of Carbonarism; and neither to write, engrave, or paint any thing concerning it, without having obtained a written permission. I swear to help my Good Cousins in case of need, as much as in me lies, and not to attempt any thing against the honour of their families. I consent, and wish, if I perjure myself, that my body may be cut in pieces, then burnt, and my ashes scattered to the wind, in order that my name may be held up to the execration of the Good Cousins throughout the earth. So help me God.

The *Carbonari* rapidly increased in numbers as they won adherents to the cause of Italian nationalism. Harried by the Austrian police, many of the members were imprisoned, exiled, or executed. By 1820 the rolls included many Italian patriots. After the suppression of the Neapolitan and Lombardian revolutions of 1821, Carbonarism was judged by the authorities to be high treason. The movement began to lose its impetus, although it was revived again in the revolutionary days of 1830.

Bibliography: Memoirs of the Secret Societies of the South of Italy, Particularly the Carbonari (London, 1831); Alberto Falcionelli, *Les sociétés secrètes italiennes: Les Carbonari* (Paris, 1936).

CARR, EDWARD HALLETT (1892–1982).   Diplomat, historian, Fellow of Trinity College, Cambridge University, and scholar of nationalism. In his book *Nationalism and After* (1945), Carr wrote that although nationalism was still strong at the close of World War II, paradoxically, certain features of the war itself seemed to mark a retrogression from the unqualified nationalism of the preceding period. "The absence of any trace of national exaltation or enthusiasm on the outbreak of the war offered in all countries—and not least in Germany itself—a striking contrast to the patriotic fervour of 1914. National hatreds have lost their old spontaneous frankness, and mask themselves delicately in ideological trappings." In other words, Carr maintained that the age of unbridled and militant nationalism was ended.

Bibliography: Edward H. Carr, *Nationalism and After* (London, 1945).

CATALAN SEPARATISM.   The idea of moderation has been conspicuously absent from Spain's political life. To the militancy of Basque nationalism (q.v.) has been added the ferocity of a second clamoring mini-nationalism—that of Catalonia. This major area of regional dissatisfaction in plurinational Spain includes the provinces of Barcelona, Tarragona, Léride, and Gerona. Some 12,000 square miles, it extends from the southeastern Pyrénées down to the Costa Brava, past Barcelona, and westward to the Ebro River. The origin of the Catalonian people is obscure, lost in the mist of time.

The Catalan language is a separate tongue and not related to any Spanish dialect. It was derived from a Latin dialect spoken by colonizing Romans. The people of the area were subjected to a series of conquests successively by Romans, Goths, Moors, and West Franks. During the feudal-manorial era, Catalans retained many of their Roman customs. In the later Middle Ages, Catalonia was a conquering country, expanding throughout the Mediterranean area and forming a powerful thalassic empire extending at one time as far east as Greece. Eventually, it became an important mercantile and industrial power in the western Mediterranean. Catalans showed their independent spirit in their *Generalitat*, a permanent executive board of Parliament that they retained for some six centuries.

In much the same way as the Basques, Catalans showed a deep sense of distaste for Madrid's centralism. Throughout five centuries as a part of Spain, they never gave up their dream of an independent

Catalonia with its own special red-yellow banner. They very nearly accomplished their goal during the brief regime of the Spanish Republic in the 1930s. Dictator Francisco Franco sent his troops into the region, but he required some three months to conquer the four provinces of Catalonia. For him it was an absolute necessity to herd both Basques and Catalans into his centralized Spain. He used his power to control the economy of Catalonia, discouraged its language, and mercilessly hunted Catalan separatists, sent them to prison, or executed them.

The reaction of Catalans to Franco's brutality was considerably less violent than that of the Basques, but it, nevertheless, existed. This proud people, adhering strongly to their regional customs and traditions, at first asserted their sense of national consciouness with biting satire, ridiculing the dictator and his efforts to control them. They would use sarcasm instead of bullets or bombs. Franco's response was to appease the unruly Catalans. He granted the regional government a measure of semi-autonomy, including the power to legislate, levy taxes, run the school system, and use its own police force.

Such concessions, while gratefully received, did not altogether satisfy the Catalans. Behind them were centuries of desire for freedom from Spain. They had no intention of relinquishing their desire for an independent state on the Iberian peninsula. Dissidents proudly sang their haunting song: "*Els Segadors*"—"Catalonia triumphant will again be rich and full!" Teenagers displayed their T-shirts with slogans calling for freedom. They flaunted their red and yellow patches proclaiming: "I'm a citizen of the Catalan nation!" Always the emphasis was upon "the Catalan nation." The people of Catalonia, while accepting the reality of their inclusion in a united Spain, always regarded themselves as free citizens of a distinct nation. They hewed to their own language and made it clear that the Spanish they were forced to speak was "the tongue of the oppressor." In many ways, Catalan separatism was the classic case of a mini-nationalism working to throw off the chains of a stronger centralism, whose tentacles had held a firm grip on a people of a "different and subjugated nation."

Although their demonstrations were muted and outside the category of Basque terrorism, Catalans made certain to let Madrid know of their own special national sentiment. They jammed their parks to celebrate their own special heroes. Typical of their approach was the greeting of several hundred thousand Catalans in October 1977 to the return home of Josep Tarradallas, a Catalan nationalist who had been in exile for thirty-nine years. The proud dissident, a former president of the *Generalitat* (which had been abolished by Franco), spoke from the balcony where the Spanish Second Republic had been proclaimed in 1931: "Citizens of Catalonia! We are here—to share your sufferings, your struggles, your sacrifices. I am here to work with you for a prosperous Catalonia in freedom."

"In freedom"—the key words for mini-nationalisms everywhere. While Madrid had restored the *Generalitat* several months before as a concession to Catalans, Tarradallas still retained his goal for Catalonia, independence. To him the mission of freedom was still unfulfilled.

Bibliography: Salvador Giner, *The Social Structure of Catalonia* (Sheffield, 1980); Oriol Pi-Sunyer, *National and Societal Integration: A Focus on Catalonia* (Amherst, Mass., 1983); Gary M. McDonogh, *Conflict in Catalonia* (Gainseville, Fla., 1986).

CAVOUR, CAMILLO BENSO, COUNT (1810–1861). Italian statesman, architect of a united Italy, and outstanding nationalist. Descended from a noble Piedmontese family, Cavour became a fervent nationalist in early life. Throughout his career he called for the regeneration of Italy. Short, stocky, recognized by his steel-rimmed glasses, he gave the appearance of a conscientious clerk, but, in fact, became one of the nineteenth century's greatest statesmen.

In 1847 Cavour founded the newspaper *Il Risorgimento*. He called for the resurrection of his country, demanded a representative system of government similar to that of England, and opposed absolutism of any kind. He denounced the use of military force to suppress political opposition. Like German Chancellor Otto von Bismarck (q.v.), he was always of practical mind; he was a master in his ability to discern the useful and possible. The Italian people gave him more respect than affection; they were more interested in the patriots Mazzini and Garibaldi (qq.v.), both of whom either ridiculed or ignored Cavour.

In 1852 Victor Emmanuel II made Cavour his Prime Minister and gave him a free hand to pursue his policies. The king was not altogether satisfied with "that pestiferous little man," but he was shrewd enough to recognize Cavour's ability and supported him in one crisis after another.

Cavour's policy of moderation was in distinct contrast to Mazzini's radicalism. As his main guidelines, he accepted the policies of British bourgeois liberalism. With his clear program, always opposed to extremism, there was never any doubt about his aims and ideals. He differed from Mazzini in that he avoided mixing national with democratic and social problems. He was careful not to paralyze the only Italian classes that could contribute to the Italian awakening. He was also careful to avoid any destructive and violent passions that might harm the Italian national state.

Cavour's work as a liberal nationalist was crucial in the critical years from 1859 to 1861. Ideologically as well as politically, he belonged to the world of John Stuart Mill (q.v.). Above all, he believed in liberty, progress, and moderation. He was against authoritarianism of any kind and opposed the concept of Jacobin authoritarian nationalism. He was not impressed with those fellow Italian nationalists who stressed the primacy of intuitive knowledge known as supernatural truth. He understood the primacy of reason, but also its limitations. He became, in effect, one of Europe's outstanding liberal nationalists. As a nationalist he was always the progressive European moderate, who contributed much to the development of Italian liberalism. True to his liberal nationalism, he opposed collectivism of any kind, as well as economic mercantilism.

As a nationalist, Cavour showed greater loyalty to a unified Italian nation than to his regional Sardinian state. He had little use for the type of integral nationalism that called for the greatness and the mission of the Italian nation. His driving goal was to expel the Austrians from Italian affairs. Above all, he wanted a unified Italy that would be devoted to liberal nationalism, not to aggression and expansionism.

Bibliography: Massimo Salvadori, *Cavour and the Unification of Italy* (Princeton, N.J., 1961); Edward Cecil George Cadogan, *Builders of Modern Italy* (Port Washington, N.Y., 1970); Denis Mack Smith, *Cavour* (New York, 1985).

CHAUVINISM.   Term originally used to denote exaggerated and unreasonable patriotism, with excessive pride in one's own country, and a corresponding contempt for other nations. It is the French equivalent of the English "jingoism" (q.v.). The word is derived from the name of Nicholas Chauvin, a soldier of the French Empire and a veteran of the *Grande Armée*. Awarded military honors and a pension for his service, Chauvin retained a lifelong, simple-minded devotion to Napoleon, Chauvin's name became a synonym for blind worship of Napoleon. His attitude was typical of the veneration of the military among those Frenchmen who had fought in the Napoleonic wars.

During the nineteenth century the term chauvinism came to express excessive nationalism or ultranationalism. In an era of strong national rivalries, it was used to glorify national consciousness, contempt for other nations and minorities, and to promote militarism, imperialism, and racism. The media of communications, from the early cheap newspapers to the later radio and television, furthered the growth of chauvinism.

Bibliography: Ottfried Nippold, *Der deutsche Chauvinismus* (Bern, 1917); Caroline Playne, *Society at War, 1914–1916* (Boston, 1931); Horace Orlando Patterson, *Ethnic Chauvinism: The Reactionary Impulse* (New York, 1977).

CHETNIKS.   Guerrillas led by the Serb, Draja Mikhailovich, in Yugoslavia. (*See* **CROATIAN SEPARATISM.**)

CHIANG KAI-SHEK (1887–1975).   General, politician, ruler of China from 1928 to 1949, and Nationalist leader. While a student in a Japanese military school, Chiang was much impressed by the teachings of Sun Yat-sen (q.v.), which became his guideline for the rest of his life. In 1911 he took part in activities against the Manchu dynasty and in 1913 and 1915 against Yuan Shih-k'ai. In 1918 he formally joined the *Kuomintang*, the Nationalist Party founded by Sun Yat-sen. The latter was attempting to overthrow the war lords who controlled China and to win the goal of national unification.

When Sun Yat-sen died in 1925, Chiang was appointed commander-in-chief of the *Kuomintang* forces in Canton. In 1926 he led the Nationalist army northward from Canton and captured Hankow, Shanghai, and Nanking. Following the original policy of Sun Yat-sen, Chiang cooperated with the Communists and accepted aid from Soviet Russia. In 1927 he dramatically reversed himself and began the long civil war between the *Kuomintang* and the Communists. Using the slogan "No parties outside the *Kuomintang*, no factions inside the *Kuomintang*," Chiang in 1927 began a grand purge of his enemies, including personal rivals, workers, peasants, and students. In 1928 he became head of the Nationalist government at Nanking and generalissimo of all Chinese Nationalist forces. Thereafter, he exercised virtually unlimited power as leader of the Nationalist government. High on his agenda was his effort to eliminate the Communists by what was then called "a white terror."

Militarized parties, such as Chiang's Nationalist Party and the Chinese Communists, both modeled on the Communist Party of the Soviet Union, tended increasingly to polarize politics in China. Chiang sought desperately to win the confidence of his people by a series of reforms. He was careful, however, to avoid any wide-ranging social and economic reforms. He proposed tariff controls and other minor changes. In general, the Chinese economy stagnated and failed to break through to self-generating momentum. Culturally, even though Sun Yat-senism, with the "Three Principles of the People"— nationalism, democracy, and livelihood, remained as a regimented doctrine throughout Chiang's years of power. During the civil war against the Communists, he supported an abortive "New Life Movement," a vague effort to change the national mood.

Chiang's consciousness of nationalism was to unify China, crush his Communist rivals, face Japanese aggression, and then later come to the matter of increasingly demanded reforms. As the suffering of the Chinese people increased, Chiang and his *Kuomintang* found themselves caught between two millstones—the Chinese Communists' demand for "a revolutionary war of popular resistance" and encroaching Japanese imperialism. Even many of Chiang's erstwhile supporters became alarmed by appeasement of the Communists and by Communist calls for a new united front. These trends lay behind the kidnapping of Chiang at Christmas time in 1936 by young officers who had been expelled from Manchuria by the Japanese. At the time it was believed that Stalin had sent orders to the Chinese Communist Party to work for Chiang's release and for a united front.

In World War II Chiang became one of the most prominent leaders of the Allies in the conflict against Germany and Japan. After the war ended, he was unable to achieve any settlement with the Communists and the confrontations with them continued. He resumed his "Extermination of Bandits" (meaning the Communists) campaign in 1947. By this time his government had become so corrupt that he lost the confidence of both the people in China and his Western allies. After a series of defeats, his troops were routed by Mao Tsetung's (q.v.) Communist army. In 1949 Chiang fled to Formosa (Taiwan) with a large entourage and became the president of the refugee regime on the island.

Chinese nationalism had originated as early as the Opium War (1839–1840), with Chinese hostility to the British. It came of age about the turn of the century after China's defeat by Japan in 1895. It became intensified under the leadership of Sun Yat-sen and the revolution of 1911. Chiang sought to carry on the nationalist zeal of his predecessor, but he was unable to control events in his politically chaotic country. Chinese nationalism was appropriated by the Communists with the advent of the People's Republic in 1949.

Bibliography: John de Francis, *Nationalism and Language Reform in China* (Princeton, N.J., 1950); Chow Tse-tung, *The May Fourth Movement* (Cambridge, Mass., 1939); William Theodor de Bary, *et al.*, *Sources of Chinese Tradition* (New York, 1960); Furuya Keuji, *Chiang Kai-shek: His Life and Times* (New York, 1981).

CHINESE NATIONALISM.   *See* **SUN YAT-SEN** and **MAO TSE-TUNG.**

CLASSIFICATIONS OF NATIONALISM.   *See* **NATIONALISM, CLASSIFICATIONS OF,** and **HAYES' CLASSIFICATION.**

COLLINS, MICHAEL (1890–1922).   Irish revolutionary leader, nationalist, and hero of the Irish struggle for independence. The youngest son in the large family of a farmer, Collins was educated in a nationalist school. From 1907 to 1916 he lived in London, where he was for a time employed in the post office and later as an accountant. During Easter week, 1916, he took part in the uprising which led to the seizure of the Dublin Post Office. Imprisoned, he was released before Christmas 1916. He was jailed again, this time for sedition. He was then elected parliamentary representative for County Cork in the republican Dáil Eireann.

Collins became an important leader of Sinn Féin (q.v.). He organized the struggle that eventually led to the breakdown of the British control of Ireland and forced London to sue for peace. He was one of the leaders of the assembly in Ireland that declared for the republic. Its elected president, Eamon de Valera (q.v.), was in prison and Collins arranged for his escape. Collins became the first Sinn Féin Minister of Finance. He also was known as Director of Intelligence of the Irish Republican Army (q.v.). The chief planner of the Irish revolutionary movement, he was wanted by British authorities, who placed a reward of 10,000 pounds on his head.

After the truce of 1921, Collins was sent to London to negotiate a peace. He signed the agreement in the belief that it was the best possible treaty that could be obtained. It gave Ireland dominion status, but its provisions for partition and for an oath of loyalty to the Crown were unacceptable to Irish republicans. With civil war seemingly imminent, Collins became head of the government. Ten days later he was ambushed by irreconcilable republicans and shot dead while motoring in west Cork.

Noted for his daring exploits, energy, and imagination, Collins was unable to overcome the mutiny by anti-treaty republicans. In the minds of most Irish, however, he is regarded as a great national hero. (*See also* **IRISH NATIONALISM.**)

Bibliography: Rex Taylor, *Michael Collins* (London, 1958); T. Ryle Dwyer, *Michael Collins and the Treaty: His Difference with Valera* (Dublin, 1981); John M. Feehan, *The Shooting of Michael Collins* (Dublin, 1982); Michael Collins, *In Great Haste: The Letters of Michael Collins and Kitty Kiernan* (Dublin, 1983).

COLOGNE SCHOOL.   In 1965 Professor Theodor Schieder (q.v.) founded his research division on nationalism at the Historical Seminar of the University of Cologne in the Federal Republic of West Germany. He led this division until his death on October 9, 1984. The aim of the research was to throw light on European national movements in the nineteenth and twentieth centuries, which despite some differences, had common elements. The concepts of nation, nationalism, and national state played increasingly important roles in European history since the French Revolution. Schieder believed that the individual nationalisms in Europe were not isolated but should be placed in a European framework. He encouraged his students to use the historical-empirical method to show that European national movements should be understood not only on ideological and political grounds, but also should be examined to reveal social, industrial, and cultural factors. As leader of his research division, Schieder took a middle position between "individual" and "typological" historical thinking.

Some fourteen books on nationalism were published under Schieder's sponsorship. These were not limited to studies of European nationalism: student guests from Canada, Australia, and Korea also contributed dissertations in the seminar. Before his death Schieder also sponsored research on the protonationalisms of the sixteenth and seventeenth centuries as well as studies on mini-nationalisms or "regionalisms" in Europe and Canada. In addition to these dissertations, Schieder also organized lectures by foreign experts and international meetings on nationalism.

The Cologne school on nationalism was influenced by the work of Karl W. Deutsch (q.v.) on a quantitative approach to the problems of nationalism. An example of the use of the Deutsch formula (q.v.) may be found in O. Dann and T. Schieder, *National Government and Social Organization* (1978). Sponsored by Schieder's seminar, the book presented comparative studies of national unification movements in nineteenth-century Europe. Peter Alter described national organizations in Ireland, 1801–1921; Hans Henning Hahn treated the organizations of the Polish Great Emigration, 1931–1947; and Gerhard Brunn analyzed the organizations of the Catalan movement, 1859–1959. (*See* **CATALAN SEPARATISM.**) All three of these Cologne studies sought to strike a balance between economic, political, and social structures, but with main emphasis upon social aspects. This accent on social organization brought a new and important element to the study of nationalism. Other scholars prefer to see nationalism as predominantly a psychological and political phenomenon.

Students who worked in the Schieder seminar on nationalism and carried on its studies included Lothar Gall, Kurt Kluxen, Wolfgang J. Mommsen, Hans Ulrich Wehler, Helmut Berding, Gerhard Brunn, Peter Burian, Dieter Düding, Elizabeth Fehrenbach, Akira Hakashima, Ulrich Lins, Klaus Papst, and Irmgard Wilharm. Among the fourteen studies published after work in this seminar were Irmgard Wilharm, *Die Anfänge des griechescnen Nationalstaats, 1833–1843 (The Beginnings of the Greek National State, 1843–1844)* (Munich and Vienna, 1973); Ulrich Lins, *Die Omoto Bewegung und radikale Nationalismus in Japan (The Omoto Movement and Radical Nationalism in Japan)* (Munich and Vienna, 1976); and Dieter Düding, *Organisierter Gesellschaftlicher Nationalismus in Deutschland, 1808–1847 (Organized Social Nationalism in Germany, 1808–1847)* (Munich and Vienna, 1986). All studies in this series were published by R. Oldenbourg Verlag.

COMMAGER, HENRY STEELE (1902–   ). American historian and along with constitutional and intellectual history a specialist in American nationalism. Educated at the University of Chicago, where he received the Ph.B., M.A., and Ph.D. degrees, Commager went on to a distinguished teaching and writing career. He served as Professor of History and American Studies at Amherst College, while remaining Adjunct Professor at Columbia University. He was Harmsworth Professor of American History at Oxford University and also taught at Cambridge University. With Richard B. Morris, he was the co-editor of the 40-volume American Nation Series.

Commager saw the War of 1812 with Britain as unfortunate, needless, and far from glorious in a military sense, but, at the same time, vital in the formation of American nationalism. Begun and continued with American discontent and bickering, it nevertheless strengthened the sentiments of patriotism and national unity. Scattered American successes, especially the naval victories, gave the American people a new sense of pride and self-confidence. Men from different states fought side by side.

According to Commager's analysis, from this time on, Americans became more and more American, they felt and acted more as a nation, and the permanency of the Union was now secured. Nationalism was irresistibly advancing, with a new national literature, a better national land system, and a national urge for internal improvements. Commerce was cementing the American people into a national unit. (*See* **AMERICAN NATIONALISM.**)

Bibliography: Henry Steele Commager, *The American Mind* (New Haven, Conn., 1950); Henry Steele Commager (ed.), *Documents of American History* (New York, 1963); Henry Steele Commager, *Jefferson, Nationalism, and the Enlightenment* (New York, 1975).

COMMUNALISM. The term "communalism" means a sense of community among ethnic or linguistic groups. The word is often used as a synonym for tribalism (q.v.). It may also denote a system of government in which communes or local communities possess a certain amount of autonomy inside a federated state. *See also* **AUTONOMY, ETHNICITY, and ETHNONATIONALISM.**

CONNOR, WALKER (1926–   ). Professor of Political Science at the State University of New York at Brockport and specialist on nationalism. Concerned that the study of nationalism is impeded by terminology, Walker devoted himself to definition as a means of clarification. He sees English-speaking societies as especially prone to careless interutilization of terms to give vastly different connotations. Because of this confusing use of key terms, Connor believes that nationalism is used to describe two different concepts that are often in conflict with one another. On occasion, it may identify loyalty to the nation in the sense of human groupings that may or may not be conterminous with a state (as for example Croatian, Scottish, or Ukrainian nationalism). At the same time, it is used more often to identify with and show loyalty to the nation, when the latter term is used to describe the state structure, without attention to the national composition of the state's population (American, Argentinian, or Filipino nationalism).

To avoid the confusion between two different and sometimes antagonistic loyalties, Connor recommended that the term nationalism be used to refer to state loyalty, and ethnonationalism to mean loyalty to the nation. In his view, nationalism and ethnonationalism both mean identity with and loyalty to the nation, while patriotism connotes identity with and loyalty to the state. This differentiation led Connor to the study of ethnicity.

Connor accepts the definition used by most American sociologists today that the term ethnic group should be used to connote "a group with a common cultural tradition and a sense of identity which exists as a sub-group of a larger society." This definition serves to make ethnic group and minority synonymous, and therefore, could not apply to the dominant people within the state (as, for example, the English or German people). In this sense, an ethnic group consists of those who conceive themselves as being alike by virtue of their common ancestry, and who are thus regarded by others.

According to Connor, the great importance that nationalism has had since the eighteenth century has been due to its linkage with political legitimacy. Whether called "the principle of nationalities" or "national self-determination," this linkage is a refinement or variant of the doctrine of popular sovereignty. Its development depends upon the appearance and spread of popular sovereignty. It will recede only when the doctrine of popular sovereignty recedes. Connor sees no evidence that such a recession is taking place in this century. (*See also* **ETHNONATIONALISM.**)

Bibliography: Walker Connor, "The Politics of Ethnonationalism," *Journal of International Affairs,* 27, No. 1 (1973), 1–21; Walker Connor, "Nationalism and Political Illegitimacy," *Canadian Review of Studies in Nationalism,* 8, No. 2 (Fall, 1981), 201–228.

CONSCIOUS NATIONALISM.   *See* **NATIONALISM, CLASSIFICATIONS OF.**

CORSICAN NATIONALISM.   Along with the mini-nationalisms of Bretons in Brittany and Basques in southwestern France, Corsican dissidents called for severance of their ties with Paris and demanded an independent homeland. Corsica is a small island of 3,352 square miles in the Mediterranean, west of Italy, north of Sardinia, and just over 100 miles southeast of France. After four centuries of colonial rule by the Genoese Republic, it became part of France in 1769. Two decades later, it was made a *département* of France. But its sense of nationalism has persisted.

The historical development of Corsica shows a long continuing sentiment favoring independence. Corsican intellectuals, in the classic tradition of modern nationalists, paid close attention to their cultural heritage. Many took pride in the career of their native-born Napoleon, even though he for a time put an end to separatist sentiment in the island and helped consolidate Corsica with the French mainland. In both World Wars, Corsica was known for its strong support of France in its times of crises.

Corsican dissenters to French rule are divided into two groups: (1) moderates who would be satisfied with more autonomy inside the French system; and (2) activists, obstreperous objectors, who refuse to settle for more autonomy and, instead, demand outright independence. Inspired by Basque guerrilla tactics in Spain and France, Corsican militants reject the slowness of democratic means to win their freedom. They call for an independent nation.

The Corsican National Liberation Front (F.L.N.C.), founded in the mid-1970s, attempted to take advantage of several areas of tension on the island. Its members were angered by the increasing numbers of Algerians who had fled their country and, with French agreement, had settled in Corsica. They were also displeased with the continued presence on their soil of 15,000 members of the French Foreign Legion. Convinced that moderation was useless, the F.L.N.C. resorted to terror to advance its cause. It believed violence to be a legitimate means of halting "colonial aggression" on their island.

The tactics of terrorists brought them the name of "wild Corsicans." They placed bombs in banks, public buildings, travel agencies, and television and radio stations, especially in Paris. In May 1979 alone they set off twenty-two bombs in the French capital. From January 1978 to July 1979, Corsican activists were responsible for some 466 bombings. Members of the F.L.N.C. made the usual claim that they were not terrorists at all but patriots fighting for the liberation of their people. They defied French officials. "Your justice is not ours. The right to resistance, to armed struggle, is inscribed in the declaration of human rights. We need to give no explanations in court to justify our actions. *'Eviva le nazione!'* ('Long Live the Nation!'), *'Francesci fuori'* ('Frenchmen go home!')."

The French public was alienated and outraged by the bomb attacks. French authorities insisted that not one inch of Corsica would be relinquished. It was the familiar case of a centralized national authority versus a particularistic mini-nationalism. To cries of *"Corsica liberta!"* Paris replied with indifference or half-hearted measures. France, they said, was a nation of patriots, not semi-patriots. Democratic dissent—yes! Independence—emphatically no! After all, Corsicans, too, shared the glory of French history. Nevertheless, in the summer of 1981 a devolution plan was inaugurated for Corsica—a new-style region of France with its own legislature, consultative councils, and cultural identity, as well as many other concessions. Moderates were appeased, but extremists rejected the new plan as unacceptable because it retained unwanted French supremacy. Corsican nationalism remains alive.

Bibliography: Dorothy Archer, *Corsica, the Scented Isle* (Boston, 1924); Ian Bentley Thompson, *Corsica* (Newton Abbot, England, 1971); Michel Labros, *La question Corsica* (Paris, 1977).

COUDENHOVE-KALERGI, RICHARD N. (1894–1972).   As research associate in history at New York University, Coudenhove-Kalergi emerged as a zealous champion of Pan-Europe to replace European nationalism. He was born in Tokyo on November 16, 1894, the son of the *chargé d'affaires* in the Austro-Hungarian embassy and Mitsui Aoyama, an upper-class Japanese lady. He grew up in Bohemia in a household that included nine nationalities. Early in life he became convinced that nationalism was a dangerous historical phenomenon, "a terrifying force" that might continue for centuries unless it was eliminated in contemporary life.

The leading spokesman for the new and defensive conception of European union, Coudenhove-Kalergi produced a long series of books from 1924 on. He urged the reorganization of the world into six autonomous units—the British Commonwealth, the Soviet Union, Pan-Europa, Pan-America, China, and Japan. There could be no united world, he warned, with a disunited Europe. He traveled throughout the world delivering lectures for his cause. He enlisted the support of such distinguished statesmen as Walther Rathenau, Thomas Masaryk, Winston Churchill, and Aristide Briand, all of whom encouraged him but would not head his movement. In October 1926, he called a European Congress in Vienna, the first of a series of gatherings. In 1947, at a meeting held in Gstaad, Switzerland, the European Parliamentary Union was founded with Coudenhove-Kalergi as Secretary-General.

Although the idea of Pan-Europa attracted the attention and support of many intellectuals, it had an underlying weakness: it lacked a mass base. Eventually, Coudenhove-Kalergi drafted a constitution for a United States of Europe. A European Parliament actually came into existence, thus realizing Coudenhove-Kalergi's dream. But it had little influence. European statesmen were quite willing to consider the benefits of economic union in a Common Market, but they resisted any political attempt to lessen their national sovereignty. Coudenhove-Kalergi's lifelong pursuit of Pan-Europa has remained an evanescent idea in the still powerful Age of Nationalism. (*See also* **PAN-EUROPA.**)

Bibliography: Richard N. Coudenhove-Kalergi, *Europa Erwacht (Europe Awakes)* (Paris, 1934); *Europeans Must Unite* (Glarus, Switzerland,

1939); *Crusade for Pan-Europa* (New York, 1943); *Pan-Europa* (Munich, 1966); *Ein Leben für Europa (One Life for Europe)* (Cologne, 1966).

CRAMB, J. A. (1862–1913).   Professor of Modern History at Queen's College, London, and one of the more assertive nationalists in pre-World War I Britain. In the spring and summer of 1900 he delivered a series of lectures on the origins and destiny of imperial Britain, which gave his listeners a vivid impression of their own greatness as a nation. Cramb's nationalism was equated with imperialism and territorial expansion. As such, it was a notable departure from traditional English liberal nationalism. In ringing phrases he called upon the witnesses of the past with the assurance that God was for Britain, and British justice and freedom would cover the globe:

> And lo! gathering up from the elder centuries, a sound like a trumpet-call, clear-piercing, far-borne, mystic, ineffable, the call to battle of hosts invisible, the mustering armies of the dead, the great of other wars—Brunanburh and Senlac, Creçy, Flodden, Blenheim and Trafalgar. *Their* battle-cries await our answer—the chivalry's at Agincourt, "Heaven for Harry, England and St. George!," Cromwell's war-shout, which was a prayer, at Dunbar, "The Lord of Hosts! The Lord of Hosts!"—these await our answer, that response which by this war we at last send ringing down the ages, "God for Britain, Justice and Freedom to the world!"

(See also **ENGLISH NATIONALISM.***)*
Bibliography: J. A. Cramb, *The Origins and Destiny of Imperial Britain and Nineteenth Century Europe* (New York, 1915).

CROATIAN SEPARATISM.   Out of the crucible of World War I came the independent succession state called the Kingdom of the Serbs, Croats, and Slovenes, all of whom spoke basically the same language. Not until 1929 was the name officially changed to Yugoslavia. The new state soon split into warring factions. In 1920 the Serbs set up a centralized government, whereupon the Croats at once demanded autonomy. From that moment on, the Croats formed a clamoring minority in Yugoslavia.

In 1928 the Croats formed a parliament of their own. King Alexander, the new monarch since 1921, responded with a dictatorship. He was assassinated by a Croatian nationalist. Croatian separatism at this time was encouraged by Hungary and Italy, both of which expected to benefit by Yugoslav factionalism. At this time the *Eustachi*, a Croatian nationalist organization, turned to terrorism (q.v.) to enforce its demand for independence. That course of action has continued to the present day.

In 1939, under the regime of Prince Paul, restive Croats were granted limited autonomy. When in March 1941 Paul signed a pro-Axis pact, he was overthrown within two days. In April the Nazis invaded Yugoslavia, whereupon the *Eustachi* proclaimed a declaration of independence. A new dictatorship was set up under Ante Pavelich, leader of the *Eustachi.*

Many Yugoslavs, angered by German domination, went underground. *Chetniks*, guerrillas led by the Serb Draja Mikhailovich, were a dedicated underground force. Josip Broz, a Croatian later to be called Tito, was supported by both the Soviet government and Great Britain. He formed a rival guerrilla outfit working to win power in Yugoslavia. Emerging triumphant after fierce infighting, Tito established his own dictatorship, which he called the Federal People's Republic of Yugoslavia. Rival Mikhailovich was executed in 1946.

Inner tensions in postwar Yugoslavia by no means disappeared during the Tito regime. The new dictator was faced with a multitude of nationalities problems. He would combine all the dissatisfied minorities into a strong centralized federal state, but that was more easily envisioned than accomplished. Any attempt to appease one nationality was met with outraged protest from others. Though himself of Croatian origin, Tito was angered by militant Croatian separatism. That fervent mini-nationalism was to be one of his most annoying problems. He urged his Croatian brothers to subjugate their aspirations in the interest of a higher Yugoslav nationalism. He was willing to grant certain autonomous rights in administration, industry, and agriculture. For Croatian separatists this was just not enough.

Although both peoples spoke similar dialects, Serbs (forty-two percent of the population) and Croats (twenty-three percent) remained bitter rivals. There was also religious differences: Serbs belonged to the Byzantine Orthodox Church, while Croats were mostly Catholic. There were also festering economic wounds: Croats claimed that the dominant Serbs treated them unfairly, especially in the allocation of profits from tourism.

As elsewhere, Croatian dissidents were divided into two major factions. Moderate Croatian intellectuals would settle for autonomy and made it a point to encourage the maintenance of Croatian culture. Emotional students began to denounce Tito's guerrillas as fat and lazy parvenus, a situation that angered the dictator loyal to his old comrades. But another group went far beyond the occasional criticisms of the moderates. These dissidents called for outright independence. In their struggle for emancipation they resorted to violence in ways that aroused the attention of the entire world. They denounced Tito as a mass murderer and turned to bullet and bomb in what amounted to a reign of terror.

Croatian extremists issued the usual claim: they were heroes engaging in a struggle for liberation, for a democratic, independent, and neutral Croatia. They operated not only in the homeland, but began a terror campaign abroad. There were some 100,000 Croatians living in Illinois and Indiana; from their ranks emerged terrorists who carried on a vicious campaign against the government of their homeland. Throughout the 1970s, Croatians from the United States, Canada, and Australia carried on a veritable war against Yugoslavia. The *Otpor* ("Resistance" in Croatian) engaged in violent actions from bombing, to highjacking, to assassination. In 1971, Croatian activists killed the Yugoslavian Ambassador to Sweden. That same year, Croatians were suspected of blowing up the main terminal at La Guardia Airport in New York City. In 1978, Croatian extremist took hostages in Chicago when West German police ordered a Croatian to be extradited to Yugoslavia.

Croatian nationalists apparently have no intention of giving up the struggle for an independent Croatia.

Bibliography: Jack Edward Fisher, *Yugoslavia: A Multinational State* (San Francisco, 1966); Franjo Tudjman, *Nationalism in Contemporary Europe* (Boulder, Col., 1981); Lazo M. Kostic, *The Holocaust in the Independent State of Croatia* (Chicago, 1981); Pedro Ramort, *Nationalism and Federalism in Jugoslavia, 1963–1983* (Bloomington, Ind., 1984).

CULTURAL NATIONALISM. A common culture is a basic attribute of modern nationalism. The people of a nation who share such a culture are able to communicate with one another usually through language, as in England, or through commonly understood languages, as in Switzerland. The critical factor is an increasing awareness of, or desire for, a national culture. In addition to a common language or commonly understood languages, cultural nationalism includes literature, education, and sometimes religion. When an individual citizen shares the national culture, he is said to belong to the nation and takes its nationality.

Although nationalism reflects the entire political, economic, and social environment of a people, it is the culture of a people that tends to hold them together in unity. Culture is a determining factor in the rise of nationalism. Human beings are not born nationalists, they are *made* nationalists. They become nationalists within special cultures. They accept the national culture because others do so; it becomes a part of their training from childhood through old age.

Throughout their lives they reflect the cultural life into which they were born. In the United States children take a pledge of allegiance to the flag, and they are taught to love their country. They are told that they are expected to defend their nation in time of crisis. Their national interest flows out of their culture.

Although people become nationalists for many reasons, awareness of their own culture remains one of the more important stimulants. In the eighteenth century, Englishmen and Frenchmen became more and more aware of being English and French. There were great writers contributing to their literature, authors who reflected the glory of the state. They became symbols of national culture. By the late eighteenth century, Paris and London were centers not only of political and economic life, but also of national cultures. Writers of genius appeared in salons to comment upon life around them. As their language and values spread, so did the national awareness of their fellow citizens. By this time the English and French languages had taken on their modern form, with new dictionaries, encyclopedias, and grammars setting standards for the languages. This coming of age of languages in England and France invited imitation throughout the world. The result of an ever-increasing attention to the national language was the fixation of nationalism everywhere. It became common to inculcate national ideas through national literatures. Cultural nationalism helped unify peoples by their common interests and made them distinct from other peoples with different ideas.

The importance of culture in national life may be illustrated by the experience of people when they emigrate from the land of their birth and settle in another country with a different culture. The case of Latin Americans who come to the United States reveals a fear of losing a culture. These immigrants are motivated not by such an abstraction as culture, but by the need for dollars, food, and often for security. Latin Americans face a predicament. They want to belong to the United States without betraying their Spanish heritage. Yet, they fear losing ground in any negotiations with the country that gives them sanctuary and the possibility of a better life. Above all, their fear is losing their culture. They come from a culture that some other Americans regard as inferior or second-rate. Their older nationalism has given them a sense of pride that they are reluctant to relinquish. They cling to their language—Spanish. They deny the value of assimilation. They prefer their home grown Hispanic-American culture, and they hope it will not be lost.

The idea of cultural nationalism has spread from Europe to other sections of the world. It has an effect everywhere, including Africa.

Thus, Aimé Césaire, who inspired a West African literary movement, attempted to place Negritude on a global basis with African cultural roots. In a paper titled "Culture and Civilization," he told of a large family of African cultures:

> I think it is very true that culture must be national. It is, however, self-evident that national cultures, however differentiated they may be, are grouped by affinities. Moreover, these great cultural relationships, these great cultural families, have a name: they are called *civilisations*. In other words, if it is an undoubted fact that there is a French national culture, an Italian, English, Spanish, German, Russian, etc., national culture, it is no less evident that all these cultures, alongside genuine differences, show a certain number of striking similarities so that, though we can speak of national cultures peculiar to each of the countries mentioned above, we can equally well speak of a European civilisation.
>
> In the same way we can speak of a large family of African cultures which collectively deserve the name of Negro-African culture and which individually reveal the different cultures proper to each country of Africa. And we know that the hazards of history have caused the domain of this civilization, the locus of this civilisation to exceed widely the boundaries of Africa. It is in this sense, therefore, that we may say that there are, if not centres, at least fringes of this Negro-African civilisation in Brazil and in the West Indies, in Haiti and the French Antilles and even in the United States.

Pioneer scholar of nationalism Carlton J. H. Hayes regarded cultural nationalism, with its limited objectives, as a blessing. He saw integral nationalism (whole or complete nationalism), because of its aggressive tendencies, as a curse, a mania, and a kind of exaggerated egoism. Where cultural nationalism reflected the best in a people, integral nationalism, he said, had a habit of carrying a chip on one's shoulder and defying another nationality to knock it off. Cultural nationalism mirrored the best in a people, but integral nationalism showed a spirit of exclusiveness and narrowness that fed on gross ignorance of others and an inordinate pride in one's self and one's nationality.

Bibliography: Carlton J. H. Hayes, *Essays on Nationalism* (New York, 1926); Aimé Césaire, "Culture and Colonization," *The First Conference of Negro Writers and Artists* (Paris, 1956); Bruce Alvin King, *The New English Literature: Cultural Nationalism in a Changing World* (New York, 1980); Philip E. Rawkins, "Nationalist Movements Within the Advanced National State: The Significance of Culture," *Canadian Review of Studies in Nationalism*, 10, No. 2 (Fall, 1983), 221–231; John Hutchinson, *The Dynamism of Cultural Nationalism* (London, 1987); Gerald Newman, *The Rise of English Nationalism: A Cultural History, 1748–1930* (New York, 1987).

D

DANILEVSKY, NIKOLAY (1822–1885). Russian naturalist, philosopher, and nationalist. Danilevsky developed a philosophy of history as a series of distinct civilizations, a concept that later influenced the thinking of Spengler and Toynbee. He is generally regarded as the founder of Pan-Slavism (q.v.). He is also credited with giving Russian nationalism a biological foundation.

Danilevsky's book, *Rossiya i Evropa* (1869), had an important effect on Russian nationalism. It was often quoted. He maintained that Russia was different from Europe because God had willed it to be. The Slavs, he wrote, were a unique species of mankind and formed one biological family, led by "Big Brother" Russia, and conforming with the spirit of God. Russia was not Europe, and Europe was not Russia. The new culture brought in from the West tended to destroy the very heart and soul of Russia, which had its own national mode of life, language, songs, attire, customs, and traditions. "On Russian soil there arises a new spring: a socio-economic stream, which satisfies the masses of people in exactly the right way. On the wide surface of Slavdom all these streams will join together to form a mighty sea." To Danilevsky, as to most enthusiastic nationalists, nationalism was a blessing. (*See also* **RUSSIAN NATIONALISM.**)

Bibliography: Robert E. MacMaster, *Danilevsky, a Russian Totalitarian Philosopher* (Cambridge, Mass., 1967).

D'ANNUNZIO, GABRIELE (1863–1938). Italian poet, novelist, dramatist, and flamboyant romantic nationalist. A man of action, as an aviator he lost an eye in World War I. In his works he repeatedly praised Italian glory, honor, and prestige. His favorite cry: "Italy or death!" A typical passage: "Of Latin pride raise thrice thy glass in honor of the race which at last is succeeding in administering the punitive police in Italian Fiume, alternating its rigors with the English bully." Many of D'Annunzio's expressions on nationalism were later copied by Benito Mussolini (q.v.) in Fascist Italy.

Bibliography: Anthony Rhodes, *The Poet as Superman: A Life of Gabriele D'Annunzio* (London, 1959); Gerald Griffin, *Gabriele D'Annunzio, The Warrior* (Port Washington, N.Y., 1970).

DAUDET, LÉON (1867–1942).   Son of noted French writer Alphonse Daudet, Léon Daudet was an author, editor, and advocate of extreme French nationalism. Bitter opponent of democracy in general, he denounced the Third Republic in scathing terms. Nevertheless, he served as deputy from 1919 to 1924, but failed to be elected as senator in 1927. In 1908, together with Charles Maurras (q.v.), he founded *L'Action Française* as a daily newspaper devoted to nationalism and reaction. He was considered to be the most violent and virulent polemicist of his generation in France. A master of insult and satire, he regarded himself as a champion of nationalism in his country.

Bibliography: Pierre Luechini, *Léon Daudet* (Paris, 1964); Jean Noel Marque, *Léon Daudet* (Paris, 1971).

DAVITT, MICHAEL (1846–1906).   Irish nationalist politician, revolutionary, and land reformer. The son of a tenant farmer who had been evicted from his land, Michael Davitt worked in a Lancashire cotton mill. In 1857 an accident resulted in the loss of his right arm. Bitterly anti-English and anti-clerical, in 1865 he joined the Fenian movement, which was designed to win political freedom for Ireland. In 1870 he was arrested in England for sending firearms into Ireland. Found guilty, he was sentenced to fifteen years imprisonment. Released after serving half his punishment, he returned to Ireland in 1879.

Davitt worked with Charles Stewart Parnell (q.v.), another Irish nationalist, in founding the Irish Land League. Its aim was organized resistance to absentee English landlords. It attempted to relieve the plight of Irish tenant farmers by what came to be known as the three Fs: fixity of tenure, fair rent, and free sale of the tenants' interests. In this work he was influenced by the land nationalization ideas of Henry George, about whom he had learned while on a visit to the United States.

Davitt was arrested again, but he was released in 1882. He was elected to Parliament in 1882, but was not allowed to take his seat because of his record as a convict. He was imprisoned again in 1883 for delivering speeches which were said to be seditious. He broke with Parnell on the question of Henry George's theories of land reform. Elected to Parliament in 1892 and 1893, he was unseated both times. For the Irish people, however, he remained an important nationalist leader and he was venerated as a patriot. (*See also* **IRISH NATIONALISM.**)

Bibliography: Michael Davitt, *Leaves from a Prison Diary* (London, 1885); Michael Davitt, *The Fall of Feudalism in Ireland* (London, 1904); M. M. O'Hara, *Chief and Tribune* (Dublin, 1919); Francis Sheehy-Skeffington, *Michael Davitt, Revolutionary, Agitator and Labour Leader* (London, 1967).

DEÁK, FERENC (1803–1876).   Hungarian lawyer, statesman, and nationalist. Leader of the political emancipation of Hungary, he was noted for his reforms as well as his role in the *Ausgleich* (compromise) of 1867, which established the Austro-Hungarian dual monarchy. He entered the Hungarian diet in 1833, and after the Revolution of 1848 he became Minister of Justice. His own sense of nationalism differed from the extremism of Louis Kossuth (q.v.), who insisted upon outright independence for the Hungarian people. Deák opposed any complete break with Austria. He withdrew temporarily from public affairs. After 1861, as new leader of the Moderates, he drew up an address to the Emperor Francis Joseph I calling for the restoration of the constitution of 1848 and the formation of an independent Hungarian ministry. From this time, Deák was the acknowledged leader of Hungary. He was primarily responsible for the *Ausgleich* of 1867, which lasted to the fall of the Austro-Hungarian Empire in 1918.

An advocate of moderate political reform, Deák's work won for him the title of "the sage of the country." Among the Hungarian people he was considered to be the spokesman for those who wanted a workable and practical solution to Hungary's political impasse. A man of modest and retiring character, he had none of the flamboyance of Kossuth and his all-or-nothing philosophy. Deák always negotiated for the attainable. His famous "Easter Article" of April 16, 1865, presented Hungary's conditions in terms that led to the *Ausgleich* of 1867. This modest man, who avoided publicity and rejected all honors, was willing to compromise his sense of nationalism and accept a status that, in the minds of Kossuth's adherents, was the wrong kind of nationalism.

Bibliography: Bela E. Kiraly, *Ferenc Deák* (Boston, 1975).

DÉROULÈDE, PAUL (1846–1914).   Poet, dramatist, politician, and extreme nationalist, Déroulède was born in Paris on September 2, 1846. When the Franco-Prussian War broke out in July 1870, he enlisted as a private, was wounded, captured, and then escaped. After the war he wrote two volumes of patriotic poems: *Chants du soldat* ("Songs of a Soldier") in 1872, followed by *Nouveaux chants du soldat* ("New Songs of a Soldier") in 1875. These emotionally patriotic poems were greeted by the French people with extraordinary popularity. A typical military poem was this one titled "Good Fighting":

> The Kroumirs leave their mountain den;
>   Sing, bullets, sing! and bugles, blow!
> Good fighting to our gallant men,
> And happy they who follow, when,
>   Brothers in arm so dear, these go.

> Yea, happy they who serve our France,
>   And neither pain nor danger fly;
> But in the front of war's advance
> Still deem it but a glorious chance,
>   To be among the brave who die!

> No splendid war do we begin,
>   No glory waits us when 'tis past;
> But marching through the fiery din,
> We see our serried ranks grow thin,
>   And blood of Frenchmen welling fast.

> French blood!—a treasure so august,
>   And hoarded with such jealous care,
> To crush oppression's strength unjust,
> With all the force of right robust,
>   And buy us back our honor fair;—

> We yield it now to duty's claim,
>   And freely pour out all our store;
> Who judges, frees us still from blame;
> The Kroumirs' muskets war proclaim;—
>   In answer let French cannon roar!

> Good fighting! and God be your shield,
>   Our pride's avengers, brave and true!
> France watches you upon the field.
> Who wear her colors never yield,
>   For 'tis her heart ye bear with you!

In 1882 Déroulède organized the *Ligue des Patriotes* (League of Patriots), whose purpose it was to avenge the defeat of France by Prussia in 1871. It called for a revision of the French constitution, and it favored an alliance between France and Russia. Déroulède used the League to support the anti-republican, reactionary General Georges Boulanger. The League was suppressed by the government. Déroulède became a member of the Chamber of Deputies in 1889, where he was notorious for the vehemence of his anti-Dreyfusard views and his noisy tactics.

In the Chamber of Deputies, Déroulède denounced the democrat and Dreyfusard Georges Clemenceau as the protégé and supporter of Cornélius Herz, a Jewish financier who was implicated in the scandal caused by the failure of the Panama Canal Company. Clemenceau claimed that Déroulède was a liar and challenged him to a duel. Neither was hurt in the fray, but Clemenceau won a lawsuit against his detractor.

Banished from France, Déroulède returned under an amnesty in 1905. He remained the irrepressible patriot, the nationalist who could see only the justice of his own cause.

Bibliography: Paul Déroulède, *Selections from his Poems,* in Warner's *Library of the World's Best Literature* (New York, 1896); Armand Plat, *Paul Déroulède, Héros national* (Paris, 1965).

DEUTSCH, KARL W. (1912–   ).   Historian, political scientist, and scholar of nationalism. Born in Prague on July 21, 1912, he came to the United States and took his M.A. at Harvard in 1941 and his Ph.D. there in 1951. He taught at the Massachusetts Institute of Technology and later at Yale University. In research he turned his interests to nationalism, especially its language and economic aspects. In 1953 he published his *Nationalism and Social Communication: An Inquiry into the Foundations of Nationality,* which presented a unique formula for the scientific access to nationalism. This book won for Deutsch a reputation as one of the outstanding American experts on the formidable -ism. (*See* **DEUTSCH FORMULA.**)

Deutsch was not altogether satisfied with the conventional study of nationalism. Admittedly, he said, there was some value in the older direct approach, which stressed the qualitative aspects of nationalism, the configuration of its symptoms, and the typical sequences of nationalistic behavior. But, at the same time, he suggested that the older views had not yielded quantitative measurements or could they lead to accurate predictions. He called for a set of tools that could open a new channel in the drive to make sense of nationalism.

Bibliography: Karl W. Deutsch, *Nationalism and Social Communication: An Inquiry into the Foundations of Nationality* (New York, 1953); Karl W. Deutsch, *Interdisciplinary Bibliography on Nationalism* (Cambridge, Mass., 1953); Karl W. Deutsch, *et al.*, *France, Germany and the Western Alliance: A Study of Elite Attitudes on European Integration* (New York, 1967); Karl W. Deutsch, and Richard L. Merritt, *Nationalism and National Development* (Cambridge, Mass., 1970).

DEUTSCH FORMULA.   In place of the conventional political, economic, and cultural factors presented by other scholars of nationalism, Karl W. Deutsch (q.v.) proposed that the test of nationality be the ability of members of the group to communicate better with their fellows than with non-members.

Noting his inspiration as coming from the scientific materialism of Hobbes and the empiricism of Locke, Deutsch offered three steps for another method of understanding nationalism: (1) He would examine the existing social sciences to find a different method of approach; (2) He would search for a new set of structural concepts; and (3) He would undertake an analysis on whether such concepts could suggest more specific and more realistic views on nationalism. In effect, this would be an entirely new method of undertaking a study of the ramifications of nationalism.

In Deutsch's view, the studies on nationalism already in existence had led to disparate and often contradictory results. The key to resolving the paradoxes, inconsistencies, confusions, and differences of opinion, could be resolved, Deutsch claimed, by placing emphasis on the role of "social communication." His past study on the nature of political power had led him to believe that such power had been dependent upon a highly uneven distribution of social communication facilities as well as economic, geographical, and cultural independence. He defined a people as a crucial unit within a cluster of intensive social communications.

Deutsch held that if one were to determine the nature of nationalism, he must turn to the communication facilities of society. These include a socially standardized system of symbols (language), and any number of auxiliary codes, including alphabets, systems of writing, and calculating. In addition, such information is stored in living memories, associations, habits, and preferences of the society's members, as well as national facilities for the storage of information, such as libraries and statutes. It is these communicative facilities that permit a common history to be experienced in common. In the long run, membership in a people consists in the ability of an individual to communicate more effectively and over a wider range of subjects with members of his own language group than with outsiders.

According to the Deutsch formula, the most important aspect of the unity of a people lies in the complementation of a relative efficiency of communications among individuals. It is something that might be called "mutual rapport," but on a much larger scale. To achieve these results, Deutsch recommended tests to establish the nature of complementarism of individuals, especially their assimilation and differentiation within the group. This kind of quantitative examination by tests and measuring devices can result not only in a quantitative analysis of nationalism but for some, even if cautious, predictions. The key is cybernetics, the comparative study of electronic calculating machines and the human nervous system, a discipline originally conceived by the late mathematician Norbert Wiener. Wiener called for interdisciplinary testing.

Deutsch was careful to recommend more research, better tools, more complete data, and more attention to refined mathematical techniques. The early tests, he admitted, were but crude indicators. More sophisticated methods would have to be used before any predictions about nationalism can be made. This kind of investigation might conceivably explain why economic growth in certain areas led to national unification, while in others it resulted in fragmentation and diversity.

It was to be expected that the Deutsch formula, radical in its approach, would be greeted with criticism, from mild to severe. Those who opposed its central thesis concentrated their attacks on the predictability factor. Nationalism, they say, is a historical phenomenon, and in both history and nationalism, spiritual and accidental factors do not lend themselves easily to predictability. Some critics contend that it is altogether impossible to measure such elements. They point out that research along quantitative lines of other movements in history have yielded sparse results, far less than the quantitative researchers claim.

The Deutsch formula attracted the favorable attention of the Cologne School (q.v.) and its founder, Theodor Schieder (q.v.). The guideline remains for those scholars who seek to clarify this baffling force in modern history.

Bibliography: Karl W. Deutsch, *Nationalism and Social Communication: An Inquiry into the Foundations of Nationality* (Cambridge, Mass., 1966).

DE VALERA, EAMON (1882–1975).   Political leader, statesman, and nationalist who dominated Irish life from 1917 to 1959. De Valera served as Irish Prime Minister for twenty-one years and as President of the Irish Free State for fourteen years. For the Irish people he stands as the personification of Irish nationalism.

Eamon de Valera was born in New York City on October 14, 1882, to a father who was a Spanish artist and an Irish mother. On the death of his father, he was sent as an infant to his mother's family in County Limerick, Ireland. He was educated at Blackrock College and the Royal University at Dublin. As a student he joined the movement to win Irish independence and became an active member of the Gaelic League. In 1913 he joined the Irish Volunteers and served as an adjutant to the Dublin Brigade when it took part in the Easter Rebellion of 1916. He was taken prisoner after this unsuccessful uprising and sentenced to death, but the verdict was commuted to penal servitude for life. He was released during the general amnesty in 1917. Unrepentant, he turned again to politics and was elected president of the Sinn Féin in 1918 and 1927.

In May 1918 De Valera was again arrested and sent to Lincoln Prison, from which he escaped in February 1919. He came to the United States, where he raised six million dollars for the Irish Independence movement. When he returned to Ireland in 1929, he found the people in a virtual war against England. Taking part in the civil war in 1922–1923, he was again arrested but was released in 1924. In 1937 he became Prime Minister of the new Irish Free State. His political decisions were intensely nationalistic and meant to remove every vestige of British influence. Throughout World War II he maintained Irish neutrality and protested Allied military activity in Northern Ireland. He intensified his personal campaign for ending the partition of Ireland, but his efforts were nullified with the outbreak of terrorism by the Irish Republican Army (q.v.).

In February 1948 de Valera's party, the Fianna Fáil, was defeated in a general election. He was succeeded by John A. Costello. De Valera then went to the United States to publicize the campaign against partition. He returned to Ireland and became Prime Minister from 1951 to 1954 and from 1957 to 1959. Handicapped by failing vision, he moved in 1959 to the less demanding post of President of the Republic.

De Valera's colorful career spanned the period of Ireland's national resurgence. He won the respect of the Irish people because of his reputation for integrity and patriotism. A wise political leader, he preferred the way of negotiation and compromise, but his work was marred by deep political divisions that arose during the civil war of the 1920s and by the rising terror of extremists. He never accepted the partition of Ireland that left the six northern counties outside Irish control. For his people he remained a symbol of national liberation and a nationalist leader of importance. (*See also* **IRISH NATIONALISM.**)

Bibliography: R. Ryle Dwyer, *Eamon de Valera: A Biography* (Dublin, 1980); Joseph Lee and Geraroid O'Tuaighaigh, *The Age of De Valera and His Times* (Cork, 1983); John Bowman, *De Valera and the Ulster Question, 1917–1973* (Cork, 1983).

DEVELOPMENT OF NATIONALISM. *See* **NATIONALISM, DEVELOPMENT OF.**

DEVOLUTION. The term "devolution" means the transference from one stage to another of property, quality, or rights, such as the devolution of a crown. When used in connection with the mini-nationalisms or ethnonationalisms, it refers to the delegation or surrender by a centralized government of its total political authority over details to regional or local governments. The granting of such rights may be minor, such as in cultural matters, or major, such as political rights of administration or augmented economic control. Most of all, devolution carries a note of moderation: to retain unity of the country, which relinquishes certain hitherto centralized laws and actions as a response to a moderate call for autonomy. Examples are the retention of Wales and Scotland in the United Kingdom by favorable concessions to moderate Welsh and Scottish nationalisms. (*See also* **AUTONOMY, PARTICULARISM, MINI-NATIONALISMS, ETHNONATIONALISM, WELSH NATIONALISM, and SCOTTISH NATIONALISM.**)

DIASPORA NATIONALISM. A form of nationalism that recognizes the national feeling of a separate group dispersed among other people and resistant to assimilation. The term "Diaspora" refers to the dispersion of the Jews after the Babylonian exile and denotes a trend of scattering. An example is the existence of Magyars in Czechoslovakia and their determination to resist their assimilation into the Czechoslovak state. (*See* **MAGYAR DIASPORA NATIONALISM.**)

DILKE, CHARLES WENTWORTH (1843–1911). British statesman, leader of the Liberal Party, and promoter of aggressive British nationalism. At the age of twenty-three, Dilke made a voyage around the world, after which he recorded in two volumes titled *Greater*

Britain (1868) his travel impressions. In this book he paid an emotional tribute to the great Anglo-Saxon "race," which, he wrote, was destined to rule the world. He held that backward peoples would inevitably be displaced by the conquering white Anglo-Saxons.

Dilke believed that the power of English laws and principles of government was not merely an English question: "Its continuance is essential to the freedom of mankind." Throughout his travels to strange new lands, he became convinced more than ever "of the grandeur of our race."

Dilke's book was successful in England, where it went through many editions. Readers were entranced to learn that everywhere countries were ruled by "an Anglo-Saxon race whose very scum and outcasts have founded empires in every portion of the globe." Dilke was said to have been considered by Disraeli as a possible Prime Minister. In 1886, at the height of his career, he was forced to retire from public life as the consequence of a citation in a divorce suit.

Bibliography: Charles Wentworth Dilke, *Greater Britain: A Record of Travel in English-Speaking Countries* (2 vols., London, 1868); Stephen Gwynn and G. M. Tuckwell, *Life of Charles Wentworth Dilke* (London, 1917).

DOOB, LEONARD W. (1909–   ).   American psychologist with a special interest in the psychology of nationalism. After study at the University of Frankfurt-am-Main in Germany from 1930 to 1932, Doob became a member of the Yale University faculty in 1934 and served as Professor of Psychology there after 1950. One of the few psychologists devoted to the study of nationalism, he published his book, *Patriotism and Nationalism: Their Psychological Foundations*, in 1964.

In his seminal treatise, Doob defined patriotism as the conviction that personal and group welfare are dependent upon the preservation and expansion of a nation's power and culture. He saw patriotism as merging into nationalism when such conviction is accompanied by a demand for action. After establishing this psychological framework, he went on to examine the justification and the demands and actions of national states and showed them to be similar from country to country. He analyzed the way in which patriots perceive and evaluate their own nation, their compatriots, and their culture, as well as other nations and peoples. The goals of patriots range from an appeal to divine sanctions to emphasis upon the need for security. (*See also* **PATRIOTISM.**)

Bibliography: Leonard W. Doob, *Patriotism and Nationalism: Their Psychological Foundations* (New Haven, Conn., 1964).

DOSTOEVSKY, FYODOR MIKHAILOVICH (1821–1881). Russian author and thinker, one of the greatest novelists in world literature, and zealous defender of Russian messianic nationalism. In his many works Dostoevsky proposed a democratic Christian nationalism under the leadership of the Russian people. Creator of the psychological novel, he was interested in and wrote about the special Russian national character. In his novel *The Possessed* (1873), he presented a famous conversation between the student Shatov, former serf, and Nikolai Stavrogin, a brilliant aristocrat. "I believe in Russia," said Shatov, "I believe in her orthodoxy. . . . I believe in the body of Christ. . . . I believe that the new advent will take place in Russia."

On June 8, 1880, speaking at a Moscow meeting of the Society of Lovers of Russian Literature, Dostoevsky delivered a passionate eulogy on Pushkin (q.v.), as a national poet. Pushkin, he said, had the peculiarly apt Russian gift of universal comprehension. Russia, he added, was the only nation in the world qualified to understand, to reconcile, and to inspire the rest of Europe:

> [Pushkin] was the first—precisely the first, and there was no one prior to him—to discern and give us the artistic types of Russian beauty directly emerging from the Russian spirit, beauty which resides in the people's truth, in our soil. . . . I merely say that among all nations the Russian soul, the genius of the Russian people is, perhaps, more apt to embrace the idea of the universal fellowship of man, of brotherly love—that sober point of view which forgives all that is hostile; which distinguishes and excuses that which is desperate; which removes contradictions.

Dostoevsky's belief in the established order, the teachings of Christ, the spirituality of the Russian Orthodox Church, and the messianic mission of the Russian people brought him acceptance by the Russian people. But Nikolai Lenin, champion of Marxism, was unimpressed by Dostoevsky's novels; he is reported to have said: "I have no time for such trash." (*See also* **MESSIANIC NATIONALISM, and RUSSIAN NATIONALISM.**)

Bibliography: F. M. Dostoevsky, *The Diary of a Writer*, trans. by Boris Brasol (New York, 1949); Ronald Kingsley, *The Undiscovered Dostoevsky* (London, 1961); David Magarschack, *Dostoevsky* (London, 1962); L. A. Zander, *Dostoevsky* (New York, 1975); Ronald Kingsley, *Dostoevsky: His Life and Work* (London, 1978); William J. Leatherbarrow, *Fedor Dostoevsky* (Boston, 1981).

DROYSEN, JOHANN GUSTAV (1808–1884). German historian, nationalist, and with Heinrich von Sybel and Heinrich von Trietschke (qq.v.), one of the leaders of Prussian historiography. Droysen began his career as a liberal nationalist, but changed later into a fervent champion of Prussia and the Hohenzollern dynasty. He would "work politically through history" ("*durch die Geschichte politisch zu wirken*"). He saw the historian's special interest as residing in ideas of national unity and national culture. Influenced by Hegel's (q.v.) theory of the supremacy of the State, he saw it as the mission of Prussia to replace Austria as the most powerful force in Germany. In his major work, *Geschichte der preussischen Politik (History of Prussian Politics)* (14 vols., 1855–1886), he contrasted Prussia's "efficiency, progress, and reform" with Austria's "emptiness, unprogressiveness, and impotency." Partial to Hohenzollern rulers, he held that they were always guided by patriotic, national motives.

It was necessary, Droysen said, that Prussia awaken to her duty and assume her destined role as the leader of the German mission. He saw three connected steps in the rise of modern liberty and nationalism—the revolt of the American colonies against England, the French Revolution, and the rise of Prussia against Napoleon. The early Hohenzollerns, he wrote, were nationalists loyal to Germany and working for the reform of the Empire. With the Reformation, Protestantism became part of the national idea. Because Austria was Catholic and cosmopolitan, Prussia became the only practical head of the German nation.

In Droysen's hands, the writing of history became highly subjective and idealized. He sought to convince Germans that Prussian leadership was absolutely necessary for them. Other German historians were not altogether convinced: they asserted that it was difficult to believe that the early German Electors advocated the German national idea.

Bibliography: Johann Gustav Droysen, *Geschichte des preussischen Politik (History of Prussian Politics)* (14 vols; Leipzig., 1855–1886); Werner Menge, *Das Volkstum in der Geschichtsschreibung (Nationality in Historiography since the War of Liberation)* (Halle, 1939).

DU BOIS, W. E. BURCKHARDT (1868–1963). American intellectual teacher, champion of black nationalism, and promoter of Pan-Africanism. Born in Great Barrington, Massachusetts, he had a brilliant teaching and a prolific writing career. As historian, he contributed much to the documentation of his race. As sociologist, he opposed the social theories associated with Social Darwinism. As propagandist, he used his poems, novels, essays, and plays to advance the cause of Pan-Africanism. Typical of his approach was his denunciation of the "separate but equal doctrine," which Booker T. Washington had approved in the so-called Atlanta Compromise. This, said Du Bois, abdicated the claim of full equality guaranteed in the Fourteenth and Fifteenth Amendments to the U.S. Constitution.

In 1905 Du Bois was one of the founders of the Niagara Movement, which called for full civil rights for Negroes, abolition of any color bar, promotion of education, and opposition to segregation in railroad trains. In 1909 he helped found the National Association for the Advancement of Colored People (N.A.A.C.P.). As editor of *The Crisis*, the association's paper, he consistently supported economic cooperation among Negro consumers and producers. He saw himself as integrally a part of Western civilization, "yet, more significantly, one of its rejected parts." The Negro, he said, was a sort of seventh son, born with a veil and gifted with second sight in the American world. The Negro was burdened with two needs—one American and one Negro, two souls, two unreconciled strivings, two warring ideals in one dark body. He had ambivalent loyalties toward race and nation.

Du Bois urged American Negroes to demand equality on the domestic scene. At a time when they were embarrassed by the "primitiveness" of their background, Du Bois called attention to their great medieval kingdoms in Africa and the sophisticated culture of African tribes. He maintained that American Negroes be proud of their earlier African culture. He held that the Negroes as a race have a contribution to make to civilization that no other race could make, that they promote Pan-Africanism, and that they establish their own businesses. Salvation would come with the leadership of an educated Negro élite. He predicted that the "talented tenth" of educated Negroes in the United States and throughout the world would regard Africa as their "greater Fatherland."

After attending the first African conference held in London in 1906, between 1919 and 1927 Du Bois called for Pan-African Congresses in Europe and the United States. Each would express the "absolute equality" of the races. At the 1921 meeting he used this specific theme in the manifesto of the Congress:

> The world must face two eventualities: either the complete assimilation of Africa with two or three of the great world states, with political, civil and social power equal for its black and white citizens, or the use of a great black African state founded in Peace and Good Will based on popular education, natural art and industry and freedom of trade; autonomous and sovereign in its internal policy, but from the beginning a part of a great society of people in which it takes its place with others as co-rulers of the world.

In 1934 Du Bois resigned from the directorate of the N.A.A.C.P. after charging that it was dedicated too much to the interests of the black bourgeoisie and that it paid little or no attention to the masses. He moved steadily leftward in his political sympathies. In 1951 he was indicted as an unregistered representative of a foreign power.

He was acquitted, but disillusioned with the United States, he joined the Communist Party, denounced his American citizenship, and moved to Ghana. He died there on August 27, 1963, at the age of 95.

As propagandist and polemicist, Du Bois was a pioneer spokesman for black nationalism and for Pan-Africanism. However, he was never able to win the kind of support that Marcus Garvey (q.v.) had achieved among the masses. Nor did African leaders respond to his version of Pan-Africanism. They saw him as a visionary with the dream of a United States of Africa, and as an impractical idealist. In their view there could be no nationalism writ large until national consciousness was stimulated at the local level. (*See also* PAN-AFRI-CANISM.)

Bibliography: W. E. B. Du Bois, *The Souls of Black Folk* (Chicago, 1903, New York, 1965); W. E. B. Du Bois, *The Gift of Black Folk* (Boston, 1924); W. E. B. Du Bois, *Black Reconstruction* (New York, 1956); W. E. B. Du Bois, The *Black Flame: A Trilogy* (New York, 1957); Dorothy Sterling, *Lift Every Voice* (New York, 1965); Rayford Logan (ed.), *W. E. B. Du Bois* (Englewood Cliffs, N.J., 1973).

DURKHEIM, ÉMILE (1858–1917).   French social scientist, founder of the French school of sociology, and scholar of empirical research on nationalism. Where fellow French sociologist Gabriel Tarde (q.v.) stressed the individual in the aggregate of people, Durkheim regarded society as a collective unity. Of Jewish extraction, Durkheim was troubled by the resurgence of nationalism in France following the defeat of Prussia in 1870–1871. This nationalism was accompanied by the anti-Semitism of the famous Dreyfus affair. Appalled by the hatred exhibited by anti-Semites, Durkheim took an active role in the campaign to exonerate Dreyfus. He left behind him a brilliant school of researchers into many disciplines, including ethnology.

Bibliography: Robert Bierstedt, *Émile Durkheim* (New York, 1966); Dominick La Capra, *Émile Durkheim: Sociologist and Philosopher* (New York, 1972); Émile Durkheim, *On Morality and Society,* ed. by Robert N. Bellah (Chicago, 1973).

DYNASTIC NATIONALISM.   While modern nationalism came of age in the late eighteenth century, its roots may be traced back much earlier. Strong dynasties, such as the Angevins and Tudors in England, and the Capetians and Bourbons in France, were constructing what would later be called national states. Dynastic nationalism, sometimes called *étatisme*, promoted what are today called basic elements of nationalism—common territory, common cultures, and common administrative and legal institutions.

Monarchs demanded the loyalty of their people. However, uppermost in the minds of the rulers was the strengthening of the power of the state to reflect their own enrichment and glory. The dynasties controlled the total political, social, and economic environment as if it were their own property. Louis XIV of France was typical of this attitude. *"L'État c'est moi!"* ("I am the State!") he is supposed to have said. His subjects, he was fond of saying, were "born to obey without question" and from them he demanded a blind obedience. He arrogated unlimited powers to himself. He did not once convene the Estates-General during the long years of his reign. He sent to prison any of his subjects who dared challenge his authority, utilizing for this procedure an ingenious system of *lettres de cachet*, documents containing charges signed with the king's seal.

While it contained some elements of later nationalism, dynastic nationalism should be regarded as a preliminary form not yet of age.

E

ECONOMIC NATIONALISM.   The intensification of national consciousness and national rivalries throughout Europe and the Western hemisphere in the 1860s and 1870s was due in large part to economic motives. Certainly, in its exaggerated form, the nationalism that leads to conflict between nations had an economic base. Economists ordinarily do not favor the word nationalism, but, instead, use the dual term economic nationalism or the professional word neo-mercantilism (nationalism working in the field of economics).

Economic nationalism is based on security for the nation-state, the idea that the people of one nation must be protected against the inroads of other peoples. The nation must be made safe in times of peace and self-sufficient in times of war. Economic nationalism means that the administration of any nation must obtain for its citizens the highest possible standard of living, that it must encourage the kind of production in which it has an advantage, and, therefore, it will depend upon other parts of the world for other products. Individual countries seek to specialize in economic activities that best coincide with their natural endowments. Therefore, in the past, the Germans worked in chemicals, optics, lithography, and potash; the English specialized in the coal industry and fiberstuffs; the French attended to wine-growing; and the Americans stressed mass production and high technology. The aim was always to increase the national gross product by emphasizing those economic areas to which the nation seems disposed.

Economic problems, like all phases of nationalism, are closely associated with the concept of power. Therefore, economic motives play a large part in national life. There are always a need of defense, the duty for military service, and the subservience of education to national welfare. Economic nationalism tends to international friction, and those who control the economic life of a nation must always be on the alert to see that economic rivalries do not descend into irreconcilable conflict. Economic policies bear within themselves the possibility of confrontation between peoples. They keep the world divided and beset by fear. The political rivalries that led to both World Wars in the twentieth century were, in part, responsible for those great wars between peoples, but economic differences played a significant role. •

Economic nationalism may be displayed in varying ways. There may be a network of national tariffs designed to maximize exports and simultaneously minimize imports. There may be import quotas and licenses, bounties for home industries, subsidized railway fares to the frontiers, restrictions on international exchange, and discouragement of the export of capital. Because of the close relations economicially in the contemporary world, economic isolation is no longer possible. Yet, the system of economic nationalism is retained as if the very existence of the nation depends on it. History, tradition, national sentiment, and the reluctance to extend world government have made the nation-state the supreme agent of economic control. Both movements, political nationalism and economic nationalism, are so closely related that they cannot be considered apart in contemporary society.

The history of economic nationalism runs closely parallel to the story of political and cultural nationalism. The great changes that took place at the end of the Middle Ages and the opening of the modern era are usually attributed by historians to the decay of medieval society associated with the introduction of gunpowder, the revival of learning in the Renaissance, and the destruction of the solidarity of the Catholic Church in the Reformation. The rise of the national state took place during the voyages of discovery to the New World, the resultant influx of precious metals, and the Commercial Revolution. With these developments, economic in essence, the new national states began to be regarded as economic units. During the Middle Ages, the main concern was local protectionism; in the early modern period, this local advocacy was succeeded by the kind of national protectionism typical of economic nationalism. National protectionism was the natural outgrowth associated with the emergence of the national economy.

Economic nationalism received its most potent stimulus during the years of the First Industrial Revolution (c. 1750–1850). At this time the factory system was introduced, transportation and means of communication were improved, and the middle class began to play a prominent role in society. Along with these new developments came the rivalries of nations for economic advantages. Factory owners, merchants, adventurers, all looked to the flag for protection, and all saw economic nationalism as important as political nationalism. Individual entrepreneurs saw their own interests as identical with those of the state and expected that the state would give them the protection they wanted. This close connection has remained in the era of nationalism.

Economic nationalism came into existence because of the existence of the self-interest of the rising middle class, the leaders of business and industry. With the Industrial Revolution, the bourgeoisie came to be the dominant social class. They identified their own interests with those of the new nation-state. They controlled production and gathered the benefits of wealth. To control both home and foreign markets it was necessary for them to have a politically united territory from which they could compete with other nationalities. They formed the backbone of the new nationalism and saw to it that nationalism would emerge in the rest of the world.

As the middle class grew in numbers and wealth in early modern times, its members turned to an alliance with the monarchs. Both sides, for varying reasons, opposed the privileged orders, the nobility and the clergy, and hence joined together to maintain their power against the enemies. The monarchs saw their strength threatened by clergy and nobility; the middle class wanted security of property and freedom of trade, both of which could be helped by the kings. They, therefore, joined together—king and bourgeoisie, for their mutual good. The national monarchs drew wealth and taxes from the bourgeoisie; the bourgeoisie obtained naval protection for their trade and protection for the domestic and foreign markets. There was no special affection in this alliance: it was based on power. The monarch got his taxes and wealth from the bourgeoisie and the latter got security for its property and the opportunity to win even greater wealth. When kings were overthrown, the middle-class propertied citizens became sovereign. They controlled the nation and nationalism represented their interests.

In the early stage of the First Industrial Revolution, economic nationalism was liberal in character and inspired by Adam Smith's idea of *laissez faire*. In the 1860s and 1870s, with the introduction of the Second Industrial Revolution, big business began to appear on the Continent and in the United States. In Europe a series of wars began as Germans, Italians, and varied Balkan peoples sought to win national unification. In the United States an intensification of nationalism came with the repression of sectionalism in the Civil War. In these developments, economic nationalism tended to swing from a liberal to an integral form. The new propaganda for economic nationalism convinced the people that their security was linked closely with their national wealth, with their industries, and a favorable balance of trade. The term "national" was used in such phrases as national resources, national productive capacity, national self-sufficiency, national system of credit, and national welfare. Economic nationalism became of extreme importance in the world. It was, in part, responsible for the two great conflicts, World War I and World War II.

Economic nationalism may be regarded as a revival of the older form of mercantilism. Economic control in the medieval era was decentralized and carefully guarded in each local district. The expansion of trade and the rise of national states in the early modern period made it necessary to desert the old restrictions of manorial and municipal administration. As economic frontiers expanded, it became necessary to find some new national control of commerce. The need for a viable set of economic principles produced a set of ideas we now call mercantilism. As European feudal society was transformed into a set of national states, mercantilism was accepted as the general economic policy. It produced a set of economic principles that governed the society of the day: the bullionist theory, which saw the precious metals as the basic form of national wealth; the merchandising theory, which believed trade to be the most desirable form of economic activity; the protectionist theory, which favored high tariffs on imports and supported home industries; and a favorable balance of trade, by which the national state sought to export more than it imported.

Mercantilism served to promote the interests of the national state at a time when foreign trade was badly organized. It helped the development of political centralization, gave power to the national monarch, and led to the prosperity of the rising middle class. By the late eighteenth century, the structure of economic control built by mercantilism began to crack. Businessmen and industrialists demanded more freedom of enterprise as expressed in Adam Smith's *laissez faire*. This came at a time when modern nationalism was beginning to be felt in Europe and elsewhere in the world. Mercantilism began to be considered as restrictive and its regulations as burdensome. However, in the nineteenth century a neo-mercantilism emerged, with principles of high tariff walls, quotas, restrictive markets, and monopolies—all in a more perfected form. The concept of industrial nationalism gained a stronger hold on popular thinking.

The early form of economic nationalism had been an attempt to insure industrial progress by *laissez faire*. However, about 1870 there was a rebirth of the mercantilist restrictions of the seventeenth and eighteenth centuries. It was this urge to promote national self-sufficiency that led to increasing confrontations between peoples and the outbreak of two world conflicts in the twentieth century.

Bibliography: J. G. Hodgson (ed.), *Economic Nationalism* (New York, 1933); Michael A. Heilperin, *The Trade of Nations* (New York, 1952); David Greenway, *Protection Again? Causes and Consequences of a Retreat from Free Trade in Economic Nationalism* (London, 1979); Otto Hieronymi (ed.), *The New Economic Nationalism* (New York, 1979); Peter Peterson, *Economic Nationalism and Interdependence* (Washington, D.C., 1984); Peter J. Burnell, *Economic Nationalism in the Third World* (Brighton, England, 1986).

EGYPTIAN NATIONALISM.   *See* **NASSER, GAMAL ABDEL.**

EJERCITO POPULAR BORICUA.   Boricuan Popular Army. Also called *Machteros*, or machete wielders, Puerto Rican group calling for independence. (*See* **PUERTO RICAN NATIONALISM.**)

EMERSON, RUPERT (1899–1979).   Professor of International Relations at Harvard University from 1948, Emerson was an expert on nationalism in non-European areas, including Africa, Asia, and the Middle East. He believed that human beings, no matter where they lived on the globe, want to build states and nations. Non-Europeans saw themselves as entitled to independent statehood, and they also were willing to grant their community a primary and secondary loyalty. African and Asian nation-states were established even before nations came into being. Both Africa and Asia were rich in nationalism but poor in nations. Emerson warned, however, that on the basis of European and other experience, nationalism was not an unmixed blessing and that it embraced within it real sins and dangers. He advised non-Europeans to do what they could to avoid the darker side of nationalism.

Bibliography: Rupert Emerson, "The Progress of Nationalism," in W. Thayer, *Nationalism and Progress in Free Asia* (Baltimore, 1956);

Rupert Emerson, *From Empire to Nation* (Cambridge, Mass., 1960); Rupert Emerson and Martin Kilson (eds.), *The Political Awakening of Africa* (Westport, Conn., 1981).

EMMET, ROBERT (1778–1803).   Irish patriot and nationalist leader, who is remembered by his countrymen as a romantic martyr. Born in Dublin, Emmet attended Trinity College, where he won a reputation as a brilliant orator. He was so fervent an Irish nationalist that he was forced to leave the college in 1798 because of his emotional outbursts. Like his brother, Thomas, a lawyer who was exiled to the United States, Robert was a member of the United Irishmen. The society was founded in 1791 by Theobald Wolf Tone (q.v.) to win the political emancipation of Roman Catholics and dissenters. From 1800 to 1802 Emmet was on the continent with exiled leaders of the United Irishmen in order to win French support for an insurrection planned in Ireland against British rule.

Returning to Ireland in the summer of 1803, Emmet planned an attack on Dublin Castle. The scheme was to seize the castle and hold the lord-lieutenant as a hostage. However, the assault was badly planned. Only a small group of disorderly men moved with Emmet on the castle and it soon turned into chaos. On the way the revolutionaries met the Lord Chief Justice and his nephew, both of whom were pulled from their carriage and murdered. Emmet, appalled by the fiasco, managed to escape and hid in the Wicklow Mountains, near his fiancée, Sarah Curran, with whom he hoped to flee to the United States. Captured on August 25, 1803, he was tried for treason, found guilty, and hanged. His defending attorney was accused of having been in the pay of the Crown. For the Irish people, Emmet was a patriot-martyr, who lost his life for the cause of Irish nationalism. (*See also* **IRISH NATIONALISM.**)

Bibliography: Leon O'Broin, *The Unfortunate Mr. Robert Emmet* (Dublin, 1958).

ENGLISH NATIONALISM.   The roots of the English nationalism that came of age in the eighteenth century may be traced to the seventeenth century. Its impetus came from the existence of English patriotism. Patriotism (q.v.) in some form has been present throughout the course of history; modern nationalism, its extension, is a relatively new phenomenon. Love of country became an essential ingredient of nationalism. In his *Richard II* (1595) Shakespeare expressed his love for England long before the modern Age of Nationalism:

This royal throne of kings, this sceptred isle,
This earth of majesty, this seat of Mars,
This other Eden, demi-paradise,
This fortress built by Nature for herself
Against infection and the hand of war,
This happy breed of men, this little world,
This precious stone set in the silver sea,
Which serves it in the office of a wall
Or as a moat defensive to a house,
Against the envy of less happier lands,—
This blessed plot, this earth, this realm, this England, . . .

English nationalism, as Hans Kohn pointed out, really began in the mid-seventeenth century, when it was established for England and was carried as its message to other nations. The seeds of modern nationalism were planted and nurtured in an essentially religious revolt. England was already territorially unified, a nation whose classes were distinguished by a sturdy patriotism. It had withstood the ravages of revolution. Battered by civil strife between religions, by conflict between King and Parliament, the English, nevertheless, retained their national spirit. Both sides—Royal England and Puritan England, professed a deep love of country. Charles I died as an honorable Englishman. Cromwell described the English as a chosen people—"to God as the apple of His eye." The English were imbued with this sense of national consciousness.

Thus, from the days it began, English nationalism preserved its special character. It has remained attached, perhaps more closely than any other nationalism, to the religious matrix from which it arose. It always stressed the role of the individual in English society. It became clothed with the spirit of liberty in the struggle against ecclesiastical and civil authority. Indeed, as popular loyalty passed from kingship to the national state, English nationalism took on a cloak of libertarianism. The English idea of liberty received powerful expression in the famous prose pamphlet of John Milton, *Areopagitica* (1644), in which he presented his basic idea: "Give me the liberty to know." "Lords and Commons of England," he wrote, "consider what nation whereof ye are, and whereof ye are the governors: a Nation not slow and dull but of a quick, ingenious, and piercing spirit, acute to invent, subtle and sinewy to discourse, not beneath the reach of any point the highest that humanity can soar to. Therefore the studies in learning in her deepest sciences have been so ancient and so eminent among us, that writers of good antiquity and ablest judgement have been persuaded that even the school of

Pythagoras, and the Persian wisdom, took beginning from the old philosophy of this island."

English nationalism in the eighteenth century took on the humanitarian tinge characteristic of the Enlightenment. By this time England was an enormously wealthy world power, respected and envied everywhere as a unified, free, and powerful national state. With its history and tradition, English nationalism became more and more stable, more tolerant, less vocal than other nationalisms. Englishmen were fully aware of their heritage and they had no need to flaunt it to the world. Certain of their power, they chose not to emphasize belligerence or aggression. English nationalism within a framework of historic liberties was studied and emulated throughout the world.

In the humanitarian nationalist tradition, every nationality was entitled to its own development consonant with its own special genius. Each nation should attend to the business of its own historical development and should have the kindest and most understanding feeling toward other nations. This was the view of Henry St. John Bolingbroke (q.v.). His aristocratically tinged nationalism was distinguished by pride in his origin.

The birth of English nationalism took place at a time when the new bourgeoisie came to political and economic power. The middle class played a vital role in this development. Its activities, its search for possibilities of trade, its accumulation of wealth, all these factors took place in the light of the new nationalism. Impelled by what it deemed to be its religious and moral duty as well as its obligations to mankind in general, English nationalism bound its own fortunes with its mission to mankind. Englishmen roamed the earth and gathered wealth and power everywhere. Even in the Age of Imperialism, English power was accompanied by a strong moral sense, fundamentally Christian and liberal, which characterized the nature of English nationalism. This has been one of the most powerful factors shaping modern civilization. Hans Kohn recognized this tendency: "English imperial politics in the nineteenth century was power-politics, but in contrast to German or Russian power politics of that day, never only power-politics. It seldom wholly lost the demand for and the promise of political and intellectual liberty and equal justice under law, and in its best representatives may always be discerned traces of the Puritan Revolution's enthusiastic hope and anticipation of a universal establishment of a universal kingdom of God on this earth."

This sense of liberty and equal justice under law remained a characteristic of English nationalism. As early as 1780, Edmund Burke (q.v.) described the theme that has remained typical of English nationalism even in the days of exploitive imperialism. "You will observe," Burke wrote, "that from Magna Carta to the Declaration of Right, it has been the uniform policy of our constitution to claim and assert our liberties, as an *entailed inheritance* derived to us from our forefathers, and to be transmitted to our posterity: as an estate specially belonging to the people of this kingdom, without any reference whatever to any other more general or prior right. By this means our constitution preserves a unity in so great a diversity of its parts. We have an inheritable crown; an inheritable peerage; and a house of commons and a people inheriting privileges, franchises, and liberties, from a long line of ancestors."

This idea of liberty as the most essential ingredient of English nationalism was held fast even during the Age of Imperialism, at a time when English power was exploitive and at times brutal. English authorities and the English people were convinced that they were bringing the blessings of liberty to subjugated peoples for their own benefit. They brought English law and introduced their own ways as a contribution to the civilization of lesser peoples. The English national character was expressed in conjunction with the humanitarian and universal character. What was good for the English was also good for the African and Asian wards of the British Empire.

On occasion, English liberal and humanitarian nationalisms were thrust into the area of integral nationalism. English nationalists were convinced that the Anglo-Saxons were destined to conquer the world. They believed that the power of English laws and principles was not merely an English question, but that their continuance was essential to the freedom of mankind. Thus, Charles Wentworth Dilke (q.v.) in *Greater Britain* (1868), paid emotional tribute to the great Anglo-Saxon extirpating "race," which was fated to win world power. The backward colored peoples would inevitably be displaced by the conquering Anglo-Saxons. Dilke wrote of "the grandeur of the English race, already girdling the earth, which it is destined eventually to overspread." "The possession of India," he wrote, "offers to ourselves that element of vastness of dominion which, in this age, is needed to secure width of thought and nobility of purpose; but to the English race our possession of India, of the coasts of Africa, and the ports of China, offers the possibility of planting free institutions among the black-skinned races of the world."

Similarly, the spirit of English national consciousness was expressed by Rudyard Kipling (q.v.), who was obsessed with the conviction of England's noble destiny. A pioneer in the modern phase of literary imperialism, he believed that patriotism was rooted in "the instinct of inherited continuity." It was England's duty, he believed, to enlighten "lesser breeds without the law." This type of assertive nationalism was favored also by J. A. Cramb (q.v.), who urged his fellow countrymen to be aware of the greatness of their own country. This Professor of Modern History at Queen's College, London, delivered a series of lectures on the destiny of Imperial Britain. In his view, every year, every month that passed, was fraught with import of the high and singular destiny "which awaits this realm, this empire, and this race." "Never since on Sinai God spoke in thunder has mandate more imperative been issued to any race, city, nation, than now to this nation and to this people. And, again, if we should hesitate, or if we should decide wrongly, it is not the loss of prestige, it is not the narrowed bounds we have to fear, it is the judgment of the dead and the despair of the living, of the inarticulate myriads who have trusted to us, it is the arraigning eyes of the unborn."

Bibliography: Edmund Burke, *Reflections on the Revolution in France* (3 vols, London, 1851); Charles Wentworth Dilke, *Great Britain: A Record of Travel in English-Speaking Countries* (2 vols., London, 1868); J. A. Cramb, *The Origins and Destiny of Imperial Britain and Nineteenth Century Europe* (New York, 1915); George Watson, *The English Ideology* (London, 1973); Nancy J. Walker and Robert M. Worcester, "Nationalism in Great Britain," *Canadian Review of Studies in Nationalism*, 13 No. 2 (Fall, 1986), 249–269; Gerald Newman, *The Rise of English Nationalism* (New York, 1987).

ERGANG, ROBERT R. (1898—1978).   Teacher, author, and specialist on the nationalism of Johann Gottfried von Herder (q.v.). Ergang took his M.A. and Ph.D. degrees at Columbia University, where he was a student in the seminar of Professor Carlton J. H. Hayes (q.v.). From that seminar came a doctoral dissertation titled *Herder and the Foundations of German Nationalism*, published by Columbia University Press in 1931. At first, Ergang taught at Columbia in the Department of Germanic Languages, then transferred to the Department of History at New York University, where he taught for two decades. A prolific author, his writings include a highly popular text, *Europe from the Renaissance to Waterloo* (1971), as well as studies on nationalism.

Bibliography: Robert R. Ergang, *Herder and the Foundations of German Nationalism* (New York, 1931); Robert R. Ergang, *Möser and the Rise of National Thought in Germany* (Chicago, 1933); Robert R. Ergang, *Emergence of the National State* (New York, 1971).

ESTONIAN NATIONALISM. *See* BALTIC NATIONALISMS.

E.T.A. (EUZKADI TA AZKATASUNA). "Basque Homeland and Liberty," an extremist movement, that demanded full independence for the four predominantly Basque provinces in Spain and eventual union of the Spanish provinces with the three in France. Madrid denounced the E.T.A. as a dangerous terrorist organization (*See* BASQUE NATIONALISM.)

ETHNIC. *See* ETHNONATIONALISM.

ETHNICITY. *See* ETHNONATIONALISM.

ETHNOCENTRISM. A technical name for the attitude in which one's own group is the center of life, and all others are rated with reference to it. Each ethnic unit sees itself as superior to others and regards outsiders with contempt. It regards its own traditions as superior to those of different nationality and rejects other cultures and traditions as inconsequential. Ethnocentrism leads the people of one group to exaggerate its own folkways while rejecting the customs and history of foreigners. This insistence upon uniqueness is universal. People draw attention to their own culture as highly desirable. They see themselves as especially gifted and denigrate others as inferior. Ethnocentrism promotes the idea of being special. It is at the root of much national sentiment.

Bibliography: R. Levine and D. Campbell, *Ethnocentrism: Theories of Conflict, Ethnic Attitudes and Group Behavior* (New York, 1972); A. D. Smith "Ethnocentrism, Nationalism, and Social Change," *International Journal of Comparative Sociology*, 13 (1972), 11–12; Roy Preiswerk, *Ethnocentrism and History* (New York, 1978); H. D. Forbes, *Nationalism, Ethnocentrism, and Personality* (Chicago, 1980); Howard J. Wiarda, *Ethnocentrism in Foreign Policy* (Washington, D.C., 1985); Vernon Reynolds *et al.* (eds.), *The Sociobiology of Ethnocentrism* (Athens, Ga., 1986).

ETHNONATIONALISM. The concepts of ethnonationalism and its closely related terms—ethnic, ethnicity, and ethnocentrism—have drawn the attention of multidisciplinary scholars in recent years. A tremendous amount of work on these subjects has engaged the attention of historians, political scientists, sociologists, psychologists and psychoanalysts. However, there has been an unfortunate tendency to avoid definitions acceptable to other scholars: each specialist either gives little or no attention to meaning or supposes that others will understand it. This has resulted in confusion thrice confounded because much of the research is devoted to a personalized jargon misunderstood by other scholars.

An attempt to remedy this semantic problem was made in 1987 by the Group for the Advancement of Psychiatry, with a membership of some 300 psychiatrists, interested in, among other subjects, the psychology of ethnonationalism. The findings of this group on definitions are presented here in summary form not as the final answer to the question of meaning, but as one contribution designed to bring some sense and order to the study of ethnicity and its relation to nationalism:

> *Ethnic.* The basic term *ethnic* is derived from the Greek *ethnos*, meaning a company, people, or nation. It suggests a gestalt of interrelated primordial bonds, kinship, affinity, attachment, and grounds for self-esteem.
>
> *Ethnicity.* Of the many differing definitions of ethnicity, the psychiatrists seem to prefer the subjective experience of ethnicity as part of the self-definition of a person. They note that each individual has shared perception of the distinctiveness of his ethnic group, and a sense of common historical experience. To this sentiment is added continuity through biological descent and the sharing of common social and cultural conditions. At the heart of ethnicity is the feeling of *being special*.
>
> *Ethnocentrism.* The generally accepted meaning of ethnocentrism is the emotional attitude that one's own race, nation, or culture is superior to all others. The psychiatrists accept this technical name for the view that one's own group is the center of everything, and that all others are scaled and rated with reference to it. Each group nourishes its own pride and vanity, exalts its own dispositions, and looks with contempt on outsiders. It exaggerates and intensifies everything in its own folkway.
>
> *Ethnonationalism.* Ethnicity and nationalism clearly have, or have historically had, some meanings in common. The word "ethnonationalism" is useful when referring to psychological processes common to ethnicity and nationalism. Birth, lineage, and kinship feature prominently in ethnicity and in nationalism, as well as in the combined term ethnonationalism. The idea of subjective psychological quality in ethnonationalism is recognized by scholars in other disciplines. Historian Hans Kohn maintained that nationalism is primarily a psychological fact.

Bibliography: Frederick Barth, *Ethnic Groups and Boundaries* (London, 1970); Nathan Glazer and Daniel P. Moynihan, *Ethnicity: Theory and Practice* (Cambridge, Mass., 1975); Uri Ra'anan (ed.), *Ethnic Resurgence in Modern Democratic States* (Elmsford, N.Y., 1980); Charles F. Keyes (ed.), *Ethnic Change* (Seattle, 1981); Louis L. Snyder, "Nationalism and the Flawed Concept of Ethnicity," *Canadian Review of Studies in Nationalism*, 10, No. 2 (Autumn, 1983), 253–270; Ken Wolf, "Ethnic Nationalism: An Analysis and Defense," *ibid.*, 13, No. 1 (Spring, 1986), 99–109; Fred W. Riggs, "What is Ethnic? What is National?," *ibid.*, 13, No. 1 (Spring, 1986), 111–121; Group for the Advancement of Psychiatry, *Us and Them: The Psychology of Ethnonationalism* (New York, 1987); Jim MacLaughlin, "Nationalism as an Autonomous Social Force: A Critique of Recent Scholarship on Ethnonationalism," *Canadian Review of Studies in Nationalism*, 14, No. 1 (Spring, 1987), 1–18.

ETHNOPATRIOTISM.   The patriotism, or love of region, by ethnic groups that have a deep regard for their own development. They are proud of their traditions, history, ancestors, folklore, and customs handed down from one generation to another. They invariably praise their own past as beautiful, good, hospitable, happy, respectable, and clean. They stress such symbols as *Heimat* (home), folk, Catholic, and Protestant. They regard the attributes of their region or state as superior. They feel that they were set apart by their territory and culture. Above all, they are intrigued by their own special character and are often subject to the exclusiveness of xenophobia. Like patriotism, itself, it is psychologically motivated and at times leads to exaggerated nationalism. (*See also* **PATRIOTISM,** and **XENOPHOBIC NATIONALISM.**)

Bibliography: Leonard W. Doob, *Patriotism and Nationalism: Their Psychological Foundations* (New Haven, Conn., 1964).

EUSTACHI.   A Croatian nationalist organization that turned to terrorism to enforce its demand for independence. (*See* **CROATIAN SEPARATISM,** and **TERRORISM.**)

EXPANSIONIST NATIONALISM.   A term closely related to imperialism. In modern times imperialism is characterized by a struggle for access to raw materials and world markets, the subjugation and control of peoples, and the establishment of colonies. In a very real sense, modern imperialism is an outgrowth of that kind of nationalism that exalts one country over another.

Imperialism has existed throughout the course of history, but in the nineteenth century it had a special import. Once a nation-state achieved its independence and unity, it could well turn its interest to expansion. As one great nation after another went this way, each provoked the fears and ambitions of others and aroused the nationalism of others. Love of country was transformed into love of more country.

There is no simple explanation for the motives of expansionist nationalism. Undoubtedly, economic drives were paramount—the urge for raw materials, more trade, more profits. But also of great concern to imperialists were the interests of their own nation as it entered into competition with other national states. The acquisition of colonies was regarded as vital for national survival. It was necessary to achieve more security, more prestige, more power. Added to economic and political factors were cultural and psychological motivations. Nationalists were convinced that their culture and civilization were great instruments for good and that they were doing an extreme favor to backward peoples by bringing to them the benefits of a superior society. Even religious fervor was added to expansionist nationalism—missionaries would bring the blessings of a better religion to unsatisfactory tribal beliefs. Critics began to describe imperialism as devoted to the issues of "Gold, Glory, and God."

Supporters of imperialism went so far as to describe acquisition of more territory outside Europe as "a matter of life and death" for the mother country. The people of Britain, the greatest imperial power, were proud of their empire "upon which the sun never set." German authorities demanded "a place in the sun" and in Berlin paraded black chieftains from their African colonies to demonstrate that Germans, too, would drive for nationalist expansion. Historian Heinrich von Treitschke (q.v.) saw German expansion as absolutely necessary in his day: "All great nations in the fullness of their strength have desired to set their work upon barbarian lands and those who fail to participate will play a pitiable role in time to come."

The clash of competing imperialisms was one of the main factors in unleashing the blood bath of World War I. The fears and ambitions of competing nations aggravated the prevailing nationalism and resulted in making the world subject to wars on a gigantic scale.

Bibliography: J. M. Robertson, *Patriotism and Empire* (London, 1900); J. A. Hobson, *Imperialism: A Study* (London, 1902); Louis L. Snyder (ed.), *The Imperialism Reader: Documents and Readings on Modern Expansionism* (Princeton, N.J., 1962).

F

F.A.L.N. (FUERZAS ARMADAS DE LIBERACIÓN NA-CIONAL). A small band of unreconciled Puerto Rican nationalists, who called for the independence of their country. Although seeing themselves as freedom fighters, they were denounced by critics as terrorists. The F.A.L.N. claimed responsibility for more than a hundred bombings since 1974 in Chicago, New York City, Miami, Washington, D.C., and Puerto Rico. (*See* **PUERTO RICAN NATIONALISM.**)

FASCISM AND NATIONALISM. *See* **ITALIAN NATIONALISM.**

FICHTE, JOHANN GOTTLIEB (1762–1814). German philosopher, first important representative of the movement called transcendental idealism, leader of the school of German Romanticism (*see* **ROMANTICISM**), and apostle of early German nationalism.

German morale descended to a low point in the winter of 1807–1808. Conqueror Napoleon had occupied Berlin, and at Tilsit, near the Russian border, he concluded a peace by which Prussia relinquished all her territory west of the Elbe. German nationalism was born in those dark days of Napoleonic despotism.

Though of Swedish descent, Fichte became a confirmed German nationalist. In 1807–1808 he delivered at Berlin his fourteen *Addresses to the German Nation*. In passionate terms he reminded his audiences that their German forefathers had refused to submit to the tyranny of Rome. German freedom, he claimed, should be established on the highest moral basis. It was vital that Germans should become aware of their great historical mission.

In these *Addresses* Fichte stated that a world of diversity is divided into nations. Language is the external and visible badge of the differences that distinguish one nation from another. It is the most important criterion of a nation: "We give the name of people," he said, "to men whose organs of speech are influenced by the same external conditions, who live together, and who develop their language in continuous communication with one another." He denounced the introduction of foreign terms into the German language because it led to confusions that could cause great harm.

The German nation, Fichte said, exists and it was worthwhile to maintain that nation. He spoke emotionally about the necessity of rallying around the nation:

> Our present problem is to preserve the existence and continuity of what is German. All other differences vanish before this higher point of view. . . . It is essential that the higher love of Fatherland, for the entire people of the German nation, reign supreme, and justly so, in every particular German state. No one of them can lose sight of the higher interest without alienating everything that is noble and good. . . .
>
> These addresses have invited you, as well as the entire German nation, insofar as it is possible at the present time, to rally the nation around a speaker by means of the printed book, to come to definite decisions, and to be of unanimous minds. . . .

Devoting himself to the practical side of idealism by denouncing Napoleonic despotism, Fichte takes rank as one of the leading champions of German nationalism in its early days. According to German historian Friedrich Meinecke, Fichte's *Addresses*, filled with the spirit of German nationalism, "have been published, read, and become famous as one of the greatest beacons of our new German history."

Bibliography: Johann Gottlieb Fichte, *Addresses to the German Nation*, trans. by R. F. Jones and G. H. Turnbull (Chicago, 1922); Hans Kohn, "The Paradox of Fichte's Nationalism," *Journal of the History of Ideas*, 10 (1949), 319–343; George Joseph Seidel, *Activity and Ground: Fichte, Schelling, and Hegel* (New York, 1976).

FISHMAN, JOSHUA AARON (1926–   ).   Educator, sociologist, and scholar of special aspects of nationalism. Fishman taught at the City College of New York, the University of Pennsylvania, and Yeshiva University, where he was dean of the Graduate School of Education. From 1944 to 1977 he edited the *Journal of Social Issues*. His main interest in nationalism is expressed in research in sociolinguistics, applied linguistics, and multilingualism. In many books and articles he wrote about a language of wider communication (English) and a language of ethnic intimacy (Yiddish).

Fishman is especially concerned about the relationship of language to nationalism. He believes local languages have attained "national" or "official" status today more than ever before in history. English, he says, continues to expand as a second language, and, indeed, has spread far beyond any previous international language. On the problem of language maintenance and ethnicity, he writes: "After two decades of modern sociolinguistic inquiry into *language mainte-nance and language shift*, and after one decade of renewed interest in the *transformation of ethnicity* in the United States, the time is probably ripe to attempt bringing these two normally separate areas of inquiry into more focussed interaction with each other." He sees a bilingual compromise as probably resorted to more and more frequently in the future. Such a compromise would not only recognize English and local standard languages as being in complementary distribution, but it would also set the stage for the recognition of even more hitherto unrecognized languages.

Bibliography: Joshua A. Fishman, *Language and Nationalism* (Rowley, Mass., 1972); Joshua A. Fishman (ed.), *Advances in the Sociology of Language* (New York, 1978); Joshua A. Fishman, "Language Mainte-nance and Ethnicity," *Canadian Review of Studies in Nationalism*, 8, No. 2 (Autumn, 1981), 229–247.

FISSIPAROUS NATIONALISM. Nationalism may be a force of union, as in the case of the national unification of Germany in the nineteenth century. Also, it may be a force for disruption, as in the case of the dissolution of the Austro-Hungarian Empire in 1918.

Fissiparous nationalism is distinguished by the quality of splitting, or reproducing, or the production of new political units by a process of fission, or division into parts. The term was first used in the national context by Prime Minister Jawaharlal Nehru, who warned that "fissiparous tendencies" might one day shatter the Indian union.

FLAGS, NATIONAL. Pieces of cloth, bunting, or similar light material, often attached to the end of a staff, with definite colors and patterns. The terms banner, standard, ensign, or signal are used as synonyms. In modern times flags serve as symbols of nationalism. They vary in size but are often square or oblong. A part of the flag is ordinarily attached by one edge to a staff or a halyard by which it is hoisted. The portion to the free end is called the fly. The quarter next to the staff and to the top is the canton.

Symbols related to flags have been used throughout recorded history. In ancient Egypt, objects mounted on poles were expected to arouse enthusiasm in battle. In China and India, cloth flags served similar purposes. The Romans preferred wisps of straws attached to a pole and later the figures of animals as similar rallying points for their soldiers. Throughout the Middle Ages, banners, standards, and emblems of various sizes were borne in battle. The variety was wide in the medieval era—gonfalons, pennons, streamers, and guidons. Use of flags was extended to trades and guilds, each of which had its special flag and, if necessary, it was borne into battle.

With the rise of national states in the modern era, the diversity of flags carried by medieval armies had to be replaced by greater uniformity with the formation of national armies. The arrangement of colors on modern national flags have varying meanings. In some cases, national flags express the coats of arms of royal dynasties, or they may imply a political or religious ideology, agricultural or maritime interests, or even national character. National flags may change with historical developments. Thus, in France the Bourbon white flag showed *fleurs-de-lis*, which, in turn, was supplanted by the tricolor at the time of the French Revolution. Symbols on modern flags often have religious connotations: many Christian countries are identified by crosses, and Israel displays the Star of David on its flag, while some Islamic nations use the crescent. In the Soviet Union the hammer-and-sickle proclaims Communism.

Modern flags are used for a variety of purposes. The international code flags enable seamen to communicate with one another regardless of language. In the armed forces, flags are used for signaling. In earlier times the black flag was used for piracy; today the white flag is used for truce, the red for revolution or mutiny, the yellow a sign of infectious diseases. When the national design is inverted, it is a signal of distress. Ordinarily, the national flag becomes for the individual citizen an object of veneration. He regards it as the prime signal of his citizenship, and he sees loyalty to his flag as one of his most important duties. The national flag is flown at half mast to signal mourning.

Some families of flags may be recognized by their similarity. Thus, the national flags of Denmark, Norway, Sweden, and Iceland, which have common cultural ties, use a similar cross and colors in their flags. Australia, New Zealand, and Canada use the British flag in the upper left of their own flags. The ensign of Great Britain is formed by the crosses of St. George, St. Andrew, and St. Patrick, national saints, respectively, of England, Scotland, and Ireland. The first flag of the United States was raised on January 2, 1776, by George Washington at Cambridge, Massachusetts. Today the United States flag, known as "Old Glory," consists of 13 red and white stripes, representing the original 13 states, with the upper inner quarter blue. It now bears one star for each of the 50 states of the union.

Contemporary scholars recognize flags as artifacts of current national states. The study of the history, etiquette, design, and manufacture of flags today is known as vexillology. It has taken on increasing interest in the current age of nationalism.

Bibliography: Whitney Smith, *Flags Through the Ages and Across the World* (New York, 1979); Kingsley Parker, *Starting with Flags* (New York, 1976); W. G. Crompton, *The Observer's Book of Flags* (New York, 1979); H. C. Barraclough and W. G. Crompton (eds.), *Flags of the World* (New York, 1981); Michael Casey, *Flags into Battle* (Boston, 1987).

F.L.B. (BRETON LIBERATION FRONT).   *See* **BRETON NATIONALISM.**

FLEMINGS.   Natives of Belgium who hold to their linguistic traditions and oppose any attempt to give second place to their language in the Belgian state. (*See* **WALLOON NATIONALISM.**)

F.L.N.C. (CORSICAN NATIONAL LIBERATION FRONT).   *See* **CORSICAN NATIONALISM.**

F.L.Q. (FRONT LIBÉRATION DE QUÉBEC).   Extremist group in Quebec, Canada, that rejected reform as inconsequential and called for independence. (*See* **QUEBEC NATIONALISM.**)

FOSCOLO, UGO (1778–1827).   Poet and patriot who helped lead the way to the *Risorgimento* (Resurrection), the Italian movement for liberation, reform, and unification from the late eighteenth century to *c.* 1870. In his *The Sepulchers* (1807), Foscolo summoned the mighty dead from their tombs to struggle again for Italy. In 1809 he was called to the "Chair of Italian Eloquence" at the University of Pavia. In his inaugural lecture, he urged his young audience to retain their literature within the framework of national growth. He spoke dramatically in presenting the essence of Italian nationalism:

> Italy! O lovely land! O temple of Venus and of the Muses! How thou art portrayed by travellers who make a show of honouring thee! How thou art humiliated by foreigners who have the presumption to seek to master thee! But who can depict thee better than he who is destined to see thy beauty all his life long? Who can address to thee a more fervent and sincere exhortation than whoever is only

honoured in honouring thee, only beloved in loving thee? Neither the barbarity of the Goths, nor the internal civic struggles, the devastation of many campaigns, the denunciations of theologians, nor the monopoly of learning by the clergy, could suffice to quench the immortal fire that animated the Etruscans and the Latins, that fired Dante's immortal spirit amidst the sufferings of his exile, Machiavelli in the anguish of his torture, Galileo among the terrors of the Inquisition, and Tasso in his wandering life, in his persecution by the philosophers, in his long unhappy love, amidst the ingratitude of courts; unquenchable the fire not in these alone, but in countless other noble souls who suffered disaster and poverty in silence. Prostrate upon their tombs, ask the secret of their greatness and misfortune, and how their love of fatherland, of glory and of truth increased their constancy of heart, their strength of mind and the benefits they have conferred upon us.

Bibliography: Antonio Cippico, *The Poetry of Ugo Foscolo* (London, 1924–1925); Ugo Foscolo, *The Sepulchers*, ed. by Ernesto Grillo (London and Glasgow, 1928); Douglas Radcliff-Umstead, *Ugo Foscolo* (New York, 1970).

FRENCH NATIONALISM. The way for French nationalism was prepared in the Enlightenment, the eighteenth-century Age of Reason. French *philosophes* defended the idea of a unified national state and praised the national character of their countrymen. Jean-Jacques Rousseau (q.v.) spoke eloquently for the cause of national sovereignty; Charles de Montesquieu (q.v.) presented scientific arguments in support of constitutionalism and the spirit of the laws; and Voltaire swept away the cobwebs of ancient superstitions and advocated a secular society. All were important progenitors of the subsequent development of French nationalism.

Journalist Henry Grunwald expressed it this way: "The most enduring legacy of the [French] Revolution is nationalism. It was certainly not invented by the Revolution, but it was elevated by it into a secular faith and put on a path to a virulent form."

French nationalism, indeed, burst into bloom during the explosive events of the French Revolution beginning in 1789. This was one of the great landmarks of history. The idea of a French nation on which the individual could focus his loyalty was harder to grasp than the traditional loyalty to a king or a provincial noble family. But Frenchmen took to the streets and barricades to fashion a new loyalty—to the spirit of nationalism and to the national state. In a sequence of dramatic events they stormed the Bastille, sent aristocrats to the guillotine, and put an end, temporarily, to the monarchy.

The budding spirit of nationalism was exhibited in the behavior of the revolutionaries. When the Estates-General was convened in 1789 for the first time since 1610, it was soon transformed into what was now called the *National* Assembly. That new body represented not the old three Estates, but the entire nation. The subsequent leveling procedure was motivated by the new consciousness of nationalism. The vestiges of feudalism, manorialism, and class privilege were abolished. Localized geographic boundaries vanished. A *national* administrative system was introduced to replace old governmental institutions. New *départements* supplanted the old provinces. Church property was confiscated in the new secular society. The Church became a national church. Where beforehand there had been division, distintegration, localism, and provincialism, now there were only nationalization and federalism. The new nationalism introduced centralized control. There were now national fêtes instead of local celebrations. The armed forces were nationalized. All schoolchildren were required to use the national language.

The new French nationalism saw the nation as composed of free individuals always protected by law. While the citizen was shielded from the abuses of government, he was expected to maintain a sentiment of loyalty to his country. He would "be born, live, and die for the Fatherland." The revolutionist Maximilien Robespierre, at the height of the crisis, boasted of the special role of France in the history of civilization: "This delightful land which we inhabit and which nature caresses with love is made to be the domain of liberty and happiness."

So convinced were the French of the desirability of their new nationalism that they were overcome with a crusading zeal to bring the benefits of their revolution to prospective converts. "What is good for France is good for Europe." The Girondins, or moderate Republicans, suffused with a passion for prestige and power, began to see ghostly opponents in foreign lands. They believed that it was necessary for French troops to force the fruits of liberty on other peoples. French revolutionaries had brought about the consolidation and reconstruction of their own country; now they would act as liberators of other peoples. From their point of view it was natural for any people who wished to be regarded as "French" to be incorporated into France. Other peoples, such as Belgians, were not too happy about the prospect. Once the process gathered momentum, good intentions were supplanted by power politics.

Napoleon Bonaparte, too, was afflicted with this urge to extend the benefits of French culture to other peoples. However, in the process he unconsciously became the traveling salesman of nationalism in Europe, the St. Paul of a new religion. He saw himself as a liberator in extending this policy of revolutionary nationalism, which he was careful to temper with a strong dose of personal and family ambitions. He erased one-third of the familiar slogan of "Liberty, Equality, and Fraternity"—he supported equality and fraternity but fell short on the element of liberty. He believed himself to be a man of benevolence, but Englishmen and Russians, among others, saw him as evil incarnate.

Instead of bringing the benefits of French civilization to other countries, Napoleon succeeded only in sowing the seeds of nationalism among those people who were subjected to his military campaigns. Germans, Italians, and Russians were angered by Napoleonic invasions; a powerful sense of nationalism was stimulated in all three countries by the hostile aggression of the French conqueror. Subjugated European peoples at long last united against him and overthrew his new order of conquest and uniformity. His fate was sealed by the resistance of other nationalities.

Napoleon, himself, said during his exile that he was interested only in eliminating European hatreds and establishing a United States of Europe, under his own control, of course:

> One of my great plans was reuniting the concentration of those same geographical nations which have been separated and parcelled out by revolution and policy. There are in Europe, dispersed, it is true, upward of thirty millions of French, fifteen millions of Spaniards, fifteen millions of Italians, and thirty millions of Germans, and it was my intention to incorporate these people each into a nation. It would have been a noble thing to have advanced into posterity with such a train, and attended by the blessings of future ages. I felt myself worthy of this glory!

Whatever his good intentions, Napoleon set an example in modern times for the potentialities of the cult of force that later found adherents in the extreme movements of nationalism. He foreshadowed those twentieth-century totalitarians (Hitler, Mussolini, Franco), all of whom regarded weakness as ignoble, laws as superfluous, democracy as weak and slow, and war as essential.

During the nineteenth and twentieth centuries, French nationalism, on the whole, retained its faith in the Declaration of the Rights of Man and the Citizen. Reverence for this document prevented France from falling into the kind of authoritarianism that was to engulf Germany, Italy, and Russia. The French sense of national consciousness remained high despite the loss of the war against Prussia in 1870–1871.

Along with French fervent nationalism went a powerful sentiment of patriotism. This was expressed in the military poems of Paul

Déroulède (q.v.) and the later integral nationalism of Maurice Barrès (q.v.) and Charles Maurras (q.v.). The latter was one of the founders of *L'Action Française* (q.v.). Even in defeat in World War II, Charles de Gaulle (q.v.) would write of his countrymen as "a race created for brilliant deeds." This extraordinary love of country was supported by the entire educational system, as witness this excerpt from a textbook for French children which went through many editions:

Moral of History
Children you have read the history of your country, the recital of its victories and defeats, its prosperity and adversity. Love your country as citizens and soldiers. As citizens you will fulfill all your duties and remain attached to the institutions which the Republic has founded. As soldiers you will perform with zeal your military service and, if the Fatherland appeals to your devotion, you will be ready to shed your blood for it. Thus, France will follow the path of its glorious destiny if all citizens are united in the same sentiment, love of the fatherland.

Bibliography: Carlton J. H. Hayes, *France, a Nation of Patriots* (New York, 1930); André Siegfried, *France, A Study in Nationality* (New Haven, Conn., 1930); Hans Kohn, "Napoleon and the Age of Nationalism," *The Journal of Modern History*, 22 (1950), 22–37; William R. Beer, *The Unexpected Rebellion: Ethnic Attitudes in Contemporary France* (New York, 1980).

FRENCH REVOLUTION.   *See* **FRENCH NATIONALISM.**

FRIEDRICH, CARL J. (1901–1984).   American professor concerned with the problems of European unification. Born in Leipzig, Friedrich came to the United States, where he became Eaton Professor of the Science of Government at Harvard University. He held posts as President of the International Political Science Association and of the *Institut International de Philosophie Politique*. In 1963 he directed a major research project, "The Political Implications of Informal Community Formation in Europe," under the auspices of the Center for International Affairs at Harvard University.

Aware of the dangers of nationalism on the European continent, Friedrich, in his book *Europe: An Emergent Nation* (1969), presented the thesis that although the optimism and enthusiasm of the early post-World War II years were gone, the hardheaded, monotonous work of moderating the weaknesses of the traditional European nation-state has continued. He saw significant and effective integration of business, labor, agriculture, communications, and education. He saw, as well, large-scale bureaucratic operations of such importance that a supranational framework of operations could be considered a reality in contemporary Europe.

Friedrich described the European community as the carrier of civilization. "Little Europe," centering in France, Germany, and Italy, is the actual as well as ideological core of the communal problem in Europe. Despite wars and bitter hatreds, thoughtful Europeans have seen the need for recreating a common political structure. In what he called his "macroanalysis," Friedrich presented a case for "a growing consensus in molding all those who live within the boundaries of a Common Market into a community possessing legitimate authorities engaged in governing and defending it." The European farmer has been mobilized successfully in support of an emergent Europe. Factory workers as well as guest workers have come to develop a sense of European community. While links between the working force are sporadic, "the bonds which unite the trade unions of the Common Market . . . are structured, formally institutionalized, and of considerable operational importance."

According to Friedrich, European local communities, which have proved to be surprisingly resistant to the pressures of totalitarian government, provide some of the genuine grass-roots support of an eventual European government. Also, growing partnership among the European universities "may prove a decisive factor in coping with these deep-seated reluctances of the academic community to abandon the familiar haven of national culture and community in which they have for so long played the central role."

Friedrich denounced the "clever talk" about the "end" of European integration, about "dead alleys," "crises," and "impending collapse." Instead, he saw what he called such realities as the continued growth of economic bonds and continuing effective integration. Europe, in his view, was bound to go forward in the direction of unification. "For such unification is the ineluctable condition for its survival as a major factor in the world that is emerging."

Friedrich's estimate of the decline of European nationalism and the rise of a spirit of European community drew an opposing point of view among other scholars. Karl W. Deutsch (q.v.) argued that European integration has slowed down since the mid-1950s and has stopped or reached a plateau since 1957–1958. Contrary to Friedrich, Deutsch predicted that the prospects for any form of European political integration appear to be fading rapidly as the Common Market encounters major obstacles. Deutsch added that the next decade of European politics will literally be dominated still further by the politics of nation-states and not by any supranational European institutions.

According to Friedrich, such views were erroneous and already proved to be mistaken by the actual course of events. He objected to Deutsch's emphasis on "élite opinions," criticized the projected relative acceptance index, and contended that there is a question of whether European integration and national sentiment can be treated as necessarily antagonistic. Friedrich also confirmed the positions of Daniel Lerner and Martin Garland, who, in their research on French and German leaders, contended that there has developed a general consensus in Europe to the effect that national answers to man's pressing problems are no longer viable. Therefore, only supranational or transnational choices will do.

In defending his views against "clever prophets," Friedrich insisted that his own views on European integration were closer to truth than the criticisms of "impatient authors." "It is now forty years," he wrote, "since Coudenhove-Kalergi (q.v.) published his *Paneuropa.* . . . Ever since then I have been a partisan of European unification. This needs to be said so that the reader may know where my heart is." (*See also* **PAN-EUROPA.**)

Bibliography: Karl W. Deutsch *et al., France, Germany, and the Western Alliance: A Study of Elite Attitudes of European Integration and World Politics* (New York, 1967); Carl J. Friedrich, *Europe: An Emerging Nation* (New York, 1969).

FROMM, ERICH (1900–1980).   German-born psychoanalyst, social philosopher, and critic of nationalism. Fromm left the Third Reich in 1934 and settled in the United States. In academic posts and in many publications, he explored emotional problems common in free societies, and applied psychoanalytic principles in the struggle to reform cultural ills and to establish what he called a "sane society." Although he attracted the interest of many social scientists, he became increasingly controversial, especially in psychoanalytical circles, because of his decidedly unorthodox views.

On the concept of nationalism, however, Fromm joined many colleagues in denouncing its evils. He called for a new world based on human solidarity:

> Only when man succeeds in developing his reason and love further than he has done so far, only when he can build a world based on human solidarity and justice, only when he can feel rooted in the experience of human brotherhood, will he have found a new, human form of rootedness, will he have transformed his world into a truly human home.

Bibliography: Erich Fromm, *The Sane Society* (New York, 1955); Erich Fromm, *The Heart of Man* (New York, 1964); Erich Fromm, *Escape from Freedom* (New York, 1968); Don Hausdorff, *Eric Fromm* (New York, 1972).

FYFE, HAMILTON (1869–1921). A British scholar, Fyfe attacked the idea of national character as an illusion that was doing great harm in the world. He denied that national characters are distinct, homogeneous, or well-defined. In his view, this was the most powerful and the most dangerous of all elements making for war.

Fyfe maintained that what is true of individuals, is more true of groups and especially of nations. No two individuals are alike and the peoples of no two nations are alike. The characteristics of a very large group cannot be ascertained accurately and set down. It is the kind of popular error and a superstition that has confused and injured mankind in the past. A nation, he insisted, is not a natural unit, such as a herd of buffalo or a pack of wolves. It is largely an accidental unit. "Men and women who easily change their minds, their sympathies, are said to be weather cocks, to lack character. Apply the same reasoning to nations and it will be seen that, since no nation can show a consistent line of action, none have national characters." (*See also* **NATIONAL CHARACTER,** and **BARKER, ERNEST.**)

Bibliography: Hamilton Fyfe, *The Illusion of National Character* (London, 1940).

G

GARIBALDI, GIUSEPPE (1807–1882). Guerrilla general, military leader in the campaign for Italian unification, and activist for Italian nationalism. An early disciple of Giuseppe Mazzini (q.v.), Garibaldi was a romantic figure and a hero of the *Risorgimento* (Resurrection). Participating in early Italian revolts, he also took part in the Austro-Sardinian War of 1859. He became convinced that the destiny of Italy was linked with that of the house of Savoy. While Camillo Cavour (q.v.) worked in the north of Italy to drive Austria from Italian affairs, Garibaldi was determined to settle accounts with the reactionary Neapolitan monarchy in the south.

On May 6, 1860, Garibaldi assembled a motley force of 1,062 Italians and five Hungarians, all wearing bright red woolen shirts and red hats. The fiery leader set sail from Genoa to invade the southern kingdom, then under the despotic rule of Francis II. Garibaldi issued a stirring call to arms to his "Expedition of the Thousand," a speech which became a classic in the annals of Italian nationalism:

> Italians!
>
> The Sicilians are fighting against the enemies of Italy and for Italy. To help them with money, arms, and especially men, is the duty of every Italian.
>
> Let the Marches, Umbria, Sabine, the Roman Campagna, and the Neapolitan territory rise, so as to divide the enemy's forces.
>
> If the cities do not offer a sufficient basis for insurrection, let the more resolute throw themselves into the open country.
>
> A brave man can always find a weapon. In the name of Heaven, hearken not to the voice of those who cram themselves at well-served tables.

Let us arm. Let us fight for our brothers; tomorrow we can fight for ourselves.

A handful of brave men, who have followed me in battles for our country, are advancing with me to the rescue. Italy knows them; they always appear at the hour of danger. Brave and generous companions, they have devoted their lives to their country; they will shed their last drop of blood for it, seeking no other reward than that of a pure conscience.

"Italy and Victor Emmanuel!"—that was our battle-cry when we crossed the Ticino; it will resound into the very depths of Aetna.

As this prophetic battle-cry re-echoes from the hills of Italy to the Tarpeian Mount, the tottering throne of tyranny will fall to pieces, and the whole country will rise like one man.

Garibaldi and his men turned first to Sicily. After escaping Neapolitan warships, the motley band of Red Shirts endured a month of forced marches, sleepless nights, and exposure to the semi-tropical sun. Finally, they entered Palermo, chief town of Sicily, in triumph. They then sailed to Naples and at the Volturno River defeated an army twice their size. Garibaldi assumed the dictatorship of Naples.

Then came an extraordinary decision. In November 1860 Garibaldi resigned and delivered his army to King Victor Emmanuel. He went back to his farm on Caprera "with a large bag of seed corn and a small handful of lira notes." This was the moment of Garibaldi's greatest statesmanship.

A master of guerrilla warfare, Garibaldi was also a powerful propagandist for Italian national unification. His message of nationalism and patriotism had a profound effect on the Italian people, who venerated him as a great national hero. Although later in life he turned to socialism and pacifism, he remained primarily what he had espoused all his life—an unbending champion of Italian nationalism.

Bibliography: George Macaulay Trevelyan, *Garibaldi and the Making of Italy* (London, 1911): Dennis Mack Smith, *Garibaldi: A Great Life in Brief* (London, 1954); Marcia Davenport, *Garibaldi; Father of Modern Italy* (New York, 1957); John Parris, *The Lion of Caprera* (London and New York, 1962); Denis Mack Smith, *Cavour and Garibaldi* (London, 1985).

GARVEY, MARCUS MOZIAH (1887–1940). Champion of black nationalism and organizer of the first significant American black nationalist movement. Born in the British West Indies, the grandson of African slaves, Garvey was raised under a color caste system— white, mulatto, and black. His early resentment against whites later became a cardinal tenet of his Back-to-Africa movement. Moving to

London, he began to support the idea of an empire ruled by black men. In 1916 he came to Harlem in New York City, where he was, at first, ridiculed as an immigrant carpetbagger, but he soon attracted attention to his views.

Flamboyant and charismatic, Garvey in 1914 founded the Universal Negro Improvement Association (U.N.I.A.). He gave his organization a set of slogans: "Back to Africa!"; "Africa for Africans!"; "Ethiopians Awake!"; "One God! One Aim! One Destiny!" He issued a program:

> The program of the Universal Negro Improvement Association is that of drawing together, into one universal whole, all the Negro peoples of the world, with prejudice toward none. We desire to have every shade of color, even with those of one drop of Negro blood, in our fold; because we believed that none of us, as we are, is responsible for our birth; in a word we have no prejudice against ourselves in race. We believe that every Negro is just alike, and, therefore, we have no distinctions to make, hence wherever you see the Universal Negro Improvement Association, you will find us giving every member of the race an equal opportunity to make good.

Garvey spoke to enthusiastic gatherings. "No one knows when the hour of Africa's redemption cometh. It is in the wind. One day, like a storm, it will be here." In his paper, the *Negro Weekly*, he paid tribute to "the glorious history" of his people. He proposed a "black economy" inside the white world and urged his fellow blacks to become independent of the grasping white businessman. He created such auxiliary organizations as the Universal Black Legion, the Universal Black Cross with its own corps of nurses, and his ill-fated Black Star Line. He took the title "Provisional General of Africa," and set up a "Court of Ethiopia." He adopted an official flag: black (for skin color); green (for hope); and red (for blood). His official anthem was titled "Ethiopia, Land of Our Fathers." In his African Orthodox Church, God, Christ, and the Madonna were all black. He promoted the manufacture of black baby dolls for black children.

U.N.I.A. membership made phenomenal growth as the stocky little nationalist leader stumped the country in a whirlwind tour. His extraordinary oratorical talent and his showmanship stimulated a sense of pride that no black intellectuals could match. Black historian Dr. William Edward Burkhardt Du Bois (q.v.) and highly respected black activist A. Philip Randolph, shocked and dismayed by Garvey's tactics, denounced him as dangerous for the black people.

Despite his mass appeal, Garvey soon encountered serious difficulties. After repeated complaints, the Federal Government investigated the Black Star Line, indicted Garvey, and put him on trial for using the mails to defraud. He was fined $1,000 and sentenced to five years in prison. His appeal was denied. Without its dynamic leader, the U.N.I.A. dissolved into quarreling factions. His Back-to-Africa movement was a failure. In 1927, after Garvey served two years in prison, his sentence was commuted, and he was deported as an undesirable alien. He was unable to revive his movement and died in obscurity in London.

While Garvey's version of black nationalism gave a new sense of dignity to American blacks, his movement foundered because the vast majority of American blacks had no intention of relinquishing their American citizenship. Historian Rayford W. Logan pronounced the Garvey movement "almost a complete failure." He saw it as widening the gulf between West Indians and American blacks, between those of dark and light skins. Other black leaders accused Garvey of creating dissension among his own people. However, in recent years black nationalists have revived an appreciation of Garvey and his movement. In his homeland of Jamaica he is praised as a national hero.

Bibliography: Roy Ottley, *New World A-Coming: Inside Black America* (Boston, 1943); Edmund Davis Cronon, *Black Moses: The Story of Marcus Garvey and the Universal Negro Improvement Association* (Madison, Wis., 1955); Theodore C. Vincent, *Black Power and the Garvey Movement* (Berkeley, 1971); Clyde Taylor, "Garvey's Ghost: Revamping the Twenties," *Black World,* 25, No. 4 (1976), 54–57.

GAULLE, CHARLES de (1890–1970).   French general, statesman, and ultranationalist. In 1910 de Gaulle entered the military academy at Saint-Cyr and was commissioned when he was 21 years old. After distinguished service in World War I, during which he was wounded several times, he taught war strategy at Saint-Cyr. Following the fall of France in 1940, he continued the struggle from London. He founded the French National Committee and assumed the title of leader of all Free Frenchmen. As President of the French Republic, he is generally credited with saving France from disaster and with restoring his country to its former leading rank among nations.

In France, called by Carlton J. H. Hayes, "a nation of patriots," de Gaulle emerged as the nationalist *par excellence.* For his country, de Gaulle had a special kind of sentiment, compounded of mysticism and romanticism. His mind was like the Louvre, filled with battle pictures in which France was always triumphant. An apostle of French nationalism, he expressed his love for country in emotional terms:

Our country, with her tinted sky, her varied contours, her fertile soil, our fields full of fine corn and vines and livestock, our industry, our gifts of initiative, adaptation and self-respect, make us, above all others, a race created for brilliant deeds.

The sword is the axis of the world, and greatness cannot be shared. (1934)

The emotional side of me tends to imagine France, like the princess in the stories or the Madonnas in the frescoes, as dedicated to an exalted and exceptional destiny. But the positive side of my mind also assures me that France is not really herself unless in the front rank; that only vast enterprises are capable of counterbalancing the divisive ferments which are inherent in her people. In short, to my mind, France cannot be France—without greatness. (1955)

During the dark days of World War II, this charismatic leader insisted that he not only spoke for France, he was France. He identified the national state with himself. In his *War Memoirs* he wrote: "And today I was at the head of a ruined, decimated, lacerated nation, surrounded by ill will. Hearing my voice, France had been able to unite and march to her liberation."

For de Gaulle, France was not only a *patrie*, it was a mystique. He would restore dignity to a country beset by humiliation, despair, and debilitation. For him this was a call from the depths of history. He believed that the instincts of the nation had led him to assume French sovereignty. He would impose law, order, and justice. He demanded that the world respect the rights of France. He would lead his nation to salvation. He was certain that France would continue to exercise in the twentieth century the major role she had played for a thousand years.

De Gaulle's unyielding nationalism had a profound effect on his countrymen. They were impressed by his faith in the permanence of national states and the desirability of purely national interests. By emphasizing national rather than supranational interests, de Gaulle and the French profoundly influenced the entire European continent. One by one, in domino pattern, the bastions of European federation fell in response to moves by de Gaulle in Paris.

Bibliography: The War Memoirs of Charles de Gaulle, trans. by Richard Howard (New York, 1961); Bernard Ledowsky, *De Gaulle* (London, 1982); Don Cook, *Charles de Gaulle: A Biography* (New York, 1983); Sam White, *De Gaulle* (London, 1984); Susan Banfield, *Charles de Gaulle* (New York, 1985).

GERMAN NATIONALISM.   In the late eighteenth century the Germanies formed a kind of "geographical expression" consisting of hundreds of kingdoms, duchies, counties, and free states. Unification was to be delayed for several centuries beyond that of England and France. The liberating waves of the Western European Enlightenment and the impact of liberty, equality, and fraternity of the French Revolution did not affect the Germanies. Where the Western rationalists were motivated by the ideas of popular sovereignty, individualism, and cosmopolitanism, the Germans were influenced by Prussianism, authoritarianism, state-worship, and historicism. Jean-Jacques Rousseau (q.v.) emphasized the critical importance of popular sovereignty, and Charles de Montesquieu (q.v.) rejected despotism in favor of democracy and constitutionalism, preferably the English model. But German national development took place within the confines of state-worship. Georg Wilhelm Friedrich Hegel (q.v.) stated: "The State represents the national life as the embodiment of a moral idea, capable of achieving whatever it may desire." German historian Heinrich von Treitschke accepted this absolute: "In the State it is not only the great primitive forces of human nature that come into play, but the State is the basis of all national life." State-worship was to become the focal point of German nationalism.

Until the early nineteenth century there had been scarcely any sentiment of German national consciousness. Goethe, the cosmopolitan, saw "all national poetry as hackneyed or would become so if it is not based upon what is universally human." The Germans as a people, from intellectuals and nobles to peasants and workingmen, saw no need to unify the combination of large and small states, each jealous of its own independence and each suspicious of any effort at unification.

When German nationalism, in common with developments throughout Europe, finally emerged, it came under distinct Prussian auspices. Such is the irony of history—the impetus for German nationalism came not from the hearts of the German people, but it was imposed from the outside, from a relatively crude, backward border state. Prussia was able by power and strength to impress its own system upon all Germany. The interloper became the head man. There was to be no synthesis of nationalism and liberalism—let the Western *philosophes* rave on about the glories of popular sovereignty, constitutionalism, social contract, liberty, equality, and fraternity— such ideas had no place in Prussian authoritarianism. The Prussian sword was to be dominant.

Historian Hans Kohn (q.v.) presented an analysis of the Prussian ideology:

> Prussianism was virtual service for a rather doubtful cause. It did not spring from the people; it sprang from the State. The Prussian concept of a power-culture

synthesis with inordinate stress upon power as the dominating element was one which gave German nationalism its indelible stamp. Where the Western rationalists placed humanity as the object and carrier of history, the Prussians substituted the State. Where the rationalists explained the founding of the State by the Social Contract, the Prussians found its sinews in politico-military power. Where the rationalists placed the State, as well as man under the law, the Prussians defined it as a social right within limits set by the State.

Intoxicated by their Faustian romanticism, the Germans were ready to accept authoritarian Prussianism even though to them it appeared to be un-German. They misunderstood its dangerous quality. Prussianism and worship of the State combined to form a time bomb that eventually would explode into the bloodshed of two global conflicts.

The real advent of German nationalism may be traced to the days when the shadow of a Corsican adventurer was cast over the whole of Europe. The heavy boots of Napoleon's troops on German soil triggered the birth of German nationalism. Neither the glory-bound French fighting men nor their egocentric Emperor were fully conscious of what they were doing. Without realizing it, they were planting the seeds of nationalism wherever they put up their tents. Subjugated peoples were shocked and angered by French invasions; they would learn that in union there was strength, the wherewithal to put an end to Napoleonic conquests. Nationalism was their response to French muskets.

The German nationalism that arose as a reaction to Napoleonic aggression was clothed with the new spirit of romanticism. To forget their humiliation and despair, Germans turned to their past when the glorious German Empire had been the fulcrum of European power. Their poets and philosphers sought for an organic folk community wrapped in the old cloak of tradition. They would mobilize their heroic past with its folk songs, fairy tales, sagas, and poetry, with an accent on imagination instead of the rationalism of the Western European *philosophes*. They would think with the blood and give free rein to all that was German.

Most of all, Germans reacted against the machinations of Napoleon. The tone was set by Johann Gottlieb Fichte (q.v.), who in his ultrapatriotic *Addresses to the German Nation* called for a higher love of the Fatherland. Poet and patriot Ernst Moritz Arndt (q.v.) demanded war to the death because there could be no honorable peace with Napoleon. Friedrich von Schlegel (q.v.), writer and critic, with intense emotion, demanded: "Awaken, Germans, from stupor and shame and ignominy! Awaken and act for the sake of German honor!" Friedrich Schleiermacher (q.v.), minister and philologist, devoted his sermons to encourage resistance to Napoleon. In the

War of Liberation a consciousness of nationalism was promoted vigorously by the *Freikorps* (patriotic volunteers), the *Turnerschaften* (gymnastic societies led by eccentric pedagogue Friedrich Ludwig Jahn (q.v.), and the *Burschenschaften* (student fraternities). The germs of nationalism were multiplying geometrically.

There was some hope in the first half of the nineteenth century that Germans would turn to the humanitarian nationalism of Johann Gottfried von Herder (q.v.), poet and philosopher, who advocated a spirit of tolerance and regard for the rights of other nationalities. German intellectuals understood the meaning of the liberal temper, but they were not successful in implanting it into the Germanies. At first, the liberal movement seemed headed for success, but after the Revolution of 1848 it was choked off and collapsed. In the minds of the German people this unfulfilled liberal revolution was stained thereafter with the odium of defeat, weakness, inefficiency, and anarchism.

For the remainder of the nineteenth century, German nationalism took on the tone of Otto von Bismarck's (q.v.) policy of iron-and-blood. When national unification was finally achieved in 1871, it came not with a liberal coating but with the trappings of an authoritarian state giving little attention to democratic forms. Bismarck's traditional nationalism was succeeded by the blustering aggressive nationalism of Kaiser William II (q.v.), who challenged Great Britain's global empire with a Big Navy of his own and a demand for Germany's place in the sun. With Adolf Hitler (q.v.), German nationalism from 1933 to 1945 went into a stage of violent frenzy—truly nationalism gone berserk.

There are different opinions about the German national character until 1945. (*See* **NATIONAL CHARACTER.**) Some observers called attention to German sentimentality, love of culture, and preference for high intellectual attainment. Others emphasized such traits as obedience to authority, acceptance of discipline, attraction to militarism, and mysticism and symbolism. British historian A. J. P. Taylor described the dual Faustian characteristics of the German people at the end of World War II in this passage:

> The history of the Germans is a history of extremes. It contains everything except moderation and in the course of a thousand years the Germans have experienced everything except normality. They have dominated Europe, and they have been the helpless victims of the domination of others; they have enjoyed liberties unparalleled in Europe and they have fallen victims to despotisms equally without parallel; they have produced the most transcendental philosophers, the most spiritual musicians, and the most ruthless and unscrupulous politicians. "German"

has meant at one moment a being so sentimental, so trusting, so pious, as to be too good for this world; and at another a being so brutal, so unprincipled, so degraded, as to be not fit to live. Both descriptions are true; both types of Germans have existed not only at the same epoch, but in the same person. Only the normal person, not particularly good, not particularly bad, healthy, sane, moderate—he has never set his stamp on German history. Geographically the people of the center, the Germans have never found a middle way of life either in their thought or least of all in their politics. One looks in vain in their history for a *juste milieu*, for common sense—the two qualities which have distinguished France and England. Nothing is normal in German history except violent oscillations.

The Taylor estimate is not applicable to contemporary Germany. The loss of two great wars in the twentieth century and especially the Nazi experience have led to a diminution of nationalism. British journalist John Artagh expressed this view: "If the continuing shame about Nazism is the main cause of wariness over national pride, this will surely ease as the years go by. It would then lead to a revival of the less pleasant aspects of German nationalism. But as yet there is little sign of this and it is important to stress that nationalism today is diluted and even transmuted by the new feeling for Europe, as it was not in the Nazi time."

Bibliography: A. J. P. Taylor, *The Course of German History* (New York, 1946); Louis L. Snyder, *German Nationalism: The Tragedy of a People* (Harrisburg, Pa., 1952, Port Washington, N.Y., 1969); Hans Kohn, *The Mind of Germany* (New York, 1960); Carole Fink *et al.*, *German Nationalism and the European Response, (1890–1949)* (Norman, Okla., 1985); Arlie J. Hoover, *German Patriotic Preaching from Napoleon to Versailles* (Stuttgart, 1986); John Artagh, *Germany and the Germans: An Anatomy of Society Today* (New York, 1987); Michael Hughes, *Nationalism and Society: Germany, 1800–1945* (London, 1988).

GIOBERTI, VINCENZO (1801–1852).   Cleric, philosopher, politician, and champion of Italian nationalism. Ordained as a Roman Catholic priest in 1825, Gioberti achieved a reputation as Professor of Theology at the University of Turin. In his prolific writings he called for a federation of the Italian states into a single nation. Such a union, he said, should be headed by the Pope. This identification of Christianity with the cause of Italy enjoyed great popularity among the Italians because it reconciled nationalism and the papacy.

As a nationalist, Gioberti was concerned above everything else with the problem of freeing Italy from foreign overlords. He called for emancipation not only from control by foreign masters, but from all modes of thought that he believed to be alien to the nation's genius and foreign to its national authority. But as a priest, that authority was always associated in his mind with the idea of papal supremacy. As early as 1843, he said:

> "I intend to show . . . that Italy alone has the qualities required to become the chief of nations, and that although today she has almost completely lost that chiefship, it is in her power to recover it. . . . The Italians, humanly speaking, have been chosen by providence to keep the Christian Pontificate, and to protect with love, with veneration, and if necessary by arms, the ark of the new covenant. . . . Let the nations, then, turn their eyes to Italy, their ancient and loving mother, which holds the seeds of their regeneration. Italy is the organ of supreme reason and the royal and ideal word. . . . It is destined to crush in its ravines, every foreign aggressor, compelling its powerful neighbors to respect the common independence of Italy."

Gioberti, like Cavour (q.v.), saw Piedmont as the leader of a great national movement that would ultimately result in a regenerated Italy. He predicted that Cavour was the man to unite the land. At first, he was partial to the radical republican Giuseppe Mazzini (q.v.), but he was careful never to join Mazzini's revolutionary movement. Later, he became a passionate critic of extreme violence as a step to Italian unity. Where Mazzini appealed to the masses, Gioberti attracted scholars, the clergy, and intellectuals. The clergy, especially, were delighted by the eloquence of one of their number, as well as by placing the Pope at the head of the national movement.

At first, the Catholic hierarchy as well as the papacy showed sympathy with Gioberti's conception of nationalism, but gradually the papacy turned against him. His fortunes were reversed when he supported popular uprisings in Venice and Milan in 1848.

Bibliography: Rupert S. Holland, *Builders of Modern Italy* (New York, 1908); Antonio Bowers, *Gioberti* (Rome, 1924); Mario Moro, *La Creazione del pensiero du Vincenzo Gioberti, 1801–1852* (Rome, 1968).

G.L.A. (GUADELOUPE LIBERATION ARMY). A militant extremist group in the Guadeloupe Islands in the Caribbean. (*See* **GUADELOUPE ISLANDERS.**)

GOGOL, NIKOLAI (1809–1852). Russian novelist, dramatist, and patriot. His great comedy, *The Government Inspector* (1836), was a merciless satire on the corrupt bureaucracy under Tsar Nicholas I. Forced to leave Moscow, he journeyed to Rome, where he wrote his masterpiece, *Dead Souls* (1842).

Gogol was also a passionate nationalist who wrote stirring paeans of praise for Russia. Like nationalists elsewhere, he spoke eloquently of his country's "mission." In his novel *Dead Souls*, he compared Russia with a *troika*, a small sleigh drawn by three horses, rushing over the hard snows toward his country's goal of world leadership.

Russia of mine, are you not also speeding like a troika which nothing can overtake? Is not the road smoking beneath your wheels, and are not the bridges thundering as you cross them, everything left behind, while the spectators, struck with the portent, stop to wonder whether you be not a thunderbolt launched from heaven? What does that awe-inspiring progress of yours foretell? What is the unknown force which lies within your mysterious steeds?

Surely the winds themselves must abide in their manes, and every vein in their bodies must be an ear stretched to catch the celestial message which bids them, with iron-girded breasts, and hoofs which barely touch the earth as they gallop, fly forward on a mission of God?

Whither are you speeding, Russia of mine? Whither? Answer me! But no answer comes—only the weird sound of your collar-bells. Rent into a thousand shreds, the air roars past you, as you are overtaking the whole world, and shall one day force all nations, all empires to stand aside, to give way to you!

Bibliography: Hans Kohn, *Basic History of Modern Russia* (Princeton, N.J., 1957); David Magarshack, *Gogol: A Life* (London, 1967); Thais S. Lindstrom, *Nikolai Gogol* (New York, 1974); Leonard J. Kent (ed.) *The Complete Tales of Nikolai Gogol* (Chicago, 1985).

GÖKALP, ZIYA, pseudonym of MEHMED ZIYA (1875/76– 1924). Sociologist, poet, and writer, one of the most important spokesmen for Turkish nationalism. He was appointed in 1912 to the chair of sociology at Istanbul University, where he developed his theories of nationalism. At first, he supported the idea of Pan-Turkism (q.v.), which aimed to unite the Turks of the world. Later, he limited his belief to an ideology that concerned only the Turks of the Ottoman Empire. In his published work, he supported the new Turkish nationalist movement and called for the modernization and Westernization of the Turkish nation.

Gökalp is considered to be the real founder of the modern Turkish nationalist movement. He paid tribute to the "new Turkish Fatherland" in an emotional poem:

A land in which the call to prayer resounds from
the mosque in the Turkish tongue,
Where the peasant understands the meaning of his prayers.
A land where the schoolboy reads the Koran in
his mother tongue,
O son of the Turk, that is thy Fatherland.

In his prose works, Gökalp attempted to educate the Turkish people about the nature of their Fatherland:

About the concept of "Fatherland." It means a sacred piece of land for whose sake people shed their blood. Why is it that all other lands are not sacred, but only that which is called Fatherland? And how does it happen that those who believe this way do not hesitate to sacrifice their lives, their families, their most beloved ones? Evidently not because of any utilitarian value. The sacredness is certainly derived from something sacred. But what can that sacred thing be?

Is it the state? The state is not a power existing by itself. The state derives its power from the nation and from the *ümmet: sharaf al-makān bil-makīn* ["the glory of the residence is with the resident"]! Thus, there are only two things which are sacred: the nation and the *ümmet* [the totality of those people who profess the same religion; the state consists of all those who are administered by the same government; the nation is composed of all those who speak the same language]. As the objects of reverence are two, their symbols of the homelands . . . of these two sacred objects should also be two: the homeland of the *ümmet* and the homeland of the nation.

In discussing the ideal of nationalism, Gökalp paid tribute to the Turkish national language, which he regarded as the best mirror of national consciousness. He believed that every national tongue must adapt itself to and express the concepts of the times. "Until the Turkish language fulfills this requirement, it will not be a modern language." (*See* **PAN-TURANISM,** and **PAN-TURKISM.**)

Bibliography: Uriel Heyd, *Foundations of Turkish Nationalism: The Life and Teachings of Ziya Gökalp* (London, 1950); Elie Kedourie, *Nationalism in Asia and Africa* (New York, 1970).

GRIMM BROTHERS, JAKOB LUDWIG KARL (1783–1863) and WILHELM KARL (1786–1859).   Pioneers in the modern science of folklore, collectors of the famed fairy tales, and fervent advocates of German nationalism. Devoted to the study of German antiquarianism, philology, and folklore, the brothers worked together all their lives. Most of their major works stressed national indigenous literature, especially their folk poetry. They published works on the history of the Germanic languages, law, and comparative mythology. They were attracted by national poetry, including epics, ballads, and popular tales.

The Grimms admitted the power of nationalism in their lives. "All my works," Jakob wrote in one of his last essays, "relate to the Fatherland, from whose soil they derive their strength." At his inaugural lecture at the University of Göttingen, Jakob said: "The love for the Fatherland is so godlike and so deeply impressed a feeling in every human breast that it is not weakened but rather strengthened by the sorrows and misfortunes that happen to us in the land of our birth." Wilhelm Grimm expressed similar sentiments.

From 1812 to 1816 the brothers Grimm collected and published their *Kinder und Hausmärchen,* generally known in English as *Grimm's Fairy Tales.* In their search for old stories, they consulted medieval manuscripts and carefully took down from dictation what German peasants remembered of the old folklore. Their two hundred stories of the collection aimed to convey the soul and imagination of the German people. They used a most readable style without changing the folkloric character of the tales. The stories received enormous attention throughout Germany as well as the world (they have been translated into more than seventy languages). Children everywhere were delighted by the fairy tales, and even adults enjoyed them.

There is evidence to show that a consciousness of nationalism played a vital role in the collecting of these fairy tales. The Grimms venerated national, anonymous folk poetry not only on esthetic grounds, but also to stimulate German national sentiment and to glorify national traditions. From the beginning of their work on the tales, the brothers took the Romantic position, closely allied with the rising German nationalism at the time. Romanticism emphasized the claims of the imagination, emotions, and feeling. Consciously or unconsciously, the brothers were motivated by a desire to glorify German traditions.

Analysis of the fairy tales show how the Grimms selected folklore that was specifically German in character. Included were qualities that are presumed to indicate the German national character (*see* **NATIONAL CHARACTER**): respect for order, belief in the desirability of obedience, subservience to authority, respect for the leader and the hero, veneration of courage and the military spirit, acceptance without protest of cruelty, violence, and atrocity, fear of and hatred for the outsider (*xenophobia—see* **XENOPHOBIC NATIONALISM**), and virulent anti-Semitism.

Several characteristics of what is said to be the German national character are emphasized in the tales. For example, the desirability of order is shown in the opening paragraph of *The Sole:*

> The fishes had for a long time been discontented because no order prevailed in their kingdom. None of them turned aside for the others, but all swam to the right or left as they fancied, or darted between those who wanted to stay together, or got into their way; and a strong one gave a weak one a blow with its tail, and drove it away, or else swallowed it up without more ado. "How delightful it would be," said they, "if we had a king who enforced law and justice among us!" and they met together to choose for their ruler the one who would cleave through the water most quickly, and give help to the weak ones.

The concept of obedience, said to be the characteristic of an apolitical people, is stressed again and again in the fairy tales. A little hare tells a musician: "I will obey you as a scholar obeys his master." When the Devil orders a father to cut off the hands of his own child, the father asks his daughter to understand his predicament. She replies: "Dear father, do with me what you will, I am your child." Whereupon she lays down her hands, and allows them to be cut off.

Still another theme of the *Märchen* was fear of and hatred of the outsider, characteristic of primitive tribalism and the xenophobia of modern nationalism. The stepmother is invariably a disgusting old woman who performs evil deeds with inhuman zest and cruelty. She works with diabolic cunning in seeking to do away with stepchildren. When a wicked stepmother is taken before a judge, she is placed in a barrel filled with boiling oil, and dies an evil death.

This fear of the outsider included German Jews. In the *Jew Among Thorns*, an honest and clever servant, who plays a fiddle, one day meets a Jew with a long goat's beard. When the Jew watches a bird in the thorn bushes, he crawls into the bushes to fetch the bird. The good servant takes up his fiddle and plays:

> In a moment the Jew's legs began to move, and to jump into the air, and the more the servant fiddled the better went the dance. But the thorns tore his shabby coat from him, combed his beard, and pricked and plucked him all over the body. "Oh, dear," cried the Jew, "what do I want with your fiddling? Leave the fiddle alone, master; I do not want to dance."
>
> But the servant did not listen to him, and thought: "You have fleeced people often enough, now the thorn-bushes shall do the same to you"; and he began to play over again, so that the Jew had to jump higher than ever, and scraps of his coat were left hanging on the thorns.

The story concludes with a courtroom scene, in which the judge "had the Jew taken to the gallows and hanged as a thief."

The military spirit is venerated throughout the tales. Again and again war is depicted as good, that fighting gives great moral courage, that bearing arms is the highest of all possible honors, and that the military instinct is a blessing. In *Iron John:* "The youth galloped thither with his iron soldiers, broke like a hurricane over the enemy, and beat down all who opposed him."

It was inevitable that German children, reading the fairy tales with delight, were affected by the sadistic social attitudes. Respect for order, obedience, love for the military, and anti-Semitism carried over into the adult years. Some of the cruel pieces in the tales were eliminated in foreign editions, as well, by authorities in the Weimar Republic. But these stories were restored in Hitler's Third Reich, where the study of German folklore was raised to a special place of honor.

Even German scholars have recognized the role of the brothers Grimm in the intensification of the spirit of nationalism in Germany. In his *Die Brüder Grimm, Ihr Leben und Wirken* (1899), Carl Franke applauded the nationalism of the distinguished folklorists:

> To the spirit of German schoolchildren the tales have become what mother's milk is for their bodies—the first nourishment for the spirit and the imagination. How German is Snow White, Little Briar Rose, Little Red Cap, the seven dwarfs! Through such genuine German diet must the language and spirit of the child gradually become more and more German. . . .
>
> Indeed the brothers Grimm have earned our innermost love and highest admiration as citizens and as men. For they belong doubtlessly in the broadest sense among the founders of the new German Reich. . . . They exhibited all the German virtues: the inner love of family, true friendship, the kindly love for the Hessian homeland, the inspiring love for the Fatherland. . . . With full right they earn therefore a place among Germany's greatest men.

Bibliography: Louis L. Snyder, "Nationalistic Aspects of the Grimm Brothers' Fairy Tales," *The Journal of Social Psychology*, 33 (1931), 209–223; Bruno Bettelheim, *The Uses of Enchantment: The Meaning and Importance of the Fairy Tales* (New York, 1977); Jack Zippes, *Fairy Tales and the Art of Subversion* (New York, 1983); John M. Ellis, *One Fairy Tale Too Many: The Brothers Grimm and Their Tales* (Chicago, 1983); Jakob and Wilhelm Grimm, *The Complete Fairy Tales of the Brothers Grimm*, trans. from the German by Jack Zippes (New York, 1987); Maria Tatar, *The Hard Facts of the Grimm's Fairy Tales* (Princeton, N.J., 1987).

GROSS, FELIKS (1906–   ).   Sociologist with a special interest in the sociology of political parties, and a critic of nationalism. Born in Krakow, Poland, he came to the United States in 1945, where he became Professor of Sociology and Anthropology at Brooklyn College in 1948. Gross saw nationalism as permeating every political philosophy be it national, pan-national, imperialistic, or international:

> The sentiment of national consciousness has entered a crusading phase so powerful that every dogma of the state and of people in general is linked with it. It has taken as complete a hold on modern thinking and attitudes as did religion and theology on the thinking of the Middle Ages.

Bibliography: Feliks Gross, *Violence in Politics* (The Hague, 1975); Feliks Gross, *Ideologies, Goals and Values* (Westport, Conn., 1985).

GUADELOUPE ISLANDERS.   Consciousness of nationalism plays a role in stimulating dissension among small colonies. France, already faced with domestic separatist movements of varying intensity by

Basques, Bretons, Corsicans, and Alsatians (qq.v.), has an additional minor problem 4,200 miles from Paris. Guadeloupe, a group of islands with 320,000 inhabitants situated in the eastern Caribbean Sea, southeast of Puerto Rico, is a *département* of France, with representation in the Chamber of Deputies.

While most Guadeloupians remain loyal to Paris and are proud of their French citizenship, a small number of dissenters present a cry for independence. The Guadeloupe Liberation Army (G.L.A.) claims that its own administration is dominated by whites, who are favored economically. Calling for freedom, the G.L.A. turned to terrorism, assassinating whites and attacking Air France planes. On January 4, 1981, extremists were accused of setting off a thunderous explosion in the Chanel fashion and perfume store in Paris. The reputation of the islands as a tourist paradise was threatened by activists who raised the familiar cry of "We are liberators, not terrorists!" (*See* **TERRORISM.**)

Bibliography: Albert Flagie, *Delinquency and Dependency in the French West Indies: The Case of Guadeloupe* (St. Augustine, Trinidad, and Tobago, 1978); Druno Lara, *La Guadeloupe dans l'histoire* (Paris, 1979); Henri Banjou, *Le Parti socialiste français face à la colonisation* (Paris, 1985).

GUIZOT, FRANÇOIS (1787–1874). Historian, statesman, and apostle of French liberal nationalism. Guizot served as Minister of Public Instruction from 1832 to 1839, and as Premier from 1840 to 1848. A devout Huguenot Calvinist, critical of the kind of popular movement that had put his father to death, he was convinced that the bourgeoisie was not simply a class but a people at its best. He opposed clerical reform on the ground that it would give political power to the economically unfit. Personally honest, he, nevertheless, was said to have countenanced graft and corruption as a means of maintaining his own power. His political life was a moderate course between reaction and revolution. He was regarded as the spokesman for political liberalism. Reformers were unable to pierce the hard rock of his ministry, which was dedicated to "peace and reform."

Guizot was convinced that the strength of French nationalism was dependent in large part upon the study of French history. As Minister of Public Instruction, he helped organize primary education, played an important role in founding the *Société de l'histoire de France*, and encouraged the publication at state expense of French medieval chronicles, documents, and archives. In his memoirs he emphasized the study of history as promoting the cause of nationalism:

Our tastes easily become manias, and an idea which has long and powerfully possessed us, assumes an importance in our estimation to which vanity often lends too much faith. Nevertheless, the more I reflect, the more I feel convinced that I have not exaggerated to myself the interest which a nation ought to take in its own history; nor the advantage it gains in political intelligence as well as in moral dignity, by completely understanding and attaching itself to this subject. In the long course of successive generations, denominated a people, how rapidly each passes away! And in that short passage how narrowly is the horizon bounded! How insignificant is the place we occupy, and how little do we see with our own eyes! We require to magnify our thoughts, that we may be able to take a serious view of life. Religion opens the future and places us in presence of eternity. History brings back the past and adds to our own existence the lives of our fathers. When we turn to them, our perceptions rise and extend. When we thoroughly know them, we acquire a better knowledge and comprehension of ourselves. Our own destiny, or present situation, the circumstances which surround and the necessities which press upon us, become more clear and natural in our eyes. We not only gratify science and imagination, by thus associating ourselves with the events and persons that have preceded us on the same soil and under the same heaven, but we take from the ideas and passions of the day much of their narrow sourness. Amongst a people interested and well instructed in their own history, we are almost sure of finding a more wholesome and equitable judgment on their present affairs, the conditions of their progress, and their chances for the future.

Bibliography: François Guizot, *Memoirs to Illustrate the History of My Time*, trans. by J. W. Cole (London, 1860); Douglas W. Johnson, *Guizot: Aspects of French History, 1787–1874* (London, 1963); François Guizot, *Historical Essays and Lectures*, ed. by Stanley Mellon (Chicago, 1972).

H

HANDMAN CATEGORIES.   *See* **NATIONALISM, CLASSIFICA-
TIONS OF.**

HASSLIED.   "Chant of Hate Against England" illustrates the effects of extreme nationalism in action. Behind this extraordinary
chant was a long building of resentment by German intellectuals
against England. They denounced what they called "the hereditary
enemy," "the most tenacious and implacable adversary." The sentiment was especially strong among German historians. Heinrich von
Treitschke (q.v.) called Britain "the shameless representative of barbarism in international law." Erich Marcks wrote: "It is certain,
England is our true mortal enemy." "None of our opponents," said
Arnold Oskar Meyer, "has made our blood boil as much as England."
"The day will come," said Friedrich Meinecke, "when people will
bless Germany's decision to enter upon a defensive war against
Britain and win the freedom of the seas."

Bitterness against England reached almost hysterical proportions
in 1914 with the publication of Ernst Lissauer's famous *Hasslied.*
During World War I, British propagandists made effective use of this
display of overblown nationalism:

> French and Russian they matter not,
> A blow for a blow and a shot for a shot;
> We love them not, we hate them not,
> We hold the Weichsel and Vosges-gate,
> We have but one—and only hate,

We love as one, we hate as one,
We have one foe and one alone.
He is known to you all, he is known to you all,
He crouches behind the dark grey flood,
Full of envy, of rage, of craft, of gall,
Cut off by waves that are thicker than blood.
Come, let us stand at the Judgment place,
An oath to swear to, face to face,
An oath of bronze no wind can shake,
An oath for our sons and their sons to take.
Come, hear the word, repeat the word,
Throughout the Fatherland make it heard.
We will never forego our hate,
We have all but a single hate,
We love as one, we hate as one,
We have one foe, and one alone—
ENGLAND!

In the Captain's mess, in the banquet hall,
Sat feasting the officers, one and all,
Like a sabre-blow, like the swing of a sail,
One seized his glass held high to hail;
Sharp-snapped like the stroke of a rudder's play,
Spoke three words only: "To the Day!"
Whose glass this fate?
They had all but a single hate.
Who was thus known?
They had one foe, and one alone—
ENGLAND!

Take you the folk of the Earth in pay,
With bars of gold your ramparts lay,
Bedeck the ocean with bow on bow,
Ye reckon well, but not well enough now.
French and Russian they matter not,
A blow for a blow, a shot for a shot,
We fight the battle with bronze and steel,
And the time that is coming Peace will seal.
You will hate with a lasting hate,
We will never forego our hate,
Hate by water and hate by land,
Hate of the head and hate of the hand,
Hate of the hammer and hate of the crown,
Hate of seventy millions, choking down.
We love as one, we hate as one,
We have one foe, and one alone—
ENGLAND!

Bibliography: Ernst Lissauer, *Hasslied,* originally published in *Jugend,* 1914. Translation by Barbara Henderson, in *The New York Times,* October 15, 1914.

HAYES, CARLTON JOSEPH HUNTLEY (1882–1964). Pioneer specialist in the history of nationalism. Hayes was born on May 16, 1882, at Jericho Farm in Afton, New York, the son of Philetus Arthur Hayes and Permilia Mary Huntley. He enrolled as a student at Columbia University in 1900, and began a career there that lasted for fifty years. Of his stay at Columbia he later wrote: "I spent seven years listening to other people and forty-three years with other people listening to me." He was awarded a B.A. degree in 1904, an M.A. in 1905, and a Ph.D. in 1909 with a dissertation on *Sources Relating to the Germanic Invasions.*

At Columbia, Hayes rose through the ranks to become full Professor of History (1919–1935) and Seth Low Professor of History (1935–1950). He also served as visiting professor at California (1917, 1923), Johns Hopkins (1930), and Stanford (1941). He was executive officer at Columbia's Department of History from 1922–1930 and 1938–1942.

Hayes became a legend on the campus of Columbia as teacher, textbook writer, and scholar on the history of modern nationalism. His lecture rooms were invariably overcrowded as students flocked to hear the popular professor. "Hayes," commented one student, "brought history from textbook abstractions to an experience lived and a problem to be faced." Tall and baldish, he presented his lectures with the skill of an accomplished actor. Glancing out the window, he would suddenly deliver some impeccably chiseled sentences, pause, and then resume in either whispers or shouts. He was especially effective in the use of sarcasm and irony. He knew the tricks of the stage. Describing the courtly manners of Louis XIV, he would pause and then dramatically draw a handkerchief from the sleeve of his coat. Students were entranced when he would wrap his double-breasted coat around himself and become either Metternich, Disraeli, or Bismarck. His audience was delighted by this kind of teacher's dynamism.

Of more importance was Hayes' seminar on nationalism, which won wide respect not only in the United States but throughout the world. Offered in the Graduate School, it was limited in size. Hayes accepted students for this seminar only after a rigid interview; there was intense competition for a seat in the special course. His students went on to carry his views on nationalism to many institutions of higher learning. Among the numerous doctoral candidates who completed their dissertations on nationalism with Hayes and went on to extend its study in their own colleges and universities were Beatrice Hyslop (France), Robert R. Ergang (Germany), John H. Wuorinen (Finland), and Oscar Janowsky (national minorities) (qq.v.). This seminar stimulated Boyd C. Shafer to devote his career to the study of nationalism.

Hayes' central thesis was that nationalism moved from an originally positive to a negative force, from "blessing to curse." He showed how modern nationalism went through several stages of development from its origins: humanitarian, Jacobin, traditional, liberal, and integral. (See **HAYES' CLASSIFICATION.**) He saw nationalism as emerging in the twentieth century with a tragic descent into aggression and expansionism.

The books on nationalism written by Hayes are regarded as classics on the subject of this important historical phenomenon. Among them are his *Essays on Nationalism* (1926), *France, A Nation of Patriots* (1930), *The Historical Evolution of Modern Nationalism* (1931), and *Nationalism: A Religion* (1960). Critics praised his "learning and grace granted few historians." Along with Hans Kohn and Boyd C. Shafer, Hayes built a reputation here and abroad as an outstanding expert on the study of nationalism.

In 1924, Hayes was received into the Roman Catholic Church, which he regarded as a spiritual and anti-nationalistic force. From then on he became a leading Catholic layman. In April 1942, in the midst of World War II, President Franklin D. Roosevelt appointed Hayes as Ambassador to Spain. In this post Hayes worked effectively to keep Spain out of the war, supported American aid to Spain, and helped discourage the sale of Spanish minerals and chemicals to the Axis.

Hayes retired in 1950 to his Jericho Farm in Afton, New York, where he continued to write and was kept busy as a self-described "dirt farmer." He died there on September 3, 1964.

Bibliography: Arthur Joseph Hughes, *Carlton J. H. Hayes: Teacher and Historian* (New York, 1970).

HAYES' CLASSIFICATION.   The best known classification of nationalism was presented by Carlton J. H. Hayes (q.v.). It has retained its validity to the present day. The formula strikes a balance between chronology and description. Following is a concise abridgment of the Hayes' classification:

(1) *Humanitarian Nationalism.*   The first systematic doctrine of modern nationalism was expounded in the eighteenth century during

the era of Enlightenment. As the name implies, humanitarian nationalism has strictly humanitarian goals: tolerance and regard for the rights of other nationalities. Its outstanding champion was Henry St. John Bolingbroke (q.v.), conservative English politician, who advocated an aristocratic form of nationalism tinged with humanitarianism; the French *philosophe* Jean-Jacques Rousseau (q.v.), who defended a democratic form of nationalism, humanitarian in spirit; and Johann Gottfried von Herder (q.v.), a German philosopher, who, unlike Bolingbroke and Rousseau, saw nationalism as a cultural rather than a political phenomenon. Humanitarian nationalists believed that every nationality was entitled to its own development consonant with its special genius.

(2) *Jacobin Nationalism.* Under the impact of the French Revolution, the earlier nationalism that had not yet crystallized into a dogma, separated into several distinct types. The democratic humanitarian nationalism of Rousseau became known as Jacobin nationalism, after the revolutionary political club dedicated to the winning of republicanism and democracy. Jacobin nationalism sought "to safeguard and extend the liberty, equality, and fraternity which had been asserted and established under humanitarian auspices in the early days of the Revolution." Jacobin nationalists, intolerant of opposition, relying upon force to achieve their ends, fanatical in their determination to succeed, and characterized by missionary zeal, gave to the present form of nationalism many of its basic qualities.

(3) *Traditional Nationalism.* The aristocratic, humanitarian nationalism of Bolingbroke emerged after the revolutionary era as traditional nationalism. The conservative and reactionary critics of the Jacobins were certain that "the quiet happiness of humanity could be assured less by the masses than by the classes." Opposed to "revolution" and "reason" as factors in national development, they turned to "history" and "tradition." In effect, this type of nationalism was a counter-movement to the forces set in motion by the French Revolution. Nevertheless, it claimed the same humanitarian motives as the Jacobins. Included among the traditional nationalists were the Englishman Edmund Burke (q.v.), the German Friedrich von Schlegel (q.v.), and the Frenchman Louis Gabriel Ambroise.

(4) *Liberal Nationalism.* Midway between Jacobin and traditional nationalism was liberal nationalism, a type neither democratic nor aristocratic, but with some of the characteristics of each one. Mainly the creation of an English lawyer, Jeremy Bentham (q.v.), liberal nationalism arose in England, the country of perpetual compromise.

It later spread to the Continent. It emphasized the absolute sovereignty of the national state, but at the same time stressed the principle of individual liberty. It held all national states responsible for the establishment and maintenance of international peace. Liberal nationalists looked to the day when all nations would enjoy opportunities for independent development.

(5) *Integral Nationalism.* Liberal nationalism persisted throughout the greater part of the nineteenth century. However, with the sharpening of rivalries among national states, with the rise of imperialism, nationalism assumed a form decidedly hostile to liberalism and humanitarianism. Integral nationalism rejected sympathy for and cooperation with other nations, promoted jingoism (q.v.), militarism, and imperialism, and opposed all personal liberties when they interfered with the aims of the State. Loyalty to the national state was elevated above all other loyalties, and all social, cultural, economic, and even religious consideration were subordinated to the ends of nationalism. Included in the general category of integral nationalists were Barrès and Maurras in France; Kipling and Rhodes in Britain; D'Annunzio and Mussolini in Italy; Treitschke, Stoecker, Wagner, and Hitler in Germany; and Pobedonostsev and Plehve in Russia (qq.v.).

(6) *Economic Nationalism.* Whereas previously only political considerations lay behind nationalism, a new tendency has been to regard the state as an economic as well as a political unit. Hayes was writing about the early twentieth century. The desire of modern states to achieve economic self-sufficiency had led to the erection of tariff barriers between nations, and to an intensified struggle for control of markets, raw materials, and fields for capital investments. Economic nationalism thus merges with imperialism as one of the most powerful factors in contemporary civilization.

Bibliography: Carlton J. H. Hayes, *The Historical Evolution of Modern Nationalism* (New York, 1931).

HAYES' DUALITY. Carlton J. H. Hayes (q.v.), pioneer scholar of nationalism, set a formula early in his career for two basic kinds of nationalism. This distinction has been accepted by most specialists on nationalism as a correct evaluation of this most important phenomenon in modern history.

According to Hayes, nationalism has a dual nature—as a force either for good or evil, as a blessing or a curse. When it becomes synonymous with the purest patriotism, it proves to be a unique blessing for mankind. Nationalism, as a historic process, has been long continued. It cannot be undone. It would be impossible to refashion all the multitudinous factors, personal and social, economic and political, religious and cultural, that during many centuries have formed city-states, imperial states, and national states. Nationalism of this sort is simply a fact. Moreover, this kind of nationalism, in its liberal or humanitarian forms, has much to recommend it, if it is based primarily on liberty or freedom.

However, in Hayes' view, nationalism *as a belief* belongs to another category altogether. It may well develop into a curse. Judged by the fruits of intolerance, militarism, imperialism, and war, nationalism as a belief is evil and must be cursed—and cured.

Hayes presented seven evils and abuses of nationalism:

1. *The spirit of exclusiveness and narrowness associated with the wrong kind of nationalism.*   It teaches the concept of a chosen people. It presents the false theory that people should prize far more what is theirs as a nationality than what is theirs as human beings.

2. *Nationalism places a premium on uniformity.*   It prescribes national modes of art, standards of thought, and norms of conduct, and it expects all citizens to conform.

3. *Nationalism increases the docility of the masses.*   Because of their upbringing and education, the masses seldom question the providential character of their nationality, their state, and their government.

4. *Nationalism focuses popular attention upon war and preparation for war.*   Military heroes outrank in the national pantheons the heroes of science, art, and learning.

5. *Jingoism (q.v.), clamoring for war or a warlike and aggressive policy, is a specific abuse of nationalism.*

6. *The evils of imperialism, a policy of expansion or territorial growth by the acquisition of foreign territory, stems from nationalism.*

7. *Intolerance is a hallmark of this kind of nationalism.*   The unwilligness to tolerate contrary beliefs or opinions goes hand in hand with the wrong form of nationalism.

Hayes warned that nationalism could be a mania, a kind of extremist egoism, indicating delusions of grandeur. If it were not mitigated, it would be an unqualified curse for future generations.

Bibliography: Carlton J. H. Hayes, *Essays on Nationalism* (New York, 1926).

HEGEL, GEORG WILHELM FRIEDRICH (1770–1831).   German idealist philosopher and innovator for the character of German nationalism. During the course of the nineteenth century, German

nationalism, as nationalism elsewhere, changed from the liberal-cultural form of Herder (q.v.) to a more integral nature. The tone was set by interpretations of Hegel, who found the highest expression of objective morality in the State. Hegel held that ideal morality was the union of the subjective (conscience) with the objective (law and tradition). In the Hegelian view, the individual was supposed to uphold and conform to rational political institutions and laws from a sense of duty. Even as Machiavelli (q.v.) in the early sixteenth century had excluded morality from politics, so did Hegel in the nineteenth century place the State above morality.

Hegel clearly stated the necessity of all citizens to abide by their duty to the all-important State:

> In the history of the World, only those peoples can come under our notice which form a state. For it must be understood that this latter is the realization of Freedom, *i.e.* of the absolute final aim, and that it exists for its own sake. It must be further understood that all the worth which the human being possesses, he possesses only through the State. For his spiritual reality consists in this, that his own essence—Reason—is objectively present to him, that it possesses objective immediate existence for him. Thus only is he fully conscious; thus only is he a partaker of morality—of a just and moral social and political life. For Truth is the Unity of the universal and subjective Will; and the Universal is to be found in the State, in its laws, its universal and rational arrangements. The State is the Divine Idea as it exists on Earth. We have in it, therefore, the object of History in a more definite shape than before; that in which Freedom obtains objectivity, and lives in the enjoyment of that objectivity. . . . The morality *[Sittlichkeit]* of the State is not of that ethical *[moralische]* reflective kind, in which one's own conviction bears sway; this latter is rather the peculiarity of the modern time, while the true antique morality is based on the principle of abiding by one's duty (to the state at large). . . . Morality is Duty—the substantial Right—a 'second nature' as it has been called; for the first nature of man is his primary merely animal existence.

Hegel's conception of the nation-state as a superpersonality, as the source of all law and ethics, and as an expression of the divine idea on earth was to have an enormous influence on the subsequent formation of the German national character. It helped mobilize national enthusiasm in Bismarck's (q.v.) drive to unify the conglomerate Germanies. The Germans, indeed, began to look to their State as a dominant element in their lives. Obedience to authority became an all-important part in the national structure. Added to these traits were respect for law and order, veneration of the military, deference for the uniform, acceptance of authority, an apolitical attitude—all these characteristics were in the Hegelian mold.

The outcome of Hegelian veneration of the State was not fortunate. There was no Kantian categorical imperative to limit state action, no international parliament to restrict State aggression. In vain did such advocates as John Stuart Mill (q.v.) plead for a doctrine of non-intervention by the State in affairs of others and that non-intervention must be a "principle of morality" to be accepted by all governments. The danger was that all governments acted as they pleased in their own interest and were limited only by superior strength. National egoism, becoming more and more intensified, came to be accepted as moral and, therefore, desirable. Hegelian emphasis on duty to the State, to "the State as the divine idea as it exists on earth," was conceived in a tone of morality and piousness. But its effects were to prove tragic for the German people. (*See* **GERMAN NATIONALISM.**)

   Bibliography: Georg Wilhelm Friedrich Hegel, *Lectures on the Philosophy of History*, trans. by J. Sibree (London, 1890); Friedrich Dittman, *Der Begriff des Volksgeistes bei Hegel* (Leipzig, 1909); M. J. Inwood, *Hegel* (London, 1983); Peter Singer, *Hegel* (New York, 1983).

HEGEMONY NATIONALISM. *See* **NATIONALISM, CLASSIFICATIONS OF.**

HERDER, JOHANN GOTTFRIED VON (1744–1803).   Poet, critic, theologian, and philosopher, Herder was also a leading figure in the early development of German nationalism. Born on August 25, 1744, he became a leader of the *Sturm und Drang* literary movement of the late eighteenth century, which extolled nature and German individualism and sought to overthrow the cult of rationalism typical of the Age of Reason. In their early years, both Goethe and Schiller were influenced by Herder's views, but later turned from the German version of Romanticism (q.v.) to become leaders of the German Classical movement.

   One of the most influential minds in German intellectual history, Herder functioned as a herald of Romanticism, the widespread European revolt against reason, authority, tradition, and discipline, which swept through Western civilization from the late eighteenth to the mid-nineteenth century. This reaction against the dominance of French culture was also a strong factor in the rise of nationalism. Herder saw the human race as a unit in which all nations should dwell in harmony "for the cultivation of humanity." Again and again he emphasized the ideas of national individuality and national character.

   In his study, *Herder and the Foundations of German Nationalism* (1931), Robert R. Ergang (q.v.) described Herder as undoubtedly one of the first, if not the first, writer of Europe to develop a comprehensive philosophy of nationalism. The social philosopher, living in an era in which nationalities were regarded as obstacles to the development of pure humanity, saw nationality as an essential factor in the progress of humanity.

Where the eighteenth century Enlightenment asserted the individuality of man, Herder claimed that only in his social context is man important. He insisted that the welfare of the individual is inseparably bound with the welfare of the group and that the individual can attain his highest development only in the life of the group as a whole. Herder presented the collectivism of the nineteenth century as an antidote to the rationalists' individualism of the eighteenth century. In effect, he advocated a philosophy of history in which the emphasis shifts from the individual to the nationality.

Always exalting nature, Herder described a nationality as a natural organic entity, and each organism as the product of a growth regulated by natural law. Human beings were not free to choose their own path, for nature had already chosen it for them. For Herder, nationality was the product of an irresistible natural force always at work molding the members of a group into a compact unit. He even clothed his concept of nationality in religious terms: nationality was "the language of God in nature," a part of the divine plan in history.

Herder saw nationality as a cultural organism. He maintained that culture must be national in form and content. The national character of culture was not only to be preferred, but it was essential. Germans, he warned, must stop imitating the culture of other nations, especially France, but must develop their own innate faculties in order to become a factor in the progress of humanity at large. Therefore, Germans must emphasize their own peculiar gifts and propensities. They must never desert their native traditions in order to build upon another nationality. The true spirit of a people is to be found in their native language "filled with the life and blood of our forefathers." The entire soul of a people is revealed in its own literature.

Herder's views on nationalism were primarily cultural and humanitarian, unlike the expansion-minded nationalism of the later nineteenth century. His nationalism was essentially humanitarian in that it was built around the principle of mankind as a whole. He discarded the idea of national superiority and rejected the glorification of one nation. Germans should cultivate their own nationality and their national group should contribute to humanity at large. Later, Herder's views of cultural and humanitarian nationalism were disregarded in the integral nationalism of Heinrich von Treitschke, Richard Wagner, and Adolf Hitler (qq.v.). (*See also* **GERMAN NATIONALISM.**)

Bibliography: Carlton J. H. Hayes, "Contributions of Herder to the Doctrine of Nationalism," *The American Historical Review,* 32 (1927), 719–736; Robert R. Ergang, *Herder and the Foundations of German Nationalism* (New York, 1931); Hans Kohn, *The Idea of Nationalism: A Study of Its Origins and Background* (New York, 1944); F. M. Barnard, *Herder's Social and Political Thought from the Enlightenment to Nationalism* (Oxford, 1965).

HERZL, THEODOR (1860–1904).   Austrian journalist and promoter of Zionist nationalism (q.v.). In 1896, embittered by implications of the then raging Dreyfus affair, Herzl published his *The Jewish State.* In this book he proposed a detailed plan for the establishment of a Jewish commonwealth in Palestine under the suzerainty of the sultan. "The Jewish question," he wrote, "is a national question which can be solved only by making it a political world-question to be discussed and settled by the civilized nations of the world in council." He demanded that the distinctive nationality of the Jews be maintained. "Our national character is too historically famous and in spite of every degradation, too fine to make the annihilation desirable."

In 1897 Herzl founded *Die Welt,* which became the official journal of Zionism. From then until his death in 1904, he maintained the long series of negotiations which, after World War II, resulted in the formation of Israel as a national state.

Bibliography: Marvin Lowenthal, *The Diaries of Theodor Herzl* (New York, 1962); André Chouraqui, *A Man Alone: The Life of Theodor Herzl* (Jerusalem, 1970); Alex Bein, *Theodor Herzl: Biographie* (Vienna, 1983).

HESS, MOSES (1812–1875).   Political philosopher recognized as one of the fathers of modern Zionist nationalism (q.v.). Fleeing from his German homeland after the Revolution of 1848, Hess lived in exile, mostly in Paris. Throughout his life he was motivated by two interests: philosophical socialism, what he called "ethical" or "true" socialism, and the plight of his fellow Jews.

As a philosopher, Hess undertook to transform Hegelian theory by conceiving man as the initiator of history rather than an observer. Though he considered himself a socialist, he was reluctant to base all human history on economic factors or the class struggle. Instead, he presented nationalities as the dominant factor in historical development.

Of greater interest to Hess was the continuous suffering of the Jews. In his twenties, influenced by his German background, he believed that Jews, having already accomplished their mission in civilization, should turn to assimilation. Gradually, he became convinced that this was the wrong road to emancipation. In *Rom und Jerusalem, die Letzte Nationalitätsfrage (Rome and Jerusalem, the Last Problem of Nationality)* (1862), which was to become a classic in Zionist literature, he wrote that the freeing and uniting of humanity was the real mission of the Jewish people. In emotional prose he called for the establishment of a Jewish state in Palestine. He admitted that in the past he had stood aloof from Judaism, but that his views had undergone a transformation. For some two thousand years the Jews had been scattered in lands into which they organically could not coalesce. Hess now began to think of his nationality as "inseparable from the inheritance of my ancestors, the Holy Land, and the eternal city, the birthplace of belief in the divine unity of life and the brotherhood of all men."

Hess urged his fellow Jews to preserve their nationality while in exile and, above all, to work for the restoration of Palestine. Again and again he returned to the main element of his thought—the indestructibility of the Jewish nationality. It was important, he believed, that Jews maintain "a center of action," which was to him a religious mission. The Jews must acquire territory in Palestine to which they were entitled. The Jewish society to be established there must function in accordance with Mosaic (in his view "socialist") principles. The guiding elements must be a combination of nationalism, the thoughts of Spinoza, and socialism.

At the root of Hess's thinking was the idea that the Jews were destined always to be a homeless people, never to be accepted by those among whom they lived. The only solution was for them to have their own country. He denounced Reform Judaism for its belief in universalism instead of nationalism, and warned that this attitude would eventually destroy Judaism. It was the messianic mission of Jews, he insisted, to win nationhood. These views of Jewish nationalism were to be supported later by such Zionist nationalists as Leo Pinsker and Theodor Herzl (qq.v.).

Bibliography: Isaiah Berlin, *Life and Opinions of Moses Hess* (London, 1939); Edmund Silberner, *The Works of Moses Hess* (Leiden, 1958); Horst Lademacher, *Moses Hess in seiner Zeit* (Bonn, 1977); Shlomo Avineri, *Moses Hess, Prophet of Communism and Zionism* (New York, 1985).

HETERO-NATIONALISM.   *See* **PAN-ARABISM.**

HISPANIDAD.   Pride in being Spanish. Both Spanish nationalists and Pan-Hispanics used the term to express their special cultural attributes. Spanish pride and dignity were to be found in a wide variety of pursuits, from music to flamenco dancing, in the distinctive art of the Prado, and in the bull ring, where calm and nobility were observed in the face of death. (*See also* **PAN-HISPANISM.**)

Bibliography: Juan Saiz Berbera, *Espana y la Idea de la Hispanidad* (Madrid, 1982).

HITLER, ADOLF (1889–1945).   Austrian-born German politician, dictator of Germany from 1933–1945, and a classic advocate of nationalism gone berserk. The apex of German integral nationalism may be found in the figure of Hitler. His rise to power had behind it the frustrated rhythm of German national pride, of national hope, and national energy. Hitler, the politician, took advantage of the surge of nationalism that swept through Germany after the close of World War I. Conscious of their heritage, of their former proud place in civilization, embittered by the accusation of sole war guilt in Article 231 of the Treaty of Versailles, the Germans sought some outlet for their enraged feelings. They found it in the career of a demagogue who was to lead them to the verge of destruction.

Hitler's autobiography, *Mein Kampf (My Struggle)* was published in 1924 after being written with the assistance of Rudolf Hess while both were incarcerated in Landsberg Prison in Bavaria, Hitler for the crime of high treason. Crude, turgid in style, the first version was filled with long words, awkward expressions, and constant repetitions. Novelist Lion Feuchtwanger called attention to thousands of grammatical errors in the original edition. Its early title was *Four and a Half Years of Struggle Against Lies, Stupidity, and Cowardice*, but publisher Max Amann shortened it to *Mein Kampf*. The innumerable errors were corrected in later editions. An enormous success in Germany, the book sold 3.2 million copies by 1939. Translated into many languages, it made its author a millionaire.

In *Mein Kampf*, Hitler presented the story of his life and political program. Regarded by the German public as the bible of the Nationalist Socialist movement, the book also presented an accurate blueprint of what Hitler intended to accomplish in the future. It is especially valuable in presenting clues to Hitler's sense of German nationalism.

"When I look back now after so many years," Hitler wrote, "I see two things of importance in my childhood. First, I became a nationalist. Second, I learned to understand and to grasp the meaning of history." And, again, he praised his own precocious nature: "When

I was but fifteen years old, I understood the difference between dynastic 'patriotism' and racial 'nationalism,' and at the time I knew only the latter." Even though he was Austrian-born, as a child he sang *"Deutschland über Alles"* with fervor. He preferred it to the *"Kaiserlied"* of Austria-Hungary, despite the warnings and punishments by his teachers. "In a short time I developed into a fanatical German nationalist."

After losing his father and mother, young Hitler left for Vienna. He was advised, after his failure to pass the entrance examinations for the Painting Academy, to follow the career of an architect. What impressed him most in Vienna, he wrote, was the lack of national pride *(Nationalstolz)* of its citizens. Here he came to the conclusion that "only he who through education learns to know the cultural, industrial and, above all, the political greatness of his Fatherland, only he is able to win and will win that inner pride which ought to go with the honor of belonging to a nation. And I can fight only for something I can love; I can love only what I esteem; I can esteem only that which I, at least know."

In 1912 Hitler went to Munich, the capital of Bavaria. "A German city," he wrote enthusiastically. "What a difference from Vienna!" Although he made a bare living by drawings and sketches for magazines, he saw these years as the happiest of his life. Here his first interest in politics was awakened. He got his first taste of Social Democracy, which he found "nationally unreliable." "I developed from a weakling, from a citizen of the world *(Weltbürger* in Lessing's conception) to a fanatical anti-Semite." From then to the end of his life, Hitler dedicated himself to the destruction of Judaism and Jews. He denounced "the Jewish teachings of Marxism" because it "disputes the importance of nationalism and race." He now believed that there was only one thing of importance for a nation—the general national necessity of existing *(allgemeine nationale Lebensnotwendigkeit).*

At the outbreak of war in August 1914, Hitler made it plain that he preferred to fight for Germany. The Austro-Hungarian Empire, with its conglomeration of peoples and the Hapsburg rulers he despised, awakened no sense of patriotism in him. He penned a note to the King of Bavaria and asked to be allowed to serve in the German Army. His application was accepted and he was sent immediately to the front. He served for four years in the thick of battle as a dispatch-bearer. The news of the fall of the Second Reich in 1918 and the formation of the Weimar Republic left him with a bitter reaction. "My brow burned with shame. . . . I, however, decided to become a politician."

For Hitler, the German Republic was "the greatest miscarriage of the twentieth century," "a monstrosity of human mechanism." He saw three prevailing conceptions of the State: the voluntary, the liberal-democratic, and the nationalistic. The State, he wrote, was always a means to an end. It must place race in the center of attention; it must keep the race clean; it must as a duty, force the practice of birth control; it must eliminate diseased and sickly persons; it must promote sport among the youth; it must make the army the last and highest school; it must stress the teaching of "racial knowledge" in schools; and it must, above all, awaken patriotism and national pride among its citizens.

Hitler's nationalism, expressed in National Socialism (q.v.), stressed racial cleanliness and economic autarchy. It was anti-Semitic, anti-democratic, anti-parliamentary, anti-Catholic, anti-Marxist, and anti-French. It was a dominantly negative philosophy. Apolitical Germans, captivated by Hitler's oratory, became his victims. Millions lost their lives in the war to get rid of him and his Third Reich.

British historian Hugh R. Trevor Roper gave an extraordinary word picture of the man responsible for the perversion of German nationalism:

> A terrible phenomenon, imposing indeed in its granite harshness and yet infinitely squalid in its miscellaneous cumber—like some huge barbarian monolith, the expression of giant strength and savage genius, surrounded by a festering heap of refuse—old tins and dead vermin, ashes and eggshells and ordure—the intellectual detritus of centuries.

Bibliography: Adolf Hitler, *Mein Kampf* (Munich, 1924); William L. Shirer, *The Rise and Fall of the Third Reich* (New York, 1960); Alan Bullock, *Hitler: A Study in Tyranny* (New York, 1964); Werner Maser, *Hitler: Legend, Myth and Reality* (New York, 1973); John Toland, *Adolf Hitler* (New York, 1976); Rudolph Binion, *Hitler Among the Germans* (New York, 1976); Louis L. Snyder (ed.), *Hitler's Third Reich: A Documentary History* (Chicago, 1981).

HUMANITARIAN NATIONALISM. See HAYES' CLASSIFICATION.

HUME, DAVID (1711–1776). Scottish philosopher and historian, innovator in the history of modern metaphysical thinking, and an early advocate of the idea of national character. Hume believed that the human mind is very imitative in nature. Men who converse together acquire a similarity of manners and communicate to each other their vices as well as virtues. There is a strong propensity to company and society in all rational creatures, as they enter deeply into each other's sentiments. Their passions and inclinations run together, as if by contagion. Attitudes of defense, commerce, and government, along with the same speech or language, as well as a resemblance of manners, lead inevitably to the formation of a common or national character.

To bolster this argument, Hume examined the annals of history and discovered everywhere signs of this sympathy of contagion of manners. He presented nine evidences of its existence:

1. Where a very extensive government has existed for several centuries, it spreads a national character over the whole empire, and communicates to every part a similitude of manners. Observe the Chinese and their great uniformity of character.

2. Even in small governments, which are contiguous, the people have notwithstanding a different character. Athenians were remarkable for ingenuity, politeness, and gaiety, as the Thebans for dullness, rusticity, and a phlegmatic temperament.

3. The same national character commonly follows the authority of government to a precise boundary.

4. Where any set of men scattered over distant nations have a closed society or communication together, they acquire a similitude of manners and have but little in common with the nations among whom they live.

5. Where any accident, such as a difference of language or religion, keeps two nations inhabiting the same country from mixing with each other, they will preserve for several centuries, a distinct and even opposite set of manners.

6. The same set of manners will follow a nation and adhere to them all over the globe. Observe the Spanish, French, English, and Dutch colonies abroad, all distinguishable.

7. The manners of a people change considerably from one age to another, either by alterations in governments or by mixtures of new people. The older Spaniards were restless, turbulent, and addicted to war; the newer Spaniards could only with difficulty be roused to arms.

8. Where several countries have a very close communication together, they acquire a similitude of manners, proportioned to the communication.

9. There may be observed a wonderful mixture of manners and characters in the same nation, speaking the same language, subject to the same government. In this respect, the English are the most remarkable of any people that ever existed in the world. (*See also* **NATIONAL CHARACTER.**)

Bibliography: David Hume, *Essays and Treatises on Several Subjects* (4 vols., London, 1753); Anthony P. Cavendish, *David Hume* (Westport, Conn., 1981); David F. Norton, *David Hume* (Princeton, N.J., 1982).

HYSLOP, BEATRICE FRY (1899–1973).   Professor of History and International Relations and specialist on nationalism. After taking an undergraduate degree at Mt. Holyoke College, Hyslop continued her education at Columbia University, where she completed her M.A. in 1924 and the Ph.D. in 1934. At Columbia's Graduate Division in History she worked in Professor Carlton J. H. Hayes' (q.v.) seminar on nationalism. As a result she turned to the study of nationalism. Her major interest was the study of nationalism in the French Revolution. She served on the staff of the History Department at Hunter College from 1936 until her retirement. In 1961 the French Government named her a Chevalier of the *legion d'honneur.*

Bibliography: Beatrice Fry Hyslop, *French Nationalism in 1789 According to the General Cahiers* (New York, 1934).

I

ICHHEISER CATEGORIES. *See* NATIONALISM, CLASSIFICATIONS OF.

IMPERIALISM. *See* EXPANSIONIST NATIONALISM.

INTEGRAL NATIONALISM. *See* HAYES' CLASSIFICATION.

I.R.A. (IRISH REPUBLICAN ARMY). A militant Irish organization devoted to the independence of the entire Irish island from British control. Claiming to be patriots fighting only for freedom, its members have waged a veritable war against England, which claimed more than two thousand lives varying from shooting British troops to the assassination of Lord Mountbatten in August 1979. Critics assailed it for its terrorist tactics and "its brutal and horrific gangsterism." (*See* **IRISH NATIONALISM.**)

Bibliography: Kevin Kelley, *The Longest War: Northern Ireland and the I.R.A.* (Westport, Conn., 1982); Eamon O'Doherty, *The I.R.A. at War* (Cork, 1985); Patrick J. Bishop, *The Provisional I.R.A.* (London, 1987).

IRANIAN NATIONALISM. Iran has a long history, filled with invasion, conquest, and assimilation. Its central location in the Middle East made it a crossroad of migration. The Iranians, or Farsis (Persians), believed to be direct descendants of the Aryans, make up over half the population. The country fairly floats on enormous deposits of oil, which became the key factor in its existence. One of its major problems is the necessity of maintaining the centralized national state while housing a hodge-podge of disparate elements, most of which demand independence.

On September 16, 1941, in the midst of World War II, the pro-German Shāh abdicated in favor of his son, Mohammad Reza Pahlavi. The new Shāh forced reforms upon the feudal Iranian aristocracy, known as the Thousand Families. More than fifteen million Iranians, nearly half the population, were given their own land. The Shāh organized a secret police, the SAVAK, to deal with opposition. He claimed that he was working for the Westernization of his country and that it had to be protected against these who would hinder the process.

Not the least of the Shāh's problems were the nationalities, which always seemed to be ready for revolt. Though its base was Persian, the population of the country was not homogeneous. Half the Iranians, living in the central and eastern part of the country, were surrounded by variegated tribal minorities. Moving clockwise from the north, these were Turkomans, descendants of the Mongols in the northern area near the Caspian Sea; Baluchis, tough warriors in the southeast; Quasqais, an indigenous tribal group living on the eastern shore of the Persian Gulf; Arabs, culturally distinct and inhabiting the north side of the Persian Gulf; Bakthiaris, a tribal group of sheepherding nomads concentrated in the Zagros Mountains; Lurs, related to the Bakthiaris; Kurds, several millions in the Zagros Mountains in the west; and Azerbaijanis, settled on the northwest frontier. All these nationalities were motivated by a strong national sentiment of their own. The central authority faced a major task in controlling these disaffected minorities.

In 1979 Shāh Mohammad Reza Pahlavi was overthrown. The Ayatollah Ruhollah Khomeini, a religious leader who had been in exile in Paris, returned to his homeland to set up an Islamic regime. The Iranian revolution led by Khomeini was marked by revolts by the ethnic minorities, all seeking either autonomy or independence, and by a struggle between the clerical forces and the Westernized intellectuals and liberals. The country descended into political chaos. Khomeini demanded that the cancer-stricken Shāh be returned to Iran to face charges of terrorism and embezzlement of funds. He blamed "the Satanic United States" for the miseries of his country. In the ensuing confusion, Iran's restive nationalities saw an opportunity to gain their independence in a country whose troubles seemed to be unsolvable.

Especially vehement in their opposition were the Kurds, an independent-minded people, whose ancient homeland, Kurdistan, is now divided between Iran, Iraq, Turkey, and Syria. Kurdish aspirations were based on the belief that they were a distinct people, who had been denied ownership and control of their share of the earth's surface by dominating outsiders. History, they said, had left them in a status of subjugation, and they had no intention of accepting this inferior status. (See **KURDISH NATIONALISM.**)

Meanwhile, Iran itself fell under the domination of Khomeini. The Islamic Constitution, drafted by the clergy, vested final authority in the Faghi, the Ayatollah Khomeini. On November 4, 1979, Iranian militants seized the U.S. embassy and took sixty-five American hostages. Despite Washington's efforts, the crisis continued. The United States broke diplomatic relations with Iran. The exiled Shāh died in Egypt in 1980. The hostage drama ended on January 21, 1981, when an accord, which included the release of frozen Iranian assets, was reached. Turmoil in the country increased. On June 28, 1981, a bomb destroyed the Teheran headquarters of the ruling Islamic Party, killing its chief and seventy-three other party members of high rank.

Added to the tensions at home created by dissatisfied minorities was the beginning of a war with Iraq. The conflict was started by Iraq and soon descended into a war raging for more than eight years. Iran soon found itself isolated from its Arab neighbors. It was in diplomatic limbo. At the June 1988 Arab summit in Algiers, the twenty-one member Arab League declared itself as "in total solidarity with Iraq and its defense of its national territories." Only Syria, which supported Iran, raised mild objections to the statement.

At the same time, Iran had to endure a series of military setbacks that served to aggravate tensions at home. The war, which caused an estimated million casualties on both sides, turned, eventually, in favor of Iraq. Iran was on the defensive after decisive defeats at the hands of the Iraqi army. In April 1988 Iraq began its strongest offensive since 1980 when it invaded Iran. Iraqi troops retook the Fao peninsula, which Iran had occupied in February. Some 20,000 Iranian troops were routed; 3,000 were killed, wounded, or captured. A day after this disaster came another conflict with the United States, which had sent strong forces to maintain the right of passage in the Gulf War. U.S. naval vessels demolished Iran's offshore oil platform near Sirri Island in retaliation for mine damage done to an American frigate. Iran lost six ships in the engagement, in addition to the offshore platform.

After eight years of Iran's fruitless war with Iraq, a United Nations cease-fire was scheduled for August 20, 1988. Ayatollah Ruhollah

Khomeini's Islamic Revolution, which once made him the most feared ruler in the Middle East, seemed to have lost it impetus. His Islamic militancy had threatened to spread far beyond the borders of Iran, but he failed to win his bloody crusade against Iraq. Shi'ite minorities in Arab countries had failed to rise up in support of Khomeini's revolution.

Khomeini died in early June 1989 and his era was brought to an end. The new problem for Iran became how his successor could control the nature of Iranian nationalism.

Bibliography: R. W. Cottam, "Nationalism and the Islamic Revolution in Iran," *Canadian Review of Studies in Nationalism*, 9, No. 2 (Autumn, 1982), 263–277; Reeva S. Simon, *Iran Between Two World Wars, The Creation and Implementation of a Nationalist Ideology* (New York, 1986); David Nissman, *The Soviet Union and Iranian Azerbaijan: The Use of Nationalism for Political Penetration* (Boulder, Colo., 1987); Ephraim Kursh, *The Iran-Iraq War: A Military Analysis* (London, 1987); George Joffe, *Iran and Iraq* (London, 1987); Frederick W. Axelgard, *A New Iraq: The Gulf War and Its Implication for U.S. Policy* (New York, 1988).

IRAQI NATIONALISM.   An oil-producing nation at the eastern end of the Arab world occupies the site of the Tigris-Euphrates valley, formerly called Mesopotamia. The Sumerian city-states of c. 3,000 B.C. began the culture later developed by the Semitic Babylonians and Assyrians. In the twentieth century Iraq has been the scene of constant turbulence. The country has been torn by political upheavals often accompanied by violence. In 1932, when the British mandated rule was terminated, Iraq joined the League of Nations as an independent country. Since that time, it has suffered continued difficulties.

Almost every part of Iraqi society, from students to workers, from civil servants to merchants, has been dissatisfied with its lot. Where their neighbors in Iran have won great economic benefits from the flow of oil, the people of Iraq have seen their government turn its own oil profits into a military machine. Iraq took part in the Arab-Israeli War of 1967, though in a minor way. At that time it broke relations with the United States.

Like Iran, Iraq has had to face a persistent problem with the Kurds, a strongly individualistic national minority that holds much of northern Iraq. The confrontation was between two nationalisms—that of the centralized Iraq administration and the Kurds, an ethnic minority forming about ten percent of the population. The Kurds have rebelled again and again against Turkish, Iranian, and Iraqi masters, all of whom used savage methods of reprisal. Only in Iraq were the Kurds able for a time to win legal recognition as a minority, but still they were dissatisfied.

On August 6, 1988, the Iraqi government at Baghdad, after forty years of effort to crush the Kurdish insurgency, began a major offensive against recalcitrant rebels. More than 60,000 Iraqi troops, using tanks, fighter-bombers, armed helicopters, and artillery attacked the Kurds. Some 50,000 Kurds fled the country into eastern Turkey. Iraq asserted its authority over an area that the Kurdish rebels had claimed to control themselves. Kurdish leaders protested to the United Nations that Iraqi forces had used chemical weapons against Kurdish camps and villages in the rugged mountains of northern Iraq. The Iraqi drive, tied to the Gulf truce, compounded the Kurdish problems. The Kurdish nationalist movement, which troubled the governments of Iraq, Iran, and Turkey, was left in disarray.

The attempt to crush the Kurds inside the Iraqi state was the outcome of the apparent Iraqi victory in its war against Iran. The conflict started in September 1980, when President Saddam Hussein of Iraq began the war. The Ayatollah Ruhollah Khomeini responded in a bloody crusade against Iraq. A United Nations cease-fire began in late August 1988, during which Khomeini sought to extend Islamic fundamentalism in the Middle East. Hussein's victory encouraged him to begin his assault on the rebellious Kurds. His goal was to eliminate the separatist Kurdish nationalism that had long caused concern in Baghdad. (*See also* **KURDISH NATIONALISM**.)

Bibliography: Dewan Berindranath, *Iraq, The Land of Arab Resurgence* (New Delhi, 1979); Saad Jawad, *Iraq and the Kurdish Question, 1958–1970* (London, 1981); Hajid Khadduri, *The Gulf War: The Origins and Implications of the Iraq-Iran Conflict* (New York, 1988); J. Anthony Gardner, *The Iraq-Iran War*, (London, 1988).

IRISH NATIONALISM. The confrontation between Ireland and England is a classic story of the conflict between two nationalisms. The antagonism between the Irish and the English began as early as 1172, when Henry II led his troops into Ireland, reduced the inhabitants to serfdom, and gave lands to his favorite barons. In this way the long struggle began that has shattered the relations between the two peoples. Ireland was to remain subservient to the British Crown for centuries. Stuart King Charles I began a carrot-and-stick approach that was to characterize Irish-English relations for many years. In

1627 he introduced reforms in order to stop the fighting in Ireland. From then on, the matter of reforms for Ireland became one of the main problems for the English. Charles I managed to antagonize English landlords who had acquired valuable lands on the island.

The Irish were additionally dissatisfied under the Commonwealth, when Cromwell decided that it was time to subdue the Irish by force. He crossed to Ireland at the head of his pious Calvinist troops in order to crush resistance and stifle plots to proclaim the son of Charles I as king. Believing that he was the servant of the Lord sent to purify the Irish and root out "papacy and episcopacy" by any and all means, he destroyed Irish Royalist garrisons and attacked Catholics at Drogheda and Waterford. "I am persuaded," he said, "that this is a righteous judgment of God upon those barbarous wretches who have imbrued their hands in so much innocent blood, and that it will tend to prevent effusion of blood for the future." In the process, many unfortunate Irish were shipped to Barbados as slaves. Inside Ireland, women, children, and priests were put to the sword in an orgy which the Irish never forgot or forgave. Driven underground, Irish dissenters rebelled repeatedly against what they called "foreigners" in their land. They especially resented the fact that Cromwell had reduced them to virtual bondage by distributing their lands among absentee Protestant landlords.

Ireland did not benefit from the Glorious Revolution of 1688, when a moderate political and religious settlement was made. In 1688 exiled James II came to Ireland from France with the aim of leading a combined Franco-Irish army against William III. The invaders prepared to attack England proper, but James was defeated at the Battle of the Boyne on July 11, 1690. The disappointed Irish settled into apathy. In 1798 they rebelled again. In 1800 Parliament passed the Act of Union, abolished the Irish Legislature, and absorbed Ireland into Great Britain.

In the nineteenth century, when nationalism began to spread throughout Europe, the conflict between the Irish and English continued as efforts were made from London to retain Ireland in the centralized state. Irish dissidents became louder and louder in their struggle for independence. The Irish saw an example in the American Revolution, when the United States fought its way to freedom. The Irish, too, hoped to win the same status for their own nationalism.

The continued struggle between England and Ireland in the nineteenth and twentieth centuries had three aspects: economic, religious, and political. By the early nineteenth century, at least six-sevenths of Irish land had been acquired by absentee English landlords. In 1846 came a terrible potato famine, which led to widespread starvation and emigration of many Irish to the United States. The first important attempt to ease the lot of the peasantry came with Gladstone's Irish Reform Bill of 1870, which protected tenants from eviction as long as they paid rent. They were also provided with loans. In 1879, Michael Davitt (q.v.), the son of an evicted tenant, organized the Irish Land League to work for the three F's—fair rent, fixed holdings, and freedom of sale. The Irish made efforts to obtain concessions from landlords, including the boycott, or refraining by concerted action from purchasing. Irish members of Parliament, using obstructionist tactics, bargained expertly with both Conservatives and Liberals; they succeeded in 1881 in obtaining a Land Act virtually conceding the three F's. The Land Purchase Act of 1903 inaugurated a fund to enable Irish peasants to purchase farms from absentee English landlords. The English Parliament was inclined to appeasement as a means of satisfying the demands of the Irish.

Added to these economic problems was a deep-rooted religious rivalry between Catholics and Protestants. The population of Ireland was mostly Catholic, with the exception of the six northern counties known as Ulster. In the early nineteenth century no Irish Catholic was allowed to vote or hold office. This was changed in 1829, when Daniel O'Connell (q.v.) was elected to a seat in Parliament under the Catholic Emancipation Act. Irish Catholics, resenting the forced payment of tithes to the Anglican Church, revolted in the Tithe Wars (1831–1838). In 1869 Parliament disestablished the Irish Church, and thereby relieved the Irish of paying tithes to support Anglicanism.

In the political field, the third aspect of Anglo-Irish relations, there was rising trouble between the two nationalisms—English and Irish. At the close of the nineteenth century, there emerged one Irish leader after another to demand more than economic or religious concessions. They would have an independent Ireland. Irish nationalists, dissatisfied with the pace of reform from London, called for a complete break with England and the formation of their own independent nation-state. One of the earliest of these dissidents became an Irish hero-martyr, Robert Emmet (q.v.), a zealous nationalist who planned to seize Dublin Castle. He was captured, found guilty, and hanged. Patriots who called themselves Young Ireland agitated for independence, only to see their leaders arrested, imprisoned, or sent into exile. Eventually, Irish emigrants in the United States formed the Fenian Brotherhood, the Sinn Féin (q.v.), to work for Irish nationalism. The movement spread to Ireland, where it was suppressed. Another Irish nationalist, Charles Stewart Parnell (q.v.), became an expert in legislative obstruction (filibustering) as a means of winning attention to Irish grievances.

Throughout the Age of Nationalism in the nineteenth century, Irish nationalists agitated for the separation of Ireland from British control and to bring relevance to a nationalism of their own. British authorities, convinced that something had to be done to meet Irish fanaticism, again tried appeasement to ease the problem. Prime Minister William Ewart Gladstone introduced two Home Rule Bills, one in 1886 and another in 1889, but both were rejected. Conservatives at the time believed that it was possible to "kill Home Rule by kindness." A third Home Rule Bill, introduced in the House of Commons in 1912, was suspended in 1914 with the outbreak of World War I.

Embittered Irish nationalists saw the war as a means of winning their own independence. Accepting German support, they rose in rebellion. The constitutional Home Rule Bill was frustrated by internal divisions and resisted by British authorities. The bill was finally superseded by the Sinn Féin movement, which was devoted to the cause of complete independence. The Easter Rebellion of 1916 was suppressed, but it was succeeded by guerrilla warfare led by Michael Collins (q.v.). The English attempted to restore order with a group of auxiliaries popularly known as the Black and Tans, who in 1920 terrorized all Ireland and, if anything, added to the strength of Irish nationalism.

In 1921 British Prime Minister David Lloyd George entered into negotiations with Eamon de Valera (q.v.), leader of the Sinn Féin, and established the Irish Free State. However, there was no new status for the six northern Protestant counties. The British decided that this area would remain with the homeland. This decision further intensified the Irish problem. The last formal ties of the Irish Free State with Britain were broken in 1948 by the Republic of Ireland Act. Most citizens of the Irish Free State hoped for eventual union with Northern Ireland, but they differed on the means to be used to bring about that union. Here again was an example of the dilemma of mini-nationalisms (q.v.)—moderation or extremism, autonomy or independence. The moderates in the Irish Free State, once a mini-nationalism that had achieved the goal of their own nationalism, believed that the English would recognize the justice of their cause. Irish extremists again turned to the way of violence.

The English policies of appeasement, conciliation, and accommodation had been successful in retaining Scotland and Wales in the United Kingdom. The case of Northern Ireland was different. The

Irish Republican Army (I.R.A.) (q.v.) insisted that the entire island of Ireland, including the six Northern provinces of Ulster, must be united as an independent state. Because of London's intention of holding on to 8,553 square miles of Northern Ireland, the I.R.A. turned to bullet and bomb in a veritable war against the British. The decision to use violence has cost some two thousand lives, brutalized the Irish spirit, and burdened it with a heritage of terror. In August 1979, terrorists assassinated Lord Louis Mountbatten, a tragedy that infuriated the British public and made British authorities more than ever intent upon holding on to Northern Ireland.

Irish nationalists believe that the occupation of Northern Ireland must be ended. They reject appeasement and compromise. They choose the way of the bullet, machine gun, bomb, and grenade as the only means to win independence. They use violence and terror as the only way to convince the English "foreigners" that they must leave Ulster. From their point of view, it is all or nothing.

Behind I.R.A. resistance is an important psychological factor added to economic, religious, and political differences. For centuries the English looked upon the Irish as an inferior people distinguished by loutishness and stupidity. English cartoonists in the nineteenth century depicted the Irish as pigs incapable of self-government, uncouth and primitive, who had not learned the ways of civilized society. This attitude carried over into the twentieth century, when jokes about the Irish were told in English pubs. The "funny little green people" were ridiculed for their lack of manners and their belief in non-existent leprechauns. The Irish reacted angrily to such stereotypes (q.v.) as unfair slurs on their national character. They denounced the English as still colonial-minded and as keeping them in bondage. This sense of inferiority, intensified by English ridicule, resulted in widespread sympathy for the I.R.A. terrorists.

The clash of nationalisms continues in a milieu of bitterness on both sides. I.R.A. extremists see themselves as liberators, as freedom-fighters representing the noblest aspirations of their people. The English, on their part, denounce the I.R.A. guerrillas as evil monsters unfit to live in a civilized world. London sent thousands of troops to Northern Ireland to maintain what they regard as a part of the United Kingdom. The situation approached a collective hysteria. Negotiation seemed to be useless, as the confrontation of nationalisms persisted.

Bibliography: Sean Cronin, *Irish Nationalism: A History of Its Roots and Ideology* (New York, 1981); Tom Garvin, *The Evolution of Irish Nationalist Politics* (Dublin, 1981); David George Boyce, *Nationalism in Ireland* (London, 1982); Clare O'Halloran, *Partition and the Limits of*

Irish Nationalism: An Ideology under Stress (Dublin, 1987); Raymond J. Raymond, "Irish Nationalism in the Twentieth Century: A Reappraisal," *Canadian Review of Studies in Nationalism*, 14, No. 1 (Spring, 1987), 19–30.

IRREDENTIST NATIONALISM. *Irredenta*, from the Italian meaning "unredeemed," refers to the territory inhabited chiefly by the natives of a specified country that formerly held it and seek to recover it. In 1878 an Italian group organized, in the name of nationalism, a movement seeking to recover for Italy adjacent regions inhabited largely by Italians and under foreign control. Such territories, they claimed, were formerly a part of Italy, and should be returned to Italian control.

Italian nationalist cries for *Italia Irredenta* flared up again during and after World War I. On April 16, 1915, Italy signed with the Allies the secret Treaty of London that promised her the Austrian provinces of Southern Tyrol (High Adige), Trieste, Istria, and Dalmatia. This program, designed to reward Italy for her turn to the Allied side in the war, went far beyond obtaining *Italia Irredenta*. It was to bring "unredeemed" Italians back to their homeland, as well as to give absolute security to Italy by putting her northern borders on the Brenner Pass and giving her complete control of the Adriatic Sea in the east. Again, in the statement of war aims on January 10, 1917, the Allies promised the "liberation of Italians from foreign domination."

Following the armistice at the end of World War I, Italy again claimed *Italia Irredenta* upon the dismemberment of the Austro-Hungarian Empire. The peacemakers were plagued by an acrimonious dispute between Italy and Yugoslavia over the control of the eastern shore of the Adriatic. Italy demanded the implementation of the Treaty of London, only to meet the determined opposition of President Woodrow Wilson. The struggle fouled the atmosphere of the peace conference more than any other question. Italian Prime Minister Vittorio Orlando, who had been demoted to a minor role in the peace discussions because his main quarrel was with Austria, not with Germany, angrily withdrew from the conference and returned only when the Italian people backed him in his confrontation with President Wilson. In the end, the conference reached an impasse on the Adriatic question. It was settled, or rather "adjourned," by two treaties: the Treaty of Rapallo (December 12, 1920), which confirmed Italy's possession of Istria and the east Adriatic Islands but not of Dalmatia, with the exception of the port of Zara. The Treaty of Rome (January 27, 1924) divided the angrily disputed port of Fiume between Italy and Yugoslavia, thus making it useless to both parties. Relations remained troubled between Italy and Yugoslavia, each of whom protested treatment of their natives in the other's country.

Italian irredentism was just one of many similar movements throughout the world. It is the essence of nationalism to demand return of citizens caught in border disputes and anxious to return with their territory to the homeland.

Bibliography: Jacob H. Landau, *Pan-Turkism in Turkey: A Study of Irredentism* (London, 1981); Giannes Koliopoulos, *Brigands With a Cause: Brigandage and Irredentism in Modern Greece* (Oxford, 1987).

ISRAELI NATIONALISM.   *See* **ZIONIST NATIONALISM.**

"ITALIA IRRENDENTA!" ("ITALY UNREDEEMED!")   *See* **IRREDENTIST NATIONALISM.**

ITALIAN NATIONALISM.   Similar to the German experience, Italian nationalism received its initial impetus at the opening of the nineteenth century as a response to Napoleonic aggression. At the time, both the Italies and the Germanies were "geographical expressions," a combination of individual states, smaller sovereignties, and city-states, each jealously guarding its own independence. Many factors making for national unification were present in the Italies— natural boundaries, common historical traditions, and the same language although in different dialects. However, there were other elements that worked against unity, such as the long, persistent struggle between Pope and Holy Roman Emperors, seemingly insurmountable differences between the industrial North and the agricultural South, and the unwillingness of such cities as Rome, Venice, Milan, Florence, and Naples to surrender their glorious pasts as city-states in favor of national unification.

The cry for liberty, equality, and fraternity, slogans of the French Revolution, crossed the Alps into the Italian peninsula. But it was the French conqueror who meddled in Italian affairs and aroused the kind of resentment that contributed to an Italian sense of national consciousness. Napoleon's standard operating procedure was geared to nepotism. He aimed to place members of his own family, as well as his trusted agents, in situations where they could hold power outside of France. He installed his agent, Joachim Murat, as King of

Naples, in reward for Murat's distinguished service on Napoleonic campaigns. The Corsican made a critical mistake here. Murat set up his own court, created a new nobility of his own, suppressed brigandage, and ended relics of the old feudal system. An angered Napoleon denounced him for his "monkey tricks." Sensing the coming of a drive for national unity, Murat presented himself to the Italians as a champion of a unified national state.

Subsequent events forced Murat out of the Italian picture. His popularity at Naples waned and his troops were routed by the Austrians. He escaped to France, where his former benefactor contemptuously refused to receive him. While attempting to recover his kingdom, he was captured, court-martialed, and shot. After Napoleon's fall, Austrian domination in Italian affairs was restored. The Treaty of Vienna gave no satisfaction to the Italians.

Meanwhile, the call for national independence from the Austrians began to be heard throughout the Italian peninsula. At first, Italian national sentiment was expressed by a small minority of poets and dramatists. Playwright Vittorio Alfieri (q.v.), who disliked the French Revolution, reacted violently against Napoleon's interference in affairs of the Italian states. The poet Ugo Foscolo (q.v.) demanded that the dead from the Italian past rise from their tombs and join the battle against the hated Austrians. Students, nobility, and bourgeoisie rallied to the cause of the national movement, which gained momentum. All Europe was permeated by national sentiment and the Italians provided no exception. They, too, wanted a unified national state.

The Italians provide a good example of how nationalism worked for unity. That hotly desired goal was achieved despite a cross fire of antagonistic interests. The urge for national unification proved to be greater than the desire of particularistic units to remain independent. Liberals called for a federation of Italian states with the King of Sardinia at the head. Radicals, led by Giuseppe Mazzini (q.v.), favored a democratic republic on the French model, a centralized Italy with Rome as its capital. Eventually, national unity was achieved by Giuseppi Garibaldi and Count Camillo Benso Cavour (qq.v.). Garibaldi provided the sword and then retired as a heroic patriot. Cavour, always partial to Sardinia as the focal point of national unity, at first sought the support of Napoleon III, who had boasted of his belief in "national sovereignty." The Sardinian outwitted the Frenchman. In 1859, on the verge of defeat, Cavour used the services of Garibaldi and, at last, was successful in uniting Sardinia, Lombardy, Parma, Modena, Tuscany, and the Papal States (except Rome) with the Kingdom of the Two Sicilies. It was a case of legerdemain accomplished with such art and adroitness that it staggered the imagination. Behind Cavour's magic was the generating influence of nationalism, which worked to bring together proud and independent-minded states and principalities. Victor Emmanuel of Sardinia emerged as the King of a united Italy. Rome and Venice held out, only to be added within a decade.

There were some blurs in the picture, as was to be expected. Several small Italian-speaking areas were left out, thereby posing a problem for the future. Trieste, Istria, and the Trentino remained under Austrian control. Ticino gravitated toward Switzerland. Nice and Corsica attracted adjacent France. These spots became known to Italians as *Italia Irredenta,* or "Italy Unredeemed," the battle cry of dissatisfied nationalists. The process had been effective as a whole in the use of national consciousness as a unifying force, but those left out resented their status as "foreigners." The inevitable result was the formation of new mini-nationalisms. (*See* **MINI-NATION-ALISMS.**)

Shortly after the end of World War I, in an era of political confusion and international anarchy, Italy, like Germany under Hitler, was to suffer the agonies of a nationalism gone berserk. Otherwise intelligent Italians fell into the abyss of Fascism under a blustering adventurer and demagogue. Disappointed by the Treaty of Versailles, which, they claimed, treated them as enemies rather than allies, Italian patriots protested vociferously. Why were they not given their expected control of the Adriatic? Where were their deserved colonial spoils in Africa and the Near East? Moreover, the country was in a miserable state: there were shortages of food and raw materials, a rapid increase in the cost of living, a dangerously unbalanced budget, and hard-to-bear currency inflation. Italian workingmen began to look to the example of the Bolsheviks in Russia and resorted to direct action by seizing factories and expelling the owners. Industry was disorganized by strikes as were essential public services. The government seemed powerless.

In this desperate situation, Italians turned to the counter-revolution led by Benito Mussolini (q.v.). An activist influenced by Hegel (*see* **HEGEL, GEORG WILHELM FRIEDRICH**) and his primacy of the state, Mussolini attempted to mold an entire nation in his own image. "Believe, Obey, Fight!" He denounced democracy as "a putrescent corpse." He called for a new élite, glorified war, and presented his people with bread-and-circuses. He gave Italians twenty-three years of tinseled glory, and then a dizzy descent into defeat and near destruction. The Italians learned the hard way about the evils of nationalism as a curse. (*See* **MUSSOLINI, BENITO, and HAYES' DUALITY.**)

Bibliography: Giuseppi A. Borgese, *The March of Fascism* (New York, 1938); S. William Halperin, *Mussolini and Fascist Italy* (Princeton, N.J., 1964); S. James Gregor, *The Ideology of Fascism* (New York, 1969); Emiliana Noether, *Seeds of Italian Nationalism, 1700–1815* (New York, 1969); Ronald S. Cunsolo, "The Fusion between Italian Nationalism and Fascism," *Canadian Review of Studies in Nationalism*, 3, No. 2 (Spring, 1976), 192–211; Alexander J. De Grand, *The Italian National Association and the Rise of Fascism in Italy* (Lincoln, Neb., 1978).

J

JACOBIN NATIONALISM   *See* **HAYES' CLASSIFICATION.**

JAHN, FRIEDRICH LUDWIG (1778–1852).   Eccentric pedagogical reformer, founder of the *Turnverein* (Gymnastic Club) movement, and passionate German nationalist. Like many other Germans, *"Turnvater"* Jahn felt humiliated by the aggressive campaigns of Napoleon. He resolved to do something about what he believed to be a national disgrace. He would restore the morale of all Germans by starting a campaign to develop their physical condition by attention to gymnastics.

Jahn believed that his countrymen had become infected with Gallic cosmopolitanism and were so soft and effeminate that they were easy victims of the French conqueror. They must turn to old Swedish exercises to bolster their physical powers. They must forget their degradation and draw strength from their own glorious past, from German art, language, and customs. Jahn believed that attention to their own great past would make Germans strong, self-confident, and assertive.

In 1811 Jahn opened his first *Turnverein* in Berlin. He taught his young gymnasts to wear their hair long and to look upon themselves as a guild to win emancipation for their country. Their dress was to be an imitation of his own—a long tunic, open collar, and prominently displayed dagger. Above all, they must show their love for the Fatherland. He emphasized those qualities that over the course of the nineteenth century came to be regarded as forming the national character of the German people—worship of the state, obedience to the authorities, support for the military way of life, belief in a national soul, and xenophobia—fear of the foreigner.

Jahn presented his theories advocating an aggressive nationalism in his work, *Das deutsche Völkstum (The German Nationality)* (1810), a kind of handbook of nationalism designed to teach the German people to love the Fatherland. In his introduction he wrote of the general life and characteristics of a people:

> *Volkstum* is the common character of a people, its inner being, its rules and life, its power of development, its power of progress. All peoples have their own peculiar thoughts and feelings, loves and hates, joys and sorrows, hopes and yearnings, ancestors, and beliefs. German means national. Our feeling of nationalism, or Germanness, has been disappearing more and more because of our own sins. We must return to the lost past and recreate Nation, Germanness, Fatherland. A nation is not made by the outer band of the state which encloses it. Much more important is what exists inside—the quiet, trustful community of interests and mutual love. Only by a study of this general inner life and characteristics of a people can we answer the questions and solve the puzzles which have remained too difficult for the mere state history. *Volkstum* is the true measuring rod of peoples, the right scale to weigh their values.

Jahn popularized the totalitarian implications of the organic *Volk* state. He demanded that the state subordinate every institution to enhancing aggressive nationalism. He played an important role in turning the nature of German nationalism from Herder's (q.v.) cultural form to support of violence. He appealed to the middle and lower classes, and especially to young students. These young men were to make lasting institutions of Jahn's dream.

Jahn, himself, writing in the third person, made the best comment on his own life:

> As a child Jahn prayed for his Fatherland in pious submission, as a boy he beamed with joy over it, as a youth he was exalted with passion and revenge for it, as a man he taught, spoke, fought, and suffered for it and served his Fatherland throughout his life as a faithful Eckhardt, held watch to turn away all things un-German and foreign *[Undeutschheit und Ausländerei]*, and led the confused back to the path of virtue and honor.

The activities of the eccentric demagogue were suppressed in 1819 and his gymnasiums closed. He was arrested and sent to prison for six years. Later, in 1848, he was vindicated when he was elected to the German National Parliament. He composed his own epitaph: "I held fast to the idea of German unity, as if it were an unhappy love."

Bibliography: Friedrich Ludwig Jahn, *Deutsches Volkstum*, (Lübeck,

1810); Peter Viereck, *From the Romantics to Hitler* (New York, 1941); Louis L. Snyder, *German Nationalism: The Tragedy of a People* (Port Washington, N.Y., 1969).

JANOWSKY, OSCAR I. (1900–   ).   Historian and specialist on nationalities and national minorities. Janowsky was born in Russia on January 15, 1900. Emigrating to the United Sates, he took his B.S. at the City College of New York, and his Ph.D. at Columbia University in 1933. At Columbia he was a member of the Hayes' seminar on nationalism. His teaching career was at the City College of New York, where he became full professor in 1948 and from 1951 to 1957 was Director of Graduate Studies. He has written widely on nationalities, Jews and minority rights, and international aspects of German racial policies.

Bibliography: Oscar I. Janowsky, *The Jews and Minority Rights* (New York, 1933); *People at Bay* (London, 1938); *Foundations of Israel* (Princeton, N.J., 1959).

JAPANESE NATIONALISM.   Nationalism in Japan was stimulated by an important event—her decisive victory over Russia in 1904–1905. This triumph demonstrated conclusively that a ''backward'' people utilizing Western techniques could win over a great military nation which up to that time had conquered more territory in Asia than any other country. Japan's victory made her a world power. At the same time, this spark set off a great series of national movements that eventually broke over Asia and Africa and swept away almost all the colonial regimes.

The nationalism that emerged in Japan was based on an idea of national polity called *kokutai*, meaning literally ''the substance, or body of the nation,'' or ''the national entity.'' The *kokutai* referred to the entire social and political fabric of the nation. But in a restricted sense it meant a basic governmental policy formed to meet internal and external problems. It could also denote a sense of national honor. According to the *kokutai* concept, the essential national polity of Japan consisted of three elements: (a) loyalty to the throne; (b) belief that the Japanese had superior inborn qualities of intellect; and (c) a sense of mission.

Veneration of the Emperor was traditional in the entire history of Japan. It can be compared to the ancient attitude of Egyptians toward the Pharaoh. In 1867, revolutionary leaders deposed the *shoguns*, the old military governors who constituted a quasi-dynasty exercising absolute rule after relegating the emperors to a nominal position.

The secular authority of the Emperor was restored and the imperial court moved to Tokyo. The new regime was called the *Meiji* (Enlightenment). *Meiji* reformers turned to the road of modernization, but retained the Emperor as the supreme symbol of national unity. He was regarded as the "Viceroy of Heaven on Earth." He was supposed to have a blood relationship with the sun goddess Amaterasu Omikami in a direct, unbroken line. His person was sacred and inviolable. Japanese were trained to turn their eyes away from the Emperor when they were in his presence to avoid being shattered by his brilliance.

The second pillar of *kokutai* was the idea that the Japanese were unequalled as specimens of humanity by any other people on earth. Every single Japanese was part of a great family, all related by blood, all achieving "cleanliness of heart" in a purifying *Shinto* rite. Behind this reasoning was the idea that the nation was similar to a tree. Its trunk was the Imperial House and its branches consisted of four family groups. From these ancient familial groups sprang millions of lesser branches and twigs. Through the entire tree ran the same sap, unifying Emperor and people.

The third element of *kokutai* was a belief in the mission of the Japanese people ordained by heaven. Japan would follow the path of expansion abroad. In doing this she was only obeying the will of the Emperor as well as a mandate imposed by heaven. Japanese nationalism, like Russian messianic nationalism (*see* **RUSSIAN NATIONALISM**), was imbued with a sense that Tokyo would give to the world the brilliance of its culture and civilization.

Nationalism in Japan was closely associated with religion. Nationalists opposed the introduction of foreign religions, especially Christianity, into Japan. "*Shinto*," said the Japanese scholar Genchi Kato, "is inseparably connected with the national ideals of the Japanese people." On August 3, 1899, came the famous Order Number Twelve, which called for instruction of state *Shinto* religion in all schools. On the following October 31 the Imperial Rescript on Education was issued, probably the most influential document in modern Japanese history.

The Imperial Rescript on Education proclaimed *Shinto* nationalism against Western and political ideals. Every Japanese was made aware of its contents:

Know Ye, Our Subjects:

Our Imperial Ancestors have founded our Empire on a basis broad and everlasting, and have deeply and firmly implanted virtue; Our subjects ever united in loyalty and filial piety have from generation to generation illustrated the beauty thereof. This is the glory of the fundamental character of Our Empire, and herein also lies the source of Our education. Ye, Our subjects, be filial to your parents, affectionate to your brothers and sisters; as husbands and wives be harmonious, as friends be true; bear yourselves in modesty and moderation; extend your benevolence to all; pursue learning and cultivate arts; and thereby develop intellectual facilities and perfect moral powers; furthermore, advance public good and promote common interests; always respect the Constitution and observe the laws; should emergency arise, offer yourselves courageously to the State; and thus guard and maintain the prosperity of Our Imperial Throne coeval with heaven and earth. So shall ye be not only Our good and faithful subjects but render illustrious the best traditions of your forefathers.

The Way here set forth is indeed the teaching bequeathed by Our Imperial Ancestors, to be observed alike by Their Descendants and the subject, infallible in all ages and true in all places. It is our wish to lay it to heart in all reverence, in common with you, Our subjects, that we may attain to the same virtue.

The 30th day of the 10th month of the 23rd year of Meiji.

(October 30, 1890)
[Imperial Sign Manual, Imperial Seal]

The national spirit of the Japanese educational system was indicated by this announcement for a teachers' convention in Kyoto:

The sole aim of education is to establish a foundation for the social system by means of the development of the abundance of our national wealth on the one hand and the expansion of the national power abroad. The spirit of patriotism which has been nourished for 2,500 years has at last found an opportunity to exhibit itself, and now there is a chance for the educators to stimulate true nationalism and nourish the national power as a grateful act of appreciation of this glorious period.

Added to religion and education was a military spirit implicit in *bushido*—contempt for death, exaltation of victory, and blind obedience. The traditions of the *samurai* warriors carried over into the modern era after the fall of the shogunate. The military was convinced of Japan's divine mission "to bring the whole world under one roof" *(hakko-ichi-u)*. This kind of ultranationalist fanaticism led to foreign adventures starting in 1931. Japanese expansionists looked in three directions—in the north to Manchukuo, in the west to China, and in the south to the rich tropical colonies of the European powers. By the time of the attack on Pearl Harbor on December 7, 1941, Japanese nationalists had outlined the Greater East Asia Co-Prosperity Sphere, a kind of oriental Monroe Doctrine. The missionary zeal of *kokutai* reached its zenith. Japanese expansionist nationalism was halted only at Hiroshima and Nagasaki in 1945.

During the first half of the twentieth century, militant nationalists ruled Japan. Its native *Shinto* religion was the core of official ideology. State Shinto emphasized the uniqueness of Japanese life and bestowed divinity on the Emperor. Those soldiers who gave their lives for their country became quasi-deities and their souls were revered at *Shinto* shrines, especially the large Yasukuni shrine near the Imperial Palace in Tokyo. This situation changed after World War II: Emperor Hirohito renounced his divinity, *Shinto* lost its official protection, and a new doctrine proclaimed the separation of church and state.

The new Japanese nationalism turned from militarism to a drive for economic supremacy. However, among a small group of Japanese, *Shinto* has been thrust back into the nationalist stage. These latter-day nationalists believe that Japan did nothing wrong when it occupied a large part of Asia in 1931. Anti-nationalists attacked this view as "a strong pressure of totalitarianism and the standardization of thought and religious belief." Right-wing groups continued to worship the war dead at the *Shinto* shrines.

Bibliography: D. C. Holton, *Modern Japan and Shinto Nationalism* (Chicago, 1947); Delmer M. Brown, *Nationalism in Japan* (Berkeley, 1955); George M. Wilson, *Radical Nationalist in Japan* (Cambridge, Mass., 1969); George Richard Storry, *The Double Patriots: A Study of Japanese Nationalism* (Westport, Conn., 1973); L. R. Oates, *Populist Nationalist in Prewar Japan* (London, 1985).

JEWISH NATIONALISM.   *See* **ZIONIST NATIONALISM.**

JINGOISM.   A term denoting excessive and belligerent nationalism, the English equivalent of the French "chauvinism" (q.v.). The origin of the word is uncertain, but it is believed to have been derived from the lines of an English music-hall song popular in 1878 and written by George Ward Hunt:

> *We don't want to fight, but by Jingo if we do,*
> *we've got the ships, we've got the men, and*
> *got the money too.*

The term "Jingoes" came to be applied as a nickname for those British politicians who supported Beaconsfield's anti-Russian policy of sending ships to help the Turks fight against the Russians. The war fever was aroused as Jingoes tried to bring their country into the Russo-Turkish War (1877–1878) on the side of the Turks. The term Jingo eventually came to mean any person who boasts of his patriotism and favors an aggressive, threatening, extreme nationalism.

Bibliography: J. A. Hobson, *The Psychology of Jingoism* (London, 1901.)

JURASSIC NATIONALISM.   Switzerland has long had a reputation as a smoothly run society, a striking example of unity in diversity. The Swiss Confederation comprises two religions (Protestant, 49 percent; Roman Catholic, 49 percent), and four national languages (German, 72 percent; French, 20 percent; Italian, 4 percent; and Rhaeto-Romansch, derived from Latin, 1 percent). The national goal is harmony, with economic factors making for strong bonds of union.

Despite this closely bound unity, Switzerland has not been altogether free from the kind of separatism appearing in most countries. Stretching along the western border is the Jura region consisting of bleak limestone folds. The inhabitants of this area, largely of Huguenot persuasion, are known for their austere faith, frugal manners, preference for the French language, and a sense of their own nationalism. Jurassic nationalists maintain that they have not been given the liberties to which they are entitled. The Jurassic Rally, a separatist organization, demands a special canton, with concessions allowing self-government. Jurassic nationalists, aware of the advantages of being attached to a prosperous Swiss state, would settle for autonomy, not independence. Above all, they want no violence such as that favored by Corsican dissenters.

Bibliography: Hans Kohn, *Nationalism and Liberty: The Swiss Example* (New York, 1956); C. Hughes, *Switzerland* (New York, 1975); Kenneth D. McRae, *Conflict and Compromise in Multilingual Societies: Switzerland* (Waterloo, Ontario, 1983); John H. G. Jenkins, *Jura Separatism in Switzerland* (New York, 1986).

K

KANT, IMMANUEL (1724–1804).   German philosopher and progenitor of modern nationalism. Kant was born at Königsberg on April 22, 1724, the son of a master saddler. He devoted his entire life to study and teaching. He never married. During his lifetime, he never traveled more than forty miles from Königsberg. He is regarded throughout the world as one of the great philosophers and thinkers of the modern era.

Königsberg during Kant's early years was a stronghold of Pietism (q.v.), and Kant was influenced by it. It remained with him for the rest of his life. A reaction against religious skepticism, Pietism retained its belief in Christianity, but disregarded any elaborate formalities associated with it. Placing emphasis upon individualism and self-determination, it helped prepare the soil for the growth of nationalism. It exalted the secular, or national, state. As a revivalist religion, it urged a new and fresh realization of gospel teachings. It was not actually nationalist, but universalist. Regarding the state as the main instrument of progress, it, in effect, acted as a stimulant for the rise of modern nationalism.

Kant's contribution to the rise of nationalism was his concept of the formal prescripts of morality. He saw the realization of duty as impossible for any being who is not thought to be free, *i.e.* capable of self-determination. In theory, freedom is not an object of cognition, but its impossibility is not thereby demonstrated. The supreme end prescribed by reason is the complete subordination of the empirical side of nature to the prescripts of morality. There is a certainty of freedom in self-determination. The Kantian concept of self-determination, in the view of later specialists on nationalism, becomes the central core of nationalism.

British scholar Elie Kedourie (q.v.) considered the emergence of modern nationalism as so important that in his study *Nationalism* (1960), he devoted his entire second chapter to Kant's analysis of the idea of self-determination. Kant discussed politics in terms of his ethical doctrine. Others later enlarged greatly on the scope of Kant's doctrine of the autonomy of the will, and from it made far-reaching conclusions. "One must be free," he wrote, "in order to learn how to use one's power freely and usefully." One never ripens into reason except through one's own experiences, and one must be free in order to undergo them. It follows that autonomy becomes the essential end of politics. "A good man is an autonomous man, and for him to realize his autonomy, he must be free. Self-determination thus becomes the supreme political good."

Kant's view helped make self-determination a dynamic doctrine. Kedourie stated that nationalism, which is largely a doctrine of self-determination, found here the greatest source of its vitality. Kant's ethical teachings expressed and propagated a new attitude of political and social questions. Moral consciousness was to be the hallmark of virtue; action could not be good unless it was the outcome of deep moral struggle. (*See also* **SELF DETERMINATION.**)

Bibliography: Immanuel Kant, *Critique of Pure Reason* (London, 1881); *The Metaphysics of Morals* (Indianapolis, Ind., 1969); Arseny Gulyga, *Immanuel Kant: His Life and Thought* (Boston, 1987).

KEDOURIE, ELIE (1926–   ).   Professor of Politics at the University of London since 1965 and prominent British scholar of nationalism. He was educated at the London School of Economics and at St. Anthony's College, Oxford, where he was a senior scholar. Editor of the journal *Middle Eastern Studies*, he has published several major works on nationalism. In his *Nationalism* (1960) he revealed his attraction for the metaphysical foundations of nationalist ideology. He showed how nationalism became firmly naturalized in the political rhetoric of the West and how it was taken over for use by the entire world. "But what now seems natural once was unfamiliar, needing argument, persuasion, evidence of many kinds; what seems simple and transparent is really obscure and contrived, the outcome of circumstances now forgotten and preoccupations now academic, the residue of metaphysical systems sometimes incompatible and even contradictory."

Kedourie's special contribution to the study of nationalism included an analysis of its development in the philosophical traditions in Europe. He was the first scholar of nationalism to show the importance of Immanuel Kant (q.v.) in the development of nationalism. The German philospher, according to Kedourie, by a kind of tortuous reasoning arrived at the concept that self-determination becomes the supreme political good. Nationalism, largely a doctrine of national self-determination, found here the great source of its vitality.

Bibliography: Elie Kedourie, *Nationalism* (London, 1960); Elie Kedourie (ed.), *Nationalism in Asia and Africa* (New York, 1970).

KENYATTA, JOMO (1898–1978). African statesman, nationalist, and the first Prime Minister of independent Kenya. Born into the Kikiyu tribe, Kenyatta joined the first Kenyan political protest movement in 1922. In 1929 he went to London to protest against a proposed union of Kenya with Uganda and Tanganyika. He studied at the London School of Economics. He helped organize the fifth Pan-African Congress in 1945. The next year he returned to Kenya to lead the Kenyan African Union and to organize a mass nationalist party. From 1953 to 1961 he was imprisoned as responsible for the Mau Mau rebellion. At the London Conference of 1963 he managed to win Kenya's independence and became that country's first Prime Minister and President.

A legend in Kenya, Kenyatta reputedly organized the Mau Mau terrorism campaign and was arrested for it. However, he was successful in having the contending African parties work for his release and for his assuming the reins of government. In his book, *Facing Mount Kenya* (1952), he expressed his sense of African nationalism:

> If Africans were left in peace on their own lands, Europeans would have to offer them the benefits of white civilisation in real earnest before they could obtain the African labour which they want so much. They would have to let the African choose what parts of European culture could be beneficially transplanted, and how they could be adapted. He would probably not choose the gas bomb or the armed police force, but he might ask for some other things of which he does not get so much today. As it is, by driving him off his ancestral lands, the Europeans have robbed him of the material foundations of his culture, and reduced him to a state of serfdom incompatible with human happiness. The African is conditioned, by the cultural and social institutions of centuries, to a freedom of which Europe has little conception, and it is not in his nature to accept serfdom forever. He realises that he must fight unceasingly for his own complete emancipation; for without this he is doomed to remain the prey of rival imperialisms, which in every successive year will drive their fangs more deeply into his vitality and strength.

Among Kenyans, Kenyatta was regarded with a religious aura. The hymn books of the Kenyan African Union saw him as enjoying special divine favor and inspiration. These books described how God "told Kenyatta in a vision 'You shall multiply as the stars of heaven, nations will be blessed because of you.' " The hymn went on: "Kenyatta will find happiness before God, for he is the foundation stone of the kingdom. He has patiently suffered pain in his heart, he is moreover the judge of the Kikiyu and will dispense justice over the House of Mumbi."

As an agitator, Kenyatta was able to exploit the grievances of the Kikiyu about their land, a large area of which had been acquired by white settlers. The most gruesome and orgiastic rites were organized by the Mau Mau, which began their campaign of terrorism in 1952. Settlers were attacked, betrayed by servants who could not resist the command to kill. Though Kenyatta was accused of working with the Mau Mau, he denied any connection with them. Thousands of Mau Mau were imprisoned. Eventually, by the end of 1955, the movement lost its thrust.

Kenyatta, who had spent his youth herding his father's goats, presided in Kenya over the complex problems of independence. He made his country economically stable and able to attract foreign investment on a large scale.

Bibliography: Jomo Kenyatta, *Facing Mount Kenya* (London, 1952); Valerie Cuthbart, *Jomo Kenyatta: The Burning Spear* (Harlow, 1982); Dennis Hepman, *Jomo Kenyatta* (New York, 1985).

KHOMEINI, AYATOLLAH RUHOLLAH.   *See* **IRANIAN NATIONALISM.**

KIPLING, RUDYARD (1865–1936).   English novelist, poet, and champion of British expansionist nationalism. Kipling represented the spirit of national consciousness and was obsessed with the conviction of Britain's great destiny. He was convinced that the British Empire was a noble institution, in which the inspiring motive was not power, as in past empires, but an institution devoted to moral force. For him, British patriotism was rooted in the instinct of "inherited continuity." His sense of nationalism, he believed, was still liberal in concept.

In 1897 Kipling wrote his famous *Recessional* to celebrate the sixtieth anniversary of the reign of Queen Victoria. He called upon the Lord God of Hosts to support the British in their great mission:

God of our fathers, known of old—
Lord of our far-flung battle line—
Beneath whose awful hand we hold
Dominion over palm and pine—
Lord God of Hosts, be with us yet,
Lest we forget—lest we forget!

Bibliography: Rudyard Kipling, *Recessional* (New York, 1898); John Leslie Palmer, *Rudyard Kipling* (New York, 1974); Hilton Brown, *Rudyard Kipling: A New Appreciation* (New York, 1974); James Harrison, *Rudyard Kipling* (Boston 1982).

KOHN, HANS (1891–1971).   Professor of Modern European History, one of the world's leading authorities on nationalism, and a pioneer in its study. Kohn was born at Prague on September 15, 1891, and earned his degree as Doctor of Laws at the German University there. In World War I he fought with the Austro-Hungarian Army and was taken prisoner by the Russians. For almost five years he was held in Turkestan and Siberia, where he witnessed the Russian Revolutions of 1917 and the subsequent Civil War. He returned to Europe in 1920 by way of Japan and the Indian Ocean. During the next eleven years he lived in Paris, London and Jerusalem.

Kohn came to the United States in 1931 under the auspices of the Institute of International Education. After lecturing at the New School for Social Research in New York City, he was appointed Professor of History at Smith College in 1934. Later he became Sydenham Clark Parsons Professor of History there. He also taught at Mount Holyoke and Dartmouth Colleges, as well as at the Universities of California, Denver, Rutgers, and Colorado. In 1949 he came to the City College of New York, where he remained until his retirement in 1962. Many students throughout his teaching career testified to his brilliance as a lecturer.

Kohn's interest in nationalism began in his youth, when he observed its triumphs and failures in his homeland. The old Austro-Hungarian monarchy, burdened by bad government, was, in effect, becoming the victim of disruptive nationalism. Aware of the unfolding tragedy, the strongly compassionate Kohn began to see his mission as a historian of nationalism, and, in the words of Robert Strausz-Hupé, "the voice of European conscience."

Kohn's interest was above all in German nationalism, on which he wrote another classic study, *The Mind of Germany: The Education of a Nation* (1960). He saw the history of modern Germany as a study in national suicide. The enormous prestige won by the Germans, he wrote, especially in scholarship, music, literature, and philosophy, was deliberately destroyed by the Germans themselves. The responsibility for the disaster must be borne by those Germans who reject the humanitarian traditions of Western Europe. (*See* **KOHN DICHOTOMY.**) Kohn excepted Goethe from this category. The great German poet, he wrote, was a cosmopolitan who spurned the cult of the Middle Ages fostered by the Romantics. Goethe suspected that this German cult inspired an abnormal interest in the "Germanness" of the Germans. The German poet Heinrich Heine had warned the French that a unified Germany, whether led by the Right or Left, would terrorize all Europe.

In this book Kohn also described the extreme nationalism of composer Richard Wagner (q.v.), as well as the surrender of liberal intellectuals to the might of Otto von Bismarck's (q.v.) Second Reich. Kohn absolved many Germans of worship of the State, but at the same time he described how an apolitical people, slavishly obedient to those who held the reins of power, allowed themselves to be led to the verge of destruction by an Austrian, Adolf Hitler, who used the tool of nationalism to bolster his dictatorship.

As an analytical historian, Kohn saw the course of German history as suffused with tragedy. The polarity in German history, he believed, had never been resolved until the emergence of the current Federal Republic of West Germany, of which he spoke highly. In Kohn's view, the major history of Germany was for a working compromise between uniformity and disruption. Uniformity was contrary to the political and cultural divergencies among Germans. There was no power strong enough to crush the centrifugal tendencies of the component parts. At no time in the past were individual parts weak enough to allow the Germans to be centralized in a highly unified body, except during the short-lived Third Reich. Further tragic elements in German history were the misconception of *Geist* (spiritual depth) and *Macht* (authoritarian power). Where other Western peoples distrusted power and feared its abuse, Germans felt an almost religious preference for it. And their sentiment of belonging, their nationalism, was raised to a dangerous level. Extreme nationalism brought the gifted German people to near-destruction in two abysmally bloody World Wars.

Kohn earned a reputation as one of the world's top experts on nationalism. Master of a gracious writing style, he was a prolific writer who published more than fifty books and scores of articles. Most of this production concerned aspects of nationalism. The following bibliography contains some of his more important books and articles specifically on nationalism.

Bibliography: Hans Kohn, *A History of Nationalism in the East,* trans. from the German by Margaret M. Green (London, 1929); *Nationalism in the Soviet Union,* trans. from the German by E. W. Dickes (New York, 1933); *The Idea of Nationalism: A Study of Its Origins and Background* (New York, 1944; 8th printing, 1960); *Prophets and Peoples: Studies in Nineteenth Century Nationalism* (New York, 1946); *Pan-Slavism: Its History and Ideology* (Notre Dame, Ind., 1953); *Nationalism: Its Meaning and History* (Princeton, N.J., 1955); *Nationalism and Liberty: The Swiss Example* (New York, 1956); *American Nationalism: An Interpretive Essay* (New York, 1957); *The Mind of Germany: The Education of a Nation* (New York, 1960); *The Age of Nationalism: The First Era of Global History* (New York, 1962); *Living in a World Revolution* (New York, 1964); *Nationalism and Realism, 1852–1879* (Princeton, N.J., 1967); *Prologue to Nation-States: France and Germany, 1789–1815* (Princeton, N.J., 1967).

Hans Kohn, "Twilight of Nationalism" *American Scholar,* 6 (1937), 259–270; "The Genesis and Character of English Nationalism," *Journal of the History of Ideas,* I (January, 1940), 69–94; "Arndt and the Character of German Nationalism," *The American Historical Review,* 54 (1949), 787–803; "Father Jahn's Nationalism," *Review of Politics,* II (1949), 419–432; "The Paradox of Fichte's Nationalism," *Journal of the History of Ideas,* 10 (1949), 319–343; "Romanticism and the Rise of Nationalism," *Review of Politics,* 12 (1950), 443–472; "The Era of German Nationalism," *Journal of the History of Ideas,* 12 (1951), 256–274; "Begriffswandel der Nationalismus," *Der Merkur* (August, 1964), 701–714; "Nationalism," in *International Encyclopedia of the Social Sciences,* 11 (1968), 62–70.

On Hans Kohn, *see A Special Issue Devoted to Hans Kohn, Orbis,* 10, No. 4 (Winter, 1967); Ken Wolf, "Hans Kohn's Liberal Nationalism: The Historian as Prophet," *Journal of the History of Ideas,* 37, No. 4 (December, 1976), 651–672.

KOHN DICHOTOMY.   In the classifications of nationalism, pioneer scholar Carlton J. H. Hayes (q.v.) presented a vertical conceptualization as he traced nationalism chronologically through its various stages. (See **HAYES' CLASSIFICATION.**) A merit of the historical approach is the possibility of observing the same set of facts from a different angle and deriving from them equally valid conclusions. Thus, Hans Kohn (q.v.), another leading pioneer scholar of nationalism, applied a horizontal measuring rod and presented an interpretation quite as enlightening as that by Hayes.

Kohn, like Hayes, saw nationalism as the outcome of a long historical process. It takes its character from the political climate as well as the historical conditions in which it is engendered. One type of nationalism, therefore, may not be the same as another. From this premise Kohn went on to present a major dichotomy in typology. He pointed to two socio-political environments in which modern nationalism made its appearance. One was the Western world, including England, the British colonies, the Netherlands, and Switzerland. The second was the non-Western world, which included Central and Eastern Europe and Asia. In each of these two areas there was a centrifugal tendency that gave a distinctive coloration to nationalism. There are dangers in generalization, for there are exceptions to any principles set up as a standard, but the Kohn prescription was nicely formulated and convincing.

Kohn organized his analysis along four lines: origins, historical motivation, characteristics, and development.

Here Kohn held views similar to those of Hayes, but he made a distinction between the origins of nationalism in the Western and in the non-Western worlds. In the West, the emergence of nationalism was primarily a political occurrence; it was preceded by the formation of the future national state or coincided with it. This is in contrast with the experience of the non-Western areas, where nationalism arose much later and also at a more backward stage of socio-political development. Nationalism in the non-Western world was a kind of spontaneous protest against the existing state pattern. Cultural contacts provided the original stimulus, and remained secondary to political exigencies.

Kohn paid close attention to historical motivation. In the early modern history of the Western world, at a time when the roots of national sentiment were being nourished, the Renaissance and the Reformation were enormously vital movements that extended far beyond either cultural or religious changes. Middle-class entrepreneurs rejected the Holy Roman Empire and all its medieval trappings, and substituted for it a society based on the needs of a national state and its prime defenders, the patriotic bourgeoisie. Nationalism in the Western world was thus a product of indigenous forces that came to fruition in the eighteenth century.

In the non-Western world, notably in Central and Eastern Europe and in Asia, the Renaissance and the Reformation did not result in profound changes. In the German states the two great movements of early modern times were more precisely scholarly and theological in nature, although there were some politico-economic overtones. But the Russian Empire, the Near East, and Asia remained virtually untouched by the Renaissance and the Reformation. The old division between Roman Catholicism and the Greek Orthodox Church, between relics of the Western and Eastern empires, still persisted. A kind of ephemeral universalism, closer akin to the Middle Ages than to modern times, remained in the non-Western world.

Kohn thus revealed a cleavage between the experiences of the Western and non-Western areas. He bolstered this view with an analysis of the characteristics of nationalism in the two worlds. His analysis of the nature of nationalism in Europe was much the same as that of Hayes. His argument can be understood best by this brief comparative chart:

The Western World

Open Society. Western nationalism was the product of the Age of Reason—the Enlightenment, *Illuminé,* or *Aufklärung.* This meant the ideas of liberty, equality, and fraternity, as well as the concomitants of constitutionalism, parliamentarianism, liberalism, democracy, tolerance, and free speech. This was the *pluralistic* or *open society.*

Reality. Nationalism in the West emphasized political reality. It responded to the challenge of building nations without too much regard for the past. The nation itself was regarded as a real, vital, existing thing. Political integration was sought around a rational goal.

Union of Citizens.
Western nationalists saw nations as unions of citizens joined by a common will expressed in the social contract and other covenants and plebiscites. The people were to work together for a common future.

The Non-Western World

Closed Society. Here the elements of the Enlightenment were rejected as unreasonable, even foolish. Nationalism meant not freedom but the duty to serve the state. This was the *authoritarian* or *closed society.*

Ideality. The non-Western mind was absorbed not by reality but by an eternal search for the ideal Fatherland. This form of nationalism was characterized by myths and dreams of the future, and not by any immediate connection with the present. The newborn nation always looked to the past and to nonpolitical and history-conditioned factors.

Folk Community. Non-Western nationalists regarded the nation as a political unit centering around the irrational, precivilized folk concept. The rallying point was not a free and rational order but the folk community. Emphasis was placed on the diversity and self-sufficiency of nations.

The Western World	The Non-Western World
Individualism. Western nationalists approved a legal and rational concept of citizenship. Individual rights were regarded as sacred. All men were to be regarded as fundamentally alike as individuals, no matter what their social class or historic nationality.	*Collectivism.* In the non-Western world the decisive appeal was not to individual but to collective rights, to peculiarities of race or class. The idea of citizenship was left purposely vague, thereby lending itself more easily to exaggerations of imagination and to the excitation of emotions.
Self-Assurance. Western nationalism, reflecting the confidence and optimism of the *philosophes* of the Age of Reason, was self-assured and positive about its virtues.	*Inferiority Complex.* Non-Western nationalism, without any real roots in socio-political reality, lacked self-assurance. Often enough its sense of insecurity was overcompensated by overconfidence and aggressiveness.
Bourgeois Support. Western nationalism was supported by the politically and economically powerful bourgeoisie.	*Aristocratic Base.* Non-Western nationalism received its main support from a combination of aristocracy and the masses, both conservative minded.

Kohn was criticized on the ground that his typology was far too favorable to the Western world. He was accused of cleansing Western nationalism of tribal impurities and of disregarding any manifestations of anti-democratic or non-Western nationalism in the Far East. Again, the criticism is unreasonable. Kohn never described Western nationalism as a complete blessing and the non-Western form as a total curse. He carefully pointed to non-Western nationalisms that accept Western forms. He gave his attention to unattractive features of nationalism in the West as well as in non-Western nations. Nowhere did he intimate that the open society is perfect or foolproof, although he did regard it as preferable to the closed society.

Both Hayes and Kohn saw nationalism as an originally humane, libertarian, and creative force that eventually was transformed into an oppressive, aggressive, and expansionist *ism.* They understood the excesses of integral nationalism and they called for its curb so that the liberating elements could function once again. Both defended that type of nationalism that combines love of country and national tradition with a sense of individual dignity.

Bibliography: See bibliography of preceding entry on **KOHN, HANS.**

KÖRNER, THEODOR (1791–1813). Patriotic poet of the War of Liberation against Napoleon in 1813, student of early nationalist

Johann Gottlieb Fichte (q.v.), and forerunner of German nationalism. Körner belonged to the school of German Romanticism (q.v.), which played an important role in the rise of German nationalism. Germans were delighted with his highly emotional poetry and triumphant battle cries glorifying the German war spirit. His death on August 26, 1813, while serving as a volunteer, made him a popular hero. Typical of his work was the *Sword Song* composed just a few days before his death in battle. Following are the opening two and the final two of the sixteen stanzas:

> Thou sword at my left side,
> What means thy flash of pride?
> Thou smilest so on me,
> I take delight in thee.
> Hurrah!

> "I grace a warrior's side,
> "And hence my flash of pride;
> "What rapture thus to be
> "The guardian of the free!"
> Hurrah!

> Then press with fervent zeal
> The bridal lips of steel
> To thine; and woe betide
> Him who deserts his bride!
> Hurrah!

> Now let her sing and clash,
> That glowing sparks my flash!
> Morn wakes in nuptial pride.—
> Hurrah, thou iron bride!
> Hurrah!

Bibliography: Theodor Körner, *The Lyre and the Sword, with a Life of the Author*, trans. from the German by W. B. Chorley (London, 1834); Christian Gottfried Körner, *The Life of Theodor Körner*, trans. from the German by G. F. Richardson (London, 1845).

KOSSUTH, LOUIS (1802–1894).   Hungarian nationalist hero, leader of extremist nationalism in Hungary, and recognized symbol of revolutionary nationalism. Kossuth was the inspiration behind Hungary's struggle for independence from Austria. He practiced law for a time at Budapest, but devoted almost his whole life to the cause of Hungarian independence. A fiery orator, he used his talents to oppose the union of the Austrian and Hungarian crowns. Arrested, he was sentenced to prison for four years. For three years he edited the *Pesti Hirlap*, the organ of the Nationalist Party. Kossuth played a leading role in the Hungarian Revolution of March 1848, but his support of Hungarian nationalism aroused resentment among such minorities in Hungary as Slavs and Germans. After a dispute arose with Austria over revolt of the Croats, Kossuth declared the independence of Hungary and took control of the government in his own hands.

Kossuth ruled Hungary as a virtual dictator, but his sense of patriotism and magnetic personality endeared him to the Hungarian public. He was able to win several victories, but Russian troops in 1849 intervened in favor of Austria. Kossuth had to resign and the republic was ended. He fled to Turkey, where he was imprisoned for a time, but later released. He went to England and then to the United States, where he was acclaimed as a champion of liberty and nationalism. He made several additional attempts in favor of Hungarian nationalism. He was grieved by the *Ausgleich* (compromise) of 1867, by which the Austro-Hungarian Dual Monarchy was created. In 1890 he was offered amnesty, but he turned it down. He spent his last years in loneliness and frustration. After he died at Turin, Italy, his body was brought back to Budapest, where he was buried as a great citizen of Hungary. Since then, he has been regarded by the Hungarian people as a symbol of their nationalism.

Bibliography: Phineas Camp Headley, *The Life of Louis Kossuth* (Auburn, N.Y., 1952); Benjamin Franklin Tefft, *Hungary and Kossuth* (Philadelphia, 1952); Istvan Deak, *The Lawful Revolution: Louis Kossuth and the Hungarians* (New York, 1979); Gyorgy Spira, *Kossuth and Posterity* (Budapest, 1980).

KURDISH NATIONALISM.   Even a people without a territorial base may well have a strong sense of national consciousness. This is the case of the fiercely independent-minded Kurds, whose ancient homeland, which they called Kurdistan, is now divided among Iraq, Iran, Turkey, and Syria. Over the years the Kurds have progressively lost parts of their territory, which were taken over and distributed among these four states. The history of the Kurds is a story of one rebellion after another, but they never have been successful in winning their emancipation from those who would dominate them. Here again is another story of a mini-nationalism unable to win a nationalism of its own.

Yet, the Kurds claim a special territorial unit as well as the status of a distinct people with common characteristics—the essence of nationalism. They claim as their own an area in the Middle East, an extensive plateau and mountainous region with 10,000-foot summits. The land straddles the frontiers between the old Ottoman and Persian Empires. Some seven million Kurds are distributed over eastern Turkey (where they are called "mountain Turks"), Iraq, and Iran, with small enclaves in the eastern extremity of Syria and some in the Soviet Transcaucasus, or Armenian S.S.R. With an economy that was mostly pastoral and agricultural, during the summers they migrated from the lowlands with their herds of cattle, sheep, and goats to the mountain pastures of the highlands. Organized along tribal lines, they owed allegiance either to chiefs, landlords, or dervish sheiks.

The Kurdish language is an Indo-European tongue, a part of the northwestern division of Aryan languages. The Kurds speak the language of the countries in which they now live. The majority of Kurds are Sunnite Muslims, unlike most Iranians, who are Shi'ites. They have fashioned their special culture over the centuries, with their own national epics and patriotic poetry. Kurdish culture was emphasized in special newspapers, literary groups, and societies. All claimed that Kurdistan has been unreasonably partitioned by usurpers and that Kurdish nationalism has been shattered unjustly by conquerors.

The Kurds have a long, common history. Unwilling to submit to dominating empires, they outlived conquests in ancient times by Sumerians, Hittites, Assyrians, and Persians. They were Aryanized by both Cyrus and Darius. From their mountain strongholds, they fought indiscriminately against Greeks, Romans, Aryans, and Turks, all of whom held them in subjugation at one time. They were conquered by Arabs from the seventh to the ninth centuries, but they were never completely subdued. They were absorbed by the Seljuk Turks in the eleventh century. Kurdish power reached its height under Saladin (1138–1193), who was himself of Kurdish origin and who eventually became sultan of Egypt and Syria. In 1187 Saladin won an important victory over the Christian Crusaders.

Kurds fought steadily against assimilation by the Turks. In 1832, dissatisfied with proposed Turkish reforms, they rose in rebellion. Turkish authorities responded by replacing the Kurds' tribal chieftains with their own administrators, a move which increased Kurdish resentment. As nationalism came of age in the nineteenth century, the Kurds became even more anxious to win their sovereignty. In

1890 Abdülhamid II began a policy of appeasement by allowing the Kurds to organize their own cavalry units. It worked for a time and Kurds became a scourge in the area. Kurdish national consciousness was curbed but not for long. Kurdish newspapers, political clubs, and literary societies, all calling for emancipation, began to appear at the opening of the twentieth century. Kurdish deputies in the Turkish Chamber and Senate worked for the cause of Kurdish nationalism.

With the defeat of Turkey in World War I, Kurdish nationalists were encouraged by Point 12 of President Woodrow Wilson's Fourteen Points (January, 1918), which mentioned "an absolutely unmolested opportunity of autonomous development" for nationalities in the fallen Turkish state. According to the Treaty of Sèvres, the Kurds won recognition of a new Kurdistan. However, there was unexpected Turkish opposition. Led by Mustafa Kemal, later Kemal Atatürk (q.v.), the Turks rose against the victorious Allies and extracted the new Treaty of Lausanne in 1923. The treaty made no mention of the formation of a new Kurdistan.

Appalled by this setback to their independence, the Kurds continued their demand for sovereignty by staging armed uprisings in Turkey, Iran, and Iraq. In Turkey there were major rebellions in 1925, 1930–31, and 1937, all of which were suppressed savagely by Turkish armed forces. Kurdish nationalists were tracked down and executed. Thousands of Kurds were transferred from their homes to the unhealthy coast of Anatolia. Turkish authorities forbade any talk of separatism and secession. They introduced a note of appeasement by recognizing Kurdish cultural interests, but they demanded an end to armed uprising and violent demonstrations.

Kurdish activists were not inclined to cease their demands. About seven percent of Turkey's people were Kurds, and of these a substantial number supported the call for independence. The Kurdish Labor Party fought for an independent state in parts of eastern and southeastern Turkey. In August 1984, Turkish dissidents began attacking military targets. Some seven hundred civilians and military personnel were killed in the process. On July 18, 1988, Prime Minister Turgut Ozal was shot in the right hand by an escaped convict as Ozal addressed a convention of the Motherland Party, which he headed. Ozal urged his fellow Turks to reject violence and said that in the last ten years political terrorists had taken 5,000 lives in his country.

Kurds in Iraq and Iran also rebelled against their masters. The first attempt to set up a separate Kurdish province in Iraq was made in the immediate post-World War I years. In accordance with President Woodrow Wilson's proposal of self-determination, with British support, a semi-autonomous regime was proposed for the Kurds in Iraq. Shiek Mahmoud, head of a local Sayyid family, led a rebellion and proclaimed himself King of Kurdistan. The proclamation was nullified when Mahmoud was ousted in a military operation and deported from Iraq.

Despite this political defeat, Kurdish resistance continued. Kurds in Iraq supported their own newspapers, historical treatises, poetry, and Kurdish grammars. They resisted the invasion of their language by Arabic words. Concerned by Kurdish intransigence, the Iraqi government in the 1930s introduced a new civil administration in the northern district of the country, where there was a heavy Kurdish population. New opposition was led by the flamboyant Mustafa Barzani, son of a Kurdish rebel hanged by the Turks before World War I. In 1943 Barzani led a guerrilla force of some 6,000 men against the Iraqi administration. Attacked by a stronger Iraqi force, Barzani and his men set out on a long march across the mountains to Iran, where they were welcomed by Kurdish nationalists. The Soviet Union, which then occupied that area of Iran, created a Kurdish republic and commissioned Barzani a major general. When the Russians left in 1947, Iranian authorities set about the task of eliminating the Kurdish movement inside its borders.

Barzani's guerrilla army, called the *Persh Merga* (Forward to Death), fought Iraqi forces to a standstill in the 1960s. In 1966 the Iraqi government said that it was willing to give a measure of autonomy to the Kurds. Kurds complained that nothing was done to satisfy their demands and began to raid valuable oil installations. Ordering a truce in March 1970, the government recognized the Kurds as a national minority with social rights in local administration, education, and law courts. There was a four-year deadline for these proposals. Just preceding the expiration date, the Kurds, dissatisfied with limited self-rule, resumed fighting. The Iraqi authorities renewed operations against the Kurds, forcibly removing them from their homes near the border with Iran, destroyed their crops, and sent them to detention centers in the south. The result was renewed Kurdish resistance.

Kurdish nationalism was also strong in Iran, where Kurdish tribal chieftains and middle-class townsmen combined to separate their northwestern area from the central government in the years following World War I. In August 1941, in the midst of World War II, Kurdish nationalists rose in rebellion and set up a "Free Kurdish State" in the mountains of northwest Iran. It lasted only twelve months. Kurdish separatists organized the Kurdish Society for the Revival of Kurdistan, which led rebellions in 1946, 1950, and 1956. Iranian authorities hunted down Kurdish leaders and condemned them to prison or execution. Unfortunately for the Kurds, there were internal rivalries that weakened their movement.

Shāh Mohammed Reza Pahlavi also used force to throttle the Kurds. Believing that, at long last, their day had arrived, the Kurds supported the overthrow of the Shāh and joined the revolution. They were soon disenchanted. The Ayatollah Ruhollah Khomeini (*see* **IRANIAN NATIONALISM**), who succeeded the fallen Shāh, had no intention of giving in to the Kurds. He made it plain that there would be no regional autonomy or independence for the restive Kurds. Kurdish separatists continued to agitate for their cause. Well-armed Kurds became walking arsenals with guns and cartridges at their hips and hand grenades inside leather pouches at their sides. Guerrillas gathered heavy equipment, including artillery, anti-tank weapons, and machine guns in the mountains and valleys. The outbreak of the Iraqi-Iranian War in September 1980 gave Kurds another opportunity to achieve their goal. Kurdish tribesmen remained fixed in their determination to transform their sentiment of separatism into a full-fledged nationalism.

In late August 1988, Iraq, undoubtedly encouraged by the success of its war against Iran, began a major offensive against Kurdish rebels in an effort to crush the insurgency once and for all. The Iraqi campaign forced more than 30,000 Kurds across the border into camps in Turkey, which already had its own problems with the Kurdish minority. The U.S. State Department formally protested to Iraq about reports that it had used poison gas against civilians in its campaign to suppress the long-standing Kurdish rebellion.

Bibliography: Margaret Kahn, *Children of the Jinn: In Search of the Kurds for Their Country* (New York, 1980); Gerard Chalian (ed.), *People Without a Country* (London, 1980); F. David Andrews, *The Lost People of the Middle East* (Salisbury, N.C., 1982); Stephen C. Pelletiere, *The Kurds: An Unstable Element in the Gulf* (Boulder, Col., 1984).

L

L.A.M. SCHOOL.   A combination of scholars—zoologist, biologist, and anthropologist—who stress similarities in the behavior of man and the lower animals especially in defending territory. By implication, the current sense of nationalism merely repeats the motivations of lower animals. Leaders of the school were Konrad Lorenz, Robert Ardrey, and Desmond Morris. The names of Lionel Tiger and Anthony Storr may also be added. (*See* **TERRITORIAL IMPERATIVE.**)

LANGUAGE, NATIONALISM AND.   Language is a basic element in nationalism, though it is not the only one. The individual in every state is born inside a group using a special language. He learns the words of his language and speaks them throughout his life. As he uses the speech of his family, he begins to think of the language as his own. He feels comfortable with it, communicates with others who understand his words, and is suspicious of those who do not use the same terms. His speech gives him a sense of community with those of his group. Meanwhile, the state, always concerned that language becomes a matter of loyalty to the nation, encourages him to see his speech as a bond of union. In this way it is an important part in the development of nationalism.

Like history itself, language is never static; it is always in a state of change. Depending upon circumstances, it may change its form and content, but it generally conforms closely to the manner of thought and expression of actual life. It was a unifying factor even before the Age of Nationalism. Almost every village and town, every trade and profession, every social class had peculiarities of speech that came to be regarded as the special attribute of the community. Languages grew out of combinations of early dialects. In early medieval France, for example, the Burgundians and Visigoths in the south used a dialect called *langue d'oc* (*oc* for yes), while the Normans and Franks in the north used the idiom *langue d'oïl* (*oïl* for yes, and pronounced like today's *oui*). These two dialects merged from the beginning of the Crusades (1096) to the death of Louis IX (1270).

A similar development of combining dialects may be noted on the German scene. Early Germans had two different dialects—Old High German (*Althochdeutsch*), used in the midlands, and Old Low German variations spoken by Germans and Scandinavians (Norsemen, Swedes, and Danes), Frisians, and Saxons (Anglo-Saxons and Dutch). Those Germanic tribes that conquered Britain in the fifth and sixth centuries, spoke Anglo-Saxon, which was mixed with Celtic, Latin, and Danish elements but remained essentially Low German. Significantly, the dialects spoken by Germans in the north are on occasion regarded by English sailors as corrupted forms of English. These dialects merged into what are today seen as modern languages.

As nations began to appear in the modern era, regional and local languages began to lose their influence. The Bible was translated into English by Wycliffe and into German by Luther. Language tended to become identified with the modern state under the impulse of new social conditions during the Renaissance and Reformation. The printing press and popular education served to help the formation of national languages. Added to this was the rise of the middle class, which identified itself with the national tongue. Although vernacular dialects remained, the critical factor was the formation of the national languages.

In modern nations, patriotism was identified with language, and the national language was brought to a stage of idolization. Language became a special symbol of national life. People began to regard their language as a major expression of their independence, of their personality, and culture. Nationalists demanded the domination of one language in their country. They suppressed the use of other languages and purified their own speech by rejecting the words of other languages. They demanded the political incorporation of the nationals of other countries who spoke their own language. They saw their own special vocabulary, syntax, word formations, and word rhythms as expressing their distinctiveness. For them, language meant that the accumulated traditions and memories were transmitted to them from their forbears. It maintained the unity of culture that distinguishes one people from another.

Throughout the eighteenth century, intellectuals and political leaders in Europe encouraged the teaching and use of the national language. This was especially true in France, where love of the *patrie* was encouraged as the dominant passion of the people because it was the *patrie* that would shape their character. Throughout the Middle Ages, Latin had been the dominant international language used for both official and unofficial purposes. Now, with the rise of the national states, it became the first and critical duty of the individual citizen to bear arms for the state and to defend what was most important and sacred for him—his nation. Where at one time the individual Frenchman had taken little interest in war unless it concerned his own village, the nation's wars became his own because he helped make up the nation's armies. From the time of the French Revolution and the Napoleonic era, armies were composed of citizen-patriots who were loyal to the nation and who spoke its language.

In France and elsewhere, citizens could understand their own language better than Latin. It was important that they have a common language to be used in their everyday life, in their relationship with others, and in business and industry. For them, Latin was a waste of time. In their minds, French was a superior language, capable of expressing clearly any facts or ideas. In fact, the French language, from the time of the French Revolution, did become the language of international diplomacy. This idea of the sacredness of the national tongue took hold elsewhere. People everywhere began to believe that each nation should have its own special language. By the end of the eighteenth century, the idea of a national language was accepted as the belief of citizen-patriots. The special language would be used throughout the national territory so that citizens could recognize one another. The concept became common—the national tongue represented the spiritual wealth of the nation and could be used only by those who understood it. There were, of course, exceptions.

The French experience penetrated throughout the Western world in more or less similar form. Thus, Herder, Fichte, and Schleiermacher (qq.v.) in the Germanies called for the use of German just as French intellectuals had insisted on a language useful to the Fatherland. Similarly, in Italy Vittorio Alfieri (q.v.) advocated the use of Italian by his people, and in the United States Noah Webster (q.v.) urged the use of an American language. The demand was always one and the same—the language of a people must be uniform. The belief was that dialects and foreign languages in the nation perpetuated the reign of fanaticism and superstition. There should be only one language, as the nation has one heart.

The idea of linguistic unity of a people is closely connected with pluralism on the basis of equality. The attachment of ethnic groups to their own individuality and their own myths and values may be too strong to be shaken by the demand for a common language. Group awareness and group attachment of an ethnic group inside the national state may be so strong that it renders units immune to the call for a common language. The state, with its dominant language, may use many different methods to force integration. Those ethnic groups speaking other tongues may hew to their own language and press for a policy of ethnic pluralism on the basis of equality. In the long run, language differences between the dominant state and its more aggressive groups may result in irreconcilable confrontations between the two.

Language plays an important and sometimes basic role in the structure of modern nationalism, especially as a determinant of national borders. Yet, its importance should not be exaggerated. It is, indeed, possible for a nation to maintain a strong national sense of consciousness even though its people may speak different languages. This is especially obvious in the case of Switzerland, where four languages—French, German, Italian, and Rhaeto-Romansch, exist in harmony side by side in the system of cantons. This is due to strict attention to the pluralistic situation and the urge to place national unity above the language question. A slightly similar situation may be noted in Canada, where Francophones and Anglophones are joined in an uneasy union for the national benefit despite sharply divergent language associations. (*See* **QUEBEC NATIONALISM.**) In Belgium, too, the same kind of union is promoted despite conflicts between Flemings and Walloons. (*See* **WALLOON NATIONALISM.**) In other words, language may well be a force for national consciousness in nations. It may also be the distinguishing mark of nationality when one language is spoken in two nations—as in Great Britain and the United States.

Some scholars of nationalism hold that the identification of a nation with a language group is not tenable. Thus, Friedrich Hertz comments that this identification conflicts with both the legal and social concept of a nation. In his view, the groups constituted by sentiment, citizenship, or language, very often do not coincide but overlap. He points out that peoples of different tongues are citizens of the same state, and sometimes regard one another as members of the same nation. Demarcation according to language, he says, is occasionally made difficult by the fact that large parts of the population speak two languages, so that is not easy to determine to which other nation they have the closest affinity.

Other scholars of nationalism hold to the line that an individual belongs to the nation if he speaks the language, and he is an outsider, or foreigner, if he does not. They hold that the language of a nation is obviously a set of habits by which members of the national community communicate with one another. In practice, what usually happened was that the language of a dominant group inside the nation became the dominant tongue, and all those who did not speak that language were pressured into using that linguistic nationality. Whether logical or not, it came to be believed that the national language in some way expressed the national character; it was desirable that everyone in the nation speak, write, and use that language in their everyday affairs. The national language usually was seen to express the desire of the people in order to maintain the national unity.

Bibliography: Otto Jesperson, *Mankind, Nations, and Individuals From a Linguistic Point of View* (Oslo, 1925); Stanley Rundle, *Language as a Social and Economic Factor in Europe* (London, 1946); Joshua A. Fishman et al., *Language Loyalty in the United States* (The Hague, 1966); Boyd C. Shafer, *Faces of Nationalism* (New York, 1972); Joshua A. Fishman, *Language and Nationalism* (Rowley, Mass., 1972); P. H. Van der Plank, "Language and Nationality," *Plural Societies,* (Fall, 1975), 9–16.

LANGUEDOC PARTICULARISM.   Added to the dissatisfaction of Bretons in Brittany, French Basques on the borders of the Pyrenees, and Corsicans on their island, there were several other even smaller mini-nationalisms in France. In southern France, bordering partly on the Mediterranean and at the foot of the Pyrenees, is the former province of Languedoc. The people living in this region have their own distinctive culture, including a language form that has become the basis of Languedoc particularism. In the early thirteenth century, the people of Languedoc chose a Manichean sect called Cathari, which Rome believed struck at the heart of Roman Catholic Christianity. Pope Innocent III (held office 1198–1216) proclaimed an Albigensian Crusade and supported an expedition of French barons led by Simon de Montfort against the Albigensians. The army ravaged Toulouse and massacred its inhabitants.

Despite this subjugation, Languedocians retained their special language, culture, and convictions. The dissent remains muted. French authorities regard Languedocian nationalism with indifference, as a kind of harmless local sentiment. Paris allowed the people of the region to retain their own cultural and social conditions, as long as they understood the privilege of sharing *la gloire* of a united France and French centralized authority.

Bibliography: Nicole Castan, *Justice et repression en Languedoc à l'époque des lumières* (Paris, 1980); Aime Vielzeuf, *Terreur en Cevenne: Chroniques la résistance en Cevenne et en Languedoc* (Nîmes, 1985).

LASKI, HAROLD J. (1893–1950).   British political scientist, educator, leading member of the British Labour Party, and critic of nationalism. Born on June 30, 1893, in Manchester, Laski attended New College, Oxford. Coming to the United States, he lectured at Harvard from 1916 to 1920. As an author he published *Authority in the Modern State* (1919), and *The Foundations of Sovereignty, and Other Essays* (1921). In these books he attacked the idea of an all-powerful sovereign state and defended the concept of political pluralism. In 1926 he accepted a post at the London School of Political Science, where he taught until his death.

A convinced Marxist, though not a Communist, Laski criticized nationalism as an extreme danger for the future of civilization. Nationalism emerging into statehood, he said, results in a world, in an egoism, that intelligent men now regard as intolerable. Either its excesses must be curbed, which to him meant the end of the sovereign state, or they will destroy civilization. The alternative to nationalism, he suggested, is the world-community, the *civitas maxima*, which must be regarded as the starting point of the social adventure. The body of law that represents the needs of the whole must bind the will of each of its constituent members. The state must be prevented from hindering the needs of the world-community from being realized. For Laski the world-community and nationalism were incompatible terms: "We must choose between one or the other; we cannot have both."

Bibliography: Harold J. Laski, *Nationalism and the Future of Civilization* (London, 1932); Bernard Zylstra, *From Pluralism to Collectivism: The Development of Harold Laski's Political Thought* (Assen, 1968).

LATIN AMERICAN NATIONALISM.   Under the leadership of such nationalists as Simón Bolívar (q.v.), a Venezuelan, and José de San Martin (q.v.), an Argentinian, Latin Americans fought for independence against Spain and won it by the end of the first quarter of the nineteenth century. Bolívar expressed the sense of the new nationalism in South America: "Venezuela," he said, "fully convinced of possessing sufficient strength to repel her oppressors, has made known by the voice of the government her final determination to fight to the death in defense of her political life, not only against Spain, but against all men, if all men had degraded themselves to the extent of a devouring government whose only incentives are a death-dealing sword and the flames of the Inquisition."

Bolívar's conception of nationalism spread throughout Latin America, which caught the idea as it progressed among European states. The growing Latin American nationalism took the form of a desire to be independent from real or alleged subservience to European Great Powers. Initially nourished by individuals in a private capacity, it was, at first, an abstract phenomenon devoid of political appeal because of its narrow audience. Eventually, nationalism was no longer confined to the abstractions of a few intellectuals but was brought to the masses in a politically charged form.

For the remainder of the nineteenth century, most Latin American countries oscillated between dictatorship and anarchy. Powerful military leaders struggled for control and set up dictatorships to maintain it. They held the native Indian population to an inferior status. This general process began to change in the twentieth century as Latin Americans, in the tradition of a new nationalism, began to discover their own past. As a century earlier in Europe, Latin Americans began to revive their early folk art and traditions. This was, in effect, a repetition of early European Romanticism, which had an important influence on the nature of European nationalism. Today, there is a great surge of determination in Latin American countries to express their own sense of nationalism. One by one, the major elements of nationalism—common traditions, common historical patterns, and common heroes—have been generated.

At the same time, nationalism in South America has been distinguished by something else in common, described by a Chilean in these words: "What unites us in Spanish America is our beautiful language and our distrust of the United States." Latin American pride, resentment, and national egoism were expressed in an attitude of disdain for the United States. In 1958 José Figueres, ex-President of Costa Rica, appeared before a Congressional Committee in Washington and issued a blunt statement to the American people explaining why Vice President Richard M. Nixon had been spat upon in Venezuela by young hotheads. "As a citizen of the Hemisphere," he said, "as a man who has dedicated his public life to the cultivation of inter-American understanding, as a student who knows and esteems the United States, and who has never tried to conceal that esteem from anyone, no matter how hostile, I deplore the fact that the people of Latin America, represented by a handful of over-excited Venezuelans, should have spat at a worthy functionary." Figueres then went on to denounce the United States for its investments in the American dictatorships. In international economic policies, he said, the United States gives the appearance of being bent on repeating certain errors of the domestic policy that did so much damage in the past. Latin Americans, he added, were tired of pointing out these mistakes. "We are not asking for handouts, except in cases of emergency. We are not people who would spit for money. We have inherited all the defects of the Spanish character, but also some of its virtues. Our poverty does not abate our pride. We have our dignity."

Arthur P. Whitaker (q.v.), Latin Americanist, then Professor of History at the University of Pennsylvania, traced the export of nationalism from Europe to Latin America and showed how the subsequent development of nationalism in Latin America reflected the great diversity of the continent. He saw the goals of Latin American nationalism as similar in many ways to those of Africa and Asia. But the Latin American states, no longer new, have been independent and already wise in the ways of nationalism. Nationalism in Latin America has been highly derivative, with Europe as the chief source. In this and in most other matters, Latin Americans have modified and naturalized their differences. Latin America has made no changes in the symbols or the vocabulary of nationalism. Latin American nationalism is no exception to the rule that the peoples of that area form a bewildering combination of diversity. As contrasted with the United States, in Latin America nationalism developed in a climate of opinion where government was regarded as neither the natural enemy of its citizens or subjects or, at best, a necessary evil. Latin Americans from the start have been disposed to regard government, at least potentially, as a friend and benefactor.

Whitaker saw four important changes in the character of Latin American nationalism since the late nineteenth century: the first in the 1890s; the second about 1910; the third in the 1930s; and the fourth starting in the 1950s. The first change was the injection of an economic content, partly under socialist influence. This was the Age of Imperialism, helped by the local corrupt oligarchy of *vendepatrias,* those who "sold out" to the imperialists. This became one of the chief weapons in the arsenal of nationalists throughout Latin America.

The second change of a broader kind was brought to focus by the centennial celebrations of independence which from 1910 on strongly stimulated nationalism in Latin America. Nationalism now provided a more effective leadership by the emergent middle class. It began to reach full flower. It was economic and cultural as well as political and military, and outward-looking instead of introspective.

The third important change in the character of Latin American nationalism began in the 1930s under Communist influence. This new type, according to Whitaker, was "negative, chauvinistic, sterile, and isolationist." The new form of nationalism was designed to separate Latin America from the United States and the rest of the Western world and to facilitate Communist penetration of Latin America by sowing discord and creating confusion among its people. Communist conspirators used Latin American intellectuals to further subversive ideas. This kind of narrow nationalism disparaged everything that tended to unite the Latin Americans with one another as well as with the United States and Europe.

Whitaker's fourth phase sees a conflict between Communists and those nationalists who resent Communist interference in Latin American affairs. On February 16, 1959, Fidel Castro took power in Cuba and converted the country into a Communist state supported by Moscow. The new Communist Cuban administration began a sweeping economic, political, and cultural program without consideration of personal liberties. On the one hand, Latin American intellectuals sought to return to the earlier form of nationalism. On the other, the United States took the position of guarding Latin Americans against any additional invasions of communism.

Since the end of World War II, the Communist campaign against the United States in Latin America has been carried on with increased intensity. It called "for peace" and denounced "Yankee imperialism." Latin American Communists described themselves as true-blue nationalists, but it was obvious that their orientation came from the Kremlin.

Bibliography: Robert J. Alexander, *Communism in Latin America* (New Brunswick, N.J., 1957); John J. Johnson, *Political Change in Latin America* (Stanford, 1958); Arthur P. Whitaker, *Nationalism in Latin America* (Gainesville, Fla., 1962); Arthur P. Whitaker and David C. Jordan, *Nationalism in Contemporary Latin America* (New York, 1966); Victor Alba, *Nationalists Without Nations* (New York, 1968).

LATVIAN NATIONALISM. *See* **BALTIC NATIONALISMS.**

LÉVESQUE, RENÉ (1922–). Canadian statesman and fervent Quebec nationalist. Coming from a farming region in Quebec, Lévesque worked first as a popular television newsman and then turned to politics. Critics described him as "a chain-smoking disorganized, hot-tempered bundle of emotional energy," but he was actually shy and self-deprecating. He advanced rapidly in politics, serving as a Liberal member of Parliament and as the country's Justice Minister and Attorney General.

Lévesque was a strong Quebec nationalist: "I am first a *Québeçois* and second, with a growing doubt a Canadian." He urged his fellow Quebecers to throw off the English yoke. In 1967 he founded the *Mouvement Souveraineté*, the forerunner of his *Parti Québeçois*. His P.Q. moved steadily forward until, in the election of 1976, he became Quebec's Premier. In this post he played down the separatist issue, but at the same time made it clear that he favored political separatism eventually "in a positive way." Carefully avoiding the term "secession," he declared that separation must be achieved peacefully and in a democratic form. The people of Quebec, he said, were a national entity with a different language and culture existing over several centuries. He paid special attention to the matter of language, which he regarded as basic:

> There are two nations here, but the *Québeçois* will make it clear what they want through a referendum. It should be as democratic and well-prepared as possible— not improvised. The Confederation has been a negative force and only force of habit has held Quebec to it. We are like two trains going farther and farther from each other. For thirty years Quebec has been moving toward self-affirmation, self-determination, and self-government, which does not mesh with the federal system. (*See* **SELF-DETERMINATION**.)

Lévesque believed that Quebec would be viable as an independent state. "In terms of potential material resources, we would be recognized as one of the most advanced and enlightened societies of the world." Francophones who dreamed of their own French state in Canada were impressed by such arguments.

Lévesque's mini-nationalism seemed on the surface to be cascading in strength. The Canadian debate was sharp, and public rhetoric on both sides threatening. The historic referendum, held on May 20, 1980, attracted one of Quebec's heaviest turnouts. The "No" vote was decisive. This federal victory meant that Quebec would go the way of Wales and Scotland in the United Kingdom—they would stay within the boundaries of the national state. Jubilant federalists cheered their victory. Lévesque's followers shouted: "We want a country." Lévesque conceded defeat, but in a final gesture of defiance urged Quebecers to "fight on until the next time."

Quebec had given its vote but not its deep sentiment to the cause of federalism. The country for the moment was relieved, but few Canadians believed the issue to be dead. In fact, it was not. The unhappy result was that Canada remained a tormented country, with national unity at stake in the continuing power struggle. An all-out Canadian consensus remains a difficult task in the face of highly emotional differences. The democratic process of referendum has not been able to heal the deep wounds. An unsatisfied mini-nationalism still threatens the structure of what was supposed to be a coherent state. (*See also* **QUEBEC NATIONALISM.**)

Bibliography: Herbert Furlong Quinn, *The Union Nationale: Quebec Nationalism from Duplessis to Lévesque* (Toronto, 1979); Graham Fraser, *P.Q.: René Lévesque and the Parti Québecois in Power* (Toronto, 1984); René Lévesque, *Memoirs,* trans. from the French by Philip Stratford (Toronto, 1986).

LIBERAL NATIONALISM.   *See* **HAYES' CLASSIFICATION.**

LIST, FRIEDRICH (1789–1846).   Württemberger scholar, pioneer German economist, and main supporter of the *Zollverein* (Customs Union) in national economics. In 1806 List entered the civil service in Württemberg. His progress was so rapid that he rose to the post of Ministerial Under-Secretary. He also became Professor of Practical Administration at the University of Tübingen. However, his private war against officialdom led to his exile for four years. Returning to Germany, he was arrested again and confined to a fortress. He was released on his promise to emigrate to the United States. Within a few years in the United States he acquired a comfortable fortune by various successful enterprises. He also became known for his attack on the cosmopolitan system of free trade advocated by Adam Smith. Strongly urging the opposite policy, he called for protection of native industry.

Returning to Germany, List emerged as an influential apostle of economic nationalism. He was the first German to advocate the importance of a national railroad system. He projected a program of protective tariffs. He called for a German merchant marine, a German navy, German colonialism, a Greater Germany, and *Mitteleuropa*. In many ways he paved the way for Germany's political and economic greatness. He never deviated from his support of the national idea. His unique contribution to German nationalism was the first expression of a systematic concept of the national idea at the economic level. His goal always was a powerful Germany unified economically and politically. "I would indicate, as the distinguishing characteristic of my system, *nationality*. On the nature of *nationality*, as the intermediate interest between those of *individualism* and of entire *humanity*, my whole structure is based."

List's career was inextricably bound up with the idea of a *Zollverein*. From his concept of a custom's union, the Germans obtained one of the most important attributes of their nationality. By appropriating the leadership of the *Zollverein* from List, Prussia managed to place herself in a favorable position to assume control of German affairs. Regarded as a major step in the direction of German national unification, the *Zollverein*, paradoxically, was originally a device utilized by Prussia to prevent a general German economic union. The Prussians were concerned lest any such union achieved through the German Confederation might result in Austrian hegemony.

List saw the *Zollverein* as a *sine qua non* for the development of a national German state. Above all, he said, the nation must be cemented by a common economic life, by a *national* economy. To reach their goal as a functioning national state, the German people must break the chains of political division. Once its national life had been molded, the German state must maintain a system best suited to its special needs. The German national state of the future should think in terms of protective tariffs until it was ready for free trade. For a moment, List warned, universal free trade worked to the disadvantage of a disunited Germany.

In his major work, *The National System of Political Economy* (1841), List placed extraordinary emphasis on the national theme, which became an *idée fixe* in his thinking. He used the term "national" in a truly wide variety of combinations:

1. national spirit	20. national intelligence
2. national point of view	21. national income
3. national independence	22. national wealth
4. national economy	23. national progress
5. national labor	24. national protection
6. national union	25. national institutions
7. national character	26. national culture
8. national industry	27. national banking
9. national self-respect	28. national freedom
10. national power	29. national body
11. national interests	30. national will
12. national consumption	31. national aims
13. national manufacturing	32. national concerns
14. national production	33. national existence
15. national commerce	34. national integrity
16. national community	35. national envy
17. national liberty	36. national territory
18. national policy	37. national war
19. national circumstances	38. national defense

39. national security
40. national economists
41. national well-being
42. national enrichment
43. national traffic
44. national capital
45. national self-sufficiency
46. national idea
47. national intercourse
48. national meaning
49. national speech

50. national consciousness
51. national manufacturing power
52. national division of labor
53. national material capital
54. national civilization
55. national confederation
56. national system of money
57. national agriculture
58. national system of credit
59. national productive powers
60. national productive ability

In his national system of economy, List expressed very much the same ideas as the literary Romanticists and the later integral nationalists. In denouncing Adam Smith's "cosmopolitanism and disorganizing particularism," List, in reality, rejected the very idea of liberalism. By directing attention to dynamic "national enrichment" over static "national wealth," he contributed to the type of thinking that was to dominate German national thought. Like the historicists, he made it plain that his economic outlook was based primarily upon political and economic considerations. The State, in his view, was always the nodal point between the processes of the spirit, an idea which he shared with Hegel (q.v.), and which was to become the theme of German political, economic, and intellectual thinking in the nineteenth and twentieth centuries. List's type of exclusive nationalism had little in common with mere patriotism. Inherent in his philosophy was the idea that Germany must drive for power despite all obstacles.

Throughout his life, List was a battered and bruised soul, the target of unappreciative German industrialists, and the prey of the Austrian secret police. He was denounced by his countrymen as "revolutionary," "Jacobin," "Republican," "demagogue," even as a "traitorous trader." Metternich called him "an heroic swindler," and "the tool of squealing German manufacturers." Yet, after List's death, when it became known that his idea of national economy was, in reality, designed as a service to the Fatherland, he was placed on a pedestal as one of Germany's outstanding patriot-heroes. Historian Heinrich von Treitschke (q.v.) described him as "a demagogue only in the noblest sense." In 1925 a *List Gesellschaft* (List Society) honored him as an economist who helped prepare the war for German national unification. He was now described as "a great German without Germany," "Germany's *verhinderten* (impeded) Colbert, an economic genius who embodied the finest thinking of Cromwell, Canning, Quesnay, Robert Peel, even Aristotle." The prophet without honor at long last achieved posthumous homage in his homeland.

On List's grave at the cemetery at Kufstein are the proud words GERMANY'S FRIEDRICH LIST. At the base of the statue is this tribute:

A DEFENDER OF HIS COUNTRY WHO TOILED WITHOUT REWARD,
A WARRIOR OVER WHOSE STRONG WILL GOLD CAST NO FETTERS,
A HERO WHO SAW BEYOND HIS OWN AGE FAR INTO THE FUTURE,
A SOWER FOR WHOM THE STARRY WORLD IS PREPARED AS A DWELL-
ING.

Bibliography: Arnold H. Price, *The Evolution of the Zollverein* (Ann Arbor, Mich., 1959); Louis L. Snyder, *German Nationalism, The Tragedy of a People* (Harrisburg, Pa., 1952, Port Washington, N.Y., 1969); W. O. Henderson, *Friedrich List: Economic and Visionary* (Totowa, N.J., 1983); Roman Szporluk, *Communism and Nationalism: Karl Marx versus Friedrich List* (New York, 1988).

LITHUANIAN NATIONALISM. *See* **BALTIC NATIONALISMS.**

LOCKE, JOHN (1632–1704). English philosopher, scientist, physician, and rationalist, who helped pave the way for the Enlightenment. Locke is generally regarded as the founder of empiricism. He believed that knowledge came from sensory experience. In *An Essay Concerning Human Understanding* (1690), he presented the idea that the mind at birth is a *tabula rasa*, a blank tablet, upon which all sensations and ultimately all thoughts are written. All knowledge begins with the receptions of sensations from without; these sensations become images; images, in turn, are elaborated in a chain; and the chain becomes intelligible thought. In effect, Locke attacked Plato's doctrine of innate ideas, that is, that ideas are inherent in the mind at birth. The importance of Locke in intellectual history is that, in demonstrating that knowledge should be based upon experience and reason, he literally created a new science of the human mind.

Locke did not write specifically about nations and nationalism as such, but he was among the rationalists who presented a secular theoretical foundation for the nation-state and its accompanying nationalism. He proposed the social contract—the idea that men created their own states by contract among themselves in order to protect and secure their natural rights of liberty and property. Men could be educated to be rational and to understand their social contract. They banded together in nations to engage in joint national enterprises. Their social contract existed throughout history and in modern form led to a national constitution and the joining together of men in nations. The nation, then, was a national group.

Locke also defended the ultimate sovereignty of the people and stressed the importance of religious liberty. For him the modern nation-state was the product of nature and, therefore, entirely rational. These views had an important effect upon the thinking of the English people and did much to shape the character of their nationalism. (*See* **ENGLISH NATIONALISM.**)

Bibliography: John Locke, *An Essay Concerning Human Understanding* (London, 1690); Maurice W. Cranston, *John Locke: A Biography* (London, 1957); John Dunn, *The Political Thought of John Locke* (London, 1969); Karen I. Vaughn, *John Locke: Economist and Social Scientist* (Chicago, 1980).

M

MACHIAVELLI, NICCOLÒ (1469–1527). Florentine statesman, author of *Il Principe* (*The Prince*), the famous book analyzing the theories by which an ambitious man may rise to sovereign power. Machiavelli may be called a precursor of Italian nationalism. Almost alone among contemporaries, Machiavelli called for an end to the unsystematic states of the medieval era. Opposed to universalism, he visualized a new Italy independent of ecclesiastical authority. In his guide for the perfect autocrat, he appealed to the wealthy Medici family to liberate Italians from the "barbarians."

Some three hundred years before the Age of Nationalism, Machiavelli issued his call for a united national state. It would be the glory of some unknown Italian hero to rid the country of its miserable condition. His countrymen, he wrote, were greater slaves than the Israelites, more oppressed than the Persians, and more dispersed than the Athenians. "In a word they are without laws, without chiefs, pillaged, torn to pieces, and enslaved by foreign powers." He urged the illustrious house of Medici, visibly favored by heaven and the Church, to lead the great enterprise of alleviating the Italians from their misery. If it had to be by war, then so be it. "Every war that is necessary is just; and it is human to take up arms for the defense of a people to whom no other resource is left."

Machiavelli's early warning was of some significance in the eventual preparation of Italian nationalism and the unification of the state in the nineteenth century. (*See* **ITALIAN NATIONALISM.**)

Bibliography: Niccolò Machiavelli, *The Prince* (London, 1872); Peter

Bondanella and Mark Musa, *The Portable Machiavelli* (New York, 1979); Leo Rauch, *The Political Animal: Studies in Political Philosophy from Machiavelli to Marx* (Amherst, Mass., 1981); Michael A. Soupios (ed.), *European Political Theory: Plato to Machiavelli* (Lanham, Md., 1986).

MACRO-NATIONALISMS.   Attempts to extend existing nationalisms into larger nationalisms based on common language, customs, traditions, history, psychological characteristics, and, on occasion, religion. They are also called pan-movements (q.v.). Specific macronationalisms, such as Pan-Slavism, Pan-Germanism, Pan-Europeanism, Pan-Ottomanism, Pan-Turanism, Pan-Turkism, Pan-Islamism, Pan-Arabism, Pan-Asianism, Pan-Africanism, and Pan-Americanism (qq.v.), have sought to push nationalism into a larger entity.

Where the nationalism of an established nation-state is expanded to a supranational form, there emerges the larger macro-nationalism. These politico-cultural movements promote the idea of a common group identification seeking a new territorial base. They may exist in small states among a people trying to link themselves with the people of another state. In most cases, however, they reflect an aggressive impulse to win alliance with another people on the basis of a territorial imperative (q.v.). There is always the concept of domination—the mother nationalism demands control of her children everywhere. Thus, macro-nationalisms become nationalisms writ large.

Most significant in the make up of macro-nationalisms is the use of a common language, which is presumed to identify a people who belong together. There may be other factors added to language affinity: messianic zeal (Pan-Slavism); territorial expansion (Pan-Germanism); religious belief (Pan-Islamism); racial unity (Pan-Africanism); or anti-colonialism (Pan-Asianism). There is no fixed pattern for the macro-nationalisms: they may be vague or well organized, or even defiant of logical analysis.

The macro-nationalisms are distinguished by common denominators in virtually all cases. There may be differences in environment, organization, methods, and goals, but there appear to be several common attributes. For example, implicit in the idea is a quality of uniqueness. Even as most religions consider their own dogmas as preferable to others, so does each macro-nationalism see itself as a favored branch of the human family. There may be actually a unique quality, or there may be an intense belief in it. Added to this sense of uniqueness is a conscious or unconscious sentiment of superiority. Here the macro-nationalisms merely reflect the sense of superiority common in established nationalisms. Both versions, nationalisms and macro-nationalisms, see themselves as destined to play a great role in history.

Though coated with intellectualism, most macro-nationalisms prefer actions over words. They may see militancy as a proper means to their goal. This militancy is geared to a move for expansion. Those who express linguistic, ethnic, and cultural ties in their aim of gathering all peoples of a common background together, often come into conflict with others who have a similar aim for themselves. In the crowded world of many nations, any attempts to expand into other territories inevitably lead to confrontation and conflict. Most macro-nationalisms are coated with this theme of aggression. It is scarcely a factor for international peace.

Macro-nationalisms may be classified in several groups: national, racial, cultural, religious, and continental. Each one has its own characteristics, but there may be overlappings. Emerging in the nineteenth century, macro-nationalisms were extensions of the existing nationalism. An example is Germany, unified by Otto von Bismarck (q.v.) after three wars against Denmark, Austria, and France. Macro-nationalists considered the unity of Germany a step toward German expansion. The unified German state would eventually be extended to include all of German background in a larger nationalism.

Some macro-nationalisms assume that a people have a common racial identity. There is no such thing as a Slavic race, but that did not prevent Pan-Slavs calling for "racial emancipation." At the same time, the racial factor is paramount in the case of Pan-Africanism, which was basically a confrontation between black and white men. In this case, the biological factor was a genuine one—black African natives versus white colonial exploiters.

Most macro-nationalisms stressed the idea of a traditional common culture rooted in past history. Historians, poets, novelists, all sought common attributes from their history—sagas, songs, costumes, stories, dances, and folklore were seen as linking a people. Ancestors had passed on such characteristics to the present. Hence, those who had these common traditions belonged together, and they must not be divided from each other by artificial boundaries. To maintain and extend the motivations of the past became the battle cry of the macro-nationalists.

Where other macro-nationalisms were mainly political in ideology, some macro-nationalisms sought to combine the people of one religious faith into a supranational state. In such combinations the lines of unity were generally vague and more theoretical than real. The most active religious movement was Pan-Islamism, which favored the union of all Muslims of a common religion, a common religious book (Koran), and a common language (Arabic). The religious community would be united under God's law as revealed to Muhammad. The followers of Islam everywhere were to be united, including those "subjugated brethren" in Europe who had failed to win the continent for Islam. The idea of pan-unity was promoted despite the political rivalries and despite the sectarian differences between Sunnites and Shi'ites.

Still another form of macro-nationalism was geographically oriented and continental in shape. Here the goal was to supersede the nation-state and organize, instead, a supranational order based on a common continental territory. In the process there was much linguistic and cultural confusion. Behind the continental macro-nationalisms was the concept of a super-territorial imperative. The problem was that geographical boundaries had already been frozen in the formation of national states. Changes could be made only by war and conquest, and the prospect of achieving a continent-wide unity was dim. An example is the Common Market in Europe, by which the continental nations agreed to economic union for the benefit of each member. However, the problem of extending the economic unity into a European political sovereignty did not attract much support in the Common Market. Not one of its members was inclined to relinquish its national sovereignty. Action stopped at this point. (*See* **PAN-EUROPA**.)

Nationalism writ large has not won its way to dominance in the contemporary world of fixed nationalisms. All have been unsuccessful in the goal of larger unity. Both Pan-Germanism and Pan-Slavism were weakened after the two World Wars. Pan-Arabism lost its thrust because of the fierce rivalries between individual Arab states: the Islamic religion was not enough to overcome political confrontations. In Africa, Pan-Africanism was limited to annual meetings at which the idea was praised, but it had to face the reality of tribal as well as new national rivalries. Intellectuals in Latin America preached the value of Pan-Americanism, but were never able to overcome the hate-the-Yankee complex. Peoples on all the continents preferred their own flags and anthems rather than a dubious continental unity.

This decline in the strength of the macro-nationalisms does not mean that the idea has disappeared. It persists in one form or another. Small intellectual groups still believe that the formation of larger unions of peoples will be a giant step in the brotherhood of man in an overcrowded planet. Nationalism, not macro-nationalisms or mini-nationalisms, remains the preferred idea in the contemporary world. The result has been continued wars with conventional weapons among peoples who are taught to believe that their greatest loyalty is to their own countries and that the duty to defend the nation takes priority over all other loyalties.

Bibliography: Louis L. Snyder, *Macro-Nationalisms: A History of the Pan-Movements* (Westport, Conn., 1984).

MAGYAR DIASPORA NATIONALISM.   Diaspora nationalism (q.v.) refers specifically to the mini-nationalism of a people dispersed inside the borders of a multi-national society and who demand either more autonomy or independence. An example is the case of the Magyars included against their will into the new Czechoslovak state after World War I.

By the postwar Treaty of Neuilly, three million Magyars were transferred from defeated Hungary and placed in three successor states—Czechoslovakia, Rumania, and Yugoslavia. Some 700,000 of these displaced Magyars were made citizens of the eastern province of Slovakia. Reacting bitterly against what they saw as a hostile environment, they resisted assimilation into a "foreign" nation. Magyars made certain to retain their own language, culture, folklore, customs, and traditions—the usual procedure of a suppressed nationality. It was *déjà vu*—the old story of a mini-nationalism flourishing in a dominant nationalism intent on absorbing it.

Magyars founded societies to maintain their own language. They opposed intrusion of Slavic or German words or phraseology. They produced books, newspapers, and literary gazettes to preserve their language, a Hungarian speech of the Finno-Ugric family. With no Magyar university, they created cultural and scholarly organizations as substitutes. They complained of political and economic exploitation—the cry of mini-nationalists everywhere. Politically, they saw themselves as second-class citizens in an unsympathetic state. Economically, they believed that they were treated poorly: in the era of industrialization, they claimed that they were pushed into agriculture. In the past they had been subjected to a variety of influences, including Turkish and German. They resented the new domination. Their sense of national consciousness was never quenched after their dispersion into the new Czechoslovak state.

Magyar nationalism reveals that both communist and capitalist states have their own problems with dissatisfied minorities. The dominant Slovaks insist that Magyars should yield to the centralized state, that in a Marxist society all antagonisms must cease, and that all subjected nationalities must operate on a class basis. Recalcitrant Magyars were warned that their own nationalism was an insane dream and that it was regarded as treason. As in anything connected with nationalism, all decisions concerning regionalism versus centralism were based on force and power.

Bibliography. Kalman Janics, "Czechoslovakia's Magyar Minority: An Example of Diaspora Nationalism," *Canadian Review of Studies in Nationalism*, 3, No. 1 (Autumn, 1975), 22–44; Vermes Gabor, *The Liberal Vision and Conservative Statecraft of a Magyar Nationalist* (New York, 1985).

MANIFEST DESTINY. *See* SULLIVAN, JOHN LOUIS.

MANZONI, ALESSANDRO (1785–1873). Italian poet, novelist, and patriot, who helped give direction to his country's national awakening (*Risorgimento* - Resurrection). While a young man, Manzoni was taken by his mother to Paris, where he was influenced by the prevalent deism. He later changed his mind and became a passionate advocate of Roman Catholicism. His historical novel, *I promessi sposi (The Betrothed)* (3 vols., 1825–1827), noted for its clear and dignified style, was a Milanese story of the seventeenth century. It brought him national and European fame. This masterpiece, especially its patriotic tenor, has remained one of Italy's most popular romances. More than 100 editions were published, and it was widely translated.

Influenced by his fellow countryman Vittorio Alfieri (q.v.), Manzoni became a leader of the Italian Romantic movement. His masterly form is judged to be a classic of pure Tuscan prose, important in the development of a consistent Italian style of writing. On his death he was given a state funeral as one of his country's great literary figures. Verdi's *Requiem* was composed in his honor.

Bibliography: Barbara Reynolds, *The Linguistic Writings of Alessandro Manzoni* (Cambridge, Eng., 1950); Umberto Manzoni, *Alessandro Manzoni* (Rome, 1985); Sante Matteo and Larry H. Peer, *The Reasonable Romantic: Essays on Alessandro Manzoni* (New York, 1986).

MAO TSE-TUNG (1893–1976). Chinese Communist dictator, leader in the Communist world after the death of Stalin in 1953, and strong apostle of Chinese nationalism. Born of a well-to-do farmer's family in Hunan province, he studied the Confucian classics at an early age and later went to Peking University. Here he became well-versed in Western philosophy and Marxism. He was elected as a Communist representative to the first national congress of the *Kuomintang* (Nationalist Party) held in Canton in January, 1924. After the Kuomintang-Communist split in 1927, Mao led the disastrous "Autumn Crop Uprising" in Hunan, for which he was dropped from the central committee of the Party. For the next several years he worked in the Chinese hinterlands, setting up Soviets and helping build the Red Army. He responded to Chiang Kai-shek's (q.v.) grand purge by organizing workers' uprisings in the big cities. In 1931 he was elected chairman of the Soviet Republic of China.

When Chiang began another of his "Extermination of Bandits," meaning Communists, Mao in 1934–1935 led the Red Army on the famous "Long March" from Kiangsi Province north to Yenan in Shensi Province. In 1935 he was elected chairman of the Chinese Communist Party. After the start of World War II, he published his treatise, *On New Democracy* (1940), in which he described in detail his plans for the economic, political, and cultural reconstruction of a new Communist China after the war. He continued his civil war with Chiang and the *Kuomintang* while at the same time fighting the Japanese invaders. In 1949, after his troops had taken most of mainland China, Mao was made chairman of the central governmental council of the newly established People's Republic of China. He was re-elected to this post in 1959.

In theory a democratic state, Mao's China was actually under his totalitarian rule. The Chinese Communist Party was his propagandizing element. He learned much from the experience in the Soviet Union—secret police, mass arrests, forced labor, brainwashing, elimination of enemies—all the familiar practices of Stalin's Russia. The entire Chinese society was communized according to the gospel of Mao. The leader was intent on transforming the country from an agricultural economy to an industrial power. Mao's first Five-Year Plan (1949–1952) was designed to rehabilitate the economy and, at the same time, redistribute land to the peasants, for whom he planned an important role. Millions of acres were taken forcibly from landlords and given to some 300 million peasants. Mao pursued his task persistently and ruthlessly. Landlords were publicly humiliated and then executed. Meanwhile, there were substantial advances in industrialization, especially in the output of coal, iron ore, and steel.

Mao started a bloody campaign against "counterrevolutionaries," a category which included anyone he suspected of being an enemy. He held public trials of "class enemies," designated as traitors. Spectators gave the verdict: "Kill! Kill!" Those accused were executed or sent to jail, their property confiscated.

When Soviet Premier Nikita Krushchev announced that there were "different roads to socialism," Mao began a movement of a new type of rule. "Let a hundred flowers bloom, let a hundred schools of thought contend." Those who were dissatisfied with the way communism was going in China believed that they were now encouraged to speak freely. Some intellectuals began to question China's close alliance with Soviet Russia. The "hundred flowers" became weeds as the critics were denounced and punished. Some were sent to labor camps, others committed suicide. Mao's rule became more oppressive than ever.

Mao's second Five–Year Plan, inaugurated in 1958, was designated the "Great Leap Forward." Because industry was outstripping agriculture, Mao decided to revolutionize agriculture by a great collectivization drive. Land recently given to farmers was simply expropriated. The peasants, in stages, were forced to join cooperatives, which paid them for the use of their land and labor. Millions of peasants were herded into 24,000 communes of 5,000 families. Each commune was supposed to cultivate some 10,000 acres. The work was organized along military lines with squads of peasants marching to and from work each day. The entire life of the farmers was organized from cradle to grave. Babies were sent to nurseries, senior citizens to "happy homes for the aged."

Mao's "Great Leap Forward" collapsed ignominiously by 1961. He blamed the failure on flood and drought, but certainly a contributory factor was peasant rebellion against the exhausting work loads and the impossibly high standards set for the communes.

From 1966 to 1969 Mao introduced what he called the "Great Proletarian Cultural Movement," a gigantic new form of political action. He identified himself thoroughly with this new upheaval designed to transform the whole spirit and structure of Chinese society. He would promote ideas simple enough to be understood by the people. But this possibly well-intended goal to increase the general level of education and culture was accompanied by simple-minded violence. Mao's followers pursued the "Cultural Revolution" by humiliating and attacking intellectuals, especially scientific experts whose skills even Mao had announced as essential to national progress. Later regimes tried to remedy the damage by reversing the ill-conceived "Cultural Revolution." Mao, himself, died in Peking on September 9, 1976.

Mao's concept of nationalism was most important for the development of the Chinese Communist state. In a sense, he recapitulated the experience of dictator Stalin. Original Marxist theory leaned toward internationalism ("Workers of the world unite! You have nothing to lose but your chains!"). Nationalism was denounced as a bourgeois phenomenon. But Stalin opted for it and saw that Leon Trotsky and his global internationalism were eliminated. Mao followed the same path.

Like Sun Yat-sen and Chiang Kai-shek (qq.v.), Mao preached the virtues of nationalism. As his predecessors, he called for a great independent, unified, and strong China. In stating his goals, Sun placed nationalism first in his Three Principles—nationalism, democracy, and livelihood. Mao presented a similar formula, again with nationalism first. He ordered his Young Pioneer Corps to be inculcated with the "five loves"—Fatherland, people, labor, science, and public property. To win power in a chaotic China, he made effective use of nationalist appeals. As early as 1939 he urged his followers: "Chinese Communists must combine patriotism with internationalism. For only by fighting in defense of the motherland can we achieve national liberation, and thus by victory help peoples of other countries." For this somewhat artificial regard for internationalism and "the peoples of other countries," Mao dropped pragmatism in favor of the mighty force of nationalism.

To what extent the "Great Leap Forward" and the "Cultural Revolution" helped to solve his country's woes is open to question. However, rightly or wrongly, they stand as landmarks in Chinese history.

Bibliography: Mao Tse-tung, *Selected Works* (Peking, 1967); Stuart R. Schram, *Mao Tse-tung* (London, 1967); Raymond F. Wylie, *The Emergence of Maoism* (Stanford, 1980); Eric Chou, *Mao Tse-tung: The Man and the Myth* (New York, 1982).

MARGINAL NATIONALISM. *See* **NATIONALISM, CLASSIFICATIONS OF.**

MARTÍ, JOSÉ (1853–1895). Cuban poet, essayist, nationalist, and symbol of Cuba's struggle for independence from Spain. As a nationalist, Martí unified the movement for Cuban independence. Exiled from both Cuba and Spain, he wrote newspaper articles, poetry, and essays, all on themes of nationalism, patriotism, and freedom. His strongly sensitive poetry and prose made him famous throughout South America. In early 1895 he accompanied a group of revolutionaries on an invasion of Cuba. He died there on May 19 in a battle on the plains of Dos Rios. His dedication to the cause of Cuban nationalism won him a reputation in all South America as a martyr for freedom.

Bibliography: John M. Kirk, *José Martí: Mentor of the Cuban Nation* (Tampa, Fla., 1973); Peter Turton, *José Martí: Architect of Cuba's Freedom* (London, 1986); Christopher Abel and Nissa Torrents, *José Martí* (Durham, N.C., 1986).

MAU MAU.   Terrorists in Kenya who began their campaign in 1952 for independence. (*See* **KENYATTA, JOMO.**)

MAURRAS, CHARLES (1868–1952).   French journalist, political theorist, and major intellectual influence on the idea of integral nationalism. (*See* **HAYES' CLASSIFICATION.**) In 1899 Maurras was one of the founders of *L'Action Française* (q.v.), a journal which claimed to represent the interests of France. In 1909, with the assistance of fellow polemicist Léon Daudet (q.v.), he changed the journal into a daily newspaper, with its columns devoted to nationalism and advocacy of royalty. For decades the paper promoted public demonstrations and riots. It was the object of many lawsuits.

In his newspaper Maurras defined integral nationalism as "the exclusive pursuit of national policies, the absolute maintenance of national integrity, and the steady increase of national power—for a nation declines when it loses military might." He saw integral nationalism as making the nation not a means to humanity, but an end in itself. He deprecated cooperation with other nations, and always spoke of the glories of France.

During the German occupation of France in World War II, Maurras supported the Pétain government, which was subservient to Hitler. In January, 1945, he was arrested and deprived of his membership in the *Académie Française*, to which he had been elected in 1938. He was released on grounds of health in 1952.

Bibliography: Michael Sutton, *Nationalism, Positivism, and Catholicism* (New York, 1982); Bertrand Renouvin, *Charles Maurras: L'Action française et la question sozial* (Paris, 1983).

MAZZINI, GIUSEPPE (1805–1872).   Italian patriot and champion of liberal nationalism. Young Italians were not discouraged by the repeated failures of the *Carbonari* (charcoal burners) (q.v.), who had been leaders of the new Italian nationalism. Among them was the twenty-five-year old Mazzini, who had joined the *Carbonari* in 1830. While living in Marseilles, he organized a new league, which he called Young Italy. He aimed to attract well-educated young men of liberal leanings for whom national unification was a holy cause.

Organizing, agitating, and educating, young Mazzini worked zealously to awaken his countrymen to the need for unity. He continued his work despite a sentence of death recorded against him in Sardinian courts. In 1837 he continued his exile in London. Nothing mattered to him except what he saw as his holy cause. He never married. He worked day and night meeting people, consulting with revolutionaries, collecting money, and making speeches for Italian national unity. He loved Italy above all earthly things. "A nation," he said, "which has been enslaved for centuries, can regenerate itself through virtue and sacrifice." He urged Italian youth to take the lead in the country's regeneration: "Place the youth of the nation at the head of the insurgent masses: there are latent strength and magic in these young men."

In his ideal state, Mazzini saw no factions or parties. His special contribution to the unification of Italy was the manner in which, by his idealism, he vitalized the struggling aspirations of the Italians. Yet, the future of Italian unification lay not with the national idealist Mazzini but with the Piedmontese monarchy and its greatest statesman Count Camillo Cavour (q.v.).

A strong historical controversy surrounds the roles of Mazzini and Cavour—Mazzini's radicalism versus Cavour's moderation, and the effectiveness of their approaches to national unity. Both leaders were nationalists, but they differed in their attitudes toward liberalism. Mazzini's vision of a united Italy was republican and democratic. British historian William Clarke praised Mazzini's lofty idealism, religious spirit, and his insistence on duty rather than rights. Other historians were not as impressed with Mazzini's nationalism. They saw his aims as idealistic dreaming and pointed to Cavour as the more successful nationalist, more statesman than thinker, more man of affairs than idealist.

Bibliography: Gaetano Salvemini, *Mazzini*, trans. from the Italian by I. M. Ranson (London, 1956); Edyth Hinkley, *Mazzini: The Story of a Great Italian* (Port Washington, N.Y., 1970); Gwilym O. Griffith, *Mazzini: Prophet of Modern Europe* (New York, 1970).

MEANING OF NATIONALISM.   *See* **NATIONALISM, MEANING OF.**

MESSIANIC NATIONALISM.   A combination of personal beliefs and political nationalism, by which one people sees itself as destined to bring to the entire world the superior attributes of its own national soul. It reflects a combination of soil and soul—the worship of the soil of the native land as well as its great national soul. It expects to retain mastery of its own territory and, at the same time, give lesser peoples the benefit of its outstanding national qualities. In some respects, messianic nationalism is the equivalent of integral nationalism and its aggressive ideology. It holds that the Fatherland or Motherland represents all that is good in human life. The nationalists of a people, proud of their superiority (which should be obvious to all the world), will graciously extend the benefits of their own superior culture and civilization to more unfortunate lesser peoples.

The most vociferous advocates of messianic nationalism appeared in the Russian Empire during the nineteenth century. In the early part of the century, Russian nationalism emerged as a concomitant of the continent-wide Romanticism. It was compounded of two seemingly diverse elements. One was the desire of Russian Westerners who looked to the West for inspiration and sought to emulate all aspects of Western society. The second was a violent, compensatory Slavic nationalism characterized by a belief in Russia's "mission" to rule the world. Where the Westerners, inspired by the Enlightenment and the ideals of liberty, equality, and fraternity, hoped to turn Russian nationalism in the direction of Herder's (q.v.) cultural nationalism, the Slavophiles hewed to their own version of Hegelianism. They borrowed from Hegel (q.v.) everything connected with "national predestination," or the mission of world leadership. Similar to Germanophilism, it feared revolutionary contagion. The deeper this fear penetrated, the coarser and more offensive Russian messianic nationalism became. Russia, it was claimed, had been spared the cancer of rationalism. But the young, virile, promising Slavs were destined to surpass the decadent and senile West. Where Western Europeans were on the road to decline, the fresh and vigorous young Slavs of Russia "have a great mission to fulfill." The victorious Russians would bring their superior culture and civilization to peoples just waiting for the global triumph of the Russian spirit.

Other nationalisms were not especially impressed by the claims of Slavophile messianism. They ridiculed Russian pretensions as expressions of a national inferiority complex, not as the existence of a great society anxious to bring its benefits to inferior peoples. (*See also* **RUSSIAN NATIONALISM, and PAN-SLAVISM.**)

Bibliography: Hans Kohn, *Nationalism in the Soviet Union*, trans. from the German by E. W. Eickes (New York, 1933); Hans Kohn, *Pan-Slavism: Its History and Ideology* (Notre Dame, Ind., 1953).

MICKIEWICZ, ADAM (1798–1855).   Poland's greatest poet and a lifelong advocate of Polish national emancipation. From the three partitions of Poland in the late eighteenth century (1772, 1793, and 1795) to the close of World War I, Polish nationalism had no territorial base. There was, however, a strong Polish nationalism and Mickiewicz was its most eloquent apostle. In 1817, at the University of Vilna, he joined the Philomaths (Friends of Learning), a secret patriotic society that called for Polish freedom. In 1824, after imprisonment for Pan-Polish activities, he was deported to Russia and was never allowed to return to his homeland. After serving as Professor of Literature at Lausanne and Paris, he took part in the revolutionary upheavals of 1848. In Constantinople during the Crimean War, he organized a Polish legion to be used against Russia, but died there of cholera.

Mickiewicz's poetry was imbued with the spirit of emancipation as well as with the national melancholy of a people who wanted their freedom. Expressing the views of Western Romanticism, it contributed powerfully to the existence of Polish nationalism at a time when the country was under foreign influence. While in Paris in 1832 he wrote, in biblical prose, *The Books of the Polish Nation and of a Polish Pilgrimage*, which helped to keep alive the consciousness of Polish nationalism. Enormously popular in his own country, he received global recognition for his art.

Bibliography: Adam Mickiewicz, *Forefathers*, trans. from the Polish by Count Potocki (London, 1945–1946); Adam Mickiewicz, *New Selected Poems*, trans. by Louis Bogan, *et al.* (New York, 1957); Maria Dernalowicz, *Adam Mickiewicz*, trans. from the Polish into English by Halina Filipowicz (Warsaw, 1981).

MILL, JOHN STUART (1806–1873). Philosopher, economist, and founder of the Utilitarian movement. Mill held that systems of laws and morals should promote "the greatest happiness of the greatest number." He believed that education is the cure for all evils and that rational argument can convince humanity in the long run of what is good. He held that nationalism, especially in its exclusive form, was barbaric. "Nationalism makes men indifferent to the rights and interests of any portion of the human species, save that which is called by the same name and speaks the same language." While he opposed the absolute application of the principle of national self-determination, he, nevertheless, became one of the most important promoters of this doctrine in England.

In his *Considerations on Representative Government* (1861), Mill wrote a famous Chapter 16 titled "Of Nationality as Connected with Representative Government." In this chapter he identified nationality and state and called for independence for the nation-state. He believed it to be a necessary condition of free institutions that the boundaries of government should coincide in the main with those of nationalities. This became a basic theme of nineteenth- and twentieth-century liberalism.

Bibliography: John Stuart Mill, *Considerations on Representative Government* (London, 1861).

MINI-NATIONALISMS.   Under political control of larger nationalisms, mini-nationalisms are supported by those dissatisfied peoples who want either more autonomy inside the structure of the national state or demand independence. They are sometimes identified as regionalisms, separatisms, or ethnic groups. The people belonging to a mini-nationalism generally see themselves as bound together by history, traditions, customs, language, perhaps religion, and believe themselves to have been incorporated unjustly into the territory of a more powerful state. People of moderate bent are willing to remain under the political control of those they regard as foreigners, provided they are given a measure of autonomy, the power or right of a certain amount of self-government. The people of Wales and Scotland take this moderate position. There are also those of revolutionary zeal who see their status as completely unfair and unreasonable and who opt for independence. Where the moderates turn to negotiation, the radicals choose bullets and bombs to enforce their demands. The Basques in Spain and the Croats in Yugoslavia are examples of the mini-nationalists who seek freedom from the centralized state by the use of extremist force.

The political units that are called modern states are held together by the cement of nationalism, which has many faces. As national states were formed in the modern era, the drive for unification almost invariably brought diverse peoples together in a nationalist mold. These were often peoples of different languages and varied cultures. They were required to accept the domination of a central authority, and they were expected to endure assimilation designed to strengthen the central authority. This was one vital trend in the construction of a larger nationalism. Added to it was a reverse movement toward disruption as the mini-nationalism emerged to demand its own special rights. These dissatisfied groups, holding a developing nationalism of their own, were banded into the framework of the national state. They either accepted their status or began to agitate for their own smaller nationalism.

Thus, a mini-nationalism is a little nationalism under the control of a larger nationalism. It is the sentiment of a people who see themselves as distinct and would prefer their own state or union with another state that they regard as having a similar history. They see themselves as held in bondage by "foreigners" against their will. They point to their own historical, linguistic, cultural, religious, and psychological ties, and believe that they are, in a combination of several of these factors, different enough to warrant emancipation from the larger nationalism. In other words, a mini-nationalism may be regarded as a nationalism that has not yet come of age. In this sense, a small or a substantially large minority inside the existing state may seek the status of a separate state. It may call for freedom from an "alien nationalism" and for the territory that it believes to be necessary for the formation of a new and independent national state.

For an already established national state composed of many different nationalities, the call by mini-nationalists for freedom presents a problem of critical importance. For example, the Soviet Union, with its multiple nationalities, regards this effort to obtain freedom as simple treason, and treats it with that designation in mind. For the Kremlin, one successful mini-nationalism would result in the domino-like effect leading to the dismemberment of the national state. For that reason the Armenians, or Latvians, Lithuanians, and Estonians were held rigidly to the central authority and allowed little autonomy and certainly no independence. (*See* **RUSSIAN NATIONALISM.**) In recent years there has been an upsurge in the demand of such mini-nationalisms for independence. (*See* **BALTIC NATIONALISMS.**)

Mini-nationalisms come into existence when a small group of local patriots begin to see themselves as a distinct nationality. They regard themselves as liberators, who point to the past of their people as reason enough to make demands on the central state. They hammer away at the claim that their linguistic aspirations have been denied in an alien society. They would have their own nation with its distinctive flag and their own national anthem. They denounce their fellow citizens as mired in apathy, indifference, or too mild support. They see themselves as chosen by destiny to lead their people out of enforced subjugation. If the process seems too slow, they turn to violence in the belief that assassinations and bombings are much more effective than words in the struggle for independence.

Thus, for the extreme mini-nationalist, the power principle is all important. He regards being controlled by a centralized authority as a violation of his rights, and he is determined to push his claims to the limit. He knows that there is no outside force able to mediate between centralization and decentralization, between the state authority and dissatisfied regionalists. He believes that any effort by such an organization as the United Nations would be deemed as interference in the internal affairs of a sovereign state. Therefore, he uses the force of his own followers to achieve what he believes to be in the best interests of his people.

Mini-nationalisms may vary in type. National minorities in older nations may feel that they have been left behind in the nation-making process (Scots in Britain, Armenians in the Soviet Union). Others may be dissatisfied in several nations and struggle for early independence (Kurds in Iraq, Iran, and Turkey). There may be unfulfilled communities that see themselves as vestiges of an independence movement or they may be separatists who want to be another nation (*Québeçois* in Canada). All such varying types want their aspirations to be recognized.

The phenomenon is global. In both the established nations and in new nations, minorities have been forced into subjugation. Following the collapse of great empires after World War I and World War II, dozens of new nations emerged. An upsurge of nationalism was to be expected as these new nations were consolidated and formed their own governments. There was no set pattern in this development: new boundaries were fixed with little or no regard for the diverse peoples inside them. Africans and Asians who had learned nationalism from their former suppressors, began to form their own process of territorialization. They put peoples of differing backgrounds together as they fashioned their national states. This was by no means a diffusion from European experience, but it was actually political parallelism.

To establish states, mini-nationalisms present a danger. Propaganda by separatist factions, far from diminishing in recent years, has increased. Separatists usually work inside the larger state, but there has begun a wide international movement. French historian Charles Seignobos suggested "a syndicate of little discontented nations," which would be set up in Paris. Eventually, several European mini-nationalists established in 1975 a small bureau with headquarters in Brussels. Whether or not this organization intended to handle the claims of regionalists as well as small nations is not altogether clear. In any event, its work has been ineffective. Disaffected small nationalisms remain everywhere throughout the world, from Sri Lanka to Spain.

Bibliography: Louis L. Snyder, *Global Mini-Nationalisms: Autonomy or Independence* (Westport, Conn., 1982): Colin H. Williams (ed.), *National Separatism* (London, 1982).

MINORITIES NATIONALISM. *See* **NATIONALISM, CLASSIFICATIONS OF.**

MISHIMA, YUKIO (pseudonym of KIMITAKE HIRAOKA, 1920–1970). Flamboyant Japanese poet, novelist, and supranationalist, destined to die tragically in a public ritual suicide. The son of a high civil servant, Mishima failed to qualify for service in World War II, which led him to a frenetic course of body-building. Devoting his energy to writing, he produced a total of thirty-six volumes, in which he discussed the themes of homosexuality, blood, death, suicide, nationalism, and rejection of the sterility of modern life. In 1960 he wrote a short story, "Patriotism," in which he glorified *hara kiri* (ritual suicide). Five years later he made a film of the story, in which he took the part of the hero, an army lieutenant who disemboweled himself. Politically, he was an agitator who resorted to violence to attain his goals.

The nature of nationalism in Japan both before and during World War II had been demonstrated by the tradition of the Japanese military to fight to the death before ignominious surrender. In the late days of the war, *kamikaze* pilots, drinking their last toast to the Emperor, went willingly to their deaths by crashing their bomb-loaded planes into American warships. Only the ultimate weapon of the atomic bombs, released on Hiroshima and Nagasaki by angered Americans who remembered Pearl Harbor, brought an end to Japanese militarism and ultranationalism.

Japanese militarists who brought their country into the war were governed by the code of *bushido*, the conduct of the *samurai* of feudal Japan, emphasizing loyalty, courage, plain living, and preferring suicide to dishonor. Intellectuals in postwar Japan disowned the military and turned their attention from aggressive nationalism to the goal of conquering the world through economics. Mishima endorsed the system of Emperor worship. Militarists had led the country into a futile war and had cost it a heavy toll of dead and a devastated homeland. Mishima tried to steer Japan back into the path of militarism, restore the Emperor to his "position of honor," and revise the Constitution to sanctify the role of the *jietai*, the armed forces.

Promoting the old Japanese art of *karate*, a system of self-defense characterized by delivering chopping blows with the open hand, and also swordsmanship, Mishima built a private army of students. Calling it the *Tatenokai* ("Shield Society"), he aimed to preserve the martial spirit and assist the armed forces in the event of an uprising by the Communists. For his one hundred members ("the smallest army in the world"), Mishima composed a stirring poem:

> The proud crest on our helmets
> Is the shield that we bear—
> To protect our loved Emperor
> From the storms of the night.
> The red glimmer of daybreak
> On our warriors' fresh cheeks
> Is the color that glitters
> On our Flag of Great Truth.
> From the night's dark corruption
> We bright youths have leapt up
> To march gallantly onward
> With our shield to the fore!

On November 25, 1970, Mishima, leading his student followers, seized control of the commanding general's office at the military headquarters near downtown Tokyo. In a ten-minute dramatic speech from the balcony to a thousand assembled servicemen, he expressed his views on nationalism to a jeering audience:

> The Japanese people today think of money, just money. Where is our national spirit today? The politicians care nothing for Japan. They are greedy for power. . . .
> We thought that the *jietai* was the soul of national honor. . . .
> The nation has no spiritual foundation. . . .
> You must protect Japan! To protect Japan! Yes, to protect Japan! Japanese tradition! Our history! Our culture! The Emperor! . . . *Tenno Heika Banzai!* ("Long Live the Emperor!")

The frenzied orator was greeted with cries of *"Bakayaro"* (an untranslatable swearword), "madman," "Shut up!" Mishima retired to an office, where he disemboweled himself with his sword. He was then decapitated by one of his student followers.

The career of Mishima is a classic example of nationalism gone berserk. The only psychologist who examined him, a Dr. Kataguchi, subjected him to Rorschach ink-blot tests eight years before his death. After Mishima's suicide, Dr. Kataguchi wrote an article describing Mishima as paranoid, psychopathic, and schizophrenic.

Bibliography: Henry Scott-Stokes, *The Life and Death of Yukio Mishima* (New York, 1974); John Nathan, *Mishima: A Biography* (Boston, 1974); Yukio Mishima, *The Way of the Samurai,* trans. by Kathryn Sparling (New York, 1977).

MONTESQUIEU, CHARLES DE SECONDAT, BARON DE LA BRÈDE
(1689–1755). *Philosophe* of the French Enlightenment, historian, and precursor of French nationalism. For twenty years he worked on his book *L'Esprit des lois (The Spirit of the Laws)*, which appeared in 1748, and which is considered to be one of the most important works of the eighteenth century. He surveyed every political system, ancient and modern, examined the principles and defects of each one, and concluded that English constitutionalism should be the model for all countries. He indicated a strong distaste for despotism, which called for the rule of one man according to his will or caprice and promoting fear among the people.

Montesquieu contrasted the despotic state with a popular, democratic one. In a democracy, he wrote, everything depends upon the political virtues of the people. When a democracy loses its sense of cohesion, its patriotism, its frugality, and its passion for equality, it is soon destroyed. The principle of democracy may grow corrupt, not only when a people loses its spirit of equality, but also when this sentiment of equality becomes excessive, with each man desiring to be the equal of those whom he has chosen to rule over him.

High on his agenda of national necessities, Montesquieu placed not only the republican form of government but also love of country. In republics, he wrote, the proper system of education should inspire a noble sentiment, "namely that disregard of one's own interest whence arises love of one's own country." "A government is like everything else; to preserve it we must love it." Montesquieu's pleas for popular government and French patriotism were effective in setting the future tone of French nationalism.

Bibliography: Baron de Montesquieu, *The Spirit of the Laws*, trans. from the French by Thomas Nugent (New York, 1900); Louis Desgraves, *Montesquieu* (Paris, 1986); Judith N. Sklar, *Montesquieu* (New York, 1987).

MORGENTHAU, HANS J. (1904–1980). Professor of Political Science and Modern European History, Morgenthau was born in Colburg, Germany, on February 17, 1904. After studies at the Universities of Berlin, Munich, and Frankfurt, he received his doctorate *summa cum laude* at Frankfurt. He came to the United States in 1937 and was naturalized in 1943. He taught international law at Frankfurt and Madrid, and political science at the University of Kansas and Brooklyn. He then transferred to the University of Chicago, where in 1963 he was appointed Albert A. Michelson Distinguished Service Professor of Political Science and Modern History. In 1968 he became

Leonard Davis Distinguished Professor of Political Science at the City University of New York, where he remained until his retirement.

A prolific scholar, writer, and activist, Morgenthau produced many books in his specialty. As a political scientist, he was concerned with nationalism and contributed much to its study. He believed that a new regionalism might possibly remedy the damage done by nationalism in the modern era. (*See* **REGIONALISM.**) He also contributed a unique view of a striking incongruity in nationalism. (*See* **THE A-B-C PARADOX.**)

Bibliography: Hans J. Morgenthau, *Politics Among Nations* (New York, 1948, 1978); *In Defense of the National Interest* (New York, 1951); *Politics in the Twentieth Century* (3 vols., New York, 1962); *Truth and Power* (New York, 1970).

M.P.L.A. (Popular Movement for the Liberation of Angola).   A Marxist group, led by Agostinho Neto, it received financial support from the Soviet Union, Cuba, and East Germany. (*See also* **U.N.I.T.A.**)

MÖSER, JUSTUS (1720–1794)   Publicist, statesman, who was posthumously awarded the veneration accorded the early prophets of German nationalism. Born in the small bishopric of Osnabrück in northwestern Germany, Möser turned to a political career as *advocatus patriae*, or state's attorney, and held other legal posts. A patriot, he devoted his research to his local homeland. He raised his voice against the cosmopolitan spirit of the Enlightenment, the Age of Reason. He agreed with Voltaire and other French rationalists that the writing of history should seek to further the welfare of the State, but he differed from them on the means to be used. Voltaire saw the salvation of the State in enlightened monarchy and, therefore, denounced the common herd as ignorant and damned by fanaticism. On the other hand, Möser took the opposing view that the prosperity of the State hinged not on a strong central government but on the freedom and security of the common landowner.

Möser also differed from Jean-Jacques Rousseau (q.v.). Where Rousseau thought in terms of a reversion to nature, he, nevertheless, recognized the evidence of urban and cosmopolitan trends as the well of civilization. Möser, on the contrary, saw in rural life the greatest possible stimulant to national strength. Where Rousseau looked to the Greek city-states for inspiration, Möser found the vital source for the great German nation in the rural life of the Middle Ages. In Möser's view, the common people knew better than the bureaucrat what is useful for them: "I notice that the farmer invents useful discoveries quickly enough when he needs them, and that one complains unjustly when he accuses them of preferring long experiences in doubtful proposals."

Möser had little regard for either princes or feudal lords. He saw in their triumph the destruction of the old freedom of the rural landowners as well as the city dwellers. He censured the German princes for their shortsighted particularism and blamed them for obstructing the development in the Germanies of a constitutional liberal state as in England. He denounced both the theory and practice of despotism and pleaded for a national organic development of the State instead of arbitrary laws imposed from above. He warned that it was of critical importance that the impetus for a strong, healthy State must come from the people, not in an egalitarian sense, but from the people organized as in the old estates and classes. It was important, he said, that the country must utilize the powerful roots of the past that had been withered by unthinking despots, selfish princes, and stupid bureaucrats.

As historian, Möser wrote not only the first German constitutional and administrative history, but for the first time he introduced the new field of social history. Until he appeared on the German scene, the writing of history had been concerned soley with kings, courts, and battles. For the first time in the Germanies he turned his scholarly attention to people, institutions, and the effects of social relationships upon historical development. Investigating political, military, legal, and social problems within a large framework, he gave direction to future German historians. Many nineteenth-century German historians followed Möser's lead, isolating and investigating many points he had made in his published works. Most important, he was among the early German historians who pointed to traditional German values in an age of political chaos and exaggerated worship of French culture. Those Germans who had thought in terms of a vague, mystical past were influenced by Möser to see real and positive values in their own past. This was, indeed, the essence of German nationalism—it was also Möser's contribution to the meaning of German nationalism.

As a small-town official, Möser saw the salvation of the German nation in its healthy, rural freeholders. "Such a man," wrote Hans Kohn about Möser, "could grow up only in the principality of Osnabrück, one of the many curiosities of the 'monstrous' empire, in which the contradictions of periods, classes, and religion mingled freely. He hated despotism, centralization, and bureaucracy; he loved independence and individual dignity; he had a clear understanding of the period of the Enlightenment in the intellectual field, but none for the political and economic changes of the epoch. He highly esteemed old things because they were old."

Bibliography: Justus Möser, *Sämtliche Werke* (10 vols., Berlin, 1842–1844); Robert R. Ergang, "Möser and the Rise of National Thought in Germany," *Journal of Modern History*, 5 (June, 1933), 172–196; W. J. Bossenbrook, "Justus Möser's Approach to History," *Medieval and Historiographical Essays in Honor of James Westfall Thompson* (Chicago, 1938), 397 ff.; Hans Kohn, *The Idea of Nationalism: A Study of Its Origins and Background* (New York, 1944, 1960).

MUSIC AND NATIONALISM.   Nationalism penetrated into the arts—literature, painting, sculpture, architecture, and music. Virtually all artistic endeavors were devoted to what was believed to be the national culture. Nationalist sentiment may be noted perhaps more in music than in the other arts. In general, music was supposed to be an international language cutting across national boundaries, but more often composers are regarded as representatives of their nationality and they see themselves as such. Biographers stress the love of great composers for their country, their consciousness of nationalism, and their fervent patriotism.

Italian composer Giuseppi Verdi (1813–1901), an artist of the first rank who transformed opera into great music-drama, was credited with expressing the very soul of the Italian people. He became the spokesman for Italian national aspirations: his early operas were specifically designed to defend Italian nationalism against Austrian domination. Verdi's name became a national acrostic for *Vittorio Emmanuele Re D'Italia*, King of Sardinia, who became the monarch of an independent Italy.

Similarly, Frédéric Chopin (1810–1849), one of music's greatest tone poets, was inspired by a strong nationalist sentiment. Though his great piano works are played everywhere, he has always been known as a "Polish" composer. As a young man, he became interested in Polish folk music, especially the mazurkas sung by peasants; later in his short life these mazurkas and polonaises were inspired by his nationalist feeling.

The Romantic interest in folk music undoubtedly stimulated nationalist tendencies in music. Throughout the nineteenth century, traditional native folk materials were injected into the general framework of musical Romanticism. Antonin Dvořák (1841–1904), Czech composer and patriot, won global recognition, along with Bedrich Smetana (1824–1884), as a founder of the Bohemian nationalist movement. Smetana's music, characteristically Bohemian, revealed the composer's deep love for his homeland. His *Slavonic Dances* (1878), a piano duet, brought him world-wide acclaim and attention for his country's music.

In France, Claude Debussy (1862–1918), though not an extreme nationalist, called for "good French music." Franz Liszt (1811–1886), Hungarian composer and a great pianist virtuoso, was delighted by the music of Hungarian Gypsies, which led to his *Hungarian Rhapsodies* and other works in nationalist style.

The Russian nationalist school of composers is noted for its passionate love of the Motherland. Nikolay Rimsky-Korsakov (1848–1908) worked assiduously for advancement of the cause of Russian nationalism in music. Aleksandr Borodin (1833–1887) reflected the character of Russian folk melodies. Modest Mussorgsky (1839–1881), composer of *Boris Godunov,* was one of the first to use Russian folk music as the basis for his music. Peter Ilich Tchaikovsky (1840–1893), great master of the classical ballet *(Swan Lake, Sleeping Beauty),* was a Russian nationalist intrigued by the stories of his nation's past. The underlying sentiment of his compositions was distinctively Russian. His emotional devotion to his country was expressed in his words: "I am Russian through and through."

Nationalism was especially evident in the work of those composers proud of their German identity; Beethoven, Bach, and Haydn are known everywhere as "German" composers. The most passionately nationalist among them was Richard Wagner (q.v.), a man of violent personal opinions who saw Germanism as his most important possession. Wagner spoke in grandiloquent terms of his Fatherland: in his mind it was the greatest of nations and one that called for eternal love and devotion. He saw his music as essentially German and as expressing the whole range of German *Kultur.* His Romanticism made him regard his music as an instrument for molding the entire philosophy and culture of the German people.

Wagner wrote not only music but German prose. His collected literary works fill many volumes, including such material as political speeches, sketches for dramas, rough chapters for a projected autobiography, aesthetic musical treatises, and polemics directed against his real or supposed enemies. One current theme may be noted in this vast body of Wagnerian prose—rebelliousness was joined to reflections on the nature of the "true German view of the world that should be valid for all humanity." "In the German *Volk,*" he wrote, "survives the oldest lawful race of Kings in the entire world; it issues from a son of God, called by his nearest kingsmen *Siegfried,* but

Christ by the remaining nations of the world. The nearest heirs of his [Siegfried's] great deed, and of the power won thereby are the Nibelungen, to whom this earth belongs in name, and for the happiness of every nation. The Germans are the oldest nation, their blue-blooded king is a 'Nibelung' and as their head he claims world leadership."

What is German? (1865) was one of Wagner's major treatises on German nationalism. The essay was a panegyric on the German Spirit, which Wagner saw as reflected in his major works. It was predestined, as he said, for the German Spirit to seize and assimilate the foreign, the primarily remote from it. "One may aver, without exaggeration, that the Antique would have stayed unknown, in its now universal world significance, had the German Spirit not recognized and expounded it." The Italians, Wagner wrote, copied and remodeled the Antique; the Frenchman borrowed from this remodelling, utilizing whatever caressed his national sense of elegance of form; but the German was the first to apprehend its purely human originality. "Through its inmost understanding of the Antique, the German Spirit arrived at the capability of restoring the purely human itself to its pristine freedom." Wagner saw everything that is noble in German art as developing out of the German *Volk* by a natural process of evolution quite different from the tyranny of the materialistic French. He coated his music with this extraordinary German Spirit.

The German Wagnerian cult that emerged saw the composer's energetic genius as leading slowly but surely from cosmopolitan confusion to the highest point of real German national drama, free from foreign color, and based on the innermost foundations of the German nature. The master composer, it was believed, had brought Germany to the peak of civilization. German art, warmth, profundity, integrity, innocence, and veracity, coupled with German strength, have torn away the mask of French falsehood. A Wagnerian enthusiast made it plain:

> Through your whole patriotic German national bent, you have kindled and sustained the flame that now stands gleaming in a mighty blaze in the German heaven. Glory to you for that also! You have inspired thousands with enthusiasm for the national cause.

Adolf Hitler, who considered Richard Wagner to be his spiritual predecessor, brooded in his eagle's nest at Berchtesgaden to the music of "the master of all the masters."

Today, virtually all the 159 nations (1987) of the United Nations have their own national anthems (q.v.), which pay homage to the national state. These songs are venerated, like the national flag, as symbolic of love for and loyalty to the state. Many national anthems call for God's blessings on the nation. They hail the nation as an unbreakable union of citizens who belong together. They refer to the glorious beauty of the land, the necessity to love it, and the duty to defend it against all enemies. The songs are generally set to martial music and the people may march to its tune. Above all, the national anthems seek to extend the claims of nationalism: the individual citizen is expected to live and die for his country. In the United States, the *Star-Spangled Banner* is played at the opening of all baseball games: both players and audience are expected to stand silent throughout the rendition. The national anthem is played on special holidays, such as July 14 in France and July 4 in the United States. It is given special attention at parades and displays of military power. (*See also* **FLAGS, NATIONAL.**)

Thus, in the arts, music is considered to be an essential ingredient of nationalism. It becomes an important asset in the arousal of national consciousness and national styles. Musical harmony and notation are international in scope and those musicians who do not understand the language of other countries still have in music what amounts to a common language, like that of mathematics. At the same time, music has become national and often reflects national consciousness.

Bibliography: Richard Wagner's Prose Works, trans. from the German by William Ashton Ellis (London 1893–1899); Ralph Vaughn, *National Music* (New York, 1935); Paul Lang, *Music in Western Civilization* (New York, 1941); Jacques Barzun, *Berlioz and the Romantic Century* (Boston, 1950); Stanley B. Kimball, *Czech Nationalism* (Urbana, Ill., 1964).

MUSSOLINI, BENITO (1885–1945).   Italian dictator, founder of Italian Fascism, and advocate of aggressive, expansionist nationalism. Five feet seven inches in height, with a bald head, prominent nose, pugnacious chin, and hefty girth, Mussolini ruled Italy from 1922 to 1944. Italians were hypnotized by the *Duce*, their leader who rolled his eyes while talking so that the white showed. A political showman and flamboyant orator, he was a master rabble-rouser. His vanity was legendary. He acquired a hold over the Italian people by a combination of effective propaganda, exaggerated promises, and the support of the army, industrialists, and landowners.

Mussolini's special type of nationalism was expressed in his Fascist movement. In his early days he was a dedicated Socialist. During World War I, he was rejected from the party when he demanded that Italy renounce her neutrality and join the Allies. Later, as editor of *Il Popolo d'Italia*, he advocated a program of violent nationalism, designed to appeal to discontented Italians. After the war, on March 23, 1919, in response to early manifestations of Bolshevism, he founded the first Fascist combat unit. Behind his movement was an eclectic set of stimulants: the blustering posturing of poet Gabriele D'Annunzio (q.v.); the economic teachings of French syndicalist Georges Sorel; the defense of the élite by Italian sociologist Alfredo Pareto; and the State as an end in itself as advocated by Machiavelli and Hegel (qq.v.).

Mussolini expressed these views on the Fascist movement:

—Fascism is a religious conception in which man is seen in his immanent relationship with a superior law and with an objective will that transcends the particular individual with a superior law and raises him in a conscious membership in a spiritual society.

—Fascism besides being a system of government is also and above all, a system of thought.

—Fascism is opposed to all the individualistic abstractions of a materialist nature like those of the eighteenth century; and it is opposed to all Jacobin utopias and innovations.

—Against individualism the Fascist conception is for the State, and it is for the individual in so far as he coincides with the State, which is the conscience and universal will of man in his historical existence.

—Liberalism denied the State in the interests of the particular individual. Fascism reaffirms the State as the true reality of the individual.

Mussolini derived the name "Fascism" from the Latin *fasces*, a bundle of rods encircling an axe, used in ancient Rome as a symbol of authority. This sign was meant to show Italian unity and to save the Italian people from the inroads of communism. All Italians would join in a united national movement—dissatisfied war veterans, the depressed middle class, hungry farmers, and radical intellectuals would be brought together in a compact political party. Most of all, Mussolini drew heavily upon an awakened spirit of Italian nationalism.

Unfortunately for his country, the dictator's brand of nationalism operated in the wrong century at a time when Italy was a prisoner of its own geography. Mussolini, a man of Calvinistic determination and Cromwellian confidence, was to see his type of exaggerated nationalism destroyed in the heat of battle. On April 20, 1945, wandering in North Italy as a Nazi puppet ruler, he was captured near Lake Como by Italian Partisans together with his mistress, Claretta Petacci, and executed. "Let me save my life," he begged his captors, "and I will give you an empire." The bullet-ridden corpses were strung up by the heels, spat upon by Italians, and then dumped like carrion on the public square in Milan, where Fascism had begun its life. (*See also* **ITALIAN NATIONALISM.**)

Bibliography: Benito Mussolini, *Fascism: Doctrine and Institutions* (Rome, 1935); Gaudens Megaro, *Mussolini in the Making* (Boston, 1938); Christopher Hibbert, *Il Duce: The Life of Benito Mussolini* (Boston, 1962); S. William Halperin, *Mussolini and Italian Fascism* (Princeton, N.J., 1984).

MUSTAFA, KEMAL.   *See* **ATATÜRK, KEMAL.**

N

NASSER, GAMAL ABDEL (1918–1970). Soldier, politician, champion of Egyptian nationalism, and promoter of Pan-Arab nationalism. Educated at the Military Academy in Cairo, Nasser served in the war against Israel in 1948. He was one of the leaders of the *coup d'état* of July 1952, which resulted in the abdication of King Farouk. Gen. Mohammed Naguib was the nominal head of the new government, but Nasser managed to hold power through the Revolutionary Command Committee. In 1954, after an attempt on Nasser's life, he became Premier of Egypt. In 1956 he was President of the Republic of Egypt in an election in which there was no opposition.

As President, Nasser nationalized the Suez Canal in the same year of his election, thereby precipitating a short-lived Anglo-French invasion that was denounced by the United States. Two years later he presented his bid to lead the Arab world, when he joined with Syria to form the United Arab Republic. He became its President. Though his leadership of the Arab cause was aggressive, he soon lost the support of the surviving Middle East monarchies, which preferred a nationalism of their own to that of an umbrella Pan-Arab nationalism led by Nasser.

More than six feet tall, weighing 200 pounds, with close-cropped graying hair, and the physique of an athlete, Nasser was a charismatic leader, who easily won the affection and support of the Egyptian people. For centuries Egypt has been ruled by foreigners: the people saw him as the first Egyptian to rule the country in several milleniums. They were entranced by his tributes to Egyptian nationalism, by his description of his fellow countrymen as "heroic and glorious," and by his promise of a brilliant future. He told them that there were no limits to how far they could go. He would help them remove rocks and obstacles in the way. That was the only duty of the Egyptians. The future was open to patriots. "It is our cherished duty, our moment of historical responsibility, thus to bring our people at long last together, and meld them in units for the future— the future of Egypt—strong and free." His appeal was a classic case of a leader using the consciousness of nationalism to bring his people to a higher level in world society.

Nasser's ambitions went even beyond the limits of mere Egyptian nationalism. In his *Philosophy of the Revolution* (1954), he presented his triple dream of becoming the leader not only of Egyptian nationalism, but also of Pan-Arabism, Pan-Africanism, and Pan-Islamism. (qq.v.). It was to be a grandiose project: there were 55 million Arabs, 224 million Africans, and 420 million Muslims. He saw the unity of his country at the center of three concentric circles:

1. *The First Arab Circle.* According to Nasser, "the first Arab circle was a part of us, and we are a part of it, our being an inextricable part of its history."

2. *The Second African Circle.* Surrounding the Arab circle was the second African circle, the continent of Africa. Egyptians, Nasser claimed, could not possibly remain aloof. They were in Africa; they gave Africans their northern gate; they were Africa's link with the outside world; and they would never relinquish responsibility for the rest of Africa. After all, Africa was vital for Egypt: the life-giving waters of the Nile flowed from its source in the heart of Africa through Egyptian territory.

3. *The Third Islamic Great Circle.* Islam was the third great circle circumscribing all the continents and oceans. Nasser called "the domain of all our brothers in faith," the common relation that linked all Arabs together, with centers of Islamic learning in Damascus, Baghdad, and Cairo. The heart of the concentric circles was Cairo, and by implication Egypt—and Nasser.

There was a need here, Nasser wrote, for a hero to perform a glorious role. All three circles surrounding Cairo presented "a wondering mission in search of a hero." For this role he nominated himself. "We alone, by virtue of our place, can perform the role." In a speech delivered at Damascus on March 11, 1959, he further described his own version of Arab nationalism:

> Fellow Countrymen: When we took it upon ourselves to raise high the banner of Arab nationalism and defend its call; when we chose the difficult, hard way, the way of defending the whole of the Arab nation, working for it in its entirety, of

Arab unity and Arab nationalism, we knew that this might be a rough one to travel, that it might be easier if we chose one of an isolationist policy, a road with a policy that was indeed selfish, a policy that was based largely on ignoring whatever happened in other Arab countries. We knew that such a policy would be easier at the outset, but that eventually it would hand over one Arab country after another to its enemies, that such a divided Arab nation would not achieve solidarity, would inevitably surrender to imperialism; so all of us, each and every one of the sons of this nation, preferred the rough, hard way, the way to Arab unity and solidarity, and resolved to raise the banner of Arab nationalism and exert every effort thoroughly to consolidate it.

Nasser's conception of Egyptian nationalism and Pan-Arab nationalism came into conflict with that of the oil-rich sheiks in Saudi Arabia and other Arab states. To expect these prosperous barons to relinquish their own sense of nationalism, as Nasser did, to accept the domination of impoverished Egypt was too much. Arab chieftains had no intention of healing their historic rivalries and submitting to the leadership of Nasser, despite all his admitted charisma. Nasser's political slogans were just not enough to meet political, social, and economic realities in the Middle East. True, Egypt had won her independence and had emerged as a national state with her own flag, national anthem, coins, and stamps. However, behind the facade of Egyptian independence were all the economic miseries of the past.

There were both positive and negative aspects of nationalized Egypt under Nasser's rule. The Aswan High Dam, which became operational in 1968 with the assistance of the Soviet Union, was a major accomplishment. Nasser promoted industrialization, introduced land reforms, and led a moderately successful campaign against the traditional corruption. He encouraged foreigners, including Frenchmen, Italians, Greeks, and Britons, to leave the country, sometimes by less than gentle means.

Against such accomplishments was a negative aspect. Egypt under Nasser's rule became a police state. There was no political democracy in the Western sense—no freedom of expression, right of assembly, or impartial justice. Nasser censored the communications media and nationalized the most important newspaper. He hand-picked all candidates for office. He sent dissenters to prison camps in the desert. There was little or no improvement in the life of the *fellahin*, the peasants and laborers.

There was little support throughout the Arab world for Nasser's version of Pan-Arab nationalism. His critics used the term "Nasserism" to describe his contention that Pan-Arabism could succeed only under his leadership. Without any central organization, Nasser's dream represented merely an emotional cause of one man rather than a regimented or co-ordinated movement. While he was able to promote nationalism among his own people and free them from foreign control, he never managed to realize his ambition of becoming the leader of his triple concentric circles of Pan-Arabism, Pan-Africanism, and Pan-Islamism. Most of all, his career suggests that when a nationalism seeks to step beyond the boundaries of its own territorial imperative, it comes into a head-on collision with other nationalisms much aware of their own identity and willing to fight to the death to preserve it. (*See also* **PAN-ARABISM**).

Bibliography: Gamal Abdel Nasser, *Egypt Liberated: The Philosophy of the Revolution* (Washington, D.C., 1956); Wilton Wynn, *Nasser of Egypt: The Search for Dignity* (New York, 1959); Robert St. John, *The Boss: The Story of Gamal Abdel Nasser* (New York 1960); Jamal Mohammed Ahmed, *The Intellectual Origins of Egyptian Nationalism* (New York, 1960).

NATION.   At the root of nationality and nationalism (qq.v.) is the word "nation." There is much difficulty in arriving at a generally accepted definition of all three terms. Some scholars consider the meaning of nation to be so complex a metaphysical fiction that they assume or explicitly state that it is not capable of scientific definition. They see it as one of those tropical jungles of thought in which politics and journalism flourish. They regard it as an organism, a spiritual entity, and conclude that all attempts to penetrate its secrets by the light of mechanical interpretation break down before the test of experience. In view of this terminological confusion, the editors of several important encyclopedias have omitted the word "nation" altogether.

Nevertheless, the editors of Websters' *Unabridged Dictionary* have tried to throw some light on an elusive term:

NATION (nā'shŭn), n. [ME. *nacioun,* fr. OF. *nacion* (F. *nation*), fr. L. *natio,* nation, race, orig., a being born, fr. *natus,* past part. of *nasci* to be born, for *gnatus, gnasci,* from the same root as E. KIN. Cf. COGNATE, INNATE, NATAL, NATIVE, NATURE, PREGNANT, PUNY, RENASCENT.] 1. *obs.* a Kindred; race; lineage. b Nationality. c A community or an aggregation of men or animals; esp., a caste or class formed by the common profession or interests of its members. d A country.

2. A people connected by supposed ties of blood generally manifested by community of language, religion, and customs, and by a sense of common interest and interrelation; thus, the Jews and the Gypsies are often called *nations. See* PEOPLE, 1.

3. Popularly, any group of people having like institutions and customs and a sense of social homogeneity and mutual interest. Most nations are formed of

agglomerations of tribes or peoples either of a common ethnic stock or of different stocks fused by long intercourse. A single language or closely related dialects, a common religion, a common tradition and history, and a common sense of right and wrong, and a more or less compact territory, are typically characteristic; but one or more of these elements may be lacking and yet leave a group that from its community of interest and desire to lead a common life is called *a nation.*

4. Loosely, the body of inhabitants of a country united under a single independent government; a state.

5. A division of students, determined by district or country of their birth, esp. in medieval universities. *Archaic.*

6. A multitude; a host.

7. One tribe of a group of Indian tribes; as, the *Six Nations.* Syn.—See PEOPLE.

This is a valiant attempt to bring some order to the use of the word nation, but it still does not solve the semantic confusion. Derived from the Latin *natio,* the basic term seems to indicate a people related by birth, and the quality of innateness would seem to be vital in its meaning. Yet, in the formation of modern nations, the exigencies of historical development caused peoples to be thrown together by factors other than ethnic relationships. However, the older Latin symbol for the nation, the *natio,* was retained as a descriptive term, even though there were variations in meaning from the original. Linguistically, the use of an earlier terminology is a common and understandable factor, necessary to avoid a multiplicity of symbols that would result in even more confusion. Much of the difficulty surrounding the word nation carries over into nationality and nationalism, as well as into such composite terms as national character, national consciousness, national soul, national will, and national self-determination.

In understanding the meaning of the word nation, we must immediately exclude the identification of nation with race. In popular thinking and especially in the view of racialists, the terms nation and race are identified as one and the same thing. This is a highly fallacious and pseudo-scientific generalization, which has no basis in fact. Most people do find it difficult to see a close unity without a physical bond and do not seem to be able to think of a common mentality without common blood. To them, an intimate solidarity between members of a nation implies a physical bond similar to the relationship between members of a family. Even the distinguished Lord Bryce expressed the view that in the thought and imagination of every civilized people "there is an unquestionable racial strain" and that "race sentiment is one of the elements that go to make up national sentiment and national pride and help to make a people cohesive." Others maintain that a common physical descent is essential if a nation is to be made a unit in the best and fullest sense. Winston Churchill, advocate of the exact word, often spoke of "the British race," though he probably did not mean it in a biological sense. Many who consciously reject the racialist position unconsciously lapse into use of the catchword race.

The French philologist Maximilien Paul Émile Littré compounded the confusion by calling a nation "a union of men inhabiting the same territory, whether or not subject to the same government, and possessing such common interests of long standing that they may be regarded as belonging to the same race." This conclusion does not take into consideration that the term nation is used in the social sciences, while race is used in natural science: the nation seems to designate historical and social characteristics that can be altered by society. Race, on the other hand, refers to hereditary, biological traits not easily changeable by education and assimilation. Race refers to a continuity of a physical type and expresses affinities of blood. The identification of nation with race is plainly scientifically inaccurate. There never was, or is there today, a German or American race, but there are German and American nations.

The consensus among all disciplines is that the term nation is tantalizingly ambiguous and that much additional study is needed to clarify it. There are differences of opinion within each discipline. All agree that a nation is not a race nor is it a state. They see language, religion, and territory as important factors in the nation, but none of them is the exclusive determinant of the nation. However, their approach to the meaning of the word nation is always determined by the demands of their own discipline.

Historians generally see the nation as the population of a sovereign state, living within a definite territory, and possessing a common stock of thoughts and feelings that are transmitted during the course of a common history by a common will. They believe that the meaning of the nation is itself subject to historical change. French historian Ernest Renan, in his famous *Qu'est-ce qu'une nation?* (1882), gave this definition: "A nation is a grand solidarity constituted by the sentiment of sacrifices which one has made and those that one is disposed to make again. It supposes a past, it renews itself especially in the present by a tangible deed: the approval, the desire, clearly expressed, to continue the communal life. The existence of a nation is an everyday plebiscite." This is the definition by Ernest Barker:

> A nation is a body of men, inhabiting a definite territory, who normally are drawn from different races, but possess a common stock of thoughts and feelings acquired and transmitted during the course of a common history; who on the whole and in

the main, though more in the past than in the present, include in that common stock a common religious belief; who generally and as a rule use a common language as the vehicle of their thoughts and feelings; and who, besides common thoughts and feelings, also cherish a common will, and accordingly form, or tend to form, a separate State for the expression of that will.

Political scientists, concerned primarily with problems of government and legislation, are interested in politics, sovereignty, and the state, and prefer to leave the concept of the nation to the disciplines of history and sociology. They distinguish a people as a group of individuals who by means of similar language, folkways, and institutions are able to communicate with each other directly and easily. They regard the state as the formal political and military organization of one or more peoples. To them a nation is the formal organization of one people. A state need not be a nation. A nation must be a state. The nation is an organic unity, the result of organic growth.

Philosophers tend to regard a nation as a unity of culture, with common history, language, literature, traditions, heroes, and sense of loyalty. Sociologists, interested especially in group behavior, regard the nation as one of the largest and most important collectives in human society. They prefer to use such terms as group, in-group, secondary group, and social unit, instead of the more controversial word nation. They believe that the one indispensable factor in the term nation is the "we-sentiment," or the feeling of oneness. When discussing the word nation, geographers point to the significance of territory, the natural center, and the environment.

The disciplines concerned with human behavior are also concerned with the meaning of the term nation. Psychologists base the existence of the nation primarily on the behavior of its individuals. They seek its meaning in terms of psychological characteristics. Consciousness and emotion, they say, form the cement that binds the nation. They have different views on the existence of a group mind, a collective mind, or a corporate consciousness within the nation. Psychiatrists, concerned with the intimacy of the relationships between the personality and the social system, see the nation as made and maintained by an emotionally sustained education in nationhood, beginning with the crucial factor of family life and extended later to the large collectivity. Psychoanalysts describe the nation as the largest of the social aggregates to which the individual ordinarily attaches his loyalty, and as the external representation of the superego (the inner, unconscious center). Some psychoanalysts hold that nations are subject to the same tensions (neurotic group ideals) as the individual, but like scholars in other disciplines, they differ among themselves on the existence of parallels between the individuals and society.

Francis Lieber, the German-born scholar who after 1856 was Professor of Political Science at Columbia University, gave a definition of the nation that has been quoted again and again to the present day:

What is a nation in the modern sense of the world? The word "nation," in the fullest adaptation of the term, means, in modern times, a numerous and homogeneous population (having long emerged from the hunters and nomadic state), permanently inhabiting and cultivating a coherent territory, with a well-defined geographic outline, and a name of its own,—the inhabitants speaking their own language, having their own literature and common institutions, which distinguish them clearly from other and similar groups of people, being citizens or subjects of a unitary government, however subdivided it may be, and having an organic unity with one another as well as being conscious of a common destiny. Organic, intellectual and political internal unity with proportionate strength and a distinct and obvious demarcation from similar groups, are notable elements of the idea of a modern nation in its fullest sense.

Bibliography: Francis Lieber, *Fragments of Political Science on Nationalism and Internationalism* (New York, 1868); Ernest Renan, *Qu'est-ce qu'une nation?* (Paris, 1882); Frederick Hertz, *Nationality in History and Politics* (London, 1951); Louis L. Snyder, *The Meaning of Nationalism* (New Brunswick, N.J., 1954); Walker Connor, "Nation-Building or Nation-Destroying," *World Politics*, 23 (1972), 319–355; E. Gellner, *Nations and Nationalism* (London, 1983); Anthony D. Smith, *State and Nation in the Third World* (New York, 1983); Carolyn M. Vogler, *The Nation-State* (Aldershot, Eng., 1985).

NATIONAL CHARACTER. The idea of national character has been defined as the totality of interests, traditions, and ideals that are so important in the life of a nation that they tend to mold its image both in the mind of the nation and that of others. Yet, there are differences of opinion as to whether or not there is any such thing as national character. There are several points of view on this matter. One holds that every nation has a specific character that is permanent and can be traced through its history. The national character, it is claimed, is a powerful element in every nationalist ideology.

Opposed to this view is the rejection of anything concerned with national character as specious and fallacious. Those who hold this concept believe that national character just does not exist. They say that the idea is wrong because it is beset with false stereotypes, generalizations, and wishful thinking. On occasion, they say, it is confounded with racialism.

Between these two extremes on the idea of national character is the proposal that it has a limited validity because its existence cannot be denied. The German historian Leopold von Ranke, known for his objective views on the course of history, presented this reserved approach when he stated that the national spirit could only be felt but not understood. It is "a spiritual air, permeating everything." Apparently, in his mind there was a close link between the national spirit and national character.

There are many examples of the differing attitudes of scholars on the concept of national character. Henry Morley believed that "in the literature of any people we perceive under all contrasts of form produced by variable social influences the one national character from beginning to last." Salvador de Madariaga held that the existence of national character is one of the obvious facts of nature, "There *is* such a thing as national character. Opinions may differ as to the influences which create or alter it. Race, climate, economic conditions, may enter for a greater or lesser part in its reception and development. But the fact is there and stares us in the face. A nation is a fact of psychology. A nation is a character." Ernst Barker spoke of national character as a reality, "a sum of acquired tendencies." He believed that national character, in its formations and manifestations, has its analogies with the character of the individual man.

Opposing this view was J. M. Robertson, who believed that "the nation considered as a continuous and personalized organism is in large measure 'a physical dream'." Francis Delaisi, turning a sardonic eye on the concept of national genius, maintained that even a cursory glance at history will show that there are between nations no watertight compartments in matters of the mind. Hamilton Fyfe (q.v.) criticized the idea of national character as an illusion that was doing great harm in the world. He denounced the commonly held view that national characters are distinct, homogeneous, and well defined. To him this was a most dangerous element making for war.

Between these extremes was the view of Francis Galton that "different aspects of the multifarious character of man respond to different calls from without, so that the same individual, and much more the same race, may behave very differently at different epochs."

The beliefs that people hold concerning their own character and that of other peoples contain a mixture of fact with exaggerations or distortions. People throughout the world believe such stereotypes as all Scotsmen are frugal and thrifty, all Germans hopelessly belligerent, all Frenchmen amorous, all Swedes cold, and all Americans naïve and aggressive. Belief in such illusions is significant because it helps produce national solidarity as well as national rivalries. Even if there may be little truth in such stereotypes, the fact that they are widely believed gives them historical meaning.

Most specialists on nationalism now reject the notion that national character persists permanently in each nation. The English, once thought to be unruly, aggressive, and revolutionary-minded, later emerged as a solid people who have great pride in the stability of their institutions. The French, at one time proud of their loyalty to the tradition of monarchy, turned on Louis XVI and sent him to the guillotine, thereby fashioning the snowball of revolution that affected all Europe. The Germans, once regarded as a musically gifted, intelligent, and peaceful people, had a global reputation in the nineteenth and twentieth centuries as a warlike community bent on conquest. Apparently, the national character of a people changes in response to varying historical stimuli. (*See also* **HUME, DAVID.**)

Bibliography: Salvador de Madariaga, *Englishmen, Frenchmen, Spaniards* (London, 1928); Ernst Barker, *National Character and the Factors in Its Formation* (New York, 1927); Francis Delaisi, *Political Myths and Economic Realities* (New York and London, 1927); Hamilton Fyfe, *The Illusion of National Character* (London, 1940); Friedrich Hertz, "War and National Character," *Contemporary Review*, 171 (1947), 274–281; Henry Steele Commager, *The American Mind* (New Haven, Conn., 1950); Hans Kohn, *The Mind of Germany* (New York, 1970).

NATIONAL MINORITIES.   By accident or design, often as a result of wars and/or revolutions, there are included in modern states peoples of differing backgrounds—history, language, traditions, customs, and religions. These peoples form minorities in the fabric of their nation. In some cases, primarily because of economic advantages, they may accept their status peaceably (Welsh and Scottish nationalisms in Britain). In other examples they may protest violently in a struggle for increased autonomy or outright independence (Basques in Spain, Croats in Yugoslavia). The term "national minorities" is often used interchangeably with mini-nationalisms (q.v.).

Among the many examples of how national minorities are created was the development of a chaotic situation following the Armistice of World War I. Four hitherto great Empires—German, Austro-Hungarian, Turkish, and Russian—were dissolved on the European scene. The peacemakers at Versailles were faced with a herculean task in making a new map of the continent. Their decisions broke up the fabric of the older states. In the process, millions of peoples of dissimilar backgrounds were banded together in new combinations. Many were transferred from one region to another, often against their will. In such artificially created nation-structures, there immediately began a struggle for domination by one people over others suddenly placed inside their borders. Along with it came friction, dissent, dissatisfaction, and vehement drives for independence. Efforts to introduce a new nationalism were met by the competition of smaller nationalisms hungering for liberation.

The settlements made at Versailles resulted in years of controversy. Decided in a milieu of confusion and bitterness, they undoubtedly sowed the seeds for another world war twenty years later. Those treaties were imperfect precisely because they represented a compromise between an ideal world society advocated by dreamers and the harsh, practical demands of some fifty sovereign states.

Characteristic of this artificial nation-building was the situation in East Central Europe. Here there were intermingled strains of Germans and Slavs, Roman Catholics and Protestants, and other rival cultures and religions. New "national states" were announced in Estonia, Latvia, Lithuania, Poland, Czechoslovakia, Austria, Hungary, and Greater Rumania. This was expected to solve the problem of discontented former subject nationalities agitating for freedom. It only aggravated the nationalities problem. In fact, the number of national minorities actually increased. In this area over the centuries the peoples had become so intermingled that it was impossible to create homogeneous national states. Forcible change of minorities in brutal fashion (Turkey and Greece) resulted only in resentful national minorities. Efforts to solve the problem by federalization failed because of the fear that federalization would lead to political dissolution. The general practice was to set up a highly centralized, bureaucratic central government and by force hold the minorities in check.

The disintegrative nature of the new nationalism exists everywhere throughout the world today. Both small and large states are subject to the problem of national minorities. There may be a single minority clamoring for freedom (Arabs in Israel) or scores of minorities, some of them highly dissatisfied (Baltic peoples and Armenians in the Soviet Union). In both these countries there are serious dissent and potential rebellion as the twentieth century draws to a close.

Israel provides an example of the troubles of a small state in dealing with its minority Arabs. In the Six Day War starting on June 6, 1967, the Israelis took the Gaza Strip, captured Old Jerusalem, Syria's Golan Heights, and Jordan's West Bank. In successive wars the

Israelis had defeated Arabs intent on driving them into the Mediterranean Sea. The only democracy in a surrounding Arab world, Israel sought to placate the Arab minority by compensation of land or cash, government-supported irrigation works, support of Arab education, active participation in the political life of Israel, and health and welfare services. These efforts were not successful. Suspicion continued to mar the relations between the two peoples.

The Arabs in Israel had suffered the shock of military defeat and especially the reduction to minority status. They felt that the old social fabric had materially disintegrated and their family units broken. Members of the Palestine Liberation Organization (q.v.) abroad maintained a steady drumfire of propaganda and even terroristic acts and sabotage to keep alive the flames of irredentism (q.v.). In 1988 there was a serious uprising in the occupied West Bank, where Israeli troops responded to rock-throwing youths first with rubber bullets followed by real bullets and beatings recorded by foreign television crews.

Since its independence in 1948, the Israeli Defense Forces proved to be formidable in five major conflicts and what seemed to be an endless guerrilla war against the P.L.O. The new mission to contain the uprising of the 1.4 million Palestinian minority unwilling to submit to the twenty-one-year rule in the West Bank and the Gaza Strip produced a crisis of conscience in Israel. The country was tormented by its inability to solve the problem of a recalcitrant national minority.

The same problem of national minorities on a larger scale exists in the Soviet Union. Since the formation of the U.S.S.R. after World War I, the Kremlin has been troubled by unrest of its minorities, some one hundred diverse nationalities and ethnic groups living in fifteen republics. Russia's rulers had dealt with restless minorities since the days of the Tsars and the problem carried over into the Soviet Union. For decades Soviet authorities used a strong hand in dealing with minorities. They equated resistance with "hooliganism" and treason. They had regarded it as an article of faith that Soviet patriotism had replaced older localized attachments. They found it impossible and highly undesirable to give independence to those minorities that clamored for it.

But nationalism refused to die among the peoples absorbed into the Soviet state. In early 1988, hundreds of thousands of Armenians demonstrated in their capital, Yerevan, demanding to be reunited with Nagordny Karabakh, a predominantly Armenian enclave in Soviet Azerbaijan. Subsequent violence resulted in the death of dissenters. (*See* **ARMENIAN NATIONALISM.**) The continuing problem of national minorities indicated some serious breaks in the Soviet monolithic facade.

Bibliography: Oscar I. Janowsky, *Nationalities and National Minorities* (New York, 1945); Warren L. Young, *Minorities and the Military: A Cross-National Study in World Perspectives* (Westport, Conn., 1982); Stephan M. Horak and Richard Blanke, *Eastern European National Minorities, 1919–1980* (Littleton, Colo., 1986).

NATIONAL SOCIALISM. The doctrines and policies of the *Nationalsozialistische Deutsche Arbeiter Partei*, the N.S.D.A.P. (the National Socialist German Workers' Party), which held power in the German Third Reich from 1933 to 1945. The word Nazi was derived from the first word in the title of the Party—N*ationalsozialistische*.

The concept of National Socialism appeared in Germany as early as 1878, when Adolf Stoecker (q.v.) founded his Christian Social Workers' Party, by which the activist pastor hoped to win the workingman away from liberal secularism to Christianity, nationalism, and anti-Semitism. In the discontent following World War I, several extremist groups arose, among them the small German Workers' Party, founded by Anton Drexler, a toolmaker, and Dietrich Eckart, a journalist. In the summer of 1919 Adolf Hitler (q.v.) became member number seven of this miniscule party. Within two years he was in control of the group under the new name of National Socialist German Workers' Party.

Hitler expressed the ideology of National Socialism in his autobiography, *Mein Kampf,* written in Landsberg Prison in 1924, where he had been sent after being found guilty of conspiring for high treason. In this wordy autobiography, Hitler presented his views on the dogma of National Socialism. Disregarding the contradiction of the very name (nationalism obviously contradicted the international aspects of socialism), the budding politician aimed to combine them both into a mighty mass movement. At the core of his ideology was the nationalism advocated by historian Heinrich von Treitschke (q.v.). A basic theme was social Darwinism: individuals and nations are both subject to a continuous struggle for life. Power was pre-eminent, and morality was foolish. Added to nationalism was the racialist doctrine of Frenchman Count de Gobineau and Englishman-turned-German Houston Stewart Chamberlain. The racially superior German people were threatened by Jews, "the plastic demons of the fall of mankind," as well as by Marxists, Bolsheviks, liberals, humanists, and humanitarians of any kind. Germany could become great again only if it waged relentless warfare against these internal enemies. Under a National Socialist dictatorship supported by the people, a new, powerful Germany would seek *Lebensraum* (living-space) denied it by external enemies. Hitler saw his fledgling movement as destined to lead Germany to a new level of greatness.

To the new National Socialist Party flocked such discontented elements as disgruntled war veterans, impoverished students, ambitious monarchists, struggling shopkeepers, dissatisfied workers, frightened industrialists, anti-Semites, anti-Catholics, anti-liberals, anti-socialists, anti-communists, and unreconciled nationalists. A hypnotic orator, Hitler promised his followers abrogation of the hated Treaty of Versailles, an end to the "war-guilt lie," restriction of citizenship rights to Aryans, expulsion of aliens from Germany, nationalization of industries, land reforms, a highly centralized government, restoration of German colonies, economic prosperity, a mighty, invincible army, and free rein for anti-Semitism.

After his release from prison, Hitler soon found that he had to make a choice between the nationalist right of his Party centered in Munich and the socialist left in Berlin led by Gregor Strasser. With his eye on support from Rhineland industrialists, Hitler opted for his own comrades in Bavaria—and nationalism. At a party conference he outmaneuvered Strasser and stripped him of any influence in the growing Nazi movement. This important choice meant the triumph of nationalism over socialism in Hitler's drive for political power.

Bibliography: William L. Shirer. *The Rise and Fall of the Third Reich* (New York, 1960); Louis L. Snyder, *The Third Reich, 1933–1945: A Bibliographical Guide to German National Socialism* (New York, 1987).

NATIONALISM, CLASSIFICATIONS OF. Scholars of nationalism have sought classification of the historical phenomenon by turning their attention to meaning through typology. Historian Carlton J. H. Hayes (q.v.) presented a vertical conceptualization following roughly a chronological pattern from the appearance of modern nationalism in the eighteenth century to its recent forms. This breakdown has enjoyed wide popularity. (*See* **HAYES' CLASSIFICATION.**) The Kohn dichotomy (q.v.), while recognizing the importance of chronology, preferred a horizontal comparison of Western and non-Western nationalism. This, too, was a major classification.

There have been additional classifications among scholars in disciplines other than history. Political scientist Max Sylvius Handman presented the following arrangement:

Oppression nationalism. This form of nationalism exists among peoples exposed to a definite regime of disabilities and subordination (Jews, Irish by the English in Ireland, Poles in Germany and Russia, Greeks and Armenians in the old Turkish Empire).

Irredentist nationalism. Peoples who demand liberation from the domination of others (Rumanians, Serbs, Bulgars, Italians).

Precaution nationalism. A type of nationalism that responds to the stimulus of competition among modern nation-states and that identifies commercial expansion with national security. Always impelled by agitated concern for the life and honor of the group, this kind of nationalism is often indistinguishable from imperialism.

Prestige nationalism. This form of nationalism emphasizes the glorious history of a people's past and demands greater respect for its beliefs [*Action Française* (q.v.)], Oswald Mosley's British Fascists).

Psychologists classify nationalism from their own special interests. They stress the real or imaginary workings of the mind, group acceptance of ideas and symbols, and community behavior. Thus, Gustav Ichheiser presented two forms:

Conscious nationalism. Members of the community profess national values in a vociferous way, consciously strive for national goals, and glorify their real or imagined peculiarities.

Subconscious (or unconscious nationalism). Those who belong to a national group, even though they do not formulate their national ideas, are, nevertheless, so influenced by naturally prejudiced concepts that they, without being aware of it, see and judge everything from a national point of view.

Sociologists, too, classify nationalisms from the viewpoint of their discipline, which concentrates its attention on group behavior. Louis Wirth based his categories on profound social conditioning and group power struggles:

Hegemony nationalism. A national group is motivated by the urge to derive advantage from consolidating smaller principalities into larger and more dynamic units (unification of Germany and Italy).

Particularistic nationalism. Based on the secessionist demand for national autonomy, the first aim of this form is divisive in character but is succeeded by a union with a more satisfactory group. Particularistic nationalism begins with a striving for cultural autonomy and then takes on political significance (the potential nationalities in the Austro-Hungarian, German, Turkish, and Russian empires before 1914).

Marginal nationalism. This type exists in frontier regions between two states, among peoples who have a mixed culture. Marginal peoples are likely to adhere to the traditions of their Motherland (such border peoples as those in Alsace, Lorraine, Silesia, Schleswig, the Saar, and the Rhineland).

Nationalities in the Minorities.   Minorities everywhere strive for recognition of their own traditional nationality and attempt to maintain their own culture while inside another nation.

Bibliography: Max Sylvius Handman, "The Sentiment of Nationalism," *Political Science Quarterly,* 36 (1921), 104–121; Gustav Ichheiser,"Some Psychological Obstacles to an Understanding between Nations," *Journal of Abnormal and Social Psychology,* 36 (1941), 427–432; Louis Wirth, "Types of Nationalism," *American Journal of Sociology,* 41 (1936), 723–737; Konstantin Symmons-Symonolewicz, "Nationalist Movements: An Attempt at a Comparative Typology." *Comparative Studies in Society and History,* 7 (January, 1965), 221–230.

NATIONALISM, DEVELOPMENT OF.   Historians generally agree that, while nationalism retained its basic elements throughout its existence, in its overall character it changed its direction during the course of the nineteenth and twentieth centuries. But it has remained one of the most powerful historical forces in the modern era.

Virtually all the important innovations of the early modern era favored the development of nationalism. Among them may be included the disruption of the medieval Church and the formation of national churches, the advent of vernacular literatures, the rise of national armies, the emergence of the middle class, and the revolutionary growth of capitalism. The middle class, the bourgeoisie, began to feel that the nation belonged to the owners of property, not to the king. National sentiment reflected this new conception. Monarchs, too, regarded the emerging nationalism as a means of perpetuating their dynasties. The language factor was important: Latin was being replaced by the vernacular tongues. Vernacular languages were elevated to the status of national languages—in England the Anglo-Saxon, in France the *langue d'oïl* of northern France, in Spain the Castilian, in the Italies the Tuscan, and in the Germanies the Saxon. The close connection between nationalism and language was retained throughout its development. (*See* **LANGUAGE, NATIONALISM AND.**)

The French Revolution accelerated the process of nationalism. Napoleon, perhaps unwittingly, became its traveling salesman and stimulated the rise of nationalism all over Europe. The idea spread throughout the continent—Englishmen, Frenchmen, Germans, Spaniards, and Italians, in addition to a host of smaller peoples, were infused with the new consciousness of nationality. All saw themselves as threatened from the outside. They expressed their xenophobia, their fear and hatred of foreigners. The result was the formation of national armies geared to what was believed to be the necessity of protecting the Fatherland or Motherland against the inroads of aggressive neighbors. Fear led to intensified hatreds as well as to greater reliance on the home government to protect its citizens from the inroads of foreigners. Peoples were united by strong bonds of community interests. Their flags symbolized national glory and prestige.

A Force for Unification (1815–1871). The early part of the nineteenth century saw nationalism as a unifying force. This was the time when Romanticism gave direction to rising nationalism. States that had outgrown feudal division moved in the direction of consolidation. Peoples who had long been split into hostile factions now began to see the virtues of unification. The Germanies and the Italies, both of which had been "geographical expressions" for centuries, began their own drives for unity and understood the advisability of union. Bismarck (q.v.) molded his national state; Cavour (q.v.) brought unity to Italy. The movement began to spread throughout the world. Simón Bolívar was motivated to free South America from Spanish control. Others continued the process.

A Force for Disruption (1871–1900). The success of the Germans and Italians in forging national unity stimulated the enthusiasm of subject nationalities in other countries. National minorities (q.v.) in Austria-Hungary, the Ottoman Empire, and other conglomerate states began to think in terms of independence. They, too, boasted of geographical unity, common language, common culture, common traditions, common history, sometimes a nonexistent "race," and they, too, believed in the virtues of nationalism. Under the banner of nationalism, Irishmen, Poles, and Hungarians began to call for nationhood or death. In this phase, nationalism became a force for breaking up or splitting the established states so that their minorities could function as independent nations.

A Force for Aggression (1900–1918). As international rivalries rose toward the end of the nineteenth century, nationalism moved closer and closer to imperialism, by which established states sought to extend their influence over what they regarded as lesser peoples. Superpatriots claimed it as their mission to bring civilization to backward peoples of the earth. Powerful nations sent their troops to Africa and Asia to obtain concessions or territory in other continents. This collision of opposing national interests was one of the factors leading to the outbreak of World War I. It was a major change in the nature of nationalism. In its early stage, it had taken on a liberal tinge, reflecting Herder's (q.v.) idea of cultural nationalisms contributing to a harmonious world order. Nationalism was transformed from blessing into curse.

Nationalism from 1918 to 1939. The factors making for nationalism were present during the Long Armistice from 1918 to 1939. The peacemakers at Versailles in 1919 attempted to remake the map of the world by granting independence to many peoples on the basis of self-determination (q.v.). Instead of solving the problem they created even more difficulties by creating new states with more dissatisfied minorities. Hitler, Mussolini, and Tojo used their own form of aggressive nationalism to turn the social order to their advantage.

A "new" nationalism emerged somewhat tamed after the end of World War II. Britain, France, and the Netherlands relinquished their overseas colonies. Added to this factor was the threat of Communist expansion, against which the Western nations formed regional confederations. Nationalism persisted in the Soviet Union and appeared in imitative form in Africa, Asia, and the Near and Middle East.

The New Nationalism was distinguished by the persistence of its major tenets. Proponents of a United States of Europe hoped that their Common Market would lead to a political unification of the continent, but this goal remained a dream. (*See* **PAN-EUROPA.**) The strength of the New Nationalism was indicated by Britain's Prime Minister Margaret Thatcher, who stated that "a centralized European government would be a disaster." And further: "We have not successfully rolled back the frontiers of the state in Britain only to see them reimposed at a European level, with a European superstate exercising a new dominance from Brussels." This attitude, general among European states, shows that nationalism, far from retreating as the twentieth century nears its end, is as strong as ever and that it is continuing as a major historical force in modern times.

Bibliography: Carlton J. H. Hayes, *The Historical Evolution of Modern Nationalism* (New York, 1931); Boyd C. Shafer, *Faces of Nationalism* (New York, 1972).

NATIONALISM, MEANING OF. The French Revolution gave to Europe the new sense of nationalism and a rising faith in liberalism. There was a nexus between the two. The cry of "Liberty, Equality, and Fraternity" gave new direction to European history. Bourgeois liberalism defended man's rights to freedom of speech, press, assembly, and religion. In political life these rights were to be assured through constitutionalism, parliamentarianism, and the franchise.

Economic activity would be governed through *laissez faire* (let people do as they please, noninterference in business and industry). During the years of the French Revolution, the rights of the individual were extended gradually to the nation as a whole. Citizens thought in terms of self-determination (q.v.), the essence of nationalism. European society was altered drastically. In earlier eras, Europeans had devoted their attachments to a dynasty, the Church, a feudal lord, a guild, or a local community. These loyalties began to change at a time when industrialism was weakening the fabric of the old society and people were drawn from rural areas to the cities.

In the late eighteenth century, citizens began to give their allegiance to the nation, to *la patrie*, to the homeland, to the Fatherland. Englishmen, Frenchmen, Russians, and others began to accept and recognize their national identity. Scholars everywhere worked assiduously in their archives to find evidence of national glory. The older agricultural nations, with their absolute monarchs, landed aristocracy, and unprivileged commoners, began to give way to industrial nations, controlled by the new industrial bourgeoisie and by parliaments, distinguished by uniform laws for all citizens. Patriotism and love for the homeland had existed for centuries, but now they were identified with the nation. Nationalism and its sense of national consciousness were beginning to flourish throughout Europe as it took its direction from France and England.

The term nationalism admits of no simple definition. It is a complex phenomenon, often vague and mysterious in character. Its most perplexing feature is that it may differ in its forms according to specific historical conditions and the special social structure of any given country. Nationalism is used in so many different senses that such figures as Mazzini, Bolívar, and Bismarck are described as apostles of nationalism along with Mussolini and Hitler (qq.v.). Nationalism may be either liberal or integral, it may be either blessing or curse. It may have a cultural tinge, or it may be promoted as an excuse for expansion. It has many faces, as Boyd C. Shafer (q.v.) contends.

Scholars of nationalism approach the matter of definition from varying points of view. The study of this elusive subject has taken on an interdisciplinary complexion: specialists in many disciplines have devoted themselves to interpreting nationalism. They include anthropologists, political scientists, sociologists, psychologists, psychiatrists, and psychoanalysts. Each approaches the matter of definition from the point of view of its special interests. The effort continue as scholars seek to unravel the mysteries of an elusive historical phenomenon.

Carlton J. H. Hayes (q.v.), Columbia's pioneer scholar of nationalism, presented four shades of meaning:

Nationalism is an actual historical process.   Here nationalism means the actual historical process of establishing nationalities as political units, of building out of tribes and empires the modern institution of the national state.

Nationalism is a theory.   Nationalism may indicate the theory, principle, or ideal implicit in the actual historical process.

Nationalism concerns political activities.   Nationalism may mean the activities of a particular political party, combining the historical process and a political theory (French nationalism, Chinese nationalism).

Nationalism is a sentiment.   Nationalism may describe a condition of mind among members of a nationality, in which loyalty to the ideal or to the fact of one's national state is exhibited in the intrinsic excellence and in the mission of one's national state.

For Hans Kohn (q.v.) nationalism was "first and foremost a state of mind, an act of consciousness, . . . the individual's identification of himself with the 'we-group' to which he gives supreme loyalty." This definition emphasized the psychological aspect of nationalism and indicated the importance of its psychological aspects. Boyd C. Shafer pointed out that men tend to seek realization of their dearest dreams, whatever they may be, within their nations. Everywhere they erect their nations into bulwarks, no matter how weak, against adversity. This devotion to the nation is called nationalism.

Karl W. Deutsch (q.v.) approached the problem of definition by devoting his attention to the communications theory and cybernetics. In place of the conventional political, economic, and cultural factors, one or more of which always seems to be missing, Deutsch proposed that the test of nationality (a term he preferred to nationalism) be the ability to communicate more effectively with fellow members than outsiders.

Some scholars used the phraseology of social psychology in seeking to elicit the meaning of nationalism. Crane Brinton wrote that "nationalism is at bottom no more than the important form that the sense of belonging to an in-group has taken in our modern Western culture." He saw nationalism as one of the facts of life, one of the observed facts no scientist can neglect. He suggested that it is most usefully studied by the social psychologist, who is as yet no more than at the beginning of his scientific work of building cumulative knowledge. Thus, nationalism becomes a form of consciousness by which the individual proclaims his supreme loyalty to the nation.

Most historians agree that nationalism is primarily a state of mind and that it is a psychological and social fact. At the same time, they are aware that it is an idea superimposed upon the natural order and that it is endowed with a questionable personality. "Each state," wrote Edward Krehbiel, "is supposed to stand for something *sui generis*, to have a personality and qualities peculiar to it and not attainable by other peoples; and its ideas for *Kultur* are supposed to be incompatible with others and to lead to conflict." From this point of view, nationalism is not chiefly a product of physical geography, but rests on traditions of politics, religion, language, war, invasion, conquests, economics, and society, which have been fashioned by peculiar and other fortuitous circumstances and which have been preserved and synthesized by great writers and other intellectuals. The motivating desire is always to increase as far as possible the consciousness of power of the dominating nationality.

Webster's New International Dictionary gives these six definitions of nationalism:

NA'TION·AL·ISM (năsh'ŭn·ăl·ĭz'm; -'l·ĭz'm;59) *n*. 1. National character or tendency to it; nationality.

2. An idiom, trait, or character peculiar to any nation.

3. Devotion to, or advocacy of, national interests or national unity and independence; as, the *nationalism* of Ireland or China. Cf. INTERNATIONALISM, 2; NEW NATIONALISM.

4. Zealous adherence to one's own nation or to its principles; patriotism.

5. A phase of socialism advocating the nationalizing of industries;—essentially the same as *collectivism*. *Chiefly U.S.*

6. *Theol.* The doctrine that the people of a certain nation or nations are God's chosen people.

The following definition may be acceptable: Nationalism is a condition of mind, feeling, or sentiment of a group of people living in a well-defined geographical area, speaking a common language, possessing a literature in which the aspirations of the nation have been expressed, and, in some cases, having a common religion. There are, of course, exceptions to every part of this definition.

Bibliography: Louis L. Snyder, *The Meaning of Nationalism* (New Brunswick, N.J. 1954); Boyd C. Shafer, *Faces of Nationalism* (New York, 1972); Peter Alter, *Nationalism* (London, 1989).

NATIONALISM, ORIGINS OF.   Nationalism in its modern form is by no means a completely new phenomenon, but rather a revival and fusion of older trends. It existed in cruder form in the tribalism (q.v.) of primitive peoples. Throughout recorded history to the eighteenth century, tribal nationalism was submerged in metropolitanism (attachment to a city-state or cultural center) or localism (loyalty to the village or region, akin to modern ruralism or regionalism). The peoples of the ancient world were faithful to their city, e.g. Athens, Sparta, or Corinth. Rome was the center of a huge empire. The city itself was the focal point of a patriotic impulse. Some elements of nationalism existed even in the medieval era among peoples with kindred languages, customs and traditions. But this sort of group cohesion was more closely related to localism than to modern nationalism.

Nationalism in its modern form was the sequel to the emergence of the nation-state as a successor to the feudal and manorial systems and the medieval concept of sovereignty. Feudal lords had given their loyalty to king, not country. Nationalism received a powerful early stimulus in mid-seventeenth-century England, the first modern nation in which linguistic, political, economic, and religious factors merged to unite the people. But the unity was still loose. The great landmark was the French Revolution, which struck down the monarchical principle and introduced the ideas of Liberty, Equality, and Fraternity for all citizens. This was the culmination of national sentiment, which began to spread throughout Europe and the world.

The French Revolution marked the breakdown of the medieval ecclesiastical authority. It also turned loyalty for the old dynasty to veneration of the state. For some time, the elements of nationalism had existed. Now they were combined in a way to mean the existence of national sentiment. Napoleon's armies extended the idea throughout Europe. The nineteenth century saw the development of nationalism into a most powerful sentiment.

Bibliography: Hans Kohn, *The Idea of Nationalism: A Study of Its Origins and Background* (New York, 1944, 1960).

NATIONALISM AND WAR. Nationalism became the seed and product of the new imperialism from the latter part of the nineteenth century to 1914. It played a dominant role in the causes and results of both World Wars. It is logical to conclude that nationalism was among the forces that led to the death of millions of combatants and non-combatants. The failure to limit the excesses of this powerful sentiment has caused untold misery among the peoples of the world.

World War I provides a case history of how nationalism can lead to bloody conflict. The war broke out partly because of many unsolved national problems. The old Austro-Hungarian Empire, composed of a conglomerate of peoples, was worried that the South Slav irredentism (q.v.) in Serbia might in the future lead to the disruption of the empire. Suppressed national groups under the Hapsburg dual monarchy, dominated by a minority of Austrians and Hungarians, called for national self-determination and independence. The government at Vienna never had any kind of national cohesion and could not control such submerged nationalities as Slovaks and Slovenes, Czechs and Serbs, Ruthenians and Rumanians. The Czechs were insistent in their demand that the old dualism be abolished and a trialism or triple union of Austrians, Hungarians, and Slavs be established in its place.

There were other dissatisfied nationalities throughout Europe. Among the national sore spots was Alsace-Lorraine, the object of Franco-German rivalry for more than a thousand years. Germany had annexed Alsace and most of Lorraine by the Treaty of Frankfurt (1871), though many of the inhabitants were French. Italy was dissatisfied with the Austrian-held but dominantly Italian district of Trentino and the cities of Trieste and Fiume. Though Italy and Austria were treaty partners (Triple Alliance, 1882), they were at odds over this question of *Italia Irredenta* (q.v.). Italian nationalists demanded the return of their "lost provinces."

Added to the sore spots was Poland, which had been destroyed as a nation by the Three Partitions of 1772, 1793, and 1795. It was reborn as a nation during the Napoleonic Wars as the Grand Duchy of Warsaw, only to be dismembered again in 1815. The Balkans, too, called "the powder keg of Europe," seethed with discontent in 1914. Greece, Serbia, Bulgaria, and Rumania, the Balkan heirs of Turkey, wanted a greater share of the spoils of the disintegrating Ottoman Empire. Pan-Germanism and Pan-Slavism (qq.v.) were to collide head on in the Balkans.

Ironically, the war triggered by these unsolved national questions led to the destruction of the Austro-Hungarian Empire (as well as three others—German, Turkish, and Russian). The triumphant Allies at Versailles hewed to the national principle as a guide in the war settlement. They would constitute the separate nationalities into new sovereign states and justify their action by applying "the principle of nationalities and the free existence of small states." President Woodrow Wilson of the United States emphasized even more the principle of nationalities as a guideline. British scholar Elie Kedourie (q.v.) showed the dismal failure of this approach:

What happened in 1919 was, in a sense, a misunderstanding. Liberal Englishmen and Americans, thinking in terms of their own traditions of civil and religious freedom, started with a prejudice in favour of the idea that if people determine the governments they wish to have, then, *ipso facto*, civil and religious freedom would be established. Possessing, for a moment, the power to bind and loose for the whole world, they were confronted by claimants and suppliants who seemed to believe in much the same things in which liberal Englishmen and Americans believed. But, in fact, they did not. The Englishmen and Americans were saying, People who are self-governing are likely to be governed well, therefore we are in favour of self-determination; whereas their interlocutors were saying, People who live in their own national states are the only free people, therefore we claim self-determination. The distinction is a fine one, but its implications are far-reaching. International conferences are, however, not the place for fine distinctions, and in the confusion of the Peace Conference liberty was mistaken for the twin of nationality.

Nationalism also played a basic role in the outbreak of World War II. After the horrors of World War I, the 1920s seemed to augur a long era of international stability, liberal constitutionalism, and economic prosperity. But the League of Nations failed to solve the continuing serious diplomatic, political, and economic problems. The Great Depression of the 1930s brought new problems to the fore and helped create an environment in which nationalism and militarism flourished.

Despite the portents for peace, Italy, Germany, and Japan remained dissatisfied nations. In all three countries a bellicose nationalism emerged that many observers judge to be nationalism gone wrong. Italians, angered by their treatment after World War I, rejected their fragile, shallow-rooted parliamentary system and turned to Fascist Benito Mussolini (q.v.). The *Duce* founded his corporate state on chauvinistic nationalism and made no secret of his territorial ambitions. In Germany a violently nationalistic Adolf Hitler (q.v.) decided to right the wrongs of Versailles by territorial expansion. Japan's new nationalism incorporated *Shinto*, emperor-worship, and glorification of warrior virtues. (*See* **JAPANESE NATIONALISM.**) It took a world-wide coalition of military power—and grievous loss of life and property—to stifle the inflamed nationalism of Germany, Italy, and Japan.

Bibliography: Louis L. Snyder, *The War: A Concise History, 1939–1945* (New York, 1960, 1964); Elie Kedourie, *Nationalism* (London, 1960).

NATIONALISM AS A RELIGION.   Carlton J. H. Hayes (q.v.), pioneer scholar of nationalism, was the first to designate nationalism as a religion. In his book, *Nationalism: A Religion* (1960), he summarized a lifetime study of what he learned about nationalism, with special regard to its story in Europe and with tentative reflections on its course in other continents.

Hayes devoted his attention to the religious sense of the term nationalism. He showed how man's religious beliefs were exemplified not only in great surviving religions such as Christianity, Hinduism, Buddhism, and Islam, but also in contemporary communism and, especially, in modern nationalism. In its original form, nationalism was simply an expression of tribalism (q.v.), but then it declined and was displaced by broader loyalties. Its resurrection occurred in modern times among traditionally Christian peoples, but its full flowering in the West and its spread elsewhere have been relatively recent.

According to Hayes, nationalism itself became a religion in Revolutionary France. It advanced from the era of Napoleon I to Napoleon III; it hardened during the period of industrialization from 1864 to 1914; and it became the seed and product of the new imperialism from 1874 to 1914. It played a vital role in the outbreak of the two World Wars.

Hayes held that against the potential pride and selfishness of the new religion of nationalism, Christianity must hold up its ideals of humility and altruism. He advised that, to limit the excesses of the new religion of nationalism, Christians must take their own religion seriously and seek to sustain it as a truly world religion superior to divisive nationalistic religion.

Bibliography: Carlton J. H. Hayes, *Nationalism: A Religion* (New York, 1960).

NATIONALITIES IN THE SOVIET UNION.   Not only the old Russian Empire, but also the Union of Soviet Socialist Republics has been plagued by a troublesome nationalities problem. The Soviet nation is constructed on the changing sands of nationalism. More than one hundred ethnic groups are bound together in a totalitarian state. Unlike the United States, with its mingling of races, religions, and nationalities, the Soviet Union is composed of different ethnic areas which cling to their own cultural and linguistic forms. The Kremlin is faced with a dangerous nationalist ferment in many of its nationalities: minorities that demand greater power over their own destinies as well as an end to control of their homelands by Moscow. While the Soviets traditionally denounce Western imperialism and colonialism, their own minorities ask why they must remain under Russian control while other empires crumble. They see themselves as restless captives.

When Mikhail S. Gorbachev introduced his new policies of *glasnost* (openness) and *perestroika* (restructuring), Soviet nationalities saw an opportunity to break the bonds of what they regarded as suppression of their own nationalism. What began to take place in the Soviet empire was the centrifugal force of nationalism tugging at the edges of Soviet unity. Cracks began to appear in the foundation of the Soviet state as clamoring minorities began to call for recognition of their own national aspirations.

In the Baltic states of Latvia, Lithuania, and Estonia, tens of thousands demonstrated in the streets to bring attention to the Stalin-Hitler Pact that led to the occupation of their countries. They see their annexation as a quirk of history that cost them their independence. They are unhappy in their present plight and want the world to know that they deserve their freedom. (*See* **BALTIC NATIONALISMS.**)

There are similar cracks in the Soviet empire elsewhere, where national consciousness rebels against the Kremlin's power. Thousands of Armenians take to the streets and demand that the Nagorno-Karabakh Autonomous Region be incorporated into Armenia. (*See* **ARMENIAN NATIONALISM.**) The Ukraine, the most densely populated of the republics, harbors dissidents who insist that the Kremlin's polycentrism infringes on their rights. (*See* **UKRAINIAN NATIONALISM.**) Many nationalities in the Soviet Union have joined the clamor for separate identities.

The thirst for independence by units of the Soviet state has presented the Kremlin with a serious dilemma. Moscow believes that its national minorities are irreversibly integrated into the Soviet Union. It regards any calls for outright independence as treasonable activity. As soon as Gorbachev permitted a degree of liberalization, oppressed nationalities registered unhappiness with their present condition. By offering a ray of hope, he stirred new demands for genuine independence, a state of affairs he had no intention of recognizing.

The Soviet problem is based upon long-standing differences among the republics. They have different histories, different cultures, and different languages. They see their own territories as legitimate nationalities, and they believe themselves to be worthy of sovereign statehood. They regard themselves as brought by force into an artificial country, and they would like to win their freedom from a centralized dictatorship.

Added to the Kremlin's problems is the increasing restlessness in the Soviet satellites. In Poland, workers go on strike and Solidarity has won recognition for a free union to share power with the despised Soviet puppet regime. In Prague thousands of demonstrators take to the streets to mark the twentieth anniversary of the crushing of Czechoslovakian liberalism by Russian tanks. Strongly nationalistic Poles and Czechs are arrested by the police to maintain the sanctity of Soviet control. In Yugoslavia, Serbs, Croats, Montenegrans, and Albanians call for recognition of their own nationalisms. (*See* **YUGOSLAV NATIONALISM.**) The more Gorbachev uses his power to open Soviet society, the more room he gives Eastern Europeans to demand recognition of their own nationalism. The idea of self-determination (q.v.) works in both capitalistic and communist nations. Frustrated nationalisms emerge in both types of societies.

Bibliography: Roman Smal-Stocki, *The Captive Nations: Nationalism of the Non-Western Nations in the Soviet Union* (New Haven, Conn., 1960); Jeremy R. Azrael, *Soviet Nationality Politics and Practices* (New York, 1982); James E. Mace, *Communism and the Dilemmas of National Liberation* (Cambridge, Mass., 1983); Robert Conquest, *The Last Empire: Nationality and the Soviet Future* (Stanford, 1986).

NATIONALITY.   Webster's *Unabridged* gives the following definitions of nationality:

> 1. State or quality of being a nation; racial, political, or institutional solidarity constituting a nation; national character; often, specif., existence as a sovereign nation; political independence as a nation; statehood; as, the *nationality* won by Greece.
>
> 2. State, quality, or fact of belonging to, or being connected with, a (or a particular) nation or state as by nativity or allegiance; as, *nationality* acquired by birth may be lost through naturalization in another country; state or quality of being generally characteristic of a nation; as, *nationality* of art usually springs from nationality of character.
>
> 3. National feeling or attachment; the feeling or sense of being one of a people bound together by common customs, language, religion, or the like; nationalism.
>
> 4. A nation; a people united by common institutions, language, etc.

Unfortunately, these notes on the meaning of nationality are not enough to understand this commonly used word. Behind it are the efforts of generations of scholars to throw light on what has become a most difficult term in the study of its concomitant, nationalism.

Perhaps we should be content with the explanation of John Stuart Mill:

> A portion of mankind may be said to constitute a nationality if they are united among themselves by common sympathies, which do not exist between them and any others, which make them co-operate more willingly than with other people, desire to be under the same government, and desire that it should be government by themselves, or a portion of themselves exclusively.

However, the concept of nationality is complex and cannot be analyzed by formula. It is an elusive idea that defies exact definition.

The factors of common territory, language, and historical traditions have been used ordinarily in defining nationality, but it has become impossible to argue *a priori* for the presence of any one of these factors in the existence of a nationality.

To add to the difficulties in meaning, nationality is often used in a concrete sense, but on occasion may be applied in an abstract or ideal sense. When used concretely, it refers to a group of people bound together by certain common attributes, or may designate an undeveloped and non-independent national group that has not yet won national sovereignty. When used in its abstract sense, it refers to an aspiration to a united existence; in the ideal sense, it means the idea of a group of people in nations or the quality of uniting the people of the same nation.

The term nationality may have a political or a cultural connotation. According to the political concept of nationality, there is a definite Swiss nationality based on membership in the Swiss state. Yet, from the cultural point of view, a German, French, or Italian nationality is attached to every Swiss individual.

To arrive at an understanding of nationality, certain false or de-monstrably inaccurate conclusions must be rejected:

1. *Nationality does not depend on race.*   The idea that race carries an unchangeable inheritance and forms the basis of nationality is a mythical concept without scientific validity.

2. *Nationality does not depend exclusively upon language.*   The Belgians speak French and Flemish; there is no Belgian tongue. The identification of nationality with language is untenable. It conflicts with both legal and sociological concepts of a nation. Many different nations can speak the same language.

3. *Nationality and state are not synonymous terms.*   A nationality may exist without a national state. After the three partitions of Poland in 1772, 1793, and 1795, there was no Polish state until it was re-established by the Treaty of Versailles in 1919. All during the hiatus, Polish nationality continued to exist.

4. *Nationality is not the result of a "World Spirit."*   Hegel (q.v.), in his *Philosophy of History* made the claim that "a world-force visits peoples in a predetermined order and endows them with exceptional vitality for some special task. While they perform the task they are moral, virtuous, vigorous." This Hegelian view impresses few schol-ars.

5. *The idea that nationality is a "folk spirit" (Volksgeist) is ficti-tious.*   This is a kind of mystical pseudo-reality proposed by en-thusiastic but mistaken nationalists.

6. *Nationality and citizenship are not one and the same thing.*   This

corruption of the term may be attributed to jurists who use nationality to indicate citizenship.

Historians see nationality as a product of the development of society, as a historical force of the utmost importance. It is not identical with clan, tribe, or folk-group. Ethnographic groups do not necessarily form nationalities. Historians, in general, see nothing especially new in nationality. It was one of the mainstays of Luther's Reformation. What is new, they say, is the transformation of the sentiment into a political idea. Historians, however, differ whether nationality is primarily political, cultural, or a combination of both. Carlton J. H. Hayes (q.v.) believed that nationality is primarily cultural and only incidentally, political. Hans Kohn (q.v.) took the position that in recent history man has begun to regard nationality as the center of both political and cultural activity and life.

Some historians recognize the abstract, or ideal, sense of nationality. Arnold J. Toynbee held that nationality, like all great forces in human life, is nothing material or mechanical, but a subjective psychological feeling in living people. Sydney Herbert described nationality as a form that binds men together irrespective of their political allegiances or opinions, religious beliefs, or economic interests. J. Holland Rose regarded nationality "as a spiritual conception." French scholar Robert Michels held that nationality does not consist necessarily in either language or religion or a common past, but in an essential single element—the will of a people. Such psychological motivations indicate that nationality is the product of a kind of mysterious instinct, consciousness, or will that leads to a union of hearts.

Lord Acton (q.v.) saw nationality as a deleterious force in modern civilization. While admitting the importance of its mission, he described it in these terms:

> Although the theory of nationality is more absurd and criminal than the theory of socialism, it has an important mission in the world, and marks the final conflict, and therefore the end, of two forces which are the worst enemies of civil freedom—the absolute monarchy and the revolution.

For Acton the greatest adversary of the rights of nationality is the modern theory of nationality itself, because it makes the state and nation commensurate with each other in theory and reduces practically to a subject condition all other nationalities that may be within the boundaries.

Karl W. Deutsch (q.v.) expressed dissatisfaction with the conventional definition of morality as a term that may be applied to a people "among whom there exists a significant movement toward political, economic, or cultural autonomy, that is to say, toward a political organization, or a market area, or an area of political or cultural exchange, within which the personnel and the characteristics of this people will predominate." All these notions involve difficulties, because some of the most frequently cited objective characteristics of a people do not seem to be essential to its unity—language, common or contiguous territory, a common condition or experience, community of character, or community of values. Instead, Deutsch presented a functional definition. What counts, he believed, is not the presence of any single factor, but merely the presence of sufficient communication facilities with enough complementarity to produce the overall result. Deutsch regarded membership in a people as consisting essentially in the ability to communicate more effectively, and over a wide range of subjects, with members of one large group than with outsiders. He, therefore, defined nationality, in the political and social struggles of the modern age as "an alignment of large numbers of individuals from the middle and lower classes linked to regional centers and leading social groups by channels of social communication and economic intercourse, both indirectly from link to link and with the center." According to Deutsch, nationality is opened to "performance tests" based on detailed analysis of the functions carried out, to measurement, and even to prediction.

Sociologists see nationality as a combination of external and internal forces (concrete and abstract senses). They admit the impossibility of developing an objective theory of nationality without the assistance of the historian and the psychologist. Psychologists regard nationality as a subjective and psychological condition of mind, a spiritual possession, a way of thinking, feeling, and living. They believe that more attention should be given to emotional factors.

Frederick Hertz described nationality as "a community formed by the will to be a nation." This simple definition combines the main interest of several disciplines—the community (sociology and psychology), the will (psychology, psychiatry, and psychoanalysis), and a nation (history and political science). Convinced that no static definition can explain completely such partly concrete, historical, and dynamic phenomena like nationality. Hertz recommended careful examination of the general characteristics of nationality as the best means of ascertaining its meaning.

We are left with the impression that a nationality derives its character not from physical geography or biological race, but from cultural and historical forces. The working definition by Carlton J. H. Hayes: "I would define nationality as a cultural group of people who speak a common language (or closely related dialects) and who possess a community of historical traditions (religious, territorial, political, military, economic, artistic, and intellectual.")

Bibliography: Louis L. Snyder, *The Meaning of Nationalism* (New Brunswick, N.J., 1954); Friedrich Hertz, *Nationality in History and Politics* (London, 1957); A. G. Bailey, *Culture and Nationality* (Toronto, 1972); T. H. Moody (ed.), *Nationality and the Pursuit of National Independence* (Belfast, 1978); G. Carter Bentley, *Ethnicity and Nationality* (Seattle, 1981); Philip L. White, "What is a Nationality?" *Canadian Review of Studies in Nationalism*, 12, No. 1 (Spring, 1985), 1–23; Robert Conquest, *Nationality and the Soviet Future* (Stanford, 1986).

NKRUMAH, KWAME (1909–1972). Political organizer, first President of Ghana, and leading ideologist of black nationalism. Born in Nkroful, Gold Coast, Nkrumah was graduated from Achimota College in 1930. He started his teaching career at Catholic junior schools, and later studied in the United States and at the London School of Economics. Attracted to the new African nationalism, he studied the work of Marcus Garvey (q.v.), who wanted to establish a black-governed nation in Africa. At this time Nkrumah described himself as a non-denominational Christian and a Marxist socialist. In his first major publication, *Towards Colonial Freedom* (1947), he presented his support for the anti-colonial struggle.

Returning to the Gold Coast, Nkrumah began a campaign of "non-violence and non-cooperation" to cripple the forces of imperialism in his country. Appealing primarily to veterans and the youth, he sought to create a mass base for the new movement. His Convention People's Party used a special technique that parodied the phraseology of Christianity in order to invest Nkrumah with a religious aura. Note this imitation of the Apostle's Creed:

> I believe in the Convention People's Party
> The opportune Saviour of Ghana,
> And in Kwame Nkrumah its founder and leader,
> Who is endowed with the Ghana Spirit,
> Born a true Ghanaian for Ghana;
> Suffering under victimizations;
> Was vilified, threatened with deportation;
> He disentangled himself from the clutches of the U.G.C.C.*
> And the same day he rose victorious with the 'verandah boys,'
> Ascended the Political Heights,
> And sitteth at the Supreme head of the C.P.P.**
> From whence he shall demand Full Self-government for Ghana.

*United Gold Coast Convention.
**Convention People's Party.

Nkrumah was a master in illustrating the nexus between leader and followers in the kind of politics of which nationalism is dominant. His organization, called *The Circle*, had a motto of three S's: Service, Sacrifice, Suffering, which was to be the revolutionary motto of the struggle for West African unity and national independence. His goal was "to make it impossible and difficult for demagogues, quislings, traitors, cowards, and self-seekers to lead astray any section of the masses of the African people." Members were to abide by these rules:

1. I will irrevocably obey and act upon the orders, commands, instructions and directions of the Grand Council of THE CIRCLE.
2. I will always serve, sacrifice and suffer anything for the cause for which THE CIRCLE stands, and will at all times be ready to go on any mission that I may be called upon to perform.
3. I will always and in all circumstances help a member brother of THE CIRCLE in all things and in all difficulties.
4. I will, except as a last resort, avoid the use of violence.
5. I will make it my aim and duty to foster the cause for which THE CIRCLE stands in any organisation that I may become a member.
6. I will on the 21st day of each month fast from sunrise to sunset and will meditate daily on the cause THE CIRCLE stands for.
7. I accept the Leadership of Kwame Nkrumah.

At the Pan-African Congress held at Manchester, England, in 1945, Nkrumah and George Padmore, a West Indian ideologist, called for African independence. By 1957 the Gold Coast has won a new status inside the British Commonwealth and Nkrumah was its leader as President of Ghana. His followers called him the Redeemer of Africa; his opponents labeled him an inflexible dictator. He was overthrown in 1966 by a police-army coup. Meanwhile, Nkrumah had won a considerable reputation as a leader for "Black Power" and as a spokesman for African unity.

Bibliography: Kwame Nkrumah, *The Autobiography of Kwame Nkrumah* (Edinburgh, 1957); Kwame Nkrumah, *Hands Off Africa!* (Accra, 1960); Timothy Barkhole, *Kwame Nkrumah: From Cradle to Grave* (Dorchester, Eng., 1981); Yuri Amertin, *Kwame Nkrumah* (New York, 1987).

O

O.A.S. (Organization of American States).   *See* **PAN-AMERI-CANISM.**

O.A.U. (Organization of African Unity).   The O.A.U. was formed in 1963 with delegates from thirty-two states, and under the chairmanship of President Sekou Touré of Guinea. A permanent secretariat was set up in Addis Ababa, Ethiopia, where heads of African states would meet each year to discuss common problems. Its goals were to resolve differences between two major factions in the Pan-African movement (the conservative Monrovia bloc and the radical Casablanca group), to promote unity among all African states, and eradicate all forms of colonialism. Eventually, all independent states of Africa with the exception of South Africa, became members of the O.A.U.

Members of the O.A.U. rarely managed to act in concert. There were far too many differences among the units, most of which were controlled by nationalist rulers. The prestige of O.A.U. declined when Idi Amin, deposed dictator of Uganda, managed to acquire temporary leadership in its affairs. Denounced as "the black Hitler," he was accused of the murder of at least 200,000 Ugandans in a barbaric blood bath. Another African leader who aspired unsuccessfully to the chairmanship of the O.A.U. was Colonel Muammar Kaddafi, Islamic fundamentalist, who was accused of using Libya's vast oil wealth to promote terrorism throughout Europe and the world.

The deterioration of the O.A.U. meant that Africa would be divided into hostile ideological camps, and that the organization would lose its credibility in international diplomacy. There was growing concern that a divided Africa would invite a new scramble for influence by foreign powers. (*See also* **PAN-AFRICANISM.**)

O'CONNELL, DANIEL (1775–1847).   Irish statesman, patriot, and nationalist. Born to an old family of Catholic gentry, O'Connell performed the historic role of bringing the native Catholics of Ireland into modern political life. In 1829, while head of the Catholic Association, he managed to extract from the Tory government the Catholic Relief Act, which, at long last, opened the Westminster Parliament to Catholics throughout the British Isles. From then until shortly before his death, he dominated Irish politics. His admirers regarded him as "the Liberator," while his English enemies called him "scum condensed of Irish bog, ruffian, coward, demagogue."

In 1840, after fighting for ten years in a disappointing effort to win London's support for ameliorating Ireland's grievances, O'Connell founded the National Repeal Association to put an end to the Act of Union and restore an Irish parliament. During 1843 he traveled extensively through Ireland addressing immense rallies. In long, eloquent speeches, he denounced the union as an obstacle to the Catholic cause. He spoke against the measure in Parliament and attacked it while claiming that the demands of Ireland had been slighted or set aside. He insisted that repeal of the union would not weaken the bond between England and Ireland. Meetings in his support were organized by the priesthood.

Early in 1844 O'Connell and his son, together with five of his chief supporters, were tried for a conspiracy to raise sedition. He and his followers were convicted and sent to prison, but they were freed after the House of Lords found a writ of error. The release was celebrated throughout Ireland with bonfires blazing across the island.

By this time, however, the spell of O'Connell's oratory had all but vanished and his health had suffered. Old and jealous of his authority, he was now confronted with the Young Ireland movement. A man of moderation and restraint, he opposed the new revolutionary tactics of the young fighters for Irish freedom. After angry disputes with his young rivals, O'Connell left Ireland on January 26, 1847. Disturbed by the revolutionary ideology, he traveled to the Continent. He died at Genoa while on his way to Rome.

Irish Catholics remained loyal to O'Connell's memory. They admired his wisdom and his cautious moderation. However, the battle he fought was not to be won in his generation. In his last year the repeal movement was in a state of collapse as famine spread throughout Ireland. (*See also* **IRISH NATIONALISM.**)

Bibliography: Robert Dunlop, *Daniel O'Connell and National Life in Ireland* (New York, 1900); Angus Macintyre, *The Liberator: Daniel O'Connell and the Irish Party, 1830–1847* (London, 1965); Raymond Moley, *Daniel O'Connell: Evolution Without Violence* (New York, 1974); Charles C. Trench, *The Great Dan: A Biography of Daniel O'Connell* (London, 1984).

OPPRESSION NATIONALISM.   *See* NATIONALISM, CLASSIFICATIONS OF.

ORGANIZATION OF AMERICAN STATES (O.A.S.).   *See* PAN-AMERICANISM.

ORIGINS OF NATIONALISM.   *See* NATIONALISM, ORIGINS OF.

ORWELL, GEORGE, pseudonym of ERIC BLAIR (1903–1950).   British novelist, essayist, and strong critic of nationalism. Educated at Eton, he served with the Indian Imperial Police from 1922 to 1927, and later underwent a period of poverty as tutor, teacher, and bookshop assistant. In 1936 he fought and was wounded in the Spanish Civil War. After World War II, he published two books that won him world fame: *Animal Farm* (1945), a biting satire on dictatorship, and *Nineteen Eighty Four* (1949), which revealed the horrors of totalitarianism.

In Orwell's pessimistic view of nationalism, he compared its victims to insects:

> By nationalism I mean first of all the habit of assuming that human beings can be classified like insects and that whole blocks of millions, tens of millions of people can confidently be labelled "good" or "bad!" But secondly—and this is much more important—I mean the habit of identifying oneself with a single nation or other unit, placing it beyond good or evil and recognizing no other duty than that of advancing its own interest.

Bibliography: Raymond Williams, *George Orwell* (New York, 1981); Bernard Crick, *George Orwell: A Life* (Boston, 1983); Averil Gardner, *George Orwell* (Boston, 1987).

O'SULLIVAN, JOHN LEWIS (1815–1895).   Jacksonian Democrat and fervent jingoist, coiner of the famous phrase "manifest destiny." In 1837 O'Sullivan founded *The United States Magazine and Democratic*

Review, an expansionist journal. His stated goal was to "strike the hitherto silent strings of the American genius of the country." He praised all things American and predicted that the United States would be the great nation of the future. In the July-August 1845 issue of his magazine he declared that foreign nations were attempting to obstruct the annexation of Texas in order to check "the fulfillment of our manifest destiny to overspread the continent allotted by Providence for the free development of our yearly multiplying millions."

O'Sullivan's expression of "manifest destiny" as vital in American nationalism (q.v.) came into national vogue after it was used in an editorial in the New York *Morning News* of December 27, 1845. The term was first employed in Congress on the following January 3, 1846, in a speech made by representative Robert C. Winthrop (Mass.). Winthrop referred to "the right of our manifest destiny to spread over the whole continent."

In an earlier edition of his magazine (1839), O'Sullivan expressed the tenor of his American nationalism by calling the United States "the great nation of futurity." The last paragraph of this editorial:

> Yes, we are the nation of progress, of individual freedom, of universal enfranchisement. Equality of rights is the cynosure of our union of states, the grand exemplar of the correlative equality of individuals; and, while truth sheds its effulgence, we cannot retrograde without dissolving the one and subverting the other. We must onward to the fulfilment of our mission—to the entire development of the principle of our organization—freedom of conscience, freedom of person, freedom of trade and business pursuits, universality of freedom and equality. This is our high destiny, and in nature's eternal, inevitable decree of cause and effect we must accomplish it. All this will be our future history, to establish on earth the moral dignity and salvation of man—the immutable truth and beneficience of God. For this blessed mission to the nations of the world, which are shut out from the lifegiving light of truth, has America been chosen; and her high example shall smite unto death the tyranny of kings, hierarchs, and oligarchs and carry the glad tidings of peace and good will where myriads now endure an existence scarcely more enviable than that of beasts in the field. Who, then, can doubt that our country is destined to be *the great nation* of futurity?

Bibliography: John Louis O'Sullivan, "The Great Nation of Futurity," *The United States Magazine and Democratic Review,* 6 (November, 1839), 2–6.

OTPOR. "Resistance" in Croatian. A Yugoslav organization fighting for Croatian independence. (*See* **CROATIAN SEPARATISM.**)

P

PALACKÝ, FRANTIŠEK (1798–1876). Historian, champion of Czech nationalism, and early apostle of Pan-Slavism, Palacký was a prolific writer on the nationalist ideal. In 1832 he began his major work on a history of the Czech nation in Bohemia and Moravia to 1526. He described the Hussite period as the central point of Czech history and as the fulcrum of the national and religious struggle. As scholar and patriot, he was influenced by Herder (q.v.), who was attentive to Slavic folklore; by Rousseau (q.v.) and his eulogy of Slavic agricultural life; and by Kant (q.v.) and his categorical imperative.

From the beginning of his work, Palacký advocated liberal nationalism. He proposed a federation of free and equal Czech nations inside the Austro-Hungarian Empire. Moderate in disposition, he eschewed revolution and violence in favor of national liberation through education and enlightenment. He favored a strong Austro-Hungarian combination of southern German and Slavic peoples, all maintaining their individual rights.

Palacký expressed his sense of liberal nationalism in a famous letter:

> I am a Czech of Slav descent and with all the little I own and possess I have devoted myself wholly and forever to the service of my nation. That nation is small, it is true, but from time immemorial it has been an independent nation with its own character; its rulers have participated since old times in the federation of German princes, but the nation never regarded itself nor was it regarded by others throughout all the centuries, as part of the German nation. The whole union of

the Czech lands first with the Holy Roman Empire and then with the German Confederation was always a purely dynastic one of which the Czech nation, the Czech Estates, hardly wished to know and which they hardly noticed.

Palacký was careful to avoid antagonizing the Russians. He proclaimed his "loyal sympathy by which this great nation within its natural borders progresses along the road to civilization." But he also expressed his distaste for a Russian universal monarchy, "not because that movement would be Russian, but because it would be universal." He believed that both Austrian and German Empires should organize themselves on a basis of equality. He cited as dangers an expansive Germany, a domineering Magyar nationalism (q.v.), and a Russian universal state. Above all, he was a man of peace devoted to democratic ideals.

Palacký's call for a federation within the Austrian Empire received much support among fellow Slavs. Yet, by mid-nineteenth century the idea of such a union collapsed. Palacký retired from active political life, but still expressed his advocacy of a Czech kingdom to include Bohemia, Moravia, and Silesia. He died at Prague on May 26, 1876, leaving a heritage as the venerated father of Czech Pan-Slavism. (*See* **PAN-SLAVISM.**) His influence on Czech nationalism was enormous. The subsequent liberal nationalism of Tómaš Masaryk owed much to Palacký's advocacy of federalism.

Bibliography: František Palacký, *Geschichte Böhmens* (5 vols., Prague, 1836–1867); Hans Kohn, *Pan-Slavism: Its History and Ideology* (Notre Dame, Ind., 1953); Joseph F. Zacek, *Palacký: The Historian as Scholar and Nationalist* (The Hague, 1970).

PALESTINE LIBERATION ORGANIZATION (P.L.O.).   Organization formed to win a territorial home for the Arab Palestinians either displaced after the formation of Israel in 1948 and living in exile throughout the Arab world or in Israel under Israeli domination. After Israel's successful war against a combination of Arab League states (Syria, Lebanon, Transjordan, Iraq, and Egypt), some 700,000 Arabs were expelled from their homeland in Palestine. The P.L.O. was formed to bring Arab refugees living in Jordan, Syria, Lebanon, and the Gaza Strip back to their homeland.

Since the 1967 war, Israel had regarded the West Bank and Gaza as essential to basic security. Contending that the P.L.O. had used terrorist tactics and that it was dedicated to the destruction of their country, Israelis refused negotiations. In late 1987, Palestinian men, women, and children on the West Bank began a stone-throwing campaign called the *intifada*, to which Israeli soldiers replied with both rubber bullets and real bullets. Scores of Palestinians died in the confrontation. The riots continued for a year.

Meanwhile, the United States, which had supported Israel since its inception in 1948, sought for some means to bring peace to the Middle East. The problem was that the P.L.O. had set its goal as the displacement of Israel by a Palestinian state. Washington made it clear to Yasir Arafat (q.v.), spokesman for the P.L.O., that negotiations for a settlement could not be started until he made two explicit public statements: (1) that the P.L.O. recognized the state of Israel; and (2) he would renounce all terroristic tactics against Israel. Make these statements, Washington urged, and the United States would end its thirteen years of diplomatic isolation. Serious discussions on how Israel might trade land for peace might then begin.

Arafat was faced with a dilemma. The P.L.O. was deeply divided under his leadership. There was no guarantee that its extremists, such as Abu Nidal, would not seek to derail the peace initiative with new acts of terror. Nevertheless, in the last weeks of the Reagan administration, Arafat spoke at Geneva and recognized the right of all parties concerned in the Middle East to peace and security, "including Palestine, Israel, and other neighbors." Then, on the matter of terrorism: "Repeat for the record that we totally and absolutely renounce all forms of terrorism, including individual group and state terrorism." Secretary of State George Schultz, who had stubbornly worn down the P.L.O. leader, announced that the United States would at last talk to the P.L.O.

The Israeli government was stunned by this unexpected development. Prime Minister Yitzhak Shamir opposed his American patrons: "The U.S. decision will not promote peace but only encourage terrorism. . . . This is a tragic mistake." The Israelis pointed out that Arafat's renunciation of terrorist acts in the past was nullified by evidence suggesting his support for their undertaking.

The issue is still unresolved. The bitter conflict reveals a kind of impossible situation when two nationalisms confront one another for control of the same territory. Israel contends that it has been attacked again and again by Arabs who lost the wars and then expected to win the fruits of victory. It sees Arafat's phased strategy as Israel's eventual liquidation. (*See also* **ARAFAT, YASIR.**)

Bibliography: Don Peretz, *Israel and the Palestine Arabs* (Washington, D.C., 1958); Cheryl Ruhenberg, *The Palestine Liberation Organization: Its Institutional Infrastructure* (Belmont, Mass., 1983); Jillian Becker, *The P.L.O.: The Rise and Fall of the Palestine Liberation Organization* (New York, 1984).

PAN-AFRICANISM.   Along with the rise of nationalism in Africa from the 1950s on went a second major movement, an attempt and an unsuccessful one to implement the call for a nationalism writ large. The thrust for this new macro-nationalism (q.v.) came from outside the continent. Behind it were two individuals: the charismatic Marcus Garvey and the intellectual W. E. Burkhardt Du Bois (qq.v.), each of whom hoped to bring the continent into a new racial federation. The ideas behind Pan-Africanism were the principle of self-determination (q.v.) and insistence upon measures to be taken to insure the social and economic betterment of all Africans.

The first stage of Pan-Africanism was under the leadership of blacks residing in the United States and the West Indies. This early form was devoted to black separatism, demanding a home in Africa for blacks no matter where they lived. The movement held that those blacks who had been brought in slavery to the United States and the Caribbean since the early seventeenth century had a homeland to which they should return. The second stage came with the decolonization of Africa after World War II. Now the leadership and character of Pan-Africanism became really African. Educated blacks who had studied abroad came back to their countries to provide new African leadership for unity. They would win real political emancipation, as well as economic prosperity and industrial modernization for their people.

In the opening stage, the idea of Pan-Africanism appeared as early as the 1870s in the United States following the era of Reconstruction. Alienated by growing racism and economic depression, American blacks began to think in terms of going back to Africa. Benjamin F. Porter, President of the Liberia Joint Stock Company of Charleston, South Carolina, claimed that he had some 150,000 exiles who wanted to return "to the Fatherland." He said that he aimed to build a nationality of Africans: "We wish to come bringing our wives and little ones with what wealth and education we have been able to acquire in the land of our exile and in the house of bondage."

Bishop Henry N. Turner demanded an indemnity "to go home to Africa." His fellow Negroes, he said, had remained in slavery for 250 years and had been free for a mere 50 years. They had been dominated by the "buckra," the white race, and were denied civil and political rights while helping to enrich the country:

The fool Negro has no more sense than a jackass, ridicules the idea of asking for a hundred million dollars to go home, for Africa is our home, and the one place that offers us manhood and freedom. . . . Every man that has the sense of an animal must see that there is no future in this country for the Negro.

The white people, he charged, are all alike. "The moment Africa is mentioned they swarm like bees and pour the vituperation and scandal upon the only spot that offers manhood and freedom."

This was said in 1900. That same year, a black barrister, H. Sylvester Williams of Trinidad, who was practicing law in London, called a Pan-African Congress. Some thirty delegates attended. For the first time the term "Pan-African" was used at the conference. This opening meeting of Pan-African enthusiasts had little impact at the time. For nearly two decades the movement remained quiescent. Then it was revived under the leadership of two advocates, the flamboyant Marcus Garvey and the quiet intellectual W. E. Burkhardt Du Bois. Both called for the independence of African peoples from their colonial masters and for the promotion of Pan-Africanism. In his brief career, Garvey, promising a black nation in the African homeland, led a popular mass movement whose goal was the migration of American blacks to Africa. He managed to transform a new hope for a black community into the largest secular organization in black American history. He gave pride and dignity to a people wounded by prejudice and injustice. However, he was less than successful in promoting the idea of Pan-Africanism. His attempts to establish branches of his movement in Africa met the opposition of both African and European leaders.

Black Americans, alienated by Garvey's bizarre behavior, turned instead to a leader whose approach was far removed from the eccentricities of Marcus Garvey. Du Bois, with a brilliant academic and writing career behind him, joined other blacks and whites in 1909 in forming the National Association for the Advancement of Colored Peoples (N.A.A.C.P.). In a memorandum sent to President Woodrow Wilson in 1919 at the Versailles Peace Conference, Du Bois urged that the then prevailing sentiment of self-determination (q.v.) be applied to Africa.

> This Africa for the Africans would be under the guidance of international organization. The governing international commission should represent not simply government, but the modern culture, science, commerce, social reform, and religious philanthropy. It must represent not simply the white world but the civilized Negro world.

The correspondent for the Chicago *Tribune* reported the details of the Du Bois memorandum of a "dream for an Ethiopian Utopia." He said, "It is quite Utopian, and it has less than a Chinaman's chance of getting anywhere at the Peace Conference, but it is nevertheless interesting." Du Bois eventually gave up in disgust and joined the Communist Party.

Between 1919 and 1927 Du Bois convened four Pan-American Congresses in Europe and the United States. All these meetings stressed the absolute equality of races. There was much enthusiastic oratory, but there were few practical results. The First African Congress, meeting in Paris in late February 1919, consisted of fifty-seven delegates from fifteen countries. The assembly drafted an appeal to the Peace Conference to give the Negroes of Africa a chance to develop unhindered by other races. Its demands made in a series of resolutions set the tone for future conferences:

1. That the Allied and Associated Powers establish a code of laws for the international protection of the natives of Africa.
2. That the League of Nations establish a permanent bureau for this purpose.
3. The Negroes of the world demand that the natives of Africa and all peoples of African descent be governed according to these principles:
   (a) The *land* and its natural resources be held in trust for the natives.
   (b) *Capital*. The investment of capital and granting of concessions shall be so regulated as to prevent exploitation of the natives and exhaustion of the natural wealth of the country.
   (c) *Labor*. Slavery and corporal punishment should be abolished.
   (d) *Education*. It was the right of every native child to read and write. The State should be responsible for higher education.
   (e) *The State*. The natives of Africa must have the right to participate in Government. If any State excludes citizens or subjects of Negro descent from its body politic, it was the duty of the League of Nations to bring the matter to the civilized world.

The Second Pan-African Congress met in London on August 28, 1921. Of the 113 delegates, 41 were from Africa, 35 from the United States, 24 from Europe, and 7 from the West Indies. Other sessions were held in Brussels and Paris. Again, Du Bois played a leading role in the meetings. The world, he said, must face two eventualities: either the complete assimilation of Africa with two or three of the great world-states, with political, civil, and social power equal for its black and white citizens, or a great black African state as a part of a great society of people in which it takes its place with others as co-rulers of the world. It was a shame, he said, that the relations between the great groups of mankind and their mutual estimate and respect was determined chiefly by the degree in which one could subject the other to its service, enslaving labor, making ignorance compulsory, uprooting religion and customs, and destroying government. All this so that the favored few could luxuriate in the toil of the many.

The Third Pan-African Congress met in London in 1923 and was continued in Lisbon later in the year. Eleven countries were represented. At the Lisbon meeting, demands were made specifically for Africans *(italics as in the original text):*

1. A *voice* in their own government.
2. The *right* of access to land and its resources.
3. *Trial by juries* of their peers and under established forms of law.
4. *Free elementary* education for all; broad training in modern industrial technique; and higher training of selected talent.
5. *The development* of Africa for the benefit of Africans, and not merely for the profit of Europeans.
6. *The abolition* of the slave trade and of the liquor traffic.
7. *World disarmament* and the abolition of war; but failing this, and as long as white folk bear arms against black folk, the right of blacks to bear arms in their own defense.
8. *The organization* of commerce and industry so as to make the main objects of capital and labor the welfare of the many rather than the enriching of the few.

The Fourth Pan-African Congress was held in New York in 1927, with 13 countries participating. There were 208 delegates from 22 American states. This time a resolution stressed six points. Negroes everywhere need *(italics as in the original text):*

1. A *voice* in their own government.
2. *Native rights* to the land and its natural resources.
3. *Modern education* for all children.
4. *The development* of Africa for the Africans and not merely for the profit of Europeans.
5. *The reorganization* of commerce and industry so as to make the main object of capital and labor the welfare of the many rather than the enriching of the few.
6. The treatment of civilized men as civilized despite differences of birth, race, or color.

For the next fifteen years the Pan-African idea lay dormant. Neither Garvey nor Du Bois had been successful in maintaining momentum for Pan-Africanism and the Return-to-Africa movement. After World War II the idea was revived when the European imperialist powers withdrew from the continent. The first Conference of Independent African States met in April 1958 at Accra, capital of Ghana. Two years later the Second Conference of independent African States convened at Addis Ababa, Ethiopia. Here the Pan-African movement split into major factions. The conservative Monrovia bloc favored a "community" of African nations rather than a union ("Africans should respect one another's sovereignty"). On the radical side was the Casablanca bloc, which leaned more to Pan-Africanism. In 1963 the Organization of African Unity was formed.

Despite the efforts of Garvey and Du Bois and the post-World War II revival, Pan-Africanism remained divided into ineffective parts.

Throughout its existence it was burdened by differences in leadership, political orientation, and nationalist ideology. There was little agreement among its supporters, except in general denunciation of white supremacy. In the United States and the Caribbean, where the concept originated, the movement collapsed under the eccentricities of Garvey and the unpopular intellectualism of Du Bois. Pan-Africanism did help somewhat to prevent the Balkanization of all Africa, but the continent remained in a ferment as each artificially created new state attempted in its own way to determine its political future. Most Africans were faced with the enormous task of developing a sense of nationhood above and beyond the loyalties of the past.

Bibliography: Rupert Emerson, *From Empire to Nation: The Rise to Self-Assertion of Asian and African Peoples* (Cambridge, Mass., 1960); Vincent D. Thompson, *Africa and Unity: The Evolution of Pan-Africanism* (Atlantic Highlands, N.J., 1969); Elie Kedourie (ed.), *Nationalism in Asia and Africa* (New York, 1970); J. A. Langley, *Pan-Africanism and Nationalism in West Africa. 1900–1945* (Oxford, 1973); Immanuel Geiss, *The Pan-African Movement* (New York, 1974); Tony Martin, *The Pan-African Connection: From Slavery to Garvey and Beyond* (Dover, Mass., 1984).

PAN-AMERICANISM. As a macro-nationalism (q.v.), Pan-Americanism has developed in three forms. Its original tenor was close to Pan-Hispanism (q.v.), a nineteenth-century movement that aimed to unite the Spanish-speaking peoples of South America. The second form was an attempt to close the gap that existed between the Spanish-American states and others such as Brazil and Haiti. In the third and best known category, emerging at the end of the nineteenth century, an attempt was made under the leadership of the United States to extend Pan-Americanism to include both South and North America. The movement was described by President Calvin Coolidge:

> In the spirit of Christopher Columbus all of the Americas have an eternal bond of unity, a common heritage bequeathed to us alone. Unless we deem the promise which his voyage held for humanity, it must remain forever void. This is the destiny which Pan-Americanism has chosen to fulfill.

Pan-Americanism differs from other macro-nationalisms in that it is hemispheric rather than continental. It has no single linguistic base: its major languages include Spanish, Portuguese, French, and English. It has little political solidarity: it remains a loose union ready for political action only if acquisitive Europeans make an effort to

Balkanize the Western Hemisphere. Similar to Pan-Europa (q.v.), it is largely economic in tone. Hemispheric solidarity is regarded as a means of promoting the economic well-being of the member states.

Actually, Pan-Americanism has few historical traditions that make for hemispheric unity. The hemisphere is divided into several distinct cultures, dominantly Anglo-Saxon in the north and largely Hispanic in the south. The sort of nationhood existing in Europe is different from that in Latin America. Mexican author and diplomat Carlos Fuentes explained it this way:

> Nationalism represents a profound value for Latin Americans simply because of the fact that our nationhood is still in question. In New York, Paris, or London, no one loses sleep asking himself whether the nation exists. In Latin America you can wake up and find that the nation is no longer there, usurped by a military junta, a multinational corporation, or an American ambassador surrounded by a bevy of technical advisers.

Behind Pan-Americanism is the Monroe Doctrine. In 1823 President James Monroe proclaimed a doctrine opposing any European attempts to control Latin American countries that had won their independence. It presented four major points: (1) the American hemisphere was no longer to be considered as open for future colonization by European powers; (2) the American political system was essentially different from that of Europe; (3) the United States considered it dangerous to its peace and safety if any attempts were made by European powers to extend their system to any part of the Western Hemisphere; and (4) the United States would not interfere with existing colonies or dependencies of European powers in the New World or would she interfere in the internal affairs of European nations. The Monroe Doctrine was a unilateral declaration coming from Washington without consultation with or approval by Latin-American states. It was the result of United States self-interest, commercial design, and neighborly altruism. The British uneasily professed support for the Monroe Doctrine.

At first, Latin Americans welcomed the Monroe Doctrine, even though it seemed to establish a kind of United States control of their affairs. Later, they began to denounce it as an arm of United States imperialism, even though the doctrine spared them from the kind of spoliation that took place in Africa and Asia during the Age of Imperialism. Latin-American criticism rose steadily in the twentieth century. Despite Washington's cautious diplomacy, Latin Americans resented preaching from the North. Politically, they wanted to make their own decisions. Economically, they saw evil effects in the existence of what they called "dollar diplomacy." Culturally, they revealed a strong anti-Yankee sentiment and preferred the mystique of an affinity with the Old World. They were not altogether attracted by the kind of Pan-Americanism modeled on the Monroe Doctrine. Yet, despite this opposition, the Monroe Doctrine was effective in eliminating from Latin America the kind of territorial penetration Europeans had brought about on other continents.

With the flowering of nationalism in the nineteenth century, several conferences were held under Hispanic-American auspices for the implementation of Pan-Americanism. The results were unimpressive. Most Latin Americans were interested only in their own national problems and had no intention of turning to a larger nationalism. Among their more important interests were the necessity of maintaining their borders against grasping neighbors, the need to thwart any attempts at recolonization by Spain, and the urge to counter any influence of the United States. In the nineteenth century, Latin-American intellectuals preached the solidarity of continental peoples, but the idea of national sovereignty appeared to be considerably more important than the prospect of continental unity.

At the end of the nineteenth century, the United States appeared as the new leader for Pan-Americanism. While European nations turned their attention to the scramble for control of African and Asian resources, the United States showed its interest in the southern American continent. The United States had no need for additional territory, but its entrepreneurs were attracted by economic advantages offered by the Latin-American states. Toward the end of the century, the term Pan-Americanism gained some attention in the United States as a counterpart to Pan-Slavism and Pan-Germanism.

In May 1888 the United States Congress authorized the meeting of a Pan-American Congress to be held in Washington in October 1889. Canada, because of its association with the British Empire, was not invited. The delegates were entertained lavishly with an expense-paid expedition to see the natural wonders of the country. About seventy sessions were held until April 1890. Before its adjournment, the Congress created the International Union of American Republics to gather and distribute commercial information for member nations. The New York *Tribune* praised its results:

> The ground has been leveled, the way has been opened for securing united action upon the part of the eighteen commonwealths which will promote the enlightened interests of each and the common welfare of all, and it now remains for the United States to take the initiative and complete a great work of high civilization. By conciliatory diplomacy, by the opportune negotiation of treaties, by energetic and

intelligent action and by perseverance and patience and tact, the State Department can accomplish great and memorable results for American civilization.

Opinion in Latin America was not altogether favorable. Cuban patriot José Martí (q.v.) condemned the Congress as "a worthless meeting, or a presidential campaign banner, or a pretext for a subsidy hunt." He saw the independent states of Latin America as being pushed to their knees by a Yankee master. Other Latin Americans denounced the United States as a juggernaut, an imperialistic monster, a dreaded foreigner, that had fixed its eyes upon the entire American family of nations. The idea of an effective Pan-Americanism under United States auspices was difficult to implement in the face of this suspicion of Washington.

Nevertheless, some ten conferences were held from 1901 to 1919, at which representatives of twenty-one American republics discussed a variety of subjects from codification of international law to financial, industrial, and commercial problems. At the Pan-American Conference held at Havana in 1928, Latin Americans, nursing their anger compounded over many years, denounced the United States in bitter terms. There had been some resentment in previous congresses, but nothing to compare with these new outbursts. Crowds in the galleries roared approval of remarks made against the United States and hissed pro-American speakers. The *Wall Street Journal* remarked:

> Here in the United States as well as throughout the Latin republics there has been a campaign as dishonest as it is determined, to picture this country as the aggressor of other republics. No proof has been adduced; the parties, instead, have relied upon the constant repetition of the falsehood.

La Nación of Buenos Aires, replied: "The high-sounding declarations often heard in Havana do not serve to erase the inexcusable acts committed in Central America which still weigh overwhelmingly and paralyze real Pan-Americanism."

A new approach to Pan-Americanism was introduced by President Franklin D. Roosevelt. In his inaugural address on March 4, 1933, he stated: "In the field of world politics, I would dedicate this nation to the policy of the Good Neighbor—the neighbor who resolutely respects himself and because he does so, respects the rights of others—the neighbor who respects the sanctity of his agreements in and with a world of neighbors." Roosevelt saw the essential qualities of a true Pan-Americanism as the same as those that constitute a good neighbor, namely, mutual understanding, and through such understanding, a sympathetic appreciation of the other's view.

Despite the tradition of Latin-American hostility to the United

States, inter-American unity was maintained, with some exceptions, during World War II. Throughout Central and South America, again with exceptions, there was opposition to the ideology and actions of Adolf Hitler (q.v.). Within seven months after Pearl Harbor in 1941, twelve Latin American states declared war on the Axis. All the rest, with the exception of Argentina and Chile, severed relations with Germany and Italy. Fear of Nazi Germany acted as a stimulant for a temporary sense of Pan-American solidarity.

On March 9, 1948, the Ninth Conference of American States was called to stabilize relations in the Western Hemisphere during the Cold War. The culmination of the Pan-American movement came with the formation of the Organization of American States (O.A.S.). The O.A.S. Charter revealed its aims:

> Convinced that the historic mission of America is to offer man a land of liberty, and a favorable environment for the development of his personality and the realization of his just aspirations;
>
> Conscious that that mission has already inspired numerous agreements, whose essential value lies in the desire of the American peoples to live together in peace, and, through their mutual understanding and respect for the sovereignty of each one, to provide for the betterment of all, in independence, in equality and under law;
>
> Confident that the true significance of American solidarity and good neighborliness can only mean the consolidation of the continent, within the framework of democratic institutions, of a system of individual liberty and social justice based on respect for the essential rights of man;
>
> Persuaded that their welfare and their contribution to the progress and the civilization of the world will increasingly require intense continental cooperation;
>
> Resolved to persevere in the noble undertaking that humanity has conferred on the United Nations, whose principles and purposes they solemnly reaffirm;
>
> Convinced that juridical organization is a necessary condition for security and peace founded on moral order and on justice. . . .

With the O.A.S. much progress seemed to have been made in the movement toward hemispheric harmony. However, despite the oratory and the expressed goals, many Latin Americans continued to interpret Pan-Americanism as merely revealing the imperialistic aims of the United States. Central and South America, they charged, had been mortgaged to the United States in a series of critical loans and investments. They would prefer a rival *Union Latino-Americana* in opposition to a Pan-Americanism dictated from Washington.

Although it has had paper successes, Pan-Americanism has been a troubled partnership, primarily because of the urge to national sovereignty. North Americans and Latin Americans have different views of individuals and society, government, justice, laws, and morality. Despite the optimism of its champions, the prospects of a viable Pan-Americanism under United States leadership grows dimmer. Anti-Yankee sentiment in Latin America seems to be much more than a reaction to superior wealth and power. To be successful, Latin-American politicians have learned that they must be loud critics of the United States. They regard American efforts at appeasements as a sign of weakness. Lawrence E. Harrison sees the movement as not only on the decline but on the verge of extinction:

> Pan-Americanism, at least under U.S. leadership as it was understood by Presidents from Franklin D. Roosevelt to Lyndon Johnson, is in its death throes, if, indeed, it ever lived. The ties that bind together the nations of North and South America became fewer and weaker; the policies and actions of the countries south of the Rio Grande became increasingly independent of U.S. influence. The vision of two great continents joined by common liberal values and aspirations as well as by geography, marching hand-in-hand into a better future for all is distorted almost beyond recognition by the events of the last several years. Many idealists and pragmatists alike among U.S. observers are alarmed, feel frustrated, and are searching for explanations.

Bibliography: Robert N. Burr and Roland D. Hussey, *Documents on Inter-American Cooperation* (2 vols., Philadelphia, 1955); Alonso Aguilar, *Pan-Americanism from the Monroe Doctrine to the Present*, trans. by Asa Zatz (New York, 1968); William O. Douglas, *Holocaust or Hemispheric Co-operation* (New York, 1971); John Edwin Fagg, *Pan-Americanism* (Malabar, Fla., 1982).

PAN-ARABISM.   The attempt to bring union of all Arabs in a giant supranational, secular-religious state. Where Pan-Islamism (q.v.) was mostly religious in content, the closely related Pan-Arabism was primarily political, but with religious, linguistic, and cultural overtones. Pan-Arabism stressed historical and cultural ties among all Arabs, linguistic affinity, and observance of the traditions, customs, and laws of Islam. It regarded Islam as a cohesive factor. It encompassed the entire Arab world, which would be fused in a common Pan-Arabic territory. Ruling Arab élites everywhere were expected to sacrifice parochial loyalties in favor of an All-Arab integration.

A sense of nationalist excitement came to the Arab world after World War I, when territory liberated from the Turks was partitioned among the British and French. As a means of weakening the Turkish enemy, the British had stimulated the revolt of Arab nationalists inside the Turkish Empire. A nationalist sentiment was promoted among the powerful Arab princes. In the peace settlements of 1919–1920, this sense of national self-consciousness was taken into consideration. Nationalism was encouraged throughout Arab territories.

Along with the new nationalism among Arabs came a struggle

between protonationalism of the Arab world and the hetero-nationalism factors among its inhabitants. This can be expressed in another way—as a conflict between integration versus differentiation. Arab integration meant that the Arab world was seeking a solid framework of its own. Arab nationalist leaders would combine the various nationalist movements in Arabic-speaking areas into one broad, if diversified, front. The whole Arab world would be combined into one nationally conscious and politically assertive community, united by a common geography, language, history, traditions, and, above all, religion. The outward symbol of this unity would be an Arab cultural renaissance. It was expected that all the ruling élites of Arab countries would join in the important task of undermining parochial loyalties and furthering the cause of Arab integration. Arabs would be expected to forget their local status and join a tremendously powerful Pan-Arab unity.

Unfortunately, there was little substance to this dream of Arab integration. Virtually every Arab people had hetero-national obligations. Self-determination (q.v.) and loyalty throughout the Arab world remained beneath even a unified national level. Few Arabs could see beyond the horizon of the tribe, the village, or Islam. There was no powerful movement to overcome differences of social structure and regional interests. There was little success in the drive to obtain mass support for political, economic, military, and cultural cooperation between Arab states. It was difficult enough for the average Arab to think in terms of nationalism. Pan-Arabism was something he just did not understand.

Not only was there a lack of mass support for the idea of Pan-Arabism, but there were differences at the upper levels which made Pan-Arabism an unlikely prospect. The atmosphere among oil-rich Arab leaders was poisoned by plots, counterplots, and assassination attempts. It was common to arrest spies and expel dangerous citizens from other Arab countries. The prospect for a unified, federate state of Arab peoples at the level of nationalism writ large was extremely difficult. Arab nationalism proved to be inestimably stronger than the urge to Pan-Arabism. Nationalism, as advocated by the educated Arab élite was far ahead of a socially effective common nationality. It wanted to be free from European rule, and it called for hatred of Israel. It had a strong xenophobic bias. Whether or not an All-Arab, or Pan-Arab, nationalist movement will result in the emergence of a common larger nationality remains to be seen.

An additional bar to the success of Pan-Arabism was the geopolitical factor. Pan-Arabists called for a union of all Arab-speaking peoples from Arabia proper across North Africa westward to the

Atlantic. The Arab super-state was to include all Arabic-speaking peoples living in Arabia and the Middle East (Iraq, Lebanon, Syria, Jordan, and stateless Palestine), Egypt, and Arabic-speaking peoples in countries west of Egypt (Libya, Tunisia, Algeria, and Morocco).

The Arab world thus consisted of eastern and western parts. The eastern half, centered in the Middle East, comprised a compact group of territories, which for centuries were Arabic in language and culture, and Islamic in religion. The western half, from Egypt to Morocco, consisted of Muslims who also saw themselves as Arabic. However, the farther they were away from Arabia proper the less was the urge for Pan-Arabic unity.

Both eastern and western spheres of Arab territory were divided by jealousies and suspicions. Arabs turned to Mecca for holy prayers, but this did not necesarily mean subjection to political domination from Arabia proper. It was an almost impossible task to unify a people torn by differences. There was one common factor—hatred of Israel, but this was just not enough to overcome local differences. A spirit of nationalism in individual states was supported not only by the educated élite but also by the masses. Nationalism had the stronger appeal precisely because it had freed the Arab world from European control. Secular-oriented societies would accept Islam as their religion, but they had little interest in a possible supra-theocratic state.

The Arab sense of differentiation seemed to emerge at critical moments. Efforts at political union were ineffective. The problem of oil served to weaken the Pan-Arabic cause. The precious fluid of modern industrialized society led to squabbling among Arab states and strengthened the bonds of economic nationalism. Oil-producing Arab nations joined in forming the Organization of Petroleum Exporting Countries (O.P.E.C.), with the goal of determining world oil prices at a high level. Its goals were economic—and national. Arab members of O.P.E.C., like members of the European Economic Union, were not attracted by the idea of submerging their economic advantages into a political union.

The Arab League (A.L.), formed in 1945 with headquarters at Cairo, was supposed to further the solidarity of Arab aspirations. However, from the beginning, it was crippled by habitual dissension. After the lightning Israeli victory in the Six-Day Arab-Israeli War in June 1967, dissatisfied A.L. members looked to Soviet Russia for assistance in the continued struggle against Israel. Nevertheless, the old rivalries persisted among Arab states. These national differences proved to be a boon to Israel.

The most charismatic of Pan-Arabic leaders was Gamal Abdel

Nasser (q.v.) of Egypt. In his *Philosophy of the Revolution* (1954), Nasser described his intention of becoming the leader first of 55 million Arabs, then 224 million Africans, and eventually 420 million members of Islam. He would direct not only Pan-Arabism but also Pan-Africanism and Pan-Islamism. To implement this goal, he formed in 1958, together with Syria, the United Arab Republic. He said:

> There are no limits beyond which we will not go. Our task is the removal of rocks and obstacles from off the way. This is our only duty. The future and all its challenge is work that is open to all patriots with ideas and experience. . . . It is our cherished duty, our moment of historical responsibility, thus to bring our people at long last together.

On March 11, 1959, Nasser delivered a speech at Damascus in which he spoke of Arab unity and Arab nationalism:

> Fellow Countrymen: When we took it upon ourselves to raise high the banner of Arab nationalism and defend its call; when we chose the difficult, hard way, the way of defending the whole of the Arab nation, working for it in its entirety, of Arab unity, and Arab nationalism, we knew that this might be a rough one to travel, that it might be easier if we chose one of an isolationist policy, a road with a policy that was indeed selfish, a policy that was based largely on ignoring whatever happened in other Arab countries. We knew that such a policy would be easier at the outset, but that eventually it would hand over one Arab country after another to its enemies, that such a divided Arab nation would not achieve solidarity, would inevitably surrender to imperialism; so all of us, each and every one of the sons of this nation, preferred the rough, hard way, the way to Arab unity and solidarity, and resolved to raise the banner of Arab nationalism and exert every effort thoroughly to consolidate it.

Nasser's words did not make much of an impression on the divided Arab world. It was too much to expect Arab chieftains to heal their historic rivalries and submit themselves to Nasser's leadership. His political slogans could not meet the reality of economic differences. Egypt, indeed, had managed to win her independence and had emerged as a full-blown national state with the proper symbols of Western nationalist traditions—flag, anthems, coins, and stamps, but behind the facade were all the economic miseries of the past. Nationalism had not solved Egypt's problems of illiteracy and poverty. It was too much to expect Arab oil barons to submit to the dominance of impoverished Egypt.

The Pan-Arab Ba'ath Party, founded by Michel Aflaq, proclaimed its support for Pan-Arabism, but it remained opposed to Nasser as a leader. In the complicated superstructure of the Middle East, the Ba'ath Party became the leading organization for the promotion of Pan-Arabism. It called for *urubah,* a semi-mystical term denoting the essence of being Arab, belonging to the overall Arab "nation," speaking Arabic, born in an Arab land, and holding precious the precepts of Islam. Ba'ath theorists saw universalism and humanism as their ultimate goals. Aflaq called for a militant Arab nationalism based on socialism. "The battle for unity," he said, "according to our doctrine and our view and our struggle—cannot be separated from the battle for freedom and liberation and socialism, nor should it be under any circumstances." He placed Pan-Arabism above Pan-Islamism. The old traditional Islam, he said, superficial worship, vague and colorless values, was being gradually Europeanized. He stated that the day would come when the nationalists would find themselves the only defenders of the true Islam. Aflaq and his followers made it plain that they saw Nasser only as a partner, not as a leader, in any proposed Pan-Arab union. Nasser, they charged, had forced upon the Ba'ath Party a struggle that had no other cause than his dictatorial tendencies.

It was this kind of difference that crippled the cause of a wide Arab unity. The idea of Pan-Arabism, "the one Arab nation with an immortal mission," never managed to win its way to dominance in the Arab world. Arab unity had been the sole publicly acceptable idea of statesmen and ideologists, but the Arabs broke down into what has been called the "normal" system of national states. Far from achieving their "immortal mission," Arabs of the Middle East fell to squabbling among themselves. The Israeli victory in 1948–1949 and the consolidation of the Israeli state traumatized the entire Arab world. It dealt a tremendous blow to Arab pride and dignity. Arabs saw the emergence of Israel not only as a defeat for the Palestinians, but also as a grievous blow for the Pan-Arab mission. This evidence of weakness against Israel was seen as out of line with past Arab glory and achievements. Arab sense of unity began to evaporate in the face of national goals. Israeli victories were discouraging blows to the idea of Arab unity.

Bibliography: Bernard Lewis, *The Arabs in History* (London, 1958); Muhammad Khalili, *The Arab States and the Arab League* (Beirut, 1962); Hisham B. Sharabu, *Nationalism and Revolution in the Arab World* (Princeton, N.J., 1966); I. Gershoni, *The Emergence of Pan-Arabism in Egypt* (Tel Aviv, 1981); Fauvic E. Farah, *Pan-Arabism and Arab Nationalism: The Continuing Debate* (Boulder, Colo., 1987); Hani A. Faris, *Arab Nationalism and the Future of the Arab World* (Belmont, Mass., 1987).

PAN-ASIANISM. Like Pan-Africanism (q.v.), Pan-Asianism is a macro-nationalism (q.v.) holding that Asiatic peoples have a common destiny and a common cause against the white race. It is not an organized movement but essentially a vague sentiment of protest against foreigners who would attempt to profit from Asiatic riches. Like other pan-movements, it seeks to extend nationalism beyond its borders and create a larger nationalism that would protect Asian peoples against foreign domination.

The concept of Pan-Asianism emerged in the late nineteenth century, in part as a response of the yellow race against the invasions of white imperialists. Like Pan-Africanism, which placed the emphasis upon black unity, Pan-Asians attempted to counter white pressure by uniting Asians of the yellow race in opposition to white foreigners. Asians hated those intruders who had little or no understanding of Asian pride and dignity. The idea never assumed great political proportions; it was supported chiefly by intellectuals. It opposed economic exploitation by foreigners and denounced their territorial acquisitions. It saw the color bar as insulting and demanding. The concept never gained a mass basis. Pan-Asians saw unity where there was actually none. There was a *tendency* toward continental union, but it was at most an ephemeral idea and never became a political reality. Like other macro-nationalisms, it did not manage to overcome the jealous sovereignties of established nationalisms.

Both ideologies—Asian nationalism and Pan-Asianism—were accompanied by a strong sense of xenophobia (q.v.), fear of and hatred of the stranger, or foreigner. Taking advantage of Asiatic countries divided by internal dissension, white imperialists intended to deprive them of the economic fruits of their own land while proclaiming the hypocrisy of advancing the cause of civilization. The process stimulated anti-European sentiment throughout the continent. An example was the Boxer Rebellion of 1900. The *I-ho-ch'uan* (righteous harmony fists), known as Boxers, was a secret nationalist society that appeared in North China in 1898. At first, the movement was aimed at Roman Catholic missionaries and converted Chinese, but it gradually grew into opposition of everything foreign. Many Chinese, old and young, flocked to the society, and organized small bands of gymnasts. Every Boxer was assured that he was immune from death or injury because his body was protected by magic from bullets or sword cuts. "Protect the country, destroy the foreigner!" The Boxers began burning, looting, robbing, and killing. They saw the gods as angry against the "Foreign Devils." They were eventually suppressed, but their sense of xenophobia remained strong in China.

Some of the most forceful advocates of Pan-Asianism were Chinese and Hindus, but it was mainly through the efforts of the Japanese that the first Pan-Asiatic Conference was held at Nagasaki in 1926, under the auspices of the Pan-Asiatic Society. Japan, like China, reacted vigorously against the West. The Japanese played an important role in the flowering of Pan-Asianism. Until this time the movement had been weak, but it gained strength from the Japanese. Until the mid-nineteenth century, the Japanese had been isolated from the West and had retreated into what historians call "a centralized feudalism." But once the country was opened, the highly educated and intelligent Japanese public began to regard the predatory West as a serious threat. They placed their political house in order as a means of meeting the unwelcome probing power of the West. They would put an end to the traditional bickering, violence, and bloodshed, and meet the West on an equal plane. To the amazement of the world, the Russo-Japanese War of 1904–1905 ended with the rout of the Russian armies at Mukden and the annihilation of the Russian fleet at the Battle of Tsushima. Not only was Japanese pride stimulated by this extraordinary victory, but the significance of the triumph was understood throughout Asia. It was a dramatic effect: an Asian people of the yellow race had successfully resisted the domination of the white West.

The First Pan-Asiatic Conference at Nagasaki failed to produce any practical results, but it did discuss plans for setting up a permanent bureau in either Tokyo, Peking, or Shanghai. A second Pan-Asiatic Conference was held near Shanghai in 1928. But disputes between Japan and China starting in the early 1930s impeded the progress of Pan-Asianism. In the long run, Pan-Asianism never achieved effective organization or recognition as a political reality. At one time it represented a common cause against the exploiting whites, but with the recession of colonialism it lost much of its vigor. It still retained some appeal in its attempt to wipe out the remnants of imperialism. However, its insistence upon a common destiny for all Asian peoples has attracted only lukewarm support. Capitalist Japan and Communist China have little interest in a common destiny.

Pan-Asianism thus remains a somewhat hazy sentiment supported by those who see a common cause where there is no common destiny. Asian realists now see that the days of protest about the color bar are gone. Despite efforts by well-meaning theorists, in the vast areas of Asia the mixture of cultures and the cross-currents of political goals have been far more important than the goal of uniting all the peoples of the continent.

Bibliography: J. Kennedy, *Asian Nationalism in the Twentieth Century* (London, 1968); Elie Kedourie, *Nationalism in Asia and Africa* (New

York, 1970); Louis L. Snyder, *Macro-Nationalisms: A History of the Pan-Movements* (Westport, Conn., 1984).

PAN-CHRISTIANITY.   In the struggle for domination in modern world society, neither class nor religion has attained the political power of nationalism. Major religions in the past, especially Christianity, have attempted to include all their adherents in a large union, but they have not been successful. Throughout most of the Middle Ages in Western Europe, attempts were made again and again to unite all the Christian world into a kind of Pan-Christianity, which would combine *all* Christians in a secular-religious state as a successor to the Roman Empire. The Holy Roman Empire, itself, was regarded as a revival of the Roman Empire under Christian auspices. Although the medieval society was fragmented, it was believed that there was, indeed, one supranational institution to which all the peoples of Western Europe, except its small minority of Jews, belonged. Actually, the medieval polity was a combination of Church and State. The individual was not a Frenchman or a German, he was a Christian. For a long time the population of Europe saw itself as a combination of the religious and the secular.

In the later Middle Ages this kind of Pan-Christianity supported by Rome began to lose its impetus. The Roman Catholic Church had been regarded as universal, as a kind of international institution. Now it began to collide with national ambitions. The papacy began to lose its awesome power by the middle of the thirteenth century. Christian religious power reached its peak during the pontificate of Innocent III (1198–1216), who had successfully extended the power of the pontificate set up by Pope Gregory VII a century earlier. The papacy saw a divine guidance: "We are established by God above peoples and realms." To maintain its authority, the papacy used the powerful weapons of excommunication and interdict.

However, eventually there emerged a strong *los vom Rome,* an "Away from Rome" movement. The papacy was not able to counteract the dissolving feature of this new development. The result was the break-up of the medieval polity and the rise of separate national states. Gradually, England, France, Spain, and Portugal began to move away from Pan-Christianity. The Pan-Christian ideal gave way to the Renaissance of the fifteenth and sixteenth centuries and to the Age of Reason in the seventeenth and eighteenth centuries. The drama of the French Revolution signaled the end of medievalism and the Pan-Christian idea. The ultimate blow came in 1806, when Napoleon announced the end of the Holy Roman Empire. This new development meant the end of Pan-Christianity, as the primacy of the nation-state spread not only through Europe but throughout the world.

The rise of Protestantism dealt a blow to Christian unity, which has not been achieved to the present day. Despite the views of Karl Marx, nationalism outstripped the class structure as a dominant force in society and moved beyond Christian unity as a basic idea in contemporary society. Christianity in its varied forms still remained powerful in world society, but its claim of a universal Christian state was relegated to a back seat in history. In the contemporary age, nationalism proved to be the more powerful force. Where Christians died on the battlefield in support of their religion, today the conflicts are dominated by the politico-economic effects of nationalism.

Bibliography: James A. Corbett, *The Papacy* (Princeton, N.J., 1956); Roland H. Bainton, *The Age of the Reformation* (Princeton, N.J., 1956); Roland H. Bainton, *The Medieval Church* (Princeton, N.J., 1962).

PAN-EUROPA.   The call for the supplanting in Europe of nationalism in favor of European integration. The idea was introduced as early as the fourteenth century by Dante and in the sixteenth century by Machiavelli (q.v.). After World War II the idea of Pan-Europa was intensified. Where Pan-Slavism and Pan-Germanism (qq.v.) had been dominantly linguistic and political, Pan-Europa was essentially geographical, dominated by economics and secondarily political. The idea was to project Europe as a third major world power after the United States and the Soviet Union. Pan-Europeans would move slowly. First, they would pool their economic resources, especially in agriculture, in a common market. The production and consumption of foodstuffs and goods would be geared for European needs. But this would be only preliminary to the political unification of the continent. A democratically elected body would present to the world a united European front.

This was the dream of Pan-Europa. After an uncertain start, the European Economic Community (E.E.C.) came into existence. The idea of working together economically was attractive and all European states would benefit. However, the proposed transfer from economic to political power was another and more difficult matter. European states duly elected delegates to the Strasbourg Parliament. At the same time, however, each member state had not the slightest intention of dropping its sovereign status in favor of a European-wide political union. Despite the exaggerated claims of its supporters, Pan-Europa has remained an unrealized dream. Europe is still existing in the era of the nation-state. Established nationalisms take precedence over the claims of macro-nationalism. The sense of national consciousness seems to be as strong as ever on the European scene.

The most stimulating voice behind Pan-Europa was that of Richard N. Coudenhove-Kalergi (q.v.), who projected his idea of a federalized Europe and extended it into a powerful one-man crusade. He presented his first draft of a program for a united Europe in 1922 in the *Neue Freie Presse* (Vienna) and the *Vossische Zeitung* (Berlin). Unable at the time to obtain sponsors among distinguished statesmen, he decided to pursue his idea alone. In October 1926 he convened a Pan-European Congress in Vienna, the first of a series of such meetings. Subsequent Congresses were held in Berlin (1930), Basel (1932), and Vienna (1935). In 1943, in the midst of World War II, Coudenhove-Kalergi, after a speech by Churchill favoring a United States of Europe, drew up a constitution for such a union and submitted it to all the foreign ministers opposed to the Axis. At a meeting held at Gstaad, Switzerland, the European Parliamentary Union was founded with Coudenhove-Kalergi as Secretary-General.

The crusader for European unity seemed to be making progress, but there was a weakness in his movement. The idea appealed to many intellectuals, but there was no mass basis. This did not deter Coudenhove-Kalergi. However, the impulse for Pan-Europa began to pass to other hands. Neither Coudenhove-Kalergi nor the European Parliament succeeded in winning wide support for his goal. Nationalism remained the power in European political affairs.

The European Economic Community, supposed to be the first step in the coming political unification of Europe, was founded in 1957. Its goals were stated in the preamble:

HIS MAJESTY THE KING OF THE BELGIANS, THE PRESIDENT OF THE FEDERAL REPUBLIC OF WEST GERMANY, THE PRESIDENT OF THE FRENCH REPUBLIC, THE PRESIDENT OF THE ITALIAN REPUBLIC, HER ROYAL HIGHNESS THE GRAND DUCHESS OF LUXEMBOURG, HER MAJESTY THE QUEEN OF THE BELGIANS:

DETERMINED to establish the foundations of an ever closer union among European peoples,

RESOLVED to ensure by common action the economic and social progress of their countries by eliminating the barriers which divide Europe,

AFFIRMING as the essential objective of their efforts the constant improvement of the living and working conditions of their peoples,

RECOGNISING that the removal of existing obstacles calls for constant action in order to guarantee steady expansion, balanced trade and fair competition,

ANXIOUS to strengthen the unity of their economies and to ensure their harmonious development by reducing the differences existing between the various regions and the backwardness of the less favored regions,

DESIRING to contribute, by means of a common commercial policy, to the progressive abolition of restrictions on international trade,

INTENDING to confirm the solidarity which binds Europe and overseas countries and desiring to ensure the development of their prosperity, in accordance with the principles of the Charter of the United Nations,

RESOLVED to strengthen the cause of peace and liberty by thus pooling resources and calling upon the other peoples of Europe who share their ideal to join in their efforts,

HAVE DECIDED to create a European Economic Community.

Eurocrats were delighted by the Common Market, which they saw as a milestone on the road to Pan-Europa. But nowhere was there a willingness to sublimate national sovereignty to the administration of a United States of Europe. In March 1982, *The New York Times,* on the 25th anniversary of the Common Market, published a report on its progress. Titled "Nationalism is Straining Europe's Economic Unity," the article stated that free trade and closer economic integration were being threatened by a new spirit of nationalism "spawned partly by the passage of time and the dimming of earlier ideals, but also by the world-wide recession." The Common Market was in deep trouble. "Those who hoped free trade would produce a political confederation of a 'United States of Europe,' have been disappointed. Instead of responding to the world economic crisis by drawing closer together, the community's members seem to be splitting apart, resisting further attempts at integration." Actually, European governments were attesting their nationalistic drives by seeking to solve their problems at the expense of others.

The idea of European integration was dealt a severe blow by Charles de Gaulle (q.v.). The French leader had no intention of relinquishing the tiniest bit of French sovereignty to a political Parliament representing Pan-Europa. He held that neither the Common Market nor the European Parliament should be allowed to challenge the existence of France as a sovereign state. He scornfully referred to "the European hybrid." European integration, he charged, actually meant "vassalage and subordination to the United States." In insisting on the permanence of national states, de Gaulle actually delivered a powerful indictment of the idea of Pan-European unity. Other European statesmen, though not gifted with de Gaulle's sense of national grandeur, felt the same way. It was fine to speak of European federation, but the idea of cutting national sovereignty appeared to them to be the height of absurdity. They would pretend to favor the idea, but they would prefer their own nationalism to Pan-Europa.

June 7, 1979, was for Eurocrats a date of fulfillment. On that and three succeeding days, 175 million Europeans voted in a single election for delegates to the first European Parliament. After decades of debate, they had made the critical move from economic to political unity. The new Council of Europe would protect human rights, bring European countries closer together, and voice the views of the European public on the important political and economic problems of the day. There were dramatic debates in the Consultative Assembly. Its members were never able to convince the Committee of Ministers to grant it any real powers. One recommendation after another was turned down. After two years of debate, Paul Henry Spaak, President of the Consultative Assembly, resigned in disgust after denouncing its members for restricting the body to mere debate instead of supporting real political action.

Critics who preferred the old nationalism denounced the Council of Europe as impractical and unable to wipe out vestiges of the still strong nationalism in Europe. They argued that no statesman could take it upon himself to diminish the sovereignty of his homeland—that would be close to treason. Europe, they contended, was not ready to transmit its national sovereignty to a Pan-European legislative body at Strasbourg. Disappointed Eurocrats, however, insisted that a new type of unity was in the air, that eventually "provincial" nationalism was certain to give way to European unity.

The issue remains unresolved. The European Parliament remains deficient in actual political power and takes a low place in European affairs, certainly when viewed against national parliaments. On the surface, this supranational and intergovernmental agency seems to provide a strong framework for national unity on the European scene. But, unfortunately for Eurocrats, political unity and the desirable pooling of national sovereignty remain in the realm of a dream. The idea of political unity has been lost in technicalities.

Responsibility for this gloomy state of affairs is varied and complex. First and basic is the ambivalence of Europe. From its early days, the European Community was burdened by a strange duality implicit in the idea itself and, in various mixtures, in all its supporters. It was a difficult and almost impossible task to reconcile former enemies as a prerequisite for continental unity as well as for world peace. In addition, from the moment of its inception there was a struggle for power inside the movement itself. The result was an ambiguity in the ultimate purpose of Western European integration.

Added to this burden was the lack of a European consensus. The idea of Pan-Europa was never able to win mass support. European peoples continued to regard themselves as patriots of their own countries, and they were inclined to accept their special flag and anthem as symbols of their nationalism. The theme of Pan-Europa continued to be held by a handful of statesmen and a minority of Eurocrats, but not by the masses.

The idea of Pan-Europa was also hurt by the erosion of governmental support. Any governmental advocacy was always conditioned by national needs. Because national policy and national traits tend to resist change, most European governments are indifferent or hostile to Pan-Europa. Invited in late September 1988 to give a speech at the College of Europe in Brussels, Belgium, Prime Minister of Britain Margaret Thatcher attacked the notion of European federalism. She rejected contemptuously any "effort to suppress nationhood and concentrate power at the center of a European conglomerate." She dealt a blow to the hope that a politically united Europe would emerge by the end of the century. The speech enraged utopian Europeanists and angered all of England's partners in the European Community.

There was also a steady competition between national European Parliaments and the European Parliament. The key issue was the proper exercise of national sovereignty. European nationalists believed that any acquisition of legislative competence by the European Parliament would be at the expense of their own legislative bodies. They believed that the European Parliament would inevitably try to exercise powers that it was not supposed to possess. They saw it as structured on intergovernmental, not federal or supranational auspices. They argued that the very idea of enforced integration at the parliamentary level was dangerous because it meant that the established national states would be divested of their previous sovereignty.

In the final analysis, Western European countries looked inward despite the survival of economic unity. European statesmen still preached the efficacy of internationalism, but they failed to practice what they preached. What exists in contemporary Europe is the maintenance of continental parochialism and the persistence of nationalism. Expectation of political unity has receded from the realm of the concrete. Coudenhove-Kalergi's great dream, which once seemed to be possible, apparently has retreated into an area of unfulfilled hopes.

Bibliography: Arnold J. Zurcher, *The Struggle to Unite Europe (1940–1958)* (New York, 1958); Richard Mayne, *The Community of Europe* (New York, 1963); Uwe Kitzinger, *The Politics and Economics of European Economic Integration* (New York, 1963); Ernest B. Haas, *The Uniting of Europe* (Stanford, 1964); Richard N. Coudenhove-Kalergi, *Pan-Europa* (Munich, 1966); Valentin and Juliet Lange, *The European Parliament and the European Community* (London, 1978).

PAN-GERMANISM.   Along with Pan-Slavism (q.v.), Pan-Germanism was one of the more important pan-movements (q.v.). Its history is briefer than that of its rival. When Pan-Slavism sought to combine supposedly related peoples of many countries, Pan-Germanism was confined to one people. Efficiently organized, it had a much larger influence than the number of its adherents. The term Pan-Germanism is derived from *Alldeutschthum* or *Alldeutscher Verband*, the Pan-German League. Based on early nineteenth-century romantic nationalism, it was developed during the foundation years of the Second Reich under Otto von Bismarck (q.v.). As an ideology, it was never explicitly defined. There are several interpretations of Pan-Germanism, ranging from the modest cultivation of German patriotism with emphasis on *Kultur* to a global Pan-German community. All versions, however, place emphasis on German national consciousness.

In its expansionist form, Pan-Germanism sought to present a united front to all potential enemies, especially Russia, Britain, and France. Its followers believed that the great industrial expansion of Germany at the end of the nineteenth century called for a more important place in the sun, to give Germany the kind of prestige that went with the British Empire, upon which the sun never set. Germany had achieved her national unity after centuries of division; now the Pan-Germanists held that the turn of history was in their favor and that they would take their rightful place in the world befitting German promise. What was once a vague, undefined program began to emerge as a combination of Anglophobia, rivalry with France, anti-Slavism, anti-socialism, and anti-Semitism. Other powerful nations had stood in the way of German progress: now the Pan-Germans would see to it that they themselves would take their rightful place in world society. They designated the *Macht*-principle—power to the strongest. Germany's new colonialism, supported by William II's Big Navy, would play its just role in world history. German nationalism would be writ large.

It was to be expected that this Pan-German principle of power would arouse opposition not only among the Pan-Slavs but also among the British, French, and Americans, all of whom resented an expansionist policy they deemed detrimental to their own security. Pan-Germanism contributed directly to the outbreak of World War I and World War II. In both these conflicts, the Allied Powers subjugated their own differences to bring an end to German pretensions. It was one thing to work for German power within the confines of German territory, but it was decidedly another matter when Germans sought to expand their borders beyond the European scene.

Eventually, the Pan-German movement was so closely and effectively organized that it was regarded by other peoples as a dangerous development. Unfortunately for Pan-Germanism, it never quite had the national support it needed to win its way to success. While most Germans undoubtedly were sympathetic to its goals, they did not participate actively in its program. Only a modest number of Germans became active in the program of Pan-Germanism and relatively few were willing to contribute funds to it.

But the government was an entirely different matter. Here the national political policy became almost at one with the Pan-German program. It promoted colonialism, militarism, navalism, and Anglophobia. William II brought his country to the abyss of World War I by asserting those policies that Pan-Germanism supported. This kind of aggression was pursued again by Adolf Hitler (q.v.), who led Germany into revolt against the Treaty of Versailles. He presented the theories of Pan-Germanism in his personal blueprint, *Mein Kampf.* He made it clear in this book that he would unite the Germans from Berlin to Rio de Janeiro in a mighty force, which William II had failed to do. It took another world-wide coalition of the Allied powers to smash the Nazi version of Pan-Germanism and throw it into the dustbin of history. Once again, world society gave notice that it had no intention of allowing any macro-nationalism to extend its power to an intolerable point.

German nationalism was stimulated in the early nineteenth century as a reaction against the designs of Napoleon. The French conqueror had looked to the east as fertile ground for his own version of glory. He would unite the many states and principalities of the Germanies, and handle them in his own way. For that purpose he formed the

Confederation of the Rhine in 1807. To his dismay this turned out to be a giant step in the promotion of German nationalism. Without wanting it, he directed German eyes to national unification. Bismarck later achieved that unity in a series of three wars—against Denmark in 1864, against Austria in 1866, and against France in 1870–1871.

By this time German nationalists were already thinking of a major extension of German power. Deep resentment against Napoleon had already led Germans to think of themselves as ready to play a greater role in world society. Johann Gottlieb Fichte (q.v.) prophesied a great destiny for Germans because, in contrast to Latins, they possessed a unique spirit of regeneration. Germans, he said, should deny submission to Napoleon. He reminded them of their own great historical mission. Similarly, Ernst Moritz Arndt (q.v.) called for a crusade against the French conqueror and urged his fellow Germans to believe that, when the final reckoning came, they must be inspired by justice and Fatherland. The way was prepared for nationalism and Pan-Germanism.

The early defenders of Pan-Germanism held fast to the belief that German *Kultur* and German *Weltanschauung* (world view) were far superior to the culture of other peoples, especially the shopkeeper Britons, the decadent French, and the barbaric Russians. They saw it as necessary that German expansion be seen as simply necessary and logical. They insisted that the continuum of history demanded such drives as national unity, leadership of *Mitteleuropa*, and global Pan-Germanism. They believed that German-ness would be elevated to the top of world society. Opposed to rationalism, they supported a biological racialism based on Teutonic supremacy. Pan-Germans would see to it that anyone who spoke German or a closely related tongue would belong in this perfect union.

In the Middle Ages, the old German Empire had promoted a "civilizing mission" of colonization; the new Pan-Germans would act in the same way. For their first step they would acquire control over *Mitteleuropa*. Their second step was to continue their mission on a global scale. All necessary means would be used to advance the cause—exploitation of irrational emotion, violence, even war as a biological necessity. Pan-Germans were aware that they would be charged with fanaticism, but they saw their cause as motivated by heroic valor. True Germans, they said, would be willing to sacrifice everything for their great cause.

Pan-Germans borrowed their ideas from varied sources—from the Machiavellian principle of power, biological racialism, rigid conservatism, popular democracy, Christian Socialism, and Marxian Socialism. It was this combination of sources that makes it difficult to define today an ideology that was never clearly or authoritatively defined in its time. Pan-Germanism adopted ideas from both Right and Left: from the Right it borrowed the concept of subservience to authority, from the Left it took the unity of State and people. It supported the power principle of a centralized authority, while at the same time calling for a democratically mobilized national sentiment. In its early stage it showed merely a desire to promote the cultural unity of all Germans, no matter where they lived. Later, in the nineteenth century, Pan-Germanism began to take on an extremist attitude. Preached in the cafes of Vienna, it attracted the attention of Hitler.

On February 25, 1885, King William I issued an imperial rescript, countersigned by Bismarck, giving governmental support and safe conduct to Dr. Karl Peters, a German colonial explorer who had won a reputation by his travels through Africa. The next year Peters convened a General German Congress *(Allgemeiner Deutscher Verband)*, to which he invited representatives of religious, industrial, and colonial organizations. This was his way of forging an alliance between Germans at home and abroad. He would sponsor emigration to new German lands abroad and at the same time maintain the spirit of German nationalism in an organization to be called the German League. When he left for Africa again, his organization, without his leadership, was dissolved.

In 1890, after the forced resignation of Bismarck, the Old German League was renamed the General German League. Again, the new organization seemed to be on the verge of dissolution. At this time the movement found a new leader in the person of Dr. Ernst Hasse, Professor of Colonial Politics at the University of Leipzig and *Reichtag* deputy. Conservative, monarchist, and zealous nationalist, Hasse became the father of Pan-Germanism. In 1894 he was elected President of what was then called the Pan-German League *(Pandeutscher Verband)*, which he led vigorously until his death in 1908. His motto for the new organization was that of the Great Elector: "Remember, you are a German!"

The new Pan-German League urged its members to do something to add to the great events of 1870–1871. It was charged that national feeling had been softened and nearly destroyed by economic interests and social problems. Other peoples had successfully defended their "race"—only the Germans failed in that critically important task. Germans must be careful, according to the League, not to place national tasks behind socio-economic ones. Kaiser William II joined the fray when he said that "Germany is justified and in duty bound no less than other nations, to take its share as a dominant power in the history of the whole world." He reminded all Germans that it was their duty to protect the many thousands of Germans in foreign countries and to link the greater German Empire closer to the homeland.

Under such guidance the Pan-German League presented its aims and policies in the introductory section of its constitution:

1. The Pan-German League seeks to quicken the national sentiment of Germans and especially to awaken and promote racial and cultural homogeneity *(Zusammengehörigkeit)* of all sections of the German people.
2. These aims show that the Pan-German League seeks:
   A. Preservation of German *Volkstum* in Europe and overseas and support of it wherever it is threatened;
   B. Settlement of all cultural, educational, and school problems in ways favorable to German *Volkstum;*
   C. Opposition of all forces that hinder national development;
   D. Furtherance of German interests in the entire world, especially continuance of the German colonial movement.
3. The League pursues its aims through:
   A. Club activities as provided for in its constitution. In countries outside of Germany, members may function under different plans and for special goals, but only with approval of the League's secretary.
   B. Publication of the periodical, *Alldeutsche Blätter.*

In addition, the Pan-German League indicated its primary concern with such problems as the Polish question, formation of a Big Navy, Anglo-German relations, reform of the citizenship laws, conditions in Alsace-Lorraine and North Schleswig, and the foreign policy of the Empire, especially in relations with Austro-Hungary. There were twenty-five other interests, including prohibition of foreign languages in clubs and meetings, funds to be used in the Fatherland for the education of sons of Germans living abroad, and Germanization of foreign words in the official language.

The Pan-German League took an active part in both domestic and foreign affairs. There was scarcely any phase of German life which did not attract its interest. It registered its opposition to any movement working against national development. It concerned itself with problems of citizenship, fiscal reforms, foreigners living in Germany, industrial politics, and emigration. Among its major efforts was a campaign of propaganda for naval supremacy. It called for a strong defense of Germany's borders. It asked for suppression of any enemies inside the Reich. In a series of Pan-German Congresses, special attention was given to Germanization of the Westmark, or

Alsace-Lorraine, which had been in contention between Germans and French for a thousand years. Its attitude toward the Nordmark, or Schleswig-Holstein, and to the Ostmark, or Posen and West Prussia, was exactly the same. It would not allow foreign nationalities to break the backbone of *Deutschtum*. Most of all, it would oppose the designs of Pan-Slavism as "nationally dangerous."

For Pan-Germans it was a matter of extreme importance to maintain the position of Germany in foreign as well as domestic affairs. Close to home were Germans who lived in the Austro-Hungarian Empire, Switzerland, and Belgium. These were Germans and to the Pan-Germans they belonged to the Fatherland. They should not be subjected to the domination of Magyars, Slavs, and Czechs. Germans living in bordering states had to have special rights and privileges because they belonged to the German entity. This again was the essence of Pan-Germanism: it would fight "with shining and clean weapons" for the goal of Germanization of all those who spoke the German language.

In its foreign affairs the Pan-German League always took a firm anti-British stand. In 1895 its propagandists excited the nation when the Jameson raid took place against the Transvaal in South Africa. They supported the Boers in their war against Britain from 1899–1902. The League used a special fund to help Germans leave the war area. It sent telegrams of support to Paul Kruger, advocate of Boer independence. In addition, wherever German interests anywhere in the world were threatened, the Pan-German League took a stand in defense of them. When Germany and the United States clashed over the Samoan Islands in the south central Pacific, the League defended German interests there with special zeal. In 1911 the League hailed with delight the dispatch of a German cruiser to Agadir to protect German interests there.

For Pan-German authorities the emigration of Germans to the United States was a serious matter of concern. Germans there must be awakened to *Deutschtum*. They must be educated to a spirit of German national pride. Pan-Germans saw it as a critical matter of importance that there be a reservoir of good will among German-Americans in the event that naval rivalry might lead to a clash between the two countries. American officials expressed their concern by what they regarded as an unacceptable Pan-German attitude toward American citizenship. The League was more successful in Brazil, where thousands of Germans had emigrated at the turn of the century. It helped repeal a German law providing that German emigrants who failed to register and pay a fee for the privilege during ten years after their emigration would forfeit their right to German citizenship.

Pan-Germanism exerted a strong appeal in Austria. Here Georg Ritter von Schoenerer became an active crusader for Pan-Germanism. A flamboyant agitator, he was the man of action who would go beyond the haze of the intellectuals. Holding that the Austro-Hungarian Empire was a fraud, he demanded that everything about it be destroyed in favor of Pan-Germanism. For him, Pan-Germanism was a glorious idea, the capstone of modern morality. Anyone standing in the way should be obliterated. He would settle for nothing less than *Anschluss* (union) between Austria and Germany.

The outbreak of World War I in August 1914 was vital for the program of Pan-Germanism, especially after the initial series of German victories. On May 20, 1915, five of six associations of Junker landowners and wealthy manufacturers, concerned that Chancellor Theobald von Bethmann-Hollweg might agree to a too early peace, presented him with a petition to keep the war going. The memorandum defended a straight Pan-German program, including its annexationist policy. The petitioners claimed that they represented the whole German people in their determination to endure to the end, notwithstanding every sacrifice "in this struggle for life and death which has been forced on Germany." They demanded that the war be continued. "No competent judge would dream of sacrificing Germany's favorable military position in order to conclude a premature peace with any of her enemies."

This stand was also taken by another petition issued by German professors, diplomats, and government officials a month later on June 29, 1915. The manifesto was circulated privately, but it soon became widely known:

> To our enemies, however, even these narrow limits and a share of the world's trade necessary to our existence seemed too much, and they formed plans which aimed at the very annihilation of the German Empire. Then we Germans rose as one man, from the highest to the meanest, realizing that we must defend not only our physical existence but also our inner, spiritual, and moral life—in short, defend European civilization *(Kultur)* against barbarian hordes from the east, and lust for vengeance and domination from the west. With God's help, hand in hand with our trusted allies, we have been able to maintain ourselves victoriously against half a world of enemies. . . .

> Let us make no mistake. We do not wish to dominate the world, but to have a standing in it fully corresponding to our great position as a civilized Power and to our economic and military strength. It may be that, owing to the numerical superiority of our enemies, we cannot obtain at a single stroke all that is required

in order thus to insure our national position; but the military results of this war, obtained by such great sacrifices, must be utilized to the utmost possible extent. This, we repeat, is the firm determination of the German people.

While denying any intention of aggression, the manifesto went on to outline an expansionist Pan-German program. It insisted that Germany must lead the way to *Mitteleuropa*. It called for a great belt of German power from the North Sea to the Persian Gulf, to include control of the Turkish Empire. The intellectuals also demanded domination of *Mittelafrika*. It was adamant on the matter of *Kultur* and power:

> The German mind is beyond all doubt our most supremely valuable asset. It is our one precious possession among all our possessions. It alone justifies our people's existence and their impulse to maintain and assert themselves in the world; and to it they owe their superiority over all other people. . . . We shall create the necessary healthy body for the German mind. The expansion of the German body which we have demanded will do the German mind no injury.

The loss of World War I dealt a devastating blow to Pan-Germanism. During the Long Armistice from 1919 to 1939, the Pan-German League went into decline, but not Pan-Germanism itself. In the hands of Hitler, Pan-Germanism took on a new and extreme form, a blend of absolute faith in Indo-European-Aryan-Nordic biological supremacy and a cult of violence to achieve its objectives. A child of Pan-Germanism, Hitler owed more to it than to any other ideology or political movement. At his trial for treason in 1924, he described himself as "Pan-German in my convictions." For more than twelve years, from 1933 to 1945, he controlled the destiny of the Germans in what was supposed to be a Thousand-Year Reich. Millions of Germans lost their lives, and billions in property were destroyed in this futile attempt to implement this version of Pan-Germanism. The idea died in Hitler's Berlin bunker on April 30, 1945. His suicide finally removed Pan-Germanism from a dream to the status of a terrible nightmare.

The story of Pan-Germanism presents a classic case of the inability of the pan-movements to extend an established nationalism beyond its borders and create a larger nationalism. Despite the enthusiasm of its champions, Pan-Germanism, like other pan-movements, was unsuccessful in its global mission. It retreated to a nationalism of more manageable proportions.

Bibliography: Roland G. Usher, *Pan-Germanism, From its Inception to the Outbreak of the War* (New York, 1914); Mildred S. Wertheimer, *The Pan-German League* (New York, 1924); Alfred Kruck, *Geschichte des*

Alldeutschen Bunds (Wiesbaden, 1954); Andrew G. Whiteside, *The Socialism of Fools: Georg Ritter von Schoenerer and Austrian Pan-Germanism* (Berkeley, 1975); Louis L. Snyder, *Macro-Nationalisms: A History of the Pan-Movements* (Westport, Conn., 1984).

PAN-HISPANISM.   A macro-nationalism (q.v.) that tried to unite Spaniards in a Greater Spain. Behind it was the idea of reviving the imperial glory of the old Spain. Like other pan-movements, Pan-Hispanism was an extension of an older nationalism, which had been stimulated by the late eighteenth-century Enlightenment, by dissatisfaction with the reactionary monarchy, and by general social and economic life. The immediate origin of Spanish nationalism was due to the Napoleonic invasion in the early nineteenth century, a move that led to denunciations of French perfidy and the rise of Spanish resentment. In 1809 a Spanish journalist wrote:

> We will recover our former customs, sing our own songs, dance our own dreams, and dress in the ancient style, [because the] nation is formed not by the number of individuals, but by the union of wills, the conformity of the laws, customs, and language, which maintain and keep them together from generation to generation.

This was, indeed, a clear expression of national consciousness. It meant that Spanish nationalism had come of age.

Beyond this early stage of nationalism, Pan-Hispanism was an extension to include all Spaniards in a revived Spain. With the accidental discovery of the New World in 1492 by Columbus, the Spanish constructed a colonial empire that for a time made them the most powerful nation in Europe. Spanish *conquistadores*, professing their overriding interest in gold, glory, and God, set out on expeditions to the New World to stake their claims. They built a Spanish Empire in the grand manner, but colored by avarice and bigotry. They struck down the prosperous Aztecs and Incas, who lay prostrate. They insisted on the right to receive tribute and services. In the process they helped build an empire that included Central and South America, the West Indies, Florida, California, and Mexico— one of the most extensive empires in history.

This great Spanish Empire was shattered by paralyzing absolutism and economic deficits. The Spanish colonial system turned out to be merely an appendage of royal absolutism. The dynasty dissipated its energies by trying to maintain a huge empire in the New World while at the same time it was overcome by burdens on the European scene—ruling the Netherlands, destroying Protestantism, and fighting the Turks. Inside Spain the masses were oppressed by taxation and inflation, business initiative was stifled, official circles were beset by bribery and corruption, and there was general economic discontent. The final blow came in 1588 when Spain's proud Invincible Armada was annihilated by a combination of superior British seamanship and an unfriendly Nature, storms that decimated their ships. The Spanish Empire went into decline.

In the New World, however, the Spanish cultural heritage remained durable. For the champions of Pan-Hispanism, the Spanish people were bound together by the bond of a common language and the existence of a Spanish culture. For them, Spanish art and literature simply meant Spanish solidarity. They would see to it that the Spanish national character, with its courage, enterprise, and dignity, would be brought together in a larger nationalism. They pointed to the medieval *Poema del Cid*, the great anonymous epic extolling the deeds of Ruy Días de Bivar, their own national hero. Filled with exaggerated fantasies and strange improbabilities, it presented Spanish sentiments of pride, honor, and pity. Another national masterpiece, *Don Quixote de la Mancha*, also stressed the enduring nature of the Spanish character. It depicts the conflict of noble dreams with the truculent world of fact. Spanish literary production provided a strong stimulus to the special Spanish traits and became the basis of structured Spanish nationalism as well as its extension into Pan-Hispanism.

Yet, despite the strength of the Spanish national character, the effort to extend it into a larger nationalism to include all Spanish-speaking peoples, has not been successful as a movement. The idea was never really organized, or was it able to win a mass basis. It gave the world a conception of the Spanish character, but it never went far beyond the stage of calling attention to Spain's myths and heroes. In this respect it was similar to other pan-movements, which stressed nationalism and the national character, but were never able to be extended into the larger nationalism.

Bibliography: Mark Jay Van Aken, *Pan-Hispanism: Its Origin and Development* (Berkeley, 1959); Richard Herr and Harold T. Parker (eds.), *Ideas in History* (Durham, N.C., 1965); Edward J. Goodman, "Spanish Nationalism in the Struggle Against Napoleon," *Review of Politics*, 20 (1968), 330–340.

PAN-IBERIANISM.   A movement designed to combine the Spanish and Portuguese peoples of the Iberian peninsula. Because Spain and Portugal share the peninsula and even a common history for a time, a small group has called for a union of the nationalisms of the two peoples. Behind this idea was the fact that the Romans, who captured most of the peninsula, had forced the combination of the early Iberian tribes with the Celts, all under Roman control. The Iberian peoples, with the exception of the Basques in the north, became thoroughly Romanized. The break into Spanish and Portuguese sections came only later. For advocates of Pan-Iberianism, these two peoples were destined for union. They believe that the entire peninsula, by historical tradition, should be united into its original form. They see the national character of the two peoples as similar. They argue that all the peoples of the peninsula represent an extension of closely allied cultures, and that by history and tradition they belong together in a greater nationalism.

This point of view is similar in all the macro-nationalisms (q.v.). In the case of Pan-Iberianism, it remains the unfulfilled dream of a small group of dedicated pan-nationalists. There is no organization devoted to the idea and it has made little or no impact on relations between the two countries.

PAN-ISLAMISM.   A movement originating from the confrontations between occidental and oriental nationalisms and imperialism. It aimed to expand an imperialist religion into a larger nationalism. Reactionary in content, it was not successful. It turned out to be a hopeless effort to combine warring factions in an effort to re-establish the caliphate.

Islam emerged in the early seventh century as a rival to Christianity. It began in 622 A.D. with the flight of Muhammad from Mecca to Yathrib (Medina, the City of the Prophet). A prosletyzing religion, it was enormously successful in its expansion, but it was unsuccessful later in seeking to unite all Muslims in a higher nationalism. The early caliphs, successors to Muhammad, first turned Islamic zeal against the Byzantine Empire. Driving westward across North Africa, the Muslims crossed to Spain and thrust at the heart of Christianity there. This move for universal power was halted only by the intercession of Charles Martel at the critical Battle of Tours in 732 A.D.

The ideology of Pan-Islamism found support in the Koran, the holy book of Islam. "Ye are the best people *(ümmet)* that hath been raised up into mankind." In the view of Islamic scholars, the term *"ümmet"* meant nation. And again: "Verily, ye are the people of one 'nation,' and I, your Lord; therefore, worship me." Arab Muslims believed: "To Islam is due the birth of a nation, the birth of a state, the birth of a national history, and the birth of a civilization." To Pan-Islamists this meant a global society based on religion. A holy war *(jihad)* was to be waged to bring Islam's value system to the world. The Koran was explicit: "And fight for the cause of God against those who fight against you: but commit not the injustice of attacking them first; God loveth not such injustice."

Pan-Islamism was dedicated to the most cherished traditions of Islam, with its ideas of religious universality, political theocracy, and exclusive sovereignty. It saw Western imperialists as infidels, who had unfairly taken advantage of Muslim brothers. It would bolster the failing fortunes of those Muslims who believed they had been unable to resist Western encroachments. If there was to be imperialism, then let it be the religious imperialism of Pan-Islamism. It saw as absolutely necessary a return to the past values of Islam.

Pan-Islamic propaganda began in the 1880s and reached its prime before the end of the century. Its chief ideologist, its intellectual philosopher and prophet was Jamāl ad-Din al Afghāni (1838–1897). Until he came on the scene, Pan-Islamism was only a vague idea, but he was responsible for solidifying agitation for a revived Islamic civilization opposed to European domination. With his eloquent tongue and facile pen, he became the leading propagandist for Pan-Islamism. Moving through the Muslim world, he preached the necessity of Islamic unity. In 1884 he published an anti-British newspaper called *The Indissoluble Link*, in which he called for the unity of all Islamic peoples and states against Western domination. In 1892, Turkish Arabs in London invited Jamāl ad-Din to settle in Constantinople on a life pension as guest of the sultan. To win prestige for his movement, he proposed to combine religion, politics, and culture in one all-embracing organization. He urged Muslims to awake. They must liberate themselves from Western domination; they must support necessary reforms; they must insist on popular and stable government; and they must cultivate modern scientific and philosophic knowledge.

Unhappy in Constantinople, Jamāl ad-Din was kept under what amounted to house arrest by the authorities. He tried many times to leave, but he was unsuccessful. He died in 1897, reportedly of cancer, but some claimed that he was poisoned by the sultan. Despite his lifetime of zealous propaganda, he was never to see his goal of Islamic unity achieved.

If Jamāl ad-Din was the intellectual leader of Pan-Islamism, its first patron was the sultan-caliph Abdülhamid II. The sultan appropriated the movement as a means of justifying his own tyrannical rule over the Turkish Empire. He proclaimed himself the defender of the Islamic social system against Western imperialism, especially against the British in the Near East and the French in Morocco. It was an article of the Islamic faith, he said, for all Muslims to combine in a holy war for the spread of Islamic ideals. Exploiter of Muslim fanaticism, he urged every Muslim, no matter where he lived, to unite with his fellow Muslims in a *jihad* against the West. The Western world tended mistakenly to regard him as a purely spiritual authority, as the Muslim "pope." It did not understand that Abdülhamid II saw himself not merely as a sultan but as the caliph of the entire Islamic world. To confuse the West, he pretended to be a supporter of constitutionalism, but he actually maintained a rigid dictatorship. For him, Pan-Islamism was the key to his own power.

In 1903 Abdullah Suhrawardy founded the Pan-Islamic Society in London. His journal, *Pan-Islam*, emphasized opposition to Western society, and used humanitarian as well as socialist phraseology to contrast "European vice" with "Asian virtue." It also dedicated itself to mending the structures between the Sunnite and Shi'ite sects, which was in itself a most formidable task.

Abdülhamid II, as curator of Islamic holy places, supported the great annual conferences of Muslims at Mecca. He provided Turkish troops as escorts for pilgrim caravans to Mecca. He helped build the Hejaz railway, which was the sole practical achievement of Pan-Islamism. On the surface, he seemed to be the ideal promoter of Pan-Islamism, but his moves were always designed to help his status as a powerful dictator.

The Young Turk Revolution not only put an end to the regime of Abdülhamid II, but it also ended the early stage of Pan-Islamism. Turkish nationalism turned out to be stronger than the internationalism of Islamism. Moreover, the alliance between Turkish nationalism and German militarism could not be reconciled with Islamic ideology. When in November 1914, the caliph proclaimed a holy war against the Allied Powers, the response in Egypt, India, and Arabia was to enlist in the ranks of his enemies. The attempts of the Berlin war office to arouse Pan-Islamic union against the Allied Powers turned out to be altogether ineffective.

When the Turkish Empire collapsed at the end of World War I, it meant the end of the original Pan-Islamic movement. A second wave of Pan-Islamism rising in India was even less enduring than the first. Several Pan-Islamic Congresses held between 1920 and 1931 were unsuccessful. On July 8, 1937, representatives of Turkey, Persia, Iraq, and Afghanistan signed a pact at Teheran designed to preserve their common frontiers. Some observers believed that this amounted to a return by Turkey to Pan-Islamism, but this was incorrect: Kemal

Atatürk (q.v.) had already cut his country off from its Oriental and Islamic past.

After World War II there was a modest revival of Pan-Islamism, when Pakistan began a center for the movement. However, this new Pan-Islamism represented a common attitude of Islamic states in meeting their economic, cultural, and social problems with emphasis upon political rather than religious questions. There were additional Pan-Islamic Congresses at Karachi (1951), Jerusalem (1953), Mecca (1954), and Lahore (1957–1958), but the heart was gone from the movement. By now the religious liberty that Pan-Islamism advocated was subordinated to political and national goals.

There was a revival of Pan-Islamic militancy starting in 1979 with the Iranian Revolution. From his house of exile in Paris, the Ayatollah Ruhollah Khomeini, Islamic religious leader, called for resistance to Shāh Pahlavi Muhammad Reza and his security police. He claimed that Iranians had turned from the true faith to the false ministrations of the Western-oriented Shāh. He charged that they had succumbed to the "American Devils" and warned that they should beware of the Russian bear bringing gifts of honey. He, Khomeini, would lead the way and awaken Iran from its long sleep. His words sparked a revolution. The Shāh left Iran on January 16, 1979, and at the end of the month Khomeini returned to his homeland to lead its regeneration. But the country descended into near anarchy. Neighboring Iraq took advantage of the chaos in Iran to assert its control over disputed oil lands. The war, which lasted until late 1988, gave evidence of nationalism and the concurrent weakness of Pan-Islamism.

Pan-Islamism turned out to be a Utopian idea that could never be successful at a time when Islamic states were suffused with nationalism. It was never implemented as a working ideology. There were far too many imponderables and inside frictions. It called for a union of disparate elements in the Age of Nationalism. The ambitions of individual rulers proved to be more powerful than the internationalization of religion. Islam found it impossible to unite its followers along religious lines. The Muslim states were enticed by the slogans of nationalism.

There were additional factors working against this failed macronationalism. Pan-Islamists were never able to overcome the bitter rivalry between Sunnite and Shi'ite factions. It was impossible for Pan-Islamism to thrive in this atmosphere of mutual hatreds. The leadership of Pan-Islamism was weak: its apostles spoke loudly for the movement and for its ideas, but the Ayatollah Khomeini and such self-appointed leaders as Libya's Muammar Kaddafi were not taken seriously throughout the Islamic world as respected leaders. Efforts to revive the caliphate as well as the shadowy Pan-Islamic movement proved to be unsuccessful. Most of all, Pan-Islamism failed to win grass-roots support among the faithful. The masses were inclined to accept religious leadership from Mecca, but not political control from any one Islamic country.

Bibliography: C. Brockelman, *History of the Islamic People*, trans. by J. Carmichael *et al.* (New York, 1947); Hazim Zaki Nussibeh, *The Idea of Arab Nationalism* (Ithaca, N.Y., 1956); Philip Hitti, *The Near East in History* (Princeton, N.J., 1961); Nikki R. Keddie, "Pan-Islam as Proto-Nationalism," *The Journal of Modern History*, 41, No. 1 (1969), 17–28; Nels Johnson, *Islam and Politics of Meaning in Palestinian Nationalism* (London, 1982); M. Ghayasuddin (ed.), *The Impact of Nationalism on the Muslim World* (London, 1983).

PAN-LUSITANISM.   A call for the unity of Portuguese people in the belief they have a community of interests, cultural reciprocity, and similar history and traditions. Pan-Lusitanism, one of the macronationalisms (q.v.), originated in Portugal, a small country with an area of 35,340 square miles occupying the southwestern part of the Iberian peninsula. At one time, Portugal played a major role in the discovery of the world's highways. The Portuguese people have long thought of themselves as descendants of the Lusitanians, who resisted Roman inroads, but adopted Roman customs and a Romance language that eventually became Portuguese.

During the early medieval period, Portugal was an obscure region of Spain and shared its history. In 1419 Prince Henry the Navigator (1394–1460) founded a school at Sagres on the southwestern tip of Portugal, where he set up a research institute with an observatory, shipyards, and classrooms. This school trained captains, navigators, pilots, astronomers, and cartographers, who moved to areas around the world. King Manuel of Portugal (1493–1521) assumed the title of "Lord of the Conquest, Navigation, and Commerce of India, Ethiopia, Arabia, and Persia," a designation confirmed by the papacy.

At a time when the Italian cities were decaying and Mediterranean trade was diminishing, the Portuguese managed to construct a great empire. Lisbon now became a center for trade in bullion, ivory, and slaves. Portuguese fleets of merchant ships came home laden with gold and slaves. For just a century the Portuguese shared with Spain a trade monopoly in the Far East. Portuguese merchants extended their efforts to the Western Hemisphere. It seemed that a long-lasting empire was in the making.

The decline of Portugal began in 1580 when Spanish troops invaded the country and controlled the people for some sixty years. The Portuguese commercial fleet was too thinly spread to meet the needs of an expanding trade. Portuguese entrepreneurs began to find themselves in the grip of German and Italian financiers. Moreover, Portuguese colonial administration was weakened by inefficiency and corruption. The restored dynasty in 1640 found itself unable to compete successfully with British, Dutch, and French businessmen, who seemed to have an unlimited supply of capital and manpower.

The process of breakdown continued into the early nineteenth century. Portugal lost her American possessions, especially Brazil, but managed to retain extensive holdings, such as the Cape Verde Islands of West Africa, Angola, Portuguese Guiana, Mozambique in Africa, and Goa in India. The Portuguese empire still had a global image, but the resources of the small country were strained by the costs of administering these faraway places. Meanwhile, the situation at home worsened. Throughout the nineteenth century, Portugal was weakened by dynastic quarrels and civil strife. Thousands of Portuguese, angered by excessive taxation and governmental misrule, emigrated, seeking better opportunities in other lands. The administration was incompetent and burdened by corruption. By the twentieth century the once-prosperous Portuguese empire was dissolved. The mighty global effort receded as one Portuguese possession after another managed to win its independence—Mozambique, Cape Verde Islands, and Angola among them.

Despite the dissolution of what was once a great empire, some Portuguese intellectuals and publicists could not forget the days of glory. For them the loss of empire was merely an inconvenient aberration. They saw the Portuguese spirit as still alive and Portuguese tradition and history as still important enough to warrant a call for unity. In common with other pan-nationalists, they held that a larger nationalism could still be won by a people whose roots went back to the Celtic Lusitanians. Tradition and sentiment, they said, called for a rapprochement of all the Portuguese, a great people who had forged a global empire and who still retained the qualities of a superior colonizing nation. They disregarded the fact that the modern Portuguese are by no means of pure Lusitanian stock, but rather a combination of Celts, Phoenicians, Greeks, Romans, Visigoths, and Arabs. Pan-Lusitanians, however, insisted that the Portuguese language was spoken by some 135 million people. It was a distinctive speech, they said, even if it was infiltrated with such foreign terms as Arabic, Germanic, and Asian. Pan-Lusitanism, they said, must include all those who spoke the Portuguese language.

Pan-Lusitanians pointed to those Portuguese literary heroes, who were doing their best to keep the national spirit alive and well. Their favorite was Luís Camòes (1524–1580), an outstanding national poet who, in his *Os Lusíadas* (1572), had praised Prince Henry the Navigator and Vasco da Gama as heroes of the Golden Age of Discovery. For Pan-Lusitanians, this epic of ten cantos called attention to their national pride and national character. There were other literary giants in the Romantic period of the early nineteenth century, whose work reflected the tenor of the rising consciousness of nationalism. Almeida Garret praised Lusitanian genius. Alexandre Herculano, the father of modern Portuguese historiography, gracefully examined the Portuguese past and found it enticing; he also introduced the historical novel in Portuguese. Antonio Feliciano de Castilho, writing in the Romantic form, was noted for the purity of his vernacular style. These three Romantics presented works that added to the national traditions and led Pan-Lusitanians to believe that there was a consistent Portuguese literature that should be revived in the imperial tradition.

Like other pan-movements, Pan-Lusitanism emphasized the heroic national past and yearned for its revival. Similar to other macro-nationalisms, Pan-Lusitanism could only dream of a larger nationalism that would encompass all the peoples of the old empire. They were emotional patriots inspired by a brilliant past, but the great days of Portuguese imperialism had long since faded. The once-prosperous empire was extinct; indeed it had now vanished. The days of exclusiveness and superiority were finished. Pan-Lusitanism was now a historical oddity, still another unfulfilled dream.

Bibliography: Harold V. Livermore, *A History of Portugal* (Cambridge, Eng., 1947); Charles E. Nowell, *A History of Portugal* (New York, 1952); Bailey W. Diffie, *A History of Colonial Brazil* (Malabar, Fla., 1987).

PAN-MOVEMENTS.   Synonym for the macro-nationalisms (q.v.), nationalism writ large, or the extension of nationalisms on the political scene. Nationalism is enlarged in meaning, influence, and scope to include all *(pan)*, who by reason of race, geography, religion, or language, or by a combination of any or all of them, are held to belong to the same category. The "we-group" sees its unity as including all those who "should" belong to the Fatherland or Motherland. The pan-movements grouped together all those holding a similar national sentiment and who believed that they belonged together.

Following is a viable definition of the pan-movements: the grouping together of and organized activities by a people working concertedly to enhance and promote their solidarity, and bound together by a common or a kindred language, the same historical traditions, and/or geographical proximity. They postulate a larger nation in the world community of nations.

There are certain common denominators for most, if not all, pan-movements. There may be differences in environment, organization, methods, and goals, but there are also common characteristics. Implicit in each pan-movement is the idea of uniqueness, or at least a firm belief in it. Pan-movements generally are distinguished by a conscious or unconscious sense of superiority. Their advocates see themselves as chosen by destiny to assume a high place in the society of nations. There is a preference for militancy and a mood for expansion.

There are several classifications of pan-movements. Some assume that they possess a common racial or ethnic identity. There is no such thing as a Slavic "race," but this did not prevent Pan-Slavs from demanding "racial emancipation." Other pan-movements stress the idea of a traditional culture rooted in the past. Historians, poets, and novelists seek common elements in their past—traditions, costumes, stories, sagas, poems, songs, dances, and folklore. Still other pan-movements direct attention to religious forms—they see primacy in the need to combine peoples of one religion into a supranational state. Another type of pan-movement is geographically oriented and continental in scope. Here the tendency is to supersede the nation-state and organize in its stead a supranational order based on a common continental territory.

Most pan-movements have been unsuccessful in winning their goals. Behind this lack of success is the familiar process of Hegelian thrust and counter-thrust. When a local pan-movement seeks status, it generally finds a counter-thrust of equal or greater strength. A classic example was the confrontation of Pan-Germanism and Pan-Slavism in World War I—two expansionist imperialisms in deadly conflict. Both emerged as considerably weakened ideologies. Despite this record of failure, the pan-movements have not disappeared. The idea persists in one form or another. The appeal seems to be much greater than the simultaneous demand for one world.

(*See* **PAN-AFRICANISM; PAN-ASIANISM; PAN-CHRISTIANITY; PAN-EUROPA; PAN-GERMANISM; PAN-HISPANISM; PAN-**

IBERIANISM; PAN-ISLAMISM; PAN-LUSITANISM; PAN-OT-
TOMANISM; PAN-SCANDINAVIANISM; PAN-SLAVISM; PAN-
TURKISM.)

Bibliography: Louis L. Snyder, *Macro-Nationalisms: A History of the Pan-Movements* (Westport, Conn., 1984).

PAN-NORDICISM.   *See* **PAN-SCANDINAVIANISM.**

PAN-OTTOMANISM.   The attempt to unite all peoples of the Ottoman Empire—Turks, Arabs, Greeks, Albanians, and Jews—into one super-Ottoman nationality. Pan-Ottomanism was the bearer of a wider Turkish nationalism. It was one of four rival factions of macro-nationalisms (q.v.) in Turkey, existing along with Pan-Islamism, which called for the union of all Muslims in one ecclesiastical-secular nation; Pan-Turkism, which sought to unite under its banner all those who spoke the Turkish language; and Pan-Turanism, which supported an alliance of all Turkish-speaking peoples living in Turan (Central Asia, the Caucasus, the lower Volga, and the Crimea). Though differing in their goals, all four were closely related, and all four were equally unsuccessful.

The major goal of Pan-Ottomanism was to revive the major Muslim power that had dominated southeastern Europe, the Middle East, and North Africa for some centuries. Osman I and his Ottoman successors had annexed Byzantine territories, took Christian Balkan states into vassalage, and conquered Constantinople. By the end of the sixteenth century, the Ottoman Empire included most of the Middle East, parts of North Africa, and almost all the Balkans. It was one of the great empires of history.

By the middle of the nineteenth century, this once important empire had faded into obscurity. It became the task of the Young Ottomans to revive its glory. In 1865 they founded a secret society, the "Patriotic Alliance," that called for one common nationality of all those who had lived in the empire in the past. Members met in London and Paris. Although their goal was clear, they broke into diversified units ranging from secularism to Islamic traditions, from conservatism to revolution, from nationalism to cosmopolitanism. Despite the arguing, they agreed on the fundamental idea that the Ottoman tradition was a superior one. It must be resurrected and the re-creation of a new Ottoman Empire would emerge as a vital, modern society.

The Young Ottomans also differed among themselves on the efficacy of Islam. However, most adhered to the basic principles of the religion and saw it as necessary for the existence of their Ottoman state. While one independent Muslim state after another was absorbed by European powers, Pan-Ottomans insisted that the caliphate had been transferred to the Ottoman sultan. They saw Fatherland *and* Islam as a dominant combination in their ideology. They adopted a condescending attitude toward the West: in their minds the best that the West had to offer was already present in Islam. As for the democratic institutions of Western society, Pan-Ottomans suggested that the idea of representative assemblies already existed in early Islamic principles. For them, the Islamic way of life was far superior to the societies of the Western world.

The idea of Pan-Ottomanism was promoted by Namik Kemal (1840–1888), who urged all the peoples living in the territories of the old empire to be loyal to the Ottoman Fatherland. He believed that indiscriminate beliefs in Western ways was the wrong approach because most of them were already present in Ottoman traditions. He called for a special constitution for the Ottoman peoples, a constitution that would reflect the greatness of the ancient empire.

Pan-Ottomanism, still another attempt to realize a nationalism writ large, was ineffective as a practical movement. It never received the type of organization that would make it a reality. The constant bickering among its members weakened the proposal and allowed it to slide into the dustbin of history. Though Pan-Ottomans dominated councils of the Young Turks, the persistent quarrels left the movement weakened. In the long run, it was unable to solve the many problems facing it. Like most macro-nationalisms, in the struggle to extend nationalism into a large unit nationalism triumphed. (*See also* **PAN-TURKISM,** and **PAN-TURANISM.**)

Bibliography: Elie Kedourie (ed.). *Nationalism in Asia and Africa* (New York, 1970).

PAN-SCANDINAVIANISM.   A movement to combine the nationalisms of five independent states in northern Europe—Norway, Sweden, Denmark, Iceland, and Finland. The history of these countries has been bound together by geography, language, and culture for more than a thousand years. The basic nations in Scandinavia are Norway and Sweden in the Scandinavian Peninsula, and Denmark is generally added to them. Some experts include Iceland on anthropological, linguistic, and cultural bases, and Finland on geological grounds. All five countries, also called Nordic states, have had common ties outweighing differences among them.

While these peoples hold fast to their sovereignties, they believe that one vigorous Nordic voice would be more effective than five weak ones. They prefer to share what they call their "transnational" character. They are linked by similar parliamentary systems, laws, education, and passion for social reform. With a combined population of twenty-two million people, the five Nordic nations present a rare unity of peoples. They form the only European bloc of nations acting as an entity at the United Nations.

The historical pattern is a common one. In 1815 the statesmen at Vienna, after the fall of Napoleon, remade the map of Europe based on "legitimacy and compensations." They recognized Sweden's annexation of Norway. Sweden was a country of large estates and tenant farmers, while Norway was inhabited by fishermen, merchants, and peasants. The union, made in the early days of European nationalism, was not altogether a happy one. Nevertheless, it lasted for nearly a century. On June 7, 1905, Norway declared the union dissolved, and the decision was ratified by popular vote. The Swedes acquiesced. The agreement provided that all disputes were to be settled by arbitration and that no fortifications were to be erected on the frontier. This peaceful separation, which was rare in European history, revealed that actually there was a close relationship between the Scandinavian countries.

In the last century the Nordic peoples have produced egalitarian states, with low levels of poverty, unemployment, and illiteracy. Dedicated to peace, they regard war as cannibalism and as an unfit procedure for European nations. The major lapse came in 1864 when the Germans, with their national revival gathering momentum, turned their attention to Schleswig-Holstein, a part of Denmark, and accused the Danes of holding these provinces under a tyrannical rule. The Danish struggle against the combined Austrian and Prussian powers was a hopeless one.

This was a blow to Nordic unity, but the idea of communion persisted. In 1952, the five countries formed the Nordic Council to arrange cooperation in legal, social, and economic matters. A common passport area was created, while working rights and social benefits were extended to citizens of the member states. The idea of the five Nordic states working together was always in the minds of their statesmen.

The five Nordic nations function as a bloc in the United Nations. They exert a collective influence on such issues as human rights and world peace. They seek more leverage by common action, as if they belonged to one family. In an informal arrangement, the five ambassadors hold weekly meetings and agree on common positions presented to the United Nations by a designated speaker. There are differences of opinion, but these are not allowed to disturb the common relationship. The image conveyed is one of fraternal unity.

In a world burdened by bitter differences between peoples, the Scandinavians presented an idea of unity. Yet, by no means does this close sense of cooperation disturb the idea of national sovereignty. Each of the five states sees itself as independent, but at the same time is willing to work closely with each other. The national identity is never submerged. This attitude is rare among the macro-nationalisms, which have remained ineffective because of rivalries among their members.

Bibliography: Brynjolf J. Hovde, *The Scandinavian Countries, 1720–1863* (2 vols., Boston, 1943); *Royal Institute of International Affairs, The Scandinavian States and Finland: A Political and Economic Survey* (London, 1951).

PAN-SLAVISM. The oldest and most important historically of the macro-nationalisms (q.v.). The idea of a union of all Slavs into a mighty coalition began in the late eighteenth century at a time when all the Slavic peoples were minorities in the Russian, Austrian, Turkish, and Prussian Empires. Economically, they were still in a primitive stage and lacked any overall culture. It was expected at the time that Slavs would work for their mutual advantage and that they would face a hostile world together. They regarded themselves as one people with a common language or dialects, as varied tribes forming one nation, and as a genuine national movement.

Gradually, over the course of the nineteenth century, it became clear to those who liked the idea of Pan-Slavism that the movement was different from what they had expected. Particularistic nationalism among the Slavic peoples was so strong that it overshadowed any extension into a broad category which would include all Slavs. Leaders began to redefine Slavism in somewhat more realistic terms. They would be content to promote mutual assistance among those Slavs who had similar languages and traditions.

Slavic national consciousness received its first notable stimulus in the work of Johann Gottfried von Herder (q.v.). The German Herder noted the Slavic national consciousness and urged a unified Slavic cult to replace the "declining Latin-German culture." Attracted by Slavic attention to their folk songs and folklore, Herder, as a disciple of French rationalist Jean-Jacques Rousseau (q.v.), praised what he called the Slavs' idyllic agricultural life. Herder saw the Latin and Germanic peoples as in decline, while the Slavs in their "uncorrupted youthfulness" were obviously the coming heroes of history. He was also influenced by the ideas of Slavs in political thought and spoke of them with genuine praise. As a humanitarian nationalist, he supported a spirit of tolerance and regard for the rights of other nationalities. Every nationality, he said, was entitled to its own development consonant with its own peculiar genius. Each nation should attend to the business of its own national development, and should have only the kindest sentiments toward other people striving for the same goals. According to Herder:

> The spirit which lives in human history wants each people to become happy in its own way as well as in its own place, but at the same time it wishes them to be ruled by a sense of reciprocity. Treat each one as you yourself would like to be treated for the human race is one whole; we work and we suffer, sow and harvest, each for all.

This attitude was regarded by Slavs as the essence of their own existence.

Herder was taken by the Slavic sense of freedom, their modesty, their sense of obedience, and their contempt for robbery and plunder. "They never wanted conquest of the world, and had no war-happy hereditary princes." Therefore, many nations, mostly those of German stock, sinned harshly against them. Where Western Europeans looked down on Slavs as backward in culture and civilization, Herder extolled them as a fine branch of humanity. He was certain that the nineteenth century would vindicate Slavs. He urged Slavic intellectuals to study their native language instead of abandoning it for French or German. Slavs should retain their heroic past by collecting their folklore and folksongs. Herder looked forward to a turn of the wheel of history to a new "garden of humanity." "It is to be hoped that there will be a halt to the increasing disappearence of their customs, songs, and legends, and that finally a complete history of these people will appear which will benefit the canvas of humanity."

This kind of understanding had an enormous effect on Slavic intellectuals. Impressed by Herder's words, they began to search their past for corroboration and to justify their position among the world's peoples. Herder's lofty estimate helped give direction to the Pan-Slavic movement. Slavs began to revise their own belief in themselves and their status in world society. They turned their eyes to an overall Slavic state, which, in fact, did not exist. Slavs of the world should unite—they had nothing to lose but their local national chains.

The first important event in the development of Pan-Slavism was the Congress of Prague held in June 1848, under the presidency of František Palacký (q.v.) There was joy in the streets of Prague as the Congress met. For the first time a minority was gathered to discuss its interests and plan for a great future. The new Slavic tricolor, blue, white, and red, was prominently displayed. Slavs, dressed in their colorful costumes, addressed one another with the catchword "Slava" instead of the customary "Heil!" They sang old Slavic songs. Palacký called for a synthesis of the Slavic character: "The freedom which we are now seeking is not a newly arrived stranger among us; it is not a scion brought to us from abroad; it is a tree which had grown of its own on our domestic soil, it is the native and first-born heritage of our ancestors." Others glorified the Slav spirit and hailed all Slavs as an important branch of mankind existing side by side with the Latins and Germans. With their unique character, Slavs were identified with humanitarianism, democracy, and peace, as examples of great humanity and pure Christianity.

Declarations of unity were proclaimed. One of them spoke of Slavic hearts beating in unison.

> The Latin and Germanic nations, formerly famous in Europe as powerful conquerors, have for centuries established their independence by the strength of the sword. . . . Only today, owing to the strength of public opinion which like the spirit of God has suddenly spread throughout all lands, the people have succeeded in breaking the fetters of feudalism and in returning to the individuals the rights of mankind. Now the Slav, long rejected, has raised his head. . . . Strong in numbers and even stronger in his will, and in his newly acquired brotherly union, he remains, nevertheless, faithful to the national character and to the principles of his ancestors; he demands neither domination nor conquest, he claims liberty for himself and for all, he asks that it be generally recognized without exception as the sacred rights of man. Therefore, we Slavs reject all domination by mere force. . . . *Liberty, equality, and fraternity* for all who live in the state is our watchword today.

These sentiments were echoed by Ján Kollár, whose *Daughter of Sláva*, glorifying the dream of Slavic unity, had brought him to the front of Slavic apostles of nationalism. He recommended the publication of a Slavic periodical, formation of a Slav Academy, a Slav library, and also both central and national committees for political and cultural affairs. Slavic unity seemed well on the way to fruition.

Yet, despite the oratory, there were few positive results of the Congress at Prague. It managed to proclaim the principle of mutuality, but there were still irreconcilable differences among the Slavs. The revolutionary radical group led by Mickhail Bakunin was loud and vociferous; it annoyed the moderates loyal to the monarchy.

Two days before the planned end of the Congress, an uprising of radical workers and students in Prague brought it to a close. Those who planned the meeting were satisfied: they, indeed, had emphasized the Slavic will to unity. All Slavs were given a tremendous psychological lift. In addition, the Congress marked the transition of Pan-Slavism from Romantic idealization to politicization. The earlier Romanticism had given way to an urge for political solidarity. The Slavs could now claim that their second-rate status was ended and they would now play their "destined role" in service for all humanity.

Russians were not pleased with the Prague Congress of 1848. Behind their own version of Pan-Slavism was the earlier ideology of Muscovite Slavophilism, a romantic idea that stressed the Russian nature of Slavic society and which called for a revival of past Slavic traditions. They wanted "Tsar, Church, and People"—under specific Russian influences. Behind anti-Western Slavophilism was a powerful religious motivation, which led eventually to the "Third Rome" doctrine: "Two Romes have fallen but the Third shall remain." That Third Rome was Moscow. From this viewpoint, Russians saw themselves as God's chosen people, unlike Western barbarians corrupted by materialism. Holy Russia was the first state in the world, and Moscow, "citadel of the true faith," would lead the peoples of the world to the paradise of true Christianity.

For the next two decades after the Prague Congress of 1848, Pan-Slavism was handicapped by internal dissensions. Russian Pan-Slavism became more dedicated to a reactionary and nationalistic policy of Russification. Pan-Slavism in the Balkans was weakened considerably by growing rivalry between Serbs and Bulgars in the Balkan Peninsula. In addition, Poles developed unifying ideas of their own. In 1867 the Society of Friends of Natural Science at the University of Moscow arranged a Slavic ethnographic exposition, to which Slavs outside of Russia were invited to attend. Some eighty-four non-Russian Slavs, including František Palacký, attended. Poles remained ostentatiously absent. Speakers lauded Tsar Alexander II as "Tsar-Liberator" and emphasized the political brotherhood which united all Slavs. One delegate proposed a theme: "Russia is no longer Russia. It is Slavonia, nay Pan-Slavonia." The heart of Pan-Slavism was being transferred from Prague to Moscow.

Differences soon arose between the Russians and their guests. The Russians demanded that their own language be the official speech of all Slavs. Russians present at the meeting greeted this suggestion with thunderous applause, but the visiting Slavs remained silent. For the latter, Pan-Slavism meant the equality of all Slavs. For the

Russian hosts, the movement was dedicated to the supremacy of the Russian language, the Orthodox faith, and the Russification of all Slavs, even those in the Balkans. Speakers tried to repair the damage by insisting that all Slavs were one nation welded together by blood and mind. Every Slav unity should develop in its own way, but there must be a common language, a treasure covering all Slavic lands from the Adriatic Sea and Prague to Archangel and the Pacific Ocean. This kind of oratory took place in an atmosphere of artificial and strained unity. The Congress ended with a display of enthusiasm shown in speeches and loud applause.

Again, practical results were minimal. The proposed next meeting in Belgrade in two years never took place. Four decades were to pass before new Congresses were held in Prague in 1908 and in Sophia in 1910. Most Slavic leaders resented Russian dominance in the movement. Pan-Slavic ideals remained hopelessly confused—a melange of mystical idealism, conservative fantasies, and political unrealism. Contradictory elements were too powerful. Anti-Russian in tone, speakers called for a union of the Western Slavs (Czechs, Slovaks, Moravians, and Silesians), Eastern Slavs (Poles and Ukrainians), and Southern Slavs (Siberians, Croatians, Slovens, and Dalmatians). The meeting was called in the atmosphere of national-liberal sentiment then popular in central Europe. Its goal was to achieve united action in democratic reforms and to strengthen the Slavic position against Germans and Magyars. While the congress failed to produce any practical results, it was important psychologically for a people who for the first time were proclaiming to all Europe the intense desire of Slavs to exist as a special people. The delegates made no secret of their anti-Russian bias, but they, nevertheless, felt it best to seek rapprochement with Russia.

When Russia was defeated in the Crimean War (1853–1856), the vague sense of Slavophilism was transformed into a militant and nationalistic Russian form of Pan-Slavism. The initiative for Pan-Slavism now passed from the minor Slav states to Russia. From then on, the Slav minorities in the Austrian Empire became known as the Little Slavs, while Russia became the "Big Slav Brother." The Little Slavs criticized the Russians, but this attitude changed after the Hungarian *Ausgleich* (compromise) of 1867, the new dual monarchy. At this time, the Czech demand for a trialism (Austro-Hungarian-Czechish monarchy) instead of a dualism was rejected. Angry Czechs now came to the support of Russian Pan-Slavism.

When in 1867 the Second Pan-Slav Congress met in Moscow, those who controlled the meeting were Russian. Pan-Slavism was regarded now as a movement to promote the political and cultural unity of all Slavs, even against their will, into a Greater Russia which was on its way to global power. The main apostle of Pan-Slavism at this time was Nikolay Danilevsky (q.v.), who urged Russians to liberate and unite all Slavs. Danilevsky was especially sensitive to European hostility to Russia and to the Slavic people. There would be an inevitable struggle, but in the end it would result in the emancipation of all Slavs and the formation of a Pan-Slavic union under Russian control.

According to Danilevsky, the Slavic type was superior and it would be the first to embody four cultural activities—religious, political, esthetic-scientific, and socio-economic. Western Europe, in his view, had degenerated into religious anarchy, with Catholicism revealing political despotism, and Protestantism presenting the foolish idea that religious truth was based on personal authority. The Slavic peoples offered a viable idea against this religious anarchy: they were the chief guardians of religious trust in Orthodoxy. Politically, Slavs were the most gifted of all peoples. Russia, said Danilevsky, was the only large state with unshakeable stability provided by peasant ownership of land. Slavs would combine to eradicate imitativeness and servility. First, however, the Russians must go about the task of liberating their "racial" brothers by instilling in them a spirit of independence and Pan-Slavic consciousness. Danilevsky was certain that the Slavs would know what to do to implement this goal.

There was some revitalization. The Czechs, impelled by their aim to create a counter-movement to Pan-Germanism, managed for a time to keep the issue of Pan-Slavism alive. In 1898, the centenary of Palacký's birth, a great Pan-Slav demonstration was held in Prague. Several Pan-Slavic Congresses met to consider the problems of economic issues, discussing the formation of a Pan-Slavic bank and the planning of future Pan-Slavic fairs and exhibitions. These goals were never achieved. Pan-Slavism was not helped by the Balkan Wars or World War I, which had its origins partly in Pan-Slavic aspirations. Pan-Slavs saw the war as the final struggle between Germans and Slavs for the supremacy of eastern Europe.

Pan-Slavism actually was ended by World War I. By now, Russia was changed into a powerful supranationalism and abandoned its interest in Slavic nationalism. Attempts were made by the peace-makers at Versailles to realize some of the Pan-Slavic dreams, as for example, the union of Czechs and Slavs in the new Czechoslovakia. However, on the whole, it became clear that the barriers between varied Slavic peoples had been accentuated rather than diminished.

New rivalries and hatreds appeared among the Slavs. National diversities and different traditions persisted. Its theory had always been vague, inconsistent, and on occasion, even incoherent. Slavic unity became more myth than fact. Behind the collapse was a combination of forces: geographical fragmentation, religious differences, psychological needs, and political bonds.

Bibliography: Robert R. Ergang, *Herder and the Foundations of German Nationalism* (New York, 1931); Hans Kohn, *Pan-Slavism: Its History and Ideology* (Notre Dame, Ind., 1953); Joseph S. Roucek, "Pan-Slavism: An Ideological Weapon," *Central European Journal*, 107 (May 5, 1969), 163–184; Louis L. Snyder, *Macro-Nationalisms: A History of the Pan-Movements* (Westport, Conn., 1984).

PAN-TURANISM. The attempt to unite in one larger nationalism the peoples who spoke Turkish, Mongol, Finnish, Hungarian, and other languages. All of them were said to have originated in "the broad and everlasting land of Turan," northeast of Persia. Pan-Turanism called for an alliance of people residing in Central Asia, the ancestral home of the Turks. Like Pan-Ottomanism and Pan-Turkism, Pan-Turanism saw itself as the bearer of a wider Turkish nationalism. Pan-Turanism, in addition, was more linguistic-minded than either Pan-Ottomanism or Pan-Turkism.

The concept of Pan-Turanism owed much to the teachings of Ziya Gökalp (q.v.), who held that the Turkish "race" originated in legendary Turan, a land described in Persian epics:

> There is, in fact, a homeland of Islam which is the beloved land of all Muslims. The other one is the national home, which, for Turks, is what we call Turan. One portion is the home of the Turks, and is at the same time a portion of Turan. Another portion is the homeland of the Arabs, which is again a part of the great Arab Fatherland.

Gökalp believed that modern Turks belonged to the Ural-Altaic group, to the Islamic *ümmet* (people of one nation), and to Western nationality. Pan-Turanism would revive the prestige of Attila, Genghis Khan, and Tamerlane. One day, according to Gökalp, a new Pan-Turanian Attila would unite Ottomans, Crimean Turks, Azerbaijani Turks, Uzbeks, Kirghis, and all other fragments of Turkism into one great Turanian nation.

Pan-Turanians regarded the old Ottoman Empire as a top-heavy multilinguistic and religious state that had to be purged of non-Turanian elements. They would delete from the Turkish language all Persian and Arabic words and see that it returned to its pure

Turanian character. They believed that Islam itself was far too wide a concept, that it was not conducive to Pan-Turanian national aspirations. They claimed that Islam was too international; it was necessary to cut through the layers of Pan-Islamism and unite the Turanian élite by emphasizing its original character, especially its sense of national pride. Religion must be confined to the status of a spiritual mood of the people, and it must steer clear of political entanglements.

According to Pan-Turanism, the people who once called themselves Turks, should, in addition, identify themselves as Turanians united by language, history, and destiny. Pan-Turanians insisted that they must repair the damage done by the fragmentation of a people who always belonged together. It was necessary, they said, that Ottoman Turks, Seljuk Turks, Mongols, and Azerbaijanis all should be joined in one great pan-movement.

Pan-Turanism called chiefly for cultural amalgamation, but it did have some political overtones. In this respect the vision clashed with political realities, because some Turks were subjected to Russian domination. Pan-Turanism gave authorities a weapon against Moscow. However, Soviet Russia considered the Turks in their society to be on the same plane as other nationalities and refused to recognize their dream of an association with Pan-Turanism.

The whole idea of Pan-Turanism slipped into obscurity after 1918, at a time when Turkish authorities turned their attention to the regeneration of Turkey proper. Pan-Turkism became the preferred macro-nationalism as the linguistic niceties of Pan-Turanism were forgotten. Some Pan-Turanians, however, continued to insist on their goal—to cut through the layers of Islamic, Persian, and Arabic cultures and combine them in one great supranationalism. That objective was not achieved, although the idea did serve as a stimulant for nationalism in Turkey proper before it began to recede. It now became obvious that complex linguistic gymnastics would not be successful in uniting a multilinguistic empire. It was far too late to combine the uncombinable. The revival of Pan-Turkism, the successor to Pan-Turanism, was the work of Kemal Atatürk (q.v.), whom the Turks regarded as the founder of their modern country. "Turkey for the Turks," he proclaimed, and that slogan became the guideline for his political life. Stressing secularism and nationalism, he concentrated on the regeneration of Turkey proper. (*See also* **PAN-OTTO-MANISM,** and **PAN-TURKISM.**)

Bibliography: Ziya Gökalp. *Turkish Nationalism and Western Civilization,* trans. and ed. by N. Berkes (New York, 1959); Elie Kedourie (ed.), *Nationalism in Asia and Africa* (New York, 1970).

PAN-TURKISM.   The concept that all Turks, no matter where they lived, as well as all non-Turks who spoke the Turkish language, should be combined in one larger nationalism. A new sense of Turkish identity emerged in the early twentieth century. The Pan-Turkish movement called for the political union of all Turkish peoples, including those in the Middle East and Asia, the Tatars of the Crimea, and those who lived in the Volga region. All, both Ottoman and Russian Turks, would be subjects of one great state.

Pan-Turkism took on an increasingly secular complexion. Even as Christians remain faithful to their gospel and the traditions of their church, and the Jews hold fast to their Scriptures and Talmud, so were Pan-Turks content with their creed, their literature, and their customs and history. But at the same time, Pan-Turkism began to turn partially from its clerical status, which it regarded as outmoded in modern society. While it veered away from Islam, it did repeat Pan-Islamic reactions against the encroachments of other nationalisms, especially Russian. Turkish nationalist Ziya Gökalp (q.v.) at first was motivated primarily by his Islamic faith and believed in religion and Fatherland. However, by the outbreak of World War I, he began to have doubts about the primacy of religion. By 1918 he became convinced that the unity of Islam was an impossible hope. He saw Islam as standing directly in the way of Turkish revival.

The idea of Pan-Turkism, the union of all Turks no matter where they lived, began in the Crimea and the Volga regions of Russia. Its outstanding spokesman was Ismail Bey Gasprinski (Gaspirali) (1818–1914), a Crimean Tatar. Influenced by the unifying linguistic aspects of Pan-Slavism, he sought to create a common Turkish language to meet the needs of his fellow Tatars. He accepted some elements of Pan-Islamism as conducive to his cause. After the Revolution of 1905, many Pan-Turks emigrated to other Ottoman lands. Among them was the Russian Tatar Yúsuf Akçuragoglu (1876–1939), who called for a union of all Russian and Ottoman Turks. In his *Three Kinds of Policy* (1903), he presented the argument that the Turkish language provided a better basis for the Ottoman Empire than either Ottomanism or Islamism. He believed that Pan-Islamism (q.v.) had passed its prime, and for that reason he was inclined to reject it.

There was an energetic propaganda campaign on behalf of Pan-Turkism in the early twentieth century. Pan-Turks took a stand opposed to Islamism and Ottomanism and expressed their views in several Muslim congresses. Those Turks who had been forced to leave Russia came to Constantinople, where they influenced the Young Turks in their direction. However, their efforts to obtain control of the Young Turk movement failed. Here, again, too many differences worked against an effective union. How to combine Tatars, Turkomans, Kazaks, Azerbaijanis, and others, all having traditions of their own, into one working union was too much to expect. A Turkish-Russian Pan-Turkism was to remain an impossible dream.

The agitation for Pan-Turkism reached its height in 1914 with the outbreak of World War I. However, the idea received a powerful blow when Turkey joined the Central Powers, while Russia turned to the Western Allies. In this way the Turks of Turkey and of Russia were split into two groups. Those Muslims who lived in Central Asia—Kazaks, Kirghiz, and Uzbeks believed themselves to be exempt from military service and rebelled angrily against the military draft.

The Russian Revolutions in 1917 and the Turkish collapse in 1918 slowed the development of Pan-Turkism. The idea was revived by Kemal Atatürk (q.v.). It was smothered in the Soviet Union, where all nationalities were subjected to Communist ideology. The Kremlin regarded any efforts by its citizens to work for union with any foreign people as simple treason. Pan-Turkism, like so many other macro-nationalisms (q.v.), lost its forward thrust and disappeared into the pages of history. Again, there was additional evidence that attempts to write nationalism on a larger scale must recede before the reality of existing nationalisms. (*See also* **PAN-OTTOMANISM, PAN-TUR-ANISM,** and **IRREDENTISM.**)

Bibliography: Elie Kedourie (ed.), *Nationalism in Asia and Africa* (New York, 1970); David Kushner, *The Rise of Turkish Nationalism* (London, 1977); Jacob M. Landau, *Pan-Turkism in Turkey: A Study of Irredentism* (London, 1981).

PARNELL, CHARLES STEWART (1846–1891).   Irish political leader, statesman, and passionate nationalist. From his mother, a daughter of Rear Admiral Charles Stewart of the United States Navy, Parnell inherited a hatred of England. A landowner and a Protestant, he was educated at Magdalen College, Cambridge University. As a young man, he spoke of his attitude to the English: "These English despise us because we are Irish, but we must stand up to them. That's the way to treat an Englishman—stand up to him!" For the rest of his life Parnell made it a point to oppose the English. A visit to the United States in 1871 transformed him from a conventional landlord into an Irish nationalist. Identified there as a poor, contemptible immigrant, he reacted by defending his Irish character. In 1877 he was elected as the head of the Home Rule Confederation, the most formidable Irish organization of its kind in Britain.

From this time on, Parnell became a champion of Irish nationalism.

In 1879 he was elected President of the Land League, which wanted to put an end to the Irish land system. He came again to the United States to raise a large popular subscription to support his movement. Present at several large Land League demonstrations, he was arrested on October 17, 1881, and lodged in Kilmainham jail. Despite his incarceration, he worked actively in the Irish cause. The Land League was dissolved, but from his cell Parnell and several fellow prisoners called upon Irish tenants to pay no rent until the government had restored the constitutional rights of the people.

On May 6, 1882, came the Phoenix Park murders, when Cavendish and Burke, the Chief Secretary and Under-Secretary for Ireland, were assassinated. Parnell was prostrated by the event. In a public manifesto to the Irish people he stated: "No act has ever been perpetrated in our country, during the exciting struggle for political and social rights of the past fifty years, that has so stained the name of hospitable Ireland as this cowardly and unprovoked assassination of a friendly stranger." The Phoenix Park murders, more than any other incident of the day, did much to frustrate Parnell's work on behalf of the Irish.

In the spring of 1897 *The Times*, London's leading newspaper, began publishing a series of articles entitled "Parnellism and Crime," which charged Parnell and several of his colleagues of conspiracy and with founding an organization that was working for the separation of Ireland from England. Letters printed in the article were proved to be the forged work of Richard Pigott, an Irish journalist. Parnell managed to vindicate himself completely by bringing an action against *The Times*. Pigott fled to Madrid, where he committed suicide. Parnell was awarded 5,000 pounds damages. In 1893 he again became a storm center in England, when he was charged with committing adultery. With no defense offered, a decree of divorce was pronounced. He and Mrs. O'Shea, the woman concerned in the charge, then married.

The adverse verdict of the divorce court caused a revulsion of feeling toward Parnell, as well as a split in the Irish Party. His political career was in decline. His scene of operations was transferred to Ireland, where he continued to fight a bitter but losing battle against his many opponents. Among them was the Catholic Church, which had never approved of the Protestant leader. Outwardly aristocratically impassive, he became a victim of restless nervousness. He died at Brighton on October 6, 1891. His remains were conveyed to Dublin, where a huge assemblage paid tribute to the fighter for Ireland. (*See also* **IRISH NATIONALISM.**)

Bibliography: Francis Stewart Leland Lyons, *Parnell* (Dublin, 1963);

Mary McAuley, *Charles Stewart Parnell: Political Paradox* (New York, 1967); Michael Hurst, *Parnell and Irish Nationalism* (London, 1968); Alan O'Day, *The English Face of Irish Nationalism* (Niagra Falls, N.Y., 1977).

PARTICULARISM. The term "particularism" refers to the divided allegiance, adherence, or devotion to a particular party, system, sect, or interest. It is on occasion used interchangeably with such terms as mini-nationalism, regionalism, or localism. In political theory it means the principle of allowing a state in a federation to promote its own interests and retain its own laws inside the nation-state. An example is the situation in Bavaria from 1871 to 1918: although it was a part of Bismarck's Second Reich, it was allowed to retain its own army and special political powers. (*See also* **NATIONALISM, CLASSIFICATIONS OF; MINI-NATIONALISMS;** and **REGION-ALISM.**)

PATHOLOGICAL NATIONALISM. The extension of nationalism into all the conditions, processes, and results of a particular disease. The rise of a pathological nationalism about ten or fifteen years after a national defeat seems to be a recurrent phenomenon. A people may go to war in an outburst of patriotic frenzy. When they are smashed on the battlefield, they retreat into glum anxiety and wonder how this great tragedy could have occurred. In time, this attitude takes on pathological overtones and the qualities of a new national disease.

Pathological nationalism may be noted in the relations of France and Germany over many years. When the Prussian troops of Otto von Bismarck (q.v.) overran the French and inflicted defeat on a proud and patriotic people, the French, stunned and bewildered by this catastrophic event, eventually turned to *revanche* (revenge) for that unbelievable tragedy. Similarly, when the Germans were defeated by the Allies in 1918, the Germans reacted in the same way and followed Adolf Hitler in an effort to mend the provisions of the Treaty of Versailles.

According to Lewis Namier, this kind of pathological nationalism develops apparently when the children of the war period attain the age of twenty to thirty. Adults may learn the lesson of war and defeat, but those who have experienced the passions of war and the bitterness of defeat while still incapable of understanding, seemed burdened with frantic, almost insane resentments. These emerge and give a pathological turn to their politics. A wave of national resentment seemed bound to sweep Germany at this time, even if the terms of the Treaty of Versailles had been different. All loss of territory was described as a "grievous wrong," a situation which had to be corrected in order to restore national honor.

Under such bitter circumstances, nationalism acts like a disease with all its implications. German love of country degenerated into strong anger against those who stood in the way of national pride.

Bibliography: Lewis Namier, "Nationality and Liberty," in *Vanished Supremacies: Essays on European History* (London, 1958); Isaiah Berlin "Nationalism," in *Against the Current: Essays on the History of Ideas* (London, 1978).

PATRIOTISM. Although the terms patriotism and nationalism are often used interchangeably and, indeed, have much in common, they are not semantic twins. Each has its own distinctive meaning. Nationalism is derived from the Latin root *natio,* referring to the people of a territory under a single government, a country, or a state. Patriotism comes from the Greek *patriōtēs,* or Fatherland, and signifies a person who loves and zealously supports his own country. The emphasis of patriotism is upon *people,* that of nationalism is upon *territory.*

Psychologist Leonard W. Doob (q.v.) of Yale University makes these definitions to distinguish between patriotism and nationalism:

> PATRIOTISM: the more or less conscious conviction of a person that his own welfare and that of the significant groups to which he belongs are dependent upon the preservation or expansion (or both) of the power and culture of his society.

> NATIONALISM: the set of more or less uniform demands (1) which people in a society share, (2) which arise from their patriotism, (3) for which justifications exist and can be readily expressed, (4) which incline them to make personal sacrifices in behalf of their government's aims, and (5) which may or may not lead to appropriate action.

Nationalism divides humanity into separate and distinct nations and claims that such nations constitute separate states. The nations are distinguished by language, culture, race, and on occasion by religion. Patriotism claims that the people of a nation must be aware of the special attributes of their own nation and must subjugate their own personalities into the greater whole of the nation. It asserts that the individual must understand and support the greater common unity for which he should be prepared to sacrifice his own life. It has had so basic an effect upon the psyche of modern men that those who reject love of country are regarded as pariahs. From this point of view, treason is considered to be the very worst of all crimes. The sentiment of patriotism is known among all men, from tribes to nations.

Patriotism is based on the emotion of love and especially on love of country. Love implies fondness, fidelity, and loyalty. Love appears to be instinctive with the human being, a natural part of his make-up and a support for social awareness among people. It is basic in relationships in families and societies. It may involve several kinds of loyalty—to individuals, ideas, localities, or larger societies. It may be concern for clan or village, lodge or church, region or state. It may well be extended to a nationality and usually becomes the main prop of nationalism.

While loyalty to the broader nation may be instinctive in nature, and while loyalty to familiar places may be natural, a sense of love for the entire country has had historically the addition of some special education and training. A country consists of a large number of areas, some of which may well be unfamiliar to the individual. For this reason, conscious efforts are made in every country to bolster a sense of patriotism. In their schooling, young children everywhere are carefully taught the importance of patriotism. They recite pledges of allegiance with hand over heart, learn quickly the words of their national anthem, and are conditioned to revel in the glories of their national heroes. Much of this training is artificially induced. In many countries, especially in dictatorships, propaganda in exaggerated form is considered to be absolutely necessary to condition citizens to what is considered to be the right kind of patriotism. In all countries civic training is seen as necessary to make people, from cradle to grave, loyal to the aggregation of countrymen, either familiar or unfamiliar, who make up the whole nationality.

Psychological motivation is basic in patriotism, as well as in nationalism. People feel, act, and pass judgment as a response to the instinct of patriotism. It is this psychological drive that convinces the patriot that his personal and group welfare is dependent upon the preservation or expansion of the country's culture and power. Patriotism merges into nationalism when the individual's conviction is accompanied by action.

Bibliography: J. Huizinga, *Men and Ideas* (New York, 1959); Leonard W. Doob, *Patriotism and Nationalism: Their Psychological Foundations* (New Haven, Conn., 1964); Morris Janowitz, *The Reconstruction of Patriotism* (Chicago, 1983).

PIETISM.   An influential religious reform movement beginning
with German Lutheranism in the seventeenth century. Its stress on
personal faith in protest against the secularization of religion drew
interest in other countries. In its early stages, the movement emphasized repentance, faith as an attitude of heart, and sanctification and
regeneration as facts. Pietists organized conventicles in various churches
to specialize in Bible study and to promote practical Christianity.
Appealing to aristocracy as well as to the bourgeoisie, they never set
up a viable organization.

Koppel S. Pinson (q.v.), pointed out the role of Pietism in the
origins of German nationalism. In his *Pietism as a Factor in the Rise of
German Nationalism* (1934), he showed how the religious movement
known as Pietism developed in the Germanies at the close of the
seventeenth century. The word "Pietist" was used in 1689 as a term
of ridicule. The word soon lost its original connotation as the movement became more widespread, and Pietism eventually took on a
serious designation. There were corresponding manifestations in
Jansenism in France, in Quakerism and Methodism in England, and
similar currents in Switzerland, Holland, and Scandinavia. There
were some informal connections between German Pietism and similar movements in other countries.

Pietism, in essence, called for a return of German Protestantism to
its original character in the Lutheran Revolt, as well as a reaction to
the Lutheran orthodoxy that later characterized Lutheranism. Pinson
saw a wide variation in the individual leaders and currents within
German Pietism, but suggested three general characteristics of all of
them. In common, these trends represented a union against the
established orthodoxy. First, Pietism was a turning toward a more
inward, emotional, and enthusiastic form of Christianity. The Thirty
Years' War had left a trail of havoc and misery. As a result, a wave
of mysticism spread over the Germanies with a reaction against
dogma, scholastic argumentation, and purity of doctrine. Hard-pressed
Germans merely wanted a simple form of religion unencumbered by
long orthodox discussions.

Second, the Pietists called for a more practical Christianity. Learning and prolonged discussions were fine, but the Pietists called for
purity of life, saintly behavior, and active Christianity. Prayer was
the mark of the good Pietists. They must turn their attention to good
works, philanthropy, and missionary zeal.

Third, the Pietists called for greater emphasis upon the doctrine
of general priesthood. There must be no chasm between the official
clergy and laymen. All classes of the people, not merely the clergy,

should turn their attention to Biblical reading and study. Pietist leaders such as Philipp Jakob Spener and August Hermann Francke distributed many thousands of Bibles, a practice which reached three million copies in the eighteenth century.

Pinson saw a special relationship between Pietism and the rise of nationalism in the Germanies. Both Pietistic religion and nationalism, in his view, were more unique and characteristic in the Germanies than elsewhere. German nationalism proceeded in quite a different manner in the Germanies from that in other European countries. Where England, France, and Spain solved the political aspect of nationalism before the eighteenth century, the Germanies remained divided until Bismarck (q.v.) achieved national unification in 1871. Until then, the Germanies had been split into many independent states and principalities. Where in England secularization led to the transference of religious concepts to the more practical questions of political power, in the Germanies the energies released by the secularization of modern life came to be focused on the problem of nationality. United Germany became the classic land of nationalism. Herder (q.v.) and the German Romanticists (*see* **ROMANTICISM**) presented a strongly developed sense of national consciousness, a concept that spread throughout Europe.

Bibliography: Koppel S. Pinson, *Pietism as a Factor in the Rise of German Nationalism* (New York, 1934).

PINSKER, LEO (1821–1891). Jewish-Russian physician, polemicist, and pioneer of Zionist nationalism. The son of a Hebrew scholar, Pinsker studied law and then medicine. In his thoughts on Judaism and the role of Jews in Russian society, he underwent precisely the same transformation as Moses Hess (q.v.), the German Jew. At first, Pinsker supported the assimilation of Jews into the society in which they lived. He changed his mind after a pogrom in Odessa in 1881, which he believed was encouraged by the Russian government.

Like Hess, Pinsker now believed that Jewish nationalism was the only solution for the suffering of Jews among other peoples. From then on, he used a pen dipped in acid to promote the cause of Jewish emancipation and the necessity for a Jewish homeland in Palestine. In 1882 he published anonymously a pamphlet titled *Auto-Emanzipation. Ein Mahnruf an seine Stammesgenossen. Von einem russischen Juden (Self-Emancipation. A Warning Addressed to his Brethren. By a Russian Jew*, Eng. trans. *Auto-Emancipation*, 1884). He expressed his views in medical terms: the Jews were infected with the virus of anti-Semitism, a social pathology. He maintained that Jews were hated and persecuted because, while they had no national existence, they continued to display the spiritual characteristics of a national entity. This kind of hatred, he wrote, was a psychosis which in 2,000 years of Jewish history had become incurable. It was impossible for Jews to find a home in any non-Jewish country, because they would be persecuted as soon as they became too populous.

According to Pinsker, the only possible restorative for Jewish health and dignity was to find a home in which they would not be strangers and to re-establish a nation of their own. They must emigrate from their European countries to a place where they could live the national life of a normal people. Pinsker warned that Jews must not rely on the humanitarianism of others, but on their own inner strength, their own historic will—or self-help, or auto-emancipation.

Pinsker's authorship of *Auto-Emanzipation* was soon discovered. The pamphlet had a strong reaction, both commendatory and critical, among Jewish leaders. The same year in which it appeared, a new Zionist group called *Hibbat Ziyyon* (Love of Zion), later to be named *Hovevei Ziyyon*—Lovers of Zion, was formed. Its members were pledged to work for a resurrected homeland in Palestine. Pinsker, who in his pamphlet stated that the new homeland need not necessarily be Palestine, was converted to the idea: he became the leader and chief theorist of the Zionist organization. (*See also* **ZIONIST NATIONALISM.**)

Bibliography: Asher Ginzburg, *Pinsker and His Brochure*, trans. from the Hebrew by H. Szold (Baltimore, Md., 1892); Yochan Block, *Judenthum in der Krise: Emanzipation, Sozialismus, und Zionismus* (Göttingen, 1966).

PINSON, KOPPEL S. (1904–1961). Professor of Modern European History and specialist on the history of nationalism. Born in Lithuania on February 11, 1904, Pinson came to the United States and took his B.A. at the University of Pennsylvania and the Ph.D at Columbia University in 1934. He first began his studies on nationalism at Columbia University, where he was a student in Professor Carlton J. H. Hayes' seminar on nationalism. His early interest was in the influence of religious currents in the seventeenth and eighteenth centuries upon the rise of German nationalism in the nineteenth century.

Where it was often alleged that the French Revolution marked the birth of German nationalism, Pinson believed that German national consciousness showed perceptible signs of growth long before 1789.

In his dissertation, *Pietism as a Factor in the Rise of German Nationalism* (1934), he showed how German Pietism began. (*See* **PIETISM.**) Philipp Jakob Spener and August Hermann Francke at the close of the seventeenth century had initiated a trend of psychological reactions and intellectual processes that eventually influenced German life. These processes formed the necessary ingredients of the sentiment and theory of nationalism. Then came the emphasis upon enthusiasm and irrationality, a sense of individuality, and an interest in popular education.

In 1935 Pinson compiled the first American bibliography on nationalism, *A Bibliographical Introduction to Nationalism*, which listed the most important books and articles on nationalism with critical evaluations.

For five years, from 1929 to 1935, Pinson served as a member of the editorial staff of the *Encyclopedia of the Social Sciences*. He was delegated the chief responsibility for all materials relating to German history, politics, and culture. He began his career of teaching at Queens College, New York, in 1937, and went through the ranks there. The promising career of a distinguished young scholar was cut short in 1961 when he was struck by a New York City bus and died of his injuries.

Bibliography: Koppel S. Pinson, *Pietism as a Factor in the Rise of German Nationalism* (New York, 1934); Koppel S. Pinson, *A Bibliographical Introduction to Nationalism* (New York, 1935).

PLEHVE, VYACHESLAV KONSTANTINOVICH (1846–1904). Reactionary Russian statesman and integral nationalist. Plehve served as Director of the Police from 1881–1884, Vice Minister of the Interior from 1884–1899, and as Minister of the Interior from 1902–1904. In all these posts he consistently followed an ultrareactionary policy and emerged as a champion of Russian nationalism (q.v.). A supporter of autocracy, bureaucracy, and class privileges, he worked incessantly to suppress revolutionary and liberal movements. He used his posts to restrain any of the many Russian nationalities that called for emancipation.

Plehve was believed to be the organizer of attacks on the Jews. He encouraged the propaganda that led to the violent pogrom at Kishinev in April 1903. As a nationalist, he was accused of helping to precipitate the Russo-Japanese War (1904–1905) as a means of forestalling revolution. He believed that this conflict could be used to stimulate Russian patriotism. In his view, a victorious foreign war would result in an intensification of Russian nationalism and at the same time turn the attention of the people from their many problems. He was assassinated in 1904 by a member of the Socialist Revolutionary Party. (*See also* **RUSSIAN NATIONALISM.**)

P.L.O.   *See* **PALESTINE LIBERATION ORGANIZATION.**

P.N.V. PARTIDO NACIONALISTA VASCA (BASQUE NATIONALIST PARTY).   Basque political party that demanded more autonomy for the Basque homeland in Spain. (*See* **BASQUE NATIONALISM.**)

POBEDONOSTSEV, KONSTANTIN PETROVICH (1827–1907). Russian jurist, statesman, and nationalist. In 1868 Pobedonostsev became a senator and in 1872 a member of the State Council. Meanwhile, he served as tutor and adviser to Emperors Alexander III and his son who became Nicholas II. In 1860 came an appointment to the high post of Director General of the Most Holy Synod of the Russian Orthodox Church.

A champion of autocracy, orthodoxy, and Russian nationalism, Pobedonostsev opposed any limitation of autocratic power, tightened censorship, and pursued a policy of Russification of all national minorities. The exclusiveness of the Russian Orthodox Church became one of his main goals. He inspired the reactionary policies of Alexander III and served as one of the most influential advisers of Nicholas II until the Revolution of 1905. Opposing social mobility, he restricted higher education to the upper classes. Pan-Slavism attracted his favorable attention. Pobedonostsev was an outstanding example in late nineteenth-century Russia of a conservative, autocratic, integral nationalist. (*See also* **RUSSIAN NATIONALISM.**)

Bibliography: Konstantin Petrovich Pobedonostsev, *Reflections of a Russian Statesman,* trans. from the Russian by Robert Crozier Long (Ann Arbor, Mich., 1965); Robert Francis Byrnes, *Pobedonostsev. His Life and Thought* (Bloomington, Ind., 1968).

P.Q. (PARTI QUÉBECOIS).   Separatist party in Quebec that hoped for independence from Anglophone Canada. (*See* **QUEBEC NATIONALISM.**)

PRECAUTION NATIONALISM.   *See* **NATIONALISM, CLASSIFICATIONS OF.**

PRESTIGE NATIONALISM.   *See* **NATIONALISM, CLASSIFICATIONS OF.**

PROTONATIONALISMS.   Movements in the sixteenth and seventeenth centuries that anticipated the later nationalism developing in the late eighteenth century. This early form had some or many characteristics of the later Age of Nationalism, but they were as yet merely indications of what later became the modern Age of Nationalism. Studies of protonationalism were made at the Cologne seminar of Professor Theodor Schieder. (q.v.). (*See also* **COLOGNE SCHOOL.**)

PSYCHOLOGY OF NATIONALISM.   Scholar of nationalism Hans Kohn pointed out again and again that because it is a sentiment, nationalism has powerful psychological overtones and that psychological investigation is necessary to explain the inconsistencies, paradoxes, and mysteries of nationalism. In definitions of the nation, nationality, and nationalism, the research of psychologists becomes of great importance. Though some psychologists have made it a point to study the implications of nationalism, it is to be hoped that current psychologists will devote more and more of their time to research on the nature of this historical phenomenon.

Social psychology, the scientific study of the individual as related to other individuals, is that branch of psychology most concerned in the quest for the meaning of nationalism. However, where sociologists are interested mainly in the group, social psychologists look at the individual in the group situation. The distinction is hard to maintain. Social psychologists are becoming increasingly aware of the importance of the group in determining the characteristics of the individual. In the continuous process, the individual joins the crowd, and the crowd becomes a nation.

Psychologists recognize the riddle of the definition of nationhood. On occasion, they use the terms nation and state interchangeably, although they are aware of the difference between the two words. They see the nation as a cultural configuration and the state as a political organization. They make this definition: a nation is a large body of persons sufficiently united by sympathy and interest to cooperate in the ways required by a common government, and who are actually organized as an independent state.

Psychologists distinguish between race as a biological concept based upon inheritable physical traits and nation as a political idea grounded on geographical boundaries. They recognize that people within a given geographical region are fashioned into a nation primarily by virtue of a common environment and quite apart from the considerable effects of a genetic intermixture. They see race as doubtfully distinct, but a nation as a cultural, linguistic, political, and geographical grouping. Historians generally agree with this view.

However, where historians speak of the traditions of the past, and where sociologists stress the activities of the group, psychologists direct most of their attention to the consciousness and emotions of the individual. They see "consciousness of kind" as the cement that binds the nation. In this view, the nation is based on the consciousness of bonds with the people to whom the subject is related. The feelings that are experienced toward one's family and closest friends are extended to others. Psychologists emphasize human emotions and the concept of the nation as an ideal center for emotions. The nation becomes a group of individuals who feel themselves as combined in a unity and who have emotions experienced in common. The nation becomes a group of people who *think* they belong together.

Psychologists today are turning their research more and more to the study of the rationale of group forms, functions, changes, and interrelationships. Social psychologists see the nation as the extension of the group. They regard earlier concepts as classificatory and hence Aristotelian, or class-theoretical. They see themselves as being forced to adapt a field-theoretical rather than a class-theoretical attack on the problems of national psychology.

Psychologists also have their own version of nationality, a term used to describe a group of persons speaking the same language and observing the same customs. They leave the concrete, or objective, sense of nationality to historians, political scientists, and sociologists, and concern themselves primarily with the abstract, or subjective, sense. For them, nationality is subjective, psychological, a condition of mind, a spiritual possession, a way of thinking, feeling, and living. In their view, nationality remains a psychological question, a form of consciousness that binds men together despite varieties of economic interests, political allegiances, and religious beliefs.

In defining nationality, psychologists favor the use of such terms as instinct, consciousness, mental state, and spirit. The emphasis is always on emotional factors. They see nationality as the personification of the unity of a nation, the mental state, or the community in behavior. To find out what nationality an individual belongs to, the simplest way is to ask him. If he speaks the truth, this is conceived by psychologists as a better criterion than history, descent, or physical measurement. Other psychologists attribute nationality to the consciousness of the members of a group and the gathering of a large number of emotional dispositions. Nationality, they say, is a configuration of citizens each of whom regards himself as belonging to the whole. Always it is the exaltation of self-consciousness through identification with the nation. Thus, it is the emotional sentiment that makes of nationality a psychological entity.

A similar approach may be noted in the attitude of psychologists to nationalism itself. They use varying approaches, but, in general, they see nationalism as motivated by a sense of belonging. (*See* **SHAFER'S SENSE OF BELONGING.**) Most psychologists regard nationalism as a form of the psychologically recognized phenomenon of individuals identifying themselves with symbols that stand for the mass. It is the response to the need for security that exists in a hostile and dangerous world. Even as the individual holds to his family relationship to obtain security in the small group, so does he identify himself with its extensity, the nation, against real or imagined dangers from other peoples.

In their definitions of nationalism, early psychologists used such terms as consciousness, feelings, state of mind, and psychic characteristics. The British social psychologist Morris Ginsberg defined nationalism as "the totality of certain fundamental psychical characteristics peculiar to and widespread in a certain people, influencing their behavior and manifested with greater or less continuity in a succession of generations." F. H. Allport defined nationalism as "the consciousness which the individual has of his nation as a whole, consisting of imagery of a vast number of people, of awareness of traditions which he supports in common with all the rest, and of present interest and ideals toward which all are disposed in the same manner as he." Bernard C. Ewer presented this meaning: "Nationalism is a state of mind, which in the individual tends to exalt the importance of the state, its opposition to other states, and its superiority to the individual." W. Ehrenstein gave the view that "nationalism is based upon the consciousness of bonds with the people to whom the subject is related; the feelings which are experienced toward one's own family and closest friends are extended to others." These early definitions of nationalism are remarkably similar to those presented by historians, political scientists, and sociologists.

Psychologists generally agree that the relationship between the individual and the collective mentality is an important factor in understanding nationalism. They see the mass mind as an integration of individual minds functioning as a unit. It may be synthetic, but it, nevertheless, exists. The motive of identification arises because the individual's thought processes are not checked at all points by the realities of the physical world; therefore, he tends to transform the boundaries of his self by his imagination. In his mind he becomes a part of the greater world, in a process known as "expansion of the ego." In identifying himself with the nation-group, the individual is better able to satisfy his material needs, feel one with the familiar group, build up a psychic reserve income, and project his hatreds upon the outsider, the foreigner.

Contemporary psychologists see it as their present task to find and measure the new master symbols that attract the emotional attachment of people in society. They are interested in describing and measuring personality norms. They assume that there is a fairly close cooperation between the common denominator of the values and attitudes of a nation's population and a personality norm. The existence of this correlation between small, culturally homogeneous, primitive societies seems to have been well established by anthropologists. Some psychologists believe that the same measurements can be applied to the study of culturally homogeneous societies within modern nations. However, their work has scarcely begun. They hope that some day, with a greater knowledge about common value-attitudes, they may be able to throw more light on various aspects of nationalism.

Bibliography: Otto Klineberg, *Social Psychology* (New York, 1940); Daniel Katz, "The Psychology of Nationalism," in J. P. Guilford (ed.), *Fields of Psychology* (New York, 1940); G. M. Gilbert, *The Psychology of Dictatorship* (New York, 1950); Ralph Linton, "The Concept of National Character," in Alfred H. Stanton and Stewart E. Perry (eds.). *Personality and Political Crisis* (Glencoe, Ill., 1951); Louis L. Snyder, *The Meaning of Nationalism* (New Brunswick, N.J., 1954); Leonard W. Doob, *Patriotism and Nationalism; Their Psychological Foundations* (New Haven, Conn. 1964); H. D. Forbes, "Two Approaches to the Psychology of Nationalism," *Canadian Review of Studies in Nationalism*, 2, No. 1 (Autumn, 1974), 172–181.

PUERTO RICAN NATIONALISM.   The demand of a small group of zealous Puerto Rican nationalists for independence from the United States. With its 3.4 million population, Puerto Rico currently (since 1952) holds the status of a free commonwealth associated with the United States. Puerto Rican nationalists have instituted a campaign to win emancipation from the United States.

Puerto Rico, or Borinquén, after the original Indian name Boriquen, was discovered by Columbus in 1493. In 1508 Juan Ponce de León conquered the island for Spain, and set up the first settlement at Caparra, across the bay from San Juan. Ruled by Spain in 1898,

Puerto Rico was occupied by the United States in the Spanish-American War and ceded to the United States by the Treaty of Paris, December 10, 1898. Spanish is the official language, but most Puerto Ricans speak English, which is compulsory in the schools. In 1900 Congress created an administration with an elected House of Representatives. In 1917 the United States granted U.S. citizenship to Puerto Ricans.

Puerto Rican nationalists were not satisfied with this situation. They regarded the new status as threatening the Spanish roots of their culture. Proud of their pre-Columbian and Spanish backgrounds, they denounced the "interference" of United States culture and values. This attitude persisted despite the fact that in the 1940s Washington no longer used denationalization tactics that had previously aroused some resistance in the island. From this point on, the United States did much to improve education, health, communications, and sanitary services. These efforts served to attract the support of both the Puerto Rican middle class and the workers. However, there were economic difficulties. Added to the ills of overpopulation were absentee ownership and a one-crop sugar economy. During the Depression of the early 1930s, when the sugar market dropped precipitously, Puerto Rican farmers became desperate. There were improvements during the administration of President Franklin D. Roosevelt's New Deal and the governorship of Rexford D. Tugwell (1941–1945). Luis Munoz Marin, the first popularly elected President in 1948, began a program of agricultural reform and industrial expansion, while at the same time maintaining cordial relations with Washington. In 1950 Puerto Rico was given the right to draft its own constitution.

These improvements did not satisfy the angry group of unreconciled nationalists. They continued to denounce the Anglo-Saxon accultural process, the political ties to Washington, and economic control by "foreigners." Beginning with nuisance raids to call attention to their existence, they soon turned to violence. On November 1, 1950, while President Harry Truman was across the street at the Blair House during the remodeling of the White House, several Puerto Rican nationalists opened fire, killing a guard and injuring a plain-clothesman. On March 1, 1954, there was a serious shooting attack in the U.S. House of Representatives. A woman walked down the aisle of the visitors' gallery, pointed an automatic pistol at Speaker Joe Martin, and shouted "Puerto Rico is not free!" Then two other nationalists sprayed the House floor with bullets. Five Congressmen were wounded. The three nationalists were quickly seized.

Puerto Rican sentiment was in three directions—assimilation, statehood, or independence. Assimilationists, headed by Marin and his Popular Democratic Party, held it to be essential that Puerto Rico cast its lot with the United States. Statehood was supported by conservative republicans. Independence remained the goal of the nationalists.

Some sixty-two percent of the island's electorate supported the commonwealth status that went into effect in 1952. About eleven percent favored statehood, while nineteen percent wanted independence. This decision was a democratic victory for the idea of commonwealth, but nationalists insisted that independence was the only solution. Among the dissidents were the *Fuerzas Amadas de Liberación Nacional* (Armed Forces of National Liberation), known as F.A.L.N., and the *Ejercito Popular Boricuda* (Borinquén Popular Army), called *Macheteros*, or machete wielders.

Puerto Rican authorities denounced terrorist attacks as the work of "fanatics or madmen." In recent Puerto Rican elections, the independence movement has drawn only six percent of the vote, although the desire for freedom seemed to be stronger than the returns indicated. The sentiment for statehood has soared to about fifty-five percent.

Despite the fact that statehood had been popular among the Puerto Ricans, the F.A.L.N. continued its drive for independence. From 1974 to 1984, the United States Government regarded the Puerto Rican separatist group as a terrorist organization responsible for forty unsolved bombings in New York City in the decade, as well as scores of other bombings around the country. F.A.L.N. dissidents held in civil contempt charged that subpoenas and court proceedings were an extension of American "colonialism" and constituted an unlawful denial by the U.S. Government "of the Puerto Rican people's human right to self-determination."

The militants see themselves as not just guerilla fighters but as heroic liberators who refuse to compromise with "Yankee tyranny." They believe that one day their fellow countrymen will regard them as saintly fighters for freedom, as liberators who had been willing to sacrifice their lives for Puerto Rican independence. For them, Puerto Rican nationalism is an absolutely necessary goal.

Bibliography: Gordon H. Lewis, *Puerto Rico, Freedom and Power in the Caribbean* (New York, 1968); Michael Sam Hornick, *Nationalist Sentiment in Puerto Rico* (Buffalo, N.Y. 1972); Marion D. Fenyo, "Puerto Rican Nationalism: A Moderate Sentiment," *Canadian Review of Studies in Nationalism*, I, No. 1 (Autumn, 1973), 120–125; Juan M. Garcia-

Passalacqua, *Puerto Rico: Equality and Freedom at Issue* (New York, 1984); Richard J. Bloomfield, *Puerto Rico: The Search for a National Policy* (Boulder, Colo., 1985).

PUSHKIN, ALEKSANDR SERGEYEVICH (1799–1837). Generally recognized as Russia's greatest poet, one of the most important figures in world literature, and accepted by the Russian people as their unexcelled national poet. Pushkin found much of the material for his poems and prose writings in Russian history. In his *Bronze Horseman,* he glorified the spirit of Peter the Great. His masterpiece, *Eugen Onegin* (1823–1831), a brilliant novel in verse, contains witty descriptions of Russian life. His works reveal a close study of Russian folklore and songs. His fellow countrymen regarded him as the creator of the Russian literary language, as "the poet of reality." As a poet-prophet, he aimed "to fire the hearts of men with his words."

Critics everywhere regard Pushkin's works as a most important expression of Russian national consciousness. Russian novelist Fyodor Dostoevsky praised Pushkin as "the first to discern and give us the artistic types of Russian beauty directly emerging from the Russian spirit, beauty which resides in the people's truth, in our soil." In the West, Pushkin is accepted as a great international poet ranking with Shakespeare, Racine, and Goethe, nationalist poets of their own countries. Inside his homeland, Pushkin was adopted by Slavophile nationalists as their supreme spokesman, a great artist who expressed the strength and spirit of Russian nationalism. (*See also* **DOSTOEVSKY, FYODOR MIKHAILOVICH,** and **RUSSIAN NATIONALISM.**)

Bibliography: E. J. Simmons, *Pushkin* (New York, 1937); Abraham Yarmolinsky, *Pushkin in English* (New York, 1937); David Magarschack, *Pushkin, A Biography* (London, 1967); A. D. P. Briggs, *Alexander Pushkin: A Critical Study* (London, 1983).

Q

QUEBEC NATIONALISM.   From the beginning of its history, Canada has been composed of two elements that never have become assimilated but have moved into a tradition of rivalry that has lasted to the present day. The confrontation between English-speaking Canadians (Anglophones) and French-speaking Canadians (Francophones) has resulted in ill-feeling between the two. Francophones, living largely in Quebec Province, have asserted their desire for independence. The union of the two peoples has been retained, but the idea of Quebec separatism persists.

The history of Canada has seen a struggle for a century and a half between two peoples, English and French, who on the European scene have long been rivals. The struggle is for control of a rich American territory. The British and French in Canada were eventually combined in a federal union that was weak from the start. The clash was between two differing concepts of what the nation was supposed to be. Anglophones favored a single federal state forming one nation, but with two languages, two cultures. Those Francophones who were dissatisfied with this idea demanded the separation of Quebec from the federation and the creation of two sovereign nations—one English-speaking with its capital at Ottawa, and the other French-speaking with its capital at Quebec City. Eventually, both were combined in a federal union that was unstable from the beginning. The possibility of a fragmented Canada remained.

Quebec is not alone in its discontent. The peoples of provinces in western Canada, notably Alberta, Saskatchewan, and British Columbia, also have a sense of alienation from the federal system. They feel that their economic progress has been too slow and they resent outside control of their rich natural resources. However, these are English-speaking provinces whose people have concerns about the protectionist tariff policies of the federal union. They have no intention of seceding from the national state. They deplore Quebec's Francophone nationalism, though they are inclined to use it as a springboard for their own aims. They see the national union as inviolate. The situation differs in Quebec Province, where many Francophones are unimpressed with the idea of two languages and two cultures inside one nation. They speak of "foreign control" by the Anglophones and they resist any policies of appeasement or accommodation. Their call is a simple one: Canada must be divided into English-speaking and French-speaking nations, two nations instead of one.

Anglo-French rivalry was traditional in Canadian history. From 1760 to 1867 Canada was a part of British North America. London had a problem in Canada—how to deal with the French-Canadians. It was considered important to work out some kind of system that would ease the antagonism felt by a people who believed that they had been robbed of their land. Early efforts at appeasement were not successful. The Quebec Act of 1774 was designed to stabilize British rule by recognizing French rights in language, religion, and civil law. English criminal law and French civil law were to exist side by side.

However, the rivalry continued in the opening years of the nineteenth century and culminated in the rebellions of 1837. Concerned, London sent Lord Durham, who had a reputation as a colonial reformer, on a mission to Canada to win back disaffected French opinion. His *Report* (1839) was highly critical of French-Canadians, but it, nevertheless, became known as the Magna Carta of the British colonial system. It provided responsible government for Canada within the framework of British colonial unity. The British North America Act of July 1, 1867, gave the French language equal status with English in the Parliament at Ottawa, in the Quebec Legislature, and in the federal courts.

The *Québecois* were not satisfied. They complained of discrimination and rejected English efforts at accommodation. They also opposed Canadian foreign policy, which they said was too submissive to Britain. Quebec, they maintained, was not a province but the homeland of a distinctive people, with separate languages, institutions, economic resources, and traditions. They were not a minority, they said, under English rule, but a distinct people of a different nation. It was the kind of mini-nationalism (*see* **MINI-NATIONAL-ISMS**) that could develop into a call for separation.

At the heart of the opposition to English control was the language problem. French-speaking Canadians make up about twenty percent of Canada's 22,998,000 people, but in Quebec the French-speaking majority runs to eighty percent. The people of Quebec thus see themselves as a French island caught in the English embrace. They argue that a common language such as theirs really provides the chief ingredient of a nation-state. A Quebec slogan illustrates the idea: "More and more in Quebec it's in French that things are happening." The French language, it is claimed, is appropriate for self-government. *Québecois* dissidents insist that any national group of substance deserves to govern itself.

For the Anglophones this attitude is a threat to national unity. The English-speaking minority in Quebec, some twenty percent in a population of 6,224,000, rejects the idea of separation and the formation of a Francophone state. The Freedom of Choice movement in Quebec, an Anglophone organization, announced that its linguistic rights had been abrogated by French-speaking fellow-citizens.

In August 1978 the linguistic clash was intensified when the Quebec government restricted the use of English. French was made the only official language in the province when the Quebec Legislative Assembly approved a law known as Bill 101. The French version of laws was officially recognized, although English translations would be provided. Governmental business was to be conducted in French; doctors and lawyers were expected to show "appropriate fluency" in French in order to practice. New residents of Quebec were limited in their right to send their children to English-speaking schools.

Anglophones reacted angrily. The Positive Action Committee announced that Bill 101 "conveyed a message to all non-French speakers in the province that is clear and unequivocal. The present government in Quebec does not respect their rights to continue as healthy, viable and creative minorities." The Quebec administration urged Anglophones "to uphold the British tradition of respect for the law." Some businesses, under the new law, had to operate in French and moved from Canada. The Quebec authorities replied that they would not settle "for a few words of French." All Quebec business enterprises were to be conducted in French. Police were ordered to arrest any strikers whose picket signs were in English. The explosive language issue soon developed into a political confrontation.

The difficulties extended to cultural activities. Cultural differences were really an extension of the language issue. There was little cultural fertilization, no fusing or melting of diverse strains. Francophones believed it to be important to maintain their own special attributes. As early as the middle of the nineteenth century there was French-Canadian literary activity at a time when Quebec nationalism was being strengthened. English-Canadian culture was largely derivative and imported from Britain. Canadian writers looked to London for inspiration; they glorified the Canadian landscape and life on farms, in towns and fishing villages, but the impulse came from across the Atlantic. Efforts were made to bridge the two cultures, but there were sparse results. The conflict extended to education from primary schools to universities. At the lower levels, parents resented the efforts to impose "foreignism" on their offspring. The hoped-for diversity in unity seemed to be an unattainable ideal.

Economic grievances also helped polarize federal and provincial relations. Many Quebecers felt that they were allowed only a secondary role in Canadian economic life. A slowing down of the Canadian economy in 1957 was followed by a severe economic recession, partly due to world conditions and partly because of the overexploitation of rich but nonrenewable resources. French-Canadian resentment increased to a point where Quebecers began to see themselves as second-rate citizens in the Canadian economy. They maintained that they had passed beyond the status of "hewers of wood and drawers of water." They began to insist on a greater share of economic security in what was supposed to be a potentially rich society. Federalists saw the economic decline as a nation-wide phenomenon running through all sectors of the national economy. The proposed secession of Quebec, they warned, would be disastrous for both sides.

Politically, most Quebec moderates hoped to see the issue decided by nonviolent means. However, from 1960 to 1970 a small group of hardliners in the *Front Libération de Québec* (F.L.Q.), rejecting reform as unsatisfactory, began a program of bombing and burning. At first, they used small devices, but later turned to powerful detonations. Most Quebecers, alienated by these violent tactics, approved harsh anti-terrorist measures by the central government.

In the late 1960s the issue of federalism or separation came to a head in the political clash between Prime Minister Pierre Trudeau and Quebec's Premier René Lévesque (qq.v.). Erudite and bilingual, Trudeau tried to persuade his fellow French-Canadians that their best hope for survival lay in the federal system. He had two goals: "One was to make sure that Quebec would not leave Canada through separation, and the other was to make sure that Canada would not shove Quebec out through narrowness." Quebecers, he said, must be masters of their own house, but it was essential that the house must be the whole of Canada. Lévesque, described as "a chain-smoking, disorganized, hot-tempered bundle of emotional energy," advanced rapidly in Canadian politics. A fervent Quebec nationalist ("I am first a *Québecois* and second, with a rather growing doubt, a Canadian"), he urged the people of Quebec to throw off the English yoke. In 1967 he formed the *Mouvement Souveraineté Association*, the forerunner of his *Parti Québecois* (P.Q.). In 1976 he became Premier of Quebec.

Meanwhile, in July 1967, came a sensational incident that gave global publicity to the Canadian problem of centralism versus separation. French President Charles de Gaulle (q.v.), on an official visit to Montreal, made a speech from the balcony of City Hall in which he shouted the phrase *"Vive le Québec Libre!—"*Long Live Free Quebec!" De Gaulle's words were unexpected—and wholly astonishing. It is possible that the French President meant this as an exaggerated but friendly salute to the second largest French-speaking community in the industrialized world. English-Canadians were not amused. Anglophone authorities informed de Gaulle that his statement was unacceptable and intimated that he was no longer welcome in Canada. Quebec's nationalists were delighted.

The Canadian debate grew sharper. The issue finally came to a head when it was given to the voters of Quebec for a referendum. The question was clear-cut:

> The Government of Quebec has made public its proposal to negotiate a new agreement with the rest of Canada, based on the equality of nations.
>
> This agreement would enable Quebec to acquire the exclusive power to make its laws, levy its taxes and establish relations abroad—in other words, sovereignty—and, at the same time, to maintain with Canada an economic association, including a common currency.
>
> No change in political status resulting from these negotiations will be effected without approval by the people through another referendum.
>
> On these terms do you give the Government of Quebec the mandate to negotiate the proposed agreement between Quebec and the rest of Canada?

The result of the referendum, held on May 20, 1980, was surprising. In one of the heaviest turnouts in Quebec's electoral history, voters rejected the call for sovereignty. The "No" vote was 2, 140, 814, or 59.4 percent; the "Yes" vote was 1, 475,509, or 40.6 percent.

Some 54 percent of Quebec's French-speaking citizens joined with 80 percent of the Anglophone minority to produce a decisive victory.

Quebec thus joined Scotland and Wales in opting for federation instead of separation. But this referendum has not really solved the issue. Canada remains a tormented country with national unity at stake on the continuing power struggle. An all-out Canadian consensus remains difficult in the face of emotional differences. Not even the democratic referendum has been able to solve the crisis. For the moment the conflict remains muted, but resentment remains strong among those who cling to the idea of Quebec separatism.

Bibliography: David Cameron, *Self-Determination and the Quebec Question* (Toronto, 1974); Richard M. Chadbourne, "Three Expressions of Nationalism in Modern Quebec Literature," *Canadian Review of Studies in Nationalism,* 4, No. 1 (Autumn, 1976), 38–51; Elliot J. Feldman and Neil Nevitte (eds.), *The Future of North America: Canada, the U.S. and Quebec Nationalism* (Cambridge, Mass. 1979); Jane Jacobs, *The Question of Separatism: Quebec and the Struggle Over Sovereignty* (New York, 1980); Dominique Clift, *Quebec Nationalism in Crisis* (Kingston, Ont., 1982); Susan Mann Trifimentikoff, *The Dream of Nation: A Social and Intellectual History of Quebec* (Toronto, 1982); William D. Coleman, *The Independence Movement in Quebec* (Toronto, 1984); Ramsay Cook, *Canada, Quebec, and the Uses of Nationalism* (Toronto, 1986).

R

REGIONALISM.   The term regionalism may be used in two senses. First, it may refer to a combination of several national states acting as a unit. From this point of view it is regarded as an alternate political system to nationalism. Second, it may refer to the division of a country into small administrative units. In this sense, it is used as equivalent to a mini-nationalism. (*See* **MINI-NATIONALISMS.**)

The late political scientist Hans J. Morgenthau (q.v.) saw the traditional state as obsolescent in view of the technological and military conditions of the contemporary world. He believed that its replacement by larger regional units would be better attuned to these new conditions and might well call forth a more effective vehicle for nationalistic competition.

Morgenthau held that since the end of World War I there has emerged a multitude of new states fashioned from the fragments of the old colonial empires. The number of new states has more than doubled. Many of these states, deficient in the essentials of nationhood, have not turned out to be viable political, economic, or military entities. They have not been able to feed, administer, or defend themselves. The disorder and threats to peace of the dissolved Turkish and Austro-Hungarian Empires have spread, in the name of nationalism, to wide areas of Africa and Asia. These new nations, many of them artificial and lacking the ethnic and historical foundations of nationhood, seem to be unable to create and maintain a workable state domestically or with their powerful neighbors.

For this dilemma, Morgenthau saw only three possible solutions:

Balkanization and anarchy, a new colonialism, or regionalism. The current fragmentation and impotence may well lead to a situation in which these new nations will have to be supported from the outside or else sink back into the anarchy of the pre-colonial days. Perhaps the present lack of viability of most of the new nations may lead to the formation of larger, more viable units. They may become pawns in the power struggle of the stronger nations.

Morgenthau further saw regionalism as likely to be a variant of the order of empire rather than the voluntary fusion of a number of autonomous political units on the basis of equality. There must be a military unit that is able to prevent recalcitrant members from destroying the unit. In the past, most regional unions have resulted from conquest both within and without, as in the cases of Austria-Hungary, Italy, and Germany.

At the same time, Morgenthau admitted that nationalism would not necessarily be mitigated by a successful regionalism. "The nations of Western Europe, for instance, are too weak to make themselves singly the effective spearhead of nationalism. The time has passed when the French or Germans could dream of making the world over in their own image. But if the nations of Western Europe were able to form a new political and military unit of very considerable potentialities, they would then have acquired the power base for a new nationalism, common to all of Western Europe, and to compete effectively with the nationalism of the two superpowers."

On another level, regionalism has achieved, indeed, a modicum of success in the military and economic spheres. The Western Powers, always interested in their own security, have worked assiduously to win military and economic unity on a regional basis. The Soviet Union, faced with what it regards as a dangerous regional threat, responded with its own regionalism consisting of unity with its satellites.

Western military regionalism originated in 1949 with the formation of the North Atlantic Treaty Organization (N.A.T.O.), with the aim of preventing any further Russian expansion into Western Europe. It was regarded as a countermove to Soviet Russian westward expansion. Taking advantage of the political vacuum in Eastern Europe at the close of World War II, the Kremlin penetrated as far westward as it could. This led to the union of the armed forces of fifteen foreign nations, all alarmed by what they felt to be Russian expansionism. N.A.T.O. provided a joint command, a common procurement system, and a unified air defense. In late 1968 Moscow was told bluntly that any intervention affecting the situation in Europe, such as interference in Rumania or Yugoslavia following the invasion of Czechoslovakia, would result in a grave crisis. In other words, in terms of diplomacy, this meant: "This far, no farther!"

There are opposing views on the value and effectiveness of N.A.T.O. Its sponsors insist that its very existence, no matter what its strength, acts as a brake on Soviet intentions of penetrating any available vacuum. Its critics describe its weakness and predict that N.A.T.O. could do very little, if anything, to prevent a Soviet sweep through Western Europe to the Atlantic. N.A.T.O., indeed, is not without internal difficulties. Charles de Gaulle (q.v.) regarded it as simply meaning American domination.

The Kremlin's response to N.A.T.O. was the Warsaw Pact (Eastern European Mutual Assistance Treaty) between the Soviet Union and six of her satellites. In 1956 Moscow crushed Hungary's attempt to leave the Soviet military regionalism. In 1968 the Kremlin led troops of all the pact members (excepting Rumania) into Prague to crush liberal dissenters in Czechoslovakia. For the Soviet Union any disposition to freedom in the satellites was bourgeois counterrevolution.

Similar attempts at regional union were made in Western Europe by the formation of the Common Market. It was comparatively easy to fashion economic integration, but there has been little success in extending it into a political combination. The so-called United States of Europe, with its common parliament, has been little more than a paper organization. The reason is clear—military or economic union means no real loss of national sovereignty. European statesmen are quite willing to work together for military or economic union, but they stop short at the boundary of political unification. National sovereignty, yes! International *political* unification, no!

In its second sense, regionalism may be used to indicate those ethnic units in a larger national state, who because of their special history and traditions want either more autonomy or even independence. The tendency here is to emphasize and value the qualities of life in a particular region and to insist that the region has been taken over by foreigners. The term mini-nationalisms has been applied to these dissatisfied peoples who believe that they deserve the blessings of self-determination (q.v.) and who want a nationalism of their own. They are not satisfied with their status as a national minority. The more obstreperous among them turn to violence as a means of telling the world that they, too, deserve to be relieved of subservience to another nationalism.

Bibliography: Hans J. Morgenthau, *Truth and Power* (New York, 1970); W. Sue Kendall, *Rethinking Regionalism* (Washington, D.C.,

1986); Roger Morgan (ed.), *Regionalism in European Politics* (London, 1986); Mark D. Rousseau, *Regionalism and Regional Devolution in Comparative Perspective* (New York, 1987).

RENAN, ERNEST (1823–1892).   French scholar, critic, and philosopher of religion, whose *Vie de Jesus* (1863) was denounced by the Church because he attributed the development of Christianity to popular imagination. In 1882 Renan presented a definition that has been widely quoted to the present day. According to Renan, it is not race, religion, language, state, civilization, or economic interests that make the nation. Instead, the nation, the *sine qua non* for nationalism, is the result of common experience, especially a heroic past, great leaders, and true glory. All of these lead to a community of will. Common grief, even more than triumphs in war, serves to bind a people together. A nation, in the final analysis, is a great solidarity based on the consciousness of sacrifices made in the past and the willingness to make further ones in the future. The very existence of a nation is a sort of plebiscite repeated daily. (*See also* **NATION.**)

Brief excerpts from Renan's famous reply to the question "What is a Nation?" indicate the tone of his response:

> A NATION is a soul, a spiritual principle. Only two things, actually, constitute this soul, this spiritual principle. One is in the past, the other is in the present. One is the possession in common of a rich legacy of remembrances; the other is the actual consent, the desire to live together, the will to continue to value the heritage which all hold in common. Man, sirs, does not improvise. The nation, even as the individual, is the end product of a long period of work, sacrifice and devotion. . . .
>
> I continue, sirs. Man is not enslaved, nor is his race nor his language, nor his religion, nor the course of the rivers, nor the direction of the mountain ranges. A great aggregation of men, with a healthy spirit and warmth of heart, creates a moral conscience which is called a nation. When this moral conscience proves its strength by sacrifices that demand abdication of the individual for the benefit of the community, it is legitimate, and it has a right to exist.

Bibliography: Ernest Renan, *Qu'est-ce qu'une nation?* (Paris, 1882). Translated by Ida Mae Brown Snyder.

RHODES, CECIL JOHN (1853–1902).   British business magnate, statesman, and integral nationalist. Coming to South Africa in 1870, Rhodes and his brother Herbert staked a claim in the Kimberly diamond mines. Cecil accumulated a vast fortune. In 1880 he combined several small companies in the Beers Mining Company. His principal objective was to create a federated South Africa under the

British flag. He decided to enhance his power by entering politics. Elected to the Parliament of Cape Colony, he held a seat there for the remainder of his life. By 1890 he was the Prime Minister and virtual dictator of Cape Colony.

As a zealous nationalist, Rhodes made every effort toward the extension of British rule and influence. He was largely responsible for the annexation of Bechuanaland in 1884. As head of the South African Company and as Prime Minister of the Cape, he was the most influential man on the African continent. He held office until the famous Jameson Raid, which he personally opposed, led to his retirement. Later, he devoted himself to the development of the country that was named Rhodesia in his honor. He died in South Africa, leaving nearly all of his great fortune to public service. He initiated the Rhodes scholarships at Oxford for the United States, Germany, and the British colonies. Imperialist as well as nationalist, his goal was to carve up Africa for British gain. He was certain that British rule was best for Africans.

Bibliography: J. G. Lockhart and C. M. Woodhouse. *Rhodes, The Colossus of Southern Africa* (London, 1963); John E. Flint, *Cecil Rhodes* (Boston, 1974); Brian Roberts, *Cecil Rhodes, Flawed Colossus* (London, 1987).

ROMANTICISM.   A movement in the late eighteenth and early nineteenth centuries that had an important effect on the rise of nationalism. Romanticism was a reaction against "the self-evident dictates of pure reason," against the Enlightenment, or the Age of Reason. In the late eighteenth century the terms "imaginative," "extraordinary," and "visionary," were becoming more and more prominent. The French *philosophe* Jean-Jacques Rousseau (q.v.) created the concept of "the noble savage," praised primitivism and sentimentality, and held that happiness and salvation could be captured only by a return to natural freedom and innocence. This view also penetrated into the Germanies, where a youthful cult called *Sturm und Drang* ("Storm and Stress") represented a combination of tendencies: intuition and mysticism, return to nature as advocated by Rousseau, and love for the vague and mysterious. At the same time, it denounced "sterile rationalism" (*Vernünftelei*) and excoriated "the pygmy French." Added to its early elements was disgust with the excesses of the French Revolution.

All these tendencies converged in the early nineteenth century in the Romantic movement, composed of a multitude of attitudes. It was never an organized sect, but revealed itself in a number of disguises, from mystic symbolism to openhearted humanitarianism. Romanticism emphasized the emotional rather than the rational side of human nature. It exalted faith and intuition instead of the intellect. The Romantics regarded their organic-genetic nature of culture as dominant. They issued a plea for the claims of the imagination, of emotion and feelings, of individualism. The new movement invaded virtually all fields of expression—culture, religion, literature, art, music, and even politics. Traditional and sentimental thinkers presented a philosophical defense of their new ideas. Romanticism in philosophy turned into a type of metaphysics known as transcendental idealism, which emphasized the emotions—ideals, spirit, and faith—with the same confidence the earlier rationalists had bestowed upon the intellectual faculties.

Politically, Romantic interest in the past soon linked up with the rising national spirit. Romantics went to history to seek evidence of "the national genius" and "the national soul." Scholars devoted their attention to the study of national laws, institutions, and languages as a means of proving that their own national culture had its roots in the past. Nationalists were intrigued by many aspects of Romanticism—its enthusiasm for history, its accent upon the familiar and the marvelous, its stress upon the dignity of the common man, and its interest in bourgeois social aspirations. All of these became tenets of the rising nationalism.

The ideals of Romanticism, especially the stress upon the consciousness of national genius, inevitably led to claims of superiority typical of the new nationalism. In the Germanies the War of Liberation against Napoleon, which stimulated the emergence of German nationalism, turned German literature from the path of classicism to Romantic exaltation of the imagination and medieval mysticism. German Romantics described the Germans as valiant, truthful, pure, and courageous, a kind of fantastic idealization of views presented long ago by Tacitus. The Germanism of Johann Gottlieb Fichte (q.v.) and the "divine mission" proposed by Johann Gottfried Herder (q.v.) served to popularize German nationalism. Poets of the War of Liberation, including Ferdinand Max Gottfried von Schenkendorf, Theodor Körner, and Ernst Moritz Arndt (qq.v.), composed passionate verses and prose about the national spirit and soul as well as odes to the German sword. This kind of Romanticism eventually led to the integral nationalism of Richard Wagner (q.v.) and the frenzied nationalism of Adolf Hitler (q.v.).

The Germanies and later Germany were not the only nations to be imbued with the union of Romanticism and nationalism. The movement, especially in the literary field, surged through the European Continent, especially in England and France. Poets and novelists sought beauty in nature, in the mountains, lakes, and forests, instead of in artificial domes and columns. Everywhere Romanticism infected the new nationalism with its mysticism, irrationalism and its accompanying political abuses, social disorder, and economic frustrations.

Bibliography: Hans Kohn, "Romanticism and the Rise of German Nationalism," *The Review of Politics,* 12 (1950), 443–472: Hans Kohn, *Prologue to Nation-States: France and Germany* (Princeton, N.J., 1967); Lillian Furst, *The Contours of European Romanticism* (London, 1979); Hugh Honour, *Romanticism* (New York, 1979); Carl Schmitt, *Political Romanticism* (Cambridge, Mass., 1986).

ROOSEVELT, THEODORE (1855–1919).   Twenty-sixth President of the United States and champion of American nationalism (q.v.). A physical weakling during his youth, he developed a rugged physique by persistent exercise. Assistant Secretary of the Navy under President William McKinley, he loudly advocated war with Spain. When war was declared against Spain in 1898, he resigned, organized the 1st Volunteer Cavalry, and took his men to Cuba. Contemptuous of army red tape and even orders, he led his "Rough Riders" up San Juan Hill, and became a national hero when his impulsive campaign was publicized.

Theodore Roosevelt became noted for his earnestness, impetuosity, and picturesque behavior. He emerged as a strongly effective preacher of national pride. Achieving a reputation for winning the confidence of Americans, he added a touch of glamor to all his actions. At the core of his political thinking was the idea that strong nations survived while weak ones perished. He believed that force was the supreme arbiter in human affairs. Quoting an African proverb, he observed: "Speak softly and carry a big stick." He used Big Stick diplomacy in the acquisition of the Panama Canal in 1903. He allowed nothing to stay in the way of this project. When Colombia balked on the cession of the necessary territory across the Isthmus of Panama, he denounced the Colombians as "contemptible little creatures," "jack rabbits," and "homicidal corruptionists." Each year as President, he asked for larger naval appropriations and urged Congress to grant him new ships. He sent the United States fleet around the world to impress one and all that his country had come of age as a leading modern power.

The consciousness of American nationalism had already come into existence in the early nineteenth century. As President, Theodore Roosevelt represented the temper of his time. At the beginning of the twentieth century, the United States was prosperous and nationalist-minded. In a very real way Roosevelt reflected the spirit of nationalism that had become rampant throughout the world.

Roosevelt became an advocate of what he called "The New Nationalism." On August 31, 1910, he delivered an address to a great crowd assembled in Osawatomie, Kansas, to witness the dedication of the John Brown battlefield. In his speech he used the term "New Nationalism" to describe his own political beliefs. A salient excerpt:

> The American people are right in demanding that New Nationalism, without which we cannot hope to deal with our new problems. The New Nationalism puts the national need above sectional or personal advantage. It is impatient of the utter confusion that results from local legislatures attempting to treat national issues as local issues. It is still more impatient of the impotence which springs from over-division of governmental powers, the impotence which makes it possible for local selfishness or for legal cunning, hired by wealthy specialists, to bring national activities to a deadlock. This New Nationalism regards the executive power as the steward of the public welfare. It demands of the judiciary that it shall be interested primarily in human welfare rather than in property, just as it demands that the representative body shall represent all the people rather than any one class or section of the people.

Bibliography: Theodore Roosevelt, *The New Nationalism* (New York, 1910); Howard K. Beale, *Theodore Roosevelt and the Rise of America to World Power* (Baltimore, 1956); G. Wallace Chessman, *Theodore Roosevelt and the Politics of Power* (Boston, 1969).

ROUSSEAU, JEAN-JACQUES (1712–1772).   Swiss-born French *philosophe*, famous figure of the Enlightenment, and progenitor of French nationalism. Rejecting aristocracy as the valued core of the nation, Rousseau believed that the more important element in society was the people themselves. He suggested that every individual should be motivated by an emotionalized, almost religious patriotism. "It is not walls or men," he said, "that make the Fatherland, it is the laws, the morals, the customs, the government, the constitution resulting from all these things. The Fatherland is in the relationships of the state to its members. When these relationships change or come to nothing, the Fatherland vanishes."

Rousseau was careful to point out how a consciousness of national unity and the arousal of an accompanying patriotism should be supported by direct governmental action. In his *Lettre à M. d'Alembert* (1758) he urged that the people be trained by simple public spectacles, pageants, and folk games to know and understand the meaning of nationalism. "The general effect of the theater is to strengthen the national character, to augment the natural inclinations, and to give a new energy to all the passions."

More than a decade later, in 1771, Rousseau expressed the same conclusions when a Polish nobleman sent him a request asking how national patriotism might be promoted. In his *Considérations sur le gouvernement de Pologne*, (published later in 1782), Rousseau wrote that national institutions inspire the people with their ardent love of the Fatherland based upon ineradicable habits. He urged that citizens be educated "from mother's milk to death" in the idea of the nation. It was absolutely necessary, he wrote, that a sense of patriotism be instilled in the public through proper education:

> EDUCATION ought to give national form to the soul of the people, and guide their opinions and tastes in such a way that they will become patriots through inclination, through passion, through necessity. A child, upon opening his eyes, must see the nation, and to the day of his death must see only that. Every real republican should absorb with his mother's milk love of his country, that is, law and liberty. This love should make up his whole existence: he should see nothing else—only his country. As soon as he is alone, he is nothing; as soon as he no longer has a country, he does not exist; and, if he is not dead, he is worse than dead.

Rousseau's advice to his Polish friend was the first systematic theory of a conscious and calculated nationalism. It became a kind of guide book for the new French nationalism, which was to emerge in the stormy days of the French Revolution and which was to become the essence of French nationalism in its development thereafter.

Bibliography: Jean-Jacques Rousseau, *Oeuvres complètes* (Paris, 1832); Ronald Grimsley, *Jean-Jacques Rousseau* (Totowa, N.J. 1983); Jim Miller, *Rousseau: Dreamer of Democracy* (New Haven, Conn., 1984).

RUSSIAN NATIONALISM.   The absolutism of late eighteenth-century Russia recognized few elements of nationalism. German influence was often more important than Russian among the dynasty, court, army, and bureaucracy. Those Russians who were fortunate enough to belong to the higher court circles were proud of their ability to speak French, which in their minds set them far apart from the bourgeoisie and proletariat. For the intelligentsia, the Orthodox Creed was of more significance than the idea of nationality. Masses of Russians knew little about or cared about nationalism. To most Russians the currents of nationalism then sweeping Western Europe were unimportant—a strange goal of an ignorant West.

In the early nineteenth century, this indifferent attitude of Russians toward nationalism began to change perceptibly. A prime cause for this transformation was found in the drive of Napoleonic despotism. Wherever the French dictator sent his troops and their unfurled standards, hatred for French arms led to strengthening of national pride and the desire to humble the little Corsican and his legions. The giant Russian bear was no exception. To pious Russians this was the real anti-Christ, who was attempting to lead the Roman Catholic West against Moscow—citadel of the true faith. It was believed that an ignominious Paris and Rome were seeking to divert Russians from their own cultural superiority and imposing new and dangerous ideas upon them.

Russians at this time had already rejected Western rationalism and the liberal cosmopolitanism which went along with it. If Napoleon wanted to impose Western ideas upon them, they would have none of it. But they understood the meaning of French nationalism and they would oppose it with a nationalism of their own. From the days of the conqueror, an uncompromising love for Mother Russia, for the *natio*, would develop in the great homeland. The Russians inflicted a humiliating defeat on Napoleon at Moscow and sent him home to Paris in disgrace. The Corsican never survived that mistaken drive into the heartland of Russia to bring home tokens of victory. What he had done was to stimulate and confirm the quality of Russian nationalism.

In Russia, even as in the West, nationalism began on a liberal note. Alexander I, grandson of the despotic Tsarina Catherine II (the Great), was a handsome, gregarious monarch who dreamed of raising the level of his backward country. The most important event of his reign was the patriotic war in 1812 against France, in which the Tsar regarded himself as an instrument of the Divine Will in the drama of Napoleon's downfall. He was aware that his vast semi-Oriental state, partly feudal, partly monarchical, lagged far behind the rest of Europe. His empire, indeed, was a huge, sprawling state, half in Europe, half in Asia, and covering one-sixth of the land surface of the globe. He would mold this great land into an enlightened, respected, and powerful state.

After 1815 Alexander I's zeal for liberal nationalism began to cool perceptibly. By 1820 he confessed to Metternich: "I deplore all that I said and did between the years 1815 and 1818. I regret the waste of time. You are right. Tell me what you want to do and I will do it." Modern history has seen few more tragic figures than Alexander I. The brilliant promise of his early years evaporated. He left Russia a legacy of tyranny, a ruined economy, a political system rotten with graft and corruption, and a festering, dangerous drift in its incipient nationalism.

During the next reactionary reign of Nicholas I (r. 1825–1855), Russian nationalism assumed a blind, ugly form. The glory of Russia became a new trinity: dynasty, Orthodox Church, and the village commune. The new nationalism of the huge state reflected the nature and character of its autocratic monarch. Because Alexander I had no children, the succession would normally have passed to his brother Constantine, but the latter, in 1822, had renounced his claims in favor of the younger brother Nicholas. In the general uncertainty, a military revolt was started by the Northern Society, a revolutionary group composed of officers inspired by the *Carbonari* (q.v.), the nationalistic Italian dissenters. The conspirators obtained the support of some 2,000 soldiers, who, on December 26, 1825, rebelled with the cry "Constantine and the Constitution." (The troops were so ignorant of what their government meant that they actually believed "Constitution" was Constantine's wife.) Nicholas I put down the revolt, hanged five of the conspirators, and sent more than a hundred others to Siberia for penal servitude.

From the time of the Decembrist revolt, Nicholas I set the tone of the new nationalism. In his thirty-year reign, he stamped out all opposition in Russia and made himself the most reactionary monarch of the nineteenth century. The "Nicholas System" meant a harsh, unending autocracy and the stamping out of all signs of liberal nationalism. Nicholas I sealed off Russia from what he regarded as the pestilential air of Western Europe. Any citizen who made the slightest dangerous remark soon found himself on the way to Siberia.

Meanwhile, during this reactionary regime, Russian patriots began to preach the glories of integral nationalism. Poets sang about the Orthodox Russian as "the most perfect citizen on earth," and Holy Russia as "the first state in the world." The term "nationalism" began to be used interchangeably with Slavophilism. Russian historians said the past belonged to a West already decadent and senile, while the future belonged to a great, young, and vigorous "race of Slavs." This new sense of nationalism was supported strongly by the rising bourgeoisie, who saw in it a reflection of their aims and desires. At the same time, there began a Russification process used against minorities, especially Ukrainians and Jews, both of whom were persecuted brutally.

During the reign of Nicholas I, a new element in Russian nationalism was introduced—the idea of the Slavic mission. Students at

Moscow University, impressed with German idealism and Hegelian dialectics, sent the same *Weltanschauung* (world view) in another direction. It was now the divine mission of the Slavs to lead the way to the future. The Slavs alone were entitled to lead such a mission, because they were young, with the future before them, while the West was exhausted and deteriorating in decay. This view was expressed by Prince Odoevsky:

> Western Europe possesses a strange, saddening spectacle. Opinion struggles against opinion, power against power, throne against throne. Science, art and religion, the three motors of social life, have lost their force. We venture to make the assertion which to many at present may seem strange, but which will be in a few years only too evident: Western Europe is on the high road to ruin! We Russians, on the contrary, are young and fresh and have taken no part in the crimes of Europe. We have a great mission to fulfill. Our name is already inscribed on the tablets of victory: the victories of science, art and faith await us on the ruins of tottering Europe.

A similar attitude was noted in 1842 by novelist Nikolay Gogol (q.v.) in his *Dead Souls*.

This strong belief in Russia's "mission" continued on to the end of the nineteenth century and the beginning of the twentieth. It was exemplified in the writings of Nikolay Danilevsky (q.v.) on the nature of Russian nationalism.

It was expected that the Marx-Lenin-Stalin trio would change Russian nationalism into internationalism and the rule of the proletariat. All held that nationalism and the bourgeois state were synonymous. Karl Marx: "The government of the national state is nothing more than a committee for the administration of the consolidated affairs of the bourgeois class as a whole." Stalin: "A nation is a historical category belonging to the epoch of rising capitalism."

The Marxist leaders did not take into account the historical fact that workers and peasants, as well as the bourgeoisie, had a stake in nationalism, which they believed gave them the protection they desired. Russian traditions of autocracy and strong leadership were unbroken in the shift from tsarism to bolshevism. The Kremlin suppressed all uprisings of the nationalities while pouring a steady stream of propaganda to the world that freedom and equality were endemic to the Bolshevist regime. Soviet leaders repeated the Marxist formula that the nation's mission had been succeeded by the class mission. Yet, under Stalin, Soviet Russian nationalism turned out to be more integral and more aggressive than elsewhere. The Russian dictator disposed of Leon Trotsky, who favored a drive to internationalism as against Soviet Russian nationalism. When, in June 1941,

Hitler invaded the Soviet Union, Stalin called for defense of Mother Russia in what he named "the Great Patriotic War." The Stalin dictatorship turned from internationalism and replaced it with national bolshevism.

Throughout the Stalin and subsequent dictatorships, the more than 100 distinct nationalities in the polyglot Soviet Union were treated with an iron fist. These restive nationalities, living in fifteen republics, had been opposed to central Moscow since the days of the tsars. Despite the whip from the Kremlin, chronic tensions and grievances among the nationalities revealed that there were cracks in the Soviet façade. In late 1987 and through 1989 nationalist demonstrations took place in the three Baltic areas annexed by Moscow—Latvia, Lithuania, and Estonia. (See **BALTIC NATIONALISMS.**) There were protests in Moscow by Crimean Tatars, who were banished to Central Asia during World War II. (See **TATAR NATIONALISM.**) Ethnic riots and demonstrations took place in the mountainous stretch between the Black Sea and the Caspian, where Christian Armenians were pitted against Muslim Azerbaijanis. (See **ARMENIAN NATIONALISM.**) It had long been an article of faith in the Kremlin that Soviet nationalism has replaced the old attachments of ethnic dissidents. Russian President Mikhail S. Gorbachev, initiator of *glasnost* (openness) and *perestroika* (restructuring), was suddenly faced with one of Russia's oldest flaws—national disunity. (*See* **NATIONALITIES IN THE SOVIET UNION.**)

Bibliography: Hans Kohn, *Pan-Slavism* (Notre Dame, Ind., 1953); Frederick C. Barghoorn, *Soviet Russian Nationalism* (New York, 1956); Roman Smal-Stocki, *The Captive Nations: Nationalism of the Non-Western Nations in the Soviet Union* (New Haven, Conn., 1960); John P. Dunlop, *The Faces of Contemporary Russian Nationalism* (Princeton, N.J., 1983); John P. Dunlop, *The New Russian Nationalism* (New York, 1985); David B. Nissman, *The Soviet Union and Iranian Azerbaijan: The Use of Nationalism for Political Penetration* (Boulder, Colo., 1987).

S

SAN MARTIN, JOSÉ de (1778–1850). Soldier, statesman, hero of independence movements in Argentina, Chile, and Peru, and leading advocate of South American nationalism. Educated in Madrid, San Martin devoted himself to the liberation of Spanish colonies in Latin America. In 1812 he offered his services to the government of Argentina in its struggle for independence. He led an army of 3,000 infantry soldiers and 1,000 cavalrymen across the Andes in January 1817, a feat comparable to Hannibal's crossing of the Alps. He played an important role in Chile's winning of independence. In 1821 he drove the Spaniards out of Chile. Threatened by jealousy among patriots, royal intrigue, and the rivalry of Bolívar, San Martin voluntarily renounced his authority and left the country. Bolívar's armies finished the task in 1824.

Bibliography: Ricardo Rojas, *San Martin, Knight of the Andes,* trans. by Herschel Brickell (New York, 1945).

SCHENKENDORF, FERDINAND MAX GOTTFRIED VON (1784–1817). German patriotic poet of the War of Liberation against Napoleon in 1813. The German public was entranced by Schenkendorf's militant verses, especially by his *The Soldier's Morning Song.* Following are two of its four stanzas:

> Thou God of endless mercy,
> Gaze from thy azure tent;
> For to this field of battle
> By thee have we been sent.

Grant we be found not wanting,
And victory accord,
The Christian flags are waving,
Thine is the war, O Lord!

A morn will dawn upon us,
Bright, balmy, and serene,
The pious all await it,
By angel hosts 'tis seen.
Soon will its rays, unclouded,
On every German beam;
O break, thou day of fulness,
Thou day of freedom, gleam!

Bibliography: The Poetry of Germany, trans. by Alfred Baskerville, (Baden Baden and Hamburg, 1876).

SCHIEDER, THEODOR (1908–1984).   Professor of Medieval and Modern History and scholar on nationalism. Schieder was born in Oettingen, and took his doctorate at the University of Munich in 1933 with a dissertation on the *Kleindeutsche* Party in Bavaria in the struggle for national unity from 1863 to 1871. From 1942 to 1976 he taught, first at the University of Königsberg, and from 1948 to 1976 at the University of Cologne. From 1962 to 1964 he was Rector of the University of Cologne. He edited the *Historsche Zeitschrift* from 1956 on.

From the beginning of his career, Schieder was interested in nationalism, upon which he wrote many books and scholarly articles. Among his publications were *Das Deutsche Kaiserreich von 1871 als Nationalstaat (The German Kaiser Empire from 1871 as a National State)* (1961); *Der Nationalstaat in Europa als historisches Phänomen (The National State in Europe as Historical Phenomenon)* (1964); and *Staatensystem als Vormacht in der Welt (The State System as Leading Power in the World)* (1977, 1982). More important for the study of nationalism, in 1965 he founded the research section of the Historical Seminar of the University of Cologne with special attention to the study of comparative nationalism. From this division there appeared some fourteen volumes on varied aspects of nationalism. Schieder's seminar on nationalism is considered to have been one of the most productive on the European scene. (*See* **COLOGNE SCHOOL.**)

Bibliography: Theodor Schieder, *Einsichten in die Geschichte: Essays (Insights in History: Essays)* (Propyläen, 1979).

SCHLEGEL, FRIEDRICH VON (1772–1829).   Author and critic, originator of many ideas of early German Romanticism, and a precursor of German nationalism. Influenced by Johann Gottlieb Fichte (q.v.), Schlegel placed great emphasis upon mythology and the imagination, characteristics of the Romantic movement. (*See* **RO-MANTICISM.**) "Poetry," he said, "can be fathomed by no theory and only intuitive criticism could presume to characterize its ideal." He was at the center of the German ideological drive against Napoleonic despotism and wrote appeals to the German people to resist the French conqueror.

Together with his older brother, August Wilhelm, Friedrich von Schlegel called for the preservation of German folk sagas. Both urged renewal of the magic power of the word Fatherland, and urged their countrymen to remember the important place of patriotism.

Bibliography: Friedrich von Schlegal, *The Philosophy of History* (London, *1835);* Hans Eichner, *Friedrich von Schlegel* (New York, 1970).

SCHLEIERMACHER, FRIEDRICH (1768–1834). Preacher, classical philologist, founder of modern Protestant theology, and German nationalist. University preacher and Extraordinary Professor of Theology at the University of Halle, he was forced to leave his post after the invasion of Prussia by Napoleon. He moved to Berlin, gave lectures to enthusiastic audiences, and traveled around the country to encourage resistance to the French conqueror. As a strong nationalist, he pleaded for the use of the German language. Like Hegel (q.v.), he idealized the national state as "an organic planetary work of art." In his sermons he declared that "Christianity demands attachment to the nation." He was emphatic: "He who does not feel the unity of the nation is an alien in the house of God."

Schleiermacher helped set the tone of the increasing sense of German nationalism:

> How little worthy of respect is that man who roams about here and there without the anchor of the national ideal and love for the Fatherland. How dull is the friendship that rests only upon personalities, similarities and tendencies, and not upon the feeling of a greater common unity for whose sake one can offer his own life. How the greatest source of pride is lost by that woman who cannot feel that she also bore her children for the Fatherland and brought them up for it, that her house and the petty things that fill up most of her time actually belong to a greater whole and take their place in the unity of her compatriots.

Bibliography: Dietz Lange, *Friedrich Schleiermacher: Theologue, Philosoph, Pedagogue* (Göttingen, 1985); David Jasper (ed.), *The Interpretation of Belief: Coleridge, Schleiermacher, and Romanticism* (Houndsmill, England, 1986).

SCOTTISH NATIONALISM.   Along with Welsh, Shetlander, and
Manx mini-nationalisms, Scottish nationalism was a separatist movement in Great Britain. Here the mini-nationalisms have been more
moderate in tone than elsewhere in Europe. Using a process of
accommodation called devolution, (q.v.), the British Government in
London has been able to appease unsatisfied regionalists and retain
them within the framework of the United Kingdom. Westminster's
concessions to local consciousness has strengthened the cause of
national unity. Movements of separatism, such as the Scottish, still
exist but they remain muted in tone.

Strains of nationalism ran deeply into Scottish history since the
union with England in 1707. For several centuries the Scots have had
their own history, their own territory, their own religious, educational, and legal institutions. They have retained a separate identity
with a rugged Highland culture. They hold their own accent and
mannerisms, characteristics of a separate nation, but they do not
possess a separate state. They show an ambivalent attitude toward
their strong neighbor to the south. Should they support the democratic way of devolution, involving an increased regional authority
against London's centralism, or should they heed the call of Scottish
nationalists to win complete independence? (*See* **REGIONALISM.**)

In its early stages, Scottish nationalism was a kind of modest,
lukewarm revolt against England's domination. It never displayed
the kind of violent attitude expressed by the Basques in Spain or
Armenians in the Soviet Union. Moderate Scottish nationalists agreed
that matters concerned with Crown, defense, and foreign affairs be
left to the Parliament in London, but expressed the hope that Scotland would have control over internal affairs, industry, public health,
housing, education, and social insurance.

More vehement Scottish nationalists insist on the Scottishness of
their culture and its difference from that of England. They boast of
a distinct culture, with their own educational system, their own
religious beliefs, and their own legal interests. Two cultural traditions
intersect in Scottish society: one was influenced by immigrants from
Mediterranean lands and the west coast of France; the other by
peoples coming from the North Sea area and the European mainland.
The two were Celtic and Teutonic. The "Highlanders" saw themselves as being of "pure" Celtic stock; the "Lowlanders" traced their
origin to Teutonic sources. Both traditions were combined in a
distinctive Scottish culture.

Of some importance in Scottish nationalism is the language issue.
Almost all Scots speak a dialect version of English. But there are
actually two Scottish tongues: the vernacular language of the Low-

lands (Scottish, Scots, or Lallans), and Gaelic, spoken in the Highlands. The Lowland Scottish is a form of English closely related to
Middle English, similar to standard English. In poetry, fiction, and
drama, Scottish writers seek the revival of the Scottish, or Lallans,
vernacular. Meanwhile, language organizations promote the use of
Gaelic, even though it has been supplanted by English. Both Lallans
and Gaelic revivals have not been successful.

The determining factor in English-Scottish relations has been an
interlocking economic situation. Scotland is rich in mineral resources
and agricultural products. The union with England in 1707 brought
a significant change as Scotland was converted from an agricultural
economy. Along with the new industrialism came a social upheaval.
The rapid growth of towns was accompanied by a grave social
problem: the new industry brought both wealth to some Scots as
well as a heritage of slums and public health problems. The twentieth
century saw an economic decline in Scotland, due in part to the
distance from important markets and high transportation costs. With
a declining market, the center of industry shifted southward to
England. Scottish entrepreneurs became dependent on their English
counterparts. Many Scotsmen began to have second thoughts about
their economic subservience to England.

The English policy of conciliation and accommodation was designed to maintain Scotland inside the United Kingdom. Westminster
was concerned not only in easing Scottish economic problems, but
also for its political life and psychological needs. Aware of Scottish
sensitivity, the English were careful to placate the Scots as much as
possible. Scotsmen were welcomed into the British armed forces and
played a most important role in British military life. Scotsmen fought
side by side with the English in Britain's wars and developed a
consciousness of sharing the British cause.

For the most part, Scottish public opinion accepted the close
relationship with England as normal and desirable. But some Scotsmen were disturbed by what they regarded as a "mentality of
dependence," a kind of inferiority complex *vis-à-vis* their English
compatriots. This sentiment, added to practical economic grievances,
gave ammunition to the cause of Scottish nationalism.

The population of Scotland is just over five million, but on October
28, 1949, a Scottish Convention issued a resolution that received
1,250,000 signatures within six months. The mood was not for complete separation from England but for more local autonomy:

> This National Assembly, representative of the people of Scotland, reaffirms the
> belief that the establishment of a Scottish Parliament with legislative authority over

Scottish affairs is necessary to the national interest of Scotland, and in order to give the people an effective means of demonstrating their determination to secure this reform, the Assembly hereby resolves to invite Scots men and women to subscribe a Covenant in the following terms:

"We, the people of Scotland who subscribe to this engagement, declare our belief that reform in the constitution of our country is necessary to secure good government in accordance with our Scottish traditions and to promote the spiritual and economic welfare of our nation . . . with that end in view, we solemnly enter into this Convenant whereby we pledge ourselves, in all loyalty to the Crown and within the framework of the United Kingdom, to do everything in our power to secure for Scotland a Parliament with adequate legislative authority in Scottish affairs."

This moderate policy was not shared by members of the Scottish Nationalist Party (S.N.P.), formed in 1928. Its goal was by no means home rule but complete independence. It rejected out of hand the concept of "loyalty to the Crown and within the framework of the United Kingdom." That idea, they claimed, was spineless acceptance of the *status quo*. To win publicity for their cause, S.N.P. members, on Christmas Day 1950, managed to steal the Coronation Stone, or Stone of Scone, from Westminster Abbey. They then deposited it in the ruins of Arboath Abbey, several yards from the spot where the signing of the Scottish Declaration of Independence in 1320 was re-enacted each year in a summer pageant. The stone was returned to Westminster Abbey several days later. Scottish nationalists regarded this episode as more than a schoolboy prank: to them it was rather a symbol of Scottish liberation. They refused to recognize the title "Elizabeth II" and regularly damaged pillar boxes bearing the Queen's cipher.

In November 1988, voters of the Govan district of Glasgow elected a Nationalist, James Sillars of the Scottish Nationalist Party, as a member of Parliament. He promised to fight for Scottish independence within the European Community. But a poll by the British Broadcasting Company in Govan on the day of the election showed that, while forty-four percent of the voters cast their ballots for Mr. Sillars, only eighteen percent of those polled thought that separation from the United Kingdom was best for Scotland.

In effect, Scottish nationalism became dissent with manners, born of irritation and frustration, and certainly not of oppression from London. It never turned to extreme violence or revolution. Scottish citizens were not impressed with those who claimed to be latter-day Mazzinis. There was much sympathy for the cause but never an overwhelming sentiment for independence. Ties with London had become too strong to be broken easily.

Bibliography: H. J. Paton, *The Claim of Scotland* (London, 1968); H. J. Hanham, *Scottish Nationalism* (Cambridge, Mass., 1969); Christopher Harvie, *Scotland and Nationalism, 1707–1977* (London, 1977); Keith Webb, *The Growth of Nationalism in Scotland* (Glasgow, 1977); Jack Brand, *The Nationalist Movement in Scotland* (London, 1978); Alan Alexander, "Scottish Nationalism: Agenda Building, Electoral Process and Political Culture," *Canadian Review of Studies in Nationalism,* 7, No. 2 (Autumn, 1980), 372–390; John A. Agnew, "Political Regionalism and Scottish Nationalism in Gaelic Scotland," *Canadian Review of Studies in Nationalism,* 8, No. 1 (Spring, 1981), 115–129.

SECESSION.   The formal withdrawing or separation of one unit in the nation-state by refusing to accept the centralized authority. An example is the withdrawal of South Carolina on December 20, 1860, when, without a dissenting vote, the State legislature voted for an ordinance declaring that "the union now subsisting between South Carolina and the other States, under the name of the 'United States of America,' is hereby dissolved." South Carolina opted for State sovereignty and justified secession on grounds of the North's attack on slavery, as well as the election of a President "whose opinions and purposes are hostile to slavery." South Carolina was followed by ten Southern States that ultimately formed the Confederate States of America. This extension of secession led to the American Civil War. Secession is regarded as a critical blow to the concept of nationalism.

Bibliography: Thomas Shepard Goodwin. *The Natural History of Secession* (New York, 1965); John Barnell, *Love of Order: South Carolina's First Secession Crisis* (Chapel Hill, N.C., 1982); James A. Rawley, *Secession: The Disruption of the American Republic, 1844–1861* (Malabar, Fla., 1990).

SELF-DETERMINATION.   The determination or decision according to one's own mind or will, or what is generally known as free will. It is behind the right of a people to decide its own form of government without coercion. A product of the thinking of German philosopher Immanuel Kant (q.v.), self-determination became the dynamic doctrine behind nationalism. In the idea of self-determination, nationalism found the greatest source of its vitality.

The concept of self-determination is derived from the principle of diversity. People differ from one another in their peculiarities and idiosyncrasies. These differences are considered to be things holy, which must be fostered and preserved. Each individual has his own special characteristics and only by considering the sum of all individuals in the state can national harmony be achieved. A common language is one means by which the individual can become conscious of his special personality. Therefore, people in the aggregate who speak a common language see themselves as having something precious in their favor. This becomes the badge that distinguishes one nation from another. It follows that people who speak the same language can form what is known as the nation. (*See* **NATION.**)

National determination thus leads to the conclusion that humanity is divided into separate and distinct nations. These nations consist of sovereign states. Every individual is expected to cultivate his own identity and make it conform to that of the nation-state. He must subjugate his own feelings into that of the great whole—the nation.

In his study titled *The Quest for Self-Determination* (1979), Dov Ronen, of the Center for International Affairs at Harvard University, set five types of self-determination as dominant at successive periods from the French Revolution to the present:

Label Reference	Type	Dominant Period	Main Geographic Location
1. nationalism	national self-determination	1830s to 1880s	Europe
2. Marxism	class self-determination	mid-19th century	Europe plus
3. Wilsonian self-determination	minorities' self-determination	1916 to 1920s	Eastern Europe
4. decolonization	racial self-determination	(1945) to 1960s	Africa and Asia
5. ethno-nationalism or sub-nationalism	ethnic self-determination	mid-1960s	Africa, Asia, Europe, North America, Far East

According to Ronen, until the time of the French Revolution, there were few advocates of the idea that man has the right to be free. Subsequently, the concept of self-determination, strengthened by the modernization process, better communication, and the impact of two World Wars, has made progress on a global scale.

Nationalism, reflecting the urge of self-determination, concerns the aspirations of a people, who believe themselves to be united, to rule themselves and not be controlled by others. The kindred ideas of nationalism and self-determination both act as forces for convergence or divergence. As a force for convergence, they inspire peoples within a given territory to create national states. Germany and Italy present examples of this urge for unification. The nation is regarded as unique and indivisible—"we" as opposed to "they." This sense of self-determination may be called "the larger nationalism."

At the same time, self-determination, like nationalism, again may act as a force for divergence—disintegrative and destructive. In this case, the varied people inside the larger nationalism refused to accept the dominance of the centralized state. They may call either for more autonomy or independence. Dissatisfied minorities hold that the political center does not respond adequately to their political, economic, and especially cultural aspirations. They want the right to rule themselves. This kind of self-determination may be called "the smaller nationalism," a mini-nationalism, sub-nationalism, or ethno-nationalism.

As always in human affairs, both forms of self-determination, the larger nationalism and the smaller nationalism, are subject to power as the deciding element. The existence or dissolution of modern states depends on the outcome of the power-struggle. If a centralized authority, such as that of the Kremlin, maintains a strong hold on its minorities, the separatist movements will remain relatively quiescent. Where the central power seems relatively weak, the mini-nationalism may turn to terror to achieve its goal (the Basques in Spain). (*See* **TERRORISM.**) In general, it may be said that self-determination is seldom achieved by logical argument. Force and power are the deciding elements.

Bibliography: Alfred Cobban, *The Nation-State and National Self-Determination*, rev. ed., (New York, 1969); A. Rigo Sureda, *The Evolution of the Right of Self-Determination* (Leiden, 1973); Lee J. Buchheit, *Succession: The Legitimacy of Self-Determination* (New Haven, Conn., 1978); Dov Ronen. *The Quest for Self-Determination* (New Haven, Conn., 1979); Edward L. Deci, *The Psychology of Self-Determination* (Lexington, Mass., 1980); Yosef Gotlieb, *Self-Determination in the Middle East* (New York, 1982); I. M. Lewis (ed.) *Nationalism and Self-Determination in the Horn of Africa* (London, 1983); James Forman, *Self-Determination* (Washington, D.C., 1984); Ralph B. Neuberger, *National Self-Determination in Postcolonial Africa* (Boulder, Colo., 1986).

SEPARATISM. The character, act, principle, or practice designed by its adherents to withdraw completely from a centralized nation-state and set up a new national government. Those dissidents and activists, who demand separatism, call for complete independence and withdrawal from the national body of which they have once been a part. Regarding themselves as patriotic liberators, separatists may prefer to win their goal without violence, but they often believe that only through terrorism can they achieve independence. They reject autonomy or semi-autonomy as weak halfway measures. They are adamant—the bullet, not the ballot.

For authorities of a centralized government, separatists are regarded as traitors who endanger the existence of the state. The Soviet Union, consisting of some 100 nationalities, throttles dissidents on the ground that granting independence to any one nationality would eventually result in a domino effect—dissolution of its state. Separatists of the Irish Republican Army wage guerrilla warfare against British control and claim that Ireland will not be completely independent until the entire island, including Northern Ireland, is free of British control. (*See also* **RUSSIAN NATIONALISM, IRISH REPUBLICAN ARMY, AND MINI-NATIONALISMS.**)

SHAFER, BOYD C. (1907–   ).   Historian and leading American authority on nationalism. Born on May 8, 1907, Shafer took his B.A. degree at Miami University in 1929, the M.A. at the State University of Iowa, and the Ph.D. there in 1932. He served as James Wallace Professor of History at Macalester College from 1963 to his retirement. From 1953 to 1968 he was editor of *The American Historical Review* and executive secretary of the American Historical Association. In 1970 he was awarded the Troyer Steele Anderson Prize by the American Historical Association for his outstanding contributions to the development of historical studies in the United States.

Shafer is the author of classic studies on nationalism. Along with Carlton J. H. Hayes and Hans Kohn (qq.v.), he is regarded as a foremost authority on the phenomenon of nationalism. (*See also* **SHAFER'S SENSE OF BELONGING.**)

Bibliography: Shafer is the author of many books and articles on nationalism: "Bourgeois Nationalism in the Pamphlets of the French Revolution," *Journal of Modern History,* 10 (1938), 31–50; "Men Are More Alike," *The American Historical Review,* 57 (April, 1952), 593–612; *Nationalism: Myth and Reality* (New York, 1955); *Faces of Nationalism: New Realities and Old Myths* (New York, 1972); *Nationalism: Its Nature and Interpretation* (4th ed., Washington, 1976); "If Only We Knew More About Nationalism," *Canadian Review of Studies in Nationalism,* 7, No. 2 (Autumn, 1980), 197–218; *Nationalism and Internationalism: Belonging in Human Experience* (Malabar, Fla., 1982); "Debated Problems in the Study of Nationalism," *Canadian Review of Studies in Nationalism*, II, No. 1, (Spring, 1984), 1–19.

SHAFER'S SENSE OF BELONGING.   Boyd C. Shafer (q.v.), American specialist on nationalism, sees as its critical element the idea of "belonging." In his view, throughout history people have belonged to varieties of groups, such as family, village, tribe, caste, class, and church, as well as to state, nation, and nation-state. This, he says, has existed as long as we have folklore and records about any kind of human experience. Throughout the course of history, the dominant groupings have constantly but irregularly changed in various parts of the world, just as people's lives, hopes, and fears have changed. "But always people have belonged, or so wished, to one or more human groups for fulfillment of their own emotional needs, for their security, for realization of their actual or imagined potentialities, for their own economic, social, and political existence and advancement, for such liberties as they have desired and been able to obtain, and because of habit and happenstance."

According to Shafer, this sentiment of belonging has motivated not only the established nations, but also the developing peoples of the world. For both it has become a way to the future. This ultimate feeling concerned belonging to the mystical concept of nation. Individuals would be at one with their *Volk*, their people. They would become Frenchmen, Americans, or Kenyans in time of crisis—because they belonged to one another. Regardless of clashing ideology, this sentiment of belonging remains powerful among peoples throughout the world.

Shafer's concept of belonging was shared by German-American psychoanalyist Erich Fromm (q.v.), who stated: "Man—of all ages and culture—is confronted with . . . the question of how to overcome separateness, how to achieve union . . . transcend one's own individual life and find at-onement." Nations and nationalism provide one way to achieve this "at-onement."

This idea of "belonging" has gained increasing currency among scholars of nationalism. The concept persists: a man belongs to the nation he thinks he belongs to, and wants to belong to, no matter what biological science or anthropology may say to the contrary. The fluidity of the national idea depends upon this irreplaceable sense of belonging. We see its protean character and indestructible diversity in the fissiparous nationalism of Europe, the anti-colonialism of Asia, the black nationalism of Africa, the politico-religious nationalism of the Middle East, the populist nationalism of Latin-America, the "melting-pot nationalism" of the United States, and the messianic nationalism of the Soviet Union (qq.v.). All of these nationalisms are distinguished by this powerful psychological sense of belonging.

Bibliography: Boyd C. Shafer, *Nationalism and Internationalism; Belonging in Human Experience* (Malabar, Fla., 1982).

SHANAHAN, WILLIAM O. (1913–   ).   Specialist on German history in the nineteenth and twentieth centuries. He was born on April 26, 1913, at Omaha, Nebraska. He took his B.A. at the University of California, Los Angeles, in 1934, and his M.A. there in 1935. He was a member of the Hayes' seminar on nationalism at Columbia University and was awarded his Ph.D. there in 1945. He held teaching posts at Columbia, Notre Dame, the University of Oregon, Hunter College, and the Graduate Center of the City University of New York.

SHEVCHENKO, TARAS GRIGORYVICH (1814–1861).   Ukrainian poet, artist, and nationalist. Using the rhythm of old Ukrainian folk songs, Shevchenko called for the independence of the Ukraine. Filled with nationalistic fervor and compassion for victims of Tsarist injustice, his work strongly stimulated Ukrainian separatism. His *Free Cossacks* (1841) told the story of a heroic uprising of Ukrainians against Polish rule.

Tsarist authorities made certain to suppress the popular poet. In 1847 they sentenced him to compulsory military service and sent him to the Urals as a private soldier. Tsar Nicholas I was said to have personally intervened in giving orders to banish the poet. Released by amnesty in 1857, Shevchenko never fully recovered his health and died in 1861 at the age of forty-seven. His work was a powerful stimulant to the emergence of national consciousness in the Ukraine. (*See* **UKRAINIAN NATIONALISM.**)

Bibliography: G. S. N. Luckyj, *Shevchenko and the Critics* (Toronto, 1980); Leonid Novchenko, *Taras Shevchenko: Ukrainian Poet* (Paris, 1985).

SIKH SEPARATISM.   A people fiercely devoted to independence, the Sikhs of the Punjab in northwestern India have long resented their inferior role in India. As early as 1845–1846 and 1848–1849 they fought two wars with the British, resulting in the conquest and annexation by Britain of the Punjab. Sikh militants fought again and again for the idea of self-determination (q.v.).

The Sikhs remained a recalcitrant minority in India and were never satisfied by an inferior role in the state. Relations between the Sikhs and the Indian Government were strained by religious differences. The Sikh religion was founded more than 500 years ago as an alternative to Hinduism and Islam. It is followed by a minority of 1.9 percent in a population of more than 670 million in a nation populated by 84 percent of Hindus. As a religious minority, the Sikhs claim that they are victims of discrimination by the majority Hindus. The hostility has persisted throughout the years.

Sikh militancy has extended into a campaign for an independent nation called Khalistan. Matters came to a head in June 1984 with a confrontation between Indian Army troops and Sikh militants at the Sikh Golden Temple in Amritsar, the most holy of Sikh shrines. Angered Sikhs had taken refuge there. It is believed that more than 1,000 people were killed in the fighting. Confrontations between Government forces and Sikh militants persisted.

Sikh militants believed that their only hope for emancipation lay in a continuation of their campaign of terror. The battle at the Golden Shrine continued. Sikh extremists continued to snipe at the paramilitary forces attacking it. The Indian police adopted a strategy of showing force in a siege to crush the rebellion. An indication of the ferocity of the clash came on October 21, 1984, when Indira Gandhi, India's Prime Minister from 1966 to 1977 and again from 1980 was assassinated by a Sikh member of her personal bodyguard.

The Sikh campaign illustrates how the clash between a small nationalism and a more powerful nationalism can merge into bloodshed when the small nationalism becomes convinced that it is useless to adopt a moderate position. Like the Basques in Spain (*see* **BASQUE NATIONALISM**) and the Irish Republican Army (q.v.), the Sikh militants see their only course as the use of terrorism (q.v.) to win their freedom.

Bibliography: William Owen Cole, *The Sikhs* (New Delhi, 1978); Mehar Singh Chaddah, *Are Sikhs a Nation?* (Delhi, 1982); Christopher Schackle, *The Sikhs* (London, 1984); Jitender Kaur, *The Politics of Sikhs* (New Delhi, 1986).

SINN FÉIN, (English "We Ourselves").   Irish Nationalist party in the period before 1922, demanding political separation from England. From the beginning its policy proposed that Irish M.P.s elected to the British Parliament should not take their seats in London, but should form a government in Ireland. Sinn Féin was later closely associated with the Irish Republican Army (q.v.) because of its militancy in the cause of a united Ireland.

The important elements of the Sinn Féin program were resistance to the British, withholding of taxes, and the establishment of independent local authorities. The party was relatively unimportant until the Easter Rebellion in Dublin in 1916. This new uprising was suppressed by the British with damage to the city and the execution of fourteen of its leaders. Until this time the Sinn Féin had won little sympathy, but with the attempt to apply conscription to Ireland in 1918, it revealed how bitter Irish feeling had become. In the general election of 1918 the Sinn Féin party overwhelmed the old Nationalist Party. The elected members of the Sinn Féin Party established an independent parliament *(Dáil Eireann)* in Dublin and organized a completely new administration for the country.

Following the formation of the Irish Free State in 1921, Sinn Féin hostility to the agreement continued because it declined to recognize the legitimacy of the new Irish Assembly. In 1926, Sinn Féin's leader, Eamon de Valera (q.v.), resigned and founded the Fianna Fáil, which took over most of Sinn Féin's membership. From then on, Sinn Féin won only a small percentage of the Irish vote. There was still some connection between Sinn Féin members and the I.R.A. In 1969 the two organizations split into "Official" and "Provisional" wings concerning the best means to win national unification of the entire country. (*See also* **IRISH NATIONALISM.**)

Bibliography: Patrick Quinlivan and Paul Rose, *The Fenians in England, 1865–1872: A Sense of Insecurity* (New York, 1982); Thomas E. Hackey, *Britain and Irish Separatism* (Washington, D.C., 1984); R. V. Comerford, *The Fenians in Context: Irish Politics and Society, 1848–1882* (Dublin, 1985).

SMITH, ANTHONY D. (1933–   ).   British sociologist and one of the few in his discipline who have devoted major attention to the problems of nationalism. In an early study, *Theories of Nationalism* (1971), Smith presented a critical examination of nationalism pitched at an abstract level. Using historical data, he defined and established an elaborate typology of nationalistic movements. He suggested that the ideology of nationalism ignited when the "defensive reformists" and "Messianic assimilationists" came together in a situation of dual legitimation. He was not altogether impressed by the argument that the European nature of nationalism is dominant. He pointed to some roots in Asian and African nationalism. Nationalism may be expected, he wrote, whenever rapid social change is accompanied by the existence of strong ethnic ties plus a threat from the outside to the traditional culture.

In his work, Smith expressed an interest in definitions, typologies, theories, stages, and consequences of nationalism. He opposed the view that nationalism would shortly be transcended and wither away. This concept, he said, is supported more by evolutionary considerations than empirical observation. He held that the survival of nationalism is likely to be maintained for some time. Since the days of "historicist" romanticism, nationalism has exhibited a powerful staying power in modern society.

In a later book, *The Ethnic Revival* (1981), Smith modified his view on ethnicity as it relates to nationalism. In his earlier work he minimized the relationship between ethnicity on the one hand and the nation and national movements on the other. In his new work he used the term "ethnic revival" to refer not to the surge of nationalism in the 1960s, but to what Carlton J. H. Hayes and Hans Kohn (qq.v.) called the Age of Nationalism. In contrast to Smith's earlier view, he now turned his attention to the study of ethnonationalism (q.v.) by analyzing its social and cultural roots and "to document its worldwide importance." At the heart of ethnic identity he now saw a sense of sharing a common origin, regardless of common geneological facts. He suggested that ethnic awareness has existed throughout history and that it was given fresh impetus during the eighteenth century Age of Reason. The intelligentsia, he believed, particularly educators, are the disseminators of the ethnonational idea.

Smith's views on nationalism have generated some criticism among other specialists. (*See* **SOCIOLOGY OF NATIONALISM.**)

Bibliography: Anthony D. Smith, *Theories of Nationalism* (London, 1971); Anthony D. Smith, *The Ethnic Revival* (London, 1981).

SOCIOLOGY OF NATIONALISM.   Sociology, the study of the structure and functions of society, deals with group behavior, the relationships among people, and the factors concerning and ensuing from these relationships. Its subject matter is variously conceived to be society, culture, race, social institutions, collective behavior, human ecology, and social interaction. Therefore, sociologists turn to the study of the nation, nationality, and nationalism as fields of interest and research.

Such senior scholars as Max Weber or Piritrim A. Sorokin commented generally on nationalities and ethnic groups (the term "group" is basic for sociologists). In his scholarly article, "Types of Nationalism" (1936), Louis Wirth made an early contribution to the study of typology, but little other work was done by sociologists at this time.

In 1952 Florian Znaniecki published a short work titled *Modern Nationalities*, which until then was the only monograph by a sociologist on the phenomenon of nationalities. This short study, however, was limited to cultural aspects of the problem. Znaniecki saw nationality as "a collectivity of people with certain common and distinctive characteristics."

As early as 1944, the British scholar Friedrich Hertz contributed a study titled *Nationality in History and Politics*, which was less clearly sociological in content. He saw political nationality as extremely complicated, so much so that it could not be observed and measured by exact methods:

> One can explore the growth and the rules of a national language or the institutions of a national State with considerable exactness, and without interrogating members of that nation which may be an extinct one as the old Romans or Greeks. National consciousness or national sentiment, however, is an exceedingly elusive thing. Its manifestations can be studied in political literature, public speeches, or national institutions, but the interpretations of such documents or objects in regard to the underlying national spirit is always more or less insecure. . . . . Legal nationality, cultural nationality, and the status of a people according to international practice can easily be ascertained. But political nationality is a very complicated matter as it depends on a sufficient degree of national consciousness which cannot be observed and measured by exact methods.

These early sociologists regarded the nation and nationality within the framework of social categories, as "great collectivities," or "human aggregates," or "in-and-out groups." They traced the evolution of society as it banded itself together for mutual protection and prosperity. They saw nationalism as a social movement that characterized the behavior of nationalities. Louis Wirth defined nationalism as "the social movements of nationalities striving to acquire, maintain, or enhance their position in a world where they are confronted by opposition or conflict." To these sociologists a key factor in the existence of nationalism was the group. In the animal world, they said, a gregarious instinct exists among herds whose members associate only with their own kind and rigidly exclude the outsider. They saw a parallel within human groups, although they warned that the instinctive factor must not be exaggerated. Znaniecki stated that organized groups of humans are more powerful socially than unorganized masses of peoples. The formation of groups follows a well-known pattern. From the group the individual imbibes traditions (patterns of behavior from the collective heritage, regardless of utility, beauty, or supernatural sanction); and interests (aims useful to the existence and well-being of the group and ideals and aims that are not the direct interests of individuals). These experiences, solidified through the process of education, eventually become organized into a system with the group as the central object. When the group becomes large and takes on a deep concern for its own honor and prestige, it becomes subject to the sentiment of nationalism.

Among the early sociologists there was some difference of opinion as to whether nationalism is a survival of primitive barbarism or the product of modern society. Those who defended the survival syndrome believed that nationalism is an assertion of the cave man within us. It arose, they said, in response to the conditions of primitive times and has been preserved in the communal mind, which exists independent of the individual mind, and as well as outside the nervous system and body of the individual. In support of this thesis, they cited numerous instances of close parallels between the behavior of primitive tribes and modern human beings, such as rejection of reason, exaltation of instinct, and irrational emotions (belief in the "mystic mass soul" and "the voice of the blood").

Friedrich Hertz and other early sociologists criticized the survival theory and contended that nationalism cannot be explained simply by harking back to or a revival of primitive barbarism and its instincts, because such instincts would be equally strong at all times and in all members of the species. There must be social factors that account for its variations according to time, nation, and class. Hertz believed that nationalism is an independent sentiment which has arisen as a response to the peculiarities of modern mass society. Not only adolescent schoolboys but also intellectuals are taken in by the intensification of nationalism.

In the last two decades, two sociologists have entered the arena and devoted their studies to the nature of nationalism. One is an American scholar, Konstantin Symmons-Symonolewicz (q.v.), and the other is an Englishman, Anthony D. Smith, (q.v.). Both are convinced that the study of nationalism thus far is unsatisfactory, that sociological work is still in its initial stage, and that it is up to sociologists to perform much of the theorizing about nationalism. In 1965 Symmons-Symonolewicz presented a new type of sociological classification of nationalism. (*See* **SYMMONS-SYMONOLEWICZ TYPOLOGY.**) His formula was based on the idea that the goals of all movements concerned with loyalty to a given group are essentially similar. He regarded it as important to search for the social group as basic in conceptions of nationalism.

In his *Theories of Nationalism* (1971), Anthony D. Smith, in conformance with the general attitude of sociologists, stressed the idea of the group in his definition of nationalism: "Nationalism is an ideological movement, for the attainment and maintenance of self-government and independence on behalf of a group, some of whose members conceive it to constitute an actual or potential 'nation' like others." He sees modern nationalism as providing the fuel for nationalist movements all over the world since the French Revolution. Smith then departs from his original definition of nationalism and presents another type with a much longer history. This type, he says, existed in the Middle Ages as well as in the ancient world. He calls the modern type "polycentric" and the earlier forms "ethnocentric." The polycentric type tries to join the family of nations to find its appropriate identity and part. For Smith, ethnocentric nationalism is quite different. It assumes the nation to be the center of the world and calls the rest heathens or barbarians, as mute instruments of God or fate. Modern polycentric nationalism, according to Smith, is more outward-looking, more self-critical, and is motivated by the idea of becoming a "nation." Smith claims that some of the confusion over the antiquity of nationalism results from the failure to distinguish between these two types.

The contrast between Smith's definition of nationalism as an ideological movement involving the conception of a nation and his extension of this idea to earlier peoples in history provoked criticism among other scholars of nationalism. Symmons-Symonolewicz considered the theory of ancient "nationalism" and asked whether there is a basis for assuming the existence of any "nations" in the ancient world. One should speak, he said, of "peoplehood," rather than "nationhood" in the ancient era. Other scholars of nationalism also criticize Smith on other grounds. For example, Boyd C. Shafer (q.v.) does not think Smith's published work is interdisciplinary, because he, for the most part, ignores historians. Shafer sees Smith's concepts as "lacking focus." "He does *not* cover 'theories' but emphasizes taxonomies—which, to paraphrase William James, "leak at the joints."

Bibliography: Louis Wirth, "Types of Nationalism," *American Journal of Sociology,* 42 (1936), 723–737; Friedrich Hertz, *Nationality in History and Politics* (London, 1951); Florian Znaniecki, *Modern Nationalities* (Urbana, Ill., 1952); Konstantin Symmons-Symonolewicz, *Nationalist Movements: A Comparative View* (Meadville, Pa., 1970); Anthony D. Smith, *Theories of Nationalism* (New York, 1971).

SOVEREIGNTY, NATIONAL.   The supreme and independent political authority, such as a sovereign state or governmental unit. It is a most important element in the Age of Nationalism. The state becomes the most powerful authority in the life of its individual citizens. They are expected to give it their loyalty, obey its laws, and respect its flag and anthem. Those who refuse to maintain their adherence are regarded as traitors.

Most scholars of nationalism believe that national sovereignty is still a powerful idea in contemporary society. Since the old powers invented the idea of the nation-state, the world has filled up with new states that hew to the same line. An example of the strength of national sovereignty may be seen in the concept of Pan-Europa (q.v.), the move to extend the Common Market from an economic to a political base. Where the member nations are quite willing to work as an economic unit, they draw back instinctively when the idea of relinquishing their political sovereignty is proposed. The pride of flag, ambassador, and vote remains powerful in contemporary social life.

Yet, there are scholars and reputable journalists who believe that nationalism, like history itself, is always in a state of flux. Thus, Flora Lewis, writer on foreign affairs for *The New York Times,* refers to "the pious principle of national sovereignty," which she sees as never having been absolute except in oratory. She admits that it did serve to provide certain standards in a disorderly world. "Now they are eroding, not just because of greed and cynicism but because of hard facts of interdependence." She believes that stubborn clinging to sovereignty has tended to undermine national capacity in Western Europe. The result, she says, has been a new spurt of enthusiasm for continental unity at the cost of national prerogatives. She quotes West Germany's Otto von Lamsdorff as saying bluntly: "National sovereignty is an anachronism which causes governments to lose power to narrow internal interests." She sees the idea of nation-states as obsolescent as the world has filled up with new states determined to assert their right of dubious value. Drug traffic and environmental pollution, she writes, are examples of how countries weigh on each other, regardless of sovereignty. The old precepts of international relations are being overtaken by the real world of inevitable ties.

The responses to these arguments hold that, on the contrary, the real world is one in which national sovereignty is a paramount force. The 1975 Helsinki agreements included provisions for human rights that the signatory states were bound to observe. The Soviet Union signed the accord but held that criticism that it was not living up to the agreements was interference with "national sovereignty." Admittedly, there may be shifting standards of national sovereignty, but the idea of nationalism remains a powerful phenomenon in modern life.

Bibliography: Richard Falk, *Human Rights and State Sovereignty* (New York, 1981); Caroline Thomas, *New States, Sovereignty, and Intervention in World Politics* (New York, 1985); Carl Schmitt, *Political Theology: Four Chapters on the Concept of Sovereignty,* trans. by George Schwab (Cambridge, Mass., 1985); F. H. Hinsley, *Sovereignty* (New York, 1986); Flora Lewis, "Shifting Standards for Sovereignty," *The New York Times,* June 20, 1988.

SPIRA, THOMAS (1923–). Professor of History at the University of Prince Edward Island and editor of the *Canadian Review of Studies in Nationalism.* Born in Bratislava, Czechoslovakia, Spira came to the United States and took his B.A. degree at The City College of the City University of New York in 1964. Later, he completed his M.A. and Ph.D. in History at McGill University, Montreal (1965 and 1970). Author of books and articles on nationalism, minority problems and related topics, Spira's main contribution to the study of nationalism was founding and editing of the *Canadian Review of Studies in Nationalism* (q.v.), the only scholarly journal devoted exclusively to the study of nationalism.

Bibliography: Thomas Spira, *German-Hungarian Relations and the Swabian Problem from Károlyi to Gömbös* (Boulder, Colo., East European Monographs, 1977.)

STEREOTYPES, NATIONAL. Fixed or conventional expressions, notions, or mental patterns on a national scale. Stereotypes concern the characteristics of an entire nation. They refer to special qualities that distinguish one people from another. The term usually carries with it an element of exaggeration. Thus, it is said that all Englishmen are polite, class conscious, and convinced of their own superiority; all Frenchmen are pragmatic, temperate, and passionate; all Italians are loud, emotional, and artistic; all Germans are hardy, theoretical, and militant; all Spaniards are proud and dignified; all Dutch are frugal and industrious; all Russians are melancholy, submissive, and frustrated; and all Americans are naïve, materialistic, and violent. Individual characteristics of some citizens are used to describe the whole population of a nation.

These stereotypes have passed into common usage. Easy generalizations hold that the people of one country merge into a common denominator: it is said that they are distinguished by a combination of permanent qualities that sets them apart from other peoples. On occasion, this kind of thinking denigrates "the others" as being different from the norm and less well-endowed. The television comedian specializing in dialect humor ridicules the "typical" Scotsman who does not want to spend the money to go to the seashore and, instead, buys a herring which he waves in his living room to bring sea air to his family. The audience accepts the false notion that all Scotsmen are thrifty and bent on saving money. Or the performer may imitate the proud, haughty, and surly attitude of a Spanish bullfighter who instantly wins recognition from his audience.

This kind of overstatement and magnifying of facts is closely related to the concept of national character (q.v.), an idea that has aroused much controversy among scholars of nationalism. Stereotypes become exaggerated versions of what contains an element of truth. On occasion, they may be used wildly to describe all the people in a nation as alike in character and in a way that admits no contradiction. Yet, the idea of stereotypes is so widespread that it cannot be rejected altogether as of no consequence. The very fact of their existence gives them historical value. Indeed, the study of national character has become a field contaminated by stereotypes about peoples and nations. It would be wrong simply to reject stereotypes as unimportant or ignore their relevance. Artificial stereotypes may well be irrational, but this does not mean that their effects on society should be abandoned.

There may be a remarkable degree of accuracy in some of the clichés people use about themselves and others. Behind the unfriendly stereotypes there are qualities that give rise to the clichés. The specificity of a nation tends to have a lasting and, on occasion, stubborn quality, and it would be unwise to pay no attention to these real or presumed qualities. Research into the characteristics of a people does show a difference in taste, temperament, and attitudes among peoples. At the root of the clichés there may well be cultural characteristics that do exist.

Stereotypes may be underestimated on the ground that "all humans are alike." If research on the determination of national character is developed, scholars may well find that the peoples of every nation are more like the peoples of other nations than they are different. Humans may differ individually and their cultures may well be diverse, but they are also much alike. It may be that human likenesses are more important than national differences. Some scholars believe that there may be divergencies in human behavior among the peoples of various nations, but that these differences should not hide similarities of behavior. Every culture has some similar practices and institutions—community organization, religious rituals, courtship, marriage, and funerals. Psychologist Lawrence K. Frank summed up this point of view:

> All men, everywhere, face the like tasks, share the same anxieties, and perplexities, bereavements and tragedies, seek the same goals in their cultures, to make life meaningful and significant, to find some security, to achieve some social order and to regulate their conduct toward values that make life more than organized existence.

The problem here is that little satisfactory work has been done on either national stereotypes or national character. What has been presented in these fields turns out to be tentative and unproved hypotheses. Whether or not such research contains vitality for the peoples of an entire nation, it probably does not do anything more than describe a minority or perhaps a few people at a given time. Apparently, some people fit the mold of a national stereotype and some do not. Does it make any sense to assume that all Italians are "passionate and excitable" because "they are warmed by the sun"? It is impossible at the present rate of study to arrive at meaningful conclusions because individual traits are so many and so changing that they defy adequate measurement. Because of the many difficulties involved in studying the ramifications of stereotypes, some scholars believe that it is advisable to maintain them in myth. As early as the eighteenth century, David Hume wrote:

> The vulgar are apt to carry all national characters to extremes, and having once established it as a principle that any people are knavish, or cowardly, or ignorant, they will admit of no exceptions, but comprehend every individual under the same censure.

Bibliography: William Buchanan and Hadley Cantril, *How Nations See Each Other* (Urbana, Ill., 1953); Harold Isaacs, *Stretches on Our Minds* (New York, 1958); Wallace Lambert and Otto Klineberg, "A Pilot Study of the Origins and Development of National Stereotypes." *International Social Science Bulletin* 2 (1959), 221–238; H. J. C. Duyker and N. H. Fryda, *National Character and National Stereotypes* (Amsterdam, The Netherlands, 1960).

STOECKER, ADOLF (1835–1909). German preacher, court-chaplain to William II (q.v.), founder of the Christian-Social Workers' Party, and proponent of political anti-Semitism in Germany. The son of an army quartermaster, Adolf Stoecker became a field chaplain at the outbreak of the Franco-Prussian War in 1870. One of his sermons on the battlefield attracted the attention of William I, King of Prussia, who later in 1874, when he was Emperor, called the young pastor to Berlin as court-chaplain. In 1878 Stoecker founded the Christian-Social Workers' Party, through which, as a conservative, he hoped "to win the workingman to national and Christian thought, and to conquer the Social Democrats for the spirit of nationalism." He held seats in both the Prussian *Landtag* and the German *Reichstag*.

Ambitious and energetic, Stoecker was always the center of controversy. As a churchman, he found it impossible to separate his ecclesiastic duties from politics. He saw no contradiction between the tenets of Christianity and his intolerance. He was certain that he had been appointed by divine providence to become a leader of the German people and to convince his countrymen of their "racial" superiority. Always in the limelight, invariably keyed for battle, he was most happy when being heckled at mass meetings. He denounced his foes in the courtroom, accused newspapers of cowardly attacks, and defiantly challenged investigators of his financial affairs.

Stoecker was the extreme nationalist *par excellence*. He was certain that the German character represented the apex of civilization. With great emotion he praised the "Germanic-Christian *Kultur* ideal." He paid tribute to "German honesty, loquacity, and conscientiousness." The German people, he said, were by nature industrious, loyal, pious, "altogether richly endowed."

> No other people have so many national songs, national tales, national customs as we. Conscientiousness, the old heritage of Germanic nature, has grown through Protestantism. One has always sung praise to German loyalty, to faithfulness between man and wife, between friend and friend, between prince and peasant. Our treasure is a serious, holy family life, respect of children for their elders, love of parents for their children. Every German possesses a feeling of duty, diligence, ability, indefatigableness—these are German attributes.

Stoecker saw his Fatherland as "blessed, beautiful, great." The word "Fatherland" became almost an obsession. In one emotional speech he used the word nine times in two sentences:

> Ten years ago much blood was spilled to win freedom and unity for the Fatherland; one cannot think enough of the Fatherland, and it is inspiring when young men give their Fatherland more than themselves, and give their blood and lives for the Fatherland. But when one makes a repulsive idol of the earthly Fatherland, when there is no heavenly Fatherland above the earthly Fatherland, then the spirit of the Fatherland remains dark; in many souls today a wrong idea of the Fatherland exists.

Stoecker clothed his sense of nationalism with a bitter dose of anti-Judaism. The foremost anti-Semite of his time, he worked energetically in the German anti-Semitic campaign. He identified Social Democracy with Judaism and attacked the National Liberals as Jewish-controlled. He led anti-Semitic delegates in the *Reichstag* in calling for the elimination of Jews from schools, abolition of equal rights for Jews, and the subjection of German Jews to laws governing foreigners. It was impossible, he said, for Jews to understand the high Christian *Weltanschauung* (world view), or the deep spirit of Germanic ideals. "Modern Judaism is a foreign drop of blood in our national body. It is a destructive power. We must nurse again the peculiarities of our national genius—German spirit, industriousness, and piety—our heritage." On the lecture platform he took delight in such inflammatory passages as this: "Ladies and Gentlemen: Recently a body was found in the vicinity. It was examined; present were the Jewish town-physician, a Jewish doctor, a Jewish coroner, a Jewish lawyer—only the body was German!" When in February 1888, a statue of Heinrich Heine, the great German poet was to be erected, Stoecker protested against the plan: "It alienates the healthy patriotism of the people. It ought to be made of mud. Heine—the Jew—was a rascal."

Called the "uncrowned king of Berlin," Stoecker fired the enthusiasm of many Germans by directing his abuse at Jews, bankers, and capitalists. Nationalism plus socialism plus anti-Semitism was the revolutionary formula that Stoecker discovered. Adolf Hitler (*see* **HITLER, ADOLF**) was to implement it in his own way. In the Third Reich it became the accepted pattern for German extreme nationalism.

Bibliography: Adolf Stoecker, *Christlich-Sozial: Reden und Aufsätze* (Bielefeld and Leipzig, 1885); Dietrich von Oertzen, *Adolf Stoecker, Lebensbild und Zeitgeschichte* (Schwerin i. Mecklenberg, 1912).

SUBCONSCIOUS NATIONALISM. *See* **NATIONALISM, CLASSIFICATIONS OF.**

SUB-NATIONALISM. Another term for a mini-nationalism or an ethnonationalism (qq.v.).

SUN YAT-SEN (Mandarin, Sun Wen-shu, 1866–1925). Chinese historian, patriot, revolutionary, and Nationalist leader. Born near Canton to a farm-owning family, Sun studied at an Anglican college in Honolulu, where he came under Western and Christian influence. Though he practiced medicine for a time, his main interest was how to improve the chaotic condition of his country. He was convinced that it was necessary to overthrow the Ch'ing dynasty and establish a stable Chinese republic. Thereafter, he devoted all his energy to this goal. In the process he became known as the father of Chinese nationalism. His greatest contribution lay in the vigor and general character of his leadership. He revitalized Chinese nationalism and made it a powerful driving force in the history of his country, first against the Manchu dynasty and then against foreign domination.

At the end of the nineteenth century, China was undergoing a depressing "Time of Trouble." The Manchu dynasty, which had ruled China since 1644, was unable to lift the country out of its backwardness and had made little progress in modernizing it. Orthodox Confucian "self-strengtheners" had attempted to introduce modern engines of power within the traditional system of values and institutions, but most of the efforts failed. The Chinese people gradually came to regard foreigners as usurpers who were harmful to them. After the defeat by "upstart" Japan in 1894–1895, the always vulnerable imperial regime went bankrupt. The country was steeped in regionalism (q.v.), with rival war lords at each other's throats.

Sun was appalled by this chaotic state of affairs. In 1894, just after the outbreak of the war with Japan, he went to Honolulu, where he founded the Society for the Restoring of China *(Hsing Chung Hui)*. Returning to China the next year, he plotted an armed uprising in the hope of capturing Canton as a base for the revolution. When the plot failed, a price was set on his head. He fled to Europe, where he stayed for two years, during which time he developed his political and social ideas. He was much impressed by the writings of Karl Marx and Henry George. Returning to China, he continued his revolutionary activities.

Central to Sun's philosophy and goals was nationalism. For him it was a precious possession, which would enable China to aspire to progress. He saw nationalism as a central political issue for China:

> Nationalism is a treasure, the possession of which causes a nation to aspire to greater development, and a race to seek to perpetuate itself. China today has lost that treasure. . . . Cosmopolitanism has been the cause of the decadence of China. . . . Cosmopolitanism will cause further decadence if we leave the reality, nationalism, for the shadow, cosmopolitanism. . . .
>
> First let us practice nationalism; cosmopolitanism will follow.
>
> If henceforth we Chinese find some way of reviving our nationalism . . . then no matter what foreign political and economic force will oppress us, our race undoubtedly will not be extinguished in a thousand or even ten thousand years.

Sun believed fervently in the future of his country, which he felt would one day play a major role in world affairs. He combined

Chinese youth in patriotic organizations, as well as several anti-Manchu secret societies. He founded the political party which had several earlier names but which finally came to be called the *Kuomintang* (Nationalist Party). His followers, ardent about anti-imperialism, put an end to the provisions of the Unequal Treaties, but they were divided about the nature and pace of the socio-economic revolution.

Sun's efforts were finally successful, when on October 10, 1899, thirteen of eighteen provinces responded to his revolutionary call and declared their independence of the Manchu dynasty. In 1912 the Nanking Assembly named Sun as President, but he resigned two weeks later in favor of Shih-kai, who had earlier supported the Manchu dynasty. The abdication of the Emperor ended 260 years of Manchu rule. From then on, there was a bitter struggle between Sun's *Kuomintang* and his reactionary opponents.

Sun's basic ideas had been formulated in the early part of the century. Now, in the early 1920s, he enunciated his views in a series of lectures, which became an important part of the Nationalist credo under the title of "The Three Principles of the People"—nationalism, democracy, and livelihood. For him, nationalism was the driving force of his country's future. "Livelihood" involved socialist principles—the regulation of private capital and the "equalization of land rights."

Although Sun continued his efforts with undiminished zeal, much of China's history at this time continued to be a confusing struggle between rival factions of war lords. The agrarian crisis deepened. Sun and his associates found it virtually impossible to bring some order to the distraught country. The *Kuomintang's* entente with the Soviet Union entailed a united front with the new and still tiny Chinese Communist Party, which became a displaced "bloc within" and eventually became strong enough to seize national power. While on a fruitless mission to unite the country under the Republic, Sun died of cancer on March 12, 1925.

Sun's dynamic personality, as well as the depth of his sense of national consciousness, endeared him to the Chinese people. His Nationalist followers called him the "Father of China." Chinese Communists revered him as "a pioneer of the Revolution." Historians see him as an apostle of Chinese nationalism as well as a symbol of Chinese modernization.

Bibliography: Sun Yat-sen, *The Principles of Nationalism* (Canton, 1924); Paul N. W. Linebarger, *Sun Yat-sen and the Chinese Republic* (New York, 1925); Abbie N. Sharman, *Sun Yat-sen, His Life and*

Meaning (New York, 1934); Harold C. Schriffen, *Sun Yat-sen and the Origins of the Chinese Revolution* (Berkeley, 1938); Marius B. Jansen, *The Japanese and Sun Yat-sen* (Cambridge, Mass., 1954); Gottfried K. Kinderman, *Sun Yat-sen: Founder and Symbol of China's Revolutionary Nation-Building* (Munich, 1982); Eugen Anschel, *Sun Yat-sen and the Chinese Revolution* (New York, 1984).

S.W.A.P.O. (SOUTH-WEST AFRICA PEOPLE'S ORGANIZATION). A Marxist guerrilla group calling for Namibian independence and an end to South African domination.

SYBEL, HEINRICH VON (1817–1895). German historian, along with Johann Gustav Droysen and Heinrich von Treitschke (qq.v.), one of the Professor-Prophets of the Prussian School of historiography. In 1856, while at the University of Munich, Sybel founded the *Historische Zeitschrift*, which became the model for succeeding technical historical publications. In 1875 he was appointed by Bismarck (q.v.) as director of the Prussian Archives. In this post, using State papers, he produced work of extraordinary value about Prussian policies from 1860 to 1866.

Moved by the political situation in the Germanies at mid-century, Sybel gradually turned to the study of German constitutional history. He soon became an advocate of Prussian leadership in German history. The Revolution of 1848 convinced him that it was necessary for the State to intervene in politics and to rescue the educated classes from attacks by lower classes. Like Droysen, he was convinced that it was the task of the historian to educate the public politically and to "the right way of thinking." He confessed that "I am four-sevenths politician and three-sevenths professor." In his work he distilled political and diplomatic details that gave a strongly partisan narrative of German unification. He attributed to Denmark, Austria, and France the responsibility for starting the three wars of German national unification. He maintained that Bismarck's editing of the Ems Dispatch in 1870 was thoroughly justified: Bismarck did not "alter" but only "shortened" that critical message. Prussia's policy, he said, was "reasonable, just, and correct."

British historians judged the work of Sybel to be marred by prejudice:

> He went through life waving a Prussian banner and waging truceless war against France, Austria, and the Roman Church. History was a vast arsenal which furnished him with a weapon of attack and defense. . . . There is no trace of genius

in Sybel or his writings. He possessed a positive, solid, powerful mind, but he lacked imagination and subtlety.

Bibliography: Heinrich von Sybel, *The Founding of the German Empire, Based Chiefly Upon Prussian State Documents,* trans. by H. S. White (7 vols., New York 1890–1898); G. P. Gooch, *History and Historians of the Nineteenth Century* (New York, 1928).

SYMMONS-SYMONOLEWICZ, KONSTANTIN (1909–1986). Born in Poland, Symmons-Symonolewicz took his master's degree at the University of Warsaw and a doctorate in sociology at Columbia University. He taught in American colleges since 1940 and spent the major part of his career as Professor of Sociology at Allegheny College, Meadville, Pa. His work is considered to be one of the most important sociological studies since Florian Znaniecki's *Modern Nationalities* (1952).

Symmons-Symonolewicz discussed nationalism as an ideology, the nation as a moral community, and national languages and national boundaries. He presented a comparative typology of nationalist movements. (*See* **SYMMONS-SYMONOLEWICZ TYPOLOGY.**) Like Hans Kohn, he was convinced that there never has been and never can be any justification for a policy of national oppression. "So long as national, or ideological, oppression exists there can be no durable peace."

Bibliography: Among the published works of Konstantin Symmons-Symonolewicz are: *Modern Nationalism: Towards a Consensus in Theory* (Meadville, Pa., 1968); *Nationalist Movements: A Comparative View* (Meadville, Pa., 1970); "Ethnicity and Nationalism: Recent Literature and Its Theoretical Implications," *Canadian Review of Studies in Nationalism,* 6, No. 1 (Spring, 1979), 98–102.

SYMMONS-SYMONOLEWICZ TYPOLOGY. In 1965 sociologist Symmons-Symonolewicz (q.v.) offered a new type of classification of nationalism. He did not attempt to present the varieties of nationalism as a sentiment, an ideology, or a political program, but, instead, limited his attention to nationalist movements. He did not include the nationalisms of the majorities or the dynamics of their development. He defined nationalism as "the active solidarity of a group claiming to be a nation and aspiring to be a state." He used the term in a neutral sense: nationalism is neither good nor bad, neither liberal nor illiberal, neither democratic nor undemocratic. "When seen as a movement, nationalism represents a series of stages in the struggle of a given solidarity group to achieve the basic aims of unity and self-direction."

Symmons-Symonolewicz distinguished between two major kinds of nationalist movements: minority and liberation. He regarded minority movements as aiming at self-preservation; they are "real minorities," groups that are so weak, or so territorially located that the aim of liberation from the majority group is for them inconceivable. On the other hand, the liberation movements are those that are able to achieve independence, or believe that they can win the fruits of self-determination (q.v.).

In his category of minority movements, Symmons-Symonolewicz drew a basic distinction between the perpetuative-segregative and perpetuative-pluralistic types. Both tend to preserve their cultural identity, but the pluralistic type seeks also for full civic equality for its members, while the other wants only to be let alone. Examples of the perpetuative-segregative type are the medieval Jewish ghettoes or the imperial Ottoman millet system. Minority rights, as in the minority treaties of post-Versailles Europe, would be a solution satisfactory to the perpetuative-pluralistic type. There is a third type—the irredentist (see **IRREDENTIST NATIONALISM**), which is limited to those border groups that seek to secede, even though they are a minority and cannot be successful on their own. They can win only when they are supported by an expansionist neighboring state that claims them as co-nationals.

In the category of liberation movements, Symmons-Symonolewicz drew a distinction in terms of historical development and the nature of unity. He defined the restorative movements as those that involve nations whose independent existence was interrupted and which were successful in retaining their social structures in relatively intact form. Examples can be found in Hungary or Poland in the nineteenth century.

In his list of liberation movements, Symmons-Symonolewicz included the following:

Revivalist Movements. This includes those ethnic communities that lost their political identities some centuries ago and which seek to rebuild both their historical traditions and social structure. Examples are Flemish, Catalan, Finnish, and Lithuanian nationalities in the nineteenth century.

Autonomist-Secessionists. These are regional entities, that, despite their ties to the mother-group, develop a distinctiveness expressed in their demand for autonomy. Eventually, they seek separation instead of autonomy. Examples are the United States and many Latin-American states. Unsuccessful examples—the Confederate States in North America and the ethnically Russian territories in Siberia.

Anti-Colonial Movements.   This type rests on opposition to, and the rejection of, colonial rule. Examples are nationalism in the Congo, Indonesia, Burma, India, and Pakistan.

Nativist Movements.   This category steps beyond the range of nationalism into xenophobic tribalism. Examples are the Caucasian mountaineers against Russia in the nineteenth century and the Riff mountaineers under Abd-el-Krim against Spain and France in the twentieth century.

The Symmons-Symonolewicz sociological formula is based on the assumption that the goals of all movements concerned with exclusive loyalty to a given group are essentially similar. Where historians are preoccupied by moral evaluations of nationalism and regard it as primarily a state of mind, most sociologists automatically search for the social group as basic to nationalism. Symmons-Symonolewicz sought a blending of both approaches.

Bibliography: Konstantin Symmons-Symonolewicz, "Nationalist Movements: An Attempt at a Comparative Typology," *Comparative Studies in Society and History,* VII (January, 1965), 221–230.

T

TAGORE, RABINDRANATH (1861–1941). Indian poet, author, mystic, and critic of nationalism. Tagore worked to introduce the best of Indian culture to the West. In 1924 he founded an international university, Visva Bharati, with the aim of bringing together men of different races and civilizations to study in an atmosphere of peace, brotherhood, and joy in work. He was the first Indian to be awarded the Nobel Prize for Literature (1913). In 1950, his poem, *Lord of the Heart of the People*, was set to music by Herbert Murrill. It became the national anthem of India.

Although he actively supported the Indian national movement, Tagore held that India's task was to show the world the way to peace through brotherly cooperation between the various races and creeds. He made a distinction between "good" and "bad" nationalism, and criticized the latter as "a terrible epidemic."

Bibliography: Rabindranath Tagore, *Toward Universal Man* (New York, 1961); George Catlin, *Rabindranath Tagore* (New York, 1964).

TAMIL SEPARATISM. The Tamil minority makes up eighteen percent of the population of Sri Lanka, formerly known as Ceylon. Consisting of 25,322 square miles in the Indian Ocean south of India, the island houses a Singhalese majority of seventy-five percent, which controls the government and armed forces. Most of Sri Lanka's aboriginals now live in remote mountain areas. The island was conquered in the sixth century by the Singhalese, who adopted the Buddhist religion. Muslim Tamils invaded the island and became a significant minority in the country. Buddhist-Muslim rivalry resulted and persisted during successive Portuguese, Dutch, and British occupations. All were attracted by the natural resources of the area. In 1948 the island won its independence with dominion status in the British Commonwealth.

In 1958, serious riots took place between the two religions, when the Singhalese called for official recognition of their language. The next year Prime Minister S. W. R. D. Bandaranaike was assassinated, whereupon his wife took power as the world's first woman Prime Minister. In 1961, the Tamil Federal Party, accused of disorder, was outlawed. Outraged Tamil leaders resorted to terrorism (q.v.) as a means of asserting their rights as a minority people. The government stepped in and arrested Tamil dissidents, some of whom were executed.

In 1972 Ceylon became the Republic of Sri Lanka, with a president, a prime minister, and a national assembly. Many Tamils opposed the new regime and demanded federal status. Ceylon Tamils had been on the island for centuries and had been granted citizenship. But the Tamils from India, who had come to the island for plantation work, were less integrated and preferred to maintain connections with their kin in southern India. Most found it difficult to choose citizenship either in Ceylon or in India. Relations between Sri Lanka and India were exacerbated.

In the north and east, where most Tamils lived, the Liberation Tigers, called Tamil Eelam, the largest rebel group, waged guerrilla warfare against the government. Like the I.R.A. (q.v.), its tactics were violent. Tamil militants ambushed buses, killed its military guards, and slaughtered the Singhalese passengers. The pattern of a dissatisfied nationalism persists.

Bibliography: Evelyn F. C. Ludowyk, *The Modern History of Ceylon* (London, 1966); Richard F. Nyrop, *et al., Tamil Culture in Ceylon* (Washington, D.C., 1971).

TARDE, GABRIEL (1843–1904).   French sociologist, criminologist, and scholar of nationalism. Tarde is regarded as one of the founders of modern social psychology. Influenced by the dialectics of Hegel (q.v.), he turned his attention to associations, crowds, and other aggregates that made up the essence of the nation. He suggested that the idea of nationalism was the product of the modern newspaper, a medium that gave a common consciousness to those who speak the same language by uniting them into a "public." In addition to this influence, the newspaper, unconsciously or unwillingly, spurred the feelings of honor and sacrifice of the masses. It succeeded in arousing the sentiment of national traditions and cherished ideals. Once awakened, nationalism led to revivals in moral life, language, literature, economics, and politics by reinforcing among its supporters solidarity, sacrifice, and struggle.

Bibliography: Gabriel Tarde, *Societal Laws: An Outline of Sociology,* trans. by Howard C. Warren (New York, 1899); Michael Marks Davis, *Gabriel Tarde* (New York, 1906).

TATAR NATIONALISM.   The Tatars are one of the Soviet Union's dissatisfied nationalisms. They demand an autonomous homeland. In 1944 Stalin ordered 250,000 Tatars, then living in the Crimea, deported on the ground that some of them collaborated with the Nazi invading forces. The Tatars claimed that almost half of the deportees died in transit or on arrival in Central Asia. The Tatar population, numbering today about 300,000, has been living in Uzbekistan and the Krasnodar region of the Ukraine. In 1967 the Soviet Government rehabilitated the Tatars and admitted that they had been treated unjustly.

In the current era of *glasnost* (openness) and *perestroika* (restructuring), Tatar protesters organized extraordinary demonstrations in Red Square, Moscow, and demanded that they be allowed to return to their homeland. Mikhail S. Gorbachev, concerned about the Tatar claims, as well as demands made by Armenians, Latvians, Lithuanians, and Estonians, set up a panel to investigate minority complaints. This commission decided that Tatars could return individually to the Crimea, but they would need the same work and residence permits that in practice limited newcomers to the peninsula. In effect, this rejected a homeland for the Tatars. From the Kremlin's point of view, major concessions to mini-nationalisms (q.v.) in the Soviet Union would encourage the many nationalities to rebel and threaten the existence of the Soviet state. Moscow would show respect for minority cultures, but it would make no territorial concessions.

Bibliography: Charles G. Halperin, *The Tatar Yoke* (Columbus, Ohio, 1986).

TERRITORIAL IMPERATIVE.   A recently developed theory that nationalism, stripped to its essentials, is merely the behavior of higher human animals in defending the territory they have staked out for themselves. It is believed that just as many species of lower animals are governed by the instinct of territorial imperative, so have human beings turned to nationalism as their version of the same drive to protect their own territory. The thesis led to confrontation among scientists and scholars of nationalism.

For years the idea of nationalism attracted the attention of historians, political scientists, sociologists, and psychologists, all of whom worked diligently to elucidate a phenomenon suffused with inconsistencies, contradictions, and paradoxes. In recent years, naturalists, biologists, and anthropologists have entered the arena in an attempt to explain the nature of nationalism. One such group combines the naturalist Konrad Lorenz, the biologist Robert Ardrey, and the anthropologist Desmond Morris. The combination has formed what may be called the L.A.M. group. Although there is no formal unity in their work, it has aroused popular attention by a series of challenging publications.

The L.A.M. thesis asserts that man, like the lower animals, is moved instinctively and unconsciously to defend his own living space. Just as lower animals regulate the distances between their members and stand aloof from other species, so are humans motivated by the same instinct. According to this theory, the ownership of land was not a human invention; it always existed among such animals as lions, tigers, wolves, eagles, ring-tailed lemurs, seals, gorillas, and many other species. They set aside specific areas as their private domain, mark it off, and aggressively attack neighbors who would dare challenge their territorial integrity. Humans as well as lower animals incorporate a regard for territory into their general behavior complex. It is claimed that the instinct may be even stronger than the sex drive.

The L.A.M. thesis further holds that man, despite his greater brain capacity, lives and acts according to the same motives that influence the lower animals. It suggests that when human beings form social groups to defend their title to the land or the sovereignty of their country, they are acting no differently from and no less innately from similar motivations in the lower animal world. It follows that the nation-state is merely an invention of man to indicate the territory of the in-group. Thus, nationalism is not a historical phenomenon whose emergence was as artificial as the building of the Panama Canal, but rather the natural expression of an innate psychological drive for security, a pursuit existing in all animals from barnyard rooster to *homo sapiens.*

An early stimulus to the nexus between the territorial imperative and nationalism came with the work of Austrian zoologist Konrad Lorenz, the founder of ethology, the study of comparative animal behavior under natural conditions of life. According to Lorenz, one particular instinct common to both animals and man is aggression.

Human behavior, especially human social behavior, far from being determined by reason and cultural tradition alone, is still subject to all the laws prevailing in phylogenetically adapted instinctive behavior. "Man's social organization is very similar to that of rats, which, like humans, are social and peaceful beings within their class, but veritable devils toward all fellow-members of their species not belonging to the community." It is claimed that human behavior runs parallel to the biological forms among the lower animals. This is true of the mechanism of territorial fighting defense in both man and the lower animals.

To Lorenz's concept of the close similarity in the behavior of man and the lower animals was added the work of Robert Ardrey, a dramatist turned anthropologist. In his major book, *The Territorial Imperative* (1966), Ardrey tried to show that man's aggressiveness is based on his "innate territorial nature." In his view, man has an inborn compulsion to defend his exclusive territory, preserve, or property. This territorial nature is genetic and ineradicable. The territorial expression is but a human response to an imperative acting with similar and equal force on both man and the lower animals. It is no less vital for the existence of contemporary man than it was to the small-brained proto-man millions of years ago. It is, Ardrey holds, an expression of the continuity of human evolution from the environment of early animals to man. Any human group in possession of a social territory will behave in accordance with the universal laws of the territorial principle. Man is a territorial species and he defends his home or his homeland for biological reasons, not because he chooses to but because he must. It follows that patriotism is a biologically innate instinct and not an environmentally produced historical phenomenon. Human xenophobia, according to Ardrey, a main component of several forms of nationalism, is close to universal animal fear of the stranger. (*See* **XENOPHOBIC NATIONALISM**.)

Desmond Morris, the third of the L.A.M. trio, is a British anthropologist who has written prolifically on biology and zoology. In his many books he supported the thesis that man is merely a higher form of animal motivated by similar drives that influence the lower animals. In *The Naked Ape* (1968), Morris analogizes between man and ape and contends that *Homo sapiens* has remained little more than the ape. While he differs in certain essentials from Lorenz and Ardrey, Morris sees the territorial imperative working in both lower and higher animal worlds. He believes that man's social behavior, apparent in such drives as nationalism, remains precisely the same as the motives impelling lower animals.

Far from attaining acceptance among scientists of many disciplines, the idea of territorial imperative fell into the whirlpool of the old heredity-environment clash. Critics accuse the L.A.M. school of oversimplification. They charge that Lorenz, Ardrey, and Morris present ideas that are shallow, ambiguous, distorted, and erroneous. This work, they claim, may be good theater but it is third-rate reporting filled with wild analogies.

Defenders of the L.A.M. school insist that, despite all such criticisms, territorial imperative is, in reality, in accord with the rapidly growing body of experimental social-psychological research. They dismiss such criticisms and call it "the usual academic bellyache." Defenders point to Galileo's difficulties with the religious authorities, and present the argument that Aristotelian "truth" was succeeded by Copernican truth.

The controversy remains unresolved.

Bibliography: Konrad Lorenz, *On Aggression* (New York, 1966); Robert Ardrey, *The Territorial Imperative: A Personal Inquiry into the Animal Origin of Property and Nations* (New York, 1966); Desmond Morris, *The Naked Ape* (New York, 1968); Louis L. Snyder, "Nationalism and the Territorial Imperative." *Canadian Review of Studies in Nationalism,* 3 (Autumn, 1975), 1-21.

TERRORISM.   Terrorism is closely related to nationalism and separatism in their most evil forms. It may be defined as the use of violence to threaten and subjugate others in the interests of a special cause such as a political weapon or policy. It also may be defined as a form of coercive intimidation. Terrorists use bullets, grenades, bombs, and hostage-taking as a way to influence individuals, groups, or nations, especially in the interest of an ethnic group demanding independence. Because terrorists are unpredictable, they spread fear and anxiety among their victims. They accept no ethical or moral limits. Innocent men, women, and children are regarded as expendable in advancing the cause. Terrorists recognize no rules or conventions, no Kantian categorical imperative to limit their excesses. They resort to savagery in a civilized society. They represent a low point in the long struggle of man for decency.

Walter Laqueur, an expert on national political violence, sees terrorism in the last several decades as taking on many different forms. Broadly speaking, he divides terrorism into several different species, dependent on whether we regard state terrorism as a separate category. First of all, there is separatist-nationalist terrorism, as for example in Ulster and the Middle East. Secondly, Latin-American terrorism takes place in a continent that has seen more civil wars, *coups d'état,* and assassinations than anywhere else. Systematic urban terror was an innovation. There are urban terrorists in North America, Western Europe, and Japan, growing out of the New Left. These terrorists assume that methods used in Latin America could be created artificially in the more developed countries. Finally, in various parts of the world there has emerged terrorism of the extreme right, or semi-Fascist in character. These groups, in contrast to those of the left, seldom cooperate with each other, nor, with few exceptions, do they have international sponsors. In all cases, apparently, the *modus operandi* remains much the same—draw attention to the cause by assassinations, bombings at busy airports, and highjacking to win media attention to the special cause.

Another category of four major types of terrorism in recent years was presented by Paul Wilkinson: (1) nationalist, autonomous, or other minority units; (2) ideological sects or secret societies calling for some form of liberation or revolutionary justice; (3) exile groups with separatist, irredentist, or revolutionary aspirations of their country of origin; and (4) transnational gangs using terrorist support from two or more countries in the name of some vague world-revolutionary goal.

Here again, in the Wilkinson set of categories, the close nexus between terrorism and nationalism is revealed. In his category four, the motivation is indistinct and does not seem to have a rational basis, but in the other three categories all are concerned in one way or another with nationalism. Wherever there is a sense of separatism and unwillingness to bow to a centralized authority, there will be either a large or a small segment of the population that will choose terrorism as its standard operating procedure. Even small factions of dissenters, no matter what their credentials, take on importance when they resort to violence.

Almost always, terrorists claim that they are speaking for the majority of their countrymen. There may be, indeed, heavy support for their objectives. Many who are unhappy with their status are unwilling to speak out boldly as do the terrorists. Activists actually do not need a mass-based following or do they require a large amount of funds. Terrorists usually are not concerned with support by a large majority of their countrymen—they are more interested in their own revolutionary zeal. Harried by the police, they may leave their own countries and operate from abroad.

The terrorist syndrome allows no use for the moderate approach of those nationalists who would settle for autonomy (q.v.). They believe that only violence can be effective. In the terrorist view, only extreme measures can put flesh on the skeleton of their ideology. Change, they are convinced, can come only through force and power. They see their ideology as sensible and intelligent. They regard their actions as logical. The more intelligent among them point to the existentialist philosophy of Martin Heidegger and Jean-Paul Sartre, who presented the idea that it is only through our own actions or will that we can escape from despair. This type of thinking had some effect on the ideology of terrorists. Under certain circumstances it could stimulate acts of terrorism.

Terrorists, especially those who work for separatist nationalism, invariably reject the name applied to them. They see themselves as heroic liberators, struggling against exploitation by powerful central- ized nationalisms that stand in the way of their legitimate rights. In their own eyes, they are romantic Robin Hoods fighting for the people in an entrenched society, the nasty establishment, that has denied them their legitimate rights. By their acts of violence they will right the injustices of history. Today, they believe, they may be regarded as dangerous animals, but tomorrow their people will see them as heroes and martyrs. They point to the case of Menachem Begin, who, they say, was once a terrorist, but later became recog- nized as a statesman and hero for the Israeli people.

The terrorist syndrome is especially strong in several areas, where violence has won global attention:

The I.R.A.   Irish nationalism did not end with the establishment of the Irish Free State in 1921. Dissatisfied nationalists resolved to continue the struggle until the six counties in Northern Ireland, or Ulster, were united with the rest of the Free State. The campaign of the Irish Republican Army (q.v.) began in the years preceding World War II with guerrilla actions across the border mostly to raid police stations or to seize army weapons. In the 1950s and the 1960s the struggle changed into outright terrorism. Behind the violence was a religious confrontation: the Catholic population was politically, so- cially, and economically underprivileged. By the late 1960s, peaceful Catholic demonstrations changed into violent confrontations when Protestant counterdemonstrations caused much resentment among Catholics. (*See* **IRISH NATIONALISM.**)

The P.L.O.   The militant Palestine Liberation Organization (q.v.) refused to accept the foundation of the Jewish state of Israel in 1948. From hit-and-run operations against Israel in the 1950s, Palestinian activists turned to violence. In 1964, before the Israeli occupation of the Left Bank, the P.L.O. came into existence. Yassir Arafat (q.v.) and Khalil al-Wasir founded *Al-Fatah*. It later became an important element in the P.L.O. and was its military arm. *Al-Fatah* emerged as the terrorist group operating under the P.L.O. umbrella. It was an implacable enemy of Israel. P.L.O. guerrillas considered it an act of war when they slaughtered Israeli athletes at the Munich Olympic Games in 1972. From then on, the violence increased in geometrical form. Each act of violence was met with equal or greater force by Israel military units. In late 1987, Palestinians on the West Bank started a rock-throwing campaign, which Israeli military units met with bullets. In April 1988, Khalil al-Wasir, the number two man in the P.L.O., was assassinated by an Israeli commando squad operating under the auspices of the Mossad, Israeli's foreign intelligence.

The E.T.A.　　The *Euzkadi ta Azkatasuna* (Basque Homeland and Liberty) was formed in the 1950s as a reaction to the dictatorship of Francisco Franco. With the exception of the I.R.A., the E.T.A. has sustained a terrorist campaign longer than any other major terrorist group in Europe. Although it claims to speak for the whole nation, it has little mass support. It demands an independent Basque state with Basque as its official language. Though its leaders differ on objectives, most E.T.A. chieftains call for a Third World, populist, and part Marxist-Leninist nation. Between 1968 and 1975, E.T.A. militants were responsible for some thirty-four assassinations. (*See* **BASQUE NATIONALISM.**)

The Armenians.　　Armenian terrorism emerged full force in the 1970s. It was a reaction to the Armenian massacre by Turks in the eastern provinces of Turkey during World War I. The fact that most Turks refused to accept the reality of the horrible measures led to such resentment among contemporary Armenians that many of them resorted to violence. Armenian terrorists were behind indiscriminate bombings at airports and assassinations. (*See* **ARMENIAN NATIONALISM.**)

In the late 1980s the character of terrorism throughout the world began to change significantly—from organized acts of individual fanaticism to skillful tactics of violence. There was greater sophistication in planning and technology. Political rationale for violence was enhanced. Unable to mount conventional warfare against real or presumed enemies, terrorists adopted new methods of procedure. To win the release of comrades jailed for acts of violence, they began to highjack planes filled with innocent passengers. Terrorist teams took along pilots able to fly a highjacked plane. They underwent briefings to meet the medical and psychological needs of their hostages. Always they made sure to win media attention to their cause. Above all, the procedure was designed to frustrate and keep normal society off balance. Authorities of attacked states were forced to use their intelligence agencies as well as new crisis management techniques to meet the assaults of separatist fanatics.

Bibliography: E. V. Walter, "Violence and the Process of Terror," *American Sociological Review,* 29, No. 2 (Spring, 1944), 245–257; B. J. Bell, *Transnational Terror* (Washington, D.C., 1975); Lester Sobel, *Political Terrorism* (New York, 1975); Desmond McForan, *The World Held Hostage: The War Waged by International Terrorism* (Wembley, 1986) Noam Chomsky, *Pirates and Emperors: International Terrorism in the Real World* (New York, 1986); Anar Kurz, *Contemporary Trends in World Terrorism* (New York, 1987); Walter Laqueur, *The Age of Terrorism* (Boston, 1987).

THIRD-WORLD NATIONALISM. Nationalism is important not only on the European scene but also throughout the Third World. In its earlier days in Europe it was a force for emancipation, a drive to organize peoples of similar language and characteristics in a given territory. Nationalism today has taken on a new meaning since the days of World War II. It becomes a problem of heterogeneity. In the Third World, it has politically and ideologically taken on a similar meaning as in Western Europe, where the rebellion of regions against the central power has certain national qualities. It is, however, still nationalism.

This does not mean that nationalism is in retreat on the European continent. Far from easing in Europe, nationalism has retained its hold on most European countries and seems to be as strong as ever. One needs only to regard the grand European dream of the Common Market. The idea was attractive—more than 300 million producers and consumers would unite economically in a European Economic Community as a prelude to the political unification of the European states. This would be followed by a European parliament. Yet, there is much to say for the contrary. Current regimes were all voted into power by *national,* not European, electorates. Most contemporary European states stress national security. They continue to place enormous emphasis upon their sacrosanct independence and upon their status as impregnable bastions of national sovereignty. There is little diminution of nationalism in Europe, where it began and where it still retains a solid hold.

In the Third World, suddenly emanicipated smaller states have been influenced powerfully by the necessity of expressing their own special awareness of nationalism. All turn to their own history and see traditions that set them apart from other peoples. They present their own flag (*see* **FLAGS, NATIONAL; ANTHEMS, NATIONAL**), national army, and national character (q.v.). They speak to the world as a sovereign force. They are guided by what is called the territorial imperative (q.v.). "This is our land and we will defend it to the death!" They see their development as natural and will brook no interference.

The emergence of nationalism among the Third World states has engaged the attention of scholars everywhere. In West Germany, however, it has received special interest. Hans F. Illy comments on the "one-dimensional imitation" of nation and state in Africa. Theodor Hanf treats secular Arab nationalism and Islamic political revivalism in the Near East. Dietmar Rothenbund analyzes questions of national integration in South Asia. These and other German scholars, especially Heinrich Winkler, see heterogeneity (*"Ungleichlichkeit"*) in the world today. There is much to say for the general idea that in the Third World, contemporary nationalism is what it was in the earlier days in Europe—that is, a force for self-determination (q.v.).

Bibliography: Heinrich Winkler, *Nationalismus in der Welt von Heute* (Göttingen, 1982); Bruno Kriesky and Humayun Gaukar, *Decolonization and After: The Future of the Third World* (London, 1987); Peter Bowden, *National Monitoring and Evaluation: Development Programs in the Third World* (Brookfield, Vt., 1988); Charles F. Andrain, *Political Change in the Third World* (Boston, 1988).

TIBETAN NATIONALISM.   A unique Central Asian Buddhist culture, Tibet has a long history of some 1,500 years. Its people are of Mongoloid origin and their religion is Lamaism, derived from Buddhism. Its capital is Lahasa, where the Dalai Lama ("Ocean Priest" or "Sea of Wisdom") resided. A land of mystery, Tibet was almost inaccessible and the exclusiveness of its inhabitants worked as a spur to explorers. In the early nineteenth century the Chinese invaded the country and placed the Dalai Lama under their control. Following the Republican Revolution of 1911, Tibet, with British assistance, declared its independence. In 1951 the People's Republic of China reconquered Tibet. A treaty was signed which cut the authority of the Dalai Lama. The Tibetans were granted the right of regional autonomy within China. A rebellion in 1959 by Tibetan nationalists led Communist China to integrate Tibet more strongly into China.

Tibetan resistance to Chinese control hinges on the person of the current Dalai Lama, Tibet's political and spiritual leader who fled the country some twenty-eight years ago. Singled out at the age of two by Tibetan monks following religious omens, he was anointed at the age of four after passing a series of obscure tests. He now lives in a hill town in northern India, surrounded by 7,000 refugees from Tibet. To his Eastern ideology of mysticism, the Dalai Lama has added the ideas of Western politics in order to win the independence of his country. He denies the right of China to exercise historical control over his people. As leader of the Tibetans, he insists that Tibet is not a part of China. His country, he charges, is occupied by force. His people do not want to live under Chinese power. At the same time, Tibet's holy man warns against violence as absolutely wrong. "Not only is it morally wrong, but practically it is almost suicidal. I tell Tibetans that first we are Buddhists and that non-violence is the only way."

Chinese response to Tibetan claims has been harsh and oppressive. Chinese occupation policy partitioned the country, transferred millions of Chinese into Tibet, moved Tibetans from their country, and burned hundreds of their monasteries. Asia Watch, a human rights monitoring group, reported that there has been abuse of every human right in Tibet and that torture is routine in prisons housing Tibetans. Again, it is the familiar story of a powerful centralized nationalism holding in subjugation a people who never in their history had ceded sovereignty to any other country.

Bibliography: Hugh Edward Richardson, *A Short History of Tibet* (Boulder, Colo., 1984); M. C. Van Praag, *The Status of Tibet* (Boulder, Colo., 1987).

TIECK, LUDWIG (1773–1853). Prolific German writer of the early Romantic movement and forerunner of German nationalism. Like his Romantic colleagues, Tieck appealed to the emotions rather than to the intellect. A close friend of the Schlegal brothers (*see* **SCHLEGEL, FRIEDRICH VON**), he parodied the rationalism of the Western Englishmen, and called for emphasis upon mysticism and the imagination. He urged his countrymen to appreciate a glorious history to emphasize their own consciousness of nationalism. He saw the plays of Shakespeare as the model for any dramatist who wished to revive the national past. Working with August Wilhelm von Schlegel, he published the great German translations of Shakespeare's plays. Tieck takes his place among the Romantics who set the tone for the development of German nationalism.

Bibliography: Klaus Gunzel (ed.), *König der Romantik: Das Leben des Dichters Ludwig Tieck in Briefen, Selbstzeugnissen und Berichten* (Tübingen, 1981); Roger Paulin, *Ludwig Tieck, A Literary Biography* (New York, 1985).

TONE, THEOBALD WOLFE (1763–1798).   Early Irish patriot, revolutionary, and nationalist. Educated at Trinity College in Dublin, Tone was called to the Irish bar in 1789, but his dislike for the practice of law turned him to politics instead. Inspired by the example of the French Revolution, with its Liberty, Equality, and Fraternity, he helped in 1791 in the foundation of the United Irish Society, which worked to unite Catholics and Protestants in the cause of opposition to English oppression in Ireland. In 1794 Tone and his United Irish colleagues, all determined to win French assistance in the struggle to overcome English rule, saw his first efforts fail. He came to the United States in 1795 to promote his cause. The next year he went to Paris, where he persuaded the Directory to organize a French invasion of Ireland. Favorably received, Tone was made an adjutant in the French army.

On December 15, 1796, Tone sailed from Brest with some forty-three ships and 14,000 men on a campaign to wrest Ireland from the English. The crews of the ships were inefficient. The flotilla, encountering bad weather, was dispersed off the coast of Ireland. Tone tried again in October, 1797, but was unable to convince Napoleon Bonaparte, the French military leader at the time, that the project was feasible. Tone was reduced in 1798 to leading small expeditions. In September he was captured along with several thousand followers. At his trial he spoke eloquently about his defiance of England and said that he was determined to wage fair and open warfare against the English in order to win Irish independence. The court-martial convicted him of treason, but on the day he was to be hanged, he committed suicide in his prison cell.

Tone's work in the revolutionary uprisings against English control was regarded by his people as high on the level of Irish calls for independence. He set a standard that was followed by Robert Emmet and Michael Collins (qq.v.) in the struggle for Irish emancipation. (*See also* **IRISH NATIONALISM.**)

Bibliography: Frank MacDermot, *Theobald Wolfe Tone: A Biographical Study* (London, 1939).

TRADITIONAL NATIONALISM.   *See* **HAYES' CLASSIFICATION.**

TRANSNATIONALISM.   A multinational network of business and industrial enterprises that operate above and below visible national controls. Those who challenge the present convention of distinct territorial units now speak of nationalism as outdated. Governments everywhere, they say, are losing their influence over the transnational flow of peoples, money, and ideas. In their view, the national state is being succeeded slowly but surely by huge corporations, which have become quasi-governmental in a union brought closer and closer together. These corporations are said to allocate revenues and privileges across the old national boundaries. Nationalism, they are certain, is being undermined by this new transnationalism.

According to those who hold to the new theory of transnationalism, such conglomerate multinational enterprises as I.B.M., Xerox, Coca Cola, and Unilever no longer operate on a national scale but, instead, have spread their operations throughout the world. Many such corporations have assets larger than most members of the United Nations. The gross national product (G.N.P.) of one giant corporation in one of the larger Western nations already exceeds that of most new African nations. Transnational entrepreneurs control corporations in many larger states. A powerful, largely private oligarchy may deal only with agencies of other governments. They may even frustrate the national policies of the home government or a host government for a corporation subsidiary. Transnational corporations have the benefit of the contemporary computer world with its high-speed communication and transportation services, as well as the instantaneous transfer of money from one country to another. Some observers believe that in this way the old nationalism is being overcome and pushed into the background.

Transnational advocates believe that all the major Great Powers are currently subjected to the strength of international conglomerates transcending the national image. They envision a society in which a few hundred interlocking giant corporations will control a major part of the world's production. Large banks and advertising agencies, they say, have already been lured into the new development. Labor unions must take into consideration the problem of bargaining with multinational enterprises. In the long run, transnationalism poses a threat to the older idea of national sovereignty. Its defenders say that the transformation process is already under way and cannot be stopped. Expressed in another way, transnationalism means the end of nationalism as we know it today.

There are, however, other scholars who are not inclined to accept the idea of transnationalism as powerful enough to end contemporary nationalism. They grant that there is a growing awareness of transnationalism. However, they say, its power remains in the field of economics. Members of the European Common Market accept the benefits of an economic Common Market, but invariably freeze at the mere prospect of political union. Political power remains substantially under the grasp of national states, not corporations. The chief factor is that international corporations remain subservient to the national state.

The realistic conclusion is that while transnational corporations may act for their own benefit, they still remain subservient to national interests. There is no transnational army to defend the interests of transnational corporations. There may be, indeed, a new interdependence based on expanding economic interests in the contemporary world, but it would be unwise to exaggerate its importance. Business may become internationalized, but not the political order. Transnationalism still operates along with the existence of the national state, but certainly, it has not displaced nationalism itself on the contemporary scene.

Bibliography: Lewis Mumford, *The Transformation of Man* (New York, 1956); Karl W. Deutsch, *Nationalism and Its Alternatives* (New York, 1969); Norman Girvan, *Corporate Imperialism: Conflict and Expropriation* (New York, 1978); Krishna Kumar (ed.), *Transnational Enterprises* (Boulder, Colo., 1988).

TREITSCHKE, HEINRICH VON (1834–1896).   Most influential of the Prussian School of professor-patriots who attempted to work politically through history *("durch die Geschichte politisch zu wirken").* Born at Dresden, the capital of Saxony, on September 15, 1834. Treitschke was descended from a line of Czechs, who, being oppressed in the Thirty Years War, emigrated to Saxony. As a precocious schoolboy, he recognized the struggle between liberalism and nationalism, and, while originally concerned with liberty, he thrust it aside in favor of a burning zeal for national unity. His fiery championship of Prussian claims was strengthened at the University of Bonn, where he, as a student in 1851, sat at the feet of the venerable, eighty-two-year-old patriot Ernst Moritz Arndt (q.v.).

When only twenty-five, Treitschke was appointed to the faculty of the University of Leipzig, where he established a reputation as a brilliant lecturer. Students flocked to hear the young Saxon. His message was simple: the Germans must reject eighteenth-century liberalism in favor of nineteenth-century nationalism. This was the German mission. The essence of the State, he said, is power, moral power, to be sure, but an authority that makes every individual subject to it. Liberty is a fine thing, but for the Germans only liberty *within* the State (not *from* or *against* the State) is permissible.

Treitschke became a devoted follower of Otto von Bismarck (q.v.). Like many other Germans, he believed that Bismarck and Prussia were the answer to Germany's need for national unification. He worked unceasingly to support the Prussian Junker in his struggle to unite the German people.

After teaching at Heidelberg University, Treitschke went to the University of Berlin in 1874. Here, as the prophet of Germany's power and mission, he became a popular national figure. On the lecture podium he lashed out against parliamentarianism, socialism, pacifism, the English, French, and Jews. Prussian monarchists, Berlin society, and starry-eyed students, electrified by his emotional lectures, flocked to hear the tall, powerfully-built professor as he denounced his enemies. Because of his deafness, Treitschke often rambled on in a high-pitched voice, gesticulating nervously, and presenting his ideas in a jerky manner. Now and then he would stop to catch his breath. To his audience this was the young Siegfried in action, breathing fire and brimstone, and rallying Germans to the flag.

German nationalism received a powerful impetus in Treitschke's lecture rooms. Although of Slavic origin, he insisted that every fiber of his being was German. "I am a thousand times more of a patriot than a professor." Germans were impressed by his glorification of Prussia, the embodiment of might, "this weapon-proud eagle land of the North." They delighted in his admonition that there was something admirable in Prussian depth of thought, idealism, and transcendent philosophy. They were pleased when he insisted that simple German loyalty contrasted remarkably with "the unchivalrous quality of the English character." They agreed with his warning that thousands of the best German manhood had turned their backs on the Fatherland and had emigrated to America. "They are lost to Germany forever."

At the core of Treitschke's teaching was the necessity for a strong State. The ultimate object of the State, he said, is always the development of a nation distinguished by its national character. The most important possession of the State, its be-all and end-all, is power. "He who is not man enough to look the truth in the face should not meddle in politics. It is the highest duty of the State to increase its power."

These views were expressed by Treitschke with clarity and with little room for misunderstanding. When World War I began, British propagandists delighted in simply publishing his works in hundreds of thousands of copies. They included Treitschke, along with Nietzsche and Bernhardi (q.v.), as one of a trio of "war-inspirers," who had prepared the Germans for a war of conquest. He was, they said, a champion of absolutism who heated the fires of chauvinism (q.v.). Hans Kohn judged the nature of Treitschke's work in these words:

> Treitschke was indisputably one of the master builders of the triumphant national edifice which seemed to stand in rocklike strength, able to weather all storms of the future. By his pen and his words he had prepared his generation for Bismarck's deed, he had anchored it to the course of preceding history and charted its road into a glorious future. He had aroused the enthusiam and deepened the faith of countless young Germans who in their turn became educators of youth and administrators of the Empire.

Bibliography: Heinrich von Treitschke, *Politics,* ed. by Max Cornelius, trans. by Blanche Dugdale and Yorben de Bille (2 vols., London, 1916); Hans Kohn, *Prophets and Peoples* (New York, 1946); Andreas Dorpalen, *Heinrich von Treitschke* (New Haven, Conn., 1957); Heinrich von Treitschke, *History of Germany in the Nineteenth Century,* trans. by Eden and Cedar Paul (New York, 1968).

TREVELYAN, GEORGE MACAULAY (1876–1962).   English historian, Regius Professor of Modern History at Cambridge University, Master at Trinity College, and critic of the wrong kind of nationalism. His books are noted for their combination of scholarship and readability. Liberal in training and personality, he showed a deep love for England, especially in his book *Must England's Beauty Perish?* (1929). More patriot than nationalist, he warned of the dangers of nationality:

> The sentiment of nationality, that most simple of ideals which appeals to the largest quantity of brute force, has in its nature no political affinity either with liberty on the one hand or with tyranny on the other; it can be turned by some chance current of events, or by cunning or clumsiness of statesmen, to run in any channel and to work any wheel.

Bibliography: George Macaulay Trevelyan, *British History in the Nineteenth Century* (London, 1922).

TRIBALISM.   Tribalism is generally defined as any group of persons, families, or clans, primitive or contemporary, descended from a common ancestor, possessing a common leadership, and forming together with their slaves or adopted strangers, a community. Members of the tribe speak a common language, observe uniform rules of social organization, and work together for such purposes as agriculture, trade, or warfare. They ordinarily have their own name and occupy a contiguous territory. Tribalism does not ordinarily apply to formations of large territorial units, or states, but denotes, instead, units composed of extended kinship groups.

Already a close similarity will be noted between tribalism and nationalism. Indeed, nationalism in its original form is sometimes considered to be an extension of the older tribalism. Carlton J.H. Hayes (q.v.) described tribalism, as it was in primitive times, as a small-scale and intensive kind of nationalism. He noted such important tribal characteristics as speech, a distinctive language, or dialect. Above all, tribalism was accompanied by a distinct, localized religion. It was prevalent throughout countless centuries and milleniums of prehistory, during the greater part of mankind's existence on earth.

According to Hayes, for fairly long periods, and in greater or lesser degree, man has broken out of narrow tribal confines and transformed tribalism into broader loyalties. With advancing and spreading civilization, tribalism—in the sense of primitive nationalism—tended in various parts of the world to be pushed into the background. What submerged that early nationalism, and long kept it submerged, was a combination of four factors: (1) conquest of various tribes by a military leader who forced them into a military, political, and economic union (ancient empires from the Egyptian to the Roman); (2) the growth and spread of a religion from some particular tribe or nationality to others (Christianity and Islam, the "world religions"); (3) linguistic and literary factors militated against nationalism and in favor of a kind of cosmopolitan patriotism, a sense of belonging to cultural societies; and (4) continuing national consciousness was by no means blotted out by military empires, world religions, or supranational languages and literature. It was submerged but not destroyed.

Thus, the concept of primitive nationalism, or tribalism, was long submerged and was revived in the eighteenth century to become one of the most powerful forces in history.

At the same time, the analogy between tribalism and nationalism should not be exaggerated. There are major distinctions between the two. British scholar Elie Kedourie (q.v.) does not feel that they are interchangeable terms, nor do they describe related phenomena:

> A tribesman's relation to his tribe is usually regulated in minute detail by custom which is followed unquestionably and considered part of the natural or the divine order. Tribal custom is neither a decree of the General Will, nor an edict of legislative Reason. The tribesman is such by virtue of his birth, not by virtue of self-determination. He is usually unaware that the destiny of man is progressive, and that he can fulfill this destiny by merging his will into the will of the tribe.

Kedourie sees self-determination (q.v.) at the core of nationalism, while tribalism places the greater accent on birth.

Whether or not nationalism and tribalism are related phenomena, the fact remains that both have persisted into the contemporary era. The case of Africa is central to the relationship between the new nationalism on the continent and the enduring continuance of the older tribalism. On the one hand, African natives were willing to accept the benefits of modernization in the Western sense; on the other hand, they were faced with the problem of their old tribal loyalty, their ancient gods, and their traditional family customs.

The conquest and exploration of Africa proceeded relentlessly in the late nineteenth century. The major European powers, assuring the world that their only mission was to "Christianize and civilize" the Africans, rushed on to acquire the resources of the rich continent. Too weak to protest, the Africans exchanged their lands and their freedom for work, taxes, and exploitation. The invading powers proceeded to partition the continent and set up new "national" states without regard for tribal allegiances.

Africans knew exactly what was happening. Resenting both paternalism and exploitation, they would later turn the tools of their own nationalism on their occupiers. They were interested in Western technology and administrative techniques, but they were not about to reject their old traditions of tribalism. The new sub-Saharan nationalism differed from the European variety. The traditional tribalism was succeeded in part by a sentiment more closely related to racialism than to nationalism. After loyalty to the tribe, the next higher loyalty was not to the new artificially created national states, but to race—to the black man as opposed to the white man. And preference for the tribe as opposed to the new nation began to assume more and more importance.

Black nationalism in Africa was beset by new problems. Africans had won liberation from European control, but not necessarily from European civilization. Almost overnight, Africans for the most part untrained for democracy, were called upon to vote, form political parties, and decide issues of national policies. Clerks became presidents, lived in palatial quarters, and rode in luxurious limousines. There was much political incompetence, much corruption in high places as the occupiers' assets and jobs were Africanized. Africans, who had believed that liberation would be followed by economic well-being, were grievously disappointed. The few European experts left behind found themselves unable to work without adequate assistance. The result—political and economic chaos. In the dilemma many Africans turned to their old tribalism.

African tribalism turned out to be a serious obstacle to national unity of the artificially created states. The core of tribalism put manners above principle, family above self, race above humanity. More important to such Africans was the old religion based on fear of the supernatural. They turned on their one-time protector and reverted to the earlier tribalism. They were motivated by a sense of resentment against those who would change their traditional beliefs. Whether they accepted the mystical formulas of tribalism or turned to the flag of nationalism, they still held the white man in contempt. Many refused to accept the artificial boundary lines set up by their nationalist leaders.

Tribal warfare in former African colonies has resulted in the deaths of many thousands as well as escapes from one territory to another. Typical of such clashes was that in the central African nation of Burundi, formerly a Belgian colony. The fighting was between the Hutu, the short and stocky majority tribe, and the Tutsi, the tall minority tribe that controlled the military and ruled the country. In 1972 the Tutsi were reported as having massacred 150,000 Hutus. The confrontation flared up again in the latter part of August 1988, when the Burundi Government said that at least 5,000 had been killed when fighting began. Members of the majority Hutu tribe attacked the Tutsi. Thousands fled into Rwanda to escape the killing.

Yet, in the ongoing conflict in Africa between nationalism and tribalism, the process of nationalism still goes on. In some cases tribalism is being eroded by increasing mobility and urbanization, by more inter-tribal contacts, and by education. Peoples of different cultural backgrounds were united in their opposition to colonial rule and developed strong bonds. The new national anthems and flags, the symbols and functions of sovereignty, give testimony to the inroads of nationalism even among peoples attracted by the old tribalism. (*See also* **AFRICAN NATIONALISM.**)

Bibliography: Carlton J.H. Hayes, *Nationalism: A Religion* (New York, 1960); Elie Kedourie, *Nationalism* (New York, 1960); William R. Bascom, "Tribalism, Nationalism, and Pan-Africanism," *Annals of the American Academy of Political and Social Science*, 342, (July, 1962), 21–29; Robert D. Hodgson and Elvyn A. Stineman, *The Changing Map of Africa* (Princeton, N.J., 1963); Thomas Patrick Melody, "The Sweep of Nationalism in Africa," *Annals of the American Academy of Political and Social Science*, 354, (July, 1964), 94 ff.; June Helm (ed.), *Essays on the Problem of Tribes* (Seattle, 1968); J. Berton Webster, "Tribalism, Nationalism and Patriotism," in Harvey Dyck and Peter H. Krosby (eds.), *Empire and Nations* (Toronto, 1969); Harold Robert Isaacs, *Power and Identity: Tribalism in World Politics* (New York, 1979); Leroy Vail (ed.), *The Creation of Tribalism in Southern Africa* (Berkeley, 1988).

TRUDEAU, PIERRE ELLIOTT (1919–   ).   Canadian Prime Minister (1968–1979) and strong opponent of Quebec separatism. The son of an oil and land investor, Trudeau took a degree at the University of Montreal and studied at Harvard University and in Paris and London. Returning to Montreal, he worked as a labor lawyer and economist and later turned to politics. Fluently bilingual, he was known as a philosopher-statesman and eventually became Prime Minister.

Even though he was a French Canadian, Trudeau was convinced that the best hope for national survival lay inside the federal system of Canada. The people of Quebec, he said, should be masters in their own house, but it was important that the house be the whole of Canada. They must be assured of equality inside the Canadian Confederation. He warned that an independent Quebec would be disastrous not only for Quebec but for the whole of Canada:

> It is a hypothesis I cannot contemplate because we would be renouncing our heritage. So for me it is unthinkable. It would be a major setback in the course of history. And the burden would be with those who would like to break up one of history's greatest achievements—the Canadian Confederation.

In Trudeau's view, sovereignty for diverse Canadian peoples would be destructive for all. He pointed to the Swiss cantonal system, with its French-, German-, and Italian-speaking autonomous cantons and the use of three official languages as a model for the people of Canada.

In his post as Prime Minister, Trudeau saw himself as the federal standard-bearer, but simultaneously he made sure to expand the role of the people of Quebec and their language in the Canadian system. He warned again and again of the dangers of independence and spoke of the advantages of confederation. Canada, he said, was already one of the most decentralized countries in the world. Trudeau's views had an important effect later when on May 20, 1980, the citizens of Quebec voted "No" on a referendum and rejected the move to sovereignty. (*See also* **QUEBEC NATIONALISM.**)

Bibliography: G. Radwanski, *Trudeau* (Toronto, 1978); Jane Jacobs, *Quebec and the Question over Sovereignty: The Quebec of Separatism* (New York, 1980).

U

UKRAINIAN NATIONALISM.   One of the many peoples of the
Soviet Union who asked to be a separate nation, the Ukrainians
believed themselves to be a distinct nation. In the southwest of
European Russia, the Ukraine, the third largest region in Europe,
spreads over 233,100 square miles. One of the Soviet Union's constituent republics and one of the four founding republics, the Ukraine
takes an important place in the Russian economy. It is the Soviet
Union's life-giving soil belt and main wheat-producing area.

The history of the Ukraine is a story of a long, unending search
for independence. One invader after another, including Goths, Huns,
and Avars, moved into the Ukrainian steppes early in the Christian
era. Russians from the north penetrated into the Ukraine and by the
early nineteenth century took control of the area. From its beginning
the Ukrainians were dissatisfied with Russian power. Their agitation
for freedom from Russia was continuous from then on. Opposition
was supported by a secret political organization called the Brotherhood of Cyril and Methodius, founded at Kiev and the new spearhead of Ukrainian nationalism. It called for a federation of Slavic
states, including Ukrainia, which would be free of Russian domination. The movement for Ukrainian separatism was led by the poet
Taras Grigoryvich Shevchenko (q.v.), who won the accolade of "the
Ukrainian Pushkin."

At first, Ukrainian national consciousness was confined mostly to
the intellectuals, but it soon gathered momentum among the masses.
There were increasing calls for independence throughout the late

nineteenth century. At the opening of the twentieth century, both the educated élite and the workers saw the best prospects for their future in a revolutionary situation. After the Bolshevik Revolution of October 1917, the *Rada,* the Ukrainian Council, proclaimed independence on January 22, 1918. Lenin, who earlier in his career had preached the desirability of recognizing the rights of national minorities, now changed his mind. He would allow no separate identity for the Ukraine. After a complicated struggle, Ukrainian independence was vetoed and the territory was absorbed into the new Soviet state.

Not even Stalinist terror was able to stifle Ukrainian nationalism. From 1936 to 1938 Stalin purged all the nationalities, including the Ukraine, and denounced them as "bourgeois nationalist deviationists." He sent Nikita Khrushchev to the Ukraine with the special task of eliminating its national leadership. When Nazi Germany invaded the Soviet Union on June 22, 1941, Hitler's forces moved into the Ukraine. Initially, the Germans were regarded as liberators, and thousands of Ukrainians, dissatisfied with Soviet rule, turned to them. But Hitler then made a critical mistake. In a basic blunder, he regarded Ukrainians as if they were Slavic beasts. Faced with a choice between two dictators, and certain that Hitler meant to enslave them, the Ukrainians returned reluctantly to the Soviet Union. Stalin welcomed them back to the defense of Mother Russia in the Great Patriotic War. By 1944 the Ukrainians were again under the rule of the Kremlin.

There was no end to Ukrainian separatism. The movement for independence from Moscow persisted and it was strongly promoted. In the 1960s a new generation of Ukrainian intellectuals renewed agitation for independence. Reviving the poetry of Shevchenko, they denounced the Kremlin's polycentrism as infringing on their rights. Behind their demands were centuries of thralldom:

1. The Ukraine was deprived illegally of its sovereignty and its people were denied the right of entering into political and economic relations with other states.
2. Ukrainian political and economic rights were harshly limited.
3. The Ukrainian language was banned in government agencies, scholarly institutions, lower schools, industry, and in the social and cultural life of the nation.
4. The Ukraine was being stifled economically by the removal of two-thirds of its natural resources to beyond its frontiers.
5. "Great Power Russian chauvinism" weighs heavily over the entire Ukrainian people.

For Soviet authorities this was bare treason and it could not be tolerated. For them, at stake was the dissolution of the Soviet Union if the more than 100 nationalities followed the demands of Ukrainian nationalists. In major arrests from 1961 to 1965, they took into custody hundreds of separatists, tried them in secret for disseminating anti-Soviet propaganda and agitation, and sent them to labor camps. Accounts of inhuman practices by Soviet secret police aroused the anger of Ukrainians who had emigrated to the West. The exiled poet, Alexandr Solzhenitsyn, sent a letter in 1967 to the Fourth Congress of Soviet writers, in which he condemned the oppression of Ukrainians. In his major work, *Gulag Archipelago* (1976), he denounced "the principles concerning our relations with the Ukraine." The Kremlin continued to suppress what it called "this ugly strain of nationalism."

The confrontation between centralized Moscow and separatist Ukrainians has continued with ill will on both sides. There is little ground for conciliation. Ukrainian nationalists insisted on their rights guaranteed by the Soviet Constitution and by the 1975 Declaration of Human Rights signed by the Soviet Union. The Kremlin replied with even more suppression of "unacceptable deviationism."

Bibliography: William Henry Chamberlin, *The Ukraine: A Submerged Nation* (New York, 1944); Alexander J. Hotyl, *The Turn to the Right: The Ideological Origin and Development of Ukrainian Nationalism, 1917–1929* (New York, 1980); Kenneth C. Farmer, *Ukrainian Nationalism in the Post-Stalin Era* (Boston, 1980); Jurij Borys, *The Sovietization of Ukraine, 1921–1923: The Communist Doctrine and Practice of National Self-Determination* (Edmonton, Canada, 1980); Bohdan Kravchenko, *Soviet Change and National Consciousness in Twentieth-Century Ukraine* (New York, 1985).

ULTRANATIONALISM.   *See* CHAUVINISM, and JINGOISM.

U.N.I.A. (UNIVERSAL NEGRO IMPROVEMENT ASSOCIATION).   Organization founded by Marcus Garvey (q.v.).

U.N.I.T.A. (NATIONAL UNION FOR THE TOTAL INDEPENDENCE OF ANGOLA).   An organization of 60,000 home-grown rebels formed to fight against Communist influence in Angola. Following the retreat of Western Europeans from the African scene, the Soviet Union began to support what it called liberation movements in Africa. Typical was the case of Angola in southwestern Africa. Stretching for a thousand miles along the Atlantic coast, twice the size of Texas, Angola was rich in natural resources. It won its independence in 1975.

After Angola received its freedom from Portugal, civil war began for control of the territory. The country was devastated. More than 200,000 Angolans were killed, tens of thousands wounded, and there were billions of dollars in war damages. The underlying dispute was a tribal conflict (*See* **TRIBALISM**). The Marxist government was controlled by 310,000 fighters loyal to President José Eduardo dos Santos, who received massive support from the Soviet Union, Cuba, and East Germany. The U.N.I.T.A., the tenacious guerrilla movement led by Jonas Savimbi, was supported by South African and United States military aid. Savimbi's units moved freely in sixteen of Angola's nineteen provinces and launched deadly assaults on government troops.

In the fall of 1988, negotiators from Cuba, Angola, and South Africa met to work out an accord to send home Cuba's 50,000 troops. Dos Santos and Savimbi, the main antagonists in the 14-year-old civil war, made an agreement to end the conflict. Dos Santos offered amnesty to U.N.I.T.A.'s 75,000 guerrilla fighters, while Savimbi continued to call for a multiparty state and free elections.

U.P.A. (UKRAINIAN INSURGENT ARMY). Guerrillas operating from the Carpathian Mountains in a large-scale campaign for Ukrainian independence from Moscow. (*See* **UKRAINIAN NATIONALISM.**)

W

WAGNER, RICHARD (1813–1883).   German composer, musical dramatist, and essayist, who created a new art form in music and who became a champion of extreme nationalism. Born at Leipzig on May 23, 1813, the young Wagner studied at the Kreuzschule in Dresden and the Nicholaischule in Leipzig. Teaching himself the piano and composition, he wrote a verse tragedy at fifteen. After three difficult years in Paris (1839–1842), he returned home and emerged as a composer of operas. Involved in the German Revolution of 1848, he was forced into exile in 1849. In 1852 he began his great tetralogy, *Der Ring des Nibelungen (The Ring of the Nibelung)*, which he completed in 1872. As a composer, Wagner is regarded as a great and distinguished artist. By force of his will and against formidable opposition, he launched his new type of opera, the music-drama, as the final art form, to which music, poetry, and even painting were to be subservient. The later history of music owed much to Wagner, either in conformance with his discoveries or in reaction against them. Cantankerous, belligerent, he allowed his personal life to become mired in scandal and continual confrontations.

As essayist and political activist, Wagner played an important role in the development of German nationalism. More than half a century had passed since the appearance of the German Romantic school, with its emphasis on anti-rationalism, its scorn of French culture, its anti-individualism, and its pro-mystical credo. Wagner revived these ideas and set his own neo-Romanticism in the framework of a mechano-materialistic world. He added to it blind worship of the state as well as a nonsensical doctrine of race. With Wagner a strong accent on the Germanic Folk-Spirit "as the true test of freedom" reached the proportions of a mania. The Jews were un-German, the press was un-German, democracy was un-German. "What is the German thing?" Wagner asked. He replied: "This must be the right thing."

Wagner was not content to wander in the limited regions of musical production. He saw music as only one great phase of the overall picture of civilization, including the whole range of German culture. Music was for him an instrument for molding the philosophy of the German nation. It was a means to exalt nationalism and to glorify German Spirit.

This important genius of German music was burdened by an astonishing polarity of character. He was at times quarrelsome, sensitive, or moody. He set one standard for others and another for himself. He was shamelessly egotistical. He informed British journalist Frank Harris: "You may yet hear it said that in orchestral harmonies the step from Bach to Beethoven is hardly longer than the step from Beethoven to Wagner." He squabbled with those close to him, argued with his supposed enemies, ran away with the wife of his best friend, and was, in general, a mass of contradictions. His sense of frustration took the form of complaining demands upon his friends and repeated threats of suicide. His deliberate rudeness and toughness may well have been a psychological compulsive hiding of personal weaknesses.

There was, indeed, more to Wagner than his music. His collected works in German fill many volumes, including such diverse materials as political speeches, sketches for dramas, rough chapters of a projected biography, aesthetic musical treatises, and especially vitriolic polemics against his enemies or supposed enemies. The significance of his writing was never as important as his contributions to music, but it played an important role in the intensification of integral German nationalism. His prose work was cluttered with ponderous phrases and a complicated, artificial vocabulary. It abounded in polemics, superlatives, and vague generalities.

Wagner attempted to solve with one mighty sweep of his baton all the heterogeneous ills of Western civilization. His was "the true German view of the world that should be valid for all humanity." Supremely confident of his learning and omniscience, he presented his kaleidoscopic views on theories of art, philosophy, and religion, and constructed a moral system based on such factors as the tragic tyranny of poverty, the unsatisfactory nutritive regime of civilized peoples and their rescue through vegetarianism, the vices of institutional religion, the regimentation of man through art, the degeneration of the Western races through evil influences, and the triumph of Western civilization through German virtue.

Three treatises written by Wagner presented his views on the national idea and the national Spirit: *Judaism in Music* (1850), *What is German?* (1865), and *German Art and German Policy* (1867). These essays give the essence of Wagner's sense of nationalism. They also throw light on the intellectual condition of the Germans affected by Wagner's extremism.

Wagner regarded the existence of German Jews as a major national problem. In his *Judaism in Music,* he revealed the extent of his anti-Semitism in a bitter, angry denunciation. While in Zürich, he decided to think about the influence of Jews in music and make clear "a closer examination of the characteristics peculiar to it." Using the pseudonym "R. Freigedank" (R. Freethought) "in order to avoid scandal," he published a pamphlet that contained two premises: (1) the Jews were aliens in thought and feeling and could not express themselves in our [*i.e.* German] art; and (2) had the Jews thought and felt like Germans, they would have succeeded no better. Germans, he wrote, have an involuntary repugnance for the nature and personality of Jews. "According to the present constitution of the world, the Jew in truth is already more than emancipated: he rules, and will rule, as long as Money remains the power before which all our doings and our dealings lose their force." The public art taste, he charged, had been brought "before the busy fingers of the Jews, who presided over an art bazaar *(Kunstwarenwechsel)."*

Wagner castigated not only the Jews' outward appearance but also the effect they produced in their un-German speech:

> The Jew speaks the language of the nation in whose midst he dwells from generation to generation, but he always speaks it as an alien. Our whole European art and civilization have remained to the Jew a foreign tongue. In this speech, this art, the Jew can only after-speak and after-patch—not truly make a poem of his words, an artwork of his doings. In the peculiarities of Semitic pronunciation the first thing that strikes our ear as quite outlandish and unpleasant, in the Jew's production of the voice-sounds, is a creaking, squeaking, buzzing snuffle *[ein zischender, schrillender, summsender und murksender Lautausdruck].* This mode of speaking acquires at once the character of an intolerably jumbled blabber *[eines unerträglich verwirrten Geplappers].* The cold indifference of his peculiar blubber *[Gelabber]* never by chance rises to the ardor of a higher heartfelt passion.

Appalled by the tenor of Wagner's strictures, critics attributed his scorn to envy of two Jewish composers, Felix Mendelssohn-Bartholdy and Giacomo Meyerbeer. Mendelssohn, he wrote, was talented but lacked "that heart-searching effect which we await from Music." He attacked Meyerbeer as "a far-famed Jewish tone-setter of our day"; "The uninspiring, the truly laughable, is the characteristic mark whereby this famous composer shows his Jewhood in music." The Jewish poet Heinrich Heine presented only "versified lies." "Heine was the conscience of Judaism, just as Judaism is the evil conscience of our modern civilization."

The second of Wagner's major treatises on German nationalism was *What is German?* The idea of *deutsch,* he wrote, is knit to the German speech and the German *ur*-homeland. From the bosom of that home there sprang for centuries the ceaseless renovation and freshening of the soon decaying outland races. Eventually, the whole Romanized Frankland passed into the power of "the purely German stock." Wagner then launched into a panegryic of the German Spirit. That Spirit, he said, is distinguished by its wondrous individuality, its strength and its meaning.

A third essay, *German Art and German Policy,* returned to the theme of the German Spirit. Everything noble and original in German is due to that incomparable Spirit. Of all Continental countries, only Germany possessed the qualities and forces of mind and spirit to bring about a noble culture, against which the French civilization would have no power any more.

Wagner's integral nationalism had an enormous effect on Adolf Hitler. The Nazi *Fuehrer* was entranced not only by Wagnerian music, but also by the composer's conceptions of art, culture, and the State. "I have discovered, with almost hysterical excitement, that anything written by this great man is in agreement with my own innermost, subconscious dormant convictions."

Bibliography: Richard Wagner, *Collected Works,* trans. by William Ashton Ellis (8 vols., London, 1892–1899); Richard Wagner, *My Life* (2 vols., New York, 1911); Jacques Barzun, *Darwin, Marx, Wagner: Critique of a Heritage* (Boston, 1941); Derek Watson, *Richard Wagner: A Biography* (London, 1979); Frank B. Josserand, *Richard Wagner: Patriot and Politician* (Washington, D.C., 1981); Alan David Aberbach, *The Ideas of Richard Wagner* (Lanham, Md., 1984).

WALLOON NATIONALISM.   Among the myriad factors that make up the content of a nationalism or a mini-nationalism is language. (*See* **LANGUAGE, NATIONALISM AND.**) Adherence to a language can result in bitter confrontations between ethnic units existing in a national state. The differences can even develop into linguistic warfare as in Belgium, where the rivalry between Flemings and Walloons has resulted in angry controversy.

The roots of competition between Flemings and Walloons ran deeply into the course of Belgian history. In the early fourth century, Salic Franks moved down from the northeast, pushed the Romans back, went southward, and settled in Gaul proper, in what is today Belgium. Those Franks who remained in the north retained a Germanic speech that later merged into Dutch and Flemish, while the Franks who moved southward accepted the language of Romanized Gaul. Separated by a natural coal forest, the two peoples, Flemings and Walloons, developed their special traditions, customs, and folkways. Most of all, they preferred their own languages, a preference that has persisted to the present day.

In 1815 the Congress of Vienna, seeking to remake the map of Europe after Napoleon's fall, paid no attention to Flemish and Walloon differences, and united them into the Kingdom of the Netherlands. The unfortunate alliance between the two communities with linguistic and religious diversities, lasted only until 1830. There was much hostility between the two peoples. The rivalry continued through the nineteenth and into the twentieth centuries. The seeds of discontent, planted deeply, grew into two full-grown competitive mininationalisms (q.v.).

A powerful linguistic wall separated Flemings and Walloons. The line between the two communities ran from east to west, just south of Brussels. North of the division, adjacent to the Netherlands, the people adhered to Flemish traditions and spoke Flemish, a language similar to German. Written Flemish was virtually identical to Dutch, and was the spoken language of the educated classes. Flemings heatedly maintained their linguistic traditions and resented any attempts to relegate their language to second place.

South of Brussels, the Walloons spoke French and preferred French cultural forms. Theirs was essentially a French dialect. They managed to maintain their linguistic distinctiveness under a succession of invaders—Burgundians, Spaniards, Austrians, French, and Dutch. In the Middle Ages the Walloon dialect was used in the famous epic *Aucassin et Nicolette*, in chronicles, religious tracts, and folklore drama. It gradually merged into French.

An important change took place in 1839, when French, the tongue of revolutionaries, was made the official language of Belgium. This was a major change in relations between the two peoples. For some ten centuries Dutch-speaking Flemings and French-speaking Walloons had lived in a common territory without relinquishing their attachment to their own languages. Official sanction given to French touched off a feud that was to last during the coming two centuries.

In Belgium the French language became the key to upward social mobility. The rivalry affected every phase of political, social, and especially economic life. French was the language of the administration as well as the professional classes. Walloons made no secret of their contempt for "peasant Flemish." They saw themselves as more progressive than backward Flemish farmers, and considered their language as elegant and far superior to guttural and coarse Flemish.

Flemings were angered by this contemptuous attitude. They resented use of French as the language of education, courts, medicine, and everyday life. Why should prosperous, French-speaking Walloons hold the most important administrative and professional posts and also dominate industrial employment? Flemings called for a renascence of the Dutch language. There must be complete linguistic equality—in business, schools, scientific research, on coins, in the military, courts, and universities.

Added to the linguistic difficulties was severe economic exploitation. Flemings in the north preferred farming and textiles, Walloons in the south chose commerce and industries. The Walloon middle class became prosperous and was more successful than the Flemings in acquiring wealth. Walloons were further enriched by the discovery of new coal basins in their territory. Then, at the time of World War I, came a rapid turnabout—Antwerp, in the Flemish area, began to win an important place in world trade. At the same time, the Walloon region suffered an economic depression due to exhaustion of the coal mines. The Flemish birth rate rose. Walloons began to bear a diminution of their favored status. They were angered by the continuing loss of their economic advantages to the "upstart Flemings." In this situation a Walloon aristocrat made it plain: "One speaks only Flemish to one's servants!"

In the late 1960s and early 1970s there were clashes between Flemish and Walloon university students. Every effort to find a solution to the linguistic problem seemed to be fruitless. However, on October 7, 1980, after years of debate, a measure of regional autonomy was achieved. Flanders and Walloonia were given their own regional assemblies and executives. New local bodies took control of public health, the economy, urban projects, and cultural matters. The federal government retained responsibility for defense, foreign affairs, education, finance, and justice. Whether or not this solution will work remains to be seen.

Bibliography: S. Clough, *A History of the Flemish Movement* (New

York, 1930); Fernand Baudhuin, *Histoire économique de la Belgique, 1914–1939* (4 vols., Brussels, 1944); F. Gunther Eyck, *The Benelux Countries: An Historical Survey* (Princeton, N.J., 1959).

WAR AND NATIONALISM. *See* NATIONALISM AND WAR.

WARD, BARBARA (1916–1981). In private life Lady Jackson, wife of Sir Robert Jackson, former Commissioner of Development in Ghana. Barbara Ward became known as one of Britain's outstanding and influential journalists. Attached to *The Economist* of London, she lectured extensively in both Britain and the United States. A specialist on nationalism, she regarded the nation-state as the real center of power in the contemporary world. She traced the origins of nationalism to the roots of human society. She held that the sense of belonging to a particular community and to no other can be found in most primitive tribes and that it coursed through an age of empires and found its ultimate expression in a world of contending nation-states. Although she credited modern nationalism with unleashing such dynamic forces of our times as democracy, industrialism, capitalism, and communism, she warned that nationalism is no longer capable of containing them within a world made small by science and technology.

Yet, Ward reported what she called a "return to nationalism":

> For ten or fifteen years after the war, the feeling in the Western world that nationalism was no longer the dominant political philosophy was fairly strong and secure. But now we are beginning to realize that nationalism has a lot of life in it still. The feelings in which nationalism is rooted and to which it can appeal are by no means dead. A revived Western Europe, a decline in Soviet belligerency, Chinese resurgence—all these changes in the world balance of power have changed emotions and reactions too. We may not yet know how general this revival is. Nor do we know whether it reaches out to a new generation. But we do know that some voices are now raised to talk once again in terms of absolute loyalty to the primacy of the nation-state.

Bibliography: Barbara Ward, *Five Ideas That Change the World* (New York, 1959); *The Rich Nations and the Poor Nations* (New York, 1962); *Nationalism and Ideology* (New York, 1966).

WEBSTER, NOAH (1758–1843). American lexicographer, philologist, and nationalist. After serving in the American Revolution, Webster was graduated from Yale University in 1778. While teaching, he became dissatisfied with textbooks that ignored American culture, and decided that he would correct that situation. From 1783 to 1785 he wrote his *Grammatical Institute of the English Language* in three parts, the first of his publications which made him the chief American authority on English. The first part, often revised, became the famous *Elementary Spelling Book,* or "Blue-Backed Speller," which was designed to standardize American spelling (e.g., center, honor). Parents taught their children to read from it, and in schools it was used as a standard textbook. The book is said to have sold more than 70,000,000 copies.

An active Federalist, Webster was a pioneer for central government. Confirming his belief that Americans must have a special language of their own, he published in 1828 his monumental *American Dictionary of the English Language,* which has since become accepted in many editions as an important American dictionary. Early editions of the book included some 12,000 words not in any other dictionary. This publication helped standardize American pronunciation. The two thick volumes, which Webster completed at the age of 70, reflected his growing conservatism and his belief in the special nature of the American language. Although always at the center of controversy, he was regarded as a powerful supporter of American nationalism.

Bibliography: Gary R. Coll, *Noah Webster: Journalist* (Carbondale, Ill., 1970); John S. Morgan, *Noah Webster* (Boston, 1975); Richard M. Rollins, *The Long Journey of Noah Webster* (Philadelphia, 1980); Richard J. Moss, *Noah Webster* (Boston, 1984).

WEIZMANN, CHAIM (1874–1952). Scientist, Jewish nationalist, leader of the World Jewish Congress, and first President of Israel. Weizmann was born in Motol, a village in the Grodno Province in Western Russia. As a youth, he studied in nearby Pinsk. In 1891, upset by university quotas restricting admission of Jews, he left Russia to study chemistry in Germany and Switzerland. He won his doctorate in 1900 and then taught chemistry at the University of Geneva. In 1904 he moved to England, where he was appointed at the University of Manchester to teach science. Meanwhile, he engaged in organic chemistry research, specializing in dyestuffs. In 1916, during World War I, the British munitions industry was in desperate need for acetone, a basic ingredient of cordite. Weizmann invented a process to extract the solvent from maize. This extraordinary achievement did much to help the negotiations with the British Government that he was conducting at the time on behalf of the Zionist movement.

From his early days, Weizmann was influenced by Jewish nationalist culture. During his teaching years, he became important as a Zionist politician. He won a reputation as the leader of the Young Zionist opposition to Theodor Herzl (q.v.), the founder of modern Zionism. In 1917 Weizmann took an important part in the negotiations that led to the Balfour Declaration, which favored the establishment of a Jewish national homeland. During that same year, Weizmann, who had been President of the English Zionist Federation, became head of the World Zionist Organization.

Throughout his life, Weizmann stood for cooperation between the Jewish people and Great Britain in the development and building of Palestine. It was a hard, thorny task for the chemist and politician. Britain, confronted by civil disorders resulting from the rising Arab nationalism, slowly retreated from its commitment to encourage a Jewish national home. The dynamic Weizmann plunged into the task of doing what he could to satisfy British politicians. In addition, he was faced with feuds by opponents inside Zionist circles. His control over the Zionist national movement was challenged when Westminster adopted policies unfavorable to the Zionist cause. In 1937 he announced his support for a British royal inquiry commission recommending that Palestine be divided into Jewish and Arab states. His opponents inside the Zionist movement furiously condemned him for what they regarded as a sell-out to British interests.

When the Republic of Israel was founded in 1948, Weizmann became its first President. His intervention led to American recognition of the newly formed state. Worn out by frail health, he died on November 9, 1952. A quarter of a million Israelis attended his state burial. He has remained a national hero in Israel. (*See also* **ZIONIST NATIONALISM.**)

Bibliography: Isaiah Berlin, *Chaim Weizmann* (London, 1959); M.W. Weisgal and Joel Carmichael (eds.), *Chaim Weizmann: A Biography by Several Hands* (New York, 1962); Jehuda Reinharz, *Chaim Weizmann: The Making of a Zionist Leader* (New York, 1985); Norman Rose, *Chaim Weizmann: A Biography* (New York, 1986).

WELSH NATIONALISM.   Wales (called *Cymru* in Welsh) occupies the central western peninsula of Britain. It is bounded on the east by England, on the north by the Irish Sea, on the south by the Bristol Channel, and on the west by St. George's Channel. The principality has an area of 8,016 square miles and a population (1985 est.) of 2,811,000. Both England and Wales are administered as a unit. Fewer than twenty percent of the people speak both English and Welsh, some 32,000 speak only Welsh. Early Anglo-Saxon invaders drove

Celtic peoples into the mountains of Wales, and called them Waelise (Welsh, or foreign).

A minority of Welshmen sees Wales as a distinct nationality. They have opted for Welsh nationalism. Their ethnic and language loyalties convinced them that they possessed an embryo of developing nationalism. Over the years, the English have regarded the United Kingdom as a unit, and consider Wales, Scotland, and Northern Ireland as component parts of the national state. In dealing with unsatisfied nationalisms in those areas, London has been careful to maintain good relations with Wales. The result has been that Wales, along with Scotland and Northern Ireland, remains within the United Kingdom and shares its successes and failures. Although Welsh nationalism remains, it is comparatively muted and does not attain the violent extremes of such mini-nationalisms (q.v.) as the Basques in Spain or the Croats in Yugoslavia (qq.v.).

Although it has never won its independence, Wales has a history and character of its own. For seven centuries, despite its distinctive environment, its life has been closely bound with that of England, its neighbor. In confrontations between the Welsh and the English, some Welshmen still regard themselves as natives, while designating the English as intruders. The peace existing between Wales and England has been an uneven one. The English introduced their own legal system throughout the principality, and slowly took control over Welsh towns and villages. Unhappy about this "foreign" penetration, Welshmen broke out in sporadic rebellions. But, in general, the Welsh gentry preferred English ways and customs. The classes clashed: the privileged gentry tended to become more and more alienated from the Welsh tenantry, who saw themselves as loyal natives and not, as the gentry proclaimed, "traitors allied with foreigners in London." Added to the class confrontation was a religious problem. The Welsh gentry remained Anglican in religion, while other Welshmen were largely Nonconformist.

Welsh national sentiment emerged in the eighteenth century. This sense of national self-consciousness was expressed in the establishment of Welsh institutions of higher learning. Aware of the national sentiment in Wales, Westminster gave Wales a large measure of control in educational matters. In 1925 the Welsh National Party, *Plaid Cymru*, was organized to win dominion status for Wales. This organization managed to attract public attention to the seriousness of the Welsh movement for autonomy.

Although quiescent, Welsh nationalism remained alive. The sentiment was expressed by the late Welsh actor, Richard Burton:

I do know that, tiny nation as we are, and being no better or no worse than any other nations, I do know that we are different and want to remain so. We don't have to have that hot rush of blood to the head 'when someone mistakes us for British, or thinks that we are one of Britain's quainter countries. We want to be uniquely ourselves and we want to keep our unique language.

Indeed, maintenance of the Welsh language is one of the dominant strains of Welsh nationalism. By the twentieth century, most people throughout the world were demanding the right to use their special national language. This was true especially among those nationalities seeking to gain their independence. Everywhere, national languages were emphasized. Patriotic societies called for the preservation of the national language and extension of its use. Welshmen, too, were proud of their special language: they believed that it was expressive and beautiful, a sacred treasure to be cherished and preserved. Regard for their speech deepened Welsh national sentiment and gave voice to the hope for an independent homeland. Oxford scholar Sir John Morris Jones described the Welsh language as "the sweetest tongue in all the world." Veneration for this old, tongue-twisting language served to accentuate the differences between Welsh insiders and English outsiders. The Welsh language, or *Cymraeg*, belongs to the wider Indo-European linguistic family, a member of the Brythonic group of Celtic languages related to Gaelic, Manx, Cornish, and Breton.

With the Anglicization of Wales in the nineteenth and twentieth centuries came a decline in the use of the Welsh language. This was due in part to the preference of the Welsh gentry for the English language. English was also used in the law courts. Yet, many Welshmen preferred their native tongue. Though succeeding censuses in the twentieth century revealed a decline in the use of Welsh, the language still remains the preference of many Welshmen and especially of those who called for separation from England. Natives who reside in the old villages prefer the Welsh tongue. The language is taught in all Welsh schools. It is used in church worship and in institutions of higher learning. Welsh nationalists believe that their own language must be retained not only in schools and administration, but also in common speech. Welsh traditionalists regard the language question as at the heart of national feeling and use it to support the movement for autonomy.

Another contributory factor to Welsh nationalism is the existence of a special culture. Welshmen admit the connection with British culture, but, at the same time, hold fast to their own institutions. Their habits have been orally oriented, as parents pass on special tales and legends to their children. The Welsh are fascinated by stories of fairies, ghosts, and spirits. They enjoy the mysterious, despite the onslaught of English materialism in literature, television, and radio. Their delight in the spoken word carries over into lyrics: Welshmen have won much acclaim for their choral singing. Both the song and the spoken word support the idea of *cynghanedd*, or solicitude for the preservation of Welsh culture.

The most effective institution working for the preservation of Welsh culture is the National *Eisteddfod*, a festival devoted to competition, and the most unique of all Welsh cultural activities. The tradition of an annual social arts competition goes back far into Welsh history. These traditional meetings became an annual festival in the early part of the nineteenth century, a patriotic event combining competitive choral singing, recitation of the Scriptures, and poetry composition. Men, women, and children wear colorful costumes and join in singing, dancing, and rituals with harp accompaniment. Prizes are awarded to the composers of the best alliterative poem in traditional meter, for the best floral dances, and ceremonies led by druids. The National *Eisteddfod* is regarded as a meeting place for the Welsh "nation." It gives notice to the English-speaking world that while Wales is closely tied to England in political, administrative, and economic matters, it proposes to maintain its identity. It will retain its own culture, even if it is allied to the English.

The Welsh economy has long been a serious problem in the relations between Wales and England. With its mountainous terrain, rainfall, and the nature of the soil, Wales is not suitable for farming. The Welsh economy rests on two extensive coal deposits, one of inferior quality in the northeast, and the other of greater value in South Wales. When the South Wales coal deposits were discovered, there was an influx of "foreign" Englishmen and Irishmen, all desperate for work in the mines. The results were unfortunate. Wales was transformed into a series of grim coal-mining valleys. The condition of housing was miserable. Wages were low. Derelict towns appeared throughout the countryside, reflecting a chronically unstable economic situation. Welshmen accused industrialists from Manchester and London of siphoning off profits from the coal mines, while, at the same time, showing little regard for the suffering of miners' families. This economic decline helped promote a sense of national consciousness among Welshmen. Westminster was aware of Welsh problems, and took special steps to improve the Welsh economy. A series of governmental grants in the 1970s amounted to about one-half the Welsh income. London encouraged the movement of new industries into depressed Wales as a means of providing work for the unemployed.

Westminster added to economic measures the politics of devolution to satisfy Welsh aspirations. Elsewhere, the British response to drives for independence or autonomy used a divide-and-rule policy. This procedure was not practical in Wales. Here the procedure was designed to discourage any possibility of dissolution of the United Kingdom. Devolution was supposed politically to meet the aspirations of Welsh moderates. Welsh militants were reluctant to accept the way of moderation. They demanded complete independence based on Welsh linguistic and cultural differences. Activists called for civil disobedience. They splashed green paint and Welsh letters over English place names. In the National *Eisteddfod* held in mid-May 1977, they disrupted the proceedings by wrecking the hall of the British Rail Exhibition because it did not use Welsh in its advertising. Most Welshmen were not amused: these tactics were in their minds either harmless exuberance or the work of lunatics. They were not inclined to promote irrational extremists to the status of national heroes. (*See also* **DEVOLUTION.**)

In late 1977 a plan was proposed for a British federation similar to that of the United States and the Federal Republic of West Germany. Wales would have its own Assembly without legislative power, while London-made laws would be administered by the principality. After a year of discussion, the plan was finally put to a vote in Wales and Scotland. The result was surprising: both Wales and Scotland turned it down, the Welsh by a 4-to-1 margin. Many feared that the practical effect of limited self-rule would be the creation of a costly new bureaucracy. The sense of cohesion turned out to be stronger than provincial regionalism. (See **REGIONALISM.**)

Welsh nativism seems quite willing to accept accommodation with British "intrusion." Welshmen apparently believe that they and the English can retain their separate identities in a union. This does not mean that Welsh nationalists see their cause as lost. They remained a passionate minority, determined that their language would survive, and were willing to break the law to make sure that it did. They destroyed vacation cottages owned by Englishmen to show the English that they were not welcome. "Sure they're extremists, those people setting the fires," said a Welsh fisherman. "But you can't help but admire the way they're standing up to the English when all that the rest of us do is talk." The Movement for the Defense of Wales, a clandestine group, insisted that it was acting on behalf of the poor in setting the fires:

> We believe that there is widespread sympathy in every area of Wales towards the burning of holiday homes, whatever the politicians and the media say. We hope that the present campaign will inspire steelworkers and miners and everyone else in Wales whose jobs and futures are being threatened terribly.

Nevertheless, such outbursts reveal that Welsh extremists, though supported by only a fraction of the people, do not intend to cast aside their concept of what must be done in Wales. Welsh nationalism remains muted, but there is a small hard core of militants who intend to keep it alive.

Bibliography: W.J. Morgan (ed.), *The Welsh Dilemma* (Swansea, Wales, 1973); R.R. Davies (ed.), *Welsh Society and Nationhood* (Cardiff, Wales, 1974); J.W. Aitcheson, *The Welsh Language, 1961–1981* (Cardiff, Wales, 1975); Colin H. Williams, "Cultural Nationalism in Wales," *Canadian Review of Studies in Nationalism*, 4, No. 1 (Autumn, 1976) 15–37; James Barry Jones, and R.A. Wilford, *The Welsh Veto: The Politics of the Devolution Campaign in Wales* (Glasgow, 1979); C.H. Williams (ed.), *National Separatism* (Cardiff, Wales, 1982); John Osmond (ed.), *The National Question Again: Welsh Political Identity in the 1980s* (Llandysul, Wales, 1985).

WHITAKER, ARTHUR P. (1895–1979). American specialist on Latin-American nationalism. Born in Alabama, Whitaker studied at the University of Tennessee, where he was graduated in 1915. A Rhodes scholar in 1917, he took his doctorate at Harvard in 1924. Teacher, writer, and historian, he served at several universities, including Harvard, Columbia, Heidelberg, San Marcos, and London. He was a former officer and consultant with the Department of State. He ended his career at the University of Pennsylvania.

In his *Latin America: Past and Present* (1962), Whitaker described nationalism as an English and Western European invention and one of Europe's most universal exports. Some forms of it have been adopted even by the newest nations still in a tribal stage of social organization. The importance of nationalism is growing in the underdeveloped countries. Latin-American nationalism early demonstrated certain characteristics such as continentalism. Despite the problems it raises, it is an asset to the United States as well as to the free world at large, because it is the most effective of all barriers against penetration of the continent by the Kremlin and the Chinese:

> Whatever the future may hold, nationalism gives no sign of loosening the firm grip it has gained in Latin America—quite the contrary. Nor does the role of nationalism there show any sign of losing its great importance to the United States. In many ways it is a serious encumbrance to this country. The Latin Americans'

economic nationalism is a bar to trade and investment; their cultural nationalism is a bar to communication; and their political nationalism has enormously complicated the problem posed for the United States by Fidel Castro's Cuba. Yet, on the other side of the ledger, their nationalism in all its aspects has been and still is, despite Cuba, in the cold war an asset to the United States and the free world at large, for it is the most effective of all barriers against penetration of the area by the Sino-Soviet bloc.

(*See also* **LATIN AMERICAN NATIONALISM.**)

Bibliography: Arthur P. Whitaker, *Nationalism in Latin America: Past and Present* (Gainesville, Fla., 1962).

WILLIAM II (1859–1941).   German Emperor of the Second Reich, last of the Hohenzollern dynasty, and promoter of aggressive nationalism. Born with a withered left arm, this grandson of Queen Victoria blamed his mother throughout his life for the accident at his birth. His character embraced a world of contradictions. Though talented and cultivated, he often acted in a highly erratic manner. He was impatient, fickle, and susceptible to the flattery of courtiers. His impulsive nature kept him from understanding the many problems he faced as Germany's ruler.

William II was convinced beyond doubt that his lofty position was entrusted to him by God. He saw it as his duty to maintain the monarchy that had been bestowed upon him by Divine Providence. "I regard my whole position," he said, "as given to me direct from heaven and I have been called by the Highest to do His work, by One to whom I must one day render an account." He informed his friend "Nicky" (Nicholas II, Tsar of Russia): "A sacred duty is imposed by Heaven on us Christian Kings and Emperors—to uphold the doctrine of the Divine Rights of Kings."

As Emperor, William II attempted to follow the policies of his Chancellor Otto von Bismarck, (q.v.), without possessing Bismarck's skill or powers of adaptability. He forced Bismarck's resignation on March 20, 1890. His chief ambitions were to build a navy rivaling Britain's, and to strengthen Germany's power in Europe by a policy of colonial expansion.

The German people regarded William II as a symbol of national greatness, who was to lead them in the vital task of counteracting the diabolical *Einkreisungspolitik* (encirclement policy) of the European powers. The German public was entranced by his stated objective of "a place in the sun." Historian Friedrich Meinecke venerated the Hohenzollern dynasty and paid tribute to William II's nationalism at an academic festival on June 14, 1913:

Our Kaiser's destiny is our destiny. . . .

From the beginning our Kaiser has worked uninterruptedly for the nation and brought her to the high seas. . . . Today we have the satisfaction of knowing that his convictions have become national convictions. Under the eyes of a powerful rival he has constructed a war fleet. . . .

We unite ourselves with our Kaiser in ardent wish that the unavoidable and natural difference between classes and confessions be resolved so that there may be national brotherhood and that our world political power not be endangered. . . .

Our hearts embrace the whole historical network of German national and State life. . . . We follow our Kaiser on the steep way to the clouds—surrounded heights of our future. God bless and protect Germany and its ruler!

William II's nationalism led the German people into the bloodshed of World War I and to a catastrophic defeat.

Bibliography: Virginia S. Cowles, *The Kaiser* (New York, 1962); M.L.G. Balfour, *The Kaiser and His Times* (London, 1964); Theo Aranson, *The Kaiser* (London, 1971); William Sidney Tyler-Whittle, *The Last Kaiser: A Biography of William II* (New York, 1977); John C.G. Rohl and Nicolaus Sombart (eds.), *Kaiser Wilhelm II: New Interpretations* (New York, 1982).

WIRTH CATEGORIES. *See* **NATIONALISM, CLASSIFICATIONS OF.**

WUORINEN, JOHN HENRY (1897–1969). Professor of History and specialist on the development of modern nationalism in Finland. Born in Vaasa, Finland, on May 10, 1897, he came to the United States, took his B.A. degree at Clark University in 1921, and the doctorate at Columbia University in 1931. At Columbia he turned to the study of nationalism in Professor Carlton J.H. Hayes seminar. Teaching at Columbia, he became full professor in 1947 and served as chairman of the History Department from 1949–1958. The Finnish Government named him Knight first class, Order of the Rose, and Commander, Order of the Finnish Lion.

Bibliography: John H. Wuorinen, *Nationalism in Modern Finland* (New York, 1931).

X

XENOPHOBIC NATIONALISM. Nationalism of an exclusive nature based on fear of and rejection of the stranger or foreigner. The term "xenophobia" is a combined form derived from the Greek *xenos*, meaning stranger, and from the modern Latin based on the Greek *phobos*, meaning an irrational, excessive, and persistent fear of some particular thing or situation. Xenophobia is closely related to frenetic chauvinism (q.v.) and rampant jingoism (q.v.). Xenophobic nationalism was directly opposite to the earlier form of liberal nationalism with its strong emotional bond, respect for tolerance, and sense of community.

Examples of xenophobic nationalism may be found in the German *Hasslied* (q.v.), the "Chant of Hate Against England," written by Ernst Lissauer in 1914:

> "We love as one, we hate as one,
> We have one foe, and one alone,
> ENGLAND!"

Xenophobia was behind the atavistic beliefs of Germany's Hitler, in the oratory of Italy's Mussolini, and in the cold brutality of Soviet Russia's Stalin. It was effective in producing social maladjustments and psychological frustrations of many peoples. Even peoples sharing the same ideology are influenced by xenophobic nationalism to the point where they bolster their borders in fear of "alien aggression." The combination of xenophobia and nationalism was responsible for much of the discontent and dangerous confrontations rampant in the world in the closing decades of the twentieth century.

Bibliography: Antonio Perotti, *Action to Combat Intolerance and Xenophobia* (Strasbourg, 1985); Vernon Reynolds, *The Sociology of Ethnocentrism: Evolutionary Dimensions of Xenophobia, Discrimination, Racism, and Nationalism* (Athens, Ga., 1987).

Y

YUGOSLAVIAN NATIONALISMS. Yugoslavia presents a case of a multinational state whose fabric is ripped by ethnic dissension. When the Austro-Hungarian Empire collapsed after World War I, the Kingdom of the Serbs, Croats, and Slovenes was formed. Its name was later changed to Yugoslavia. But this artificial union had within it rival ethnic units that demanded their own nationalisms.

Of a population of 23,284,000 (1986 estimate), the Serbs form 26 percent, Croats 22 percent, Slovenes 8 percent, and Montenegrans 3 percent. Other minorities include Albanians, Hungarians, Turks, Slovaks, and Gypsies. It was the task of Josip Broz, known as Tito, leader of the Yugoslav Partisans who fought against Hitler in World War II, to keep these disparate ethnic groups under control. In order to maintain unity of the country, he divided it into "republics"—Serbia, Croatia, Slovenia, Bosnia-Herzegovina, Macedonia, and Montenegro. He also attempted to reduce the power of the Serbs by forming two autonomous regions—Kosovo and Vojvodina out of prewar Serbia. When he was elected first President of Yugoslavia in 1952, his new constitution was designed to unite all nationalities of Yugoslavia into a joint and equal community.

Tito managed by sheer force of personality to keep the rival factions of his country in a national union. When he died in 1980, the central authority began to break down. Ethnic strife arose, especially between Serbs and Croats. (*See* **CROATION SEPARATISM.**) In the late summer of 1988, Serbs in the southern province of Kosovo protested mistreatment by ethnic Albanians predominant in the area.

The attacks on Serbs by Montenegrans aroused the country's Serbs in a fever of anger. Other ethnic units believed that any further gains by the Serbs would result in bitter resentment throughout the country. Clashes between Serbian protestors and military police became common. Paramilitary forces clubbed and tear-gassed demonstrators in Titograd, the capital of Montenegro. Protestors shouted: "We will return the beatings."

These were unprecedented major challenges to Communist leaders. Regional authorities were toppled. The situation revealed that Yugoslavia was a fragile community of potential disunity. Tito had managed to unify the country into a socialist federation, but since his death ethnic and territorial divisions intensified. Added to the country's difficulties was economic chaos. Yugoslavia owed $21 billion to Western countries and depended upon them for further credits. The annual inflation rate was 217 percent. A million people were unemployed. The grave economic situation produced deepening disenchantment with the Communist Party leaders. There were more than 800 strikes in 1988, and workers stormed the legislature in June. Nationalism and economic chaos were a dangerous mixture.

It remains to be seen if Yugoslavia's current political leaders can replace Tito or even win dominance over the entire country. The decentralized state that was Tito's legacy is on the verge of civil war. His efforts to unite diverse factions have not been continued successfully. Current officials of the Communist Party's Central Committee warned that "the passion, vengefulness, and aggressiveness" of the protestors were harming the country's position before the world.

This kind of bitter parochial ethnocentrism means a difficult future for plurinational Yugoslavia. The unity of the federation seems on the verge of collapse. The situation reveals the extreme difficulty of unifying peoples who do not want to be unified. This kind of disruptive nationalism exists all over the world. Peoples combined artificially against their will are not inclined to peaceful coexistence, nor are they willing to recognize and tolerate each other's ethnicity.

Bibliography: Ivo Banac, *The National Question in Yugoslavia: Origins, History, Politics* (Ithaca, N.Y., 1984); Nora Beloff, *Tito's Flawed Legacy* (London, 1985); Bruce J. McFarlane, *Yugoslavia: Politics, Economics, and Society* (London, 1988).

Z

ZIONIST NATIONALISM.   A movement to restore and maintain Palestine as a national Jewish state. It is the modern, organized expression of the Jewish love for Zion, the original homeland, and the hope for the gathering of Jews from the *Diaspora* (dispersion). From the end of the seventeenth century, varied proposals were suggested for the return of Jews to their ancestral homeland, but it was not until the late nineteenth century that practical steps were taken for a modern nationalist movement.

Behind modern Zionism was the long-time yearning of Jews for an end to their position as outsiders in Western society and for a restoration of their homeland. There was a powerful religious fervor behind the movement. In ancient times the Jews were one of the few peoples animated by a strong sense of national consciousness. For more than two thousand years the call for a return to Zion had been paramount in Jewish life. Daily prayers constantly reminded Jews of the necessity for the return to Zion; philosophical and legal teaching were devoted to the idea. Religious and national lives were inextricably bound together, and both were regarded by Jewish leaders as forming a tight union. In the modern era, when nationalism spread throughout Europe and eventually all over the world, it intensified the demand for a national home. The romantic impulse to Zionism was emphasized by the treatment of Jews in Europe. They were subjected to political humiliation, economic strictures, and social misery. The longing for a return to Zion persisted in the

Age of Nationalism and became a powerful movement for the re-establishment of Israel as a national state.

During the first half of the nineteenth century, European Jewish intellectuals believed that their problem might be settled by political emancipation and the assimilation of Jews into the political, economic, and cultural life of the countries in which they lived. Eventually, it became obvious that assimilation was no answer except in special individual cases. Some Jewish families of enormous wealth might penetrate into society and be well received, but for the masses this was an impossibility, especially in Eastern Europe. Most Jews did not have the opportunity to be assimilated and most did not want it. Assimilation had succeeded to a greater extent in Western Europe, where Jews had entered into the economic and cultural life of the nations. The possibility of assimilation was lessened by the influx of Eastern Jews to the West, by those who came to the large urban areas where they could enjoy a better economic life. Their rise in commerce, finance, and industry led to recurrent anti-Semitic movements, which acted as a bar to assimilation. The idea of absorption had failed.

Zionism emerged in Western Europe among Jewish intellectuals, but it received its mass support among Eastern and Oriental Jewish masses. It was, indeed, a combination of these two factors, the goal of secularized Western intellectuals and the medieval religious Zionist zeal, that led to the formation of modern Zionist nationalism. The opening stimulus came from Moses Hess (q.v.), who in 1862 published his *Rom und Jerusalem, die Letzte Nationalitätsfrage (Rome and Jerusalem, the Last Problem of Nationality)*, the first important book on modern Jewish nationalism. Hess was dominated by the need to maintain Jewish values and the necessity of regarding the proposed Jewish homeland in Palestine as the long-awaited fulfillment of the messianic promises of the French Revolution. Hess remained a solitary voice for two decades, until in 1882, Leo Pinsker (q.v.), a Jewish physician in Odessa, published his *Auto-Emanzipation (Self-Emancipation)*, by which he hoped to rescue the Jewish people from their misery. He insisted that Jews must look to their own force and their own will and that they just could not depend on existing European governments to help them. In this direct appeal to Jewish nationalism, Pinsker applied the historic tendencies of the nineteenth century to the Jewish people. He would seek a home for Jews either in Palestine or elsewhere.

A new and important impetus to Zionism was made by Theodor Herzl (q.v.). A Viennese journalist and playwright, Herzl published in 1896 a pamphlet titled *The Jewish State,* in which he supported the idea of an autonomous Jewish nation as the only solution to the Jewish question. The next year he convened a Congress in Basel to consider the project. With some 200 delegates from over the world, the Basel Congress adopted as the program of the new movement the goal of Zionism: "The aim of Zionism is to create for the Jewish people a home in Palestine secured by public law." The conference also founded a global organization, with headquarters in Vienna, which would organize and stimulate work for Zionism.

Herzl developed his idea of political Zionism and raised the Zionist movement out of its previously dominant religious role. He knew little about traditional Jewish values or about the problems of Eastern Jews. His concept of Zionism was intensified by the rising anti-Semitism then existing in Western Europe as a result of the Dreyfus case in France. His idea of Zionism was purely political, but at the same time his detachment from Judaism enabled him to give Zionism its modern form and set it up as a democratic, nationalist political movement. A zealous propagandist, he made Zionism the first organization of its kind in Jewish history.

During Herzl's life, all work within the Zionist Organization was done without remuneration. The organization was maintained by means of the *Shekel,* an annual contribution paid by members throughout the world. In 1901 the Jewish National Fund was set up for the purchase of land in Palestine as the possession of the Jewish people. After Herzl's death in 1904, a bureaucratic apparatus was created, which, after World War I, expanded to a great extent and controlled the organization. The period from the death of Herzl to the outbreak of World War I in 1914 was an era of little success for Zionist nationalism, but there was a strong intellectual life and the insistent cry for a return to the homeland in Palestine. In 1911 the headquarters of the Zionist Congress, which met every two years, was moved to Berlin, where it remained until the beginning of World War I.

During World War I, the attitude of Zionists on the belligerents was divided, but eventually the movement followed the lead of Dr. Chaim Weizmann (q.v.) and Nahum Sokolow. These two Zionist leaders set up new headquarters in London and pinned their hopes on an Allied triumph. Appointed Director of the Admiralty Laboratories engaged in research work on behalf of the Foreign Office, Weizmann made a critical discovery of a process for the manufacture of acetone, the basis for high explosives. In his role as President of the World Zionist Congress, he was mainly responsible for the political relationship between the Colonial Office and the Jewish Agency in Palestine. In the midst of the war came a decisive turn for Zionist nationalism, when the Balfour Declaration of November 2, 1917, was declared. The British Government announced its sympathy with the cause of Zionism in a letter from Foreign Secretary A.J. Balfour to Lord Rothschild. The Declaration stated:

> His Majesty's Government view with favour the establishment of a national home for the Jewish people, and will use their best endeavours to facilitate the achievements of this object, it being clearly understood that nothing shall be done which may prejudice the civil and religious rights of existing non-Jewish communities in Palestine, or the rights enjoyed by Jews in any other country.

This Balfour Declaration was incorporated into the Palestine Mandate committed to Great Britain by the League of Nations in 1922.

The Balfour Declaration was intentionally vague and did not altogether fulfill the ambitions of Zionists for the establishment of a national Jewish homeland in Palestine. However, it did arouse hopes among many Jews, especially those of wealth who had remained aloof from Zionism, that there was a practical solution to the long, difficult Jewish question. Zionism now entered a troubled existence. Jews, from the extremely Orthodox to the Socialist *Bund* in Poland, condemned Zionism. The movement split into political and religious factions. Weizmann's leadership was challenged in this chaotic era. The relationship of Zionists with the British Government became progressively worse, as London attempted to reconcile the Balfour Declaration with its own commitments to Arab nationalism.

However, Zionism had shown excellent colonizing achievements in Palestine, even if from the beginning it was faced with the serious problem that Palestine was populated by Arabs who had their own sense of national consciousness. In 1947 the United Nations voted to partition Palestine into an Arab and a Jewish state. The British withdrew in May, 1948. On May 14, 1948, Israel was declared an independent state. Rejecting partition, Egypt, Jordan, Syria, Lebanon, Iraq, and Saudi Arabia invaded Israel, but did not succeed in destroying the new Jewish state. The fighting ended in 1949 with Israel in possession of almost fifty percent more land than originally granted. Armistice agreements, but no peace treaties, were signed with the Arab countries.

The defeated Arab nations were not willing to recognize the existence of Israel as an independent national state. After a series of terrorist attacks, Israeli armies invaded Egypt on October 29, 1956, helped originally by British and French forces. There was an uneasy truce supervised by a U.N. Emergency Force until May 19, 1967. The Six Day War started June 5. The Israelis stormed the Gaza Strip, occupied the Sinai Peninsula to the area of the Suez Canal, and took Old Jerusalem, Golan Heights, and Jordan's West Bank. But there was to be no halt in Arab goals. On October 5, 1973, (among Jews this was Yom Kippur, the most solemn religious day of the year), Egypt and Syria, supplied by massive Soviet air lifts, again attacked. Israel, supported by air lifts from the United States, counterattacked. The Syrians were driven back, and the Israelis crossed the Suez Canal. After the cease-fire, Israel withdrew from the Canal. Since then, relations between Israel and the Arabs have worsened with the *intifada,* a rebellion of Arabs in the West Bank and Gaza.

Behind the success of Israel in overcoming its Arab enemies were the persistence of Zionist nationalism and the support of the United States. The building of Israel into an independent state revealed the organizing and constructive abilities of the Jews, even as farmers and farm workers. The achievements of Zionism in political, economic, and cultural life are outstanding in the history of modern nationalism. Zionism gave the Jews a new pride in their history and a new consciousness of what was in store for them. For many Jews from all areas of the world it provided a revived homeland. Israel still struggles for its existence: the Palestine Liberation Organization (q.v.) has made it plain that it intends to destroy the Jewish state and it supports a program of terror which the Israelis counter with forces of their own. It remains to be seen whether or not this tiny state, in the center of an Arab world, will be able to maintain its existence in the face of continuing opposition.

Bibliography: P. Horowitz, *The Jewish Question and Zionism* (London, 1927); Stephen S. Poppel, *Zionism in Germany, 1897–1933: The Shaping of the Jewish Identity* (Philadelphia, 1977); Paula Hayman, *The Kibbutz Community and Nation–Building* (Princeton, N.J., 1982); Conor Cruise O'Brien, *The Siege: The Saga of Israel and Zionism* (London, 1986); David Vital, *Zionism: The Crucial Phase* (New York, 1987).

ZOLLVEREIN.   *See* **LIST, FRIEDRICH.**

Bibliography

READINGS ON NATIONALISM

Abraham, W., *The Mind of Africa* (Chicago, 1962).

Aksim, Benjamin, *States and Nations* (London, 1964).

Alba, Victor, *Nationality Without Nations: The Oligarch versus the People in Latin America* (New York, 1968).

Anderson, Eugene N., *Nationalism and the Cultural Crisis in Prussia, 1801–1815* (New York, 1930).

Antonius, George, *The Arab Awakening: The Story of the Arab Nationalist Movement* (New York, 1965).

Ardrey, Robert, *The Territorial Imperative* (New York, 1966).

Arendt, Hannah, *The Origins of Totalitarianism* (New York, 1931, 1966).

Armstrong, J.H., *Ukrainian Nationalism* (New York, 1963).

Aveneri, Shlomo, *The Meaning of Modern Zionism* (New York, 1981).

Bailey, Samuel L. (ed.), *Nationalism in Latin America* (New York, 1971).

Barclay, Glen St. J., *Twentieth Century Nationalism: Revolution of Our Times* (New York, 1972).

Barghoorn, Frederick C., *Soviet Russian Nationalism* (New York, 1956.

Barker, Ernst, *National Character and the Factors in its Formation* (London, 1927).

Barker, Ernst, (ed.), *The Character of the English* (London, 1947).

Baron, Salo W., *Nationalism and Religion*, (New York, 1947).

Barzun, Jacques, *Race: A Study in Superstition* (New York, 1937, 1965).

Bell, Wendell and Walter E. Freeman (eds.) *Ethnicity and Nation-Building* (Beverly Hills, Calif., 1974.

Bendix, Reinhard, *Kings and People: Power and the Mandate to Rule* (Berkeley, 1978).

Benedict, Ruth, *Race, Science, and Politics* (New York, 1940).

Berlin, Isaiah, "The Bent Twig: A Note on Nationalism," *Foreign Affairs*, 51, No. 1 (October, 1972), 11–30.

Birch, A.H., "Minority Nationalist Movements and Theories of Political Integration," *World Politics*, XXX, No. 3 (April, 1978), 325–346.

Blausten, Albert P., "New Nationalism," *American Journal of Comparative Law*, XXX (1982), Supplement, 377–388.

Bossenbrook, W., *Mid-Twentieth Century Nationalism* (Detroit, 1965).

Buchheit, L.C. *Secession: The Legitimacy of Self-Determination* (New Haven, Conn., 1978).

Buchman, William, *The Rise of Integral Nationalism in France* (New York, 1937).

Buchman, William and Hadley Cantril, *How Nations See Each Other* (Urbana, Ill., 1953).

Cameron, D., *National Self-Determination and the Quebec Question* (Toronto, 1971).

Carr, E.H., *Nationalism and After* (London, 1945).

Carter, Gwendolen M. (ed.), *National Unity and Regionalism in African States* (Ithaca, N.Y., 1966).

Cecil, Lord Hugh, *Nationalism and Catholicism* (London, 1919).

Chadwick, H.M., *The Nationalities of Europe and the Growth of National Ideologies* (Cambridge, England, 1945).

Cobban Alfred, *National Self-Determination* (London, 1945).

Cobban, Alfred, *The Nation-State and National Self-Determination*, (rev. ed., New York, 1969).

Cohen, Israel, *The Zionist Movement* (New York, 1946).

Commager, Henry Steele, *The American Mind: An Interpretation of American Thought and Character Since the 1880s* (New Haven, Conn., 1950).

Connor, Walker, "Self-Determination: The New Phase," *World Politics*, XX, No. 1 (October, 1967), 30–53.

Connor, Walker, "The Politics of Ethnonationalism," *Journal of International Affairs*, XXVII, No. 1 (1973), 1–21.

Connor, Walker, "Nationalism and Political Illegitimacy," *Canadian Review of Studies in Nationalism*, VIII, No. 2 (Fall, 1981), 201–228.

Coudenhove-Kalergi, Richard N., *Europa Erwacht (Europe Awakens)* (Paris, 1934).

Coudenhove-Kalergi, Richard N., *Europe Must Unite* (Glarus, Switzerland, 1939).

Coudenhove, Kalergi, Richard N., *Crusade for Pan-Europa* (New York, 1943).

Coudenhove-Kalergi, Richard N., *Kampf um Pan-Europa (Struggle for Pan-Europa)* (Zürich, 1949).

Coudenhove-Kalergi, Richard N., *Die europäische Nation (The European Nation)* (Stuttgart, 1953).

Coudenhove-Kalergi, Richard N., *Eine Idee erobert Europa (One Idea Conquers Europa)* (Munich, 1958)

Coudenhove-Kalergi, Richard N., *Pan-Europa* (Munich, 1966).

Coudenhove-Kalergi, Richard N., *Ein Leben für Europa (One Life for Europe)* (Cologne, 1966).

Copelund, Miles, *The Game of Nations* (New York, 1969).

Coupland, Reginand, *Welsh and Scottish Nationalism* (London, 1954).

Cowan, Laing Grey, *The Dilemma of African Independence* (New York, 1984).

Cowie, H.R., *Nationalism and Internationalism in the Modern World* (Melbourne, Australia, 1979).

Cox, Richard Hubert Francis, *Pan-Africanism in Practice* (New York, 1964).

Cunsolo, Ronald S., *Italian Nationalism: From Its Origins to World War II* (Malabar, Fla, 1990).

Curti, Merle, *The Roots of American Loyalty* (New York, 1946).

Dangerfield, George, *The Awakening of American Nationalism, 1815–1828* (New York, 1965).

Davies, Wallace, *Patriotism on Parade* (Cambridge, Mass., 1955).

Delaisi, Francis, *Political Myths and Economic Realities* (New York, 1927).

Deutsch, Karl W., "The Trend of European Nationalism: The Language Aspect," *American Political Science Review*, XXXVI (1942), 533–541.

Deutsch, Karl W., "The Growth of Nations: Some Recurrent Patterns of Political and Social Integration," *World Politics*, V (1952), 168–196.

Deutsch, Karl W., *Nationalism and Social Communication: An Inquiry into the Foundations of Nationality* (2nd ed., Cambridge, Mass., 1966).

Deutsch, Karl W., *Nationalism and Its Alternatives* (New York, 1969).

Deutsch, Karl W., *Tides Among Nations* (New York, 1979).

Deutsch, Karl W. and W.J. Foltz (eds.)., *Nation-Building* (New York, 1963).

Dilke, Charles Wentworth, *Greater Britain* (London, 1868).

Doob, Leonard W., *Patriotism and Nationalism: Their Psychological Foundations* (New Haven, Conn., 1964).

Du Bois, W.E., Burghardt, *The Conservation of Races* (Washington, D.C., 1897).

Du Bois, W.E., Burghardt, *The Souls of Black Folk* (Chicago, 1903).

Du Bois, W.E. Burghardt, *The Negro Church* (Atlanta, Ga., 1903).

Du Bois, W.E. Burghardt, *The Negro* (New York, 1915).

Du Bois, W.E. Burghardt, *The Gift of Black Folk* (Boston, 1924).

Du Bois, W.E. Burghardt, *Color and Democracy* (New York, 1940).

Du Bois, W.E. Burghardt, *Autobiography* (New York, 1960).

Du Bois, W.E. Burghardt, *The World and Africa* (New York, 1965.

Du Bois, W.E. Burghardt, *Black Reconstruction* (Millwood, N.Y., 1976).

Duggan, Laurence, *The Americas: The Search for Hemispheric Security* (New York, 1949).

Duijker, H.C. and N.H. Frijjda, *National Character and National Stereotypes* (Amsterdam, Holland, 1960).

Earle, E.M. (ed.), *Nationalism and Internationalism: Essays Inscribed to Carlton J.H. Hayes* (New York, 1950).

Eban, A., *The Tide of Nationalism* (New York, 1959).

Edwards, Owen Dudley *et al.*, *Celtic Nationalism* (New York, 1968).

Emerson, Rupert, "An Analysis of Nationalism in Southeast Asia," *Far Eastern Quarterly*, V. No. 2, (1940), 208–215.

Emerson, Rupert, "Paradoxes of Asian Nationalism," *Far Eastern Quarterly*, XIII, No. 2 (1954), 131–142.

Emerson, Rupert, *From Empire to Nation: The Rise of Self-Assertion of Asian and African Peoples* (Cambridge, Mass., 1960).

Enlow, C., *Ethnic Conflict and Political Development* (Boston, 1973).

Ergang, Robert R., *Herder and the Foundations of German Nationalism* (New York, 1931).

Essian-Udom, E.U. *Black Nationalism: The Search for Identity in America* (Chicago, 1962).

Fagg, John Edwin, *Pan-Americanism* (Malabar, Fla., 1982).

Fishman, Joshua, *Advances in the Sociology of Language* (New York, 1950, 1978).

Fishman, Joshua, *et al.*, *Language Loyalty in the United States* (The Hague, 1966).

Fishman, Joshua, *Language and Nationality* (Rowley, Mass., 1972).

Forbes, H.D., "Two Approahes to the Psychology of Nationalism," *Canadian Review of Studies in Nationalism*, II, No. 1 (Fall, 1974), 172–181.

Friedrich, Carl J., *Europe: An Emergent Nation* (New York, 1969).

Francis, E.K., *International Relations* (New York, 1976).

Fyfe, Hamilton, *The Illusion of National Character* (London, 1940).

Gibbons, H.A., *Nationalism and Internationalism* (New York, 1930).

Ginsberg, Asher, *Nationalism and the Jewish Elite* (New York, 1962).

Girardet, Raule, *Le nationalisme française, 1871–1914* (Paris, 1966).

Glaser, Nathan and Daniel P. Moynihan, "Why Ethnicity?" *Commentary*, LVIII, No. 4 (October, 1974), 33–37.

Glaser, Nathan and Daniel P. Moynihan, *Ethnicity: Theory and Practice* (Cambridge, Mass., 1975).

Glenn, Edmund S., "The Two Faces of Nationalism," *Comparative Political Studies*, III, No. 3 (October, 1970), 347–366.

Gökalp, Ziya, *Turkish Nationalism and Western Civilization*, trans. and ed. by N. Berkes (London and New York, 1959).

Gordon, D.C., *Self-Determination and History in the Third World* (Princeton, N.J., 1971).

Gotleib, Yosef, *Self-Determination in the Middle East* (New York, 1982).

Gross, Feliks, *European Ideologies* (New York, 1948).

Grumer, Rebecca, *American Nationalism, 1783–1832* (New York, 1970).

Hahn, L., *North Africa: Nationalism to Nationhood* (Washington, D.C., 1960).

Haim, S., *Arab Nationalism* (Berkeley, 1962).

Hanham, H.J., *Scottish Nationalism* (Cambridge; Mass., 1969).

Hatch, John, *Africa Emergent* (Chicago, 1974).

Hayashi, C., *A Study of Japanese National Character* (Tokyo, 1961).

Hayes, Carlton J.H. Hayes, *Essays on Nationalism* (New York, 1926).

Hayes, Carlton J.H., "Contributions of Herder to the Doctrine of Nationalism," *The American Historical Review*, XXXII (1927), 719–736.

Hayes, Carlton J.H., *France, A Nation of Patriots* (New York, 1930).

Hayes, Carlton J.H., *The Historical Evolution of Modern Nationalism* (New York, 1931).

Hayes, Carlton J.H., *A Generation of Materialism, 1871–1890* (New York, 1941).

Hayes, Carlton J.H., "The Church and Nationalism," *Catholic Historical Review*, XXVIII (1942), 1–12.

Hayes, Carlton J.H., *Nationalism: A Religion* (New York, 1960).

Hertz, Friedrich, *Nationality in History and Politics: A Study of the Psychology and Sociology of National Sentiment and Character* (London, 1944).

Hertzberg, Arthur (ed.), *The Zionist Idea: A Historical Analysis and Reader* (New York, 1966).

Hinsley, F.H., *Nationalism and the International System*, (London, 1973).

Hodgkin, T., *Nationalism in Colonial Africa* (London, 1956).

Holland, W.I., (ed.), *Asian Nationalism and the West* (New York, 1953).

Hoover, Arne J., *The Gospel of Nationalism* (Stuttgart, 1983).

Huntington, Samuel P., *Political Order in Changing Societies* (New Haven, Conn., 1968).

Isaacs, Harold R., *Idols of the Tribe: Group Identity and Political Change* (New York, 1975).

Janowsky, Oscar I., *Nationalities and National Minorities* (New York, 1945).

Jesperson, Otto, *Mankind, Nation and Individual from a Linguistic Point of View* (Oslo, 1925).

John, H., *American Nationalism* (New York, 1957).

Kamenke, Eugene (ed.), *Nationalism: The Making and Evolution of an Idea* (Canberra, Australia, 1973).

Kann, Robert A., *The Multinational Empire: Nationalism and Reform in the Hapsburg Monarchy, 1848–1918* (2 vols., New York, 1950, 1964).

Kann, Robert A., *The Hapeburg Monarchy: A Study in Integration and Disintegration* (New York, 1957).

Kautsky, John A., *The Political Consequences of Modernization* (New York, 1972).

Kedourie, Elie, *Nationalism* (London and New York, 1960).

Kedourie, Elie (ed.), *Nationalism in Asia and Africa* (New York, 1970).

Kennedy, J., *Asian Nationalism in the Twentieth Century* (London and New York, 1968).

Kleinberg, Otto, "A Science of National Character," *Journal of Social Psychology*, XIX (1944), 147–162.

Knapp, W., *Unity and Nationalism in Europe Since 1945* (London, 1969).

Kohn, Hans, *A History of Nationalism in the East*, trans. from the German by Margaret M. Green (London, 1929).

Kohn, Hans, *The Idea of Nationalism: A Study of Its Origin and Background* (New York, 1944, 1960).

Kohn, Hans, *Prophets and Peoples: Studies in Nineteenth Century Nationalism* (New York, 1946).

Kohn, Hans, "Arndt and the Character of German Nationalism," *The American Historical Review*, 54, (July, 1949), 787–803.

Kohn, Hans, "Father Jahn's Nationalism," *Review of Politics*, II (1949), 419–432.

Kohn, Hans, "Romanticism and the Rise of German Nationalism," *Review of Politics*, XII (1950), 443–472.

Kohn, Hans, "The Era of German Nationalism," *Journal of the History of Ideas*, XII (1951), 256–274.

Kohn, Hans, *Pan-Slavism: Its History and Ideology* (Notre Dame, Ind., 1953).

Kohn, Hans, *Nationalism: Its Meaning and History* (Princeton, N.J., 1955).

Kohn, Hans, *Nationalism and Liberty: The Swiss Example* (New York, 1956).

Kohn, Hans, *Prologue to Nation-States: France and Germany, 1789–1815* (Princeton, N.J., 1967).

Kohn, Hans and Wallace Sokolsky, *African Nationalism in the Twentieth Century* (Princeton, N.J., 1965).

Laqueur, Walter Z., *Communism and Nationalism in the Middle East* (New York, 1986).

Lemberg, Eugen, *Nationalismus* (2 vols., Hamburg, 1964).

London, K. (ed.), *New Nations in a Divided World* (New York, 1968).

Masur, Gerhard, *Nationalism in Latin America: Diversity and Unity* (New York, 1966).

Mboya, Tom, *The Challenge of Nationhood* (London, 1970).

McGiffert, Michael, *The Character of Americans* (Homewood, Ill., 1974).

Meier, August, *The Emergence of Negro Nationalism* (New York, 1949).

Meinecke, Friedrich, *Cosmopolitanism and the National State* (New York, 1930).

Minogue, K.R., *Nationalism* (New York, 1967).

Namier, Lewis, *Vanished Supremacies: Essays in European History* (London, 1958).

Noelther, Emiliana, *Seeds of Italian Nationalism, 1700 to 1815* (New York, 1951).

Nussileh, Hazim Zaki, *Arab Nationalism* (Ithaca, N.Y., 1956).

Paliakov, L., *A History of Racist and Nationalist Ideas* (New York, 1974).

Palumbo, Michael and William O. Shanahan, (eds.), *Nationalism: Essays in Honor of Louis L. Snyder* (Westport, Conn., 1981).

Payne, Stanley G., *Basque Nationalism* (Reno, Nev., 1973.

Pipes, Richard, *The Formation of the Soviet Union: Communism and Nationalism, 1917–1923* (Cambridge, Mass., 1954).

Platt, W., *National Character in Action* (New Brunswick, N.J., 1961).

Rawley, James A., *Secession* (Malabar, Fla., 1990).

Rich, Norman, *The Age of Nationalism and Reform, 1850–1870* (New York, 1977).

Roberts, Kenneth, "Social Communication and Mass Nationalism," *Canadian Review of Studies in Nationalism*, II, No. 1 (Fall, 1974), 148–151.

Romein, J., *The Asian Century: A History of Modern Nationalism* (New York, 1962).

Ronen, Dov, *The Quest for Self-Determination* (New Haven, Conn., 1979).

Rotberg, Robert, *The Rise of Nationalism in Africa* (Cambridge, Mass. 1965).

Royal Institute of International Affairs: *A Report by a Study Group of the Institute* (London, 1939).

Rustow, D., *A World of National Problems of Political Modernization* (Washington, D.C., 1967).

Schapiro, Leonard B., *Racism and Nationalism in Russian Nineteenth Century Thought* (New Haven, Conn., 1967).

Seton-Watson, Hugh, *Nation and States* (London, 1977).

Silvert, K.H., *Expectant Peoples: Nationalism and Development* (New York, 1963).

Shafer, Boyd C., *Nationalism: Myth and Reality* (New York, 1955).

Shafer, Boyd C., *Faces of Nationalism: New Realities and Old Myths* (New York, 1972).

Shafer, Boyd C., *Nationalism: Its Nature and Interpretation*, American Historical Association Pamphlet 701 (Washington, D.C., 1976, 3–58.

Shafer, Boyd C., *Nationalism and Internationalism: Belonging in Human Experience* (Malabar, Fla., 1982).

Sharabi, H.B., *Nationalism and Revolution in the Arab World* (Princeton, N.J., 1966).

Sigmund, Paul, (ed.), *The Ideologies of the Developing Nations* (New York, 1963).

Smith, Anthony D., *Theories of Nationalism* (London, 1971).

Smith, Anthony D., "Ethnonationalism, Nationalism, and Social Change," *International Journal of Comparative Sociology*, 13, No. 1 (March, 1972), 1–28.

Smith, Anthony D. (ed.), *Nationalist Movements* (London, 1976).

Snyder, Louis L. *German Nationalism: The Tragedy of a People* (Harrisburg, Pa., 1952, Port Washington, N.Y., 1969).

Snyder, Louis L., (ed.), *The Dynamics of Nationalism* (Princeton, N.J., 1964).

Snyder, Louis L., *The New Nationalism* (Ithaca, N.Y., 1968).

Snyder, Louis L., "Nationalism and the Territorial Imperative," *Canadian Review of Studies in Nationalism*, III, No. 1 (Fall, 1975), 1–20.

Snyder, louis L., *Varieties of Nationalism: A Comparative Study* (New York, 1976).

Snyder, Louis L. (ed.), *Roots of German Nationalism* (Bloomington, Ind., 1978).

Snyder, Louis L., *Global Mini-Nationalisms: Autonomy or Independence* (Westport, Conn., 1982).

Snyder, Louis L., *Macro-Nationalisms: A History of the Pan-Movements* (Westport, Conn.,, 1984).

Strayer, Joseph. *On the Medieval Origins of the Modern State* (Princeton, N.J., 1979).

Sugar, Peter and Ivo Lederèr, *Nationalism in Eastern Europe* (Seattle, 1969).

Sun Yat-sen, *The Three Principles of the People* (Shanghai, 1929).

Symmons-Symonolewicz, K., *Modern Nationalism: Toward a Consensus in Theory* (New York, 1968).

Symmons-Symonolewicz, K., *Nationalist Movements: A Comparative View* (Meadville, Pa., 1970).

Symmons-Symonolewicz, "Ethnicity and Nationalism," *Canadian Review of Studies in Nationalism*, VI, No. 1 (Spring, 1979), 98–102.

Talmon, J.L., *Political Messianism: The Romantic Phase* (New York, 1961).

Thayer, P.E., *Nationalism and Progress in Free Asia* (Baltimore, Md., 1956).

Tudjman, F., *Nationalism in Contemporary Europe* (Boulder, Colo., 1981).

Ward, Barbara, *Five Ideas That Change the World* (New York, 1959).

Ward, Barbara, *Nationalism and Ideology* (New York, 1966).

Waterman, A.M.C., "Nationalism, Sovereignty, and Economic Policy," *Canadian Review of Studies in Nationalism*, II, No. 1 (Fall, 1974), 1–18.

Whitaker, Arthur P., *Nationalism in Latin America: Past and Present* (Gainesville, Fla., 1962)

Young, Crawford, *The Politics of Cultural Pluralism* (Madison, Wisc., 1072).

Zea, L. *The Latin American Mind* (Norman, Okla., 1963).

Znaniecki, Florian, *Modern Nationalities: A Sociological Study* (Urbana, Ill., 1952).